Decision Analysis
for the Professional

Peter McNamee
John Celona

FOURTH EDITION

SmartOrg, Inc.
www.smartorg.com

Decision Analysis for the Professional
Peter McNamee
John Celona

Printed in the United States of America

00000000000

ISBN 0-9710569-0-0

Publisher: SmartOrg, Inc.

Editors: Mimi Campbell, Bill Roehl, Mary Story

Typography and Layout: Don Creswell and T/D Associates

Cover Design: Rogodino & Associates

Dedication

We would like to dedicate this book to a number of very special people—Tereza, Patrick, Christina, and Andrew McNamee, and Karen Schwartz, who endured computer widowhood and orphanhood during the long weeks, weekends, and months while this book was first being written. Without their constant support and indulgence, this project would have never come to fruition.

Preface

In the thirteen years since the first edition of this book, the authors have seen a dramatic evolution in the practice of decision analysis. The number of companies using decision analysis as an approach to problem solving has grown rapidly. Our experience during this period has shown that practical as well as analytical skills are needed for successful implementation of a decision analysis program.

As a problem-solving approach, decision analysis involves far more than the use of decision trees as a calculational tool. It is a process of framing a problem correctly, of dealing effectively with uncertainty, of involving all the relevant people, and, above all, of communicating clearly. Accordingly, in addition to the analytical techniques used in decision analysis, this book presents material that the authors hope will assist the reader in integrating these techniques into a practical and effective problem-solving process.

The dialog decision process (DDP) and the language of decision quality have emerged as a powerful tool in the application of decision analysis in a world of delegated decision making and cross-functional teams. The team process combines with the analytical clarity of decision analysis to produce decisions which can be accepted and implemented by the organization.

This third edition splits the material into four major sections. The first section addresses the tools of decision making and decision analysis. The second section then shows how these tools can be applied in the complex corporate environment. The third section is new and presents the process and language that has been developed for dealing with teams and delegated decision making. The fourth section deals with more advanced topics which are of interest to the more advanced practitioner.

The book has been rewritten so that it is independent of software. In several examples and problems, we use hand calculations to teach readers what the computer programs do. In principle, this text could be read (and many of the problems done) without using computer software.

However, as everyone knows, it is impossible to do much in decision analysis without the aid of supporting software. Descriptions of how to use some software packages such as Supertree are available from the authors. A free student version of Supertree can be downloaded from the www.supertree.net website.

We hope this book will lead the student to develop an appreciation of the power, practicality, and satisfying completeness of decision analysis. More and more, decision analysis and the dialog decision process are becoming accepted as the best way to address decision problems. Being a decision facilitator is an exciting and satisfying occupation. This text is designed to emphasize this. Furthermore, since texts tend to remain on students' shelves, we hope this book will be of assistance long after the course is done.

The text is intended for a short course in decision analysis in business schools. It could also be part of an analytical methods course. The general philosophy of the book, however, is more consonant with extending the course by having the student apply decision analysis to more complex cases, perhaps based on real data or problems supplied by local businesses.

Decision analysis is both young enough that its founders are alive and active in the field and old enough that the literature on the field has grown large. We have chosen not to write a book bristling with footnotes. Rather, we have chosen to list in the bibliography several books in different areas for readers interested in those topics. We ask our colleagues not to take offense if their names or works are not explicitly referred to in this book. We gratefully acknowledge their contribution of accumulated wisdom and knowledge, which has made decision analysis a useful and powerful management tool.

We especially thank all the people who contributed their useful comments and constructive suggestions, including Charles Bonini, Max Henrion, and Myron Tribus. Dr. Bonini kindly allowed us to use the IJK Products and Hony Pharmaceutics problems that appear in Chapters 4 and 7, respectively. We are also indebted to Dr. Udi Meirav for assistance in the discussion of Options and Real Options. We also thank Yong Tao, who assisted in constructing problems for the book. We are particularly indebted to Ronald A. Howard and James E. Matheson for contributions and insights, which appear throughout this book.

Peter McNamee
pmcnamee@smartorg.com
Menlo Park, California

John Celona
jcelona@sbcglobal.net
San Carlos, California

Contents

Chapter 3 – Decisions Under Uncertainty 41

Chapter 4 – Probabilistic Dependence 75

Chapter 7 – Typical Corporate Applications of Decision Analysis 187

Part III: Corporate Decision Making

Chapter 8 – A Decision Making Process 223

Chapter 9 – Decision Quality 253

Part IV: Advanced Topics

Chapter 10 – Probability Theory 267

1

Introduction

Origins of Decision Analysis _____

Decision-making is one of the hard things in life. True decision-making occurs *not* when you already know exactly what to do, but when you do not know what to do. When you have to balance conflicting values, sort through complex situations, and deal with real uncertainty, you have reached the point of true decision-making. And to make things more difficult, the most important decisions in corporate or personal life are often those that put you in situations where you least know what to do.

Decision science evolved to cope with this problem of what to do. While its roots go back to the time of Bernoulli in the early 1700s, it remained an almost purely academic subject until recently, apparently because there was no satisfactory way to deal with the complexity of real life. However, just after World War II, the fields of systems analysis and operations research began to develop. With the help of computers, it became possible to analyze problems of great complexity.

Out of these two disciplines grew decision analysis: the application of decision science to real-world problems through the use of systems analysis and operations research. Decision analysis is a normative discipline, which means it describes how people should logically make decisions. Specifically, it corresponds to how (most) people make decisions in simple situations and shows how this behavior should logically be extended to more complex situations.

This book is divided into four parts, as described in the following pages. The first part develops the tools of decision making. The second part describes how these tools can be applied to complex problems. The third part presents a process for using decision analysis in today's corporate setting. Some specialized topics are dealt with in the fourth part.

Decision Making _____

Imagine a decision-maker struggling with a difficult decision problem. The decision analysis approach provides a normative approach that can support the decision-maker.

Decision analysis functions at four different levels—as a philosophy, as a decision framework, as a decision-making process, and as a decision-making methodology—and each level focuses on different aspects of the problem of making decisions.

Part I of this book lays the foundation for all four levels.

A Philosophy

As a philosophy, decision analysis describes a rational, consistent way to make decisions. As such, it provides decision-makers with two basic, invaluable insights.

The first insight is that uncertainty is a consequence of our incomplete knowledge of the world. In some cases, uncertainty can be partially or completely resolved before decisions are made and resources committed. However, in many important cases, complete information is simply not available or is too expensive (in time, money, or other resources) to obtain.

Although this insight may appear obvious, we are all familiar with instances in the business world and in personal life in which people seem to deny the existence of uncertainty—except perhaps as something to be eliminated before action is taken. For example, decision-makers demand certainty in proposals brought before them. Twenty-year projections are used to justify investments without any consideration of uncertainty. Time and effort are spent to resolve uncertainties irrelevant to the decision at hand. And this list could, of course, be greatly extended.

The second basic insight is that there is a distinction between good decisions and good outcomes. Good outcomes are what we desire, whereas good decisions are what we can do to maximize the likelihood of having good outcomes. Given the unavoidable uncertainty in the world, a good decision must sometimes have a bad outcome. It is no more logical to punish the maker of a good decision for a bad outcome than it is to reward the maker of a bad decision for a good outcome. (Many types of routine decisions have little uncertainty about outcomes; thus, in these cases, it is not unreasonable to associate bad outcomes with bad decisions.)

This insight, too, may seem obvious. Yet how often have we seen corporate "witch hunts" for someone to blame or punish for unfortunate corporate outcomes?

A Decision Framework

As a framework for decision-making, decision analysis provides concepts and language to help the decision-maker. By using decision analysis, the decision-maker is aware of the adequacy or inadequacy of the decision basis: the set of knowledge (including uncertainty), alternatives, and values brought to the decision. There is also a clear distinction between decision factors (factors completely under the decision-maker's control) and chance factors (uncertain factors completely outside the decision-maker's control). Moreover, the decision-maker is aware of the biases that exist in even the most qualitative treatments of uncertainty. He or she knows these biases exist because people are not well trained in dealing with uncertainty and because they are generally overconfident in describing how well they know things.

A Decision-Making Process

As a decision-making process, decision analysis provides a step-by-step procedure that has proved practical in tackling even the most complex problems in an efficient and orderly way. The decision analysis cycle provides an iterative approach that keeps the focus on the decision and that enables the decision facilitator* to efficiently compare the decision alternatives. Modeling, both deterministic and probabilistic, reduces the problem to manageably sized pieces and allows intuition to function most effectively. Knowledge of the biases in probability estimation enables the decision-maker or facilitator to take corrective action.

A Methodology

As a methodology, decision analysis provides a number of specific tools that are sometimes indispensable in analyzing a decision problem. These tools include procedures for eliciting and constructing influence diagrams, probability trees, and decision trees; procedures for encoding probability functions and utility curves; and a methodology for evaluating these trees and obtaining information useful to further refine the analysis.

It is a common mistake to confuse decision analysis with constructing and manipulating influence diagrams and decision trees. The real contribution and challenge of decision analysis occur at the much more general level of defining the problem and identifying the true decision points and alternatives. Many decision analyses never reach the point of requiring a decision tree. Nonetheless, obtaining a full understanding of the philosophy and framework of decision analysis requires some familiarity with the methodology, including trees.

Dealing with Complex Problems

Imagine a decision-maker struggling with a decision problem that involves a complex set of interactions. A decision may affect several products in several different markets. There may be many different alternatives which should be under consideration. Information may be difficult to obtain and may be of uncertain validity.

---

*The term *decision facilitator* is used throughout this book rather than the more traditional *decision analyst* to emphasize the many roles the individual must play in bringing clarity to a decision.

There is a temptation in problems of this type to go to either of two extremes in using decision analysis. Either the analysis is done at a superficial and often simplistic level, resulting in inadequate insight for the decision-maker and perhaps in incorrect conclusions. Or the analysis attempts to include all possibly relevant detail, resulting in the ultimate abandonment of decision analysis because it is perceived as lengthy and expensive.

Part II of this book presents a method to steer between this version of Scylla and Charybdis. The method helps the facilitator discover the real problem, keep the analysis manageable, and find the insights.

Discovering the Real Problem

Finding the real problem is often the most crucial task facing the decision-maker and the decision facilitator. Problems worth extended analysis often come to the surface because many people see only parts of a problem or opportunity. There is confusion as to how things interact, what the possibilities are, what the threats are, what is important and what is irrelevant to the decision. Information is fragmentary, alternatives have not been thought out, consequences have not been fully identified.

The decision basis provides a structure that cuts through much of the confusion and helps identify the real problem. The decision basis is composed of the answers to three questions: What are the possible alternatives? What information do I have to describe these alternatives? What value (decision criterion) do I want to use to choose between the alternatives? When the decision basis is developed, the underlying problem is usually well identified.

The decision analysis cycle then refines the decision basis through a series of approximations. Start with a simple analysis and use the tools of sensitivity analysis to discover what is important and what is irrelevant. With one or two iterations, the problem is almost always clearly identified.

Keeping the Analysis Manageable

People involved in the decision-making process will usually keep the facilitator from falling into the trap of making the analysis too simple. But what will keep the facilitator from making the analysis too complex? The decision analysis methodology provides guidance.

The decision analysis cycle not only guides the direction in which the analysis grows, but also contains the rules for judging when the analysis should stop and the decision made.

In each iteration of the cycle, various forms of sensitivity analysis determine what information is important and why one alternative is better than another. This guides the next iteration of the analysis, and helps the facilitator avoid the addition of irrelevant detail and complexity.

But when does the process stop? When is the level of detail sufficient? The process should stop when the cost of further refinement (sometimes money, more often time) is greater than the benefit the refinement would provide to the decision-maker. Value of information and control provide the key concepts used to identify this cost/benefit trade-off.

Finding the Insights

The purpose of the analysis is not to obtain a set of numbers describing decision alternatives. It is to provide the decision-maker the insight needed to choose between alternatives. These insights typically have three elements: What is important to making the decision? Why is it important? How important is it?

The various forms of sensitivity analysis and probabilistic analysis readily identify which factors are important in making a choice and which are not. The decision analysis cycle iteratively focuses the analysis on the important factors and develops an understanding of why these factors matter to the decision and how much they contribute to the difference of value among the alternatives.

Dealing with Complex Organizations

Imagine a set of decision-makers trying to identify a set of alternatives, choose between them, and create the conditions required for successful implementation in a multi-organizational environment. Many decisions in the modern corporate world are cross-organizational. They involve decision-makers within the organizations, information shared between organizations, and implementation tasks in each organization.

Part III of this book outlines a decision process that gets the analysis done well, and also manages the organizational dimension in such a way that a decision choice will be implemented effectively. Essential elements of this process are a team approach, structured dialogs, and the concept of decision quality.

The Team Approach

The most effective means of dealing with cross-organizational problems and opportunities appears to be the cross-organizational team. The team normally has someone from each organization to present the information and concerns of that organization. Team members are ordinarily detached from their ordinary duties (either part- or full-time) for a fixed length of time to achieve some well defined goal.

The Dialog Decision Process (DDP) has been developed to combine the decision analysis approach with the team approach. This is important from the decision analysis point of view because the information and alternatives need to come from the organizations, and teams are an effective means of accomplishing this. The team structure is important from the cross-organizational point of view because team interaction and understanding will contribute to the successful implementation of the decision.

The DDP sets up two teams. A decision team is composed of the effective decision-makers. A project team is composed of the people who will supply the information and perform the analysis. A schedule is set up to determine the points of interaction between the teams.

Structured Dialog

The DDP is based on a structured dialog between the decision team and the project team. At several points during the project, the two teams will meet for a specific purpose. At these meetings, the project team members present the results they have developed up to that point and request input from the decision team members.

Several important goals are achieved in the ensuing dialog. First, the developing understanding of the problem can lead to redefinition of the project or redirection of the efforts of the project team. Second, the experience and knowledge of decision team members can contribute to the analysis in a timely fashion. Third, the decision team members will be exposed to the concerns of the other organizations, and this shared understanding will be important later during implementation,

Decision Quality

A single decision-maker can decide when the time has come to stop the analysis and make the decision; decision analysis can provide some guidance, but it is really up to the decision-maker to decide when the decision is "good"—logically consistent with the decision-maker's decision basis (alternatives, information, values).

However, in the cross-organizational, multi-decision-maker environment it is not so easy to determine when a decision is "good." A more detailed language is needed to facilitate the discussion and indicate when the team is decision-ready.

The language of Decision Quality has been developed to fill this need. It describes both the quality of the analysis and the quality of commitment to action. Decision Quality is measured by a number of quantitative estimates which, although subjective, are less ambiguous than purely verbal descriptions. And Decision Quality can be monitored periodically during the course of a DDP and corrective actions can be taken if required.

Advanced Topics

Clarity of thinking and common sense are the most important skills required of a decision facilitator. As will be seen in the first three parts of this book, many applications of decision analysis do not require complex mathematics or very specialized interviewing skills.

Of course, there are some decision analysis problems that soar into the realms of mathematical complexity and form the substance of Ph. D. theses.

And the ability to deal sensitively with people and facilitate group meetings is essential for anyone involved in the decision process.

Part IV of this book is intended to take the facilitator a short way along these paths in three areas: dealing with uncertainty, dealing with complex informational relationships, and obtaining reliable information.

Dealing with Uncertainty

Clarity of discussion through the language of probability is one of the hallmarks of decision analysis. We must confront the reality of uncertainty and be able to describe it, and probability is the natural language to describe uncertainty.

This section develops the concepts and language that facilitate discussion of uncertainty and the linkage between uncertainty and probability. Some of the more important rules for calculating with probabilities are reviewed. The most used representations of probability are defined and motivated. Finally, some hard-to-find results on cumulants are recorded for the expert.

Dealing with Complex Informational Relationships

Influence diagrams are used throughout this book to describe our state of information. Influence diagrams are an intuitively clear way of representing this knowledge, even when states of information are related in a complex fashion.

Influence diagrams are mathematical constructs that obey strict mathematical rules. Definitions and rules that are of practical importance are presented and illustrated through several examples.

Obtaining Reliable Information

One task that faces every decision facilitator is obtaining information about uncertainty. And experience has shown that expressing our state of knowledge about uncertainty is not something that we do well.

The decision facilitator must learn to deal with the problems that occur in eliciting information about uncertainty. The causes of the problems are reviewed, and means of correcting for the problems are discussed. A process for conducting a probability encoding interview is described.

Focus of This Book

Since its birth in the 1960s, decision analysis has developed into several different schools, though differences in schools are mostly differences of emphasis and technique. One school focuses on directly assessing probabilities and the different dimensions of value and spends much effort exploring the trade-offs between the uncertain outcomes. Another school focuses more on the art of bringing an assembled group of people to choose a course of action.

This text concentrates on the approach that grew out of the Department of Engineering-Economic Systems at Stanford University and that was pioneered as a practical methodology at SRI International. This approach is characterized by models that take the burden of estimating values and outcomes in complex situations off the individual's shoulders. A computer model is constructed to reduce a complex problem into manageable components. An influence diagram or decision tree is used to divide uncertainty into subfactors until the level has been reached at which intuition functions most effectively. This modeling approach is especially appropriate in business decisions, where the expertise of many individuals and groups must be combined in evaluating a decision problem.

This book begins with the archetypal decision problem: a single decision-maker using the knowledge of a number of "experts" to make a business decision based on a single principal value (money). The single decision-maker requirement is then relaxed somewhat to describe decisions in organizations. True multiple decision-maker problems, however, go beyond the scope of decision analysis and bring in elements of game theory.

There are other types of problems to which decision analysis has been applied with some success. These applications tend to fall into three areas— personal, scientific, and societal. All three areas are beyond the scope of this book.

Personal decision-making frequently involves difficult and sometimes complex value considerations, such as the life-death-pain-resources trade-offs found in medical decisions.

Scientific decision-making (e.g., the choice of experiments to be funded) also involves special value considerations, since it involves making a controversial comparison of the worth of different scientific results and of the resources required to obtain these results.

Societal decision-making, finally, provides one of the most frustrating and fascinating applications of decision analysis. Not only is there no single decision-maker (but rather a decision-making process), but there is also no single set of values that characterizes society. Rather, conflicting sets of values characterize groups within society. There are even values attached to the process used to make the decision.

In these problems, as in all decision analysis applications, the analysis aims at providing insight into the problem, at opening channels of communication, at showing where differences in values or information do or do not affect decisions, and at directing future efforts in ways that will most improve decision-making.

Problems and Discussion Topics

1.1   Describe the difference between good decisions and good outcomes.

1.2   Describe your own approach to making important decisions. Do you use a systematic approach in making them? Do you try to make decisions in a consistent manner? Have you been satisfied with the major decisions you've made so far (or just happy or unhappy with the outcomes)?

1.3   How did you make your decision on which college to attend? Does hindsight reveal any shortcomings in the decision process?

1.4   What concerns would you like a decision-making methodology to address?

1.5   Describe a decision you currently face in which uncertainty is an important factor. Will you find out the outcome of the uncertainty before or after you make your decision?

1.6   Can an uncertainty be an important factor in a decision when the outcome may never be discovered? Describe why or why not and give an example.

Part I

Decision Making

2

Uncertainty and Probability

Probability: A Language of Uncertainty

Uncertainty is a fact of life in the modern world. Both in business and in personal life, there is an almost universal realization that few things can be counted on as certain, at least in the long run. In the business world, recessions come and go, competition comes up with new and unexpected challenges, consumer preferences change (sometimes seemingly at random), accidents or labor problems unexpectedly interrupt business, lawsuits threaten the existence of the company, and so on. And this is true in personal life as well. How will a new job or personal relationship work out? What are suitable investments against the future? In both areas, the list of uncertainties can be expanded indefinitely.

Thinking clearly about these uncertainties—whether to plan better, to make better decisions, or to communicate better about plans and decisions—is important. The key to thinking and communicating clearly about uncertainty is the use of probabilities to describe uncertainty. Fortunately, probability language reflects intuitive concepts of uncertainty. A review of the aspects of probability theory that we will use can be found in Chapter 10. Most readers, however, will find that reading Chapter 10 is not a prerequisite to following the development of ideas in this book.

In this chapter, we concentrate on describing and communicating about uncertainty. In Chapter 3, we deal with how to make decisions under uncertainty.

Along with precise language about uncertainty, we will use two equivalent graphic representations that make it easier to express and to communicate about complex uncertainties. The first of these is the influence diagram. Influence diagrams are an efficient, compact, and intuitive way of representing the uncertainties in a problem and the relationships between the probabilities that describe these uncertainties. At the beginning of this chapter, we use influence diagrams to describe uncertainty.

Later in this chapter, we introduce another representation for uncertainty—the probability tree. These two representations serve complementary purposes. Influence diagrams are a natural way to develop and understand the overall picture; probability trees provide a framework that facilitates calculations with probabilities and the development of insight into the solution of a problem.

The example we will use throughout this chapter and the following three chapters is the semifictional one of Positronics, a manufacturer of sophisticated scientific instruments. This example contains elements from many different cases the authors and their colleagues have worked on. It would be rare for one case to exhibit all these elements. All Positronics discussions are set in italics.

Positronics had decided to bid on supplying MegaCorp with 100 instruments. Positronics estimated it could build them for $4,000 each; the president of Positronics decided to offer the 100 instruments for $500,000. Positronics' only real competitor was Anode Industries, a company with the same reputation for reliability and quality as Positronics. For this reason, the president of Positronics was sure the order would be given to the lower bidder.

Positronics had formed a team to discuss allocating resources to filling the order should its bid be accepted. At the team's first meeting, it became apparent that everyone was worried about the possibility of losing the bid. The head of marketing put himself on record as saying that it was quite likely that Anode would come in with a bid higher than Positronics'. During the discussion, someone noticed the head of production was looking a little uneasy. Some questioning revealed that he was by no means certain of the costs to produce the instruments and that a winning bid of $500,000 might well make Positronics lose money.

The team leader decided that there was a deeper problem here than had been expected. To focus the discussion, she elicited from the group an agreement on what they were worried about: everyone was worried about the uncertainty in the profit resulting from the venture. The team leader took a large sheet of paper and wrote the word "Profit" with an oval around it (Figure 2–1a); the oval indicates that profit is an uncertainty. This was the beginning of the "influence diagram" for the problem, a diagram that starts with and focuses on the ultimate, key uncertainty in the problem.

The team proceeded to look for other uncertainties relevant to (influencing) the uncertainty on profit. Most important in most people's minds was the uncertainty in Anode's bid: if Anode were to bid less than $500,000, Positronics would lose the bid. The team leader added an oval to represent Anode's bid and drew an arrow from the Anode Bid oval to the Profit oval to represent the fact that learning Anode's bid would help answer the question of what profit could turn out to be (Figure 2–1b).

The team then asked if there were other relevant uncertainties. The head of production reminded the team of the uncertainty on production cost. Accordingly, another oval was added to represent the uncertainty on Positronics' cost, and an arrow was drawn from the Cost oval to the Profit oval (Figure 2–1c). At this point, the oval representing Profit was doubled to indicate that, given Anode's bid and

―――――――――――――――― Figure 2–1 ――――――――――――――――

Development of the Influence Diagram of the Positronics Bid Venture

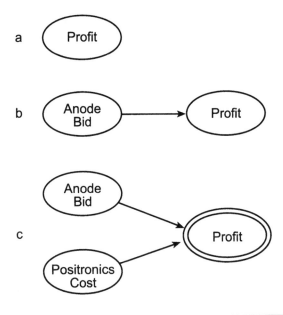

Positronics' cost, there would be no remaining uncertainty—it would be simple to calculate profit.

The meeting made it clear that there were two key areas of uncertainty to work on: the size of Anode's bid and the amount of Positronics' costs. It was also apparent that if preliminary analysis warranted, the team's task might be extended to finding the optimal level of Positronics' bid. All the other concerns (contingency plans, hiring policy, etc.) would fall into place after these three areas were better understood.*

The influence diagram is a very useful representation of problems involving uncertainty. Not only is it a concise statement of the problem, but it also gives the analyst a valuable tool for finding the structure of problems, for organizing the tasks of an analysis, and for eliciting the data and judgments necessary to analyze an uncertainty. Further, as we will see in Chapter 3, it is straightforward to extend the use of influence diagrams to problems that involve decisions as well as uncertainties.

Three elements of the influence diagram were introduced in the preceding example and are defined below.

- An oval represents an uncertainty. Inside the oval is written

_____

*The experienced reader might correctly object that things almost never happen this way. Meetings of this sort are often filled with worries and discussions that turn out to be irrelevant to the problem at hand, while the true uncertainties and decisions are often hidden and discovered only by the careful work of someone who listens, observes, and avoids common prejudices and preconceptions.

a descriptor (or variable name) to identify the set of events (or the quantity) about which we are uncertain or a question to which we would like an answer. Uncertainties are one of several types of "nodes" that we use in influence diagrams.

- An arrow represents relevance. The arrow between the Anode Bid oval and the Profit oval is read as "Anode Bid is relevant to Profit." This simply means that if we knew what Anode's bid turned out to be, it would help us determine what our profit would be. The concept of "relevance" is an important one and will be made more precise in succeeding chapters.

- A double oval represents an uncertainty that ceases to be uncertain once we know how all the uncertainties turn out in the nodes that have arrows pointing to it. This is a "deterministic" node since its value is determined by the nodes that influence it.

The remaining elements concern decisions and will be introduced in the next chapter.

Terminology concerning influence diagrams has shifted during the 1990s. If there is an arrow between two uncertainty nodes, A and B, current best practice is to say "A is relevant to B." Formerly, common usage was to say "A influences B;" the use of the word "influence" in this context is discouraged because it has the connotation of causality, which is not necessarily present. Influence diagram terminology will be more fully discussed in Chapter 4.

The steps for drawing an influence diagram are summarized below.

1. Determine the one key uncertainty you would like resolved— that is, that you would like an answer to. Write it down and put an oval around it.

2. Ask whether there is another uncertainty that—if you knew how it turned out—would help you resolve the uncertainty you identified in step 1. If there is another uncertainty, write it inside an oval and draw an arrow from this oval to the oval drawn in step 1.

3. Repeat step 2 until all *important* uncertainties influencing the key uncertainty (identified in step 1) are identified. An uncertainty is important in this context only if resolving its uncertainty helps resolve the uncertainty in the key variable. As you repeat step 2, check whether arrows should be added to or from all the uncertainties.

4. Ask whether there are uncertainties that would help resolve the uncertainties identified in step 2. If there are, add them to the diagram. Terminate the process when adding another oval does not help you understand the problem.

5. Check whether any of the uncertainties you have identified are completely resolved (determined) if you have all the information indicated by the arrows. Add another oval around these determined nodes to make a double oval.

Influence diagrams are used throughout this book, and their properties will be introduced as needed. The reader desiring a preview or review of influence diagram theory should consult Chapter 11.

Why Bother with Probabilities?

People often claim that they deal adequately with uncertainty through the ordinary use of language and that the quantitative methods we propose are much too elaborate and unnecessary for any problems except very technical and complicated ones.

However, if we ask people to define just what they mean by such common describers of uncertainty as "probably" or "very likely," we usually find a great deal of ambiguity. The authors and their colleagues have demonstrated this ambiguity in seminars attended by high-ranking executives of many of the country's large companies. The executives are asked to define a number of terms, such as "likely," "very likely," or "probably," by assigning a range of probability to each term (e.g., "likely" means 60 percent to 80 percent probability). Although the exercise is not rigorously and scientifically conducted, two results occur so consistently that they warrant attention.

1. If we compare the probability ranges of the group for any one term, the ranges vary greatly. If we form some sort of composite group range spanning the individuals' ranges, there is very little difference between such terms as, for example, "likely" and "very likely."
2. In any moderate-size group, we find people who assign nonoverlapping probability ranges to the same word. For instance, one person might state that "unlikely" means 20 to 30 percent while another might put it at less than 5 percent. While these people may think they are effectively communicating about the likelihood of an uncertain event, they actually have quite different judgments about the likelihood and are unaware of the differences.

Positronics was just beginning to use decision analysis and had just discovered how differently participants at the meeting were using the same terms. It turned out that when the head of marketing said it was "quite likely" that Anode would bid higher than Positronics, he had meant that there was a 60 to 80 percent chance Anode would bid higher. When the president of Positronics heard this, he was more than a little disturbed, since he had assumed that "quite likely" meant something on the order of 90 to 95 percent. The lower probability argued either for more contingency planning by the production staff or for a lower bid. Of course, a lower bid would increase the likelihood of the newly perceived possibility that high production costs could lead to a loss for Positronics.

Verbal descriptions of uncertainty tend to be ambiguous or ill-defined, but numerical probability statements clearly and unambiguously describe uncertainty. Yet many people are overwhelmed with the idea of using probability. After all, probability is a rich and complicated area of study.

However, conducting a decision analysis requires knowing only a few simple properties. While applying probabilities in decision analysis is at times subtle, common sense and careful reasoning are usually more useful than technical sophistication.

What Are Probabilities?

Before we proceed further, let us pose a somewhat philosophical question: what do probabilities represent and where do they come from?

Probabilities represent our state of knowledge. They are a statement of how likely we think an event is to occur.

This simple but profound concept can be illustrated by the example of three people considering an oil-drilling venture in a new area. One person is the president of the company. He has been around for a long time, and his experience tells him that there is a 20 percent chance that there is recoverable oil in the area. The second person is a technical expert who has just finished studying the most recent seismic and geological studies on the area. She assigns a 60 percent probability that there is oil there. The third person is someone out at the drilling site; they have just struck oil, and he would assign a 100 percent probability to finding oil.

Who is right? They *all* are right, assuming that they all are capable of processing the knowledge available to them. (Fortunately, decision-makers in business situations are rarely incompetent or incorrigibly optimistic or pessimistic.) The general acumen of the president, the technical and statistical data of the analyst, and the simple observation of the person at the site—these are different sets of knowledge.

This view of probability as an expression of a state of knowledge has profound consequences. We comment on it in one way or another in every chapter of this book. This perspective on probabilities is called the Bayesian point of view.

Frequently, the nervous decision-maker will ask, "What are the correct probabilities?" Unfortunately, there are no "correct" probabilities. Probabilities represent the decision-maker's state of knowledge or that of a designated expert source of knowledge. Probabilities thus represent a person's judgment and experience and are not a property of the event under consideration. We can worry about whether the expert has good information, whether the probabilities represent the information adequately, whether the state of information should be improved, or whether efforts should be made to elicit the probabilities better. These questions examine the quality of the probabilistic information, but they are not attempts to get the "correct" probabilities.

We do not, however, imply that data are irrelevant. One of course wants the best data and statistics available and to consider the advice of the most experienced people available (another form of data). Unfortunately, the hard decision problems usually involve uncertainties for which definitive data are either not available or not completely relevant. And, when the decision needs to be made, the decision-maker must consider how relevant even the best data are to predicting the future.

Using Intuition Effectively

The "Divide and Conquer" Approach

To help the individual think about uncertainty, decision analysis makes judicious use of the "divide and conquer" approach. To do this, the overall uncertainty is divided into a reasonable set of component uncertainties (and, as we will see in Chapter 3, decisions), which are then treated individually. We have seen an example of this approach in the development of the influence diagram for the Positronics case.

This approach reduces the complexity and scope of the problem to a level at which intuition can function effectively. This is important because, as discussed above, probabilities are statements derived from a person's state of knowledge. It is very difficult (if not impossible) for a person to give meaningful probabilities on an uncertainty that is complex or that includes factors beyond his or her immediate knowledge and experience.

Dividing the uncertainty is also useful in helping different people in a company communicate about the uncertainty and contribute to the analysis. Since different people bring different expertise and experience to the decision-maker or decision-making process, dividing the uncertainty into small pieces enables each individual to contribute precisely within his or her area of expertise.

In the case of Positronics, the problem already showed a natural division into two subcomponents: the uncertain size of Anode's competitive bid and the uncertain cost of production if Positronics won the contract. It seemed natural that the uncertainty in the production cost would be best estimated by someone from the manufacturing or production staff, while the uncertainty on the size of the competitive bid would best be estimated by someone from marketing or upper management. Assignments for further study were made accordingly.

Passing the Clairvoyance Test

One of the most common barriers to the use of intuition and to effective communication is lack of clarity in defining the event to which we are assigning probabilities.

To test the clarity of definition, we use the clairvoyance test. The clairvoyant is a hypothetical person who can accurately answer any question, even about the future, but who possesses no particular expertise or analytical capability. Thus, for instance, when asked about production costs in the year 2010, the clairvoyant might "look" at a company's annual report for the year 2010 and report the answer he sees there.

The clairvoyance test is a mental exercise to determine if the clairvoyant can immediately tell us the outcome of a chance node or if he needs to know other things first. An immediate prediction means that the uncertainty is clearly defined. If the clairvoyant would have to ask some questions first, then we have not clearly laid out exactly what the uncertain quantity is.

For instance, imagine we ask the clairvoyant what production costs will be in the year 2010. The clairvoyant would have to ask whether the costs are in today's dollars or 2010 dollars; whether they include or exclude depreciation, fixed costs, and allocated expenses; whether they are given in terms of an advance in technology or an evolution of the product; etc. Our response, of course, is to define better what we mean by production costs so they more nearly pass the clairvoyance test.

The clairvoyance test is surprisingly difficult to pass. Yet if it is not passed, we will find that uncertainty compounded with an ill-defined quantity yields results of dubious quality at best. The problem becomes even more acute when information obtained from different people is compared. The time spent in taking—and passing—this test is well rewarded by a lack of confusion and greater insight later on.

The Positronics staff agreed on definitions for the uncertainties that passed the clairvoyance test. Cost was a well-defined measure that excluded depreciation, allocated costs, and truly fixed costs. Anode's bid was interpreted strictly in terms of the deliverables called for in the request for bids.

Assigning the Numbers

Using Trees

To put explicit values on probabilities, we use drawings called "distribution trees" to represent the data in the nodes of the influence diagram—the information on how each uncertainty may turn out. It is called a distribution tree because it has a line (branch) for each possible outcome. In statistical terms, this is the distribution of possible outcome. The data in this form are then combined into a "probability tree" that both graphically describes and numerically analyzes the problem. Each uncertainty node we have identified in the influence diagram becomes an uncertainty or chance node of the probability tree.

What does a distribution tree look like? Shown in Figure 2–2 is the skeleton of a three-branch distribution tree. At the branching point on the

Figure 2–2

Skeleton of a Three-Branch Distribution Tree

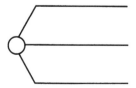

left is a circle to indicate that this is an uncertainty or chance node. Associated with each branch is an outcome. The set of outcomes describes all the different events that could occur at that node—all the ways the uncertainty could be resolved.

The set of outcomes at a chance node must be mutually exclusive and collectively exhaustive. That sounds more complicated than it really is. Mutually exclusive means that the way an uncertainty turns out must correspond to only one of the outcomes (i.e., there is no overlap in the list); collectively exhaustive means that the way the uncertainty turns out must correspond to one of the outcomes (i.e., all possible outcomes are included in the list).

The Data in the Nodes

After some work, the Positronics staff came up with the following probability assessments to represent their perception of the uncertain future. To keep things simple, the staff judged it sufficiently accurate to divide both quantities (Anode's bid and Positronics' cost) into three ranges, thus creating three discrete outcomes for each node.*

First, the three possible states representing Anode's bid were chosen. The Anode bid could be less than $500,000, between $500,000 and $700,000, or greater than $700,000. The marketing personnel used their judgment to assign the following probabilities: a 35 percent chance the Anode bid will be less than $500,000, a 50 percent chance it will be between $500,000 and $700,000, and a 15 percent chance the bid will be greater than $700,000. These definitions and probabilities can be thought of as being contained "inside" the Anode Bid oval in the influence diagram. Shown in tree form (Figure 2–3), the outcomes are on each branch, the probability of the branch occurring is at the left of each branch,

———————————————— Figure 2–3 ————————————————

The Anode Bid Node

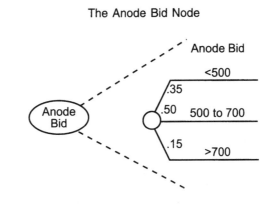

———————————————————————————————

*Chapter 12 gives much more careful procedures for eliciting probabilities. The informal process used here is appropriate only when an uncertainty is unusually well understood.

and the circle at the branching point indicates that it is an uncertainty node. To keep notation compact, all values in the figures are shown in units of thousands of dollars—e.g., $500,000 is shown as 500.

Similarly, Positronics' cost could turn out to be less than $300,000, between $300,000 and $500,000, or greater than $500,000. There is a 25 percent chance Positronics' cost will be less than $300,000, a 50 percent chance it will be between $300,000 and $500,000, and a 25 percent chance it will be greater than $500,000 (Figure 2–4).

The range of values assigned to Positronics' cost is very large, with about a factor of two (<300 to >500) uncertainty. It is rare to find so great an uncertainty on costs, except in one-of-a-kind construction or in very large projects.

Drawing the Probability Tree

All these data now are put together to create a "probability" tree. This probability tree represents all the different combinations of events that can occur and their probabilities. How are the data joined together to create a probability tree?

Pick an order in which to display the two uncertainty nodes. The order is arbitrary for the present example. The rules applicable in more complicated cases are presented in the next chapter. In Figure 2–5, we choose Anode Bid to be the first node and Positronics Cost to be the second. The deterministic node, Profit, will be at the right-hand side of the diagram.

At the end of each of the branches of the first node (Anode Bid), attach the second node (Positronics Cost), as in Figure 2–6. We will deal with the deterministic node (Profit) shortly.

The final column in Figure 2–6 has been added to clarify the meaning of the tree. The probability of each of the nine scenarios (paths through the

--- Figure 2–4 ---

The Positronics Cost Node

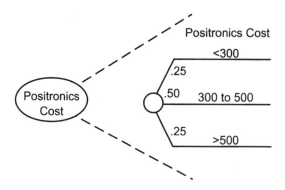

─────────────────────────── Figure 2–5 ───────────────────────────

Influence Diagram Prepared for Drawing the Tree

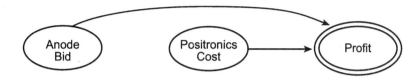

─────────────────────────── Figure 2–6 ───────────────────────────

Probability Tree Displaying the Probability of Each Path Through the Tree

Anode Bid	Positronics Cost	Probability of Path Through Tree
	<300	.0875
	.25	
<500	.50 300 to 500	.1750
	.25 >500	.0875
.35		
	<300	.1250
	.25	
.50		
500 to 700 .50 300 to 500		.2500
	.25 >500	.1250
	<300	.0375
	.25	
.15		
>700 .50 300 to 500		.0750
	.25 >500	.0375
		─────
		1.000

tree) has been calculated by multiplying the probabilities that occur at each branching. These products are referred to as joint probabilities. Thus, the scenario of Anode bidding less than $500,000 and Positronics' cost being less than $300,000 (the topmost path through the tree) is $.35 \times .25 = .0875$. The sum of all the joint probabilities is 1, as it must be.

We can see that however difficult it is to assign the probabilities for each chance node, it would be much more difficult (if not impossible) to directly assign the joint probabilities. The "divide and conquer" technique reduces scope and complexity so that judgment and intuition work effectively.

You can conserve space by drawing the tree in the more compact form shown in Figure 2–7. This form of the tree is often referred to as a "schematic tree." Drawing the tree with nodes following each other like this means that each branch of the left node leads to the next node on the right. Thus, the implication is that each node is duplicated as many times as necessary to produce the full tree structure.

A refinement has been added in Figure 2–7. The outcomes on each branch are now single numbers that represent the ranges of the original outcome. For instance, the Anode bid can be $400,000, $600,000, or $800,000. We have approximated the original ranges by discrete values, resulting in the Anode bid having only three values. (The procedure for doing this is described at the end of this chapter.) Clearly, the more branches we have, the narrower we can make the ranges and the better a single number can represent the range. On the other hand, the more branches, the larger the tree.

A Value Function

We still have not dealt with the deterministic (double oval) node, Profit, which appears in the Positronics influence diagram (Figure 2–5). This is the node for which there is no remaining uncertainty, once we know the outcome of the nodes that influence it. Its value is determined by the outcomes of the influencing nodes. Thus, unlike the other two nodes, the profit node needs only a value function (a formula) that translates the

―――――――――――――――――――― Figure 2–7 ――――――――――――――――

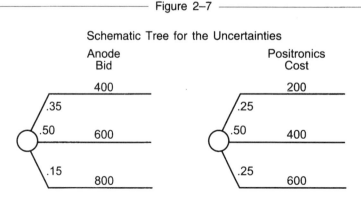

Schematic Tree for the Uncertainties

Figure 2–8

Influence Diagram Showing Equation "Inside" the Profit Node

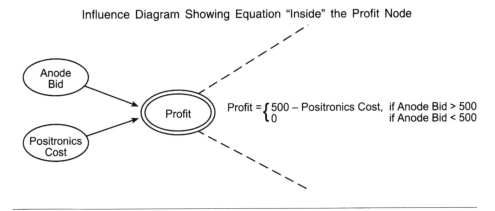

$$\text{Profit} = \begin{cases} 500 - \text{Positronics Cost,} & \text{if Anode Bid} > 500 \\ 0 & \text{if Anode Bid} < 500 \end{cases}$$

uncertainties in the chance nodes into the uncertainty on the value of interest to the decision-maker. (We discuss value functions in detail in Chapter 3.)

Positronics had decided that profit was the prime value in this case. The deterministic node for profit can therefore be thought of as having an equation "inside" the node (Figure 2–8).

The completed probability tree is shown in Figure 2–9.

The values in the column on the right are needed to complete the probability tree and allow analysis. Sometimes the value model comes from a subjective assessment where the values for each scenario are assessed directly rather than calculated. Sometimes the value model is a simple relationship (as in the Positronics case) where the value can be calculated by a single equation. However, most often the value model is implemented as a computer program (or spreadsheet) that calculates how revenues and costs develop over time, figures tax effects, calculates a cash flow, and so forth.

Analyzing the Tree

Now that the tree has been completed, we will determine what information can be drawn from it. First, we will examine how the component uncertainties have translated into uncertainty on the value of ultimate interest to the decision-maker.

Because a cumulative probability plot (like the one shown in Figure 2–10) is the most efficient means of presenting information for decision analysis, we use it throughout this book. The plot is worth studying closely, since it answers most of the questions the decision-maker will ask.

The plot gives the probability (the vertical axis) that the venture's value will turn out to be less than or equal to the value shown on the horizontal axis. Thus, the plot shown in Figure 2–10 indicates that there is:

- No probability of the venture being worth less than –$100,000

——————————————————— Figure 2–9 ———————————————————

Completed Probability Tree

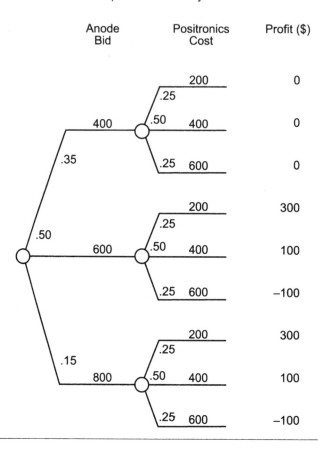

Anode Bid	Positronics Cost	Profit ($)

The data beneath the tree:

- A .1625 probability of its being worth less than or equal to –$100,000 (.1625 that it is equal to –$100,000)
- A .5125 chance of its being worth less than or equal to $0 (.1625 that it is equal to –$100,000 and .35 that it is equal to $0)
- A .8375 probability of its being worth less than or equal to $100,000
- A 1.0 probability of its being worth less than any value above $300,000.

The data for this graph is contained in Figures 2–6 and 2–9. The procedure for constructing the cumulative graph is simple:

1. Create a list of the values in the tree, ordering them from smallest to largest. For Positronics, Profit is the value.
2. Next to each value, put the probability associated with the value. Some values may occur several times in the tree; for these, add the probabilities together.

Figure 2–10

Cumulative Plot of Probability Distribution on Profit in the Positronics Venture

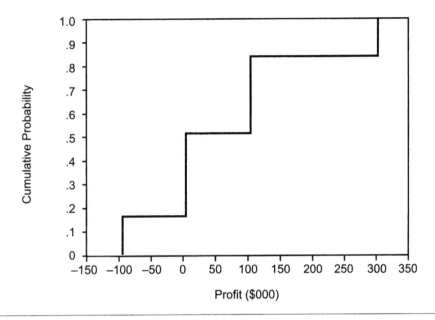

3. In the space labeled cumulative probability, enter the sum of the cumulative probability immediately above and the probability to the left. For the top row in the list, use zero for the cumulative probability immediately above. (The cumulative probability is the sum of all the probabilities on and above each line.)

Value	Probability	Cumulative Probability
–100,000	.1250 + .0375 = .1625	.1625
0	.0875 + .1750 + .0875 = .3500	.5125
100,000	.2500 + .0750 = .3250	.8375
300,000	.1250 + .0375 = .1625	1.0000

4. Create a graph with Profit on the horizontal axis and probability on the vertical axis.
5. For each line in the list, mark the point corresponding to that value of Profit on the horizontal axis and the corresponding cumulative probability on the vertical axis.
6. For each line in the list, mark the point corresponding to that value of Profit on the horizontal axis and the cumulative probability for the *previous* value of Profit on the vertical axis. For the first value of Profit in the list, use zero as the cumulative probability for this point.
7. Join the points with horizontal and vertical lines.

The staircase nature of the graph is, in this case, imposed partly by the discrete approximations used to turn an originally continuous range of bids and costs into nine (3 × 3) different cases. If the ranges had been broken into more segments, the distribution would have been smoother. But there would still have been a step at $0 corresponding to the probability that the bid was lost.

There is another way to represent the probability distribution for the venture's value: the histogram plot. In a histogram plot, the horizontal (value) axis is divided into a number of equal-sized ranges or bins. The height of the bar drawn for each bin is the probability (vertical axis) that the value falls in the bin.

The histogram in Figure 2–11 has five bins ranging from –$100,000 to $400,000. The plot reveals that there is:
- A .1625 probability of the bin ranging from –$100,000 to $0
- A .35 probability of the bin ranging from $0 to $100,000
- A .325 probability of the bin ranging from $100,000 to $200,000
- A .1625 probability of the bin ranging from $300,000 to $400,000.

The data for this graph is contained in Figures 2–6 and 2–9. The procedure for constructing the histogram is simple:
1. Define the equal-size ranges for the value and create a list with as many lines as there are ranges.
2. Determine the range into which the value at the end of a branch falls. By convention, a value falls with a bin if its value is greater than or equal to the lower bound and less than the upper bound.

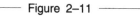
——————————— Figure 2–11 ———————————

Histogram of Probability Distribution on Profit in the Positronics Venture

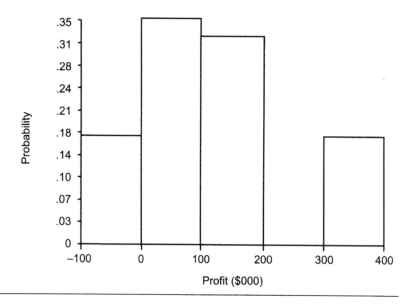

3. Add the probability for the branch to the line in the list for the range.

Lower Bound	Upper Bound	Probability
–100,000	0	.1250 + .0375 = .1625
0	100,000	.0875 + .1750 + .0875 = .3500
100,000	200,000	.2500 + .0750 = .3250
200,000	300,000	0
300,000	400,000	.1250 + .0375 = .1625

4. Create a graph from these ranges and probabilities.

How Much Detail Is Enough?

In an actual case, the value model might be more complex, and there might be more nodes in the tree or more branches on the nodes. While such complexity may be appropriate, more detail may not add insight. Hence, the results shown in the cumulative and histogram plots may be close to representing the essentials of the situation. Before succumbing to the temptation to make an analysis more complicated, we should pose the following questions:

- Will a more complicated value model really change the values that much?
- Will more nodes or more branches at a node really change the probability distribution that much?
- Will the added detail really add insight?
- Is the focus shifting from "a model adequate to make a choice" to a "good model of reality"?

Often, the essential insight into a decision problem is conveyed by results almost as simple as those shown here. That a decision has proved much simpler to grapple with than one would have supposed is an insight a decision-maker really appreciates.

With the initial analysis completed, the decision analysts were preparing to present their results to the president of Positronics. They decided to avoid puzzling him with the complications of understanding a cumulative probability graph and instead used the histogram. During the presentation, the president began asking questions like "What's the chance we will make a substantial profit?" and "What's the chance we will lose money?" which the analysts realized could be read directly off the cumulative probability graph. Being experienced presenters, they had a copy of the cumulative probability graph ready in the set of backup materials they had prepared for the presentation.

To everyone's astonishment, the president was genuinely surprised by the results. After some discussion, everyone agreed that he was surprised because the explicit judgments inherent in the probabilities had opened up new channels of clear communication. For one thing, the president had not appreciated just how worried production was that the cost of producing the instruments might be much higher than expected. The analysis also enabled the president to see how the uncertainties in cost and in Anode's bid combined into an overall uncertainty. Looking at the cumulative and histogram plots, he now had a good idea of the uncertainty and risk in his current bid strategy. He did, however, ask whether there was a single number that could be used to characterize the worth of the venture when he was comparing it with other ventures or speaking to members of the board (who were probably not interested in details of this rather minor facet of the business).

Certain Equivalent and Expected Value _____

One of the goals of decision analysis is to give a single number that characterizes a probability distribution. This number is called the certain equivalent and is the value that, if offered for certain, would represent to the decision-maker an even exchange for the uncertain venture described by the probability distribution. (This topic is discussed extensively in Chapter 5.) There is, however, a quantity closely related to the certain equivalent but easier to use and understand: the expected value. The uncertain venture is described by a probability distribution—a set of possible outcomes and the probability that each outcome occurs. Figures 2–10 and 2–11 show the probability distribution for profit in graphical form. The expected value of a probability distribution is obtained by multiplying each outcome by its probability of occurring and then by adding the products. The data plotted in figures 2–10 and 2–11 are shown in the trees in figure 2–9.

The data in these trees can be combined in what is called the "roll-forward" evaluation (Figure 2–12). The roll-forward evaluation rolls all the information forward—i.e., to the right-hand side of the tree. This means that for each path through the tree, there is a value and a probability (Figure 2–9). Multiply the value by the probability at the end of each path and add the results to obtain the expected value.

The expected value can also be obtained through the "rollback" evaluation, a much more general technique that is easier to use. In the rollback, we start at the right-hand edge of the tree and replace each chance node with its expected value. (Multiply the value on each branch by its probability and sum the products.) We then move to the left and continue the process, except that what was the rightmost column of nodes has now been replaced by expected values. This procedure continues until all the nodes have been replaced and we are left with the expected value of the tree (Figure 2–13).

In Figure 2–13, we see how the Cost node expected values are the branch values for Anode Bid, which lies to the left of Cost. For instance, the branch with Anode Bid equal to 800 replaces the Cost node with its expected value, which is calculated below.

$$(300 \times .25) + (100 \times .50) + (-100 \times .25) = 100 \qquad (2\text{--}1)$$

The expected value of the Anode Bid node is then:

$$(0 \times .35) + (100 \times .50) + (100 \times .15) = 65 \qquad (2\text{--}2)$$

Figure 2–12

Expected Value Determined Through Roll-Forward Evaluation

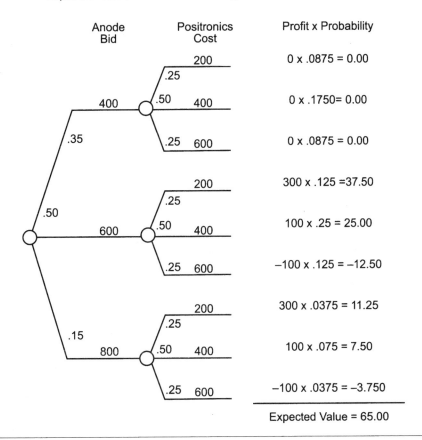

Anode Bid	Positronics Cost	Profit x Probability
	200	0 x .0875 = 0.00
400	400	0 x .1750= 0.00
	600	0 x .0875 = 0.00
	200	300 x .125 =37.50
600	400	100 x .25 = 25.00
	600	−100 x .125 = −12.50
	200	300 x .0375 = 11.25
800	400	100 x .075 = 7.50
	600	−100 x .0375 = −3.750

Expected Value = 65.00

Given a large number of identical uncertain ventures, the average value would be the expected value. For instance, in a coin toss that yields a prize of $1, the expected value is:

$$(.5 \times \$1) + (.5 \times \$0) = \$0.50 \tag{2–3}$$

We would expect to be about $50 richer after flipping the coin 100 times. Of course, the problem is that we are often presented with one-of-a-kind situations. For the coin toss example, if we are offered a single coin flip with a prize of $1, we will either walk away with $1 or with nothing. Still, it is not unreasonable to value the opportunity at the $0.50 expected value for decision-making purposes. For much larger values (e.g., a single coin flip with a prize of $1,000), the expected value may not adequately give us the value of the uncertain venture. If it does not, we should use the probability distribution. For most problems we will encounter in practice, the certain equivalent will not be very different from the expected value. In addition, the

Figure 2–13

Expected Value Determined Through Roll-Back Evaluation

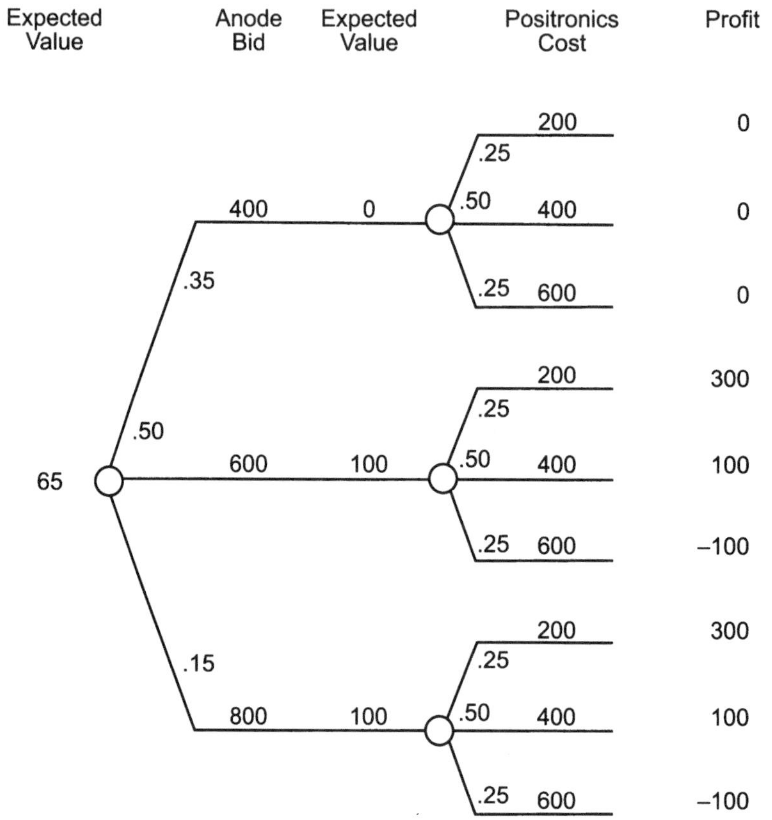

Expected Value	Anode Bid	Expected Value	Positronics Cost	Profit
			200	0
			.25	
	400	0	.50 400	0
.35			.25 600	0
			200	300
			.25	
.50	600	100	.50 400	100
65			.25 600	−100
			200	300
.15			.25	
	800	100	.50 400	100
			.25 600	−100

methods of tree evaluation are similar for both measures. Thus, it will prove simple to make the transition from one measure to the other.

Encoding Probabilities[*]

How does one obtain probabilities in practice? Obtaining probability distributions for use in decision analysis is no easy task. People are not trained in thinking about uncertainty, so the exercise of assessing probabilities can be uncomfortable and difficult. In this section, we briefly describe the encoding process and how to discretize the resulting continuous distributions. In Chapter 12, we further discuss the encoding process and give an actual procedure to follow. We also further discuss the commonly encountered biases that must be counteracted (as much as possible) to obtain accurate information.

To obtain probabilities, a tree can be set up and people can be directly asked to write probabilities on it. Another quick way to get a probability

[*] Reading this section may be postponed until after Chapter 5 has been read.

distribution is from existing "range data." Unfortunately, while both these procedures are easy and take relatively little time, they can yield "bad" probabilities if the analyst does not take some care to counteract common biases. Earlier, we emphasized that probabilities represent a person's state of knowledge and that there are no "correct" probabilities. Biased probabilities are those that do not adequately represent what a person really knows; something prevents him or her from using or expressing this knowledge correctly.

The most common types of bias cause people to think they know things better than they do. In other words, their probability distributions are usually much too narrow and understate the uncertainty. The best way to counteract this bias is, if possible, to address extreme outcomes ("How high could the value be? What would have to happen for the value to be even higher?") before getting base case, best guess estimates.

Another type of bias occurs because most people are unfamiliar with probability theory and make false analogies or draw false conclusions about probability. The best way to counteract this bias is to be clear and explicit in drawing influence diagrams and trees.

Obtaining the Data

In a complete encoding of continuous numerical variables, the decision facilitator usually assesses the cumulative probability distribution directly. This process will allow the facilitator to counteract the biases during the assessment. The cumulative probability graph is obtained by plotting responses to such questions as "What is the likelihood that costs will be less than $500,000?" or "Less than $650,000?" (Actually, it is best to ask these questions using a reference device such as a probability encoding wheel— see Chapter 12.) The result of such an assessment process will be a set of points and a smoothed curve such as the one in Figure 2–14 for Positronics' cost.

Discretizing the Data

In tree analysis, we usually make a discrete approximation by setting up nonoverlapping (mutually exclusive) ranges that encompass all possible values (collectively exhaustive), by finding the probabilities that the values fall in these ranges, and by then choosing a value to represent that range. (This is the approximation.) By doing this, we have converted a continuous variable to a discrete variable and a probability density function to a probability mass function.

Given a continuous probability distribution such as the one shown in Figure 2–14, how does one perform this approximation? One widely used technique is to select the number of outcomes and the values of the probabilities you want and then draw a horizontal line at these probabilities. In Figure 2–15, we have chosen the number of outcomes to be three. We have also chosen the probabilities .25 for the lower range (line at .25), .5 for

Figure 2–14

Cumulative Probability Distribution for Positronics' Cost

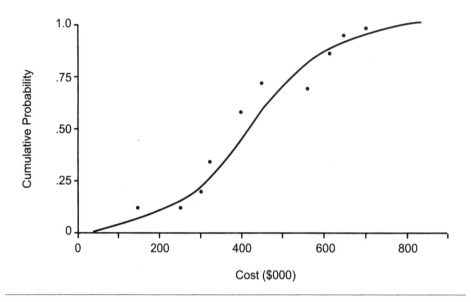

the middle range (line at .25 + .50 = .75), and .25 for the top range (line at .25 + .5 + .25 = 1).

Figure 2–15

Approximation of Discrete Probability Distribution for Positronics' Cost

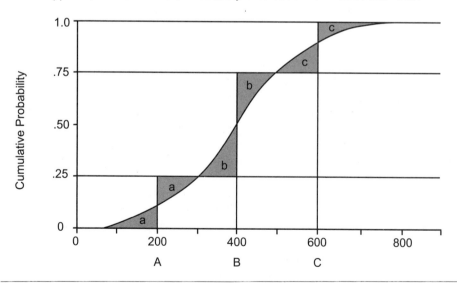

Figure 2–16

Discrete Probability Distribution in Tree Form

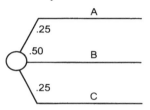

Next, we draw a vertical line at A, choosing point A so that the shaded area to the left of the vertical line is equal to the shaded area to the right. (The eye is surprisingly good at doing this.) These two areas are marked by the letter "a." Then we pick a point, B, at which to draw a vertical line with the shaded area to the right being equal to the shaded area to the left. Finally, we pick the third point, C, at which to draw the vertical line balancing the two shaded areas.

The procedure sounds much more complicated than it is in practice. The result is that we now have approximated the continuous probability distribution; the discrete probability distribution is shown in tree form in Figure 2–16. The actual values are A = 200, B = 400, and C = 600. These values are used for Positronics' cost in this chapter. In general, the values for A, B, and C will not come out evenly spaced.

The reason the procedure works is that we divided the continuous probability distribution into ranges with associated probability when we drew the horizontal lines. In Figure 2–17, we see that the first range was from negative infinity to x and had probability .25. The second range was from x to y and had a probability of .5. The third range was from y to infinity and had a probability of .25. (For this example, x = 300 and y = 500, corresponding to the ranges in Figure 2–4.) Picking point A in such a way that the shaded areas are equal is a visual way of finding the expected value, given that you are in the lowest range. (Proving that the expected value makes the shaded areas equal is a nice exercise in calculus in problem 2.15.) Choosing the expected value to represent the range is a natural approximation and is commonly used. There are, however, other possible choices.

Using Range Data

We see that the final result was three numbers, with probabilities of .25, .50, and .25. There is a shortcut for assessing these values directly. This method is frequently used in the early stages of analyzing a problem when you have obtained ranges within which the values of variables are expected to fall. (See Chapter 6 for a discussion of Sensitivity Analysis.) The ranges are typically defined by best guess (50 percent chance it could be less), low value (10 percent chance it could be less), and high value (90 percent

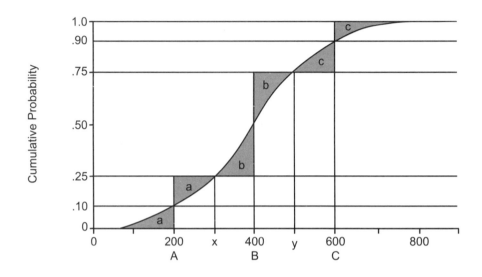

Figure 2–17

Ranges Associated with Approximate Discrete Probability Distribution for
Positronics' Cost

chance it could be less or 10 percent chance it could be greater). As a quick
way of setting up a tree, these three values can be used for B, A, and C,
respectively. But remember that you want to encode probabilities more
carefully later on!

Figure 2–17 shows why this procedure works. There is about a 10
percent chance the value will be less than A and about a 10 percent chance
that the value will be greater than C—and this is how we defined the
ranges! (This property is almost exact for a Gaussian or normal distribution
and is quite good for most of the distributions you find in practice.) Finally,
the best guess can be used for B unless you know the distribution is very
asymmetric. Thus, in summary, we can take the "10 percent, best guess,
90 percent" range numbers and use them in a tree with .25, .50, and .25
probability, respectively.

Beware, however, of "best guesses" that come from a business plan and
are far from the median value. Also, be alert for ranges that are too narrow
or are given without sufficient thought and reflection.

Summary

Probabilities are a precise way of expressing a person's information about
an uncertain event. Judicious use of the clairvoyance test and the divide
and conquer approach make the use of probabilities an intuitive as well as
precise process.

Influence diagrams and probability trees constitute a framework to hold and process probability statements. The influence diagram is a powerful tool for structuring a problem. The probability tree is the tool used most often for calculating with probabilities.

The primary output of the analysis is the probability distribution on value. This information can be represented graphically by a cumulative probability plot or by a histogram. For the Positronics case, the graphs showed the uncertainty in profit.

A single measure to represent the value of an uncertain venture is the expected value of the probability distribution. For the president of Positronics, this number provided a starting point for putting a value on his uncertain venture.

Finally, care and skill are required in the assignment of probabilities. A simple example showed how information on Positronics' cost can be used for input to the probability tree.

Problems and Discussion Topics _____

2.1   Consider today's weather forecast. Are the chances of rain or sunshine expressed verbally or with probabilities? What is your probability of rain given that weather forecast? If your probability is different from the forecast, is the difference because you and the forecaster have different states of knowledge or because of some other reason?

2.2   In the section "What Are Probabilities?" are statements like "Probabilities represent our state of knowledge." Such statements are sometimes misinterpreted to mean that probabilities are arbitrary numbers between 0 and 1. In fact, probability is a well-defined concept with very strong implications. For example, if two people have exactly the same information (knowledge) about an event, they should assign the same probability to this event. Furthermore, if new relevant information becomes available, the prior probability assignment will have to be changed (updated).

What else can you infer from the statement "Probabilities represent our state of knowledge"?

2.3   Why is an influence diagram (or similar method) necessary for understanding complex uncertainties? How do the procedure and graphical form of an influence diagram deal with the problem?

2.4   What is the relationship between each component of an influence diagram (arrows, ovals, and double ovals) and the components of a probability tree?

2.5   Can you draw a probability tree directly without first drawing an influence diagram? When would this be a bad or good idea? Does your answer depend on the level of expertise of the person doing the analysis?

2.6   In the section "Using Intuition Effectively", we discussed how to define uncertainty clearly and the role of the clairvoyant in the clairvoyance test. How can the clairvoyant help you? Can the clairvoyant change your future?

2.7   What do you do when an uncertainty fails the clairvoyance test? How might this change your influence diagram? How might this change the structure of your probability tree?

2.8   The expected value is sometimes described as the mean value you would expect to achieve if you undertook the same venture many times. Unfortunately, since many decisions are one-of-a-kind decisions, there is no opportunity to repeat them and establish a historical mean. Suppose, though, that a venture had just been resolved (all the uncertain events had happened) and you were now faced with an identical one. Would your prospective expected value for the second venture be the same as it was for the first? Why or why not?

2.9   You are going to the movies tonight with a new date. You plan on treating, but your date may want to go Dutch treat (each person pays) or treat you. You figure the three outcomes are equally likely. The cost for the movie is $5 per person. You plan to at least buy popcorn if your date wants it (with a 4 out of 5 chance that he or she will). However, you have forgotten how much the large popcorn costs. You would give 5 out of 10 that it costs $2 and split the rest of the probability between $1.50 and $2.50.

You just discovered that you only have $10 cash right now. What is the expected cost of going to the movie tonight? What is the probability that it will cost you more than $10? What is the probability that it will not cost you anything?

2.10   Your prize Rapid Ripe tomato plant has flowered and is ready to start producing fruit. If all goes well, your plant will produce tomatoes by the end of the week. It will then produce a new set of flowers and blossoms next week. Unfortunately, your area is subject to blossom wilt, which causes the tomato flowers to fall off. If the blossoms fall off, a new set of blossoms will not emerge until next week, and tomatoes will not be ready until the end of that week.

Luckily, each time blossoms fall off, the plant builds up its resistance; the probability of each succeeding blossom falling off is then only half as much. You estimate that the probability of this first set of blossoms falling off is .40.

   a. Draw the influence diagram for this problem and then draw the probability tree.

   b. What is the probability tomatoes will be ready in the third week?

c. What is the expected number of weeks you will have tomatoes over the next three weeks?

d. What is the probability you will lose the blossoms one or more weeks of the next five weeks?

2.11 You have discovered the lights on Van Ness Avenue in San Francisco are synchronized, so your chances of getting a green light at the next intersection are higher if you have not been stopped by a red light at the last intersection. You estimate that there is a 4/5 chance of getting a green light if the previous light was green. Similarly, there's only a 1/4 chance of getting a green light if the last light was red. Because Van Ness is a major throughway, you estimate there's a 2/3 chance of the first light being green.

a. Draw the influence diagram for this problem and then draw the probability tree.

b. What is the probability that the second light will be green?

c. Out of the first three lights, how many lights can you expect to be green?

d. What is the probability of the third light being green when the first one was red? (Hint: draw a tree with three nodes representing the first three lights.)

2.12 An excess probability distribution plots the probability that the value is greater than a given number. Plot the excess probability distribution for the initial Positronics tree (Figure 2–9). What is the probability the value is greater than $130,000?

2.13 Plot the probability mass function for the initial Positronics tree (Figure 2–9). What is the difference between the mass function and the histogram? (The probability mass function is defined in Chapter 10.)

2.14 Suppose the closing trading price for platinum on the world markets today was $550 per ounce. (Does this pass the clairvoyant test?)

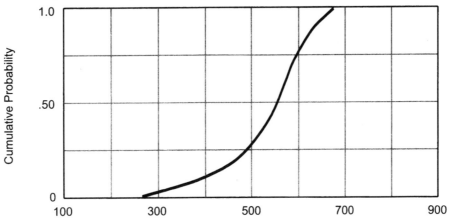

Trading Price of Platinum One Year from Today ($ per ounce)

Toward the end of the day, you put in an order to your broker to purchase one, two, or three contracts to sell 100 ounces of platinum one year from now, depending on how many contracts were available. Given the low volume in platinum contracts recently and given how late you called in, you figure there is about a .3 chance you got one contract, a .6 chance you got two, and a .1 chance that you got three.

You decide to seek out further information on the future of platinum prices. A very nervous metals broker gave you distribution on the closing trading price one year from now.

a. Draw the influence diagram for this problem. Is there any information not reflected in the influence diagram, and, if so, how does the influence diagram relate to it?

b. Discretize the distribution into a chance node whose branches have probabilities of .25, .50, and .25. What is the expected price of platinum one year from now?

c. Put together the complete probability tree describing your profit if you hold on to however many contracts you get until fulfillment. Assume you can buy the platinum you need to fulfill the contract(s) just before you need it. What is your expected profit from holding the contract(s)?

d. Discretize the distribution again, but this time into a two-branch node with probabilities of .5 and .5; then incorporate this node into the complete probability tree. Now, perform probability sensitivity analysis on the probabilities for platinum price by systematically changing the pair of probabilities—for instance, (1, 0), (.9, .1), (.8, .2), and so on. At what probability of the high level of platinum price does your expected profit from holding the contracts become negative?

e. Is this insight reflected in the influence diagram? Why or why not?

2.15 Show that balancing areas in the discretization process is equivalent to choosing the expected value given that you are in the range. The expected value, given you are in the range $a \leq x \leq b$, is:

$$\frac{\int_a^b xf(x)dx}{\int_a^b f(x)dx}$$

where f is the probability density, and the cumulative probability density is

$$P(x)_{\leq} = \int_{-\infty}^x x'f(x')dx'$$

(Hint: you will probably need to do an integration by parts.)

3

Decisions Under Uncertainty

What Is a Good Decision? _____

One common way people distinguish good decisions from bad ones is by looking at the results of the decision. Most people, however, realize this criterion is not very satisfactory. For one thing, while the results may not be apparent until much later, we would like to immediately characterize the decision as good or bad. In addition, all we see are the results of the chosen alternative—there is usually no way to see the results that would have occurred if a rejected alternative had been chosen and, thus, no way to see whether we have really chosen the better alternative. Most troublesome, however, is evaluating the situation when someone "lucks out" with what seems to us undeservedly good results. Should you call the decision "good" in this case and reward the decision-maker accordingly?

One of the fundamental benefits of decision analysis is that it can distinguish good decisions from bad ones. Furthermore, it provides a criterion for establishing whether a decision is good or bad.

Decision analysis starts by defining exactly what a decision is—the commitment of resources that is revocable only at some cost. If we do not commit resources, it is almost meaningless to say we have made a decision. The alternative "Do nothing" is a commitment of resources in the sense that an opportunity has been rejected.

Decision analysis, then, clearly lays out the four elements of rational decision-making (Figure 3–1). The first element is information, or "What do I know about the world and the business or personal opportunity under consideration?" An important component of this knowledge is an assessment of uncertainty (or "What *don't* I know?") The second element is alternatives, or "What courses of action are open to me?" The third element is values, or "What do I want?" Finally, there's logic, or "How do I put knowledge, alternatives, and values together to arrive at a decision?"

Figure 3–1

The Elements of a Good Decision Analysis Process

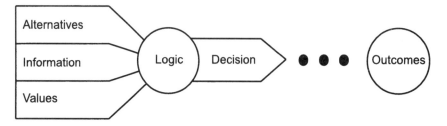

Given these elements, we can now characterize a good decision as one that is logically consistent with the alternatives, information, and values brought to the decision. In the decision analysis process, we can explicitly record the principal inputs to the decision-making process and establish that a good decision was made *before* the results of the decision are known. This minimizes the problem of "Monday-morning quarterbacking," which can have an insidious effect on the morale of a company. Furthermore, in decision analysis, you can disagree with the information or values the decision-maker brings to the problem to the extent that you would have chosen another alternative—and still say that the decision-maker made a good decision. In corporate practice, other sets of information (and values, if appropriate) can be substituted in the evaluation for the decision-maker's. By doing this, we can test not only whether the same alternative would be chosen, but also what the loss in value would be from choosing the other alternative. These results could then be filed as sort of a minority report to the record of the decision.

Why is it important to be able to determine whether a decision is good or bad? For one thing, the decision-maker will sleep better realizing that, given the time and resources available, he or she has done the best job possible. In addition, in corporate decisions (such as those made by electric utility companies), it may later be necessary to justify to stockholders, regulators, or other stakeholders that a good decision was made, even though a bad outcome ensued. Finally, we like to identify people who make good decisions so that they can be rewarded and promoted. Judging by results rather than by good decisions discourages people from taking a course of action with any risk in it—unless the results will not be known until the distant future!

One frequent objection to this definition of a good decision is, "That all sounds fine, but, in reality, it's results that count, and you can't tell me that in the real world a decision that leads to bad results is a good decision!" For operational decisions, there is much truth in that objection. However, there is seldom significant uncertainty in operational decisions. Consequently, if we correctly process the information available to us and follow up diligently, our decisions will usually lead to good results. It is in decisions involving significant uncertainty (typically strategic decisions) that the distinction between good decisions and good outcomes becomes important.

A second objection is that uncertainty represents inadequate knowledge and that a decision made with inadequate knowledge cannot be a good one: garbage in, garbage out. While the quality of the available information is certainly an important consideration, waiting for more information is frequently not advisable. Specifically, while the option of waiting and gathering more information to reduce the uncertainty should be included among the alternatives considered, information-gathering requires money (incurring information-gathering costs) and time (risking competitors' actions, opportunity lost, revenue lost). Furthermore, information-gathering will usually be incomplete and resolve only some of the uncertainty. Finally, some uncertainties cannot be resolved, either in principle or in practice, until the actual results occur. Decision analysis addresses these concerns explicitly with the value of information and value of control concepts and calculations, which are described in this chapter.

Recasting the Problem As a Decision Problem

Decision and Value Nodes

The president of Positronics was by now becoming uncomfortable with his decision to bid $500,000. Correction—He had not yet submitted the bid and committed himself, so he had not yet really made the decision! To ease his discomfort, he requested the analysis be redone for different bids. The facilitator suggested rephrasing the problem in terms of a decision tree, which would not only automatically handle different potential bids, but would also allow further analysis to clarify the decision. The facilitator first added the decision to the influence diagram, using a rectangle to denote it. Then she drew an arrow from the decision node to the profit node, since the level of bid affects the profit. Finally, she changed the double oval around the Profit node to a double octagon to denote the fact that profit is the criterion to be used when making the decision.

——————————— Figure 3–2 ———————————

Influence Diagram of the Positronics Bid Decision

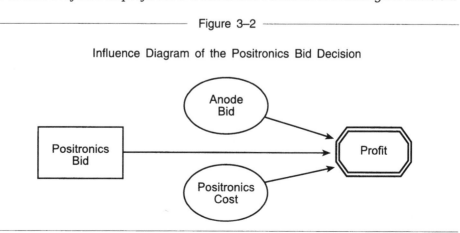

In Figure 3–2, we have introduced the remaining elements of influence diagrams. In Chapter 2, we saw the uncertainty node (represented by an oval), the deterministic node (represented by a double oval), and influences (represented by arrows.) Here, we introduce the decision and value nodes and extend the concept of influence.

A *rectangle* represents a decision. Inside the rectangle is a descriptor (or variable name) to identify the set of events (or the quantities) among which the decision-maker is choosing.

An octagon represents a value node, inside which is a descriptor of the value measure. The value measure is the quantity that the decision-maker uses in making decisions; as discussed later in this chapter, the decision-maker will choose the alternative that maximizes some function of the value measure. The value node is just a chance node drawn with a special symbol to represent its special role.

A *double octagon* represents a value node that has ceased to be an uncertainty because all the uncertainty has been expressed in the nodes that influence it. It is just a deterministic node with a special role with respect to decisions.

The arrow now has added meaning. The basic concept of an arrow is flow of knowledge: the person providing the probability distribution for the node at the head of the arrow has information about what happened at the node at the base of the arrow. In addition, when decision nodes are involved, this information flow implies a chronology. The following are the four ways in which an arrow can be used:

- *Uncertainty Node to Uncertainty Node*—The outcome of the uncertainty at the base of the arrow is provided when probabilities are assigned for the node at the head of the arrow. This means that the probabilities at the node at the head of the arrow are conditional on the resolution of the uncertainty at the base of the arrow. (Conditional probabilities are treated extensively in Chapter 4.) For the special case of a deterministic node at the head of the arrow, the influence means that the resolution of the uncertainty at the base of the arrow provides a value to be used in the deterministic node.
- *Decision Node to Uncertainty Node*—The alternative chosen at the base of the arrow is provided when probabilities are assigned for the node at the head of the arrow. This means that the probabilities at the node at the head of the arrow are conditional on the alternative chosen at the base of the arrow. This means that the decision is made *before* the resolution of the uncertainty.
- *Uncertainty Node to Decision Node*—The outcome of the uncertainty at the base of the arrow is known when the decision is made. This means the uncertainty is resolved (and the results learned) *before* the decision is made.
- *Decision Node to Decision Node*—The alternative chosen at the base of the arrow is known and remembered when the deci-

sion is made at the head of the arrow. This implies that the decision at the base of the arrow is made *before* the decision at the head of the arrow.

"Information flow" means that information is available to the person providing the probabilities or making the decision. Thus, we could have a node "Sales, 2005" influencing "Sales, 2003." This would not imply backward causality in time! Rather, it would mean that the person providing probabilities for Sales, 2003 would be given information on the Sales, 2005 outcome: "If you knew Sales, 2005 were high, what would be the probability distribution for Sales, 2003?"

Rules for Constructing Influence Diagrams

To construct an influence diagram, follow the procedure outlined in Chapter 2. Two elements must be added to this procedure. First, decision nodes (drawn as rectangles) are to be identified in addition to the uncertainties as we work back from the one key uncertainty. Second, one uncertainty should be enclosed in an octagon to indicate its role as the value measure for decision-making.

Four rules must be obeyed if you wish to construct meaningful influence diagrams.

1. *No Loops*—If you follow the arrows from node to node, there must be no path that leads you back to where you started. This is most readily understood in terms of the information flow indicated by the arrows.

2. *Single Decision-Maker*—There should be just one value measure (octagon) and all decisions should be made to maximize the same function (expected value or certain equivalent) of this value.

3. *No Forgetting Previous Decisions*—Each decision should be connected to every other decision by an arrow. This will establish the order in which the decisions are made and indicate that the decision-maker remembers all his previous choices.

4. *No Forgetting Previously Known Information*—If there is an arrow from an uncertainty node to a decision node, there should be an arrow from that uncertainty node to all subsequent decision nodes.

Constructing the Decision Tree

After some discussion, the Positronics staff identified four different alternatives for analysis—three levels of bid ($300,000, $500,000, and $700,000) and the alternative not to bid. The square at the branching point in the tree in Figure 3–3 indicates a decision node, and each branch is an alternative. There are no probabilities associated with the branches because the node represents a decision, not an uncertainty. The value node now needs some modification because it is influenced by the decision node.

——————————————————— Figure 3–3 ———————————————————

Data Describing Positronics' Decision

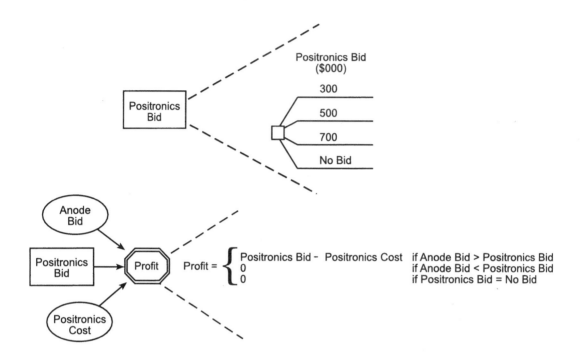

To join the pieces in a tree, we must be a little more careful than we were in the approach described in Chapter 2. The following procedure will transform an influence diagram into a decision tree.

1. Arrange the decision nodes such that all arrows with a decision node at their base or head point to the right-hand side of the page. Arrows pointing to or emanating from decision nodes imply a chronology that must be followed in decision trees. By convention, the chronology of decisions in a decision tree flows from left to right, and therefore, these arrows must point from left to right.

2. Arrange the uncertainty nodes so that no uncertainty node is to the left of a decision node unless there is an arrow from that node to the decision node. In a decision tree, the outcome of a node to the left of a decision node is known to the decision-maker when he or she makes the decision; in an influence diagram, this means there is an arrow from the uncertainty node to the decision node.

3. Arrange, insofar as possible, the uncertainty nodes so that all arrows point to the right. This will cause conditional probabilities to be displayed simply on the tree.

4. Make the deterministic value node a tree endpoint node. This will usually involve calculations to find the value associated with each combination of events at the nodes that influence the value node.
5. Now convert the diagram to a decision tree. Draw the content of the leftmost node in tree form. To obtain the complete tree, draw the content of the next node at the end of each branch of the preceding node, and repeat this process until all the nodes are drawn. To obtain the schematic tree, draw the contents of the node in order, with the understanding that each branch of a node leads to the node to its right.

Figure 3–4 is the rearranged influence diagram for Positronics and the schematic tree. Some common sense modification of this last step is needed in asymmetric situations. For instance, the No Bid branch of the decision need not be joined to the Anode Bid node or the Positronics Cost node, since both these nodes are irrelevant if no bid is made.

Figure 3–4

Translating the Influence Diagram into a Schematic Decision Tree

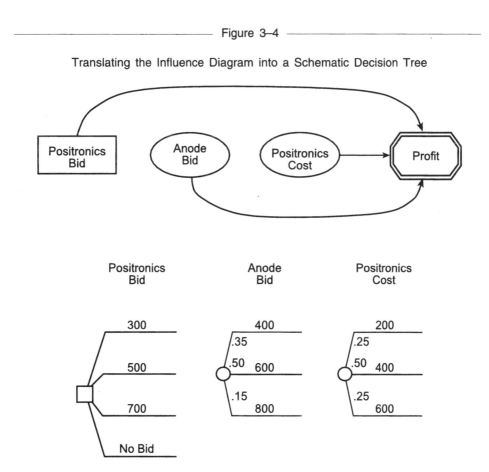

Decision or Uncertainty?

Graphic conventions are important in forming both influence diagrams and decision trees. As we have noted, a decision node is represented graphically by a square or rectangle, while chance nodes are represented by circles or ovals. This graphic convention helps to avoid confusion about what is a decision variable (completely under the decision-maker's control) and what is an uncertainty (or chance) variable (completely out of the decision-maker's control).

The distinction between decision and chance variables is occasionally not as clear cut as we might think. Sometimes the facilitator can choose which variables are decision variables and which are chance variables. For instance, the price of a product and the volume of sales cannot normally *both* be decision variables. You can set the price and then let the market determine the quantity sold or you can set the volume sold and then let the market determine the effective price realized. If nothing in the structure of the problem dictates which is the decision variable, the facilitator must decide. In making the choice, the facilitator should consider the impact of the choice on modeling the problem and on assessing probabilities. What is the easy or natural way to model? How do people think about the problem? How will it be easiest to assess probabilities?

There are several important differences in handling decision nodes and probability nodes. A decision node does not have any probabilities associated with the branches. Consequently, for the rollback procedure for tree evaluation introduced in Chapter 2, instead of replacing the node with its expected value (as we do with a chance node), we replace a decision node with the value of the branch that has the maximum value to the decision-maker. In other words, at a decision node we choose the alternative (branch) that gives us the most of what we want.

The order of nodes in the probability tree was fairly arbitrary, dictated mainly by the requirements of how people think best about the uncertainties. In a decision tree, however, the ordering of nodes implies a sequence of events. Time proceeds from left to right in the tree. If two decisions occur in a tree, the decision to the right is made after the one to the left; and the decision-maker remembers the choice made in the first decision when making the second decision. In addition, the uncertainty of any chance nodes that occur to the left of a decision node is resolved before the decision is made. That is, the decision-maker knows what actually happened before having to make the decision. However, node ordering is important only relative to the decision nodes. The ordering of the chance nodes relative to one another is still arbitrary. Thus, in Figure 3–4, Positronics makes its bid decision before it knows Anode's bid and before it knows what its own costs will be.

The outcomes or branches of a decision node should be a list of significantly different alternatives. Unlike the outcomes at a chance node, the list of alternatives at a decision node need not be mutually exclusive and collectively exhaustive (mutually exclusive: you cannot choose more than one branch; collectively exhaustive: every possible alternative is represented by a branch). However, if the alternatives are not mutually exclusive, confusion may arise. It is very important to have a list of significantly different alternatives. (A collectively exhaustive list of alternatives is impossible for all but the simplest problems.)

Finding even a few truly different alternatives requires creative thinking before and during the decision analysis process. All too often, the decision process is hobbled by a lack of genuinely innovative possibilities. In the Positronics bidding case, we are looking only at different bid levels. Other alternatives might involve forming a joint venture to bid with another company more experienced in building this kind of instrument, performing some cost studies before bidding (we consider this later in the chapter), or exploring the possibility that MegaCorp would accept a bid of some fixed markup on cost (with appropriate safeguards against irresponsibility in cost overruns).

Building the Tree

We have already done most of the work required to build the tree. The schematic tree has been created (Figure 3–4) and the value to be placed at the end of each of the branches has been determined. The complete tree is shown in Figure 3–5.

Each bid decision branch has its own probability distribution on Profit. Using the method developed in Chapter 2, we can construct the cumulative probability distributions for our decision tree (Figure 3–6). The staircase appearance is a result of the discrete approximation used in constructing the tree. If more branches had been used, the curves would be smoother. The data in Figure 3–6 show the "risks and rewards" associated with each of the alternatives. The decision-maker now has the data needed to make the decision.

Which alternatives are risky and which are conservative? Often, the high bids ($700,000 in this case) are considered safer or more conservative because there is no possibility of losing money. However, we could also view the high bid as being the less conservative course of action: we are seeking to make a great deal of money, but since we probably will not make any money at all (because we probably will lose the bid), we are undertaking a great risk.

Notice the ambiguities in the preceding paragraph. "Risk" has so many ill-defined meanings that it is often better to avoid the word entirely. We will, however, use it in several well-defined contexts such as "risk attitude" and "risk penalty," as discussed in Chapter 5. Another problem word is "conservative," the meaning of which depends on our viewpoint and on the relevant values. When applied to estimates, conservative means a number the estimator thinks will result in a safe or conservative decision—according to his or her viewpoint. There is no point in giving "conservative" estimates for chance variables; they give an inaccurate estimate of the total uncertainty and often distort the results in unanticipated ways. It is much better

────────────────────────── Figure 3–5 ──────────────────────────

Completed Decision Tree

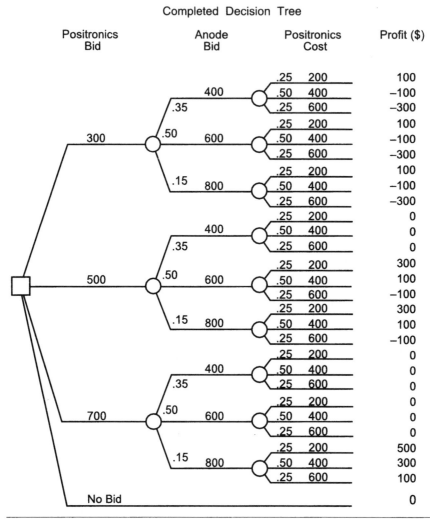

Positronics Bid	Anode Bid	Positronics Cost		Profit ($)
		.25	200	100
	400	.50	400	−100
	.35	.25	600	−300
		.25	200	100
300 .50	600	.50	400	−100
		.25	600	−300
		.25	200	100
.15	800	.50	400	−100
		.25	600	−300
		.25	200	0
	400	.50	400	0
	.35	.25	600	0
		.25	200	300
500 .50	600	.50	400	100
		.25	600	−100
		.25	200	300
.15	800	.50	400	100
		.25	600	−100
		.25	200	0
	400	.50	400	0
	.35	.25	600	0
		.25	200	0
700 .50	600	.50	400	0
		.25	600	0
		.25	200	500
.15	800	.50	400	300
		.25	600	100
No Bid				0

to put in the best information through the probability distribution and to let the decision-maker make the decision.

Decision Criterion ─────────────────────────────────────

How do we make decisions under uncertainty? For a simple tree with a single decision node (such as Figure 3–5), the decision-maker can stare at the probability distribution on value associated with each of the alternatives and make the decision. Figure 3–6 shows the results of combining all the information logically and consistently. Because only three branches were used for Positronics' Cost, the graph is difficult to read. If the underlying data from Figure 2–14 were discretized into very many branches, the second graph in Figure 3–6 would result.

Figure 3–6

Probability Distribution on Profits for Alternative Bid Decisions

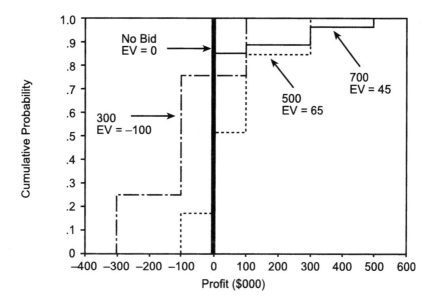

Probability Distribution on Profits for Alternative Bid Decisions
With Many Branches for Positronics Cost Node Discretization

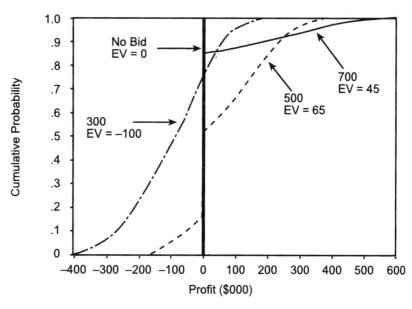

However, for more complicated trees with multiple decision nodes, this procedure is impractical. We need a decision criterion that indicates the best choices and that helps the decision-maker choose consistently. The decision-maker's true decision criterion is embedded in the values he or she brings to the decision. Thus, the decision criterion is highly personal. But there are common characteristics that can help the decision-maker (and the decision facilitator) model these values and obtain a systematic decision criterion.

In most business and personal financial decisions, money is the primary value and maximizing wealth is the principal decision criterion. To express the value function completely in monetary terms, however, we must be able to express nonmonetary items in monetary terms. To do this, we must deal with the following three subjects:

- The value of nonmonetary, intangible goods
- The value of future money
- The trade-off between certainty and uncertainty.

The Value of Nonmonetary, Intangible Goods

When the principal value function of a tree is given in monetary terms, all values to be included in the tree must also be in monetary terms, including such intangible items as goodwill, worker safety, and laying off workers. Usually, obtaining estimates of monetary equivalents for these so-called intangibles is not difficult, though the decision-maker might not want the value needlessly publicized.

Many items that are referred to as intangibles are not really intangible, but rather are difficult to put a value on. For instance, increased goodwill may result in direct economic effects from increased sales or decreased transaction costs. This is not an intangible but rather an effect that is difficult to estimate. After this has been separated out, you can address the intangible part of the value that stockholders and managers attach to goodwill.

Establishing values for intangibles is not an attempt to disguise moral or social irresponsibility. Moral and social responsibility should be built into the initial choice of acceptable alternatives. Nor are intangible value trade-offs an attempt to put a price on intangibles such as happiness. The goal is to appropriately represent the trade-offs people make in practice in order to include them in economic decision-making.

In most business decisions, intangibles with even the most generous trade-offs have little effect on the value of the decision alternatives. In the rare case in which intangibles are important in the problem, the decision-maker must examine his or her values with much more care than outlined here.

In societal decisions, determining the value function is much more difficult. Societal decisions, such as road design or worker safety legislation, typically involve a trade-off between resources measured in monetary terms and in terms of human life and welfare. While there are a number of ways to deal with these decisions rationally, they are beyond usual business decision analysis practice.

The Value of Future Money

In the previous section, we expressed the value function in monetary terms. This reduces multiple time-varying uncertain results to a single time-varying uncertain result. This result is typically expressed as a stream of money stretching many years into the future. The value of money received in the future is not the same as that of money received today. Some people have immediate, productive uses for their capital while others do not; and if they do not, they can always lend (invest) their money to someone else for a fee (interest). Banks and other financial institutions establish a marketplace between present and future funds. The relationship between present and future funds is expressed in terms of a discount rate or an interest rate. The present value of cash, c_i, received years i from now is:

$$\frac{c_i}{(1+d)^i} \tag{3–1}$$

where d is the discount rate the decision-maker wishes to use when trading off between present and future. (We discuss in Chapter 5 values that might be appropriate for the discount rate.) Using the present value formula, we can reduce the time series of cash extending m years in the future to a net present value (NPV):

$$NPV = \sum_{i=1}^{m} \frac{c_i}{(1+d)^i} \tag{3–2}$$

thus eliminating time from the decision criterion.

Our decision criterion is to maximize the NPV of future cash flows. We could also maximize the NPV of other monetary measures, but cash flow is ordinarily a very good measure of the net change in wealth of a company or an individual. Other monetary measures (net income, earnings per share, dividends, payback period, return on investment) tend to focus only on parts of the problem and can lead to bad decisions if used as criteria without sufficient care.

The internal rate of return (IRR) criterion, although similar to the NPV criterion, is difficult to apply meaningfully in an uncertain situation. This criterion can be used to choose the best alternative given certainty (i.e., the same choice as from an NPV), but it does not show how much more valuable this preferred alternative is than the others—and in choices under uncertainty, we *must* be able to balance how much we might win against how much we might lose.

The Trade-off Between Certainty and Uncertainty

In the preceding two steps, we have reduced multiple time-varying uncertain outcomes to an uncertain NPV. As we saw in Figure 3–6, uncertainty means that there are many possible NPVs with associated probabilities. How can we now choose between alternatives with different probability distributions on NPV?

In Chapter 2, we discussed the expected value: the sum of probabilities multiplied by their respective values. The expected value represents the average return we would expect to receive if we were engaging in many identical but uncorrelated ventures. If the stakes are not very high, it makes sense to use the expected value as the value of a probability distribution. As the stakes go up, most people begin to show risk-averse behavior: the value they assign to a probability distribution is less than its expected value. (This behavior is discussed in Chapter 5.) Most business decisions, however, are not really that large relative to the total value of the company, and maximizing the expected value of the NPV of cash flow is a good approximation of the actual decision criterion.

The president of Positronics had become rather befuddled during the discussion of values and trade-offs. It had been a long time since he had been forced to examine just what he was trying to accomplish in running Positronics. However, it turned out that the simple value function used in the tree was substantially correct. Winning the bid would not greatly alter the probability of obtaining future work with MegaCorp, so there was no follow-on value to be added. Losing the bid would not entail any layoffs, because managing the normal labor turnover would be sufficient. The job was routine enough that no intangibles, such as added reputation, were attached to winning the bid. The job would be done within a year, so discounting was not a problem. Finally, at least for the time being, the president was willing to use expected value of profit as a decision criterion. After all, the possible profits or losses from the job were not that important to the company's long-term success.

Analyzing the Tree _____

The complete tree is shown in Figure 3–7. The rollback procedure has been used to present the expected value for each of the decision alternatives. What should happen at the decision node? If expected value is the chosen decision criterion, then the decision rule is to choose the alternative with the maximum expected value. For this decision criterion, the best alternative is to bid $500,000. Note the arrow to indicate the chosen alternative.

We have said that there is no such thing as a "correct" probability. The only worry is whether the probability assessment adequately reflects the decision-maker's state of knowledge. Nevertheless, there is a natural desire to know how important a probability assessment is in the choice of the alternatives in the decision problem. To show this, you can perform probabilistic sensitivity analysis (also known as stochastic sensitivity

Figure 3–7

Rollback Evaluation of Tree

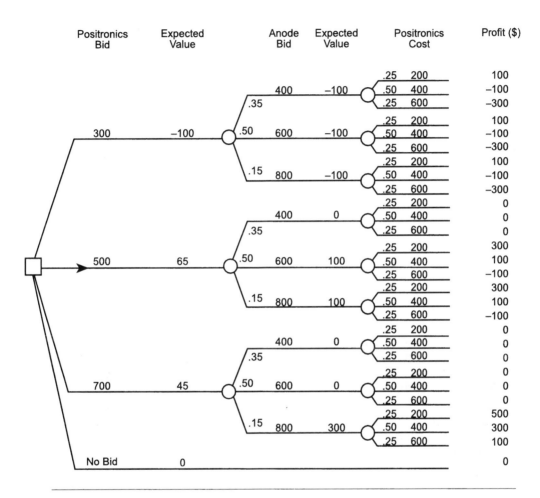

Positronics Bid	Expected Value	Anode Bid	Expected Value	Positronics Cost		Profit ($)
				.25	200	100
		400	−100	.50	400	−100
			.35	.25	600	−300
				.25	200	100
300	−100	.50 600	−100	.50	400	−100
				.25	600	−300
		.15 800	−100	.25	200	100
				.50	400	−100
				.25	600	−300
				.25	200	0
		400	0	.50	400	0
			.35	.25	600	0
				.25	200	300
500	65	.50 600	100	.50	400	100
				.25	600	−100
		.15 800	100	.25	200	300
				.50	400	100
				.25	600	−100
				.25	200	0
		400	0	.50	400	0
			.35	.25	600	0
				.25	200	0
700	45	.50 600	0	.50	400	0
				.25	600	0
		.15 800	300	.25	200	500
				.50	400	300
				.25	600	100
No Bid	0					0

analysis). In Figure 3–8, the horizontal axis is the probability assigned to the first (top) branch of node Positronics Cost; the rest of the probability is assigned to the bottom branch, and the middle branch is given zero probability. This two-branch approximation is used for ease of interpretation. There are other approximations which are sometimes appropriate. For instance, the probability of one branch can be varied while keeping the ratio of probabilities of the other branches fixed, as in the probability for Anode Bid in the two-node sensitivity example below.

The plot in Figure 3–8 shows that when the probability of low cost ($200,000) is high, the $500,000 bid is preferred. Below about 40 percent probability of low cost, the $700,000 bid (alternative 3) becomes preferred because the losses associated with the $500,000 bid become much more likely.

Figure 3–8

Probabilistic Sensitivity Plot

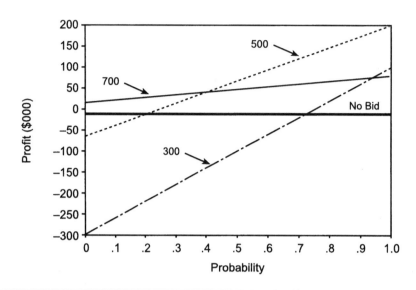

Probabilistic sensitivity to two nodes can be evaluated by systematically changing the probabilities at two nodes to determine the probability at which the decision choice switches.

Positronics felt that the relative likelihoods of the $800,000 and $600,000 values for the Anode bid were reasonable. The staff was much less certain about the probability of the low bid ($400,000). Some thought a bid this low was not typical of Anode; others thought Anode had enough experience in this area that it could hold costs very low and hence afford to bid low. To see how changes in the relative likelihood of the $800,000/$600,000 bid level and the $400,000 bid level affected their decision, they decided to do a probability sensitivity analysis with the constraints shown in equations 3–3 and 3–4.

We use the notation $p(X|S)$ to indicate the probability that X occurs, given the state of knowledge S. However, in performing probabilistic sensitivity analysis, we are continuously varying probabilities—implying that we are similarly varying the underlying state of knowledge S on which a probability depends. Because the state of knowledge is varying, we have replaced the S notation here by S' to indicate that a different state of knowledge is implied by each different probability.

$$\frac{p(AnodeBid = 600|S')}{p(AnodeBid = 800|S')} = \frac{.5}{.15} \tag{3–3}$$

$$p(PositronicsCost = 400|S') = 0 \tag{3–4}$$

In the display of sensitivity results (Figure 3–9), the X marks a point corresponding to the current state of information. [Since Positronics Cost has been changed from a three-branch node to a two-branch node, we have set p(Positronics Cost = 200 | S') = .5 to get the same expected value as the original tree.]

The graph shows that when p(Positronics Cost = 200 | S') is less than .4, bidding $700,000 is preferred. When p(Positronics Cost = 200 | S') and p(Anode Bid = 400 | S') are both high, bidding $300,000 is preferred.

Probabilistic sensitivities are often useful to settle arguments or to obtain consensus. If the same decision alternative is optimal for everyone's set of probabilities, then there is really no argument about what to do. If someone's probability indicates that he or she would choose a different alternative, then the plots show how much is "lost" by choosing the "wrong" alternative.

The Value of Perfect Information

The president of Positronics was satisfied by the results he had seen so far. He requested that the facilitators add more branches to the tree so he could zero in on the optimal bid. However, the facilitators suggested that they first examine other insights available from the tree: the value of information and the value of control.

One of the powerful features of decision analysis is the ability to show the value of resolving an uncertainty *before* making the decision. The simplest approach is to calculate the value of perfect information (also called the value of clairvoyance). Imagine that we had some means of obtaining information to completely resolve an uncertainty before we made our decision. (Perhaps a clairvoyant's services were available.) What is the

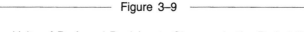

Figure 3–9

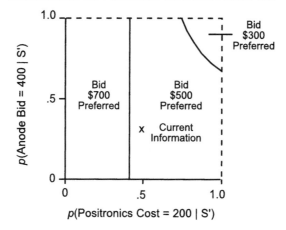

Sensitivity of Preferred Decision to Changes in the Probability Assessments for Positronics Cost and Anode Bid

maximum we should pay for this information? This value, which turns out to be easy to calculate, is the upper limit of the amount we should be willing to spend on any information-gathering effort, which generally yields imperfect rather than perfect information. Incidentally, we often find companies spending more on information-gathering than it is worth.

To calculate the value of perfect information on Anode's bid, Positronics introduced a new decision at the front end of the tree (Figure 3–10). The first node in this tree is the decision whether or not to obtain the perfect information. If Positronics does not obtain the information, it faces the tree following the "No" branch, which is identical to the tree evaluated in Figure 3–7. Thus, for the "No" branch, Positronics already knows it should choose to bid $500,000, resulting in an expected value of $65,000.

If the company decides to obtain the information (the "Yes" branch), it must pay the cost of the information. It then faces a tree similar to the original one, but with the first and second nodes reversed, because Anode's bid is known before the decision is made. A way to represent this subtree at the end of the "Yes" branch is to add an arrow from the Anode Bid node to

Figure 3–10

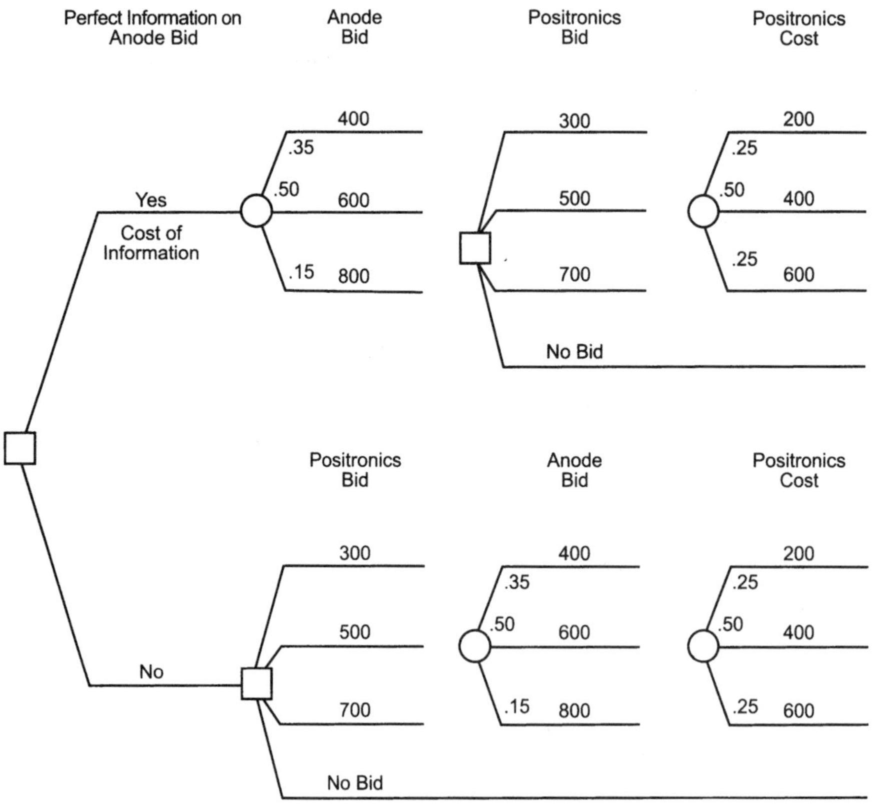

Decision Tree to Determine the Value of Perfect Information on Anode's Bid

the Positronics Bid node in the influence diagram (Figure 3–11). This indicates that the uncertainty on Anode's bid is resolved before the Positronics bid decision is made. The corresponding tree is shown in Figure 3–12.

Note that the probabilities for Anode Bid are the same as before—if we thought there is a 35 percent chance of Anode's bid being $400,000, then we should think there is a 35 percent chance that the perfect information-gathering activity (or the clairvoyant) will reveal that Anode's bid is $400,000. The tree in Figure 3–10 could be evaluated for varying costs of information until the expected value of the "Yes" (obtain information) alternative is equal to the expected value of the no-information alternative. This would then reveal the value of obtaining the (perfect) information—the maximum cost Positronics would be willing to incur to obtain it.

However, there is a simpler approach. The expected value of $95,000 for the tree in Figure 3–12 is the value of the venture with perfect information. We can then calculate the value of the perfect information as follows:

$$
\begin{aligned}
\text{Value of Information} &= \text{Value with Information} \\
&\quad - \text{Value Without Information} \\
&= \$95,000 - \$65,000 \\
&= \$30,000
\end{aligned}
\tag{3–5}
$$

Similar calculations show that value of the venture with perfect information on Positronics' cost is $85,000 (Figure 3–13). The value of perfect information on Positronics' cost can be calculated to be $85,000 – $65,000 = $20,000.

Note that the value of information on two or more variables is *not* the sum of the values of information of each variable separately—it can be smaller or greater. In this case, the sum of the values of information on both variables separately is $30,000 + $20,000 = $50,000. This is smaller than $51,300, the value of information on both variables simultaneously.

We can gain further insight into the value of information by examining the portion of the tree as it would appear for the "Yes" branch of Figure 3–10. This subtree is displayed in Figure 3–12. Note that the only change

—————————————— Figure 3–11 ——————————————

Adding an Arrow from Anode Bid to Positronics Bid

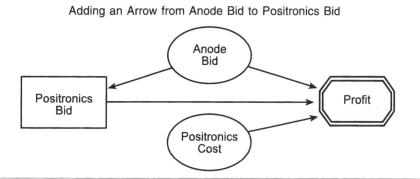

──────────────────────── Figure 3–12 ────────────────────────

Subtree for "Yes" Branch for Perfect Information on Anode Bid

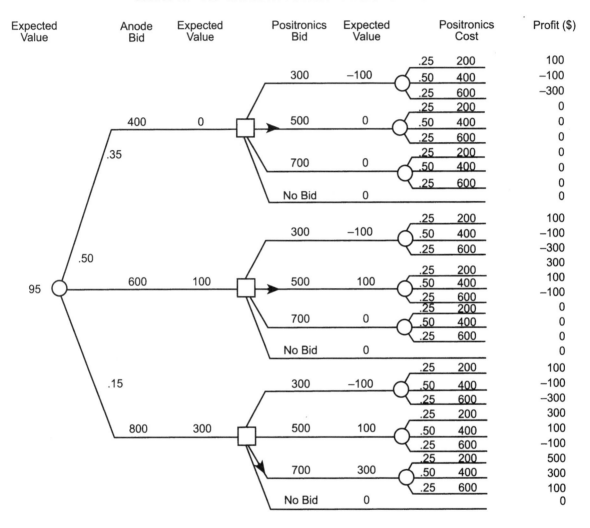

Expected Value	Anode Bid	Expected Value	Positronics Bid	Expected Value	Positronics Cost		Profit ($)
					.25	200	100
			300	−100	.50	400	−100
					.25	600	−300
					.25	200	0
	400	0	500	0	.50	400	0
					.25	600	0
	.35				.25	200	0
			700	0	.50	400	0
					.25	600	0
			No Bid	0			0
					.25	200	100
			300	−100	.50	400	−100
					.25	600	−300
	.50				.25	200	300
95	600	100	500	100	.50	400	100
					.25	600	−100
					.25	200	0
			700	0	.50	400	0
					.25	600	0
			No Bid	0			0
					.25	200	100
	.15		300	−100	.50	400	−100
					.25	600	−300
					.25	200	300
	800	300	500	100	.50	400	100
					.25	600	−100
					.25	200	500
			700	300	.50	400	300
					.25	600	100
			No Bid	0			0

that Positronics would make would be to change its bid from $500,000 to $700,000 if it knew that Anode were going to bid $800,000. Making this change in bid changes the expected value in that case from $100,000 to $300,000, for a net improvement of $200,000. But there is only a .15 chance of finding that Anode will bid $800,000. Therefore, the expected improvement in value is .15 × 200,000 = $30,000. This is the value of the information for Anode Bid—the same answer as obtained above.

Thus, information has value if knowing the results could lead us to change our decision. If none of the possible information-gathering results change the decision, there is no value to the information.

——————————————— Figure 3–13 ———————————————

Subtree for "Yes" Branch for Perfect Information on Positronics' Cost

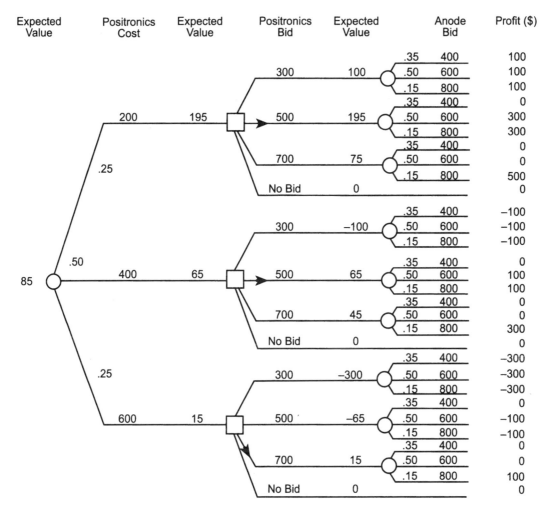

Expected Value	Positronics Cost	Expected Value	Positronics Bid	Expected Value		Anode Bid	Profit ($)
					.35	400	100
			300	100	.50	600	100
					.15	800	100
					.35	400	0
	200	195	500	195	.50	600	300
					.15	800	300
	.25				.35	400	0
			700	75	.50	600	0
					.15	800	500
			No Bid	0			0
					.35	400	−100
			300	−100	.50	600	−100
					.15	800	−100
	.50				.35	400	0
85	400	65	500	65	.50	600	100
					.15	800	100
					.35	400	0
			700	45	.50	600	0
					.15	800	300
			No Bid	0			0
					.35	400	−300
	.25		300	−300	.50	600	−300
					.15	800	−300
					.35	400	0
	600	15	500	−65	.50	600	−100
					.15	800	−100
					.35	400	0
			700	15	.50	600	0
					.15	800	100
			No Bid	0			0

The value-of-information tree illustrates a number of powerful concepts. We believe that for many people, a change in perspective must occur
before they understand the value of information calculation. ("Oh, is that
what you mean?!") Understanding the concepts behind value of information is crucial to understanding and effectively using decision trees.

Positronics' president was impressed with the ideas implied in calculating
the value of information. Since new information on Anode's bid was not
obtainable by any ethical means, value of information was of only academic
interest; most sources of information, such as information on prior bids, publicly

available information on Anode's backlog, etc., had already been used in the probability estimates. Some information on what Positronics' cost might be was obtainable for considerably less than the value of perfect information of $20,000. This information would be obtained by using some off-the-shelf components to build a prototype instrument. The president encouraged production to go ahead with its prototype, provided the cost of the program was well under $20,000.

The Value of Perfect Control

Decision trees produce one more piece of information: the value of control (also called the value of wizardry). If a clairvoyant (someone who can foresee the future) is valuable to us, a wizard (someone who can change the future) is even more valuable. The effect of perfect control is that we could pick which one of the future (or otherwise unknown) possibilities (branches) we wanted to happen. Thus, the value with perfect control for Positronics' cost can be obtained by inspecting the tree with the Positronics Cost node moved to the front of the tree (Figure 3–13).

Inspecting the top branch shows that if there were some way to force Positronics' cost to be $200,000, it would yield an expected value of $195,000. (A more straightforward but time-consuming way of obtaining this result is to change the probability that Positronics' cost is $200,000 to 1.0 and then roll back the tree.) The calculation of the value of perfect control is similar to the calculation of the value of information.

$$
\begin{aligned}
\text{Value of Perfect Control} \ &= \text{Value with Perfect Control} \\
&\quad - \text{Value Without Perfect Control} \\
&= \$195,000 - \$65,000 \\
&= \$130,000 \qquad\qquad\qquad (3\text{–}6)
\end{aligned}
$$

How can we interpret the value of perfect control? The probabilities for cost were obtained under the assumption that Positronics would use its normal cost control procedures. Control might, therefore, correspond to the alternative of instituting some extraordinary cost control procedures to make sure costs stay as low as possible. The value of perfect control gives an upper limit on the amount Positronics should be willing to spend on such cost control procedures.

Summary

Given our understanding of uncertainties and their different possible outcomes, it is possible to define a good decision as one that is logically consistent with the information, alternatives, and values brought to the decision.

We introduced a decision on the bid level into the Positronics example and showed the probability distributions on profits for each bid level. It is clear that whatever bid level is chosen, there is some possibility of a bad outcome; and yet it would seem wrong to characterize a bid of $500,000 or $700,000 as a bad decision. The problem is choosing the better of the two levels.

We then discussed criteria for making a decision, including the value of nonmonetary, intangible goods; the value of future money; and the trade-off between certainty and uncertainty. (The trade-off between certainty and uncertainty is discussed at greater length in Chapter 5.)

By defining these valuations and trade-offs, we were able to calculate the preferred decision for the Positronics decision tree and to examine the sensitivity of the value of the preferred decision to changes in the probability assessment.

The analysis was expanded by the introduction of the value of perfect information and of perfect control. As illustrated by the modified trees used to calculate these values, information or control only has a value when it changes the preferred decision from what it otherwise would have been.

For Positronics, a small information gathering exercise on cost appeared justified. Much more valuable would be a cost control program.

Problems and Discussion Topics _____

3.1   It is very common for people to judge the quality of a decision by looking at its outcomes. Is this an unbiased point of view? How can you best deal with uncertainty to make a decision?

3.2   A good decision is defined as one that is logically consistent with the information, alternatives, and values brought to the decision. Give an example from your own experience (or perhaps from history) of a good decision/bad outcome and bad decision/good outcome. How could the bad decision have been improved? Remember that a good decision only has to be consistent with the information available at the time of the decision, though value of information should reveal the importance of the things you do not know.

Possible examples from history are: good decision/bad outcome—sailing on the Titanic (Who would have thought that the safest ship afloat would sink on its maiden voyage?); bad decision/good outcome—assigning Michelangelo to paint the Sistine Chapel (Who would have thought that a sculptor could paint on such a vast scale?).

3.3   Describe the information, alternatives, values, and logic you used in deciding where to eat dinner the last time you went out. Afterwards, were you satisfied with the decision? Was the outcome good or bad?

3.4   How is getting the expected value different for decision trees than for probability trees?

3.5   Net present value (NPV) and expected value are abstract concepts in that people usually will not get the NPV of a cash flow (unless they are buying or selling an annuity) or the expected value of a lottery. NPV is usually understood as the result of a trade-off between future value and present value; expected value is regarded as a way to deal with or evaluate an uncertainty that is unresolved.

Write a short definition of each term. How are these concepts implemented in decision tree calculations?

3.6   List two radically different alternatives to getting your homework done (other than doing it yourself). Are these alternatives worth pursuing further? Why or why not? (Relate them to your values, the probability of getting caught, and the consequences of getting caught; to the effect when you take the midterm exam; etc.)

3.7   Today, liability for damages is usually settled with a cash sum, whereas in the past, the rule was often blood for blood. (Consider Oedipus, for instance.) One rationale is not that the victim is being bought off (i.e., that money is equivalent to his or her pain), but rather that given that the incident has already occurred, the victim can use the money for some purpose whose value to him or her can help compensate for any losses. In addition, there are sometimes punitive damages to punish the malefactor.

Do you agree with this concept of trading money for pain and suffering? Do you find it more, less, or just as moral as the earlier method of compensation? Another alternative is no compensation. Suppose you are a victim. Do these two types of compensation mean anything different for you? Why or why not?

3.8   Anyone lending money at interest is establishing a marketplace between present and future money. The relationship between present and future is described by the interest rate. The marketplace works because some people have capital that would otherwise be unproductive if they did not lend it to people with a better use for it. List at least three reasons why people (or companies) might have different time values of money (discount rates).

3.9   As with discount rates, people can have different attitudes to trading off certainty and uncertainty. List at least three reasons why people might have different attitudes toward risk. For instance, some people have dependents and some don't. Why might a person's risk attitude change over time? Can education play a role in this?

3.10 List some of the principal values that must be considered in making decisions in a profit-making, publicly held hospital. Suggest the structure of a value model that establishes trade-offs between the values (at a deterministic level). State the limitations of the model. Are there ethical questions that cannot be simply resolved?

3.11 Explain how (if at all) the purpose of an influence diagram is different from that of a decision tree. Would it ever make sense to draw a tree and *then* the influence diagram? If so, when?

3.12 Can an equivalent decision tree *always* be drawn from an influence diagram and vice versa, or are there structural and/or informational differences that would make it impossible to do so without changing the problem or adding information? If there are differences, illustrate them with examples.

3.13 There are two main reasons for doing probabilistic sensitivity analysis in a decision-making process. First, probability assignments could change because of new information or could be different if there is more than one decision-maker. In each case, we need to know how the decision will change given changes in probabilities (information).

Second, probability sensitivity can distinguish the major uncertainties that are most influential to the decision from those that are less influential. This may increase understanding of the decision, provide directions for further information-gathering activity, etc.

Interpret Figure 3–8, the probabilistic sensitivity plot. If there are crossover points between alternatives, how do you interpret the corresponding crossover probabilities?

3.14 Draw an influence diagram that corresponds to the tree in Figure 3–10. (Hint: Introduce a deterministic node called Information Learned About Anode Bid.)

3.15 Suppose you are going skiing this weekend for the first time. However, you are worried about the possibility of breaking your leg during your first time out. Your alternative is to go to the beach. After thinking about the possibilities, you have decided that you value a weekend of skiing with no mishaps at $1,000 and that you value a broken leg at –$5,000. Going to the beach instead is worth $500 to you. Finally, after talking to other people, you peg the chance of breaking your leg at 1 in 100.

   a. Draw the influence diagram for this problem.
   b. Structure the decision tree for this problem. What is the preferred decision and expected value?
   c. Calculate the values of information and control on breaking your leg. To do this, you will have to symmetrize the tree so that the uncertainty on breaking your leg follows both the ski and beach alternatives.
   d. What impact might the values of information and control have on your choice of weekend?
   e. For what probabilities of breaking your leg do you prefer going to the beach?

3.16 You are considering four different restaurants for dinner with a group of friends tonight. However, before deciding whether or not to eat at a restaurant, you'll want to look at the menu and see what they have. At that point, you can either stay and eat or move on to the next restaurant. You value the cost of gathering everybody up and driving to the next restaurant at $20.

When you look at a menu, you have a scale in mind for rating it. You'll assign a score of A, B, or C and value the scores for their contributions to the evening's enjoyment as follows.

Score	Value
A	$100
B	$50
C	$0

You judge your four possible choices as equally likely to get any of the three scores.

- a. Draw the influence diagram and decision tree for this problem.
- b. What is the best strategy for picking a restaurant, and what is the overall expected value?
- c. Suppose you can buy a restaurant guide for $20 that will alert you to any C restaurants. Modify your influence diagram and tree to reflect this choice. Should you buy it?

3.17 Raquel Ratchet is working on a Volkswagen Beetle to be sold at a collectors' car sale on Saturday. If she finishes it in time, she'll be able to sell it for $1,000, at a cost of $100 in parts. (She got the car from a junkyard.) She thinks there's a 60 percent chance of being able to do this.

She also has the option of installing a turbocharger and intercooler in the car, which would quadruple the horsepower and enable her to sell it for $10,000. This would cost an additional $1,000 in parts. She thinks there's only a 20 percent chance of being able to finish this amount of work by Saturday. If she misses the collectors' sale on Saturday, Raquel figures she can only sell the car for $400 ($1,400 with turbocharger and intercooler).

Suddenly, the Wizard appears in the form of a good salesman and tells her that he can increase the selling price to $20,000 if she installs the turbocharger and intercooler. What is the maximum Raquel should be willing to pay the Wizard to do this? What is the maximum amount she should be willing to pay him on a contingency basis (if he makes the sale)?

- a. Draw the influence diagram and tree for this problem.
- b. How much should Raquel pay in advance (nonrefundable) if there's only a .8 probability of his making the sale?

3.18 Samuel Steelskull is thinking about whether or not to wear a helmet while commuting to work on his bicycle. He figures his chances of dying in an accident during the coming year without the helmet are about 1/3,000. The odds of dying go down to 1/5,000 with the helmet.

Sam figures it is worth about $80 to him for his hair not to be messed up when he gets to work during the coming year, and he is pretty much indifferent between wearing and not wearing the helmet.

    a. Draw the influence diagram and tree for this problem.

    b. What's the implicit value Sam is putting on his life (i.e., a value that might be used in very small probability situations)?

3.19 Your company has recently developed Chewsy, a new sugar-free gum that contains fluoride. Not only does it taste good, it's also good for your teeth. You are faced with the decision of whether or not to introduce Chewsy to the market.

The total sales of chewing gum are expected to be about $200 million over the next 10 years.

Your marketing personnel feel that with their best efforts and with a front-end marketing expenditure of $4 million, your company could capture from 2 percent to 10 percent of the chewing gum market with Chewsy. They have given you the following probabilities.

Market Share	Probabilities
High (10%)	.30
Medium (6%)	.50
Low (2%)	.20

Your financial advisors point out that the profit margin on Chewsy is quite uncertain because of unusual manufacturing requirements. They say that there is a 40 percent chance that the profit margin will be only 25 percent of sales revenue and a 60 percent chance it will be 50 percent of sales revenue. The manufacturing requirements will be known before the marketing decision needs to be made.

    a. Draw the influence diagram for this problem.

    b. Structure the decision tree for Chewsy. What is the preferred decision and expected value?

    c. Plot the probability distribution for profit for the Chewsy decision. What are the expected values for both alternatives?

    d. What is the value of information on market share? On profit margin? On both?

    e. What is the value of control on market share? On profit margin? On both? Are there any possible ways of achieving further control over either of these uncertainties?

f. Does the preferred decision vary with the probabilities for market share or margin? What decisions are preferred for what ranges of probability?

3.20 The Southern Power Company is planning to submit a major rate increase request to the state Public Utilities Commission. The Commission has assured Southern Power that it would approve a request for a moderate rate increase. With this moderate rate increase, Southern would receive $40 million in additional revenues during the next few years (relative to no rate increase).

However, the company is also considering a riskier course of action—requesting a high rate increase that would yield $100 million in additional revenues, if approved. If the high rate increase is not approved, there is still some chance the Commission would grant Southern a low rate increase, which would mean $30 million in additional revenues. Of course, the possibility exists that the Commission would simply refuse any rate increase whatsoever if Southern asks for the high increase.

The best information within the company indicates a 70 percent probability the Commission would disapprove the high rate increase request. Given that it does so, the chance it would then grant a low rate increase is believed to be 60 percent.

a. Draw the influence diagram for Southern's problem.
b. Draw the decision tree for Southern's decision problem.
c. Find the expected value of each alternative.
d. Draw the probability distribution on profit for each alternative.
e. Calculate the value of perfect information on:
  • Whether or not the Commission approves the high rate increase
  • Whether or not the Commission would grant a low rate increase given that it does not approve the high rate increase
  • Both of the above.

3.21 Your company markets an all-purpose household glue called Easystick. Currently, a sister company in another country supplies the product at a guaranteed delivered cost of $2.00 per unit. You are now thinking about producing Easystick locally rather than continuing to import it. A staff study indicates that with a projected sales volume of 4 million units over the product's life, local production would cost an average of $1.50 per unit.

However, two things could significantly affect this cost. First, the government in your country is considering imposing a heavy tax on the primary raw material of Easystick. This would increase the average production cost of Easystick to $2.25 per unit. You think there is a 50/50 chance the government will impose the tax.

The second factor is a newly developed improvement in the production process that uses the expensive raw material more efficiently. This new process would reduce the average production cost of Easystick as shown below.

	Average Cost Per Unit	
	Old Process	**New Process**
No tax on raw material	$1.50	$1.25
Tax on raw material	$2.25	$1.75

Unfortunately, local conditions may make it impossible to implement the new process. Your staff estimates a 60 percent chance of being able to use the new process.

Should you continue to import or switch to local production?

  a. Draw the influence diagram for this problem.

  b. Draw the decision tree for this problem and calculate the expected value for each option. (For the outcome measure, use the total savings in cost relative to importing Easystick.)

  c. Draw the probability distribution on profit for each option.

  d. Calculate the values of perfect information and control on:

  • Whether or not the tax will be imposed on the raw material

  • Whether or not the new production process can be used

  • Both of the above.

  e. Do a probability sensitivity analysis to determine the preferred decision for different ranges of probabilities.

3.22 It is 1986 and Shipbuilder, Inc., has decided to take a long, hard look at its telephone needs. Its present system has one major problem: it is very costly to make moves or changes. A task force has identified the most attractive alternative: Fone-Equip can install a system that will enable moves and changes to be made at almost no cost.

The five-year lease on the current system is up for renewal for the period 1987–1991. Another renewal of the lease would be made in 1991 for the period 1992–1996. Fone-Equip's system is available only for outright purchase. Under any alternative, Shipbuilder will be in the same position in 1996 (a completely new phone system will be needed), so costs beyond 1996 can be neglected.

Shipbuilder is planning a shipbuilding program called Program A, which will entail considerable phone moves and changes in the years 1987–1991. Under the present system, these changes would cost

$2 million per year. However, if Program A does not materialize, there will be very little in the way of phone moves and changes in this period.

Similarly, Program B would entail $4 million per year in costs for phone moves and changes in the years 1992–1996. However, if Program B does not materialize, there will be very few moves and changes in this period.

All costs were estimated in 1986 dollars, with the effects of inflation removed. The costs for the present system are $1.5 million per year lease and $0.5 million per year recurring costs. Fone-Equip's system has a purchase price of $14 million (including installation) and $1.0 million per year recurring cost.

Shipbuilder judged that Program A has a 50 percent chance of occurring. The 1986 telephone decision will be made before Program A's fate is known.

Program B is judged to have a 60 percent chance of occurring if Program A does occur, but only a 30 percent chance of occurring if Program A does not occur. If there is a telephone decision to be made in 1991, it will be made before Program B's fate is known.

There is also a 20 percent uncertainty on what Fone-Equip's system would cost in 1991.

The decision-maker insisted on using a discount rate of 10 percent. At this rate, the net present value in 1986 is:

- $1 expense in 1987—$0.91
- $1 expense in 1992—$0.56
- $1 expense per year for 1987–1991—$3.79
- $1 expense per year for 1992–1996—$2.12.

   a. Draw the influence diagram and decision tree for this problem.

   b. What is Shipbuilder's best strategy? Show the probability distribution on costs for the alternatives.

   c. What is the value of delaying the 1986 decision until Program A's fate is known?

   d. What is the value of delaying the 1991 decision until Program B's fate is known?

   e. Suppose Shipbuilder could obtain perfect information on Program A and Program B before the 1986 decision is made. What would this information be worth?

   f. Show how the expected values associated with the 1986 decision vary with the probability of Program A occurring.

3.23   The pharmaceutical division of Dreamland Products has been the world leader in the area of soporific drugs. Its major product, Dozealot, is approaching the end of its patent life, and already sales have fallen significantly from the peak because of the inroads of new and superior competitive products. However, Dozealot sales are still quite significant and are considered to be of strategic importance for maintaining the sales of the entire product line of soporific drugs. Therefore, the research and development (R&D) department has defined two alternative approaches to improve the product quality and, thus, future sales prospects.

One approach, which is quite conventional, is simply to reformulate the product to minimize an undesirable side effect that exists in the current galenical form. The manager in charge of galenical development has created a number of new formulations since the original introduction of Dozealot that have the desired characteristic, but even such a simple change in the formulation will require a development expenditure of 500,000 Swiss francs. By estimating the increase in sales of both Dozealot and the rest of the soporific product range, the product manager for soporific drugs has estimated the value of this improvement. Taking into account the production cost of the new formulation and the minor investments required, the improvement in Dreamland's cash flow would be substantial and yield a net present value (NPV) of 2.5 million Swiss francs (not including the cost of development).

The second approach, which is riskier but potentially more rewarding, involves a new controlled-release technology based on differential microencapsulation. This approach, if successful, would not only eliminate the undesired side effects but would also substantially improve the product efficacy. Market forecasts and cash-flow analyses indicate that this product, B, would be four times as profitable to produce and market as the more conventional product A, described above. The drawbacks, however, are that the microencapsulation development project would cost 3 million Swiss francs and still might fail because of an inability to control the differential layering process within tolerances specified by Good Manufacturing Practice. After a recent review of the microencapsulation process development efforts, the R&D director concluded that there is 1 chance in 2 of being technically successful within the deadlines imposed by the patent life of Dozealot.

   a. Draw the influence diagram and decision tree for Dreamland Products considering it could separately pursue the development of A or B or even pursue both to reduce the risks involved in B. In the latter case, it would naturally market B and not A if B were a technical success.

b. Compute the expected value of each alternative, assuming B has 1 chance in 2 of being successfully developed. Based on the criterion of expected value, what should Dreamland do?

Since the probability of successfully developing product B is difficult to determine, Dreamland's managing director would like to know how sensitive the best decision is to this probability assignment.

c. Compute the expected NPV of developing B alone and of developing A and B simultaneously as a function of p_B, the probability of technical success of B.

d. Graphically represent the expected value of the three alternatives as a function of p_B and determine for what range of values of p_B each alternative is best.

Resolving the technical uncertainties surrounding the microencapsulation project early could be achieved by immediately conducting a few critical experiments at an additional cost of 1 million Swiss francs.

e. Compute the expected value of perfect information on whether microencapsulation could be successfully accomplished, assuming an initial probability of success of .5.

f. Compute and graphically represent the expected value of the entire project given perfect information about whether or not microencapsulation would be feasible as a function of the initial probability of success p_B. Graphically show the expected value of perfect information and determine over what range of initial probability of success p_B this value exceeds 1 million Swiss francs.

3.24 The internal rate of return (IRR) of a venture is the value that, if substituted for the discount rate, makes the net present value (NPV) zero. There are several difficulties in using IRR as the sole criterion in choosing between alternatives.

Consider the following two ventures:

A: Invest I in year 0, receive positive cash flow, C, in all years from year 1 to infinity.
B: Invest I in year 0, receive positive cash flow, K, in year 1, nothing in succeeding years.

a. Solve for $c = C/I$ and $k = K/I$ in terms of $n = \text{NPV}/I$ and d, the discount rate. Use the sum

$$\sum_{i=1}^{\infty} \frac{1}{(1+d)^i} = \frac{1}{d}$$

b. Assume that both ventures have the same investment and the same NPV. Plot the IRR value against n for the two ventures. (Take the discount rate d to be .1.)

c. For equal n (equal value to the decision-maker), how do the IRR values of long-term and short-term investments (A and B) differ? Is IRR an adequate decision criterion? What assumptions do you have to make concerning use of funds after year 1 for investment B?

3.25 A venture with an NPV of zero is acceptable to the decision-maker. Why is this true? What problems in interpretation does this cause for the decision-maker unfamiliar with the concept? What steps would alleviate these problems?

3.26 If financing is available at an interest rate equal to the decision-maker's discount rate, a venture with a positive NPV can be transformed into a venture with an infinite IRR.

a. How can this be done?

b. Does a similar situation exist for leasing alternatives?

c. For existing businesses, one alternative usually involves no major new investments. What is the IRR for this strategy? Compare the type of results you might expect for NPV and for IRR for "Invest" and "No New Investment" strategies. In what situations might you prefer NPV or IRR as a decision criterion?

4

Probabilistic Dependence

Dependence and Independence

The probabilities in the preceding chapters were simpler than those one finds in most real decision problems. There was no probabilistic dependence; it made no difference to the person providing the probabilities at one node if he or she learned what happened at another node. Real decision problems usually start with a set of variables for which the probabilities are very interdependent. One of the subtler skills in influence diagram and decision tree construction is finding a set of variables for the nodes that have independent probabilities and that are natural and meaningful. But it is not often that this can be done for all the variables in the problem.

Usually the facilitator faces a situation described by variables that are far from independent. How are uncertainties related? How will resolving uncertainty on one variable affect the uncertainty in another area? Questions like these frequently lie just below the surface of many deliberations, but they can be extremely difficult to enunciate. One of the advantages of influence diagrams and decision trees is that they provide a language that makes dialog in this area possible and relatively easy.

This chapter deals with three related topics. First, the Positronics case is used to demonstrate why and how dependent probabilities are used in real decision problems. Second, dependent probabilities are used to combine new information with prior information. The process for doing this is called Bayes' Rule. Third, Bayes' Rule and decision trees are used to show how to calculate the value of imperfect information.

Dependent Probabilities _____

Obtaining the Data

Achieving clarity when dealing with dependent probabilities is often both difficult and important, particularly when information from different people needs to be combined. This is illustrated in the Positronics example.

After a presentation on the MegaCorp bid, the Positronics production manager came to the decision facilitator. After seeing the presentation and learning more about how the probabilities were used, he had reconsidered the probabilities that he had provided for Positronics' costs. If he knew what Anode's bid was, he would assign different probabilities to Positronics' costs. He had great respect for the production staff at Anode and had heard it had much more experience than Positronics in making instruments of the type being bid on. Thus, Anode should have higher quality information and much less uncertainty about costs than Positronics. Positronics should have the same costs as Anode, except that Anode's experience would give it a small cost advantage. The facilitator tentatively drew an arrow from the Anode Bid node to the Positronics Cost node to show this influence (Figure 4–1a). Using this diagram, the production manager would provide the probabilities for the distribution tree and the marketing department would give the probabilities for Anode Bid.

After some thought, however, the facilitator realized they had it backwards. It was the probabilities for Anode's bid that should be reassessed. The original assessment on Anode's bid was done without any real input on Anode's cost and would be a meaningless starting point for an assessment of anyone's cost. However, the production manager had added two crucial pieces of knowledge: Anode will know its costs accurately when it makes its bid, and Anode and Positronics both have approximately the same costs because they use the same process. Thus, given a particular level of cost, the real uncertainty is how much over cost Anode would bid. The people who would best know how much Anode wanted the business and how much of a margin it would figure in were in marketing. Accordingly, the arrow was reversed, and the probabilities in Figure 4–1b for Anode's bid were obtained from the marketing department.

A discussion such as this would be very difficult without the language of influence diagrams and probability trees. Most people untrained in probability theory or decision analysis find it difficult to communicate information concerning uncertainty; interdependence among uncertain factors is almost impossible to talk about. The graphical structures of influence diagrams and trees give a visual, simple, and systematic way of discussing structure and data in this area.

Using the Data

When we have chosen the order of nodes and assessed a set of dependent probabilities, we will have a set of probabilities that depends on the branch or outcome of another node. The second node is "relevant" to the first node.

—————————————— Figure 4–1 ——————————————

Structuring the Problem and Identifying Data Requirements

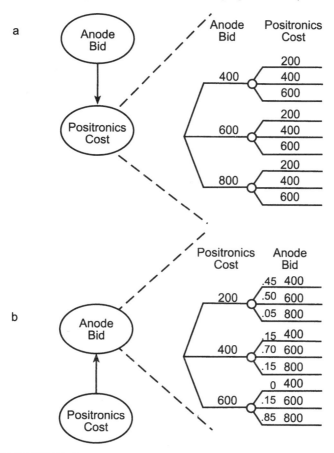

The second node is called the "conditioning" (or, in older terminology, the "influencing") node and is the one at the base of the arrow in the influence diagram.

It is easy to input these dependent probabilities in a tree. Figure 4–2 shows the tree in completely rolled back form, with expected value used as the decision criterion. Because of the order in which the probabilities were assessed (Figure 4–1), the Positronics Cost node is to the left of the Anode Bid node. Later in this chapter, we will see how to reverse the order of these nodes.

The cumulative probability distributions for this tree are shown in Figure 4–3. Comparing this with the previous cumulative plot (Figure 3–6), we see that the risk has been intensified: there is a larger probability of losing money if Positronics wins the bid. This makes sense, because the dependent probabilities tell us that if Anode bids high, Positronics wins the bid but its costs are likely to be high.

Figure 4–2

Decision Tree Given Dependent Probabilities

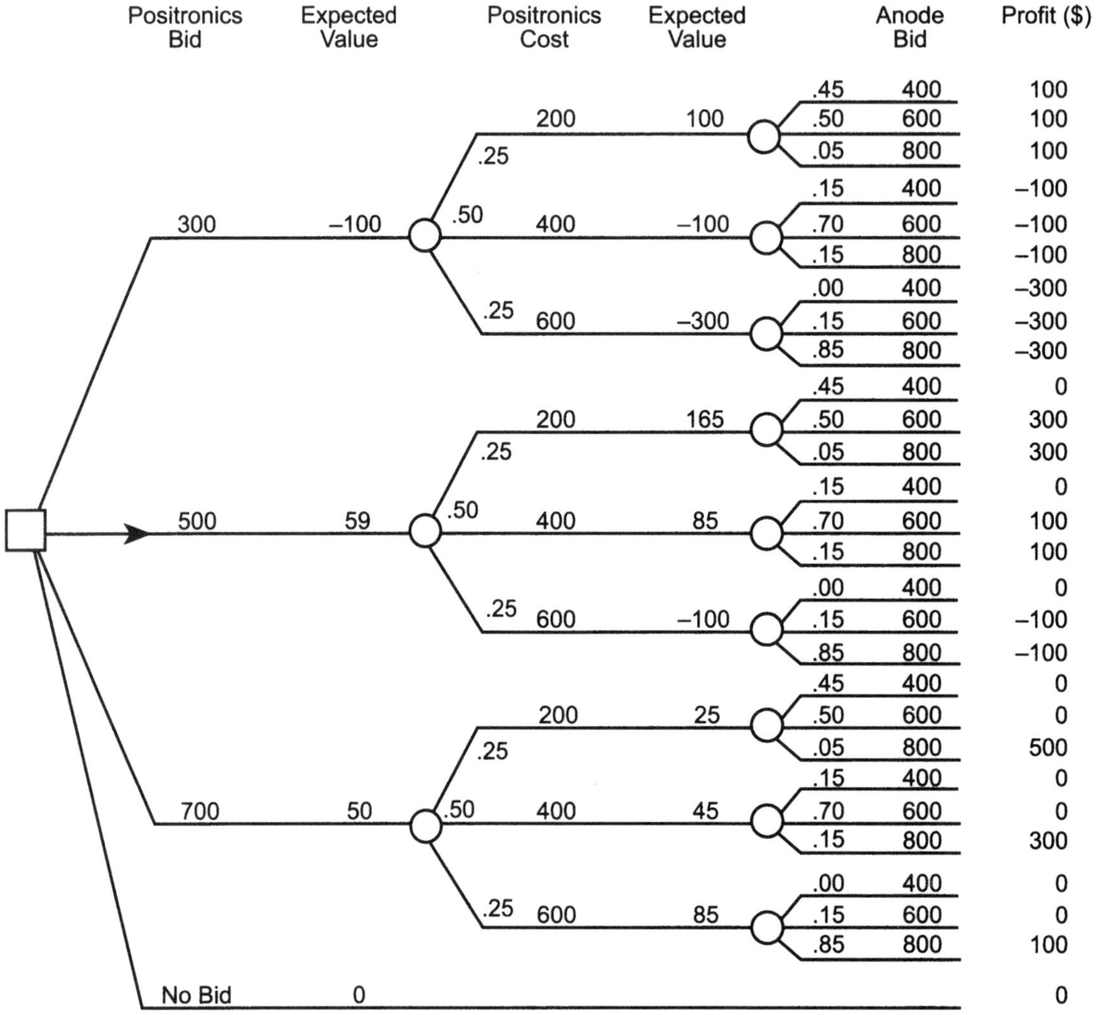

Positronics Bid	Expected Value	Positronics Cost	Expected Value		Anode Bid	Profit ($)
		200	100	.45	400	100
				.50	600	100
		.25		.05	800	100
		.50		.15	400	−100
300	−100	400	−100	.70	600	−100
				.15	800	−100
		.25		.00	400	−300
		600	−300	.15	600	−300
				.85	800	−300
		200	165	.45	400	0
				.50	600	300
		.25		.05	800	300
		.50		.15	400	0
500	59	400	85	.70	600	100
				.15	800	100
		.25		.00	400	0
		600	−100	.15	600	−100
				.85	800	−100
		200	25	.45	400	0
				.50	600	0
		.25		.05	800	500
		.50		.15	400	0
700	50	400	45	.70	600	0
				.15	800	300
		.25		.00	400	0
		600	85	.15	600	0
				.85	800	100
No Bid	0					0

This effect would have been missed if the probabilistic dependency were missed. A common pitfall for the novice decision facilitator is missing the interdependence or relevance between uncertainties. These interdependencies can often dramatically increase or decrease the uncertainty in the value measure. The use of influence diagrams helps avoid this problem; arrows indicate probabilistic dependence or relevance, and most people deal naturally and easily with these arrows.

—————————————————————— Figure 4–3 ——————————————————————

Probability Distribution on Profits Given Dependent Probabilities

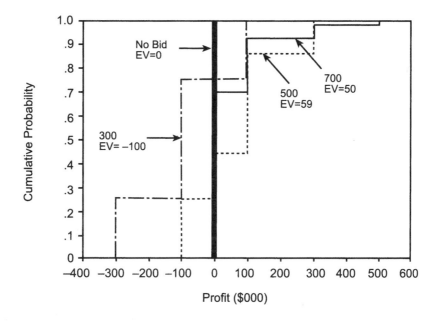

Dependent Outcomes

Obtaining the Data

The next morning, the marketing people returned to the decision facilitator and said they were really uncomfortable with the probabilities they had supplied the previous day (the dependent bid probabilities shown in Figure 4–1). After thinking about them, they wanted to be able to systematically change the outcomes rather than the probabilities. They presented the decision facilitator with the distribution tree shown in Figure 4–4.

Dependent outcomes are another way of representing dependencies among uncertainties. In this case, it is not the probability of an outcome that changes, but the outcome itself.

Having dependent outcomes is another way of representing probabilistic dependence for continuous variables. In our discrete approximation, we chose ranges and then assigned probabilities to those ranges. Probabilistic dependence means that the probabilities assigned to these ranges change depending on which branch of the conditioning node we are on. Alternatively, we can readjust the ranges (as we move from branch to branch of the conditioning node) to keep the probabilities the same.

In our experience, using dependent outcomes is frequently a sign of systematic considerations in the thought process of the person supplying

—————————————————————— Figure 4–4 ——————————————————————

Structuring the Problem on the Basis of Dependent Outcomes

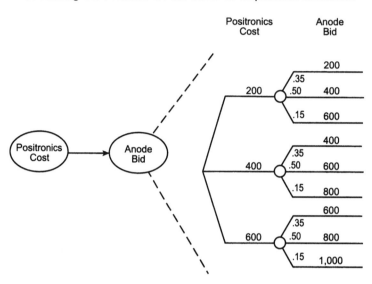

the data. To promote clarity of thought and communication, we can use the deterministic value model (rather than probabilistic dependence) to capture this systematic consideration in a deterministic way. For instance, dependent outcomes might result from a thought process like "Shift the value up by X in that case and then put a 10 percent uncertainty in either direction." Remembering our divide and conquer technique, we can improve the accuracy of the assessment by separating these two effects and assessing them individually.

Using the Data

Entering dependent outcomes in the tree is not difficult. Figure 4–5 show the tree rolled back for the expected value criterion. The cumulative probability distributions associated with this tree are shown in Figure 4–6.

We see that the risk has intensified (as indicated by the higher probabilities of low and high outcomes), and the even larger probabilities of losing money lead to an expected value of only $38,800. The preferred alternative has shifted from a bid of $500,000 (Figure 3–7 and 4–2) to one of $700,000 (Figure 4–5). The $500,000 option has an expected value that has dropped to $18,800.

Nature's Tree ————————————————————————————————

Dependent probabilities are important in dealing with a problem we address informally in our daily lives: How do we incorporate new information into our current information base?

—— Figure 4–5 ——

Decision Tree Given Dependent Outcomes

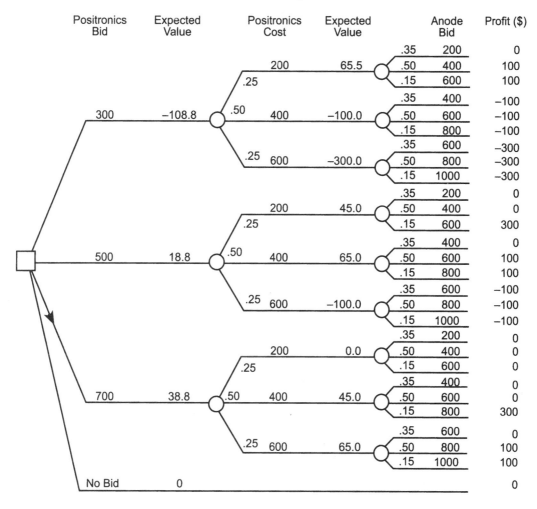

Positronics Bid	Expected Value	Positronics Cost	Expected Value		Anode Bid	Profit ($)
				.35	200	0
		200	65.5	.50	400	100
		.25		.15	600	100
				.35	400	−100
300	−108.8	.50 400	−100.0	.50	600	−100
				.15	800	−100
				.35	600	−300
		.25 600	−300.0	.50	800	−300
				.15	1000	−300
				.35	200	0
		200	45.0	.50	400	0
		.25		.15	600	300
				.35	400	0
500	18.8	.50 400	65.0	.50	600	100
				.15	800	100
				.35	600	−100
		.25 600	−100.0	.50	800	−100
				.15	1000	−100
				.35	200	0
		200	0.0	.50	400	0
		.25		.15	600	0
				.35	400	0
700	38.8	.50 400	45.0	.50	600	0
				.15	800	300
				.35	600	0
		.25 600	65.0	.50	800	100
				.15	1000	100
No Bid	0					0

Indicators and States of Nature

In the section "Dependent Probabilities", we stressed the importance of drawing the relevance arrow correctly when encoding dependent probabilities. There is one type of situation in particular where correct ordering is imperative and where people frequently make mistakes, both in daily life and in decision analysis: when people describe the relationship between an imperfect indicator and the state of nature (e.g., the relationship between medical symptoms and the actual state of health). To establish this relationship correctly, we follow a two-step process. First, we track the indicator to see how accurate its predictions are. Second, these results are incorporated into a tree, which is used to predict the state of nature, given an indicator result.

Figure 4–6

Probability Distribution on Profits Given Dependent Outcomes

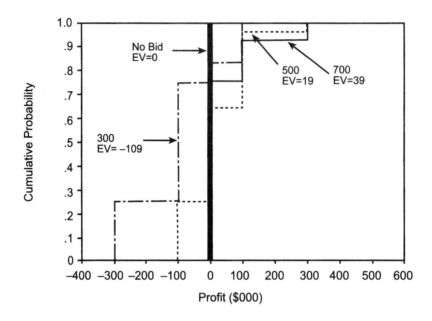

The following are examples of state of nature/indicator pairs that occur in business situations.

State of Nature	Indicator
Market size	Market survey
Number of future competitors	Articles in business journals
Amount of recoverable oil	Seismic study
Economic climate	Leading indicators
Production costs	Prototype costs
Drug safety and efficacy	Clinical trials
Software stability	Beta tests

An Example from Medicine

Let us use a simple medical example. Through either experience or a controlled test, we track the number of people with and without measles who have spots on their face. Using this and other data, we can find the probability that someone who has spots on his or her face has measles. Unfortunately, people make mistakes all too often when they try to go through this process. The problem is that they do not correctly combine their prior information with the indicator data. For instance, assume that most people with measles have spots on their face and that few people without measles have spots on their face. If you know (prior or general information) that there is a measles epidemic, spots on a person's face would lead you to put a high probability on measles. If, on the other hand, there has not been a case of measles in the city for months, spots on a person's face would lead you to put a much lower probability on measles.

How do we correctly mix our prior or general information with the data (indicator results and track record of the indicator)? The rule for performing this process correctly is to first construct Nature's tree. In the influence diagram corresponding to Nature's tree, the state-of-nature node is relevant to the indicator result. The data then supply the probabilities for the indicator results, given the state of nature. We have to supply our subjective (prior, general information) probabilities for the state-of-nature node.

Suppose a doctor has tracked the correlation between the state of health and the indicator for her patients. Suppose she has come up with the Nature's tree in Figure 4–7. (The probabilities in this distribution tree are for illustration only.)

Now let us assume there has been a measles epidemic, and the doctor judges that the next patient who walks into her office has a 20 percent chance of having the measles (Figure 4–8).

In the probability tree (Figure 4–9), the column of joint probabilities (that is, the probability that both events will occur) has been calculated by multiplying the probabilities at each branching for a path through the tree. For instance, the topmost path (Measles, Spots on Face) has a probability of .19 (.20 × .95).

—————————————————— Figure 4–7 ——————————————————

Probabilities for Indicator

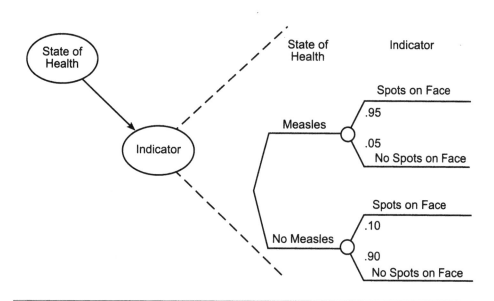

Figure 4–8

Probabilities for State of Nature

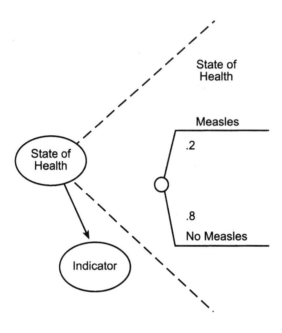

Figure 4–9

Probability Tree for Medical Example

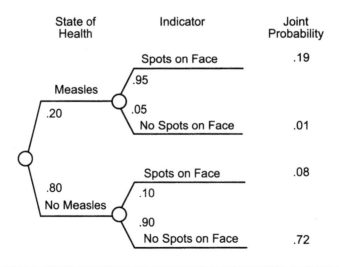

Bayes' Rule

To find the probabilities in the order needed for most decision-making, we use Bayes' Rule to reverse the order of nodes, putting the indicator node first and the true state of nature second. Thus, we can read off the probability of the true state of nature given an indicator result.

To apply Bayes' Rule to trees, we first calculate the joint probabilities from Nature's tree. Second, we draw the tree with the nodes in reversed order and transcribe these probabilities to the ends of the appropriate paths in the reversed tree. Then we can find the probabilities for the node on the left by adding the probabilities of all paths passing through that branch. The probabilities for the branches of the node on the right are found by dividing the joint probability at the end of the branch by the probability for the branch of the node on the left. The process is fairly simple but tedious.

For the measles example, we can use this process to reverse Nature's tree (Figure 4–10). Thus, we see that if a patient with spots on his or her face walks into the doctor's office, there is a $19/27 = .70$ chance the patient has measles. There is a 27 percent chance that the next patient who walks in will have spots on his or her face.

The probabilities in Nature's tree have traditional names (Figure 4–11). In Nature's tree, the probabilities of the state of nature are called the prior probabilities; the probabilities of the indicator (the second node) are called the likelihood function. The rule for reversing the order of nodes in the tree is called Bayes' Rule. Reversing the order of nodes in the tree is indicated in the influence diagram by reversing the arrow between the nodes. The probabilities of the second node of the reversed tree (the state of nature) are

---

Figure 4–10

Applying Bayes' Rule to Reverse the Tree Shown in Figure 4-9

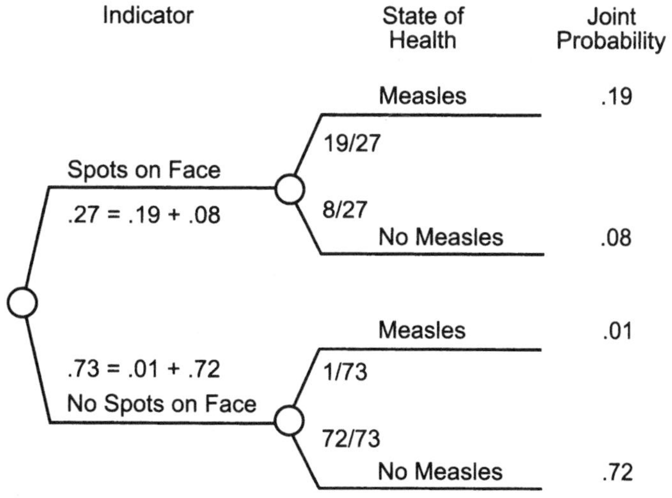

--------------------------------- Figure 4–11 ---------------------------------

Names of Probabilities in Nature's Tree

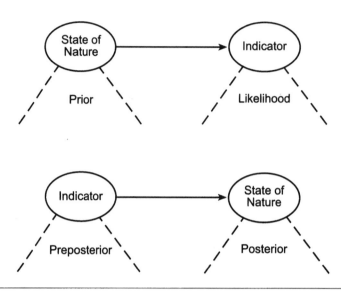

called the posterior probabilities; the probabilities of the first node in the reversed tree are called, believe it or not, the preposterior probabilities.

Why is Bayes' Rule so important? It gives the method for correctly adding data and new information to an existing subjective state of information (the prior). This information can then be used to construct the posterior distribution, which represents an updated state of information. People commonly make mistakes in using new information. Although it appears rather formal, Bayes' Rule is the best method for avoiding mistakes in judgments that often have great importance.

In summary, when dealing with indicators, first draw Nature's tree: the tree with the state of nature first and the indicator second. Then, enter the data into this tree. Only in this way will we be able to correctly separate our expectations about what the future will bring from how good the indicator is. The process of reversing the tree is important when we wish to find out how knowledge of an indicator result changes our expectations of what the future will bring. This procedure will become clearer in the next section, "The Value of Imperfect Information."

A Prototype As an Indicator

The production engineer suggested that Positronics could resolve some of the uncertainty on production costs by building a prototype instrument and carefully monitoring the cost of the steps that went into building it. The cost of the prototype would be an indicator for the state of nature, the actual costs. In Nature's tree for this procedure, the first node is the actual costs and their probabilities, as used earlier. The next node is the prototype cost, which was felt to be best described as inexpensive or expensive. (The production engineer gave a technical specification for these rather vague terms.) Given the difference between prototypes and real production, the engineer estimated the probabilities for prototype cost, as shown in Figure 4–12.

We emphasize that the probabilities must be assessed in this order, although there is a real and constant temptation to assess them in the reverse order. The reason for using this order is that it clearly separates expectations about what the future will bring (the probabilities on the first node) from the reliability of the test (the probabilities of the second node). Assessing probabilities with the nodes in the opposite order completely mixes the two sets of ideas.

The Value of Imperfect Information

One of the most important uses of Bayes' Rule and Nature's tree is in obtaining the value of imperfect information. If we obtain imperfect information, we know the outcome of the imperfect indicator before we make a decision—and before we learn the true state of nature. This order requires reversing Nature's tree.

The president of Positronics was well aware that perfect information is seldom available. Most often, the choice is whether or not to undertake a study to reduce the uncertainty. Figures were now available (Figure 4–12) that would permit more quantitative analysis of the value of building the prototype instrument to reduce the uncertainty on cost (see Chapter 3, "The Value of Perfect Information").

──────────────── Figure 4–12 ────────────────

Influence Diagram for Cost of a Prototype

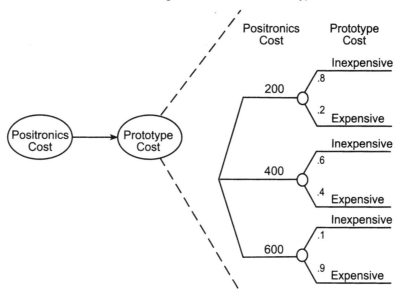

─────────────────────── Figure 4–13 ───────────────────────

Influence Diagram Depicting the Positronics Prototype Build Decision

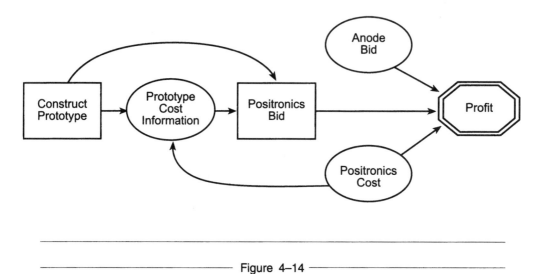

─────────────────────── Figure 4–14 ───────────────────────

Distribution Tree of Prototype Cost Information Node

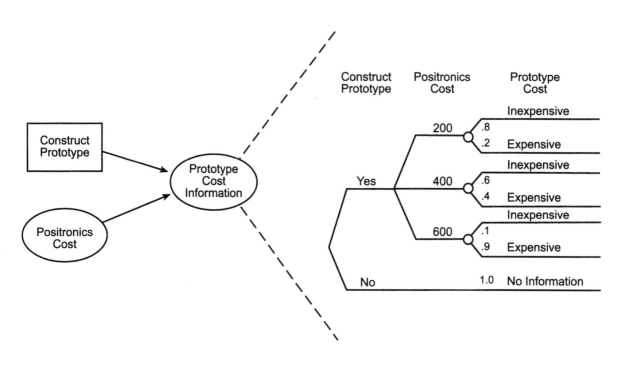

Figure 4–15

Decision Tree of Prototype Construction Question

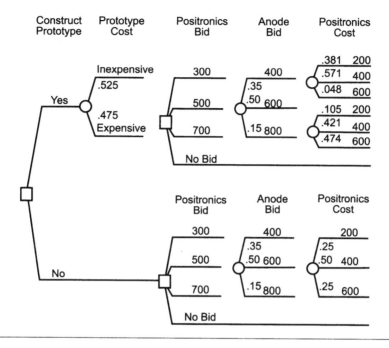

Figure 4–16

Probability Tree for Prototype Example

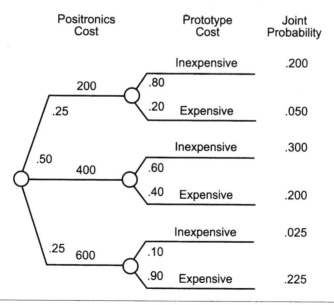

One way to represent this extended decision problem is shown in Figure 4–13.

The Construct Prototype node contains the alternatives "Yes" and "No." The distribution tree contained in the Prototype Cost Information node is shown in Figure 4–14.

The decision tree (Figure 4–15) is constructed according to the rules given in the section "Recasting the Problem as a Decision Problem" in Chapter 3. Note the difficulty in representing the probabilities in this tree: For the "Yes" branch of the tree, the upper node for Positronics Cost corresponds to the "Inexpensive" branch of Prototype Cost, and the lower node to the "Expensive" branch.

Where did the probabilities for Positronics Cost in Figure 4–15 come from? Just as with the medical example, we have to use Bayes' Rule to reverse the order of the nodes. Figure 4–16 shows Nature's tree, and Figure 4–17 shows the reversed tree. The probabilities in Figure 4–17 are in the form needed for the tree in Figure 4–15.

The easiest way to find the value of imperfect information is by just evaluating the subtree following the "Yes" branch in Figure 4–15. We can do this by adding the node on Prototype Cost onto the front of the existing tree and by then comparing its value with that of the original tree (the subtree at the bottom of Figure 4–15). This tree is shown in Figure 4–18.

The expected value with the imperfect information is $73,000. We follow the same calculation method we used for the value of perfect information.

——————————— Figure 4–17 ———————————

Applying Bayes' Rule to Reverse the Tree Shown in Figure 4–16

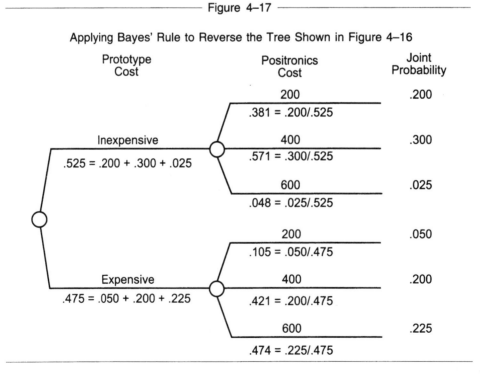

Prototype Cost	Positronics Cost	Joint Probability
	200	.200
	.381 = .200/.525	
Inexpensive	400	.300
.525 = .200 + .300 + .025	.571 = .300/.525	
	600	.025
	.048 = .025/.525	
	200	.050
	.105 = .050/.475	
Expensive	400	.200
.475 = .050 + .200 + .225	.421 = .200/.475	
	600	.225
	.474 = .225/.475	

Figure 4–18

Decision Tree with Imperfect Information

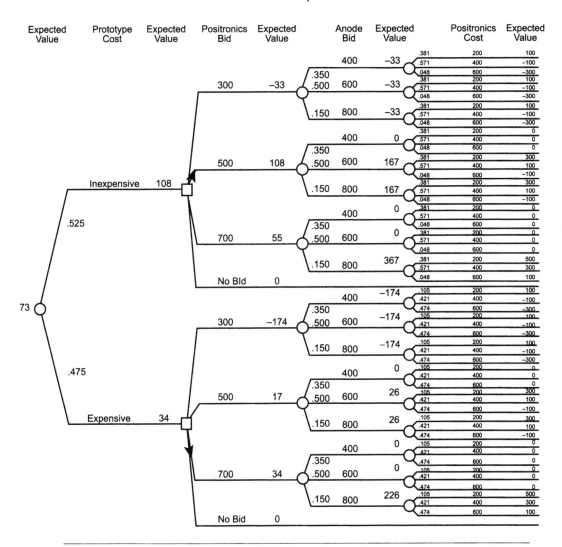

Value of Imperfect Information = Value with Imperfect Information
– Value Without
= $73,000 – $65,000

= $8,000   (4–1)

Thus, the prototype program should not be undertaken if it costs more than $8,000.

As with perfect information, there is an alternative method for calculating this value. From Figure 4–18, you can see that about half the time (probability .475) the prototype information will lead you to switch your bid

--------------------------- Figure 4-19 ---------------------------

Influence Diagram Showing Probabilities Dependent on a Decision Node

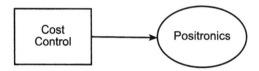

(hence, the information has value). If the prototype is expensive, we switch the bid from $500,000 to $700,000. This improves the value by $33,900 – $17,100 = $16,800. The expected improvement is then $16,800 × .475 = $8,000.

The Value of Imperfect Control

The value of imperfect control is much simpler to calculate. Assume that a feasible cost control program is put into effect. Obtain the probabilities for Positronics' costs given this cost control program. Presumably, the probability of the high-cost branch is smaller than before. Find the expected value of the tree using these new probabilities. This is the value with control for this (imperfect) cost control program. As before, the value of control is the improvement in value.

Value of Imperfect Control = Value with Imperfect Control
                              – Value Without Imperfect Control
                                                        (4–2)

Common Interpretive Problems with Reordering the Tree

Care must be taken in reordering decision trees. The decision facilitator is normally concerned with decision-dependent probabilities or decision-dependent outcomes. The information in this section will help you in these cases.

Decision-Dependent Probabilities

Probabilities can depend on a decision node. For instance, suppose we introduced a decision on whether or not to institute stringent cost control measures. The probabilities for Positronics' costs would then depend on which branch of the cost control decision node we were on (Figure 4–19).

Suppose we now decide to move the cost node in front of the cost control decision node in the decision tree. This would be equivalent to drawing an arrow from the Positronics Cost node to the Cost Control node. Decision analysis theory would object that this was not a valid order for the tree because of decision-dependent probabilities.

There are three ways to understand why the reordering is not allowed. The first way is operational. To reverse the order of nodes with dependent probabilities, use Bayes' Rule. However, a decision node has no probabilities to insert into Bayes' Rule!

The second, more fundamental way of understanding the problem is to realize that this would create a loop in the influence diagram. Since arrows represent a flow of information, a loop makes no sense. This conclusion is reinforced by the chronology implied by arrows into and out of decision nodes. (See Chapter 11.)

The third way of understanding the problem is the second way reexpressed in decision tree language. If the Positronics Cost chance node occurs before the Cost Control decision node, it means we know what our costs are going to be before we make the decision. However, knowing that costs were low, for instance, would argue that we are probably going to make the decision to implement the stringent cost controls, which will make costs low. This gets us into a logical loop. No matter how we put it, decision trees will not allow us to interchange the order of a decision node and a chance node whose probabilities depend on the decision node.

Putting all influence diagrams in the Howard Canonical Form (see Problem 11.10) would avoid all arrows leading from decisions to uncertainties. In this case, the oval for Positronics Cost in Figure 4–19 would be replaced by several ovals, Positronics Cost under Cost Control alternative X, one oval for each alternative. In this formulation, the state of knowledge is clearly separated from the choice of alternative, and the problem of decision-dependent probabilities does not occur.

Decision-Dependent Outcomes

For chance nodes whose outcomes depend on a decision node, we would expect the same problem as with decision-dependent probabilities. After all, dependent probabilities and dependent outcomes are both ways of characterizing dependent probability distributions. However, there is an interpretation of dependent outcomes that allows us to interchange the nodes.

The interpretation is that we learn whether we are on the high branch, the middle branch, or the low branch (assuming there are three branches) before we make the decision. We do not know the value of the outcome, only whether we are on the top branch, the second branch, or the third branch. This interpretation is consistent with the observation that dependent outcomes often represent a deterministic shift combined with uncertainty in estimation. The information gained in interchanging the nodes is on the uncertainty in estimation. This interpretation is illustrated in the influence diagram in Figure 4–20.

Summary

A dependency can be expressed with dependent outcomes or with dependent probabilities. These forms are equivalent, and the selection of form

—————————————————————— Figure 4–20 ——————————————————————

Influence Diagram Illustrating Handling of Uncertainty in Estimation

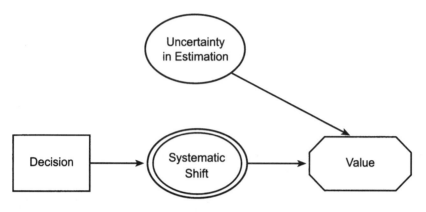

usually depends on how the source of information thinks about the uncertainty. This was illustrated in a probabilistic dependence that increased the riskiness of Positronics' bid decision.

We also discussed how correctly handling dependencies is a common problem that arises when dealing with tests or information gathering (Nature's tree). We then applied this to the calculation of the value of the imperfect information that could be obtained if Positronics were to build a prototype.

Finally, we discussed some interpretive difficulties that commonly arise when reordering trees with decision-dependent probabilities or decision-dependent outcomes.

Problems and Discussion Topics _____

4.1   What are joint probabilities? How are these different from conditional probabilities?

4.2   Suppose your interview with a decision-maker has revealed a dependency between two uncertainties. How do you determine which uncertainty depends on the other for assessment purposes? What does this imply for the order of assessment?

4.3   "Flipping the tree" refers to reordering the nodes in a tree or part of a tree (reversing them if there are only two nodes). Since the flipped tree represents the same state of knowledge (uncertainties) as the original tree, the principle of flipping a tree is that the probability of any event derived from the original tree should be the same as the probability of the same event represented by the flipped tree.

Consider the medical example in Figures 4–7 and 4–8. Suppose a medical expert assigns a probability that 50 percent of the total population currently has measles, and that given a person has measles there is a chance of 85 out of 100 that the person has spots on his or her face. If a person does not have measles, there is a .95 chance that the person has no spots on his or her face.

What is the conditional probability that someone who has spots on his or her face has measles? What is the conditional probability that someone who does not have spots on his or her face has measles?

4.4   We already know that changing the order of two chance nodes (called flipping the tree) does not change the knowledge represented by that tree. What happens if we move a chance node from the right of a decision node to the left of it? And vice versa?

4.5   The radiator in your car tends to overheat, but you have not fixed it because it is still winter and cold outside. The radiator overheats only 5 percent of the days it is used in cool weather. However, it overheats 70 percent of the time in warm weather. The weather report has just predicted a 1 out of 5 chance of warm weather today.

   a. Draw the influence diagram for these relationships.

   b. What is the chance your radiator will overheat today?

4.6   After having had pizza delivered at 11 p.m. several times a week for a number of years, you decide that there is a 70 percent chance that a pizza with a visible amount of cheese has a visible amount of pepperoni. You also figure that the probability that a randomly selected pizza will have visible amounts of cheese and pepperoni is .40.

   a. Draw the influence diagram for these relationships.

   b. What is the probability that a randomly selected pizza has a visible amount of cheese?

4.7   Using first dependent probabilities and then dependent outcomes, write down your probabilities on the temperature outside given that it is 9 a.m. or 9 p.m. Assume a .5 probability that the observation is made at either time and make your chance node on temperature have three branches.

Compare the expected temperature from each method (dependent probabilities or outcomes). How different are they? Which method enabled you to give the better estimate and why? What does this tell you about the underlying process affecting the temperature? What does it tell you about your thought process?

4.8   An expected-value decision-maker faces the short-term investment in a given stock shown in the tree below:

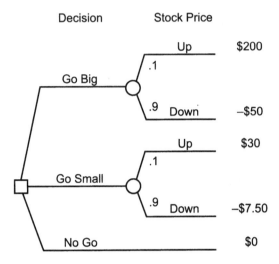

a. Draw the influence diagram. Do you have enough information to do so?

b. Calculate the expected value of this decision.

c. What is the maximum amount the decision-maker should
pay for perfect information on the stock price?

d. Suppose there is a test that can predict the stock price with
an accuracy of .9. Draw the influence diagram for this. What
is the maximum amount the decision-maker should pay for
this test?

e. Suppose the test says the stock will rise and this information is given to the decision-maker for free. Now what is the
value of perfect information on the stock price?

f. Suppose a wizard comes along. He can make any possible
outcome happen the decision-maker desires. Draw the
influence diagram for the value with the wizard. What is the
maximum amount the wizard should be paid?

4.9   Ursa Major Movies (UMM) has been trying a blind test on all its movies
before releasing them. The test labels a movie as a "Hit" or a "Dud."
To make the test blind, UMM released all movies regardless of the test
result. The test result and the actual history of the movies are shown
in the following table.

	Test Result	
	"Hit"	**"Dud"**
Broke box office records	5	1
Run of the mill	13	7
Disaster	8	9

    a. Draw the influence diagram for the test and movie results. Is it in the order of Nature's tree? Why or why not?

    b. What is the probability that a film chosen at random out of the studio's past movies was a disaster? Run of the mill? Broke records?

    c. What is the probability that a disaster had previously been labeled a "Hit"? What is the probability that a box office record breaker had been labeled a "Dud"? Is the test better at detecting good or bad movies?

    d. The producer thinks that a new movie is really quite good (a 5 in 10 chance of being a box office hit, a 3 in 10 chance of being run of the mill). After learning that the test came up "Dud," how should the producer revise her probabilities?

    e. The president thinks that this new movie is like all the others, meaning that the historical frequencies above apply. What should he think after learning that the test result for this movie was "Dud"?

    f. Assume a record breaker gives the company a net profit of $20 million; a run of the mill, $2 million; and a disaster, a net loss of $2 million. What value would the producer place on the new film before learning the test results? After learning the test results? How about the president?

4.10 C. Thompson, the credit manager of IJK Industrial Products, considered extending a line of credit to Lastco Construction Company. Lastco was a new company and was definitely considered a credit risk. Drawing on his experience, Thompson said, "There is about a 30 percent chance Lastco will fail within the year, which means a severe credit loss. And the way these construction companies operate, I would say there is another 25 percent chance Lastco will run into serious financial trouble." After being further questioned about other possibilities, Thompson said, "If they don't run into financial problems, there still is less than a 50/50 chance of Lastco becoming a regular customer. I would say the odds are about 5 to 4 that Lastco will end up being a sporadic customer." Thompson also made the following predictions:

    • If Lastco failed completely, it would average purchases of $1,500 before failing but leave an average unpaid balance of $800, which would be totally lost.

    • If Lastco had severe financial troubles, it would lose its credit but only after purchases of $2,000, including an unpaid balance of $1,000, of which $500 would ultimately be collected.

- As a sporadic customer, Lastco would average purchases of only $500 (with no credit losses). However, as a good customer, it would average purchases of approximately $6,000.

IJK was concerned about granting credit to Lastco. On the one hand, if it did not extend credit to a potential customer, business was lost. On the other hand, there was a substantial risk of nonpayment (as described above), and since IJK made an average profit (price minus variable cost) of only 20 percent of sales, this exacerbated the problem. In addition, there were collection costs of $100 per customer for those that failed or were in financial trouble.

a. Draw the influence diagram for this case.

b. Construct the decision tree for this case.

c. Should IJK grant credit to Lastco?

d. Suppose a credit rating company could somehow provide perfect information on a potential customer for $200. Should IJK buy it?

e. Suppose the fee of the credit rating company was only $50, but the company could provide only "good opinions" (not perfect information) about potential customers. Suppose also that Thompson has some experience with credit rating companies, which he says applies to the Lastco decision. His rating experience is summarized below as credit ratings by customer classification (percent of total.)

Rating	Failed	Financial Troubles	Sporadic Customer	Good Customer
Good	0	10	40	40
Medium	40	50	50	50
Poor	60	40	10	10
	100	100	100	100

Note: The table should be interpreted as follows: For example, in similar situations of companies that failed, none had been rated good, 40 percent had been rated medium, and 60 percent had been rated bad.

Would it be worthwhile to use the credit rating company? Illustrate your answer with a revised influence diagram.

4.11 Most market surveys give imperfect information. The example below shows a symmetric situation—a fraction, q, of product successes had positive survey results, and a fraction, q, of failures had negative survey results. The prior probability of a product success is given as p.

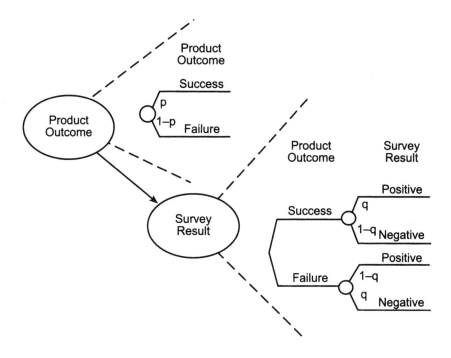

a. Flip the tree and calculate the posterior probabilities for Product Outcome and the preposterior probabilities for Survey Result in terms of p and q.

b. Plot the probability of a product success given a positive survey result against the value of p. Do this for q = .5, .6, .7, .8, .9, and 1.0. Why are values of q less than .5 and greater than 1 not needed?

c. How useful is the survey result for values of p near 0, .5, and 1.0? How does this depend on the value of q? Explain qualitatively what this means in terms of uncertainty and certainty and the accuracy of surveys.

5

Attitudes Toward Risk Taking

The Inadequacy of Expected Values _____

As noted previously, the expected value is not always an adequate decision criterion, especially for decisions that involve uncertainty and that are truly important to people or companies. Usually (but not always) people shy away from risk and uncertainty.

For example, in seminars to upper-level executives from many of the country's largest companies, participants were asked to bid for the rights to toss a coin where the prize was $200. Because we are dealing with a coin toss, the expected value is, of course, $100. It is surprising how few people bid anywhere close to $100. Most bid in the $40 to $60 range—and these were not the people who objected in principle to gambling.

The exercise shows how easy (but often wrong) it is to think of expected value as an adequate decision criterion. When there is money on the table, we find we are anything but expected-value decision-makers. The seminar also revealed that few people behave consistently when making decisions involving risk. If they carried the attitude used in the coin toss over into other decisions, they would be very conservative investors indeed!

Most people and companies exhibit an aversion to risk taking. While they are willing to play the averages for small stakes, they are willing to give up a part of the expected value to avoid the uncertainty and risk for larger stakes. Thus, this attitude should be incorporated in the decision criterion. The effects of risk attitude can be quantified in terms of the certain equivalent, which, as we recall, is the certain amount the decision-maker would accept in exchange for the uncertain venture. This certain amount of cash is thus the venture's minimum selling price.

One way to see the effect of a risk-averse attitude is to look at the risk penalty (or risk premium)—the difference between the expected value and certain equivalent. As the amount at risk increases (e.g., as the prize in the

Figure 5–1

Relationship Between Risk Penalty and the Amount at Risk

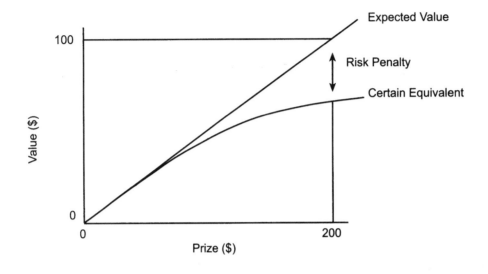

coin toss increases), the risk penalty increases and the certain equivalent becomes a smaller fraction of the expected value (Figure 5–1).

Furthermore, the decision criterion should have the certain equivalent decreasing the most (relative to the expected value) when the uncertainty is greatest. For instance, experience shows that if we hold the prize constant, but vary the probability (*p*) of winning the prize, we will see the greatest difference between the expected value and the certain equivalent in the region where the uncertainty is greatest (*p* around .5). (See Figure 5–2.)

Toward a Consistent Risk Attitude

The decision-maker could, in principle, stare at the probability distribution on value for each alternative of each venture, arrive at a set of certain equivalents, and then make the decision. Indeed, this is what we all do informally when faced with a decision under uncertainty. However, this approach has three problems. It is virtually impossible to be consistent from decision to decision, it is difficult to delegate effectively, and it is time-consuming and exhausting when many decisions must be made.

For these reasons, the decision criterion should enable the decision-maker to make explicit this most personal of values. The criterion should be applicable to all decisions, simple to apply in calculations, simple to communicate, and based on solid grounds—not just a rule of thumb of limited applicability.

Fortunately, we can take a series of certain equivalents the decision-maker has given for different ventures and produce a criterion for making other decisions consistently. The argument goes as follows:

- If we choose to behave according to a few reasonable behavioral rules, there is a utility function that describes our attitude toward risk taking.
- This utility function can be used in a simple way to obtain our certain equivalent for any probability distribution.
- The utility function is obtained by asking what our certain equivalent is for a few simple uncertain ventures.
- Over a reasonable range of outcomes, most people's and companies' utility functions for money can be fit by a function with one parameter, the risk tolerance. This makes it simple to speak of and compare attitudes toward risk.

The behavioral rules are shown below. We give a mathematical formulation for each rule and then explain how each relates to the way we actually

---

Figure 5–2

Relationship Between Certain Equivalent and Uncertainty

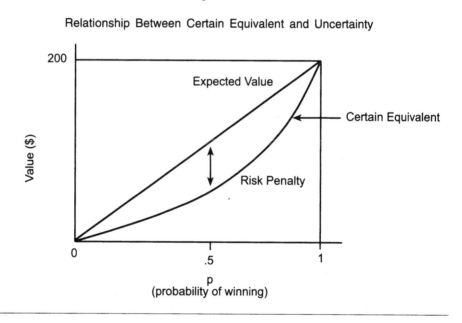

---

behave—or wish to behave. Note that in the context below > means "preferred to" and an arrow in the tree drawing indicates this preference.

Order Rule

If A > B and B > C, then A > C.

The order rule states that if we prefer A to B and B to C, then we prefer A to C. For instance, if we prefer a Mercedes to a Ford and a Ford to a Volkswagen, then we prefer a Mercedes to a Volkswagen. If we were to violate this rule, an unscrupulous car dealer could turn us into a "money pump": have us trade in our Volkswagen and buy a Ford; trade in our Ford and buy a Mercedes; trade in our Mercedes and buy (at a higher price) a Volkswagen. In the end, we have returned to our original state, but are poorer. Objections to this rule usually err in focusing on only one attribute of the outcomes.

Equivalence Rule

If A > B > C, then there is some value, p, for which the decision-maker is indifferent between the alternatives in the tree shown in Figure 5–3. (The double arrow means indifference between the two alternatives.)

Figure 5–3

Equivalence Rule in Tree Form

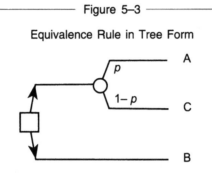

The equivalence rule says there is some value for the probability, p, at which we are indifferent between choosing a Ford and choosing the alternative where we might win a Mercedes or we might win a Volkswagen.

Substitution Rule

Given this indifference, B can be substituted for the uncertain venture in the top branch of the tree shown in Figure 5–3 without changing any preferences.

The substitution rule is really here for mathematical purposes. In behavioral terms it means, "Do you really mean it?" Are you willing to use the value p obtained in the preference statement of the equivalence rule as a probability in calculations? You must be able to substitute a certain venture for an uncertain venture with the same certain equivalent without changing any preferences.

Choice Rule

If A > B, then the choice shown in Figure 5–4 is true only if p is greater than q.

The choice rule says that we prefer the venture with the greater probability of winning the Mercedes.

────────────────────────── Figure 5–4 ──────────────────────────

Choice Rule in Tree Form

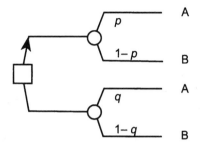

Probability Rule

The decision-maker is indifferent between the two alternatives shown in Figure 5–5. (Note that the probabilities of outcomes A and B are the same for both alternatives.)

The probability rule is fundamental in that it says that we wish to act rationally and consistently, at least to the level of being willing to use probabilities in our decision-making.

This rule is sometimes called the "no fun in gambling" rule. It states that multiple ventures can be replaced by equivalent single ventures because the decision-maker finds no intrinsic value in the ventures themselves. Much of the "fun in gambling" occurs because multiple ventures spread the excitement out over time. If we can put this entertainment value of gambling into the value function, then even the gambler may be able to satisfy this rule.

We can prove that if we subscribe to these rules, a utility function exists that can be used to find our certain equivalent for any uncertain venture. We will postpone the proof for the existence of the utility function until the end of this chapter.

────────────────────────── Figure 5–5 ──────────────────────────

Probability Rule in Tree Form

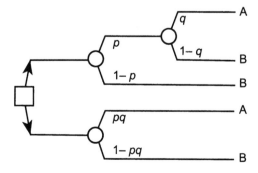

For convenience, we will restrict the values to a single continuous variable (money), although the utility function can treat discrete variables and multiple attributes. As we discussed in Chapter 3, this restriction will cause no problem for most business decisions.

What Is a Utility Function?

A utility function is a means of describing how much a particular outcome is worth to you. For instance, winning $1 million probably means something different to you than it does to the Sultan of Brunei (unless you are the Sultan of Brunei), and this difference would be reflected in your respective utility functions. A utility function measures worth by translating values (such as $1 million) into a measure called utiles or utility values.

Your utility function has the following two properties that, as we will see in a moment, make it useful in establishing a decision criterion:

- You prefer the alternative with the largest expected utility.
- Because utility values have no intrinsic meaning, you can arbitrarily assign the utilities of any two outcomes. This allows you to set a scale that determines the utility value of any other number, much like the way water freezing at 0°C and boiling at 100°C sets the centigrade scale.

These two properties can be seen in the proof of the existence of a utility function in the section "Deriving the Existence of a Utility Function."

Before it can be used, a utility function must first be created. For example, let us continue with the case of someone who is willing to bid a maximum of $60 for the chance to flip a coin for a prize of $200. Using tree notation, we can illustrate a very similar situation where the decision-maker is indifferent between accepting a sure $60 and accepting the coin flip (Figure 5–6). Another way to state the situation would be to say that the decision-maker's certain equivalent for the coin flip is $60—sixty percent of the expected value of $100.

———————— Figure 5–6 ————————

Tree Showing Coin Flip Decision

	Value ($)	Utility Value ($)
Win	200	u(200)
Lose	0	u(0)
Take the Sure Thing	60	u(60)

Play .5 / .5

We can write the utility of an outcome, x, as $u(x)$. Then the (expected) utility of the second alternative is simply $u(\$60)$. The expected utility of the first alternative is computed in the same manner as the expected value: multiply the probabilities by the utility values and sum the results. Thus, the expected utility of the first alternative is $(.5 \times u(\$200)) + (.5 \times u(\$0))$.

If we always prefer the alternative with the largest expected utility, indifference means that the two alternatives have the same expected utility.

$$u(\$60) = (.5 \times u(\$200)) + (.5 \times u(\$0)) \tag{5-1}$$

Using the second property from above, we can arbitrarily assign two utility values.

$$u(\$0) = 0 \tag{5-2}$$

$$u(\$200) = 2 \tag{5-3}$$

Now we can calculate $u(\$60)$.

$$u(\$60) = (5 \times 2) + (5 \times 0) = 1 \tag{5-4}$$

We can then graph these three points and sketch in a smooth curve (Figure 5–7). (A procedure for assessing the curve more carefully is given in the section "Encoding a Utility Function.")

How can we interpret this curve? In the positive direction, the curve flattens out so that, for instance, going from $200 to $220 produces less

Figure 5–7

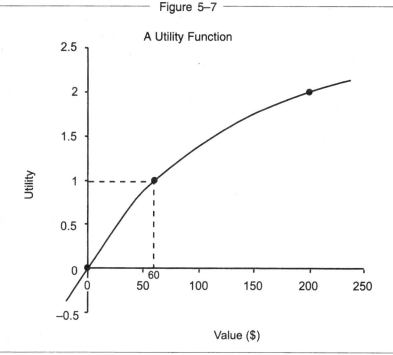

A Utility Function

increase in utility value than going from $0 to $20. In other words, going from $200 to $220 means less to us than going from $0 to $20. In the negative direction, the curve becomes ever steeper, indicating that additional decreases in value become ever more significant.

Utility curves have some general properties that help in understanding them.

- Utility curves should generally be monotonically increasing. A utility function that sometimes decreases would mean that getting more of what you want would sometimes be undesirable!
- It is the curvature of the utility function that is important. The shape of the curve in Figure 5–7 (concave downward) indicates that the certain equivalent is less than the expected value. Upside potential means less (the curve flattens in the positive direction) than downside risk (the curve grows steeper in the negative direction). Having a certain equivalent smaller than the expected value is characteristic of risk-averse behavior. The more risk averse you are, the more curved (concave downward) your utility function is.
- The reader can easily verify that risk-neutral behavior (with the certain equivalent equal to the expected value) is described by a straight-line utility function. Utility curves for expected-value decision-makers are straight lines.
- Risk-seeking behavior is possible. Risk seeking implies certain equivalents greater than expected values. Utility curves for risk-seeking individuals would be concave upward. Significant risk seeking (not just buying a state lottery ticket) is ordinarily found in individuals whose aspirations are blocked by lack of fair markets. For instance, a man who needs $100,000 to start a small business and cannot find any backing may be willing to risk all his $50,000 capital in a desperate gamble whose net expected value is much less than $50,000, but which has a possible outcome of $100,000. Clearly, this type of behavior is very special and will not be considered further in this book.

Using a Utility Function _____

How do we use the utility curve? Suppose, for instance, that the person whose utility curve we plotted above is faced with a venture with smaller stakes, such as a coin flip for only $100. We can use the utility curve to determine this person's certain equivalent (maximum bid) for the new coin flip. As in equation 5–1, the utility of the maximum acceptable bid is equal to the expected utility of the coin flip. We could draw a tree similar to the one for the first flip, but the following steps more directly accomplish the same calculation (finding the certain equivalent):

--- Figure 5-8 ---

Probability Tree

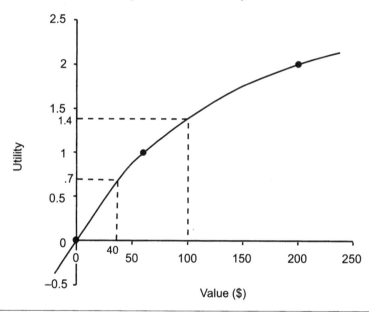

	Value ($)	Utility Value
Win	100	1.4
Lose	0	0

Expected Utility = .7
Certain Equivalent = $40

--- Figure 5-9 ---

Reading Values from a Utility Curve

1. Use the utility curve to find the utility values of the outcomes.
2. Calculate the expected utility.
3. Use the utility curve to find the certain equivalent value corresponding to the expected utility.

This calculation is illustrated in the tree in Figure 5–8 describing a coin flip for a $100 prize. The values used in this tree are obtained from the utility curve shown in 5–9.

Note that with an expected value of $50, the certain equivalent is now 80 percent of the expected value, whereas in the first coin flip the $60 certain equivalent was only 60 percent of the $100 expected value. With smaller amounts at stake, the certain equivalent becomes a higher percentage of the expected value. Another result the reader can verify is that the certain equivalent value becomes equal to the expected value as the probability of winning (or losing) approaches 1.0.

After some discussion, the president of Positronics consented to an interview in private by the decision facilitators. In the interview, the facilitators assessed a utility curve for the president. Reluctantly, he allowed his utility curve (Figure 5–10) to be shown the next day at the analysis group meeting that had by now begun to be scheduled on a regular basis. At first, he was a little hesitant to allow people to see what his attitude to risk was. The facilitators also presented a few examples to show some implications of the utility curve. Upper level management was a bit surprised that the examples showed the president willing to take much greater risks than they had thought he would. They had previously discarded ventures as too risky that they now perceived might be interesting to him. Some rather frank discussion revealed that although the president was willing to take risk, he frequently rejected ventures not because of the risk but because he thought the optimists who presented the decision to him had overstated the probability of success.

Figure 5–10

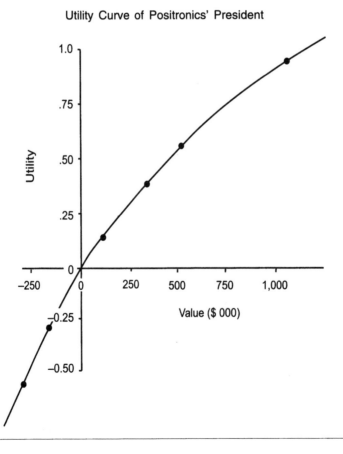

Utility Curve of Positronics' President

By examining the curve (Figure 5–10), we can see that, like most people, the president is risk averse. As mentioned above, this means that his utility values drop off ever more sharply for large negative numbers and flatten out for large positive numbers.

We saw above how to use a utility function in a simple situation. A similar procedure is used for more complicated situations (and more complicated trees). As the proof in the section "Deriving the Existence of a Utility Function" shows, the procedure for using the utility function starts by first converting all the values at the endpoints of the tree into utiles. Then, in the rollback procedure, chance nodes are replaced by their expected utility (instead of expected value) and decision nodes by the alternative with the greatest (expected) utility. The utility curve can then be used in reverse to convert the expected utility into the certain equivalent of the overall tree, or even to convert the expected utility into the certain equivalent at any point in the tree.

Positronics applied this procedure to the decision tree (Figure 5–11). The utility values at the end of the tree were calculated and rolled back through the tree to obtain the expected utility at each node.

The choice is still to bid $500,000, with a utility of .088. Although it is difficult to tell from the encoded utility function (one reason why we will go to a computerized function), we can estimate that the certain equivalent corresponding to the utility is quite close to the expected value of $65,000.

Value of Information with an Encoded Utility Function

One thing to remember when using a directly encoded utility function is to be particularly careful about doing value of information calculations. To calculate the value of information, you should use the full value of information tree (Figure 3–17) rather than just reorder the nodes.

To find the value of information, put in different information costs as (negative) rewards on the "Yes" branch until you have found a cost level for which the value of the two alternatives is equal. This cost is the value of information. This iterative procedure is necessary because different costs shift us to different regions of the utility curve where the utility/value trade-off may be different.

However, when using an exponential utility function such as the one discussed below, we can calculate the value of information as we did for expected-value decision-makers—there is no need for this iterative procedure.

An Exponential Utility Function _____

Within a reasonable range of values, many personal and corporate utility curves can be approximated well by an exponential function:

$$u(x) = a - be^{-x/R} \tag{5–5}$$

where x is the value (such as dollars), R is the risk tolerance, and a and b are parameters set by the choice of two points in the utility curve. The

——————————————————— Figure 5–11 ———————————————————

Using the Utility Function in the Positronics Tree

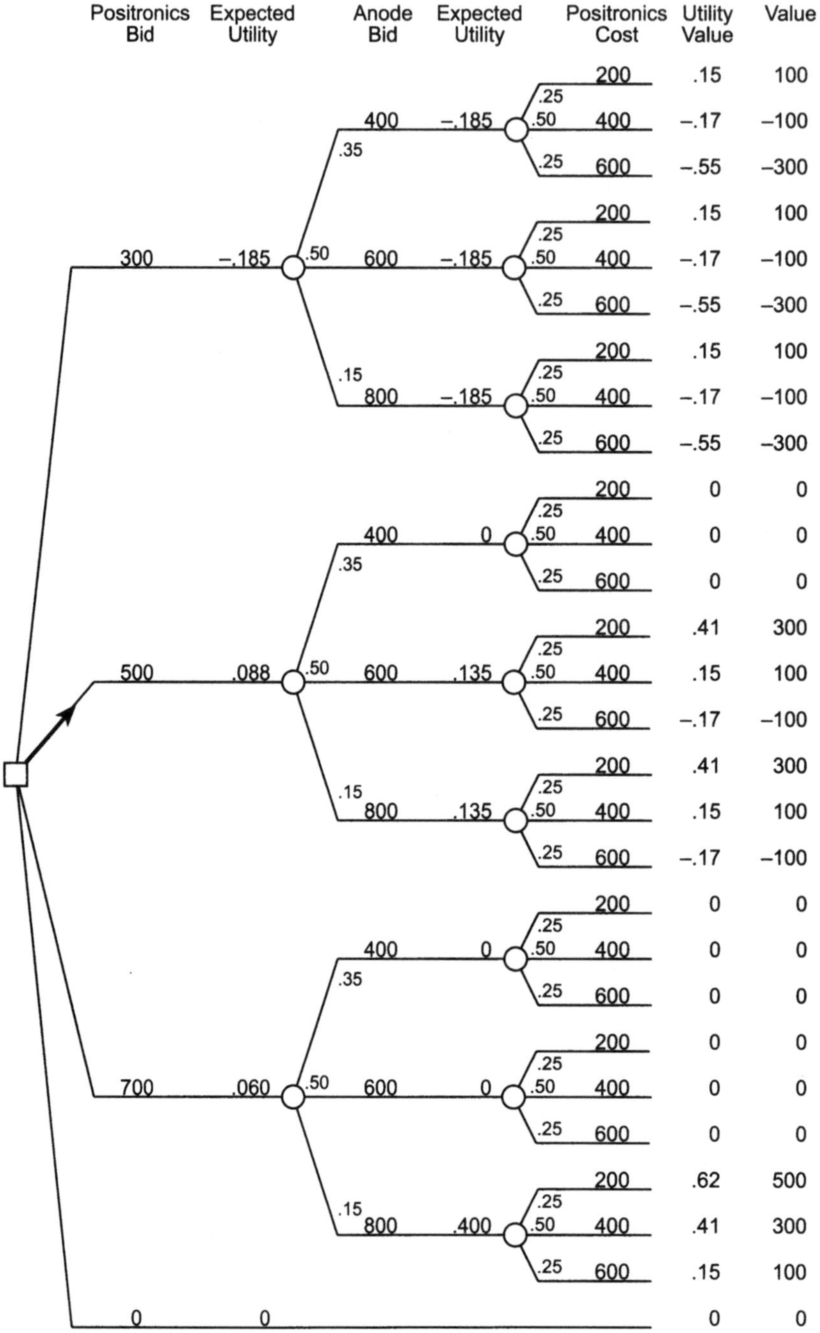

Positronics Bid	Expected Utility	Anode Bid	Expected Utility	Positronics Cost	Utility Value	Value
				200	.15	100
		400	−.185	400	−.17	−100
				600	−.55	−300
				200	.15	100
300	−.185	600	−.185	400	−.17	−100
				600	−.55	−300
				200	.15	100
		800	−.185	400	−.17	−100
				600	−.55	−300
				200	0	0
		400	0	400	0	0
				600	0	0
				200	.41	300
500	.088	600	.135	400	.15	100
				600	−.17	−100
				200	.41	300
		800	.135	400	.15	100
				600	−.17	−100
				200	0	0
		400	0	400	0	0
				600	0	0
				200	0	0
700	.060	600	0	400	0	0
				600	0	0
				200	.62	500
		800	.400	400	.41	300
				600	.15	100
0	0				0	0

Figure 5–12

Exponential Utility Function Curves

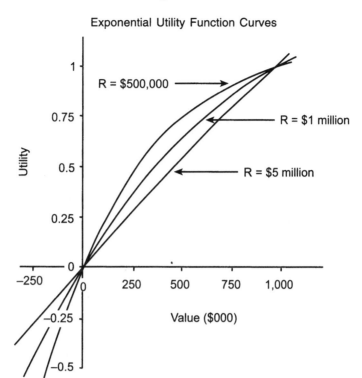

parameter *b* must be greater than zero. The risk tolerance is the parameter that describes the curvature of the utility curve and is expressed in the same units as the values. One sometimes sees reference to the risk-aversion coefficient, which is defined as $1/R$.

The facilitator graphed exponential utility functions for several different values of risk tolerance and compared these functions with the curve encoded from the president of Positronics. * *As he saw in Figure 5–12, the utility function encoded from the president was well described by an exponential utility function with a risk tolerance of about $1 million. Further, within the range over which the curve was encoded, he saw that Positronics was not far from an expected-value decision-maker (which would mean a straight-line utility function and imply infinite risk tolerance).*

The facilitator decided to use the exponential utility function with a risk tolerance of $1 million. Tree calculations could be done more quickly and consistently using this function rather than the encoded curve. In addition, the facilitator decided to show certain equivalents rather than expected utilities in the tree drawing (Figure 5–13).

* The two arbitrary points in the encoded curve were $u(\$0) = 0$ and $u(\$1 \text{ million}) = 1$. The exponential utility function that goes through these points is

$$u(x) = (1 - exp(-x/R)) / (1 - exp(-1,000/R))$$

where R is the risk tolerance and x and R are expressed in units of thousands of dollars.

——————————————— Figure 5–13 ———————————————

Positronics' Decision Tree with a Risk Tolerance of One Million Dollars

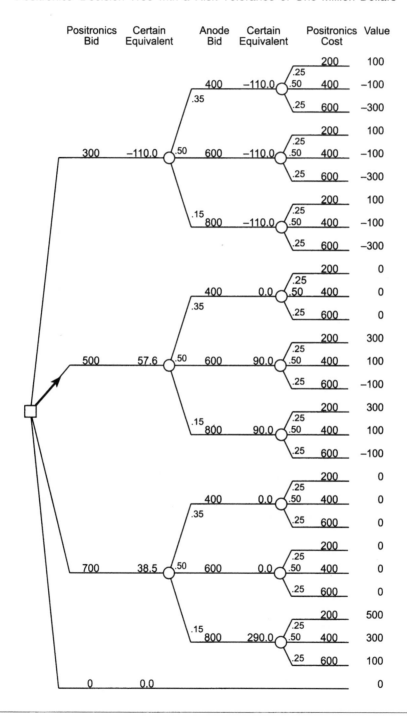

As the facilitator saw from the tree drawing, the certain equivalents for each alternative were quite close to the expected values. The difference is small because none of the possible outcomes in this decision problem posed a significant risk to the business. The risk premium was only $65,000 – $57,600 = $7,400.

There are several quick ways of estimating risk tolerance. The proofs of these estimating techniques are in problems 5.14 and 5.15. First, you can consider the uncertain venture illustrated by the chance node in Figure 5–14. To make it more concrete, imagine that an acquaintance needs backing to start a small business and offers to "double your money in a short period." You judge there are 3 chances in 4 he will be able to pay off.

——————————————— Figure 5–14 ———————————————

Use of a Venture to Estimate Risk Tolerance

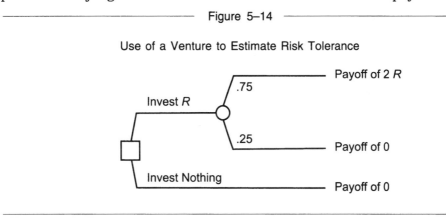

The question, then, is what is the largest sum of money you would be willing to lend your friend? In other words, what is the largest investment, R, you would consider making in a venture that has a .75 chance of paying 2R in return and a .25 chance of paying nothing in return?

An equivalent way of posing this question is shown below. Suppose you had an opportunity to take the chance illustrated in Figure 5–15 or pass. What is the largest value R for which you will accept a .75 chance of winding

——————————————— Figure 5–15 ———————————————

Would You Take the Chance or Pass?

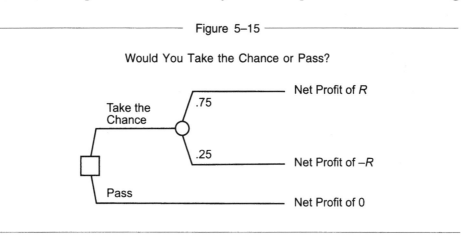

up R richer and a .25 chance of winding up R poorer? (This question just combines the investment and return from the Figure 5–14.) R is approximately your risk tolerance and should be the same in both cases.

You can also use another venture (Figure 5–16) to estimate your risk tolerance without having to consider the possibility of such severe losses.

———————————————— Figure 5–16 ————————————————

Use of Another Venture to Estimate Risk Tolerance

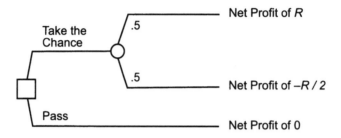

What is the largest value of R for which you will accept a .5 chance of winding up R richer and a .5 chance of winding up $R/2$ poorer? Once again, R is approximately your risk tolerance.

Value of Corporate Risk Tolerance?

In the relatively rare event of assessing corporate risk tolerances from top management in the corporation, we have used the encoding methods described at the end of this chapter rather than the quick estimates discussed above. However, there are several rules of thumb for estimating risk tolerance. One rule of thumb is to set risk tolerance about equal to net income for companies that generally take moderate risks. Another rule of thumb is to set the risk tolerance equal to one-sixth of equity, or to one-fifth of market value. Compare these rules to the figures in the following table, which shows the risk tolerance obtained in the 1970s from the top management in three real companies.

| | Company | | |
Measure ($ millions)	A	B	C
Net Sales	2,300	16,000	31,000
Net Income	120	700	1,900
Equity	1,000	6,500	12,000
Market Value	940	4,600	9,900
Risk Tolerance	150	1,000	2,000

These three companies are large capital-intensive oil and chemical companies. Individual companies and different types of companies vary widely in the ratio of risk tolerance to net income, company size, stockholders' equity, or other measures. One would expect the ratio of risk tolerance to equity or market value to translate best between companies in different industries.*

However, there is a basic question whether publicly traded corporations should have a utility function and exhibit risk aversion. Standard corporate finance argues that corporate officers should maximize share price in their decision-making. Given that the shareholder has diversified holdings, the shareholder sees only the overall market risk and not project risk. Following this logic, projects should be evaluated at their expected value with market risk incorporated in the cost of equity.

How can we reconcile this conclusion with the fact that corporations appear to act in a risk-averse way? One suggestion is that there are hidden costs created by uncertainty—hidden in the sense that they are usually not completely modeled in project analysis. A corporation is the nexus for a set of contractual relationships among many individuals: shareholders, directors and officers, debt holders, employees, suppliers, distributors, customers, and government. Because many of these individuals are exposed to project risk (e.g., officers, employees, suppliers, and distributors), a risk premium may be required in executing risky projects; these risk premiums can effectively create a corporate utility function.†

In practice, most decisions do not pose serious "risk" to the corporation. Also, in practice, most corporations do exhibit risk aversion when faced with "risky" ventures. Clarity in corporate decision making is usually achieved by displaying probability distributions for their expected values.

An Approximation to the Certain Equivalent

Once we have assessed a risk tolerance, the following approximate formula is a quick way to approximate the certain equivalent for a given probability distribution:

$$\text{Certain Equivalent} = \text{Expected Value} - \frac{1}{2}\frac{\text{Variance}}{\text{Risk Tolerance}} \qquad (5\text{--}6)$$

---

* There is some descriptive evidence that divisions within corporations act as if they had even smaller risk tolerances (are more risk-averse) than described here. See, for instance, "Risk Propensity and Firm Performance: A Study of the Petroleum Exploration Industry", M. R. Walls and J. S. Dyer, *Management Science*, 42, 7 (1966), 1004–1021.

† "The Corporate Contractual System and Normative Corporate Risk Attitude", James Eric Bickel, Ph. D. thesis, Engineering-Economic Systems, Stanford University, June 1999.

This approximation comes from the Taylor series expansion of the utility function and of the probability distribution (problem 5.22). The variance characterizes the width (uncertainty) of the probability distribution, and the risk tolerance characterizes the risk attitude embodied in the utility function. The second term on the right is just the risk penalty (Figures 5–1 and 5–2.) To estimate the variance, take the width from the .1 to the .9 points on the cumulative probability curve, square it, and then divide by 6.6. This works because that width is 2.56 times the standard deviation for a normal (Gaussian) distribution. (This value can be seen in the graph of the normal distribution in Figure 10–17.) Since the variance is the square of the standard deviation, when we square the width, we get $(2.56)^2 = 6.6$ times the variance. For distributions that are not normal distributions, this is, of course, only an approximation of the variance.

What is a reasonable range of values for which the exponential function is adequate? Normally, a reasonable range is one for which none of the values (positive or negative) are much larger than the risk tolerance. There are a number of other functional forms that fit well to utility functions with a wider range of values but that are not as convenient to work with. Furthermore, our experience shows that probability distributions should be explicitly examined by the decision-maker when they involve a range of values so great that the exponential utility function is inadequate; decision-makers will not rely solely on the decision implied by a utility function when so much is at stake.

The president of Positronics had tried all these techniques and obtained values for the company risk tolerance that, although well within an order of magnitude of each other, varied considerably. Part of the problem was that he had never worked with an explicit representation of uncertainty, so he was on unfamiliar ground. Furthermore, risk attitude is difficult to express quantitatively because it involves very personal values. To help him with his decision, the president asked the facilitators to evaluate the tree for a number of values of risk tolerance and see if it changed the preferred decision.

The tree was reevaluated using a number of different values for risk tolerance, and the results are shown in Figure 5–17. The horizontal axis is linear in 1/risk tolerance, which is the risk-aversion coefficient. The leftmost values are for infinite risk tolerance, which is equivalent to the expected value. The certain equivalents are plotted for each alternative for each value of the risk tolerance.

We see that the $500,000 bid is optimal for risk tolerances down to around $120,000. Below that value, the $700,000 bid becomes preferable.

The risk attitude sensitivity is a very powerful tool. Frequently, decision-makers do not feel they have been consistent in encoding their risk tolerance and, thus, would not want an important decision to hang on such a difficult number. Also, in large companies, it is often difficult to interview decision-makers long enough to encode a utility curve. One approach is to estimate a risk tolerance for the company from the ratios above and then use the sensitivity to find out if a more exact determination of the risk

Figure 5–17

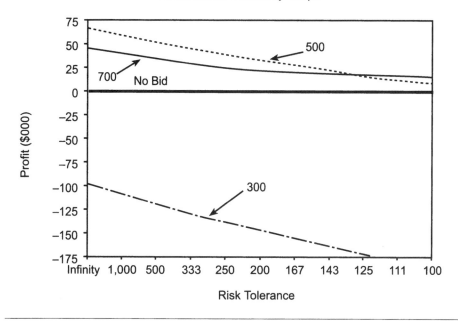

Risk Attitude Sensitivity Graph

tolerance is called for. The risk tolerance sensitivity frequently shows that, for any reasonable range of risk tolerances, the decision is clear.

Encoding a Utility Function

Encoding a utility function is not particularly complicated for a single continuous attribute such as money. First, arbitrarily set two points on the utility scale. A common practice is to set the utility of $0 value to be 0: $u(\$0) = 0$. Pick another point (say $10,000 for a personal utility curve) and let it be 1: $u(\$10,000) = 1$. Next, construct a simple two-branch venture with these two values as outcomes (Figure 5–18.)

Figure 5–18

Simple Two-Branch Venture

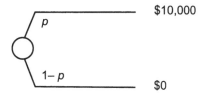

Choose a probability p and ask the decision-maker what his or her certain equivalent is. Suppose the probability p were .7 and the decision-maker responded with a certain equivalent of $5,000. We would then be able to plot a third point on the utility curve by using the basic utility property: indifference between the sure $5,000 alternative and the uncertain alternative means their expected utilities are equal.

$$u(\$5,000) = \left[.7 \times u(\$10,000)\right] + \left[.3 \times u(\$0)\right]$$

$$u(\$5,000) = (.7 \times 1) + (.3 \times 0)$$

$$u(\$5,000) = .7 \qquad\qquad (5\text{--}7)$$

We can now either change the probability, p, or construct a new simple venture from the values for which we have utility values. We then request that the decision-maker furnish a certain equivalent for this venture, which is used to find the utility point of still another value.

The process of encoding the utility points is thus fairly straightforward. However, the process of giving the certain equivalents is very unfamiliar and difficult. The first try at a utility function may produce a set of points that do not fit on a smooth curve.

The person encoding should be alert for discontinuities in slope occurring at $0. People frequently get unduly alarmed by numbers with a negative sign, no matter how small. One technique to iron out this problem is to ask the decision-maker to consolidate this venture with another (certain) venture. This does not change the problem, but it does shift the place where the zero occurs. By doing this several times, you should obtain smooth continuity through the zero point.

In corporate decision problems, the utility function should be encoded from the top management of the company—often the president or CEO. However, since top management time is valuable, it is often best to estimate an appropriate risk tolerance for the company, perhaps using the ratios mentioned earlier in this chapter. You can then find out if the problem requires going beyond the expected value and risk sensitivity. For many business decisions, expected value turns out to be adequate. Only the largest and most uncertain problems require careful use of the utility function.

Deriving the Existence of a Utility Function _____

The behavioral rules discussed in the section "Toward a Consistent Risk Attitude" can be used to show that a utility function exists that has the desired property: decisions are made to choose the alternative with the greatest expected utility. The following seven-step proof derives this property from the rules. To keep things simple, we will present the proof for a finite number of discrete outcomes. The outcomes need not all be monetary and can represent a mix of different values.

1. The order rule is used to order the outcomes as R_1, R_2, ..., R_n, where $R_1 > R_2 > ... > R_n$.
2. Any uncertain venture, P, can be reduced by the probability rule to the form shown in Figure 5–19.

Figure 5–19

Representation of Uncertain Venture P

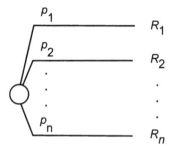

3. The equivalence rule is used to find, for each R_i, a probability u_i such that R_i is equivalent to the uncertain venture shown in Figure 5–20.

Figure 5–20

Using the Equivalence Rule

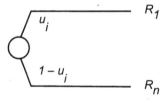

4. The substitution rule can be used to substitute the results of step 3 of the tree in step 2 (Figure 5–19) and obtain the tree in Figure 5–21.

Figure 5–21

Using the Substitution Rule

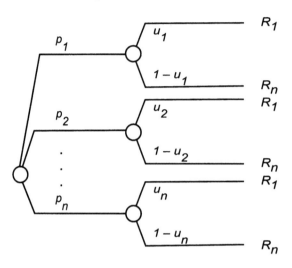

5. The probability rule can be used again to simplify this tree, as shown in Figure 5–22.

Figure 5–22

Probability Rule Used to Simplify the Tree

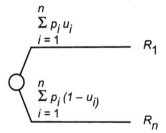

6. Another uncertain venture, Q, can be represented by the tree in Figure 5–23 (as P was in step 2), and, by the same procedure, put in the form shown in Figure 5–24.

——————————————————— Figure 5–23 ———————————————————

Representation of Uncertain Venture Q

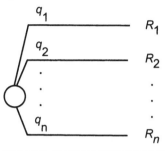

——————————————————— Figure 5–24 ———————————————————

Revised Form

7. If P is preferred to Q, then the choice rule states that

$$\sum_{i=1}^{n} p_i u_i > \sum_{i=1}^{n} q_i u_i \qquad (5\text{–}8)$$

Believe it or not, we have achieved the desired result. If we define u_i to be the utility of R_i, then we prefer the alternative with the larger expected utility. (Remember that p_i and q_i are the probabilities associated with the alternatives P and Q.) We have constructed a utility function with the desired property.

Incidentally, you can easily see that when the utility values are transformed by a linear transformation

$$u'_i = a + b u_i \qquad (5\text{–}9)$$

(with $b > 0$), the decision criterion that P is preferred to Q if $\Sigma_i p_i u'_i > \Sigma_i q_i u'_i$ is still maintained. The two parameters a and b are set by arbitrarily choosing the utility of any two values (provided the utility of the preferred value is greater than the utility of the other value).

Risk-Free Discount Rates

The choice of a discount rate is important in almost any business decision. Making a proper choice involves both the finance department and the decision analysis team and is one of the thornier questions a facilitator faces. It is often difficult to find people who really understand the considerations in choosing a discount rate and who will commit themselves to a particular rate. In this section, we describe some of the considerations and pitfalls in choosing a discount rate.

In Chapter 3, we mentioned that we accounted for time in the value function by discounting future cash flows to obtain the net present value. In this chapter, we have shown how to account for risk. For this reason, a risk-free discount rate should be used in the evaluation. What is an appropriate value for a risk-free discount rate? One risk-free investment opportunity is U.S. Treasury bills. Examining interest rates on these bills over the last 50 years or so has shown that, in real terms (excluding inflation effects), these bills return less than 4 percent (Figure 5–25).

Note that if d is the real interest rate (excluding inflation effects), i is the inflation rate, and d' is the nominal interest rate (including inflation effects), then $(1 + d') = (1 + i)(1 + d)$.

Figure 5–25

Real Average Annual Returns on Common Investments
Real Average* Annual Return (%)

Series	1926–98	1940–89	1960–89	1980–89
Common stocks	—	7.4	5.4	12.4
Large company stocks	7.9	—	—	—
Small company stocks	9.1	—	—	—
Long-term corporate bonds	2.6	0.4	2.0	7.9
U.S. Treasury bills	0.7	–0.2	1.4	3.8

* Geometric mean, net of inflation

Source: Roger G. Ibbotson and Rex A. Sinquefield, *Stocks, Bonds, Bills, and Inflation*. 1990 Edition, Institute of Chartered Financial Analysts, Charlottesville, Virginia; *Stocks, Bonds, Bills, and Inflation, 1999 Yearbook*, Ibbotson Associates, Chicago, Illinois

However, the situation that most projects face in the corporate world is that funding can not be obtained at the U.S. Treasury bill rate. Rather, capital is available at the Weighted Average Cost of Capital (WACC) rate. For corporate decision-makers, this often represents the "risk-free" corporate time preference. Whether this is appropriate is a matter of ongoing debate.

In business evaluations, an internal rate of return (IRR) criterion is often used. To account for risk, a minimum acceptable value for the IRR is established. In Chapter 3, we showed why the IRR criterion is inappropriate for dealing with situations in which uncertainty is important.

Another commonly used decision criterion is to apply a risk-adjusted discount rate and then to check for a positive present value. This criterion addresses uncertainty and risk indirectly by adding several percent to the discount rate to account for risk. However, as shown below, this approach contains many potential pitfalls, since it mixes considerations of time and risk, which are not necessarily connected.

In contrast to the risk-adjusted discount rate approach, the certain equivalent accounts for risk explicitly in the risk penalty, and the discount rate separately accounts for time with a risk-free rate. With the certain equivalent approach, when the certain equivalent for any uncertain venture falls below zero, the venture becomes undesirable (Figure 5–26). This is determined by the risk tolerance, a number that is determined once and then used for all decisions.

With the risk-adjusted discount rate approach, on the other hand, the venture is desirable for all values of the discount rate for which the NPV of some base case is greater than 0. The adjustment to the discount rate, however, has to be estimated for each alternative, taking into account the uncertainty of each venture. The Capital Asset Pricing Model (CAPM) is one approach to determining the discount rate for risky ventures.

The basic problem is that there is no intrinsic relationship between time and risk; thus, why try to evaluate risk by a discount rate? Several simple cases where blindly applying risk-adjusted discount rates produces spurious results illustrate this problem, as shown below. The certain equivalent method discussed in this chapter always works.

1. For any ventures where the uncertainty is resolved almost immediately, virtually no discount rate is high enough for the risk-adjusted discount rate method to make a risky venture appear undesirable. Ventures of this type include coin tosses, foreign currency exchanges, options, and opportunities arising because of acquisitions and divestitures.

2. For ventures with long time horizons, risk-adjusted discount rates tend to discourage ventures with any amount of uncertainty. This is one of the reasons why some companies spend too little money on long-term activities like research and development. Ironically, much of the uncertainty in research and development is usually resolved in the short term with the technical success or failure of a project.

—————————————————— Figure 5–26 ——————————————————

Certain Equivalent and Risk-Adjusted Discount Rate Approaches

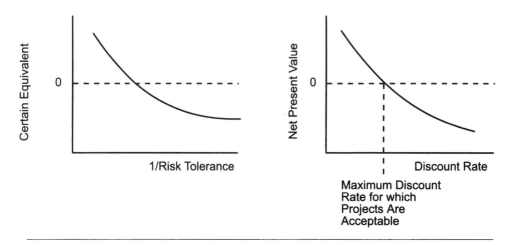

3. For ventures with unconventional cash flows (profits occurring before payment), the higher we adjust the discount rate, the better the risky venture looks. However, higher discount rates are intended to discourage risky ventures! Examples of such "fly now, pay later" ventures occur in litigation (settle now or wait to see if the courts will declare you liable), in long-term financing, and in nuclear power plant construction (initial investment followed by operating profit followed by decommissioning costs).
4. A last example shows how the certain equivalent approach is sensitive to the size of the amounts involved, while the risk-adjusted discount rate approach is not. Consider Venture A and Venture B; B is identical to A except that it has all A's

—————————————————— Figure 5–27 ——————————————————

Sensitivity of Certain Equivalent and Risk-Adjusted Discount Rate Approaches to Size of Amount at Risk

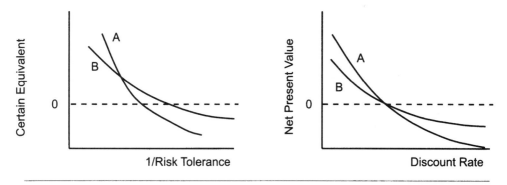

outcomes cut in half. B could be, for instance, a 50/50 joint venture of A. The certain equivalent approach shows that below some value of the risk tolerance, the larger venture A becomes too risky and B is preferred (Figure 5–27). (This is one of the reasons for engaging in joint ventures.) However, the risk-adjusted discount rate approach will always prefer the larger Venture A for values of the discount rate where the NPV is positive. Venture B is only preferred for discount rates for which the NPV of both A and B is negative—the "lesser of two evils." This characteristic depends only on the time pattern of the cash flow and not at all on the size of the alternatives, even though A is obviously riskier than B because it is bigger. Different risk adjustments must be used for the discount rates for Ventures A and B to make the risk-adjusted discount rate approach work.

Summary

Expected values are often an inadequate criterion for decision-making. People often exhibit an aversion to risk that leads them to different choices than looking at expected values would indicate. This behavior can be accounted for by substituting certain equivalent values for expected values. Certain equivalent values can be assessed directly for each probability distribution, but this procedure is cumbersome and difficult to do consistently.

Certain equivalent values for a decision-maker can be calculated consistently and easily by using a utility function. If the decision-maker is willing to accept a reasonable set of behavioral rules, it can be shown that he or she has a utility function with the desired properties. The utility function can be used to translate a probability distribution on values into the certain equivalent value.

A utility function can be encoded directly. However, an exponential utility function often provides a good approximation of actual behavior for most individuals and corporations and is analytically much easier to use. An exponential utility function can be characterized by a single parameter, the risk tolerance.

Finally, we briefly discussed why it is better to account for risk by using a utility function and a risk-free discount rate rather than by using risk-adjusted discount rates.

Problems and Discussion Topics

5.1 Consider several decisions you have made, ranging from minor importance to major importance. Was there implicit or explicit risk aversion in the way you went about making these decisions? Do you think your risk attitude was consistent across these decisions? Give examples and say why or why not.

5.2   Do the behavioral rules adequately describe the way you would like to make certain types of decisions?   Are there cases that do not fit the way you would like to make a decision? If so, give an example.

5.3   What factors contribute to the difference between using the expected value and using a utility function with risk aversion? Under what circumstances would the expected value and the certain equivalent value be the same?

5.4   Suppose you have a certain equivalent, CE, for a venture with probabilities $(p_1, p_2, ..., p_n)$ and prizes $(x_1, x_2, ..., x_n)$. The Delta Property states that if we add some arbitrary amount Δ to all the prizes such that the venture is now for prizes $(x_1 + \Delta, x_2 + \Delta, ..., x_n + \Delta)$, then your certain equivalent for the new venture will be CE + Δ. Furthermore, if you subscribe to the Delta Property, then your utility function is exponential or linear.

Describe a situation where the Delta Property would not apply to you.

5.5   Use one of the two methods described in the text to assess a risk tolerance for yourself. Have the rewards or losses used in this assessment be paid immediately.

Now consider that the money you invest or lose can be paid monthly over a thirty-year period. For instance, at 10 percent you would pay roughly $1,000 each month for the next thirty years to pay off $100,000. Reassess your risk tolerance. Is it any different? Why or why not? What if interest were included on the balance?

5.6   Use the method described in the text to encode a utility function for a classmate. Then, directly assess his or her certain equivalent (minimum selling price) for a 1 in 5,000 chance of winning $10,000. Compare the result with the certain equivalent from using the utility function. What does this tell you about your classmate's risk attitude for this kind of opportunity?

5.7   Peter Portfolio faces a decision for a short-term investment based on the prospective movement of a stock. The possibilities are shown below.

Peter has an exponential utility function with a risk tolerance of $5,000.

a.   What is Peter's decision? What is his certain equivalent for the venture?

b.   Peter is not sure if his risk tolerance is exactly $5,000. For what range of risk tolerance should he "Buy"?

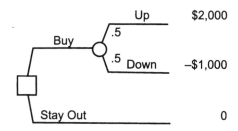

Decision   Stock Price

c.   Sheba Sisters brokerage firm has investigated the stock and offers Peter perfect information on whether the stock price will go up or down. What is the maximum he should pay for the information?

5.8   Your regular morning radio show has awarded you the uncertain venture shown below.

You have an exponential utility function with a risk tolerance of $2,000. You are indifferent to selling the venture for $700. What is the probability p?

$1,000

p

$1-p$

-$500

5.9   J. K. Kay faces a short-term investment decision on stocks A and B whose performance is correlated.

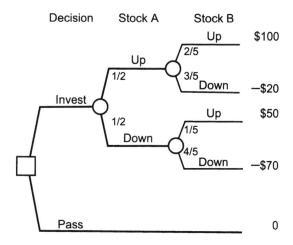

Decision   Stock A   Stock B

    a.   If JK is an expected-value decision-maker, how much should he pay the clairvoyant for perfect information on whether stock B goes up or down?

    b.   If JK is risk averse and has an exponential utility function with a risk tolerance of $500, what is the most he should pay for the perfect information on stock B?

5.10 Compare the certain equivalents from using the exponential utility function for some problems in previous chapters with the certain equivalents obtained from the following approximation:

$$\text{Certain Equivalent} = \text{Expected Value} - \frac{1}{2}\frac{\text{Variance}}{\text{Risk Tolerance}}$$

where

$$\text{Expected Value} = \sum_{i=1}^{m} x_i\, p(x_i|S)$$

$$\text{Variance} = \sum_{i=1}^{m} (x_i - \text{Expected Value})^2\, p(x_i|S)$$

5.11 Je has the following utility function:

$$u(x) = \ln(1 + x / R)$$

where R = $200. His utility is set so that outcomes x are measured as differences from his present wealth. There is an uncertain venture, L, shown below.

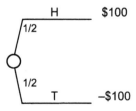

Assume that Je can borrow money at no cost.

    a.   Suppose that Je does not own the venture. What is the maximum he should be willing to pay for this venture?

    b.   Assume that he owns the venture. What is the lowest price that he should be willing to sell it for?

5.12   There are extreme situations in which people may behave differently than normal. Some of these situations can be explained by a special utility function.

Mr. Sam Spade, after a night of partying in San Francisco, suddenly realizes that he has only a $10 bill left in his pocket. Unfortunately, the train fare home for him is $15. Then he observes a wild gambler in the nearby corner who offers him the three opportunities shown below, each at a certain cost:

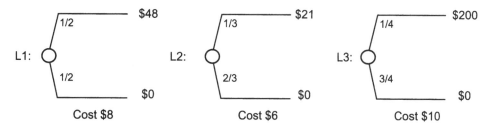

Right now, all Sam cares about is getting home. What is his special utility function for this situation? Which opportunity should Sam choose?

5.13   Missouri Tubing, Inc., is a manufacturer of specialty steel and copper tubing. Its production facility is located adjacent to the Missouri River and is protected from the waters by a 20-foot-high dike. Extremely heavy rains in recent weeks have raised the level of the river dangerously close to the top of the dike. Several other areas near the river have already been badly flooded and the weather forecast is for continued rain.

The risk manager of Missouri Tubing estimates that there is a 20 percent chance that the river will top the dike in the coming weeks and flood the factory. If the factory is flooded, there is a 50 percent chance the damage will be heavy, costing about $20 million to repair, and a 50 percent chance it will be light, costing about $10 million. Furthermore, flooding of the factory will force it to shut down while repairs are made. If damage is heavy, the factory will be closed for four months. If damage is light, there is a 60 percent chance the shutdown will last four months and a 40 percent chance it will last only two months. For each month the factory is closed, Missouri Tubing will lose $25 million in profits.

The risk manager now regrets that he recently cancelled the company's insurance policy covering flood damage. However, his insurance agent has decided to help him out by offering him a special emergency flood insurance policy. The policy provides coverage of both property damage and business interruption (i.e., lost profits) from flooding for a period of six months. The premium for the policy is $30 million. Another policy providing only the business interruption coverage is also available for a premium of $25 million.

a.   Draw the influence diagram for Missouri Tubing's problem.

b.   Structure the decision tree for Missouri Tubing's problem and calculate the expected value of each alternative.

c.   Calculate the value of clairvoyance for an expected-value decision-maker on whether or not the Missouri Tubing factory is flooded.

d.   Calculate the certain equivalent for each alternative assuming that Missouri Tubing's risk tolerance is $50 million.

e.   Calculate the value of clairvoyance with risk aversion on whether the Missouri Tubing factory is flooded.

5.14   Suppose that a decision-maker agrees on the five utility rules. We then know that there exists a utility function for the decision-maker. If he or she also agrees on the Delta Property, then we know further that the utility function is exponential and can be characterized by a single number, the risk tolerance. (See problems 5.4 and 5.17.)

One way to approximate the risk tolerance is to find the largest number X for which the venture shown below is still acceptable to the decision-maker. Show that X is within about 4 percent of the true risk tolerance.

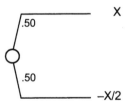

5.15   Show that the largest value X for which the venture shown below is acceptable is within 10 percent of the risk tolerance (assuming an exponential utility function).

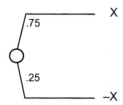

5.16 In general, the risk tolerance function can be defined as

$$\rho(x) = -u'(x)/u''(x)$$

where x is the increment to current wealth of the person in question (wealth = x + current wealth), u' is the first derivative of the utility function, and u'' is the second derivative. Some people agree that if they had more wealth, they would probably tolerate more risks. To a first approximation, this can be captured by:

$$\rho(x) = \rho_0 + Kx \quad \text{where} \ K \geq 0,$$

which says that risk tolerance would increase if wealth increased. At the current level of wealth, $x = 0$ and the risk tolerance is just ρ_0. What are the values of K and ρ_0 for the following utility functions?

a. $u(x) = a - be^{-x/R}$

b. $u(x) = a - \dfrac{b}{(1 + cx/R)^{(1-c)/c}}$

c. $u(x) = a + b\ln(1 + x/R)$

d. $u(x) = a + bx$ (expected - value decision - maker)

The utility functions in (b) and (c) go to negative infinity when $x = -\rho_0/R$.   What does this mean behaviorally? Is it meaningful to use these utility functions for values $x \leq -\rho_0/R$?

5.17 If someone owns a venture, then the selling price for that venture should be such that the owner is indifferent between having the venture and having the selling price. The buying price should be such that the person is equally happy (has equal utilities) before and after giving up the buying price and getting the venture.

a.   Show that for a particular person the selling price of a venture is, by definition, equal to the certain equivalent of that venture.

b.   Show that if a person agrees to the Delta Property (which implies an exponential or linear utility function), then the selling price and buying price for a venture are the same for that person. (See problems

5.4 and 5.14 for a discussion of the Delta Property.)
Does this result make sense to you?

5.18 A decision-maker is confronted with an uncertain venture, A, with outcomes x_i and associated probabilities $p(x_i|S)$.

   a. Justify the statement that if the decision-maker already owns A, then the minimum selling price, S, of the venture is equal to the certain equivalent.

   b. Justify the statement that the maximum buying price, B, of the venture is a number such that if the decision-maker wishes to acquire A, his certain equivalent for A with outcomes set to $x_i - B$ is zero.

   c. Show that S = B for a linear utility function $u(x) = a + bx$.

   d. Show that S = B for an exponential utility function $u(x) = a - be^{-x/R}$.

   e. Explain why if the stakes are large enough, the decision-maker can logically have S > B.

5.19 Value of information can be viewed as the largest amount the decision-maker would be willing to pay to get the information. It is, therefore, really the buying price of the information. Show that the value of information is given by

   Value of Information = Value with Information
                                        – Value Without Information

   for a straight line or exponential utility function. Explain behaviorally why this is not generally the case.

5.20 Assume that you own two uncertain ventures, A and B, with outcomes x_i and y_j, respectively. There are no synergies between the ventures, so the net outcome to the company is the sum of the outcomes for each venture. The probability distributions for A and B are independent.

$$p(x_i, y_j|S) = p(x_i|S)p(y_j|S)$$

   a. For a straight-line utility function $u(x) = a + bx$, show that the certain equivalent of A and B together is the sum of the certain equivalents for A and B separately.

   b. Repeat (a) for an exponential utility function $u(x) = a - be^{-x/R}$.

   c. Explain in behavioral terms why the certain equivalent for A and B together can logically be less than the certain equivalents for A and B separately (e.g., for cases when (a) or (b) above do not apply).

It is the property in (a) and (b) above that lets the decision facilitator work on a decision problem without too much concern for the resolution of other decision problems within the company.

5.21 You are given an uncertain venture with outcomes $x_i (i = 1, 2, ..., n)$ and probabilities $p(x_i | S)$.

    a. Show that if the utility function is straight line $u(x) = a + bx$, then the certain equivalent of A is equal to its expected value.

    b. If the utility function is exponential $u(x) = a - be^{-x/R}$, show that the certain equivalent of A is

$$CE(A) = -R \ln \left[\sum_{i=1}^{n} p(x_i | S) e^{-x_i / R} \right]$$

and is independent of the choice of values for a and b (provided that b is not equal to 0).

5.22 Given the results of the previous problem, prove that for an exponential utility function there is the following approximate expression for the certain equivalent.

$$\text{Certain Equivalent} = \text{Expected Value} - \frac{1}{2} \frac{\text{Variance}}{\text{Risk Tolerance}}$$

Hint: Use the following Taylor Series approximations, which are valid for small x.

$$e^x = 1 + x + x^2 / 2! + x^3 / 3! + ...$$

$$\ln(1 + x) = x - x^2 / 2 + x^3 / 3 - ...$$

5.23 You have the venture shown below and your certain equivalent is zero.

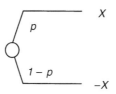

    a. If your utility function is $u(x) = a - bw^{-x}$, show that $w^x = p/(1-p)$. The value of $p/(1-p)$ is often called the odds.

    b. If your utility function is $u(x) = a - be^{-x/R}$, show that your risk tolerance is $R = x / \ln(p/(1-p))$.

Part II

Dealing with Complex Problems

6

The Complexity of Real-World Problems

Up to now, we have dealt with problems that are relatively simple and easy to structure and analyze. Actual decision problems, however, are usually complicated and thorny. Furthermore, they never come to the decision facilitator in simple form. The professional decision facilitator sees only the problems that are complicated and often poorly described; frequently, it is unclear what the problem is and what decisions need to be made.

Fortunately, the techniques for dealing with simple problems are virtually the same as those for dealing with complex problems. The most important rule for dealing with both kinds of problems is "Keep it simple!" Unnecessary complexity makes the analysis more difficult without offering additional insight.

Throughout this chapter, we use an example to illustrate how decision analysis applies to the complicated problems (and short time frames) typically encountered in practice. This example is based on an actual analysis performed in a week. However, the example has been modified. Medequip and Diagnostics, the companies in the example, are fictitious. The products in the original analysis were *not* medical diagnostic equipment.* And the analysis itself has been modified and simplified.

Diagnostics was a relatively small company in the medical diagnostics equipment business. From the start, it had chosen to supply high quality products at a reasonable price to health care facilities such as hospitals. A well informed sales force and an excellent service and maintenance department had contributed to an excellent reputation for the limited number of products it offered.

Medequip was a large company offering a wide variety of equipment in the medical area. During a strategic review, Medequip's management realized that there was an area in which Medequip was weak: diagnostic equipment. And

---

*The products in this example are not real products, and the input and results contained in this example do not describe real products.

there was an obvious tie-in between diagnostic equipment and the rest of the Medequip line. With diagnostic equipment, Medequip would have the advantage of being a supplier of a larger fraction of the hospitals' equipment needs. And the attractiveness of Medequip's products could be enhanced by software and hardware links between the diagnostic equipment and other Medequip products.

For many reasons, Medequip chose to acquire a diagnostic equipment company rather than develop these products internally. They acquired Diagnostics to form the core of the new Diagnostics Division. Several months after the acquisition, Medequip's company-wide budgeting process had reached the point of requiring input for the following fiscal year. And the new Diagnostics Division realized that it had to solve a problem that had been postponed during the turbulent times before and after the acquisition.

Diagnostics had two instruments that were used to monitor a certain characteristic of a patient's blood. These instruments were designed to be kept at the patient's bedside and to provide instant readout to doctors and nurses. One instrument, DiagStatic, used a static electric field to separate elements in blood samples. The other instrument, DiagRF, used a radio-frequency electric field to perform a similar function. Some tests could be done by one instrument and not the other, some tests could be done by both.

DiagStatic was a low margin, low market share product. It was an old product and both sales and margin were eroding rapidly; hospitals were switching over to a competitor's product at an alarming rate. If nothing were done, the product would be discontinued in five years. With a radically new design, new features would allow enhanced performance and also interconnection with other equipment.

DiagRF, on the other hand, was a high margin, high market share product in a smaller segment of the industry. It was based on a newer design and was selling reasonably well, but was also threatened by competition. An upgrade using the current design would enhance sales and prolong the life of the product.

At the time of purchase by Medequip, Diagnostics had the people and resources to develop only one new product at a time, and development was estimated to take two to three years. Which product development should Diagnostics choose to include in its budget request? Or should it choose to focus its budget requests in other areas? Or should it think big and ask for development for both products?

Budget submission was due in two weeks, but Laura, the head of Diagnostics Division (former CEO of Diagnostics), wanted results in one week so that consensus could be built during the following week. And amid all this turmoil, someone came up with a new alternative: a piece of equipment used in the operating room could be modified so that, when needed, it could fill the function of both DiagStatic and DiagRF at the patient's bedside. And then someone suggested that a small company had a design for a DiagStatic replacement that might be available for purchase. And then somebody mentioned that the consumables used by DiagStatic and DiagRF might be a profitable market for Diagnostics to enter—the current supplier was doing very well.

——————————————— Figure 6–1 ———————————————

The Decision Analysis Cycle

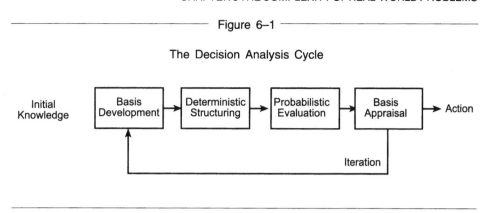

A Cyclical Approach _____

To deal with complex real-world problems, decision analysis uses a cyclical approach (Figure 6–1). The phases of this approach are illustrated in detail in this chapter. In this section, we give an overview of the process.

To start with, we bring some initial knowledge to a problem. Then, in the basis development phase, we gather data, generate alternatives, and identify values for making the decision. In the deterministic structuring phase, we build a model of the decision, develop base-case input to the model, and perform deterministic sensitivity analysis to find the crucial uncertainties in the problem. (Many uncertainties are relatively unimportant.) Then, in the probabilistic evaluation phase, we encode probability distributions for these variables, construct the decision tree, and evaluate the alternatives. Finally, in the basis appraisal phase, we examine the results obtained from the decision tree, revisit the information, alternatives, and values used in the evaluation, and reexamine the model. Based on this appraisal, we decide whether to act or to return to the beginning and start the cycle again.

Drawing on years of experience using the approach, we have developed several rules of thumb for how many times to go through the cycle and for how long to spend on each phase of the cycle. In general, there should be at least two to three iterations through the decision analysis cycle. Through each phase, the analysis should be successively developed and refined until it reflects the best judgment and expertise of the facilitator and personnel involved, keeping in mind that the level of effort should be commensurate with the size and importance of the problem.

In an analysis lasting several months, a preliminary iteration should take place in the first weeks (possibly even in the first few days) to give a feeling for the overall scope and structure of the analysis. Depending on the situation (and to a certain extent on the decision facilitator), another iteration might be performed before the full-scale analysis (when the major work is done). At the end, there should be time for a final iteration to recheck the problem formulation and results and make any final modifications.

Using the cyclical approach minimizes wasted time and effort. For instance, while the initial pass does not produce definitive results, it does give us a sense of how much additional information will be required and of how to further structure the model. And making multiple passes minimizes the practical errors that often arise: treating the wrong problem, focusing on the wrong factors, using the wrong model, gathering the wrong information, and using the wrong people.

Most of the hard analytical and data-gathering work is done during the main pass through the cycle, which, of course, varies tremendously in terms of time spent. In a typical analysis, the main pass might consume 50 percent of the time, with 25 percent of the time spent in the initial passes and 25 percent spent in a final pass and in preparing the presentations. During the main pass through the cycle, the effort is usually split fairly evenly between constructing the model and gathering the data to use in it.

Typically, there is one presentation after the main deterministic structuring phase and one presentation at the end of the analysis. A presentation after the basis development phase, however, is often an excellent investment of time and resources. In recent years, the Dialog Decision Process (DDP) described in Chapter 8 has been used as the process of interaction with the decision-maker(s), and the decision analysis cycle has been used for the back-room analysis effort. In DDP terms, a presentation at the end of the basis development phase would be called a Framing and Alternatives Dialog, a presentation after the main deterministic structuring phase would be an Analysis Dialog, and the final presentation would be an Analysis and Decision dialog.

The total amount of time and effort spent in each of the phases varies with the type of problem. Basis development ranges from 10 percent of the effort in a well-defined problem to 50 percent for a strategy project involving many people and complex alternatives. Basis appraisal can vary from 5 percent of the effort for clear problems with clear solutions and a single decision-maker to 25 percent for problems involving many people and many divisions within a company. Finally, deterministic structuring usually takes about twice the effort required for probabilistic evaluation.

Laura, the head of Diagnostics Division, realized that she had to sort through all these possibilities within the week and arrive at a budget request that the division could live with. In addition, Medequip was a rather staid company, not used to taking gambles—and in the DiagStatic/DiagRF area, technology and competition were changing so rapidly that all courses of action (including doing nothing) were a gamble. She needed to make a choice and be able to justify it during this first budget review with the new parent company.

She therefore called in one of her staff who had done decision analyses in the past, explained to him the need for fast turnaround, authorized him to assemble a small team for two or three meetings during the coming week, and sat down with him to start working on the decision.

Basis Development _____

The basis development phase determines the scope, method of approach, requirements, and objectives of the analysis. This phase is especially critical because all the successive phases depend on it. When something really goes wrong in analyzing a problem, the roots of the difficulty usually lie in the problem structure that came out of the basis development. Similarly, when a problem is exceptionally well analyzed, it is usually because the analysis was well structured from the beginning.

The most common errors in structuring are analyzing the wrong problem or analyzing the correct problem in an overly complicated manner. While there is unfortunately no procedure to follow that guarantees success in structuring a problem—problem structuring is a skill learned by doing— most successful analyses have a number of common elements.

Starting the Process

The process starts with identifying a decision facilitator and establishing the roles of decision-maker, decision facilitator, project team, and subject matter key personnel/experts.

The decision-maker should almost certainly be involved at some point in the basis development phase, because the analysis will be much smoother if from the start it addresses at least the alternatives the decision-maker sees as viable, the uncertainties or worries he or she thinks critical, and any special values that may be important.

The decision facilitator must be given sufficient authority and expertise to direct the analysis effort, though he or she may be relatively unfamiliar with the problem at hand (as is usually the case when acting as a decision consultant). The decision facilitator must have the courage to ask questions about the obvious and the perspective to see the forest, not just the trees. Furthermore, the facilitator must have at least occasional access to the decision-maker. Finally, the decision facilitator must be (and be perceived to be) neutral concerning the choice between alternatives; if not, biases easily arise (or are thought to arise) in the analysis.

It is very difficult for a decision facilitator to work alone. A project team should be identified to assist him or her. The project team does not have to be as neutral as the decision facilitator, but the team should be balanced. How many team members? Enough to represent the principal stakeholders (e.g., design, manufacturing, marketing, sales), though one person can often represent different constituencies. How often need the team meet? Once or twice a week appears to be a natural frequency.

Key personnel and experts are the people who need to be consulted during the decision process. Some of these people have the knowledge that the decision-maker wishes to use in making the decision. Other have a crucial role in implementation and need to be consulted and kept informed.

——————————————— Figure 6–2 ———————————————

Decision Hierarchy

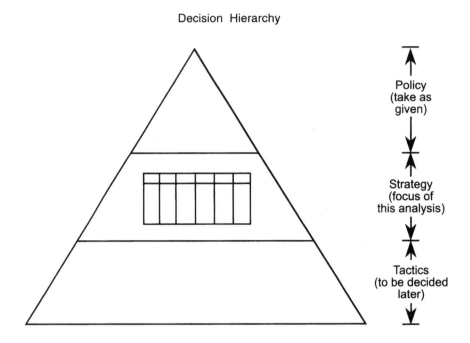

Using Decision Hierarchy

The Decision Hierarchy (Figure 6–2) helps people sort through the different types of decisions. This hierarchy distinguishes between three types of decisions. *Policy* decisions are those decisions made at a "higher" level within the organization; more loosely, they are the "givens" of the problem. *Strategy* is the name given to the decisions that are under consideration in the analysis; the symbol in the middle section of the decision hierarchy stands for the strategy table dealt with below. *Tactics* are the decisions to be taken later, after the strategy has been chosen.

Initial meetings and interviews with key personnel should focus on identifying the key policy and strategy decision or decisions. All too frequently, the initial focus is on operational, tactical, or "how-to-do-it" decisions rather than on the underlying strategic or "what-should-we-be-doing" decisions. One way to identify the key decisions is to elicit a short description of the problem, such as, "Explain to an interested stranger what all the effort is about."

When the principal policy and strategic decisions have been identified, a number of operational or tactical decisions can be dropped from the analysis. This must be done in a realistic manner. Usually, it should be assumed that these decisions will be made using the expertise available to the company. To avoid losing the goodwill of important personnel, the process of eliminating "how-to-do-it" decisions from the analysis must be done delicately.

Because this was the first time through the budget process with Medequip, Laura was not really sure what conditions corporate headquarters would impose on the division. She and the facilitator put together the following list of what she thought were the policy decisions, the "givens" of the problem. This list would furnish a starting point for the analysis.

- *Diagnostics Division could not obtain more resources than they already had, so at most one new product could be developed.*
- *Purchase of the DiagStatic replacement from another company was not a possibility. Medequip was not in a position to purchase anything for some time, given its recent acquisition of Diagnostics.*
- *Diagnostics could not enter the market for consumables for these products.*

Laura promised to phone corporate headquarters and get some clarification of these policy statements within a few days. As it turned out, the list was substantially correct.

She was less definite about the division between strategy and tactics, but she stated that she wanted a clear statement of what needed to be developed. The team could work out the level of detail needed to achieve clarity in that decision.

Using Strategy Tables

In the decision hierarchy, the policy decisions and the strategy decision areas were identified. Now the decision facilitator needs to develop several strategic alternatives that are significantly different.

The first problem that often arises in finding strategy alternatives is tunnel vision, where companies evaluate only a few fundamentally similar alternatives. By using processes ranging from simple heuristics to extensive group exercises, companies can stimulate the creativity needed to generate these alternatives. One simple exercise that often elicits creative responses is to imagine we are looking back from some future point (perhaps retirement) and critically examining this portion of our life.

The second problem that arises in finding strategy alternatives is often the multiplicity of alternatives. In many problems, there is a bewildering number of alternatives simply because choices must be made in several decision areas, and each decision area has several possibilities to choose from—the number of possible combinations increases rapidly with the number of decision areas. Creativity exercises may have dramatically enlarged the number of possible alternatives. The challenge now is to pick several alternatives (three to five alternatives, so that the analysis is feasible) that are significantly different (so that the analysis is creative). The decision analysis cycle will allow subsequent refinement of alternatives that appear most attractive.

The strategy table is a convenient and powerful technique for dealing with alternatives. The strategy table consists of a column for each decision area, with all the possible choices for that decision area listed in the column.

A strategy alternative (a complete set of decisions) for the problem can then be specified by making a choice for each decision area.

In practice, forming a strategy table is often a group exercise. Different people contribute the decision areas they feel are important and then help to list all the choices in that decision's column. Initially, all the decision areas relevant to the problem are included, whether strategic or operational, important or unimportant. The group then discusses which decisions clearly do not belong in the strategy table.

Next, the group identifies a set of strategy alternatives to be developed. One way to begin developing an alternative is to pick a strategy theme or to make a choice in a key decision area. Then the alternative is developed by making one choice in each decision column. One of the alternatives should describe how things would have happened on their own—this might be the "momentum" or "do nothing" alternative, depending on the context.

Tables for major strategic studies can start with as many as 40 or 50 columns. For tables this large, explicitly identifying the elements of major alternatives often shows that what at first appeared to be a good alternative is a poor or unfeasible one. In addition, some decision areas may be perceived to be mainly tactical or operational. Finally, some decision areas may have choices dictated by the choice made for a more important strategic decision area. Through these kinds of considerations, the complexity of even large strategy tables can be reduced to a conceptually manageable level.

Although it is not a quantitative tool, the strategy table is a surprisingly effective way to apply intuition and experience to a highly complex situation. When used correctly, the table can also be used to eliminate most of the possible strategies that are inconsistent, inferior, or undesirable.

The decision facilitator called a meeting of four people who were responsible for most aspects of the products under discussion. Two were development engineers, one was in charge of manufacturing, and one doubled as the head of sales and of marketing.

The facilitator quickly described the problem, the time frame, and the desires of the division head. He then stated the purpose of the meeting was to identify the key decisions that would have to be made in choosing a course of action. As the facilitator listened, he noted all the decision areas and the options in these areas. The team then organized these into a simple strategy table (Figure 6–3) with four decision areas:

- *If they chose a new DiagStatic, should they concentrate on product features for competitive advantage or should they work on adding links to other Medequip devices?*
- *If they chose a new DiagStatic, should they integrate graphic output capabilities or should they continue with the current OEM add-ons?*
- *What target average selling price should be used in designing the devices?*
- *What about that operating room device? Should they design in Static and RF capability so that it could also be used at bedside?*

-- Figure 6–3 --

Initial Diagnostics' Strategy Table

DiagRF		DiagStatic				Other
New DiagRF	Target Selling Price	New DiagStatic	Competitive Advantage	Output Graphics	Target Selling Price	Operating Room Device
None	$10,000	None	Features	OEM add-on	$10,000	No change
Upgrade current design	$15,000	Upgrade current design	Features + links to other equipment	Proprietary add-on	$15,000	Add Stat+RF capability for bedside use
	$20,000				$20,000	
	$25,000	New design		Integral dedicated	$25,000	

At this point, they called Laura in and asked her if the strategy table fairly represented the choices the division faced. She agreed that for this quick analysis, they had the right level of decision in the table. She thought that the operating unit device decision was not really relevant—operating unit devices were expensive and dedicated and would never be available for bedside use. But she thought that the column should be left in the table so that the issue could be discussed before being dismissed.

Using this table, Laura and the group discussed the different possible alternatives. The problem was simple enough that the group readily came up with three alternatives (Figure 6–4):

- *Milk Existing Products: Keep both DiagStatic and DiagRF on the market as long as feasible and then discontinue them.*
- *DiagRF Plus: Upgrade the current DiagRF to DiagRF Plus using current product technology and design. Keep DiagStatic on the market in its current state.*
- *New DiagStatic: Develop a completely new design for DiagStatic, DiagStatic New, including links to a number of Medequip devices. Keep DiagRF on the market for as long as feasible, and then abandon the static segment of the market.*

Everyone thought that, once they understood the differences between these three alternatives, they would be able to refine the best alternative and make a choice.

Using Influence Diagrams

As soon as possible, the decision facilitator should develop a list of the uncertainties that will probably be important. Although this list will be revised during the analysis, it lays the groundwork for developing a deterministic model. The model will need to contain as explicit variables the major uncertainties identified and should be suitable for analyzing the alternatives that have been developed.

─────────────────────────── Figure 6–4 ───────────────────────────

Diagnostics' Alternatives

	DiagRF		DiagStatic				Other
Strategy Theme	New DiagRF	Target Selling Price	New DiagStatic	Competitive Advantage	Output Graphics	Target Selling Price	Operating Room Device
Milk existing products	None	$10,000	None	Features	OEM add-on	$10,000	No change
	Upgrade current design	$15,000	Upgrade current design	Features + links to other equipment	Proprietary add-on	$15,000	Add Stat+RF capability for bedside use
DiagRF Plus		$20,000			Integral dedicated	$20,000	
DiagStatic New		$25,000	New design			$25,000	

Earlier, we developed the basic tools and theory of influence diagrams. In this section, we focus on using influence diagrams in fairly complicated analyses involving many people in an organization and, later, on how deterministic sensitivity analysis identifies the most crucial of these uncertainties.

There are two ways to begin an introductory session using influence diagrams. One way is to start from a simple influence diagram that the facilitator is fairly sure represents the "backbone" of the problem. This has the advantage of cutting short the initial phases of the discussion and the disadvantage of not allowing the session participants' understanding to grow while the diagram grows.

The opposite approach is to start with the value function on one side of the page and a decision node on the other and to gradually break the value function uncertainty into its components; near the end of the process, the decision variable becomes connected to the growing diagram. There are three advantages to this approach.

1. It focuses attention and demands agreement on the value function at the outset. It is surprising how much confusion in a decision problem arises because the decision criterion is not explicit and agreed on.
2. It focuses attention on the future and its attendant uncertainty rather than on the immediate concerns of selecting and implementing an alternative.
3. It allows all the participants to join in the thought process. This is valuable for obtaining enthusiastic implementation of the alternative that is finally chosen.

Most often, a modification of the second approach is used. The facilitator begins the process, creating several nodes. Fairly soon, the participants get the idea and begin to contribute. People who are not quantitative often find themselves contributing enthusiastically and productively at this stage of the analysis.

----------------------------------- Figure 6–5 -----------------------------------

Influence Diagram for Diagnostics

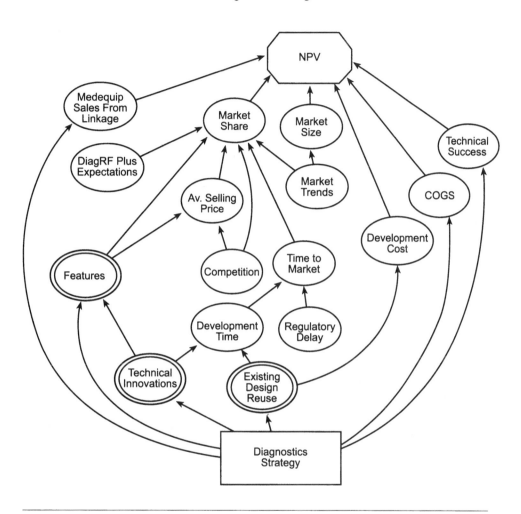

Occasionally, a tree is a more natural tool than an influence diagram for opening the structuring session. This can occur when the sequential nature of the problem is very important. For instance, some litigation and R&D problems are more readily described by trees in the early stages of structuring. (See Chapter 7.)

The group used an influence diagram to structure their problem (Figure 6–5.) They first created the topmost node NPV (net present value of cash flow) as the fundamental uncertainty. If they knew the probability distribution on NPV for each alternative, it would be easy to make the decision. Since this was the value function, it was drawn as an octagon.

Next, the facilitator asked what would the group would most like to know to reduce the uncertainty on NPV, given that they could not determine the distribution on NPV for each alternative directly? The group immediately replied "Market Share." The facilitator classified this response as an uncertainty, wrote it down in an oval, and drew an arrow from it to NPV. He mentioned to the group that the oval was really shorthand for two ovals: the Static and the RF market shares.

The facilitator next asked what the group would most like to know to reduce the uncertainty on market share. He got five immediate answers: Average Selling Price, the state of competition, the features in the devices, the date the new device arrived in the market, and market trends (RF might take some of the Static market).

The facilitator started a discussion around Average Selling Price. Target Selling Price appeared in the strategy table (Figure 6–3 and 6-4). After some discussion, some clarity was reached. In the development process, design and marketing reached agreement on the set of features to be included and a target selling price and a target cost to manufacture. When the device appears in the market several years later, the actual selling price is set by market considerations, and it is this actual selling price that is the uncertainty.

Some additional questioning revealed that Features and Competition both influenced Average Selling Price. Further questioning revealed that Features was not really an uncertainty but was determined by the strategy decision, so it was put in a double oval and an arrow drawn to it from the Diagnostics' Strategy decision rectangle. At this point the head of Marketing/Sales added an additional uncertainty called DiagRF Plus Expectations—the upgrade to DiagRF had already been announced, and he was uncertain whether the market would react unfavorably if the upgrade did not take place.

At this point the facilitator thought the Market Share uncertainty was quite well developed. So he asked what other uncertainty was important to NPV. Market Size, Development Cost, Cost of Goods Sold (COGS) were all identified and included in the diagram. One design engineer pointed out that the new design that would be attempted for DiagStatic was not that easy, and there was a possibility that, after some initial development effort, they would be forced to abandon the effort—this resulted in a oval labeled Technical Success. Finally, somebody suggested that if links were established to other Medequip equipment, there might be some additional sales of that Medequip equipment, so one final oval was added to the influence diagram.

Was the decision facilitator correct in allowing each oval to stand for two markets/devices? An alternative approach would be to duplicate each oval, once for Static and once for RF and to ask what arrows should be drawn from Static to RF bubbles. In reality, that is what is going to happen when the time comes to obtain input and assess probabilities. Given that discussions had indicated that interaction between the two markets/devices was weak, the influence diagram in Figure 6–5 is probably a reasonable communication tool. But the facilitator must remember to ask about interactions between Static and RF when obtaining data.

When do we stop adding to the diagram? When we reach a level of detail where we can use intuition and judgment to make meaningful assessments. In practice, we sometimes add another level of decisions and uncertainties beyond this point, which are discarded later on as too detailed. Typically, an influence diagram for a complex diagram can grow to 50 or 60 decisions and uncertainties, can then be reduced to 10 or 20 by general considerations, and can be finally reduced to 5 to 10 by sensitivity analysis. (See "Sensitivity Analysis" below.)

The chief value of constructing the influence diagram is that it forces people to think hard about the decisions and uncertainties and their interrelationships. Specifically, people can contribute their thoughts and argue with others' conceptions, areas of investigation can be identified and responsibility established, and probabilistic dependencies can be elicited and examined.

Deterministic Structuring: Modeling the Problem

Most corporate decision problems are complex enough to require using a model, usually implemented on a computer, to determine the value of each alternative. The models used today tend to be simpler than those used when decision analysis was first routinely applied to real-world problems. This change has come with the realization that the model does not need to depict the real world with absolute accuracy, but rather mainly needs to differentiate between the possible alternatives. However, in recent years, a rising level of sophistication and expectations appears to have resulted in larger, more complex models than were common a decade ago.

The basic rule of decision analysis is "keep the model as simple as possible—and no simpler."

Preexistent corporate models are rarely useful for decision analyses. They tend to be too complex, take too long or are too complicated to run, and usually focus on quantities important to running the company but not really relevant to making major decisions. For this reason, decision facilitators almost always create a new "throwaway" model that simply and clearly describes the problem at hand. Once the decision is made, much of the model becomes irrelevant to future operations. What remains can sometimes be used as the core of a model for future business.

The primary criterion for the model is that it be accurate enough to distinguish between the alternatives. The large value swings caused by uncertainty will make the accuracy of the model relatively unimportant. The cyclical decision analysis approach enables us to successively refine the model as we go through iterations of the decision analysis cycle (Figure 6–1), which means the model does not have to be perfect the first time used.

One frequent comment is that "the model has to be complete and detailed enough to convince the decision-maker and others of its accuracy." Such logic is poor justification for building an overly complex model. To the contrary, decision-makers are often suspicious that very complex models are black boxes hiding all sorts of errors or incorrect assumptions. A well-wrought model is seldom rejected for being too simple. Because they are easier to understand, simple models also have the advantage of yielding insight into a problem that helps generate new alternatives.

Today's spreadsheet programs (e.g., Microsoft Excel) furnish the capability for simple logic and easy output, making it easy to understand and validate the model and to understand the results. Whatever the modeling language chosen, it should be accepted within the organization, familiar to those involved in the analysis, and compatible with the tools of decision analysis.

To analyze the options, the facilitator built a spreadsheet model. The model had to relate together all the quantities indicated on the influence diagram (as either data inputs or calculation results) and had to be able to value all the different alternatives indicated in the strategy table. Most of these relationships could be expressed as simple financial calculations.

A basic model for market share for the new products (DiagStat New or DiagRF Plus) is shown in Figure 6–6. A five parameter model of this type facilitates discussion and is surprisingly efficient in modeling many different situations.

After much discussion, the project team simplified the influence diagram to the one shown in Figure 6–7. Medequip sales linked to the new products were thought to be small and, given the time available, the team decided to neglect this added value; the new products would have to stand on their own. Other nodes were judged to be useful in thinking about variables, but were not used directly in the model.

Many of the nodes in the original influence diagram do not wind up as explicit variables in the model. Some nodes are eliminated at a qualitative level as being interesting, but not worth modeling because the effect is too small; "Medequip Sales from Linkage" is an example. Other nodes are not explicitly modeled, but encourage systematic thinking about the uncertainties that are modeled; "Competition" is an example. This latter type of node is sometimes called an "evocative node."

–––––––––––––––––––––––––––––––––––––– Figure 6–6 ––––––––––––––––––––––––––––––––––––––

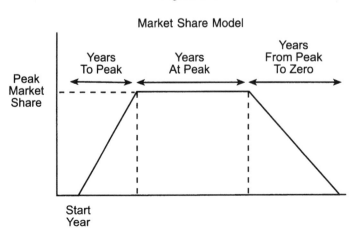

Market Share Model

Figure 6–7

Diagnostic's Final Influence Diagram

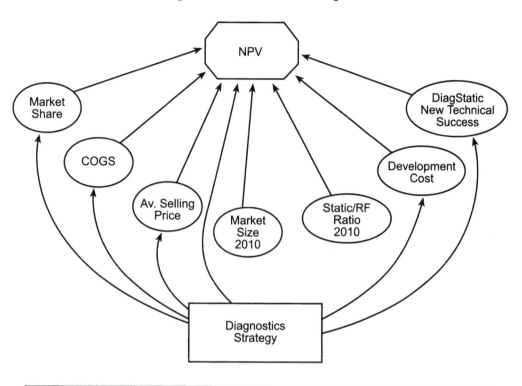

Note that the facilitator separated the spreadsheet into a data input section (Figure 6–8) and a calculation section (Figure 6–9.) The data input section contains all the input numbers for the spreadsheet for both constant and uncertain parameters. The input that is actually used in the calculations is contained in the shaded cells, mostly in the "In Use" column.

The calculation section contains only equations, though, of course, the results of these calculations appear as numbers. By setting up the spreadsheet this way, the facilitator has automatically parameterized the inputs for later analysis and made sure that he can easily scan down the complete list of data inputs.

Some programmers, especially those who use spreadsheets, are accustomed to entering a string of numbers to represent a time series, such as estimates of sales volumes for the next 10 or 20 years. To model the uncertainty and to help understand the results, these strings of numbers should be parameterized. For instance, for sales volume, we could enter an initial value and a growth rate instead of 10 or 20 numbers. Thus, decision analysis may require programmers to change their style of programming, especially if spreadsheets are used.

--- Figure 6–8 ---

Input Section for Diagnostics' Spreadsheet

Alternative Table		DiagRF		DiagStatic			
#	Name	Device	Target Price	Device	Comp. Adv.	Graphics	Target Price
1	Milk Exisiting Products	Current	$20,000	Current	Features	OEM	$10,000
2	DiagRF Plus	Upgrade	$25,000	Current	Features	OEM	$15,000
3	DiagStatic New	Current	$20,000	New	Link+Features	Integral	$10,000

INPUT

Description	In Use	Range Name	Low	Base	High	Units
Alternative	3	Alternative				1, 2, 3
Market						
Total market, 2000	3,500	Mkt_00		3,500		units/year
Total Market, 2010	4,500	Mkt_10	4,000	4,500	5,000	units/year
RF Fraction of Market, 2000	17%	Mkt_RF_fr_00		17%		percent
RF Fraction of Market, 2010	25%	Mkt_RF_fr_10	20%	25%	35%	percent
DiagStatic						
DiagStatic, Market Share, 2000	10%	MS_00_DSt		10%		percent
DiagStatic, Market Share growth rate	-20%	MS_gr_DSt	-25%	-20%	-15%	percent
DiagStatic, Year Discontinued	2005	Yr_DSt_stop		2005		year
If DiagStatic New is introduced before this year, DiagStatic is discontinued at that time						
DiagStatic, Price, 2000	$9,500	ASP_00_DSt		$9,500		$/unit
DiagStatic, Price CAGR	0%	ASP_gr_DSt	-5%	-1%	1%	percent
DiagStatic COGS, 2000	$4,500	COGS_00_DSt		$4,500		$/unit
DiagStatic, COGS CAGR	2%	COGS_gr_DSt	0%	2%	3%	percent
DiagStatic New						
DiagStatic New, Technical Success	Yes	tech_succ_DStn	No	Yes	Yes	yes/no
DiagStatic New, Start Year	2003	Startyr_DStn		2003		year
DiagStatic New, Years to Peak	3	Yrs_to_pk_DStn		3		years
DiagStatic New, Years at Peak	8	Yrs_at_pk_DStn		8		years
DiagStatic New, Years from Peak to 0	7	Yrs_to_0_DStn		7		years
DiagStatic New, Market Share at Peak	20%	MS_pk_DStn	10%	20%	40%	percent
DiagStatic New, Price, start year	$14,000	ASP_sy_DStn	$12,000	$14,000	$15,000	$/unit
DiagStatic New, Price CAGR	0%	ASP_gr_DStn	-3%	0%	1%	percent
DiagStatic New, COGS, start year	$4,800	COGS_sy_DStn	$4,600	$4,800	$5,200	$/unit
DiagStatic New, COGS CAGR	2%	COGS_gr_DStn	0%	2%	3%	percent
DiagRF						
DiagRF, Market Share, 2000	40%	MS_00_DRF		40%		year
DiagRF, Market Share growth rate	-10%	MS_gr_DRF	-20%	-10%	-5%	percent
DiagRF, Year Discontinued	2008	Yr_DRF_stop		2008		year
If DiagRF Plus is introduced before this year, DiagRF is discontinued at that time						
DiagRF, Price, 2000	$17,000	ASP_00_DRF		$17,000		$/unit
DiagRF, Price CAGR	0%	ASP_gr_DRF	-4%	0%	1%	percent
DiagRF, COGS, 2000	$4,500	COGS_00_DRF		$4,500		$/unit
DiagRF, COGS CAGR	2%	COGS_gr_DRF	0%	2%	3%	percent
DiagRF Plus						
DiagRF Plus, Start Year	2001	Startyr_DRFp		2001		year
DiagRF Plus, Years to Peak	2	Yrs_to_pk_DRFp		2		years
DiagRF Plus, Years at Peak	6	Yrs_at_pk_DRFp		6		years
DiagRF Plus, Years from Peak to 0	5	Yrs_to_0_DRFp		5		years
DiagRF Plus, Market share at Peak	40%	MS_pk_DRFp	25%	40%	45%	percent
DiagRF Plus, Price, start year	$19,000	ASP_sy_DRFp	$17,000	$19,000	$23,000	$/unit
DiagRF Plus, Price CAGR	0%	ASP_gr_DRFp	-3%	0%	1%	percent
DiagRF Plus, COGS, start year	$4,800	COGS_sy_DRFp	$4,600	4,800	$5,300	$/unit
DiagRF Plus, COGS CAGR	2%	COGS_gr_DRFp	0%	2%	3%	percent
GLOBAL VARIABLES						
Base Year	2000	BaseYear		2000		year
Discount Rate	10%	DiscountRate		10%		percent
Tax Rate	38%	TaxRate		38%		percent
Sales, General, Administrative	10%	SGA		10%		% of unit sales
Working Capital, 1999	$3,000,000	Wcap_99		$3,000,000		$
Working Capital	29%	Wcap		29%		% of revenue

R&D Investment ($000)			2000	2,001	2002	2003
DiagRF Plus		RD_DRFp	500	1,500		
DiagStatic New, pre-success		RD_pre_DStn	1,800	1,800		
DiagStatic New, post-success		RD_post_DStn		400	1,900	1,100

--- Figure 6–9 ---

Calculation Section for Diagnostics' Spreadsheet

Alternative		DiagRF			DiagStatic							
# Name	Device	Target Price		Device	Comp. Adv.		Graphics		Target Price			
3 DiagStatic New	Current	$20,000		New	Link+Features		Integral		$10,000			
	1999	2000	2001	2002	2003	2004	2005	2006	2007	2008	2009	2010
Market Units Sold												
Static		2,905	2,950	2,996	3,042	3,088	3,135	3,182	3,230	3,278	3,326	3,375
RF		595	639	685	732	782	833	887	943	1,001	1,062	1,125
Diagnostics' Units Sold												
DiagStatic		291	236	192	156	0	0	0	0	0	0	0
DiagStatic New		0	0	0	0	206	418	636	646	656	665	675
DiagRF		238	230	222	214	205	197	189	180	172	0	0
DiagRF Plus		0	0	0	0	0	0	0	0	0	0	0
Revenue ($000)												
DiagStatic		2,760	2,242	1,821	1,480	0	0	0	0	0	0	0
DiagStatic New		0	0	0	0	2,882	5,852	8,911	9,044	9,178	9,314	9,450
DiagRF		4,046	3,910	3,771	3,630	3,488	3,346	3,206	3,067	2,931	0	0
DiagRF Plus		0	0	0	0	0	0	0	0	0	0	0
Cost of Goods Sold ($000)												
DiagStatic		1,307	1,083	898	744	0	0	0	0	0	0	0
DiagStatic New		0	0	0	0	1,008	2,088	3,242	3,356	3,474	3,596	3,722
DiagRF		1,071	1,056	1,038	1,020	999	978	956	933	909	0	0
DiagRF Plus		0	0	0	0	0	0	0	0	0	0	0
Financial Results ($000)												
Revenue		6,806	6,152	5,592	5,109	6,370	9,199	12,117	12,112	12,110	9,314	9,450
Costs		2,378	2,139	1,936	1,763	2,007	3,066	4,198	4,289	4,384	3,596	3,722
Gross Margin		4,428	4,013	3,656	3,346	4,363	6,133	7,919	7,822	7,726	5,718	5,728
SG&A		681	615	559	511	637	920	1,212	1,211	1,211	931	945
R&D Expense		1,800	2,200	1,900	1,100	0	0	0	0	0	0	0
EBIT		1,947	1,198	1,197	1,735	3,726	5,213	6,707	6,611	6,515	4,786	4,783
Tax		740	455	455	659	1,416	1,981	2,549	2,512	2,476	1,819	1,818
Earnings		1,207	743	742	1,076	2,310	3,232	4,159	4,099	4,039	2,967	2,966
Working Capital	3,000	1,974	1,784	1,622	1,482	1,847	2,668	3,514	3,512	3,512	2,701	2,741
Change in Working Capital		-1,026	-190	-162	-140	366	820	846	-2	-1	-811	40
Cash Flow		2,233	932	904	1,216	1,944	2,412	3,312	4,101	4,040	3,778	2,926
Cumulative Cash Flow		2,233	3,166	4,070	5,286	7,230	9,642	12,954	17,055	21,095	24,873	27,799
PV Cash Flow		2,233	847	747	913	1,328	1,498	1,870	2,104	1,885	1,602	1,128
Cumulative PV Cash Flow		2,233	3,081	3,828	4,742	6,070	7,567	9,437	11,541	13,426	15,028	16,156
NPV ($ million)												
Cash Flow 2000-2010		16										
Terminal Value		10										
Total		27 NPV										

The following paragraphs contain modeling suggestions that may appear obvious to some. However, we have noticed that oversights in these areas are surprisingly frequent.

Modeling Profit

Care must be taken in modeling how revenue and cost change over time. Because profit is a small difference between these two larger numbers, it is extremely sensitive to the details of modeling. For many businesses, it is better to estimate costs and margin (or revenue and margin) rather than revenue and costs directly.

Sunk Costs

It is surprising how much confusion arises if investments have already been made in the area of the decision problem. This money is spent (it is a "sunk cost"), and the decision problem is what to do in the future, given present assets and experience. One approach is to exclude all sunk costs from the evaluation of the problem; the other approach is to include the sunk costs in all alternatives, including the "do nothing" alternatives.

Shutting Down the Business

Models should have a cutoff in them so that when margins are negative for more than a few years, the business shuts down. Models should also have checks to prevent unrealistic or impossible situations, such as a market share exceeding 100 percent. Remember that the decision tree will evaluate the model for a number of extreme cases and that unexpected values may occur in these cases, thus distorting the overall results.

Inflation

It is usually better to model in constant dollars, because you can then avoid simultaneously modeling both the systematic changes of prices and costs and the change from inflation. Remember, however, to deflate such items as interest payments, undepreciated capital, and working capital to account for the effects of inflation on them.

Terminal Value

Even when the model explicitly considers 10 to 15 years, as much as 50 percent of the net present value of a business may arise from the period beyond that modeled. This occurs especially for new product introductions and for research and development. It is therefore usually important to explicitly include a value for the business beyond the time period of the model. This value might be estimated as a sale value (perhaps expressed as a multiple of cash flow in the final year considered) or as a salvage value (estimated from assets, including working capital). In estimating this value of ongoing business, remember that no business lasts forever and that migrating to new forms of the business may require substantial new capital investments.

Diagnostics decided to focus on the NPV of cash flow. There were no sunk costs to worry about. There would be no cost associated with eliminating old products if DiagStatic New or DiagRF Plus were not developed; the resources devoted to these products could be gradually migrated to other areas of the business. Inflation effects were included in the estimates for price and cost.

The terminal value for the analysis was the cash flow from operations in the final year (2010) divided by the discount rate. This value is the NPV of operations that continue in perpetuity with the same cash flow as 2010. In this case, the terminal value arises only from new products (DiagStatic New or DiagRF Plus) which have sales beyond 2010. Because terminal value in this case is a small fraction of total NPV, this approximation was acceptable.

Deterministic Structuring: Sensitivity Analysis

One of the main tasks in the deterministic structuring phase is to sufficiently develop the model to produce credible base-case results. The base case is a set of input parameters used as a starting point for further analysis. If the decision alternatives are very different, it may be necessary to establish a base case for each alternative. If there is an underlying uncertainty of success or failure (as with a new product introduction), the base case should usually be estimated given success. Too much effort should not spent in establishing base-case values, since they are just a starting point. On the other hand, the values should be reasonable enough not to stir up unnecessary controversy.

Ideally, the base-case parameters should all represent a median value, which means that in most people's judgment there is a 50/50 chance that the true value will be above or below the value. In practice, however, base-case parameters are often developed from an unduly optimistic or pessimistic business plan. As the analysis progresses, some effort should be spent establishing a set of base-case parameters close to most people's median value.

For all important variables, a range of values should be established in early interviews: the base-case value, a low value (10 percent chance that the value will turn out to be lower), and a high value (10 percent chance that the value will turn out to be higher). The next task is to identify the crucial uncertainties, which is accomplished using deterministic sensitivity analysis. Frequently, this process shows that uncertainties originally thought to be important are relatively unimportant.

Deterministic sensitivity analysis starts by evaluating the model with all variables set to their base-case values, which gives the base-case value of the model. Then, for each of the variables in turn, the model is evaluated at the low value of the variable and then at the high value of the variable (with all other parameters kept at their base value), thus yielding low and high values of the model. The difference between the low and high value of the model is a measure of how sensitive the problem is to the uncertainty in that variable.

The project team developed ranges for the data inputs for the spreadsheet (Figure 6–8) in the columns labeled Low, Base, and High. They then calculated the sensitivity for the Alternative 3, DiagStatic New. The results are shown in Figure 6–10.

The results shown in Figure 6–10 are plotted in what is called the "tornado" chart. The variables are arranged so that those having the largest swing are at the top. The vertical line shows the position of the base case. The horizontal bars show the size of the swing for each variable or joint

---

Figure 6–10

Initial Sensitivity Analysis for DiagStatic New Alternative

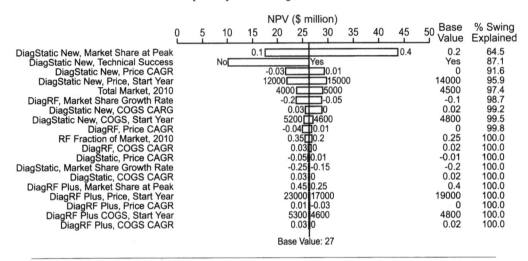

	NPV ($ million)	Base Value	% Swing Explained
DiagStatic New, Market Share at Peak	0.1 — 0.4	0.2	64.5
DiagStatic New, Technical Success	No — Yes	Yes	87.1
DiagStatic New, Price CAGR	-0.03 — 0.01	0	91.6
DiagStatic New, Price, Start Year	12000 — 15000	14000	95.9
Total Market, 2010	4000 — 5000	4500	97.4
DiagRF, Market Share Growth Rate	-0.2 — -0.05	-0.1	98.7
DiagStatic New, COGS CARG	0.03 — 0	0.02	99.2
DiagStatic New, COGS, Start Year	5200 — 4600	4800	99.5
DiagRF, Price CAGR	-0.04 — 0.01	0	99.8
RF Fraction of Market, 2010	0.35 — 0.2	0.25	100.0
DiagRF, COGS CAGR	0.03 — 0	0.02	100.0
DiagStatic, Price CAGR	-0.05 — 0.01	-0.01	100.0
DiagStatic, Market Share Growth Rate	-0.25 — -0.15	-0.2	100.0
DiagStatic, COGS CAGR	0.03 — 0	0.02	100.0
DiagRF Plus, Market Share at Peak	0.45 — 0.25	0.4	100.0
DiagRF Plus, Price, Start Year	23000 — 17000	19000	100.0
DiagRF Plus, Price CAGR	0.01 — -0.03	0	100.0
DiagRF Plus COGS, Start Year	5300 — 4600	4800	100.0
DiagRF Plus, COGS CAGR	0.03 — 0	0.02	100.0

Base Value: 27

---

sensitivity; the swing is the largest of the absolute values of the differences between the high, low and base values of the model for that variation.

Those variables with the greatest swing are the crucial uncertainties that dominate the problem. As such, they will be treated as explicit uncertainties in the decision tree, while the remaining variables will be set to their base-case values (but may change with the decision alternatives).

Sometimes it is not reasonable to vary two or more variables independently—they are correlated. When one is high, the other is high (or low if they are anti-correlated). For these variables, it is appropriate to set up a joint sensitivity. The variables in the joint sensitivity are varied jointly, i.e., at the same time. Even if these variables individually appear low in the sensitivity analysis table, their joint effect may be large enough for them to be included in the tree. These variables may be entered in the tree as separate nodes (with dependent probabilities) or as a single joint node that sets the values for two or more variables on each branch.

The project team realized that not all these variables were independent. The ovals in the influence diagram represented uncertainties for multiple products, and the uncertainties were linked. For instance, the compound annual growth rate (CAGR) for costs reflected underlying economics of the business, and would be correlated for all the products under consideration—if one were at its low (or high) value, all would be at their low (or high) values. Similarly, the CAGR for average selling price reflected the forces pressing for reductions in medical expenses, and would be the same for all the products. So these variables were grouped into two "joint sensitivities" rather than being varied individually, as shown in Figure 6–11. The sensitivities were then recalculated for all three alternatives, and are shown in Figure 6–12.

─────────────────── Figure 6–11 ───────────────────

Joint Sensitivities

Joint COGS Growth Rate Sensitivity

Product	Variable	Low	Base	High
DiagStatic	COGS_gr_DSt	0	2%	3%
DiagStatic New	COGS_gr_DStn	0	2%	3%
DiagRF	COGS_gr_DRF	0	2%	3%
DiagRF Plus	COGS_gr_DRFp	0	2%	3%

Joint Average Selling Price Growth Rate Sensitivity

Product	Variable	Low	Base	High
DiagStatic	ASP_gr_DSt	–5%	–1%	1%
DiagStatic New	ASP_gr_DStn	–3%	0	1%
DiagRF	ASP_gr_DRF	–4%	0	1%
DiagRF Plus	ASP_gr_DRFp	–3%	0	1%

As mentioned above, when two or more variables are varied jointly, they often appear higher in the tornado than the variables varied independently. However, the effect was small for the DiagStatic New alternative.

Some variables in the sensitivity analysis table may be decision or value variables (such as the discount rate). These variables may have been included in the sensitivity analysis for general interest, but they should not be confused with the critical uncertainties that will go into the tree as chance nodes.

Often, the largest uncertainties affect all the alternatives in the same way, causing the model result for each alternative to vary up or down about the same amount. Usually, the uncertainties that affect all the alternatives this way are underlying macroeconomic variables. To conserve tree size and leave space for the uncertainties that distinguish between alternatives, these macroeconomic variables can be combined into one or two nodes. Each branch of the combined node would then represent a scenario in which several macroeconomic variables are set.

Since ordinarily a few uncertainties really do dominate the problem, we should not be afraid to limit the number of uncertainties in the tree to several with the largest swing in the sensitivity analysis. However, we need to examine our assumptions and results a little more closely to understand how to recognize this dominance. The basic assumptions are listed below.

1. The certain equivalent is the measure that takes into account the uncertainty of a venture. We can therefore determine how important a variable is to the overall uncertainty by determining how important it is to the certain equivalent value.

2. As mentioned in Chapter 5, we can approximate the certain equivalent using the following equation:

$$\text{Certain Equivalent} = \text{Expected Value} - \frac{1}{2}\frac{\text{Variance}}{\text{Risk Tolerance}} \qquad (6\text{--}1)$$

Since the variance accounts for the way uncertainty affects the certain equivalent, the variance is the measure of uncertainty we are looking for.

Figure 6–12

Joint Sensitivities

DiagStatic New

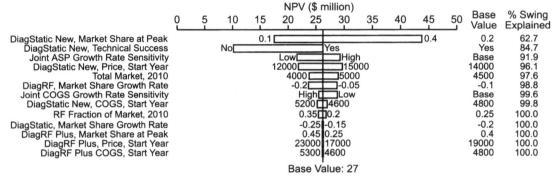

NPV ($ million)

	Base Value	% Swing Explained
DiagStatic New, Market Share at Peak	0.2	62.7
DiagStatic New, Technical Success	Yes	84.7
Joint ASP Growth Rate Sensitivity	Base	91.9
DiagStatic New, Price, Start Year	14000	96.1
Total Market, 2010	4500	97.6
DiagRF, Market Share Growth Rate	-0.1	98.8
Joint COGS Growth Rate Sensitivity	Base	99.6
DiagStatic New, COGS, Start Year	4800	99.8
RF Fraction of Market, 2010	0.25	100.0
DiagStatic, Market Share Growth Rate	-0.2	100.0
DiagRF Plus, Market Share at Peak	0.4	100.0
DiagRF Plus, Price, Start Year	19000	100.0
DiagRF Plus COGS, Start Year	4800	100.0

Base Value: 27

DiagRF Plus

NPV ($ million)

	Base Value	% Swing Explained
DiagRF Plus, Market Share at Peak	0.4	28.0
DiagRF Plus, Price, Start Year	19000	53.3
RF Fraction of Market, 2010	0.25	77.8
Joint ASP Growth Rate Sensitivity	Base	95.0
Total Market, 2010	4500	98.1
Joint COGS Growth Rate Sensitivity	Base	99.3
DiagRF Plus, COGS, Start Year	4800	99.9
DiagStatic, Market Share Growth Rate	-0.2	100.0
DiagRF, Market Share Growth Rate	-0.1	100.0
DiagStatic New, Technical Success	Yes	100.0
DiagStatic New, Market Share at Peak	0.2	100.0
DiagStatic New, Price, Start Year	14000	100.0
DiagStatic New, COGS, Start Year	4800	100.0

Base Value: 24

Milk Existing Products

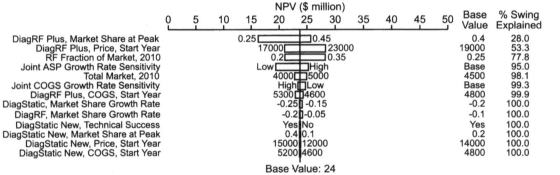

NPV ($ million)

	Base Value	% Swing Explained
DiagRF, Market Share Growth Rate	-0.1	62.0
Joint ASP Growth Rate Sensitivity	Base	83.6
RF Fraction of Market, 2010	0.25	96.6
Total Market, 2010	4500	98.3
Joint COGS Growth Rate Sensitivity	Base	99.4
DiagStatic, Market Share Growth Rate	-0.2	100.0
DiagStatic New, Technical Success	Yes	100.0
DiagStatic New, Market Share at Peak	0.2	100.0
DiagStatic New, Price, Start Year	14000	100.0
DiagStatic New, COGS, Start Year	4800	100.0
DiagRF Plus, Market Share at Peak	0.4	100.0
DiagRF Plus, Price, Start Year	19000	100.0
DiagRF Plus COGS, Start Year	4800	100.0

Base Value: 13

3. To obtain the variance, we recall the statistical result that, for probabilistically independent variables and for small variations of these variables, the total variance is the sum of the variances for each variable. The variance for each variable is the square of the standard deviation, which is, in turn, proportional to the width of the distribution or swing for each variable. (Recall that the swing is obtained by evaluating the model for the 10 percent and 90 percent points for each variable and see Figure 10–17.)

4. Thus, the square of the swing for a variable determines how important it is to the overall uncertainty.

Accordingly, one easy way to compare the importance of uncertainty in the variables is to square the swing and express it as a percentage of the sum of squares of all the swings. The final column in Figures 6–10 and 6–12 show this swing. (Technically, the variation for Technical Success for the DiagStatic New alternative is not a 10/50/90 variation and distorts the overall uncertainty figures shown in the final column.)

Thus, we see that, for the DiagRF Plus alternative, the top four variables (peak market share, initial price, RF fraction of market in 2010, and average selling price) account for 95% of the uncertainty. In most problems with more variables and complex models, we find that the top three or four variables capture 80 to 90 percent of the effects of uncertainty.

Remember, though, that for this approximation to be valid, we need to use probabilistically independent variables. With dependent variables, use the joint sensitivity as illustrated above. This joint sensitivity must then be probabilistically independent from the other variables listed.

Probabilistic Evaluation: Building and Pruning the Tree

Even after deterministic sensitivity analysis, it is often difficult to limit the tree to a reasonable size. If there are, for instance, n nodes in a tree and each node has three branches, a symmetric tree will have 3^n paths. For example, for seven nodes, we would have 2,187 paths. If the model takes 1 second to calculate an answer (not untypical of a large spreadsheet model on a personal computer), the evaluation command will take a little over half an hour to execute. If we add several more nodes, change a node from three to four branches, or construct a more elaborate model, we will have a tree that is impractical to evaluate on a personal computer.

How large a tree is reasonable? This depends greatly on the type of problem (and on the opinion of the facilitator). However, we feel that for most problems, 50 to 200 paths per alternative is sufficient. This number of paths allows us to include the three generic uncertainties that often affect an alternative: uncertainty about the growth of the market, uncertainty in competitive action or reaction, and uncertainty in how well we will fare. At three branches a node, we have 27 paths per alternative, leaving room for several other nodes if called for. After the full-scale analysis is complete, we will probably find that around 20 paths per alternative are enough to draw all the conclusions. Reducing the tree to this size is often important for clarifying the results and drawing the tree for the final presentation to the decision-maker.

How can you make your tree small enough to evaluate? By reducing the number of branches at each node, by reducing the number of nodes, and by creating asymmetric trees. Simplifying the model can also help by reducing the time required to evaluate the tree. We consider each of these options in turn.

What is a reasonable number of branches at a node? Our experience indicates that chance nodes are usually well approximated by three branches. Going to four or more branches seldom perceptibly affects the overall profit distribution. While we can use two branches for uncertainties that deterministic sensitivity analysis shows to be less important, there is no central branch in a two-branch node to trace the effect of the base case. With decision nodes, we can use the preliminary evaluation to eliminate the inferior alternatives and narrow down to the three or four really distinct and most promising alternatives.

What is a reasonable number of nodes in a tree? A good number to aim for is five or six nodes. Normally, there are too many nodes in the initial version of the tree, and the tree has to be pruned before it can be evaluated. In pruning the tree, four types of nodes compete for a place on the final tree: decision nodes, chance nodes with effects common to all alternatives, chance nodes with effects that distinguish between alternatives, and chance (or decision) nodes that are not really important to the tree but should be included for political reasons.

By using the results of the deterministic sensitivity analysis, we can usually manage to discuss and eliminate the politically important nodes from consideration. Indeed, this may be one of the important insights from the analysis. If necessary, chance nodes with effects common to all alternatives can be combined into one or two nodes whose branches represent scenarios (combinations of events). If there are still too many nodes, we must be creative in combining variables, restructuring the tree, and using further sensitivity analysis to narrow down the number of important uncertainties even more. In cases of real necessity, we may have to run a separate tree for each alternative. If we do this, we will have to do some calculations by hand to reorder the tree (i.e., to obtain value of information), but we can still have software do most of the work for us.

Creating asymmetric trees is another way to reduce tree size. For instance, when uncertainty is important for one alternative but not for another, we can have the chance node for this uncertainty follow only the alternative for which it is important. Similarly, an uncertainty may be important only for certain branches of a chance node, in which case you can have the node follow only those branches.

Finally, we can simplify the model to shorten its running time and, thus, the time required to evaluate the tree. Models can be simplified by eliminating calculations of quantities that were initially of interest but that are not necessary for calculating the net present value of cash flow. Models can similarly be simplified by replacing complicated calculations with simplified ones that produce approximately the same results.

In general, beginning with a small version of the tree is better, even if you are using a software program to evaluate the tree. Nothing is as discouraging as starting off by running up against multiple errors from hardware/software limitations—correcting one error, waiting a long time for the tree to reevaluate, and then finding another error.

After examining the sensitivity analysis results in Figure 6–12, the team drew the schematic decision tree shown in Figure 6–13. These seven uncertain variables account for almost all of the uncertainty in the three alternatives. All other variables were set to their base-case values or determined by model calculations. The decision node occurs before (to the left of) all the uncertainty nodes because information on the resolution of these uncertainties will not be available until after the decision is made.

The team started to more carefully examine the uncertainty on the variables in the tree. The previous ranges were fine for sensitivity analysis, but now the facilitator wanted to assess complete distributions to obtain better quality information for the tree. (See Chapter 12 for more on this process.) After some careful thought, however, the team judged that the information prepared for the

───────────────────────── Figure 6–13 ─────────────────────────

Schematic Tree for Diagnostics

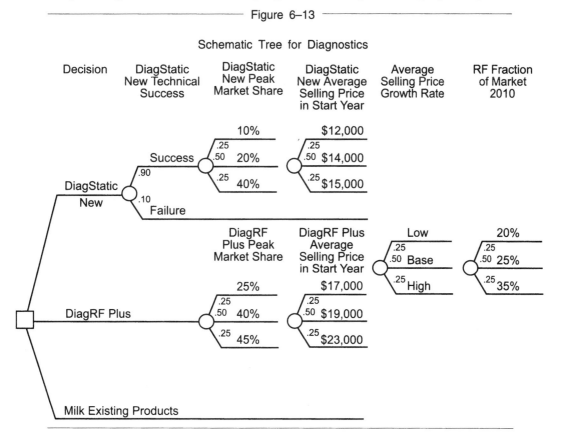

sensitivity analysis represented their best state of information. They assigned .25/.50/.25 probabilities to the values used in the 10/50/90 ranges in the sensitivity analysis—see Chapter 2 for a justification of this process.

The one probability they were missing was the probability of technical success for DiagStatic New development. A lengthy discussion of technical hurdles with the design staff established that the probability of technical success was 90 percent.

Basis Appraisal: Obtaining Information from the Tree _____

The facilitator began analyzing the tree by plotting the probability distributions (Figures 6–14 and 6–15). The distributions were shown in two forms.

Figure 6–14 shows the cumulative probability distributions for each of the alternatives. Figure 6–15 shows a plot of the 10-90 percentile range around the expected value for each alternative. For each bar, there is a 10 percent chance the value falls to the left of the bar and a 10 percent chance it falls to the right; the star near the center marks the expected value; the lines on either side of the bar show the full limit of the distributions. This simpler plot contains the essential information needed to compare the risk and return of each alternative. Because they are so simple and intuitive, plots like Figure 6–15 are frequently used in presentations.

The expected values showed the DiagStatic New alternative was preferred, with an expected value of $25 million. The DiagRF Plus alternative was a close second, with an expected value of $22 million. The Milk Existing Products alternative had an expected value of only $13 million.

However, as illustrated by the width of the distributions, The DiagStatic New alternative was also the most uncertain, with potential values ranging from $9 million ($2 million lower than $11 million, the lowest value for Milk Existing Products) and $55 million ($16 million higher than $39 million, the highest value for the DiagRF Plus alternative.)

On an expected value basis, Diagnostics should go with the DiagStatic New alternative. In terms of the budget request, it seemed clear that creating a new product (DiagStat New or DiagRF Plus) was $9–13 million better than doing nothing (Milk Existing Products.)

Besides getting expected values (certain equivalents) and probability distributions on profit for the alternatives, we can get a wealth of information to help us glean all possible insights from the tree.

Conditional Distributions

First, we can look at the distributions and expected values (certain equivalents) at points other than the first node in the tree and see if these conditional values hold any surprises.

To better understand where the potential risks and profits came from, the facilitator decided to look at what the distributions for the alternatives would be, given technical success or failure of DiagStatic New (Figure 6–16). For technical

Figure 6–14

Cumulative Probability Distributions for Diagnostics' Alternatives

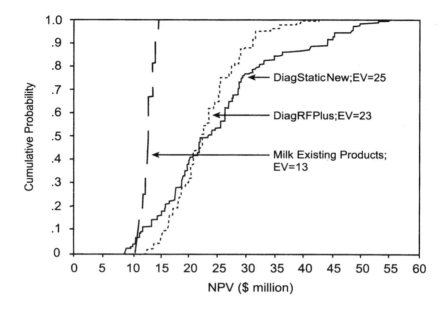

Figure 6–15

10–90 Bars for Probability Distributions for Diagnostics' Alternatives

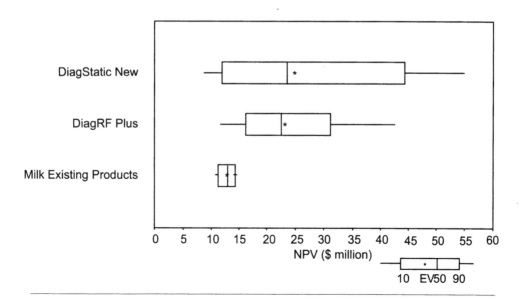

success, DiagStatic New is clearly preferred to the other alternatives; for technical failure, DiagStatic New reverts to the Milk Existing Products alternative less the $3.6 million R&D investment incurred before failure is known.

He then plotted the conditional distributions for DiagStatic New for Peak Market Share (Figure 6–17), which shows dramatic differences between the three values; note that the lowest 10 percent of the distribution shows no difference, corresponding to technical failure. Figure 6–18 shows DiagStatic New for the uncertainty on the compound annual growth rate on Average Selling Price for all the products. Figure 6–19 shows DiagStatic New for the different values of the Average Selling Price in DiagStatic New start year, 2003. Figure 6–20 shows DiagStatic New for the different values of RF fraction of total market in 2010.

Value of Perfect Information

Besides looking at conditional distributions, we can calculate the value of perfect information for each uncertainty. If possible information-gathering efforts have costs comparable to these values, we can formulate the decision for gathering imperfect information and see if it is worthwhile.

The facilitator rolled back the tree with the chance nodes brought one by one in front of the decision node and then took the difference between the resulting expected value and the original expected value to obtain the values of information (Figure 6–21).

Peak Market Share for DiagStatic New has the largest value of information, even more than Technical Success. RF Fraction of Total Market, 2010, has a

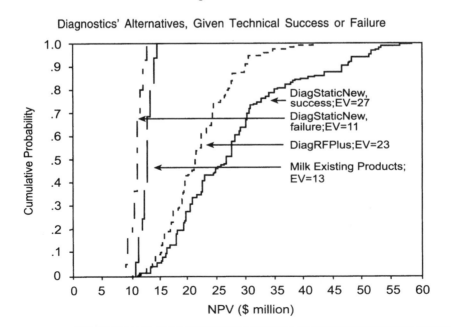

Figure 6–16

Diagnostics' Alternatives, Given Technical Success or Failure

Figure 6–17

DiagStatic New, Given Different Peak Market Share

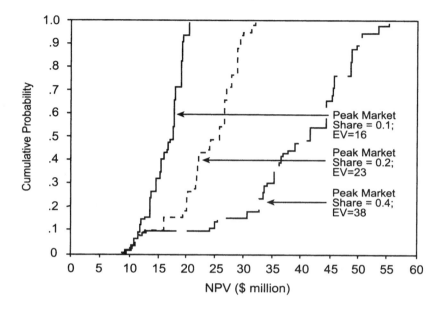

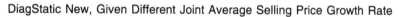

Figure 6–18

DiagStatic New, Given Different Joint Average Selling Price Growth Rate

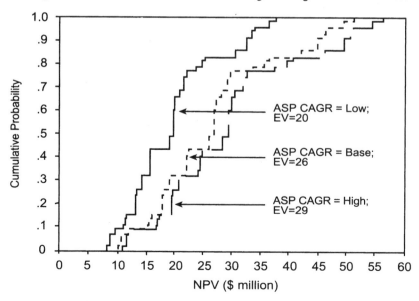

──────────────── Figure 6–19 ────────────────

DiagStatic New, Given Different Average Selling Price in the Start Year, 2003

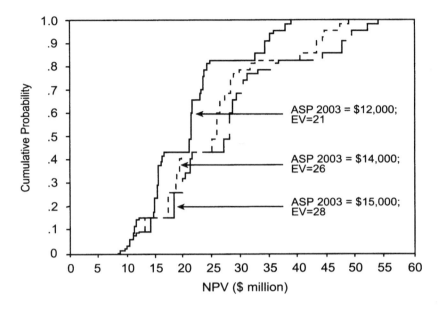

──

──────────────── Figure 6–20 ────────────────

DiagStatic New, Given Different RF Fraction of Total Market, 2010

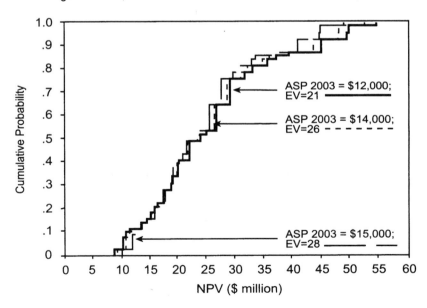

larger value of information than one would have expected from Figure 6–20; although DiagStatic New is not very sensitive to this variable, DiagStatic Plus is quite sensitive (see the sensitivity bars in Figure 6–12), creating the relatively large value of information.

The value of perfect information on all uncertainties together is $3.42 million, less that the sum of the value of information for each uncertainty separately, $4.96 million.

Given the very short time allotted to the analysis, no realistic information gathering activities were possible concerning the market. However, it was noted for the record that discussions with potential customers might shed some light on the market uncertainties.

When the design staff saw the value of information for technical success in developing DiagStatic New, they commented that they could clear up most of this uncertainty with a few weeks of concerted effort at a very small cost.

Laura could not wait the few weeks requested by the design staff before submitting the budget request. However, she planned to include this information in the request for DiagStatic New along with a contingency request if design staff indicated that DiagStatic New was technically infeasible.

Value of Perfect Control

Another insight we can glean form the tree is the value of perfect control. If there are feasible control procedures of reasonable cost, we can generate the new alternative of using these control procedures and reevaluate the tree.

To obtain the values with perfect control, the facilitator displayed the tree with the uncertain nodes brought to the front of the tree one by one; then he picked the best expected value for that node and took the difference between it and the original expected value (Figure 6–21).

—————————————————— Figure 6–21 ——————————————————

The Values of Perfect Information and Perfect Control for Diagnostics

Uncertainty	Value of Perfect Information ($ million)	Value of Perfect Control ($ million)
Technical Success, DiagStatic New	1.22	1.60
Peak Market Share, DiagStatic New	1.70	12.61
Peak Market Share, DiagRF Plus	.28	1.10
Average Selling Price CAGR	0	3.39
Average Selling Price 2003, DiagStatic New	.43	2.78
Average Selling Price 2001, DiagRF Plus	.57	2.26
RF Fraction of Total Market 2010	.70	2.12
All seven uncertainties	3.42	29.88

Peak Market Share for DiagStatic New has the largest value of control, even larger than control of Technical Success. The value of control on all seven uncertainties was $55.07 million, considerably greater than the sum of the value of control for each individual uncertainty, $25.89 million.

As for controlling these uncertainties, the facilitator suggested long-term favorable contracts with customers might achieve the higher market share levels with modest price adjustments.

Sensitivity Analysis to Probabilities, Risk Attitude, and Value Trade-offs

We can use the tree to perform sensitivity analysis to probability, risk attitude, and value trade-offs (such as the time value of money captured in the discount rate). We can also form new sensitivity displays by picking two values for the axes of a graph, such as the probabilities for two different uncertainties, and by showing which alternative is preferred in which region of the graph.

Sensitivity analysis results like these can suggest areas for refining estimates; show the consequences of using different, conflicting estimates from experts; and avoid potential "Monday morning quarterbacking."

The facilitator had already done a form of probabilistic sensitivity by looking at the conditional probability distributions in Figures 6–16 to 6–20. Now, however, he systematically varied probabilities to see if the preferred decision would change with changes in the probabilities for a particular uncertainty.

If there are more than two branches at a node, there are many ways to vary probabilities for a sensitivity analysis. One method is to put a probability *p* on the top branch and the rest of the probability (1-*p*) on the bottom branch, and then systematically vary *p*. If the top and bottom branches are the "best" and "worst" outcomes, you are varying in a systematic way between best and worst.

This is the method used in Figures 6–22 to 6–28. The original state of information had the probability symmetrically distributed around the middle branch; when we go to the two-branch approximation, this translates into assigning 50 percent probability for the top and bottom branches. The one exception is Technical Success, which was originally a two-branch node with 90 percent probability on the top "Success" branch and 10 percent on the bottom "Failure" branch.

The probability sensitivities show that all of the uncertainties (except for Average Selling Price CAGR) have the potential to switch the best alternative from DiagStatic New to DiagRF Plus.

For Technical Success, Figure 6–22 shows that for probabilities of technical success over 70 percent, DiagStatic New is the preferred alternative. Everyone agreed that the probability was in the 90 percent range, so there was no concern about this probability.

The remaining probabilities (Figures 6–23 to 6–28) had fairly general agreement that, in the two-branch approximation, each branch had about a 50 percent probability.

So the conclusions appeared to be quite robust against differences of opinion concerning probabilities.

Figure 6–22

Sensitivity to the Probability of Technical Success for DiagStatic New

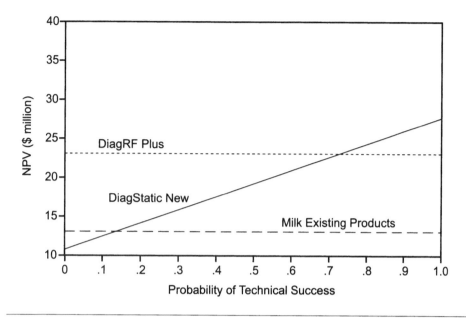

Figure 6–23

Sensitivity to the Probability that DiagStatic New Peak Market Share Is Low

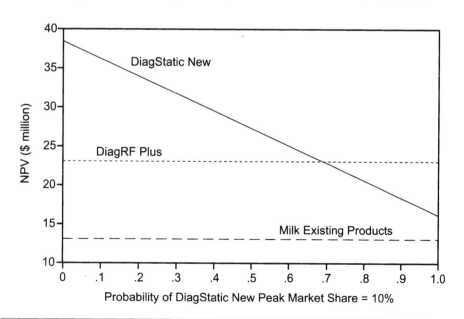

—————————————————— Figure 6–24 ——————————————————

Sensitivity to the Probability that DiagRF Plus Peak Market Share Is Low

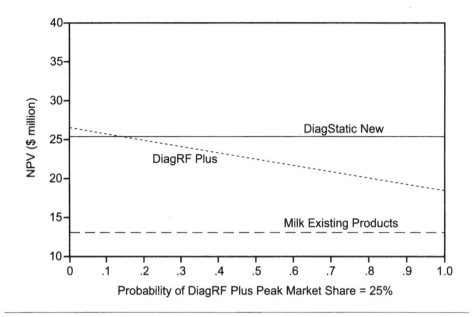

—————————————————— Figure 6–25 ——————————————————

Sensitivity to the Probability that Average Selling Price Growth Rate Is Low

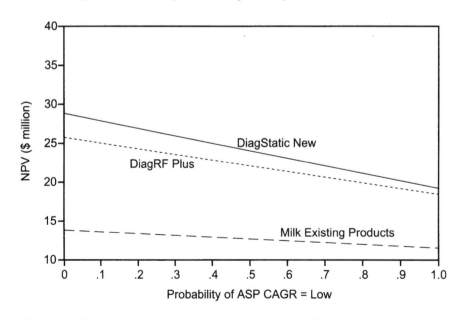

Figure 6–26

Sensitivity to the Probability that DiagStatic Price in 2003 Is Low

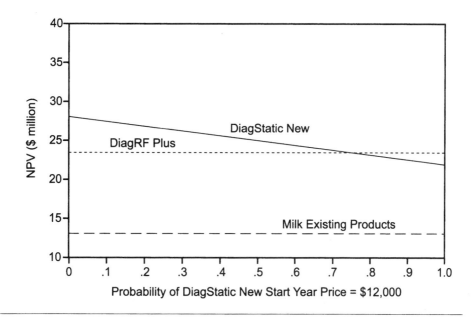

Figure 6–27

Sensitivity to the Probability that DiagRF Price in 2001 Is Low

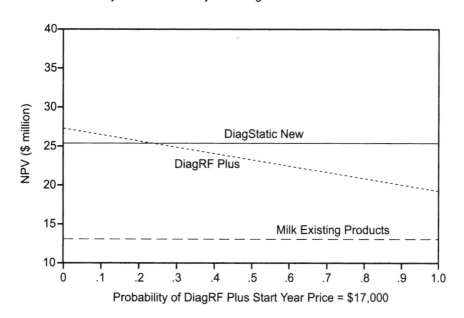

———————————————————————— Figure 6–28 ————————————————————————

Sensitivity to the Probability that RF Fraction of Total Market in 2010 Is Low

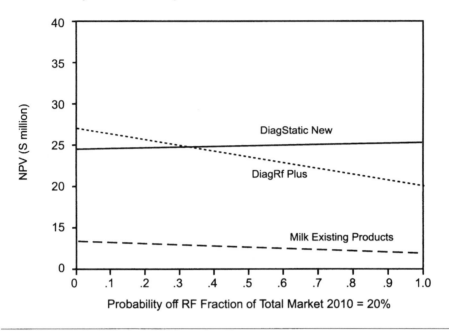

———————————————————————— Figure 6–29 ————————————————————————

Sensitivity to the Probabilities of Peak Market Share

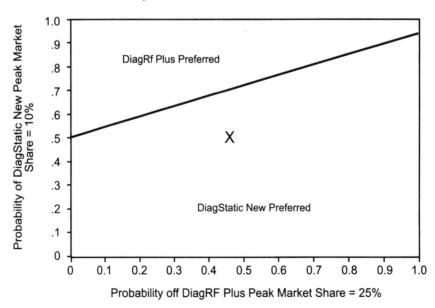

The facilitator put together several sensitivity plots against pairs of probabilities, such as the one shown in Figure 6–29. In this plot, the vertical axis is the probability that the peak market share for DiagStatic New is Low (10%) and the horizontal axis is the probability that the peak market share for DiagRF Plus is Low (25%). In the two-branch approximation, the current state of information is that both of these are 50 percent, the point marked X in the plot. If someone were to choose a different set of probabilities, they could refer to this plot. If the point is above the line, DiagRF Plus is preferred, and if it is below the line, DiagStatic New is preferred.

Finally, the facilitator heard someone refer to DiagStatic New as "risky." He immediately did a sensitivity to risk attitude, as shown in Figure 6–30. Unless the risk tolerance of Medequip is less than $3 million, DiagStatic New is preferred. Using the rules of thumb described in Chapter 5, the facilitator estimated that Medequip's risk tolerance should be on the order of $1,000 million. Clearly, this was not a "risky" choice from Medequip's point of view.

Policy Matrix

If there are decisions at other than the first node in the tree, we can generate a policy matrix to show what they would be. A policy matrix lists all paths through the tree that lead to the final decision node and the alternatives that would be chosen for that path. The policy matrix shows the importance (or lack of importance) of explicitly considering the decision in the analysis and may help in establishing a monitoring program and contingency plans. The simplest way to obtain the policy matrix is to display the tree for all the nodes up to and including the rightmost decision node.

—————————— Figure 6–30 ——————————

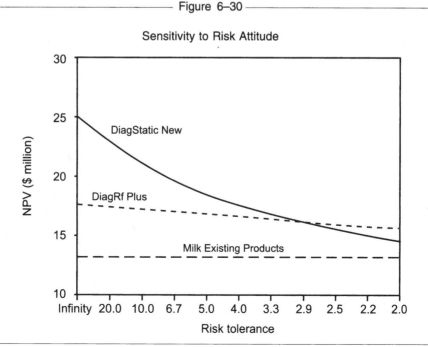

Sensitivity to Risk Attitude

For Diagnostics, the only decision node was in the front of the tree. However, if Diagnostics did choose to seek out imperfect information on the uncertainty with the highest value of perfect information (peak market share for DiagStatic New), they might get the policy matrix of Figure 6–31.

The analysis had reached the point in the decision analysis cycle (Figure 6–1) at which Basis Appraisal is complete. Now it was time to decide whether to act (decide on a budget request) or iterate the analysis.

Laura and the facilitator pondered further improvements to the analysis. The most glaring omission was not explicitly considering the alternative of developing two products for both the Static and RF market. They knew that no amount of sensitivity analysis would reveal the value of an alternative that was not included in the analysis.

An alternative with two products appeared quite attractive, but developing both would put quite a strain on the development staff. Both products could not be developed on the time schedule allotted for each when developed singly. In addition, there would be effects on pricing and market share if products were introduced in both the Static and RF market. Perhaps a platform could be developed which would support both markets.

These new alternatives violated the policy that had been developed at the beginning of the cycle—but they both knew that one of the most valuable outputs of an analysis can be results that suggest that policy should be violated.

The facilitator also suggested they might include the profit from the service part of the business. Diagnostics had a service force that kept its products in working order and made a modest profit. This source of profit was deliberately excluded from the analysis because Medequip was not certain that it wanted to keep the service organization or whether it wanted to sell it.

While Laura could see how added refinement might provide more insights into the decision, she was rather more worried about preparing a good presentation for the budget request. If the budget request succeeded, there would be ample time to refine the analysis and optimize the decision.

Figure 6–31

Hypothetical Policy Matrix for Diagnostics

Seek Imperfect Information on Peak Market Share for DiagStatic New	Peak Market Share for DiagStatic New	Decision
No	None	DiagStatic New
Yes	10% 20% 40%	DiagRF Plus DiagStatic New DiagStatic New

Time to Prepare and Present

A final, equally important phase of the analysis takes place after the last pass through the cycle and the last tree analysis. The facilitator and project team members should set time aside to explore the information contained in the analysis, obtain insight into the real-world problems and questions the analysis was intended to answer, and make sure the analysis addresses all the decision-maker's concerns. The insights and results then need to be packaged for effective communication to the decision-maker. (See the end of Chapter 8 for details.)

An all-too-frequent mistake is to continue the analysis until the last possible moment. There is not sufficient time for the careful preparation necessary for synthesizing, summarizing, and presenting the conclusions. As a result, the report or presentation can be a haphazard one that may omit crucial points, may contain analytical errors, and may (worse yet) be difficult to understand. Such a report may fail to cogently address the decision-maker's concerns and thus fail to provide motivation for action—which relegates the results to a file rather than establishing them as a basis for action.

Laura presented the results at the budget meeting. Because she knew the board would want to see some of the nuts and bolts that went into the numbers, she presented a base-case run of the spreadsheet model for each alternative and then the tree results. The board was very impressed with the thoroughness of the analysis and with the way Laura produced a reasonable picture of Diagnostics' opportunities.

Not surprisingly, the board asked Laura to have the design group do some work on the technical feasibility of DiagStatic New before they gave final approval. Rather surprisingly, however, the board also requested that she look into alternatives that would capitalize on the opportunity in both the Static and RF markets. The two opportunities looked attractive, and the board was willing to stretch the budget rather than leaving profits sitting on the table.

Summary

The decision analysis cycle makes it possible to tackle complex, real-world problems by breaking the decision analysis into four stages: basis development, deterministic structuring, probabilistic evaluation, and basis appraisal.

In the basis development stage, the problem is described, a value measure is chosen, the important decisions and uncertainties are identified, and the relationships between these decisions and uncertainties and the value measure are sketched out.

In the deterministic structuring stage, these decision and chance variables are related together in a deterministic model that calculates a value for any combination of these variables. Deterministic sensitivity analysis is then used to identify the key decisions and uncertainties.

In the probabilistic evaluation stage, these crucial decisions and uncertainties are structured into a decision tree, which is then analyzed.

In the basis appraisal stage, the results of the previous three stages are used to review the analysis for relevance and insight and to formulate recommendations (that may be for action or for further study).

When applied correctly, this cyclical process makes most decision problems tractable. In the case of Diagnostics, the two-week limit allowed only one real pass through the cycle. But the structured approach ensured that at the end of the week, the best possible results were available for decision-making.

Problems and Discussion Topics

6.1   A friend has come to you for help in deciding how to maximize his grade point average. What steps would you go through in developing a basis for the decision? What would you have at the end of the basis development? What are the next steps?

6.2   In the decision analysis cycle, there is a deterministic structuring phase. This phase often includes deterministic sensitivity analysis. In Chapter 3, there is a discussion of probabilistic sensitivity analysis. What are the differences between the two kinds of sensitivity analysis? What effects (or functions) does deterministic sensitivity analysis have in dealing with complex problems? Compare these two sensitivities with the sensitivity to risk tolerance seen in Chapter 5.

6.3   The complexity of a real-world problem is also reflected in its dynamic nature. The process of analyzing a decision problem can create new decision problems and add to the complexity of the original problem. A typical decision faced by the decision-maker (company) after the preliminary or pilot analysis is whether to proceed with the recommendation from the analysis or gather further information. Fortunately, the decision analysis cycle provides a framework with which to make this decision. Frequently, there are even preliminary numerical results available, such as the values of information.

What other complexities can arise in the course of analyzing the decision problem? (Hint: consider the elements of the decision basis.)

6.4   The ways of making decisions can be divided into normative methods and descriptive methods. Normative methods describe what people should do in a given situation. Descriptive methods focus on what people typically do.

For instance, if you face a decision on whether to hold on to a stock or sell it, a decision analysis (normative method) would tell you what you should do. Descriptively, many people make this kind of decision by asking their spouse, broker, or friends to effectively make the decision for them.

Is it possible to reconcile the two methods of decision-making? Provide an argument and example to support your judgment.

6.5   The framing of a decision problem describes how the decision is stated. An example is describing the effects of a new, dangerous, and relatively untested drug in terms of either net lives saved or net lives lost. Decision-makers are often affected by the framing of the problem. For example, the information they provide and preferences they express will vary with the framing of the problem. Many of these framing issues are believed to be psychological in origin. What could you do to avoid these problems?

6.6   Innovative Foods Corporation (IFC) is a wholly owned subsidiary of Universal Foods Corporation (UFC). UFC is a major Fortune 500 company in the food processing industry. IFC is in the market of supplying specialized processed foods for human consumption. In 1979, the total market for specialized processed foods amounted to $600 million and is growing.

IFC's leading products are dehydrated and processed foods targeted at two consumer groups: people on a special diet and people who are recovering after a serious illness. IFC has been using a well-known additive in its food processing, Divit, which is a recognized food additive in the food processing industry.

By carefully researching and testing its products, IFC has established a secure but small market share. IFC has a reputation as a good and reliable company and anticipates a $2 million net yearly cash flow after taxes for the next 20 years.

In the last year, IFC management has become acquainted with some troublesome experiments carried out by its research division. The results of these experiments indicate a high probability that Divit is carcinogenic when applied in very high concentrations to the skin of mice. The carcinogenic properties when Divit is ingested by humans are by no means certain. IFC believes its competitors may be on the same track. If Divit turns out to be carcinogenic, the FDA will surely ban it, thus bringing about a major decrease in IFC's earnings and probably the loss of most of IFC's hard-earned market share.

However, IFC management has also been informed about another option. Its research division has developed another additive, Biovit. The research director believes Biovit is an excellent food additive that will have none of the problems of Divit. At present, the manufacturing costs of Biovit are uncertain. To process its food with Biovit, IFC will have to invest around $150 million. IFC management must make an important decision: should it continue to use Divit and face its potential banning or should it invest in new facilities and start using Biovit?

Assume you are a member of IFC's executive committee. How would you structure your thinking about this problem? Are there ethical considerations?

6.7   Plastic Co. is a fairly large company that manufactures bulk plastics for a large variety of uses. It has an extensive network of customers—companies that turn the bulk plastic into items that are then sold to the end-user.

Tech Co. is a European company that owns a process for formulating a special plastic that is useful for making bearings for high-speed centrifuges. There are several other potential high-tech applications for this special plastic. The same production equipment can also be used for making a common, low-margin type of plastic, which, it turns out, is not a plastic that Plastic Co. currently makes.

Tech Co. does not want to enter the U.S. market and is offering Plastic Co. an exclusive license for the manufacturing technology. The asking price is a $500,000 license fee plus 5 percent of sales for 10 years.

Plastic Co. has determined that the equipment could come in a small size (3 million pounds per year) or a large size (10 million pounds per year). The respective costs for the equipment are $3 million and $7 million. Tech Co.'s experience has been that production costs are $0.20 per pound.

a. Begin to develop the decision basis for this decision. What are the alternatives? What are the uncertainties? What is the value? What information do you have? What information do you still need?

b. Designate someone to be the decision-maker. She will be the president of Plastic Co. Review with her the work you have done so far and finish structuring the decision. Assess any further information you may need.

c. Analyze the decision and produce a recommended course of action. Review the recommendation with the decision-maker. (Does she need to know the details of the analysis?) Is your recommendation useful to her? Does she believe and understand it? Why or why not?

6.8   Form a group to analyze a decision about whether or not to add a salad bar to a pizza parlor. Designate at least one person to be the client and one person to be the facilitator. (You may have more than one of each.) Make a pass through the decision analysis cycle as described below.

a. **Background**. Develop an image of the pizza parlor that is as realistic as possible for whoever is playing the client. (This will greatly aid in the assessments.) How large is the place? How old is it? Who owns it? Who runs it? What kind of an area is it located in? What kind of clientele does it have? What is currently on the menu? What is the monthly sales volume? How many customers does it have daily? What are the peak hours? What kind of decor does it have?

b. **Basis Development**. Develop the basis for the decision. If you like, you may use an influence diagram for this step. What decisions must be made? What are the significant uncertainties? How do they relate to one another? What are the values on which the decision will be made? Try to keep the problem description simple.

c. **Deterministic Structuring.** Develop a model to determine the value for any scenario the tree might generate. The model may be assessed values or a spreadsheet model. Use sensitivity analysis, if necessary, to reduce the number of variables in the tree. Focus on modeling to help your understanding of the problem and to distinguish between alternatives.

d. **Probabilistic Evaluation.** Build and analyze the decision tree. For simplicity, try to keep the number of nodes down to four or five. You may start with a larger tree and then eliminate the nodes that do not distinguish between alternatives. Examine profit distributions, expected values, tree drawings, probability sensitivities, etc. Check that the results are consistent with your understanding of the problem.

e. **Basis Appraisal.** What is the preferred decision? How do its expected value and risk compare with those of the other alternatives? Is the preferred decision sensitive to changes in probabilities or risk attitude. What are the values of information and control? Would the client feel comfortable acting at this point, or would further study be advisable?

f. **Action.** Prepare a list of requirements for implementing the recommended alternative. These may include allocating funding, hiring personnel, hiring contractors, etc., or there may be no requirements if the recommendation was to do nothing. Has the analysis shed any light on the steps required for implementation? Is there any value to updating the analysis periodically to provide further guidance?

6.9 Form a small group to perform a decision analysis of a case study you have previously worked on. Assign roles. You will need at least one facilitator and one client who can supply structure and probabilities. Complete at least one pass through the cycle, perhaps limiting the exercise to two or three hours. Spend most of the time structuring the problem and preparing a final report.

6.10 Insitu Corp., an energy company, had developed a new technology for oil drilling in cold climates. The technology involved injecting a heated chemical solution into the well field at one location and waiting for the solution to percolate through the oil-bearing formation. Then, the solution was pumped out of the well field at another location and the oil was extracted in a processing plant.

Insitu had proven this technology on a pilot scale and was considering whether to build a full-scale project on its Whalebone property in Alaska. One of the major uncertainties was the capital cost of constructing the complex, consisting of the plant, pipeline, and well field. An engineering and design firm had estimated a base cost of $320 million. To obtain financial backing for the project, Insitu felt it needed to verify this cost.

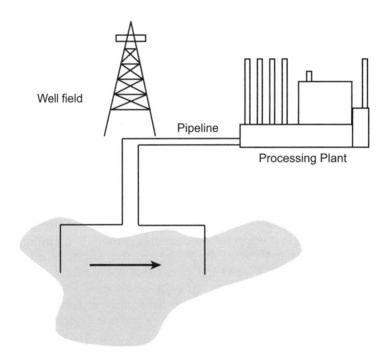

A team assembled in September to review the cost estimate identified two major risks in the estimate. First was the question of the efficiency of the new technology. In the pilot plant, a flow rate of 500 gallons per minute had produced a solution 30 percent saturated with oil. However, if the full-scale process were less efficient and produced, say, only 10 percent saturation at a flow rate of 1,000 gallons per minute, additional equipment would be required for the volume of oil produced to remain constant. Engineering estimates the additional equipment would add 15 percent to the base cost.

The second major risk was the productivity of the union workers. The largest influence on productivity was the unemployment rate in the area. If unemployment were high, then the workers would be less likely to strike and would work harder. Unemployment, in turn, depended on the number of large pipeline and energy projects competing for workers and, ultimately, on energy prices. Changes in energy prices in recent years had been correlated with productivity variations as large as +30 percent. The team decided to include in its estimate a contingency to reflect these risks in the capital cost.

As the team was about to adjourn, someone asked if there were any other reasons the base cost could be exceeded. An inexperienced staffer, Ms. Pessi Mist, asked whether they were sure the construction would be finished on time. Since wage and materials rates were escalating at almost 25 percent a year, she felt a late construction schedule would increase costs. Her question was met with disbelief. The venture manager explained that most of the construction had to be completed before the spring thaw date, because heavy equipment could not be operated on the muskeg once it thawed in June. The EPA was very unlikely to allow summer construction on the fragile muskeg. In addition, a June 1 expected completion date had already been announced publicly by the president of Insitu. No one had to mention the company's unblemished record of completing projects within the allotted time once construction was under way. Because of the cost of interest on funds expended during construction, Insitu had made this its trademark.

Undaunted, Ms. Mist pursued the question of what remained to be done before the three-month construction schedule could begin. A cost engineer explained that the board of directors had taken the position that it would not meet to review the project unless the native claims issues were settled for the pipeline route. Without board approval, a contract could not be let. If the contractor did not arrange for materials delivery to the site by March 1, the start of the project would be delayed. In addition, the board required a minimum of one month for deliberation, and two months each were required to let contracts or deliver materials.

Sparked by the mention of the EPA, another young staffer, Enviro Mann, asked what would happen if the EPA did not allow the spent solution to be pumped back into the mine shaft as planned. The environmental engineer assured him that a waste pond would cost only $5 million to build. The possibility that recycling of the solution would be required was very remote.

a. Draw an influence diagram for the total capital cost of the complex in current dollars.

Slightly unsettled by the questions of Ms. Mist and Mr. Mann, the team assigned them the job of developing a better picture of the risks in the capital cost. Mist and Mann interviewed a number of people in the corporation. From the engineering manager, who knew the most about scaling up chemical processes, they assessed a 75 percent chance that the full-scale plant would work as efficiently as the pilot plant. From the regulatory affairs department, they assessed a 50 percent chance that the spent solution could be put in the mine shaft. There was only a 20 percent chance that recycling would be required. However, if this additional step were required in the process, $120 million of equipment would be added. The manager of regulatory affairs was uncomfortable about whether the EPA would allow summer construction on the muskeg. He could remember only five winter Alaskan projects that had been delayed until summer. Of these, only one had been allowed to proceed before the September 1 freeze date. For the four events necessary to begin construction, the following probabilities were assessed.

Event	Probability
Native claims issues settled for pipeline route by October 1	.70
Board of Directors approval by November 1	.50
Contract let by January 1	.90
Materials on site by March 1	.25

The probability distribution below was assessed for worker productivity. Ms. Mist noted that labor costs were only 35 percent of the total construction costs.

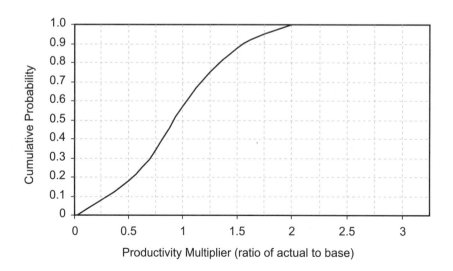

b. Draw a probability tree for the total capital cost of the project in current dollars. Label the branches and put in the probabilities.

c. Write an equation for the cost model to calculate the total capital cost of the project.

d. Calculate a probability distribution on the total capital cost of the project in current dollars. How do you explain its shape?

e. Perform a sensitivity analysis to determine the most important risks in the total cost. Calculate the following quantities.

   • The change in total expected cost when each individual variable changes from its lowest to its highest value. This answers the question, "How much difference does this variable make in the expected cost?"

   • The expected change in the standard d eviation of the total cost if perfect information were available on each variable. This answers the question, "How much does this variable contribute to the risk?" Why can't we do ordinary value of information calculations?

f. What conclusions, insights, and recommendations would you make for risk management and cost control?

7

Corporate Applications of Decision Analysis

In the previous chapters of this book, we used simple examples to illustrate decision analysis techniques. In this chapter, we discuss several of the most important corporate applications of decision analysis—examples that provide some general outlines and points to consider when approaching a problem for the first time.

Because of the tremendous variations encountered in practice, these examples should not be viewed as templates, much less as cookbook formulas for analysis. A decision tree formulation is seldom appropriate for any problem other than the one it was designed for. Thus, the reader should concentrate on the process of understanding and structuring the problem that leads to the tree formulation.

New Product Introduction

One of the classic applications of decision analysis is introducing new products to the marketplace. Such problems have a large amount of uncertainty. Will the market accept the new product? How will the competition respond? How long will the product last? What will the margins be? If the product introduction requires large amounts of investment (such as capital for production equipment, promotion, or advertising), the decision may be a source of substantial risk to the company.

For many products, the model to evaluate the cash flow can be based on a simple product life cycle model (Figure 7–1).

This simple model requires only five parameters (year of introduction, length of introduction phase, maturity phase, decline phase, and market share at maturity) and, given the large uncertainties involved, is usually a sufficiently accurate description.

Figure 7–1

A Simple Product Life Cycle Model for Evaluating Cash Flow

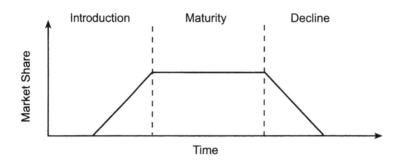

To complete the calculation of cash flow, we also need the size and growth rate of the market, fixed and variable costs, capital investment, the cost of ongoing research and development, the margin realized, and the value of possible follow-on business.

One of the most difficult aspects of analyzing new products is determining precisely how to model revenues and costs. Many products are sold like commodities in that prices are determined by some markup or margin over cost, usually the cost of the highest-cost producer. As a new entry to the market, our cost may be high if we have not moved down the learning curve or low if we have the latest, most efficient means of production. The first possibility can sometimes be handled by including a start-up cost. In the second case, we should consider the possibility that our margins decline over time. Specifically, either the competition strives to match our cost or new competitors enter the market and drive out the old high-cost producers, thus reducing prices.

Other types of products have some differentiation from competing products, at least at the time of introduction. In this case, modeling price over time will be quite difficult. One possibility is to make the absolute price (e.g., $7 each) or relative price (e.g., 20 percent over competition) a decision variable and let market share be an uncertainty, with probabilities depending on the pricing decision. Alternatively, we could make market share a decision (e.g., hold 30 percent of market) and let realized price be an uncertainty, similarly depending on the share decision. In any case, the model should check that margins do not become unreasonably high or low over any extended period.

Two aspects of competition should be considered: (1) What will the competition do over time, perhaps in response to our entry into the market and our pricing? and (2) Is there a possibility of some competitive breakthrough that will completely change the market? We might include these considerations by assessing the price necessary to hold a particular market share given different competitor actions or product introductions.

The influence diagram (Figure 7–2a) shows one way of relating all these factors. This influence diagram is a disguised and simplified version of one used in an actual application. We see that the product introduction

Figure 7–2

Critical Uncertainties and Decisions in a New Product Introduction

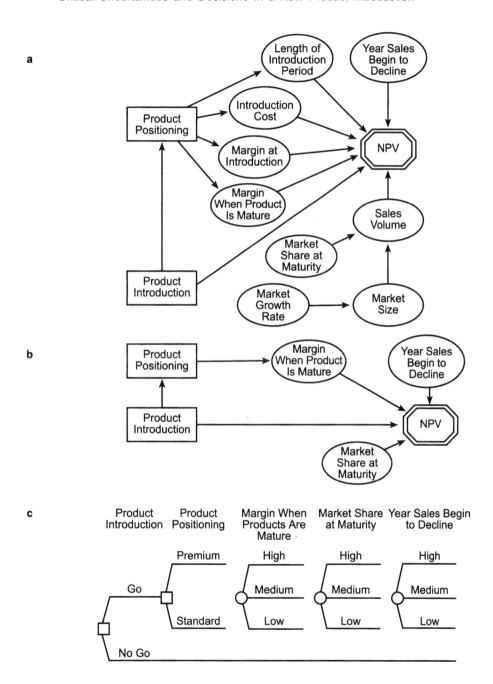

affects sales volume (because there are no sales if the product is not introduced) and product positioning. Product positioning in turn influences margins, costs, and some aspects of the product life cycle, which, together with market size, share, and sales volume, determine the net present value (NPV) for the product.

A model was used to capture the relationships in this influence diagram, and sensitivity analysis was then applied to determine the critical uncertainties and decisions. Those uncertainties and decisions are shown in influence diagram form (Figure 7–2b) and in tree form (Figure 7–2c).

The first node is a decision about whether to introduce the product, with the Go option requiring a major capital investment. The second node represents a decision on how the product is positioned relative to existing competitive products, which affects the size of the introduction costs, the length of the growth period, and the initial margins. The third node represents the margins achieved during the maturity period of the life cycle. These margins depend on the product positioning decision. Thus, probabilities for different levels of margin vary according to the product positioning decision; in this case, the company was a market leader, and its initial actions would help set later prices (and margins).

The fourth node represents uncertainty in market share during the maturity phase. The probabilities of this node were independent of the other nodes, since the company and the product were judged important enough that the initial product positioning would not affect the mature market share. The final node is the year the decline phase begins in the product life cycle. The probabilities for this node were also judged probabilistically independent of the previous nodes, implying that in no case is the product so successful (or unsuccessful) as to accelerate (or delay) competitors' introduction of the next generation product.

Litigation Decision Analysis

Litigation is an area in which uncertainty is extremely important and where the stakes may be large enough to pose a serious risk to a company if it loses a suit or provide a significant opportunity if it wins one.

In one common kind of litigation decision, a company is being sued and has the opportunity to settle out of court. Thus, it has to decide on whether to settle the case or to continue in litigation (Figure 7–3). If the company chooses to litigate, there is an uncertainty concerning what the judgment will be and the size of the judgment if the company is found liable. If the company chooses to settle, there is some uncertainty about the final settlement cost. Presumably, however, the plaintiff's counsel has indicated the size of potential settlements. There is a question mark on the arrow between the Settlement Cost node and the Settle/Litigate Decision node to indicate that the arrow should be there if the settlement cost is known and should not be there if it is still an uncertainty.

—————————————————— Figure 7–3 ——————————————————

Critical Uncertainties and Decisions in a Litigation Question

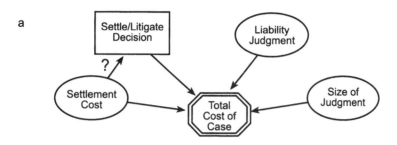

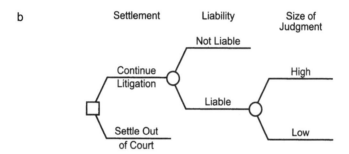

The decision tree formulation for this problem begins with a decision node on whether to litigate or settle. The litigation branch is followed by uncertainties on the verdict and on the size of the judgment if the company is found liable. The Settle Out of Court alternative branch will be followed by an uncertainty in Settlement Cost if the questionable arrow in the influence diagram does not exist.

One implicit assumption in this tree is that this is the company's last opportunity to settle out of court. If this were not the case, there should be another decision about whether to settle out of court later, perhaps after something has been learned to change the probabilities for liability or size of judgment.

Modeling in litigation tends to be simple. However, it is important to discount future values and to include the cost of the proceedings since large cases tend to last a long time. It is also important to include in all the outcome values the cost or value of setting a precedent.

Other litigation decision problems can be examined with decision analysis. For instance, the value of pretrial work and investigation can be analyzed. The value of this work is either value of information (the trial strategy can be chosen better) or value of control (the probability of a favorable outcome can be increased).

Litigation problems can be difficult for the facilitator. Lawyers are often highly resistant to the notion that someone (the facilitator) is telling them how to do their job. Lawyers, like doctors or polymer chemists or nuclear physicists, are quite right in thinking that their years of training and practice have made them facile with complexities and language to which the ordinary facilitator is not privy.

This impression is perhaps reinforced for lawyers by the special legal monopoly accorded their profession and by their traditional independence from clients in all decisions except those decisive to the outcome of a claim (such as whether to accept a particular settlement offer).

Therefore, it is especially important that a legal decision analysis meet two important goals. First, it should reflect the counsel's best judgment about the law and precedent that bear on the client's prospects. Second, it should forcefully direct that judgment to the value measure of importance to the client.

To meet the first goal, analyses will often be very detailed at the influence diagram stage, reflecting alternative legal theories and perhaps even evidentiary issues bearing on what the judge or jury will see.

The second goal of forcefully directing the analysis toward the value measure is accomplished by framing the analysis in terms of what the judge or jury will actually consider and base the decision on.

Decision analysis can dramatically improve the quality of communication about legal questions. Without it, the difficulties in communicating about legal complexities and uncertainties often remove effective control from the hands of the president or CEO of the company—a serious condition since the suit may have major implications for the company's future. In addition, explicitly considering risk attitude through decision analysis can enable management to make litigation decisions in a manner consistent with regular business decisions.

Bidding Strategies

Bidding is another area in which uncertainty plays an important role. The difficulties in bidding problems are twofold. First, we are uncertain about how our competitors will bid and thus about whether we will win the bid or not. Second, as the number of serious competitors increases, competition becomes keener and the likelihood of winning decreases. In these highly competitive bidding situations, the winning bid can yield the winner little profit (and even a net loss).

Addressing all the costs and uncertainties associated with losing or winning a particular contract is essential. Assuming there is no cost associated with losing a contract, Figure 7–4 is a good representation of a typical bidding problem. We can look at how some of the quantities described by this tree vary by plotting them (Figure 7–5).

We have superimposed three graphs, with the horizontal axis for each being the size of the bid (the first node in the decision tree). The first line plotted is the probability of winning the contract as a function of the bid size. It obviously decreases as the size of the bid increases. The second line plotted is the expected value of the business, given we win the bid. This line rises, because, as we bid more for the same job, our profit margin increases. The third line is the expected value of the business multiplied by the probability of winning the bid, which is the expected value of the bid. The optimal value of the bid for an expected-value decision-maker is the peak of this third line. This optimal bid maximizes the expected value of the bid. (Note that because of differing vertical scales, there is no relation between

---
Figure 7–4

Critical Uncertainties and Decisions in a Bidding Problem

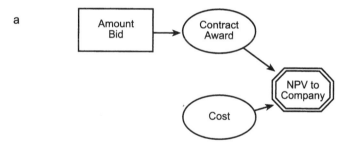

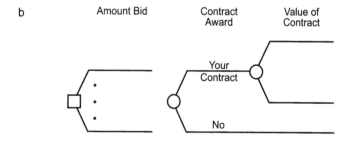

—————————————————— Figure 7–5 ——————————————————

Values in a Bidding Problem as a Function of the Amount Bid

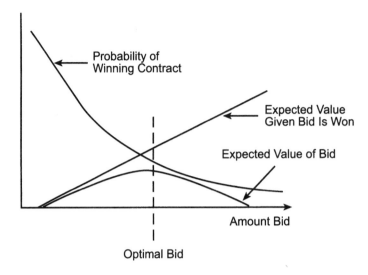

the position of the "Optimal Bid" and the bid value where the "Probability of Winning Contract" and "Expected Value Given Bid Is Won" lines cross.)

For this type of problem, the bid that maximizes the certain equivalent is frequently somewhat lower than the bid that maximizes the expected value. Risk avoiders prefer to bid lower and increase the probability of getting the business. The higher chances of loss with a lower bid may counteract this tendency, however, and push the risk avoider's bid higher.*

Investment and Investment Rollover Decisions —————————————

Many investment decisions are extremely difficult to analyze because of the variety and liquidity of available investment instruments and because of the many points when a decision can be made. As a result, attempts to model investment decisions in their most general form can produce an unmanageable decision tree. However, once the choice of investments and the time frame have been restricted, decision analysis formulations can be applied.

For instance, banks frequently sell 90- or 180-day certificates of deposit (CDs) to maintain some of their funds in relatively short-term, liquid form.

---

*For an interesting analysis of oil company bids on leases, see E.C. Capen, R.V. Clapp, and W.M. Campbell, "Competitive Bidding in High-Risk Situations," *Journal of Petroleum Technology* (June 1971): 641-653. Reprinted in *Readings on the Principles and Applications of Decision Analysis*, ed. R.A. Howard and J.E. Matheson, 2 vols. (Menlo Park, California: Strategic Decisions Group, 1984), 2: 805–819.

In the CD investment decision, the first decision is whether to buy 90- or 180-day CDs. If we choose 180-day CDs, that decision will take us to the end of the time period considered (Figure 7–6).

However, if 90-day CDs are chosen, we have to decide what to do with the money in 90 days when the CD matures. At that time, we will know what the 90- and 180-day CD rates have gone to, though this is an uncertainty now.

Finally, we need to be able to value the investment decisions made in each scenario. For the initial choice of a 180-day CD and for any choice of a 90-day CD, the value is simply the face value at maturity. However, if we choose 180-day CDs 90 days from now, they will only be halfway to maturity at the end of the 180-day time horizon. At that point, the 180-day CDs will have 90 days to go and, therefore, will be valued as if they were 90-day CDs. Thus, to value the 180-day CDs bought 90 days from now, we need to know what the 90-day CD rates will be 180 days from now (Figure 7–6).

—————————————————————— Figure 7–6 ——————————————————————

Critical Uncertainties and Decisions in an Investment Question

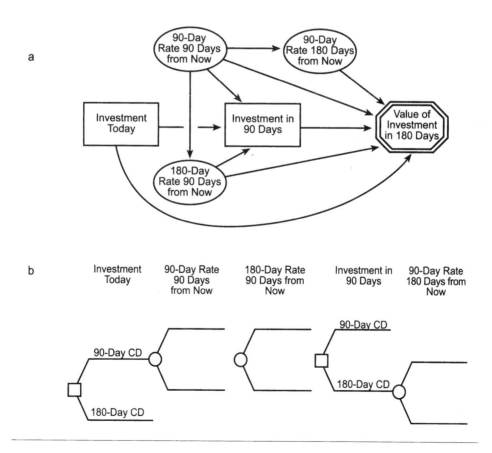

Options _____

The stock market would appear to be a natural place to use the tools of decision analysis. Decisions, uncertainty, risk are all there. We will demonstrate how decision analysis can be applied to a very simple choice between buying a stock, buying an option on a stock, and not investing. Then we will give the reasons why analysis of financial investments of this type can not be described in one section of a book.

A stock option is a contract that gives the owner the right, but not the obligation, to buy ("call") or sell ("put") the underlying stock at an agreed-on price, the "strike" price. The option can be exercised at any time up to the expiration date (an "American" option) or only on the expiration date itself (a "European" option). In the example below, we will consider a European call option.

When the time comes to exercise this option, the owner knows the price of the stock. If the price of the stock is greater than the strike price, he or she will purchase (exercise the option) at the strike price and take the difference between actual stock price and the strike price as profit—the stock could, in principle, be bought at the strike price and sold immediately at the actual market price. Of course, if the price of the stock is less than the strike price, he or she will refuse to exercise the option.

As an example, take the case in which an investor is interested in buying a stock today at purchase price S and holding it for a year (Figure 7–7a); the uncertainty is in S', the price of the stock one year from now (Figure 7–7b). Another alternative is to purchase an option today with strike price $30 at purchase price C; the value of this option is shown in Figure 7–7b, given that the option would not be exercised if stock price were less than the strike price of $30. Using the expected values (or certain equivalents), the investor is faced with the tree in Figure 7–7c; now it just a matter of comparing the present value of the outcomes (including transaction and tax costs) with the purchase prices S and C. Note that funds not used in the investments in this simple example are kept in accounts with no return— under the mattress!

To pursue this example a little further, we might adjust the alternatives so that they are approximately of equal magnitude. To do this, we can change the options alternative so that it has an expected value equal to that of the alternative to purchase the stock. The stock purchase alternative had an expected value of $35.0; the option on one stock with strike price $30 had an expected value of $6.6. We change the alternative to an option for 5.27 (35.0 / 6.6) stocks; stocks being traded in large lots, there is no problem in having a fractional multiple. This venture is shown in Figure 7–8.

What about the purchase prices?* For the stock, let us assume that the investor and the market share a common estimate for the future value of the stock and that, for the purposes of this example, the investor and the

---

*For an excellent introduction to investment topics, see David G. Luenberger, *Investment Science*,   New York: Oxford University Press, 1998.

Figure 7–7

An Investment Decision for One Stock

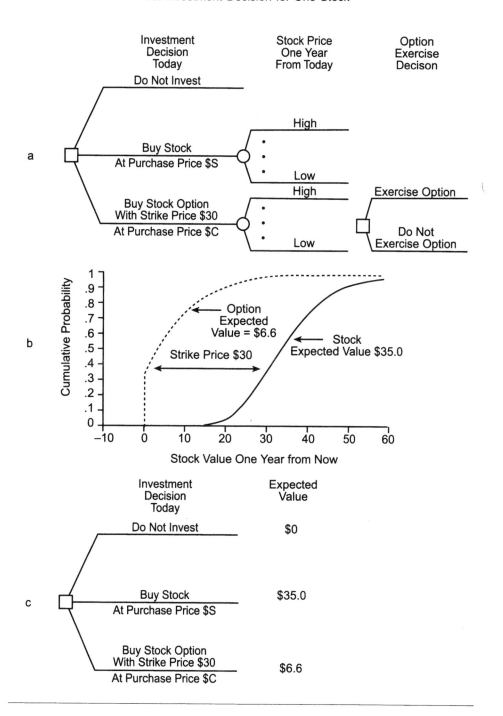

Figure 7–8

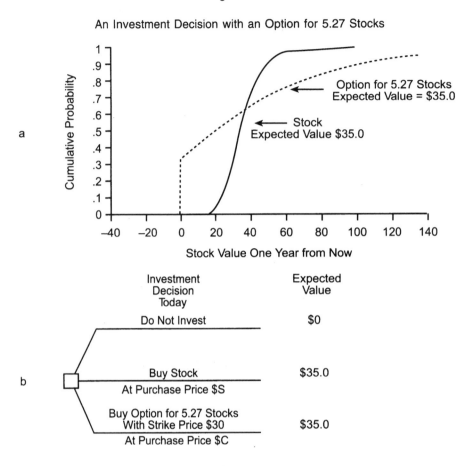

An Investment Decision with an Option for 5.27 Stocks

a

b

market both want a 15 percent expected profit during the year. The purchase price of the stock is then S = $30.4 = $35 / 1.15.

What about the purchase price of the option? In 1973, Black, Scholes, and Merton developed a theory for valuation of this type of asset in an efficient market; for this work, Merton and Scholes won the Nobel prize in 1997. They recognized that portfolios of investments could be constructed which perfectly replicate the payoffs of the option. The value of this replicating portfolio determines a fair market price of the option.

A common application of this methodology to place a market value on a European call option is given by the Black-Scholes formula. This formula has two major assumptions: that the markets are efficient and that stock prices perform "geometric Brownian motion," namely, a random walk superimposed on a constant exponential rise. This implies that the uncertainty in S', the stock price a year from now, is lognormal (see Problem 7.5.)

Inputs to the Black-Scholes formula for a European call option are current stock price (S), strike price (K), time to expiration of the option (t), the stock's volatility (σ), and the risk-free discount rate (r). The option price is C, where:

$$C = N(d_1)S - N(d_2)Ke^{-rt}$$

(7–1)

The "probabilities" $N(d_i)$ are the cumulative normal distribution (in Microsoft Excel, you can calculate $N(d_i)$ as $NORMDIST(d_i, 0, 1, TRUE)$), with

$$d_1 = \left(\ln(S/K) + (r + \sigma^2/2)t\right)/\sigma\sqrt{t}$$

(7–2)

$$d_2 = d_1 - \sigma\sqrt{t}$$

(7–3)

The example supplies the values S = \$30.4, K = \$30, and t = 1 year. For the purposes of this illustration, take the risk free discount rate, r, to be 7 percent.

How can we estimate the volatility? The volatility is the standard deviation for the probability distribution for $ln(S')$, the logarithm of the stock price one year from now. It is a parameter that you can estimate from the past performance of this stock or similar stocks, assuming the future will be like the past. But for this example, we can estimate it from the data given. As shown in Problem 7.5, the volatility is approximately the standard deviation of S' divided by the expected value of S'; the standard deviation of S' can be approximated as the 10–90 fractile width of the distribution for S' divided by 2.56 (see Chapter 10, Figure 10–17). Inspection of the distribution in Figure 7–7b gives a 10–90 width of approximately 25 and a standard deviation of 9.8 = 25 / 2.56. The expected value is \$35. Thus the volatility is approximately .28 = 9.8 / 35.

Putting this all together, we find the Black-Scholes formula yields an option price of C = \$4.61 (70 percent of the expected value of \$6.6) for one stock or a purchase price for an option for 5.27 stocks of \$24.3 = 5.27 × \$4.61. The results are shown in Figure 7–9 net of purchase price. The options alternative is much "riskier" (more uncertainty for approximately the same expected value) than the simple stock purchase.

Why is this simple picture too simple? Because there are many decision alternatives that have not been considered in Figure 7–7. The most obvious alternatives concern the timing, size, and nature of investment: the investor can sell the stock or the options during the course of the year or acquire more of the stock or options during the course of the year. In addition, the investor need not restrict investments to this particular stock and can invest in any of myriad other investment possibilities.

Real Options

The idea of real options is that many business decisions create not only a stream of cash flows, but also future investment opportunities that management can later choose whether or not to exercise. As such, these opportu-

—————————————— Figure 7–9 ——————————————

An Investment Decision with an Option for 5.27 Stocks Net of Purchase Price

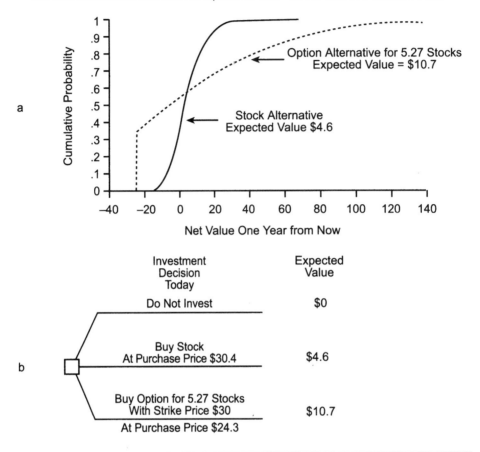

nities are valuable and must be considered part of the value delivered by the immediate investment.

Clearly such real options are analogous to stock options, which once purchased by an investor, create a future opportunity to make another investment (namely, to buy the underlying stock).

Introducing this terminology into a decision-analytic framework can stimulate ideas and help uncover hidden issues, possibilities, and sources of value. More than that, it can point to deficiencies in many analyses. Decision analyses all to often tend to focus on uncertainties and up-front decisions; the value of a rich set of downstream decisions (decisions to exercise options) is sometimes slighted. By explicitly thinking about options, we can add an element of quality control to the process.

A topic beyond the scope of this book: From options valuation and from a number of other sources comes the idea of "risk neutral valuation" or "options valuation."* In this valuation, future cash flows are always discounted at the *risk-free borrowing rate* rather than the actual borrowing rate (e.g., weighted average cost of capital, WACC) or any other risk-adjusted rate. To the extent that there is a securities market whose risks are correlated with the risks associated with the project, the "probabilities" for future scenarios are deduced from the current market price of these securities. These probabilities are called *risk neutral probabilities*. While they are not the subjective probabilities discussed in this book, they are used as probabilities and take into account the non-diversifiable risks associated with the overall market. This topic is too deep and controversial for further discussion in this book. At the moment, the approach appears to be mostly theoretical and academic. However, the decision facilitator should be able to recognize the topic if it should occur and know when to seek assistance.

A problematic application of the Black-Scholes formula: Sometimes people try to take the analogy to stock options a step further and use the powerful methods developed for stock-option pricing in the real option setting. The essential idea is to apply the Black-Scholes formula to evaluate capital investment and long-term business ventures. Consider a situation in which we can make a modest initial investment, acquiring the right to making a major investment several years from now to enter a new business; R&D is an example of this type of situation. The probability distribution on the value of the new business gives the current value S (expected value) and the volatility σ; the major investment is K, the strike price; the time until the major decision is made is t, and the risk free discount rate is r. *Voilà*, the value of the venture, to be compared to the modest initial investment.

There are a number of profound problems with this application of the Black-Scholes formula. The formula is formally applicable only under fairly stringent assumptions about the stochastic nature of the underlying stock; these assumptions are almost certainly not met by most business ventures. Furthermore, it implies that the value of the stock is accurately known on the date of exercise, which is definitely not the case for the value of a new business opportunity. It also assumes we have an efficient market that will trade any position on the underlying stock and provide low-interest loans for leveraging positions; again, this is not easy to do for most new business opportunities. From a decision-analysis perspective, the use of the Black-Scholes approach to place a value on real options should be taken as a helpful *qualitative* tool to bring to light the drivers of value in a real option.

In summary concerning real options: Make sure to think carefully and creatively about "downstream" decisions and incorporate them, as appropriate, in the analysis. Sometimes downstream decisions will be built into the model, sometimes into explicit tree/influence diagram structure. If their use is required, use stock option tools (e.g., Black-Scholes formula) with caution and only as an indicator for defining or refining an analysis.

---

*For an introduction to real options, see Martha Amram and Nalin Kulatilaka, *Real Options: Managing Strategic Investment in an Uncertain World*, Boston: Harvard Business School Press, 1999.

R&D Decisions _____

Research and development (R&D) is one of the most obvious areas for applying decision analysis in the corporate sector, because R&D decisions usually have large and unavoidable uncertainty. Any evaluation of whether a project justifies its cost must deal with this uncertainty. Though decisions on individual R&D projects usually do not involve large enough costs to pose significant risk to a company, the existence of an adequate portfolio of R&D projects is frequently critically important to the company's continued well-being.

General research without any specific application (also called "blue-sky" research) is difficult to evaluate, no matter what methodology is used. It is usually best to restrict analysis of research to laboratory work with an identified application or applications. An example of research with an identified application could be work on a coating both to reduce corrosion in chemical plant pipes and also to coat nonstick cookware.

Staged Decisions: In an R&D project where an application has been identified, there are a series of decisions: research, development, scaleup, and commercialization. Luckily, not all these decisions are relevant for every R&D project. For research, we can start or not start the research (or continue or terminate it if it is already in progress). For development, we can abandon development or continue engineering to develop a practical product or process. For scaleup, we can abandon scaleup or build a pilot plant. For commercializing a product, we can abandon commercialization, introduce the product, replace an existing product, or wait until the competition introduces a similar product. For commercializing a process, we can abandon the process, use it ourselves, license it to others, or sell the rights to the process outright.

Pharmaceutical R&D: Pharmaceutical R&D* lends itself well to this type of analysis. Regulation requires a staged set of clinical trials to prove the safety and efficacy of new compounds. These stages provide a natural setting for reviewing the project and making decisions concerning the next stage. Because only 20% of the new compounds that begin clinical trials make it through to registration, it is essential to deal with uncertainty adequately in decision making.

Products and Processes: Products and processes require quite different modeling techniques. Products have a commercial value modeled identically to the new product introductions described at the beginning of this chapter. Process R&D usually targets cost reduction though new catalysts, material substitution, simplification of production steps, and the like. New processes have value when they replace an existing process and lead to more efficient operations; their value usually disappears when they themselves are replaced. So modeling of process improvements is normally modeling cost reductions in an existing business.

_____

*For an example of pharmaceutical R&D analysis, see Paul Sharpe and Tom Keelin, "How SmithKline Beecham Makes Better Resource-Allocation Decisions," *Harvard Business Review* (March-April, 1998): 45-57.

Figure 7–10

Critical Uncertainties and Decisions in an R&D Project

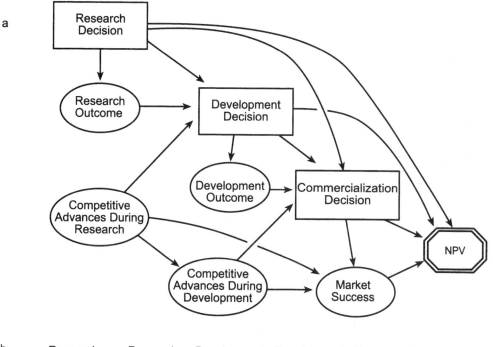

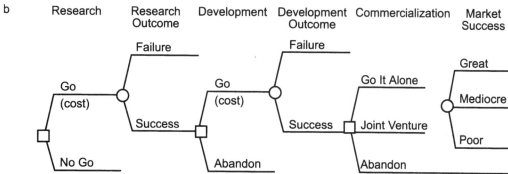

Technical Success: A difficulty often arises in defining exactly what it means for research to be technically successful. It may be necessary to model several different levels of technical success, with branches in a chance node corresponding to each possible level. Furthermore, it may be desirable to separate into distinct nodes the various technical hurdles that must be surpassed for overall technical success. These nodes might then be collapsed into a single composite node for entry into the tree.

A typical influence diagram for an R&D problem (Figure 7–10a) shows the different decisions that must be made and the uncertainties that must be resolved before an R&D project can be valued. First is the decision of whether or not to conduct the research, followed by an uncertainty on the success or failure of the research. Then follows the decision of whether or not to undertake development of the product, followed by an uncertainty on the success or failure of development. The final decision is of whether or not to commercialize the product, which, in turn, leads to an uncertainty on market success if the product is commercialized. The arrows from each decision to the final net present value show how all the decisions and the market success must be known before the research can be valued.

The influence diagram might have more arrows than shown if, for instance, there were different potential levels of market success depending on the development program chosen (which would mean an arrow from Development Decision to Market Success) or if the level of research affected market success, perhaps because of timing changes in product introduction (which would similarly mean an arrow from Research Decision to Market Success).

In the decision tree for this influence diagram (Figure 7–10b), an initial research decision is followed by a node for the success or failure of the research. (The competitive advances nodes were dropped for simplicity in showing the tree, but should be included in the analysis.) Given research success, there is a development (engineering) decision node and a chance node for the outcome of development. Finally, there is a decision on commercialization, followed by the uncertainty on the market value of the product. At each decision point, there is a cost associated with proceeding.

A typical probability distribution from an R&D decision tree has a vertical line corresponding to the probability of R&D failure, which occurs at a negative value—the cost of performing the unsuccessful research (Figure 7–11). The rest of the distribution corresponds to various outcomes given research success. The distribution shows some probability of outcomes worse than research failure: research success followed by market failure so great that market entry costs are not covered.

Frequently, one of the main benefits of using decision analysis on R&D projects is improved communication between the research and business departments. In particular, research can use the precise language of probability to communicate its hopes and fears about the technical success of different research projects, and the business side can use probability distributions to communicate its knowledge about future markets in a nonthreatening manner. Without this kind of communication, research could work on projects with little commercial potential, and business could have overly optimistic or pessimistic expectations for research results.

R&D Portfolio

Decision analysis can also help the company manage the portfolio of research projects. The decision hierarchy for R&D decisions (Figure 7–12) involves communication across organizational boundaries. Ideally, R&D strategy should be made in the context of the policy contained in the overall

Figure 7–11

Probability Distribution from an R&D Decision Tree

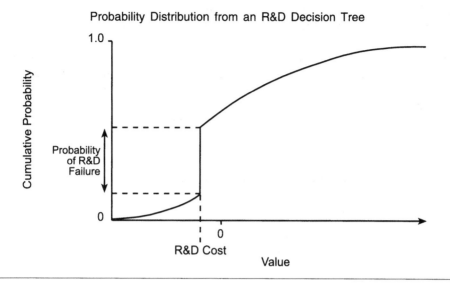

business strategy. However, not all things are possible, and the R&D director needs to work with the business director to make sure that business goals are consistent with the feasibility of the R&D required to achieve those goals.

Figure 7–12

Decision Hierarchy for R&D Decisions

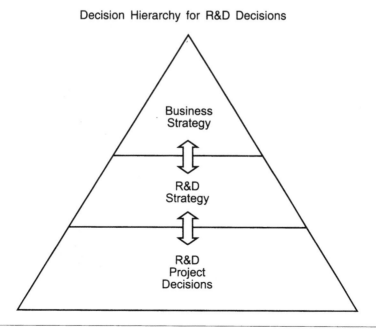

R&D strategy and R&D project decisions are similarly coupled. Projects should be chosen to further the R&D strategic goals. The R&D goals must be set in light of the probabilities, cost, and time to success of the R&D projects.

For the R&D director, the most important project metrics are the probability of research success and the expected value given research success. The product of these two numbers is the expected commercial value of the R&D project, which should be greater than the expected cost of beginning or continuing the research. We can use a graph to display how each research project fits into the portfolio (Figure 7–13a). The graph shows

---

Figure 7–13

Assessing the Value of an R&D Portfolio

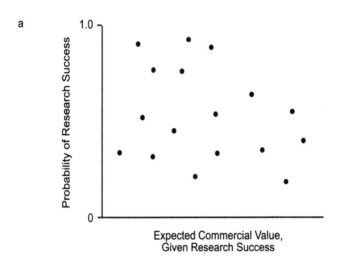

a

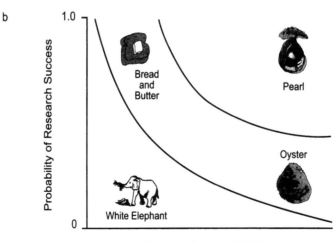

b

probability of research success versus expected commercial value given research success; each dot represents an R&D project.

The regions of the graph can be characterized according to the value of the projects that fall within them. The curved lines in Figure 7–13b are lines of equal expected project value. (Expected project value is the probability of research success multiplied by the expected commercial value given research success.) The white elephants are low-probability, low-value projects that consume resources but do not contribute much to the portfolio—white elephants were treated with veneration and not used for work. Bread-and-butter projects are low-value but high-probability projects; often routine product or process improvements, they are desirable because of their high probability. However, a portfolio unduly weighted in this area can lead to long-term strategic weakness for a company—nothing new and great is on the way. Oysters are the high-value, low-probability projects that typically represent early research into potential product or process breakthroughs—there is probably not a pearl in the oyster, but if there is…! While these projects are desirable, a portfolio unduly weighted in this area tends to perform erratically. Pearls (high in value and probability) are the things every R&D director would love to find. Unfortunately, they are rare.

Characterizing R&D projects as in Figure 7–13 may help the R&D director balance the R&D portfolio in terms of consistency of output (Bread and Butter projects give a regular pattern of success, while Oysters succeed only rarely) and long-term strategy (Bread and Butter projects support today's business, Oysters provide for tomorrow's business.)

The output shown in Figure 7–14 can help the R&D director in the difficult and contentious task of allocating limited resources (budget and people). Imagine that R&D projects were analyzed and projects A through F were characterized by Probability of Technical Success, Expected Commercial Value (if technically successful), and expected R&D Cost to perform each project. From these values, we can calculate the Expected Project Value (Probability of Technical Success multiplied by Expected Commercial Value) and Productivity (Expected Project Value divided by R&D Cost)—a "bang for the buck" measure.

If we fund projects in the order of decreasing productivity, we obtain the line in Figure 7–14b showing the most efficient use of R&D funds. If the budget for R&D were $70 million, we would fund Projects A, D, E, and F; if the budget were increased to $80 million, we would add B. When the incremental productivity drops below 1, no more projects should be funded (benefit is less than cost), and so Project C should not be funded.

Of course, the R&D director will not blindly use the results of either Figure 7–13 or 7–14. There may be conflicts between meeting the strategic needs of the company and maximizing productivity. There may be constraints imposed by the availability of qualified researchers. Decision analysis can provide tools that help make the portfolio decisions more aligned with the goals of the company and more understandable by those affected by the decisions.

Figure 7–14

Maximizing Value of R&D Portfolio for Limited R&D Cost Budget

Project	Probability of Technical Success	Expected Commercial Value	Expected Project Value	R&D Cost	Productivity
A	90%	$60	$54.0	$5	10.8
B	90%	$15	$13.5	$10	1.4
C	50%	$35	$17.5	$25	0.7
D	35%	$300	$105.0	$20	5.3
E	35%	$200	$70.0	$25	2.8
F	40%	$100	$40.0	$20	2.0

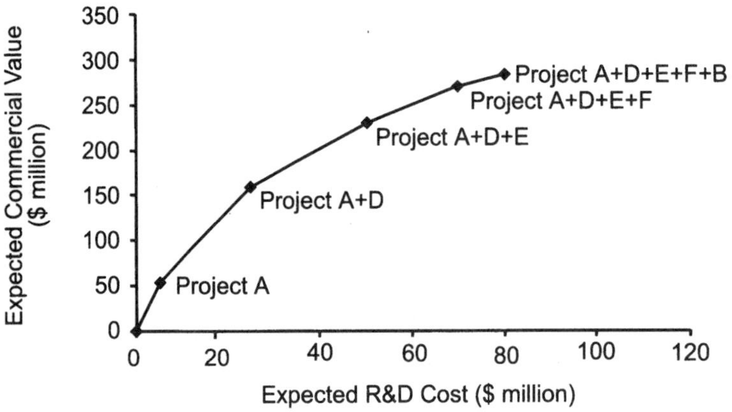

Corporate Strategies and Business Portfolios _____

OneLarge businesses must often evaluate strategic options that affect many or all of their component businesses or business units. Since these strategies commonly involve decisions for the company as a whole, decisions in the individual business units, uncertainties that affect all the business units, and uncertainties that affect only certain business units, the problem formulation may be very large. Business Portfolio evaluation involves a number of elements that require special attention.*

Business Assessment: Business portfolio decision often take the decision-makers out of their "comfort zone" in terms of the underlying state of knowledge required for a decision. Mergers, acquisitions, and divestitures in a rapidly changing world require deep and current assessments of potential candidates and where they will fit in tomorrow's world. One of the most important (and sometimes lengthy) tasks in the Basis Development steps of the decision analysis cycle (Figure 6–1) is a thorough assessment of the business environment.

---

*See, for example, Michael S. Allen, *Business Portfolio Management: Valuation, Risk Assessment, and EVA Strategies*, New York: John Wiley & Sons, 2000.

Alternative Generation: Creating decision alternatives for business portfolios is another task that is very important and time-consuming, given the size of the strategy table—there are many fields the company could be in, and many candidates in each field. More important, however, is the need for qualitative thought of high quality in developing alternatives. Before any evaluation, you have to make sure that the alternatives are compelling, coherent, and complete. Will the cultures, core competencies, strategic goals and processes of the business units fit together? How will suppliers, customers, and competitors react? What synergies (or dissynergies) will occur?

Strategic Flexibility: There is a tendency to think of a strategy is something chosen now and followed forever. The typical decision tree has one decision point at the beginning of the tree. The value of strategic flexibility must be incorporated in the definition of the alternatives, the spirit of the evaluation, and the possibility of inserting a "downstream" decision.

Uncertainty: While decision analysis tools and concepts are exceedingly valuable in evaluating business portfolios, the resulting influence diagram may be very large and the actual decision tree may be difficult to manage. But the tree must be analyzed because the uncertainty characterizing business portfolios may be significant to the corporation.

To construct a decision tree for evaluating strategic alternatives for multiple businesses, we put the decision node for the different alternatives first and then the chance nodes for the uncertainties that affect all businesses—uncertainties that are usually economic or environmental factors, such as energy prices or interest rates (Figure 7–15). Then we have the uncertainties specific to each of the business units. All business-unit uncertainties must appear on each path through the tree so that a model

Figure 7–15

Critical Uncertainties in Deciding on Business Strategies

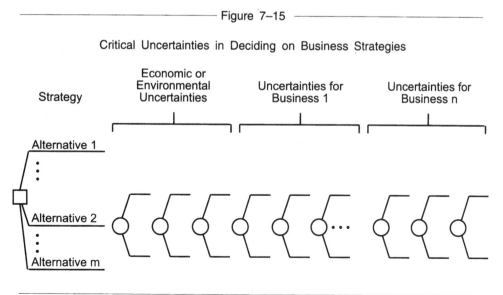

at the end of the tree can calculate the value of each business unit and combine these values to obtain the value of the whole company for each scenario.

As we can see, this tree is impossibly large. However, by using a three-step process, we can reduce the tree to a more manageable size.

1. We construct a tree for each business unit that has the uncertainties particular to that unit. This tree allows us to calculate the probability distribution for each business unit given a particular alternative and set of economic uncertainties (Figure 7–16a). The result of this step is a set of probability distributions. For each business unit, there is a probability distribution:
   - for each alternative
   - given each alternative, for each set of economic or environmental uncertainties.

2. Discretize each of these probability distributions into a two or three branch tree and restructure the tree by stringing these nodes together as in Figure 7–16b.

3. Evaluate this much smaller tree.

While this tree is significantly smaller than the original tree, it is still probably too large to evaluate if the portfolio has more than several business units or if there are many alternatives and economic or environmental uncertainties. Therefore, we can reduce the tree size again by adding a step between step 2 and step 3:

2.5 Combine the distributions for the business units for each alternative/environmental scenario to produce a combined distribution for the business uncertainty for each scenario (Figure 7–17). We can do this by tree evaluation.

The non-technically inclined may wish to skip the rest of this section!

There is a different way to accomplish this task using moments (defined in Chapter 10) to manipulate probability distributions. This section assumes that there is some easy way to obtain the cumulants of probability distributions, such as a computer program for analyzing decision trees.

The basic tool for the method is to use moments and cumulants to characterize and combine probability distributions. Cumulants are combinations of moments. For example, the first three cumulants are the mean (expected value, first raw moment), the variance (second central moment), and skewness (third central moment.) The two fundamental results we need are:

- If two or more ventures are probabilistically independent and if their values are additive, we can add the cumulants of their probability distributions to obtain the cumulants of the combined venture. For the first two cumulants this reduces to the familiar statement that we can add means and variances if probability distributions are independent and additive.

Figure 7–16

Combining Uncertainties of Business Units

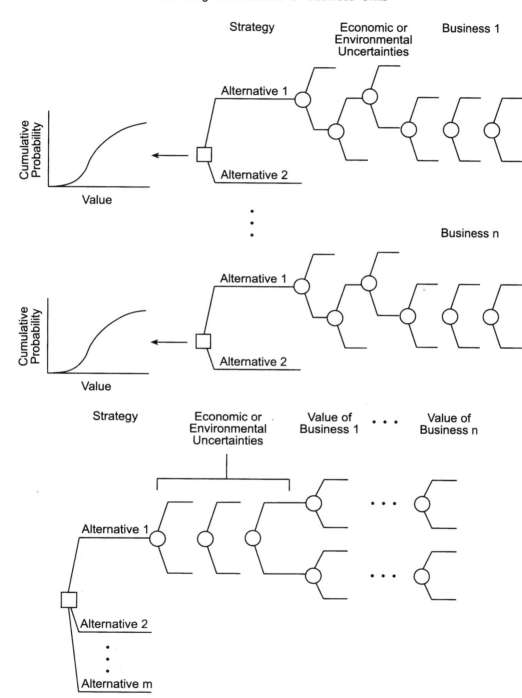

Figure 7–17

Combining Business Uncertainties

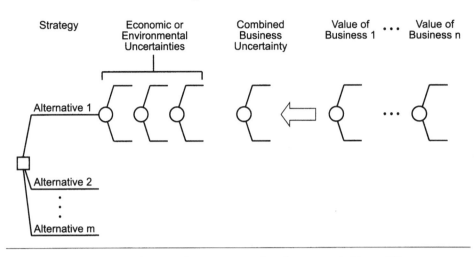

- At an uncertainty node, we can take the expectation of the raw moments describing the probability distribution at the end of each branch to obtain the raw moments of the probability distribution at the node.

For the moment method, the steps are:

1. We construct a tree for each business unit that has the uncertainties particular to that unit. This tree allows us to calculate the probability distribution for each business unit given a particular strategy and set of economic uncertainties (Figure 7–16a). The result of this step is a set of probability distributions. For each business unit, there is a probability distribution:
   - for each alternative
   - given each alternative, for each set of economic or environmental uncertainties.

2. Obtain the cumulants for each of these probability distributions. How many cumulants? Two would give a mean and variance approximation, which may capture most of the problem. Three is probably the practical limit: mean, variance, and skewness. Restructure the tree by replacing the probability distributions with these cumulants, as in Figure 7–18a. Here, j is the alternative, k the environmental scenario, i the order of the cumulant, and l the business unit.

3. Add the cumulants (sum over l) to obtain the cumulants of the combined business distribution, as in Figure 7–18a. The reason we can do this is because the business-unit distributions are independent of each other. We formulated the problem that way.

Figure 7–18

Using Moments to Combine Business Uncertainties

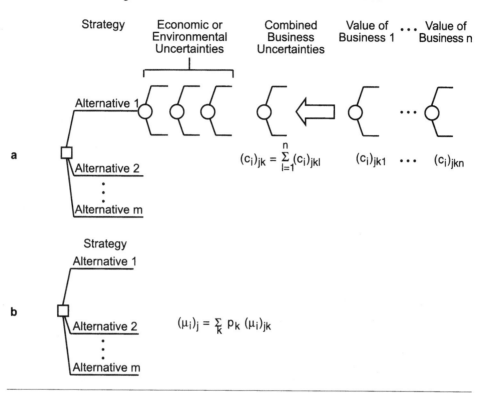

4. Convert the cumulants c to the raw moments μ, using Equations 10–48.

5. Now take the expectation over the economic or environmental uncertainties, as in Figure 7–18b: Expectation $(\mu_i)_j = \Sigma_k p_k (\mu_i)_{jk}$, where j is the alternative, k is the environmental scenario, and p_k is the probability of that scenario, and i is the order of the raw moment.

6. Now reconstruct a probability distribution that has these raw moments. This is not trivial. The best way is to use a named distribution with the moments as parameters. For instance the normal (Gaussian) probability distribution (Equation 10–50) has two parameters which are the first two moments. The lognormal distribution can be used to fit a distribution for three moments: mean, variance, and skewness—see Problem 10.24.

Though it is cumbersome to evaluate a portfolio of businesses using either of these methods, few other options exist for problems this large. While we could simply truncate the tree to a manageable size, we would lose much of the accuracy, believability, and insight necessary for handling decisions this large and this important. We could also use a Monte Carlo simulation to estimate the value of the full tree, but again at the cost of some lost insight.

Fortunately, strategic portfolio evaluations do not need to be done often and can be updated fairly easily once they have been done the first time. Considering that the direction of a multibillion-dollar business may be at stake, the effort is well worth it.

Summary

In this chapter, we discussed several of the most common applications of decision analysis to business problems. These examples are not intended as models for other problems, but rather to illustrate the considerations and process that go into structuring an influence diagram and decision tree. Most problems should be individually structured and analyzed to ensure that the analysis is relevant, useful, and insightful.

Problems and Discussion Topics

7.1   Huntenpeck Company manufactures typewriters, and Huge company has requested a bid on a contract for 10,000 new typewriters, which cost $1,000 to manufacture. Huntenpeck would very much like the contract, especially since the publicity would lead to additional sales to Huge's subsidiaries. On the other side of the coin, losing this large contract would introduce a competitor with the potential to cut into Huntenpeck's sales of dictaphones to Huge Company. The secondary impact of winning or losing the contract would be felt for about five years.

a. Begin structuring the problem and decide what information you need. Make sure you draw an influence diagram.

Huntenpeck decided to make its decision on purely economic factors and to be an expected-value decision-maker.

After heated discussion, Huntenpeck estimated that if it won the contract, it would sell between 1,000 and 1,400 extra typewriters a year to Huge's subsidiaries over the next five years, with equal probabilities of the high and low figures. These typewriters would be sold at $2,000 (in 1986 dollars). If it lost the contract, it would lose about $1 million profit a year in dictaphone sales over the next five years. After even more heated discussion, Huntenpeck decided to use a discount rate (time value of money) of 10 percent for constant dollar analysis.

Concerning the contract itself, there seemed to be two principal competitors: Carboncopy and Misprint. No one was sure what their bids would be. However, their typewriters were similar enough to

Huntenpeck's that it was certain that Huge would accept the lowest bid. Probability distributions were encoded for both competitors' bids.

Bid Level ($ per typewriter)	Probability of Competitor Bidding Lower	
	Carboncopy	Misprint
1,200	.01	.00
1,300	.05	.00
1,400	.20	.05
1,500	.50	.45
1,600	.80	1.00
1,700	1.00	1.00

b. Finish structuring the problem and draw the decision tree for it.

c. What is Huntenpeck's optimal bid ($ per typewriter)?

d. What are the values of information for the crucial uncertainties? Are there circumstances under which the optimal bid would be different given perfect information?

e. If Huntenpeck had a risk tolerance of $10 million, what would its optimal bid be?

7.2 The ABC Construction Corporation is being sued for damages as a result of an accident in which the plaintiff fell from a second-floor balcony. The open side of the balcony had been closed off only by a pair of chains held in place by hooks at each end. The plaintiff was leaning against the chains when one of the hooks snapped. He incurred serious injuries in the subsequent fall. In his complaint, the plaintiff charges ABC Construction Corporation with negligence in designing the balcony and the Wisconsin Hook Company with negligence in manufacturing the hooks and asks for $2 million in damages, including pain and suffering.

ABC has a $3 million policy covering this kind of claim with United Insurance Company. United's attorneys have told the claims supervisor that a jury might find ABC negligent in this case. Furthermore, they have said that independent of the jury's finding about ABC's negligence, the hook manufacturer could be found negligent. If both defendants are found negligent, each would have to pay 50 percent of the total damages awarded to the plaintiff. If only one is found negligent, that defendant would have to pay the full award. It is believed that the jury would probably award only $500,000 or $1 million, but there is some chance of the full $2 million award.

United Insurance Company has been approached by the plaintiff's counsel and been given the opportunity to settle out of court for $500,000. Should the offer be accepted?

a. Structure the litigate/settle problem as an influence diagram and then draw the decision tree.

b. Assign dollar outcomes to all endpoints of the tree.

Noticing that litigation could produce losses substantially in excess of the $500,000 settlement offer, the claims supervisor realized that he should quantify the likelihood of the various outcomes. After a long, rigorous discussion of the legal and damage issues, the lawyers provided the claims supervisor with the following probabilities.

There is a 50 percent chance of a jury finding ABC negligent, but only a 30 percent chance of it finding the hook manufacturer negligent. If both defendants are found negligent, there is 1 chance in 5 the full $2 million will be awarded. The $500,000 and $1 million awards are equally likely. If only one defendant is found negligent, on the other hand, the probability of the full $2 million award is cut in half, and there is a 60 percent chance of the $500,000 award and a 30 percent chance of the $1 million award.

c. Find the expected value of each of United Insurance Company's alternatives.

d. Draw the profit distributions for United Insurance Company's alternatives.

The attorneys were surprised to hear that the claims supervisor was going to reject the settlement offer. Because they felt that a little more pretrial discovery could greatly reduce their uncertainty about whether the hook manufacturer would be found negligent, they urged the claims supervisor to briefly delay his decision until they could complete some additional pretrial work.

e. Determine the expected value of perfect information about whether the hook manufacturer will be found negligent.

7.3 Hony Pharmaceutics is a manufacturer engaged in developing and marketing new drugs. The chief research chemist at Hony, Dr. Bing, has informed the president, Mr. Hony, that recent research results have indicated a possible breakthrough to a new drug with wide medical use. Dr. Bing urged an extensive research program to develop the new drug. He estimated that with expenditures of $100,000 the new drug could be developed at the end of a year's work. When queried by Mr. Hony, Dr. Bing stated that he thought the chances were excellent, "about 8 to 2 odds," that the research group could in fact develop the drug.

Dr. Bing further stated that he had found out that High Drugs, Hony's only competitor for the type of product in question, had recently started developing essentially the same drug. He felt that working independently, there was a 7 out of 10 chance that High would succeed. Mr. Hony was concerned about the possibility that High would be able to develop the drug faster, thus obtaining an advantage in the market, but Dr. Bing assured him that Hony's superior research capability made it certain that by starting development immediately, Hony would succeed in developing the drug before High. However, Dr. Bing pointed out that if Hony launched its development, succeeded, and marketed the drug, then High, by copying, would get its drug on the market at least as fast as if it had succeeded in an independent development.

Worried about the sales prospects of a drug so costly to develop, Mr. Hony talked to his marketing manager, Mr. Margin, who said the market for the potential new drug depended on the acceptance of the drug by the medical profession and the share of the market Hony could capture. Mr. Hony asked Margin to make future market estimates for different situations, including estimates of future profits (assuming High entered the market shortly after Hony). Margin made the estimates shown below.

Market Condition	Probability	Present Value of Profits ($)
Large market potential	.1	500,000
Moderate market potential	.6	250,000
Low market potential	.3	80,000

Mr. Hony was somewhat concerned about spending the $100,000 to develop the drug given such an uncertain market. He returned to Dr. Bing and asked if there was some way to develop the drug more cheaply or to postpone development until the market position was clearer. Dr. Bing said he would prefer his previous suggestion—an orderly research program costing $100,000—but that an alternative was indeed possible. The alternative plan called for a two-phase research program: an eight-month "low-level" phase costing $40,000, followed by a four-month "crash" phase costing $80,000. Dr. Bing did not think this program would change the chances of a successful product development. One advantage of this approach, Dr. Bing added, was that the company would know whether the drug could be developed successfully at the end of the eight-month period. The decision would then be made whether to undertake the crash program. In either case, the cost of introduction and marketing would be $50,000.

Mr. Hony further consulted Mr. Margin about the possibility that more market information would be available before making the decision to introduce the drug or to complete the crash development program if that strategy were adopted. Mr. Margin stated that without a very expensive market research program, he would have no new information until well after the drug was introduced.

Mr. Hony inquired about the possibility of waiting until High's drug was on the market and then developing a drug based on a chemical analysis of it. Dr. Bing said this was indeed possible and that such a drug could be developed for $50,000. However, Mr. Margin was dubious of the value of such an approach, noting that the first drugs out usually got the greater share of the market. He estimated the returns would only be about 50 percent of those given in the table, but that the cost of introducing the drug would be only $20,000; for the One-Phase or Two-Phase strategy, the cost of introducing the drug would be $50,000. Mr. Hony thought briefly about the possibility of going ahead with development after High had failed, but quickly realized that the chance of Hony's success under such circumstances would be much too low to make the investment worthwhile. The chances of a successful development by High after Hony had failed in its development attempt were considered so remote (1 percent) that the "imitate-and-market" strategy was not considered once Hony had failed.

   a. Draw the influence diagram for this case.

   b. Draw the decision tree for this case.

   c. Determine the best decision, assuming risk indifference.

   d. Draw the profit distribution for each alternative.

   e. Determine the best decision, assuming the payoff on each terminal node is certain and that Mr. Hony's risk tolerance is $100,000.

Consider a clairvoyant so specialized that he could perfectly predict market outcomes but not development or competitive outcomes. Distinguish this case of partial perfect information (perfect information on only one of the uncertain variables) from the case of imperfect information.

   f. Determine the value of market clairvoyance for a risk-indifferent (expected-value) decision-maker.

   g. Determine the value of market clairvoyance for a risk-averse decision-maker using Mr. Hony's utility. Assume that the cost of information is zero.

7.4   Mr. Able is the president of Blackgold, a petroleum distribution and marketing company that supplies refined products to a number of customers under long-term contracts at guaranteed prices. Recently, the price Blackgold must pay for petroleum has risen sharply. As a result, Blackgold is faced with a loss of $480,000 this year because of its long-term contract with a particular customer.

Able has consulted his legal advisers to see if this supply contract might be relaxed in any way, and they have advised him that it contains a clause stating that Blackgold may refuse to supply up to 10 percent of the promised amount because of circumstances beyond its control (a force majeure clause). Able's marketing staff estimates that invoking the clause and selling the contested 10 percent at prevailing market prices would turn a loss of $480,000 into a net profit of $900,000.

However, the lawyers caution that the customer's response to Blackgold's invoking the clause is far from certain. The marketing staff claims there is a small chance that the customer will accept the invocation and agree to pay the higher price for the 10 percent. If the client does not agree to pay the higher price, the lawyers feel it might sue for damages or it might simply decline to press the issue. In either case, Blackgold could then immediately sell the 10 percent on the open market at prevailing prices. A lawsuit would result in one of three possible outcomes: Blackgold loses and pays normal damages of $1.8 million, Blackgold loses and pays double damages of $3.6 million, and Blackgold wins. If it loses, it must also pay court costs of $100,000, but it need not deliver the oil.

a. Draw the influence diagram for Mr. Able's problem.

b. Structure the decision tree for Mr. Able's problem.

c. Assign dollar outcomes to all endpoints of the tree.

Noting that invoking the clause could lead to a profitable outcome, Able has asked his staff to assess the likelihood of the various outcomes. After a great deal of discussion, they report that their best judgment indicates 1 chance in 5 the customer will agree to pay the market price for the contested 10 percent and, if it does not agree, a 50/50 chance it will sue Blackgold for damages. Based on past experience with cases of this type, the lawyers believe there is only a 10 percent chance of Blackgold's winning the lawsuit, an 80 percent chance of losing normal damages, and a 10 percent chance of losing double damages.

d. Find the expected value of each of Blackgold's alternatives.

e. Draw the profit distribution for each of Blackgold's alternatives.

Distressed by Mr. Able's persistence in pursuing what they regard was an extremely risky course, the legal and marketing people propose two investigations with the hope of delaying any "reckless" actions. These include $2,000 for wining and dining the customer's executives to sound out whether they might accept a revocation and $10,000 to have an objective outside survey team gather information on the possibilities of a lawsuit.

f. Determine the expected value of perfect information about whether Blackgold's customers would agree to a price increase under the 10 percent clause and about whether they would sue if they did not agree to the increase. In each of these determinations, assume that only one of these two uncertainties can be resolved. How would you advise Able about the proposed studies?

One further investigation that could be conducted is a $15,000 study by an outside legal firm on the likelihood of the possible outcomes of the lawsuit.

g. Determine the expected value of perfect information about the outcome of a lawsuit (assuming this is the only uncertainty that can be resolved). How would you advise Able about the above study?

h. Determine the expected value of perfect information (simultaneously) about all three uncertainties facing Blackgold.

7.5   The assumption behind the Black-Scholes formula is that stock prices perform "geometric Brownian motion." This implies that the probability distribution for the stock price S at some future time, t, is lognormal:

$$f(S) = \frac{1}{\sqrt{2\pi}\,sS} e^{-\frac{1}{2}\left(\frac{\ln(S)-m}{s}\right)^2}$$

In this formula, m and s are *not* the mean and standard deviation of S, but rather of ln(S). For stock prices, s is $\sigma\sqrt{t}$, where σ is the stock's volatility; in this problem, we reserve σ for the definitions below.

The mean, μ, and variance, v (square of standard deviation σ) of S are given by the formulas (see Problem 10–24)

$$\mu = e^{m + \frac{1}{2}s^2}$$

$$v = e^{2m + 2s^2} - \mu^2$$

Show that the volatility, s, is approximately

$$s = \frac{\sigma}{\mu}\left(1 - \frac{1}{4}\left(\frac{\sigma}{\mu}\right)^2 + \ldots\right)$$

Hint: Use the approximations for $-1 < x < 1$:

$$\ln(1+x) = x - \frac{1}{2}x^2 + \ldots$$

$$(1 \pm x)^n = 1 \pm nx + \ldots$$

Part III

Corporate Decision Making

8

A Decision Making Process

In Chapters 6 and 7, we have seen some of the techniques, considerations, and philosophy necessary to conduct an insightful and successful decision analysis of a business problem. In this development, we have used a simplifying frame:

- There is a single decision-maker.
- The decision problem is fairly well defined.
- The decision maker can rely on trusted sources of information.
- There is adequate time to iterate the analysis.
- The decision-maker controls the resources to implement the decision.

For many important decisions, this frame does not describe the reality of modern corporate life.

- Decision making is often delegated to the extent that effective decisions require the cooperation of several decision-makers. Effectively, there are multiple decision-makers.
- The decision problem is not well defined. Each group in the organization sees the problem differently. Not infrequently, values and goals differ among the groups involved.
- Important decisions need cross-organizational teams to address all the facets of the problem. Team members often do not fully understand or trust information developed by team members from other organizations.
- A team approach usually calls for a linear work plan, with little possibility for an open-ended, iterative approach.

- When a decision is made, it is not a foregone conclusion that the chosen alternative will be implemented. Needed resources may lie outside the decision-maker's control. Lack of understanding and commitment by lower-level management may lead to inadequate or postponed implementation.

Needless to say, solutions to all these problems have been developed. Otherwise, decision analysis would have remained an academic curiosity applicable only to a small number of problems in the modern world. This chapter and Chapter 9 will describe techniques for dealing effectively with decision making in the corporate environment.

Decision Projects

Within a large organization, work is commonly organized as a *project*. The project is intended to accomplish a particular goal and then to terminate. Our focus is on designing projects intended to arrive at a decision and lay the groundwork for implementing that decision.

There are three essential processes in a project (Figure 8–1) that are beyond the scope of this text:

- Creating the Project: The need for a decision must be identified, communicated, and "sold" within the organization.
- Managing the Project: People, budgets, and timelines must be managed.
- Implementing the Decision: Implementation of decisions is a topic of vast proportions. Implementation can be simple, but often it involves profound changes and efforts in the organization.

The other two processes, Project Design and Conducting the Decision Process will be discussed below.

Should There Be a Project?

Before designing the project, the decision facilitator should first ask whether there should be any decision project at all! The first question is whether the decision-makers are comfortable with decision-making in an

---

Figure 8–1

Processes in Decision Projects

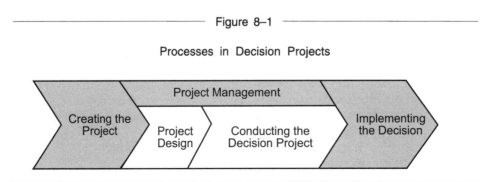

open, collaborative forum. Some organizations prefer decision-making behind closed doors—perhaps to preserve secrecy, perhaps as a management tool, perhaps to engage in back-room politics. A group process might not be acceptable for decisions in this type of organization.

Given that an open decision process is acceptable, further questions like the following should be asked:

- Is there a decision to be made?
- Has the decision already been made?
- Is the project a political ploy?

If the answer to any of these questions is "yes," the decision facilitator would be wise to decline to commit to a decision project. At best, it would be a waste of valuable time and resources. At worst, the dynamics designed into decision processes would lead to "project meltdown" and organizational dissatisfaction with the whole process—and perhaps with the process leaders.

Instead, the decision facilitator might endeavor to discover the underlying needs of the person requesting the process and to suggest ways of meeting that need. Suggestions might range from information-gathering studies to group processes leading to alignment.

Choosing the Decision Process

Given the desirability of a decision process, we need to design the process. Experience has shown that the most important factors in choosing a decision process are organizational complexity and analytical complexity, as shown in Figure 8–2.

— Figure 8–2 —

Possible Decision Processes

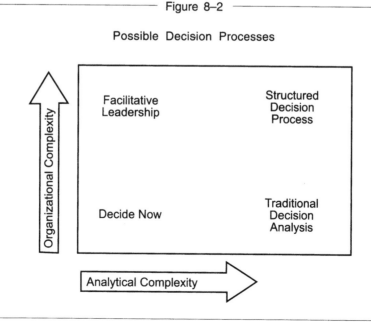

Organizational complexity ordinarily rises with the number of people and organizations that have a stake in the decision. Measurement is subjective, but organizational complexity is usually proportional to the number of the following which are true:

- There are many parties involved in the decision.
- They have differences in values, desires, and motivation.
- They have differences in initial convictions.
- They have fundamentally different frames.
- They have very different personalities and competencies.
- They have different degrees of power and resources.

Analytical complexity arises from factors which should be familiar to the reader:

- Uncertainty is important to the decision.
- Many interrelated factors need to be considered.
- Dynamic relationships exist among uncertainties and decisions.
- Multiple alternatives need to be considered.
- Multiple interrelated decision criteria have been proposed.

Possible decision processes are suggested in the four quadrants of Figure 8–2. The decision processes that are appropriate to the four quadrants are quite different, as seen below.

Low organizational and low analytical complexity: Make the decision using the tools ordinarily used by the organization. Most organizations have developed a variety of methods for dealing with routine decisions.

High organizational and low analytical complexity: The methods presented in this book are probably not required to sort out which is the best course of action. In this quadrant, the need is to develop "UAS"—Understanding of the situation, Acceptance of the conclusion, and Support of the decision—among all the parties involved. One way to accomplish this goal is through the process of facilitative leadership: a group of interested parties is created, and a skilled facilitator helps them work through their issues and concerns and arrive at consensus and alignment. Facilitative skills are beyond the scope of this book.

Low organizational and high analytical complexity: The single-decision maker perspective of traditional decision analysis works nicely for this case. The major task is discovering the best alternative; once this is known, it should not be hard to get everyone "on board" and proceed to implementation. Chapters 6 describes a case of this type.

High organizational and high analytical complexity: This is, of course, the subject of this chapter. Analytical complexity requires the tools and skills described in previous chapters of this book. But these tools and skills must be incorporated into a structured decision process which includes elements to address and resolve the people issues.

The remainder of this chapter will deal with the structured decision processes which are appropriate for situations of high organizational and analytical complexity.

Structured Decision Process

A structured decision process is required to achieve success in making a decision in situations of high organizational and high analytical complexity. Experience has shown that some elements that should be part of the process are:

- The process should be a group process.
- Decision-makers (and potential decision-blockers) should play a role in the process.
- Representatives of the all the parties with a stake in the decision should play a role in the process.
- Someone with analytical skills should play a role in the process.
- Constant communication is essential both in the group(s) and to the rest of the organization.
- Predetermined deliverables and milestones are needed to help the group through unfamiliar territory.

The form of the structured decision process will vary. For instance, the process used to decide on a major investment in an unfamiliar technology will be different from the process used for R&D portfolio management. For the remainder of this chapter, we will focus on the Dialog Decision Process, a process that has been developed to deal with major, one-of-a-kind decisions that cut across organizations within a company. Many other decision processes can be developed by selecting and modifying tools from this process.

Dialog Decision Process

Many decisions in the modern corporation are made in a team context. A cross-organizational or cross-functional team is formed to bring varied expertise together to address opportunities or problems that face the corporation. This team develops a solution that capitalizes on the opportunity or solves the problem. The solution is then presented to a management team for approval.

One of the problems with this type of team-based decision making is that there is not enough formal communication. The decision-makers commission a team to work on the problem. The team analyzes the situation (sometimes in parallel subteams), creates a solution, and at the end presents this solution to the decision-makers. There is no formal communication between decision-makers and project team during the process, only at the beginning and the end. All too often, the project team presents only a single alternative as "the answer" to the problem. At this point, the decision-makers can approve, disapprove, or send the problem back for more work.

What can go wrong in this approach? Working on the wrong problem, choosing alternatives because they are not controversial, and proposing a solution that no one outside the team is committed to.

——————————————— Figure 8–3 ———————————————

Dialog Decision Process

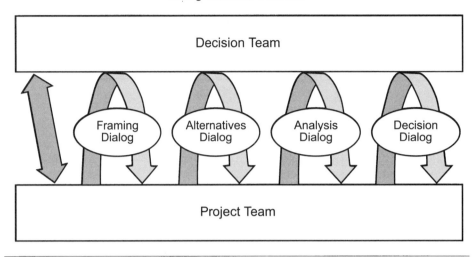

The process encourages advocacy rather than collaboration—"the answer" needs to be right the first time, otherwise the project team has its work disapproved or sent back for repairs. This encourages developing conventional solutions and hiding any problems with the solution. The decision-makers have only a critical role ("prove it") and little opportunity to use their collective wisdom and experience to collaborate in creating a great solution.

A process has been developed to bring the power of decision analysis to team-based decision making (Figure 8–3). It has been named the Dialog Decision Process because of its emphasis on systematic dialog between the two groups: the team that makes the decisions, and the team that develops the basis for the decision. This process grew out of the marriage of strategic planning and decision analysis first at SRI International and later at Strategic Decisions Group (SDG) in the late 1970s and early 1980s. A version of the process was christened "Dialog Decision Process" at GM during the late 1980s and early 1990s and was adopted as GM's decision making process.*

An essential part of the Dialog Decision Process is four formal dialogs during the course of the project. The dialogs are in response to the following questions:

- Framing: do we all see the same problem and see it in the same way?
- Alternatives: have we identified a good set of alternatives to choose from?

———————————————

*The role of this process at GM has been described by Vincent P. Barabba, *Meeting of the Minds: Creating the Market-Based Enterprise*, Boston: Harvard Business School Press, 1995.

- Analysis: what have we learned about the alternatives?
- Decision: what do we choose to do?

The decision dialog does not always occur as a formal dialog, especially if the final decision needs to be made by decision-makers higher in the organization than the decision team.

The decision team is composed of the people who allocate the resources and who represent those who have a stake in the decision. Decision team members also tend to be people who have valuable experience, broad understanding, and little time.

The project team is composed of people with profound knowledge and a stake in implementing the decisions. They tend to be people with more time for thought, gathering information, and formulating strategy.

"Dialog" may appear to be a pretentious word for a meeting, but the emphasis really is on sharing of information, not just presentation of material. Part of the dialog is between the decision team and the project team: The project team presents the information it has developed and the decision team offers direction on what more needs to be done. Equally important is the dialog within the decision team itself: The decision-makers share their insights and concerns long before the moment the decision need be made.

To illustrate the concepts of this chapter, we will take the fictitious example of FoodMachines, a rather small company producing food processing equipment. FoodMachines was considering producing and marketing a new line of can opener. This was a new product line for the company, and involved a substantial investment. Stakeholders in the product were North American and European marketing, distribution, and sales, product design, engineering, and manufacturing. The company decided to use the Dialog Decision Process to deal with the organizational complexity of the problem as well as the uncertainties surrounding the introduction of a new product.

This example combines elements from many different cases. The level of detail has been kept at a very simple level. The example is intended to illustrate the process, not the actual case.

Framing Dialog

What precisely is framing? Framing is making sure the right people are treating the right problem from the right perspective. There are three key dimensions to framing a problem well: purpose, scoping and perspective.

When a team begins to work on a decision, its members rarely agree on what has to be done. A clear purpose must be established and agreed to before the team begins to work.

The scoping dimension of framing is usually straightforward and easily understood. It establishes the boundaries of the problem, the dimensions of the solution, the sources of information that will help determine the solution, and the criterion to be used in the choice.

The perspective dimension of framing is much harder to describe. We all have a method of dealing with the flood of information presented to us. One analogy is that each person has established a filter: some information is classified as irrelevant and discarded early in the perception process. Another analogy is a picture frame: we place a frame around a problem, excluding some things from the picture, including others. The engineer focuses on the features of a new product, with little thought for the benefits the marketer may see; neither engineer nor marketer may be sensitive to the interplay of investment, price, variable cost, and volume that is important to the financial analyst. When a cross-functional, multidisciplinary problem arises, the filter must be revised and the frame enlarged. It is impossible for a team to think strategically or to commit to implementation unless all of the members share the same frame.

Success in framing has proved to be critical for decision quality. Studies and analyses that have failed to achieve acceptance or implementation often prove to have failed in framing the problem correctly. Perhaps it is easiest to describe the purpose of framing in terms of the following challenges to the team:

- Develop a shared understanding of the opportunity or challenge being addressed.
- Create an awareness of the different perspectives of the group members and expand the thinking of each individual in the group.
- Create a respect for the legitimacy and importance of others' perspectives.
- Surface unstated assumptions that could affect the project.
- Explicitly formulate and communicate the problem to be solved.

Warning: During the preparation for the framing dialog, there is an "opening" of perspectives, a creation of new visions, a discovery of new possibilities. This can be difficult for members of the team who feel "the answer is obvious" and "let's get on with it!" These people must be led along carefully.

The principal processes and deliverables of the framing dialog are:

Issue Raising: Perhaps the most straightforward way to start the framing task is free-form issue raising from the project team, the decision team, and from any other important stakeholders. Issue raising is usually a group process in which team members state whatever comes to mind as being important or of concern to the decision. Issue raising in a group has three purposes: it surfaces much of the material to be dealt with during the process; it exposes the members of the team to each other's frames; it develops a sense of team ownership of the decision to be addressed.

The list of issues is usually not a deliverable of the process. Rather, once the issues have been recorded, they can be sorted into categories by their underlying content: decisions, uncertainties, values, or process issues. This information can be used in developing the deliverables for the framing dialog. The issues can also be used later to check that the analysis treats everything that was thought important.

Project Vision Statement: The project vision statement is developed from the answer to four simple questions about the project: What are we going to do? Why are we doing this? How will we know if we are successful? How could we fail? When, in the course of the project, the team begins to wander off course, this statement will help refocus efforts. (Remember that the vision statement applies to the decision process, not to the outcome of the decision that will be made at the end of the process.)

The FoodMachines project team developed a vision statement that incorporated the following points:

- *The team was going to investigate the attractiveness of the new product (can opener) using existing manufacturing and distribution channels.*
- *The current product line was growing weak and business projections did not look good. The new product would stimulate distribution channels and would help rejuvenate the product line.*
- *Project success could be measured by the endorsement of the new product (assuming the financial projections looked good) by the sales and distribution managers.*
- *Failure in the project could occur if sales, distribution and manufacturing were not closely involved in decisions concerning features and pricing.*

Decision Hierarchy: Nothing is quite as wasteful as finding an elegant solution to the wrong problem. The decision hierarchy (Figure 8–4) is a clear way to establish the boundaries of the problem.

During framing, a list of policy decisions should be identified. Strategy decisions are usually dealt with by the strategy tables described in Chapter 6. Although tactics are normally not dealt with explicitly, the concept is very

Figure 8–4

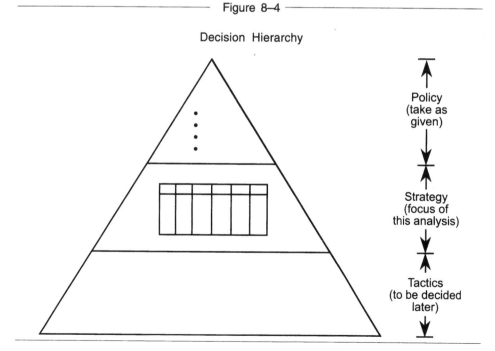

Decision Hierarchy

Policy
(take as
given)

Strategy
(focus of
this analysis)

Tactics
(to be decided
later)

important when simplifying the strategy table—when a column is dropped from the table, it is organizationally important to acknowledge that, although it is not a decision that will be dealt with at the moment, it will be important later on.

The FoodMachines project team identified several policy decisions that were relevant to the new product decision:

- *Existing distribution channels must be used.*
- *Product manufacturing should utilize only existing, idle capacity.*
- *FoodMachines' cost of capital is the discount rate for the analysis.*
- *The product should not be marketed outside North America or Europe.*
- *Investment should not exceed $40 million.*

The project team was not sure about the last two policy statements, but decided to write them down and test them with the decision team at the framing dialog.

Strategy Table: The strategy table is a tool for sorting through a complex set of decisions (Chapter 6). It lets the decision-maker keep track of many decisions simultaneously. It helps separate the important from the unimportant and the strategic from the tactical. It also provides a framework for coordinating a set of decisions into a coherent strategy. During framing, the task is to develop the skeleton of the strategy table: the decision areas (column headers) and some of the principal choices in these areas (entries in the columns). Strategy tables for complex corporate decisions may have ten to one hundred columns at this stage.

The project team developed a strategy table (Figure 8–5) to describe the possible courses of action open to the company. First, during issue raising, the team discovered that two models of can opener were possible, A and B; B was

---

Figure 8–5

FoodMachines' Strategy Table

Product	Distribution	Price
A	N. America	$12/Unit
B	Europe	$15/Unit
A and B	N. America and Europe	$17/Unit

an upscale version of A and required considerable additional investment. Second, distribution could be in North America or Europe, or both. Pricing could be set at various levels and were effectively fixed over the short life cycle of the product.

Influence Diagram: Uncertainty makes decision-making difficult. In most cases, a good outcome cannot be guaranteed. The quality of decision-making depends in part on the treatment of uncertainty. The influence diagram is a tool that keeps track of decisions, uncertainties, and their interrelationships. Influence diagrams for complex corporate decisions will be much larger than the one shown in Figure 8–6. The influence diagram is very important for developing the project team's understanding of the problem and in managing tasks. However, it is rare that anyone outside the project team will need to invest the time to understand a large, complex influence diagram.

The influence diagram developed (Figure 8–6) showed some modeling decisions based on the team's understanding of the market and of the company. The principal market was judged to be in North America, and North American Volume was entered as an uncertainty. European distribution system was smaller and less developed, and people were most comfortable estimating European Volume as a multiple of North American Volume.

Decision Criterion: Before a decision can be made, the criterion by which the decision will be made must be established and agreed to. As discussed in Chapter 3, the principal criterion for most decisions should be

---

Figure 8–6

FoodMachines' Influence Diagram

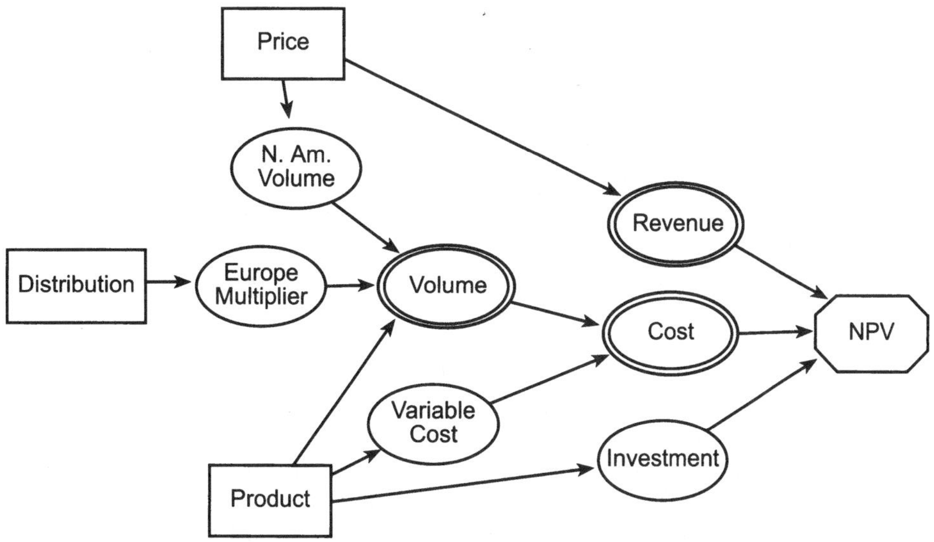

net present value (NPV) of cash flow over the time horizon of the project. Part of the task of the framing phase is to surface and discuss the inadequacy of management goals such as market share or production throughput as criteria for decision-making.

The project team had decided to use NPV over the five year life of the product. Manufacturing representatives on the team had been thinking that their task was to utilize idle capacity. Distribution representatives had been concerned about the health of the distribution network. But the team came to realize that first it had to find the right, profitable product.

Typical framing dialogs tend to center around the deliverables. Are the policy decisions correct? What is the boundary line between policy and strategy? Can the project team challenge any of the policies? Has the project team taken on too broad (or too narrow) a challenge in the strategy table? Is the decision criterion good? Are there relevant constraints, either organizationally or financially?

The decision team agreed that the project team had framed the project well. They agreed to let the project team violate some of the policy decisions in trying out alternatives. The decision team had a long discussion on the health of the product line and the distribution system—some thought things were going well, some thought that there were growing problems. The information shared did not solve any problems, but it did make some of the decision-makers aware of the importance of this opportunity.

Alternatives Dialog

The framing dialog defines the dimensions of the problem; the alternatives dialog defines the dimensions of the solution to the problem. The framing dialog creates a team with a shared frame; the alternatives dialog proposes different approaches within this shared frame.

The alternatives phase provides the following challenges to the team:
- Find creative, fresh alternatives that go beyond variations of "business as usual."
- Do not be satisfied with a few look-alike alternatives. Find significantly different alternatives that cover the complete range of possibilities.
- Do not squander resources on evaluating undoable, unacceptable alternatives.
- Challenge the common perception of what is acceptable and what is not, what is possible and what is not.
- Look at the problem from a corporate and stockholder perspective. Look to the long term.
- Do not lose mutual respect or the common, shared frame.
- Be enthusiastic about and energetic with all the alternatives.

Warning: During the preparation for the framing and alternatives dialog, there has been an "opening" of perspectives, a creation of new visions, a discovery of new possibilities. This can be difficult for members of the team who felt "the answer is obvious" and "let's get on with it!"

However, many of these people are beginning to get excited by the new perspectives. Prepare these people for the "closing down" which will begin in the analysis dialog.

The principal deliverable for the alternatives dialog is a set of three to five significantly different alternatives, each with:

Theme: A one- to four- word name that characterizes the alternative. This name should be catchy and descriptive—it will be used repeatedly and will come to represent the alternative in everyone's mind.

Path through the strategy table: A path through the strategy table makes the alternative actionable—a choice in each decision area. The path through the strategy table should be all that is required to instruct the right people in the organization to begin implementation. Of course, implementation will require many tactical decisions, but the direction should be set in the strategy table.

Rationale: The rationale is a brief statement of why the alternative is coherent, compelling, and complete. The purpose of the rationale is to enhance the quality of creative thought and of communication.

- **Coherent**: The choices made in each decision area are consistent with each other and with the strategy theme. Each choice is aimed to achieve the same overall goal.
- **Compelling**: The theme and the choices made in each decision area come together in a way that can motivate people, that can generate a movement toward successful implementation.
- **Complete**: The alternative includes all the elements needed for beginning a successful implementation.

The project team worked with the strategy table and brainstormed a number of strategy themes. It then divided into subgroups, each developing one of these themes in terms of a path through the strategy table and a rationale for that path (Figure 8–7). An alternative called momentum was developed which aimed at minimizing investment (one product) and marketing expenses (only the larger North American market) with a relatively high price. Another alternative was much more aggressive, developing two products, aiming for market share by lowering price, and marketing to both North America and Europe.

During the alternatives dialog, the decision team indicated that two other alternatives (not shown in Figure 8–7) should not be pursued further. One of these alternatives involved a joint venture and was rejected as against current company policy. The other rejected alternative involved distribution through the company's Far East distribution channels (an alternative that tested a policy decision). The head of Far East marketing indicated that the product was not well suited to that market.

———————————————————— Figure 8–7 ————————————————————

FoodMachine's Alternatives

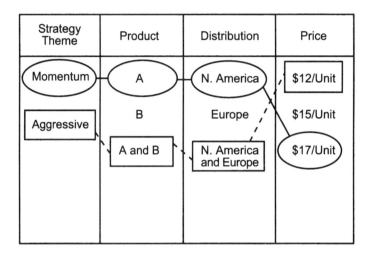

Analysis Dialog

At the analysis dialog, the decision team is presented with a quantitative evaluation of the alternatives. There is a wealth of material that can be presented at this meeting, and the project team should think carefully about what it wishes to present.

It would be a mistake to think of the analysis dialog as the time when numbers and a computer model are used to find the right answer to a problem. The analysis dialog has a much more ambitious set of goals: understanding, insight, and communication.

- Better understanding is achieved because the model keeps track of complex relationships and uncertainties, something that cannot be done in our heads.
- Organized thought about data, relationships, and results yields insight into the benefits and drawbacks of alternatives.
- Quantitative analysis can be used to communicate to the decision-makers and others the reason why one alternative is preferable—the decision-makers obtain the understanding and insight needed for confidence beyond a gut feel, and they have the financial projections to justify the decision.

The principal challenges in the analysis phase are:

- Never lose sight of the purpose of the model. Start simply and build in complexity by detailing factors that matter to the decision. Maintain simplicity by excluding factors that do not matter to the decision.

- Model to the level of complexity that is required for organizational buy-in, remembering that buy-in is ultimately achieved by insight, not detail.
- Produce insights, not answers. Look to the analysis for insight, not for a machine-made, machine-blessed solution.
- Quantify "intangibles," "ghost stories," and issues people avoid talking about.

Warning: During the preparation for the analysis dialog, the "closing down" process begins as alternatives are discarded and as hard reality shows that exciting possibilities are not realistic. This can be difficult for many members of the team. Let the results and insights speak for themselves and gradually convince those unwilling to give up favorite alternatives.

The deliverable for the analysis dialog is the same as for any good decision analysis: insight to help the decision-makers choose among alternatives. Analytic results should be presented only insofar as they illustrate and support these insights. Possible analytic results include:

Base Case Evaluation of Alternatives: What does the deterministic model show for the NPV of each alternative? If the project had to stop at this point, it might be reasonable to choose the alternative with the highest NPV.

The project team found that the base case NPV for the momentum alternative was $21 million while the base case for the aggressive alternative was $18 million.

Sources of Value: Why is one alternative better than another in the base case? The identification of sources of value provides basic insight into the nature of the decision problem. The "waterfall" chart in Figure 8–8

Figure 8–8

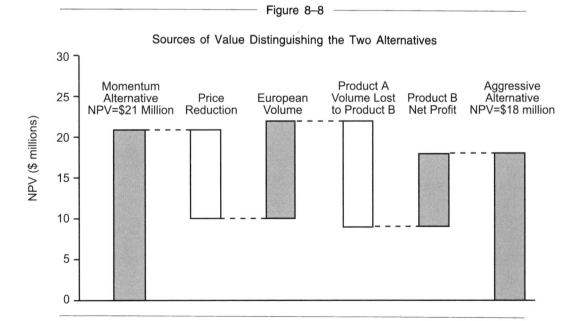

Sources of Value Distinguishing the Two Alternatives

shows how the various changes in going from Momentum to Aggressive affect the NPV. (Note that changes happen cumulatively from left to right in this chart.)

The team identified that, in the price reduction in Product A (required to enter the European market) was not offset by a sufficient volume increase, and therefore led to a loss in NPV; this loss, however, was almost completely compensated for by profits from adding the European market.

Product B cannibalizes volume from Product A and does not generate enough profit to compensate for this lost volume.

Deterministic Sensitivity to Uncertainty: This sensitivity identifies the uncertainties that have the largest effect on the alternative and which consequently should appear in the decision tree. These are also the uncertainties for which there is often a high value of information.

The "tornado" charts for the Momentum and Aggressive alternatives are shown in Figure 8–9. Price, cost, volume and investment for Product B were estimated as a fraction of those for Product A. As had been expected, the uncertainty in the size of the North American market dominated. However, even with the worst outcome, the NPV was still positive, which was an encouraging sign. Uncertainty in unit cost and on how much volume B would take from A were somewhat less important, as was the uncertainty on the size of the European market. The results on uncertainty in investment were important because people

Figure 8–9

Sensitivity to Uncertainty for Alternatives

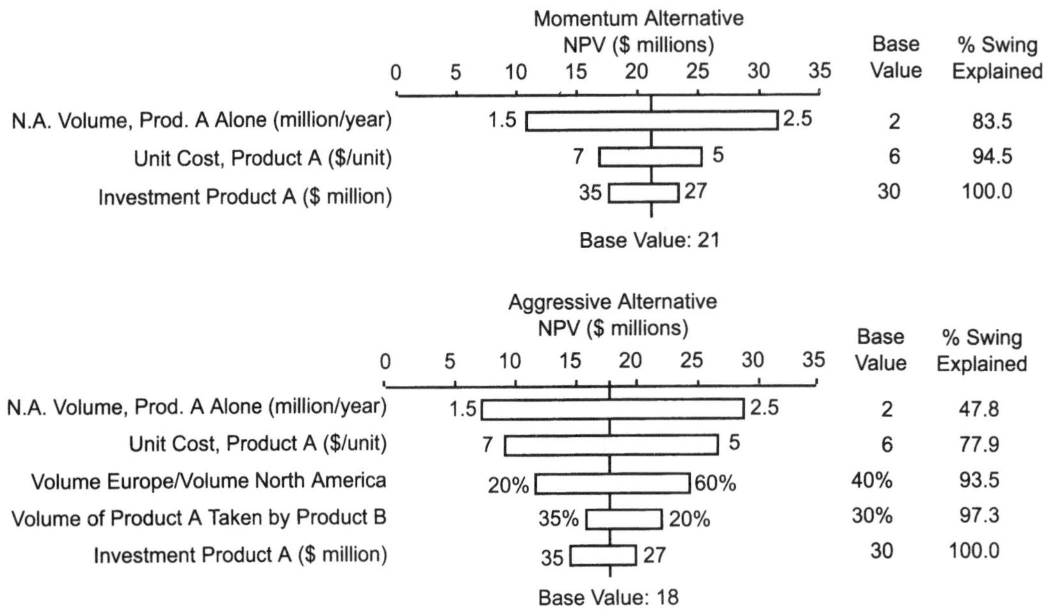
Momentum Alternative
NPV ($ millions)
0 5 10 15 20 25 30 35
Base Value
% Swing Explained
N.A. Volume, Prod. A Alone (million/year)
1.5
2.5
2
83.5
Unit Cost, Product A ($/unit)
7
5
6
94.5
Investment Product A ($ million)
35
27
30
100.0
Base Value: 21
Aggressive Alternative
NPV ($ millions)
0 5 10 15 20 25 30 35
Base Value
% Swing Explained
N.A. Volume, Prod. A Alone (million/year)
1.5
2.5
2
47.8
Unit Cost, Product A ($/unit)
7
5
6
77.9
Volume Europe/Volume North America
20%
60%
40%
93.5
Volume of Product A Taken by Product B
35%
20%
30%
97.3
Investment Product A ($ million)
35
27
30
100.0
Base Value: 18

were concerned about the lack of experience in manufacturing with this type of product. (Uncertainty in investment is typically low in the tornado chart.)

Deterministic Sensitivity to Decisions: It is often useful to perform a deterministic sensitivity by varying each of the entries in the strategy table over the range of options in that column. The columns with the largest swing are those decision areas with a high value of control. Although many of the combinations of choices do not make sense, the output of this sensitivity has often suggested modifications to alternatives that has substantially increased the value of the alternatives.

Figure 8–10 shows this sensitivity for the Momentum alternative. This plot showed that not much value was created by introducing both products A and B in North America. It did make a lot of sense, even without product B, to add the European market. The price sensitivity included the increase in volume caused by the price reduction; once this was made clear, the decision team understood just how sensitive the venture was to price and the team became very interested in estimating the reaction of the market to pricing.

Probabilistic Analysis: The final step in the analysis phase is to bring everything together in a decision tree/influence diagram analysis. Examples of output from the probabilistic analysis shown in Chapter 6. The list of possible outputs includes: a simple tree with probabilities; probability distribution of the alternatives; sensitivity to probabilities; value of information; value of control; sensitivity to risk tolerance.

Figure 8–11 shows the probability distribution on NPV for FoodMachines' two alternatives in two forms: the cumulative probability distribution and the simpler form showing the 10 and 90 percentiles around the expected value. The latter was used in the presentation materials. It was clear that the Aggressive

Figure 8–10

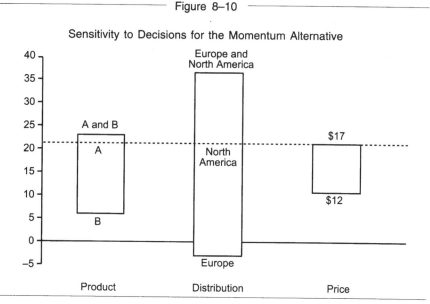

Sensitivity to Decisions for the Momentum Alternative

--------------------------------- Figure 8–11 ---------------------------------

Probability Distribution for FoodMachines' Alternatives

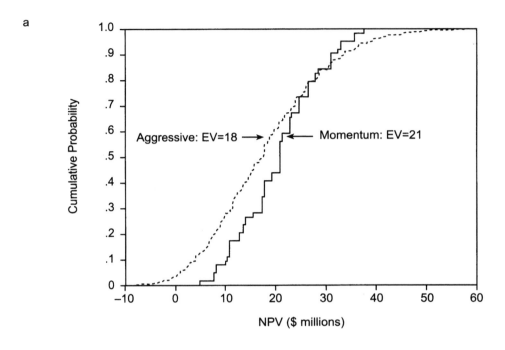

a

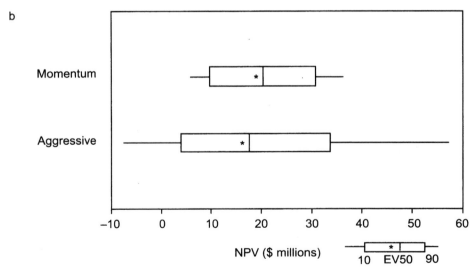

b

alternative was not very desirable—it had lower expected value and more downside potential than the Momentum alternative.

During the analysis phase dialog, insights often occur that lead to a better alternative. This alternative is created out of the alternatives that have been analyzed, using information from the various sensitivity analyses and from the combined wisdom of the teams. This new alternative is often called a "hybrid" alternative, and it is not unusual for this alternative to be much more valuable than any of the alternatives that were originally considered. For instance, the results shown in Figure 8–10 suggest a hybrid of the Momentum alternative in which Product A alone was offered in both North America and Europe.

The decision team tried to absorb this avalanche of information. It was clear that there was considerable uncertainty, but that both alternatives were attractive—neither of the alternatives had a substantial chance of losing money.

The project team indicated that some preliminary analysis showed that the problem with the Aggressive alternative was in the low pricing. With some reasonable assumptions on market behavior, higher pricing made the Aggressive strategy a clear winner. The decision team requested the project team to analyze a hybrid alternative: the Aggressive strategy with somewhat higher prices. In addition, the project team was requested to use a less investment-intensive form of B in the alternative. Finally, several additional sources of information were identified to help clarify some of the market issues.

Finally, the decision team indicated that, if the analysis of the hybrid alternative worked out well, it would be in a position to make a decision at the next meeting.

It is not uncommon for a second analysis dialog to be needed. The first set of alternatives may not be optimal (it is necessary to hold them constant during the analysis phase in order to gather a consistent set of data), and a really complex problem may require the decision-makers to review the analysis more than once.

Decision Dialog

Corporate decisions are not made in a moment, nor are they made once the analysis has been presented. The results need to be discussed, criticized, tested, and assimilated. Often, private discussions need to happen.

The decision dialog has still another purpose. During the project, the team has worked to share a frame, understand a problem, and develop the insights that result in a choice. But the choice will never produce results unless it is related to the larger world of the corporate organization. Both the decision team and the project team must begin to communicate their frame, their insights, and their enthusiasm to the people who will initiate, implement, and live with the chosen alternative. If this does not happen, the chosen alternative may never be implemented or, even worse, may be badly implemented by a recalcitrant, unenthusiastic, or misunderstanding organization.

The decision phase poses the following challenges:

- Choose an alternative.
- Communicate the frame so that all involved see the full picture.
- Communicate the insights so that all involved see the reason for the choice.
- Communicate the robustness of the choice so that participants can see why their favored alternative may not have been chosen.
- Communicate enthusiasm for and commitment to the chosen alternative.
- Obtain organizational ownership of and commitment to the decision.
- Get the implementation started.

Warning: Some team members may feel depressed that what turned out to be a "fun" and exhilarating project is drawing to a conclusion. Rather than let the project end on a flat note, encourage the participants to be disciples of the process and to encourage the creation of more projects.

The deliverable for the decision dialog is simply a well thought out presentation of the chosen "hybrid" alternative—or of several "hybrid" alternatives, if there is still a significant choice to be made. This presentation may contain the elements of an implementation plan and of a plan to communicate the decision to the rest of the company.

FoodMachines' decision dialog was almost anticlimactic. The hybrid alternative turned out pretty much as had been expected after the analysis dialog. There was some discussion whether the product was worth the marketing cost for European distribution, given the relatively low volume expected in Europe, but the head of European distribution made an impassioned plea for this product. In the end, the hybrid alternative was chosen and a product leader was appointed to begin implementation.

DDP and the Decision Analysis Cycle

The tools and deliverables of decision analysis appear throughout the DDP. But how does the DDP relate to the decision analysis cycle introduced in Figure 6–1 of Chapter 6?

The apparent mismatch arises because the DDP involves teams, and these teams are ordinarily composed of people pulled aside from their regular duties for the purposes of this special project. Organizationally, this requires a fixed beginning and end to the effort, with milestones at fixed points during the project. The decision analysis cycle, on the other hand, is structured to "continue the work until the decision-maker is ready to act."

In practice, there are two correlated projects: the group process with its fixed schedule, and the analytical cyclical process going on in the "back room" (Figure 8–12). The analyst starts early, gets input from the project

Figure 8–12

DDP and the Decision Analysis Cycle

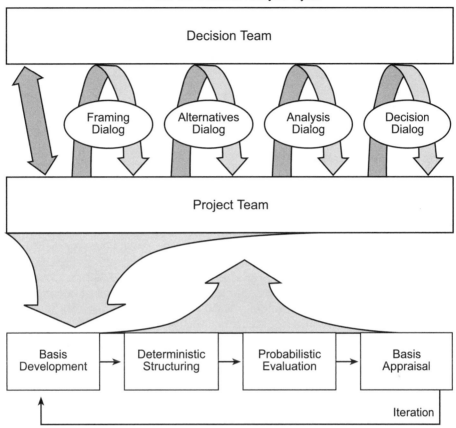

team and other sources, and makes sure that there are results available for the analysis dialog. Further iterations can (and will) be made for the decision dialog.

Project Staffing and Timing

Who is on the decision team? Most important corporate decisions cross one or more corporate boundaries. For instance, a new product decision will involve resources from marketing, design, engineering, manufacturing, sales, and finance. It would make sense to have representatives from all involved organizations on the decision team.

Who should be on the project team? Normally one would expect roughly the same composition as on the decision team. In addition, the decision facilitator(s) should be on the project team. Often, the decision facilitator serves as the neutral moderator of project team meetings.

How long should the process take? If the full process with four dialog meetings is followed, four calendar months is typical, although the duration varies a great deal in practice.* Among other things, decision-makers' calendars are typically too crowded to arrange meetings more than once a month. The schedule should allow time for reflection and off-line discussion on the part of the decision team and for analysis and preparation of presentation materials by the project team. Four months may appear an inordinately long time for decision-making, but usually the decision is made at the end of the process and not revisited later. Corporate decisions that are made more quickly have often been reopened and remade, leading to a net expenditure of more time and effort and in the loss of opportunities.

Presenting Decision Analysis Results

One of the most important tasks in a decision analysis or Dialog Decision Process is presenting the analysis results simply and convincingly. Decision analysis is supposed to help the decision-making process, and the findings are of little use unless they are well communicated. Unfortunately, in some cases, not enough effort is spent preparing the presentation insights and materials.

The first consideration in preparing a presentation is its purpose. Is it solely intended for the decision-maker(s)? Or is it intended as a communication tool and consensus builder—perhaps serving to make others appreciate the rationale behind the decision and build their enthusiasm for a course of action that they might not originally have championed? In the first case, the presentation should emphasize the conclusions and qualitative insights that came out of the analysis and discuss the next steps. In the second case, emphasis should be placed on how information derived from many different sources within the company comes together in the conclusions.

A second consideration in preparing the presentation is the appropriate level of detail. A good rule of thumb is that the higher in the organization the audience, the less the audience's interest in *how* the analysis was done. Rather, senior managers need to be convinced the work was well done, dealt with their major concerns, and has intuitively reasonable conclusions or recommendations.

In preparing the actual report or presentation, avoid concentrating on the methodology of the probabilistic or deterministic analysis. Generally, the decision-maker is interested only in the overall flow from believable input to reasonable conclusions. Presentations should not contain (unless particularly relevant or necessary) explanations of risk attitude, value of information and control, the techniques of tree evaluation, and the like.

---

*Major strategic decisions appear to take two to four months in corporations, regardless of the process used. See Kathleen M. Eisenhardt, "Strategy as Strategic Decision Making," *Sloan Management Review*, Spring 1999, pp. 65-72 and C. J. G. Gersick, "Pacing Strategic Change: The Case of a New Venture," *Academy of Management Journal*, volume 37, February 1995, pp. 9-45.

Nor should the facilitator talk too much about the model. In many companies, those attending the presentation will tend to concentrate on what is familiar from most other presentations within the company: deterministic detail. The presenter must be skillful in leading the discussion smoothly but reasonably quickly through the deterministic phase and into the probabilistic phase. Again, the speaker should avoid (unless relevant or necessary) discussions of the discount rate, details of depreciation and tax treatment, undue concentration on the early years of the cash flow, and similar details.

A short presentation might have the following set of slides as a backbone for the presentation for the analysis dialog for a Dialog Decision Process:

- Introduction
- Principal alternatives
- Graphical description of deterministic model (if relevant)
- Base-case input and results for the Momentum alternative—a graph or table of financial and performance results for the first five or ten years is often an efficient way to present model logic and input data
- NPV for the base case for the principal alternatives
- Sources of value—by choice in the strategy table, by product, by region, by whatever yields insight
- Deterministic sensitivity analysis results
- Key probability assessments and information sources, perhaps shown in an abbreviated tree with probabilities
- Probability distributions for the alternatives
- Conclusions
- Value of information or control, probabilistic or risk sensitivity analysis, and the like, only if relevant.

Decision analysis results lend themselves well to graphic rather than tabular presentation—e.g., sensitivity analysis plots, trees, and probability distribution plots. Graphics have been shown to be the most effective way of ensuring both immediate comprehension and subsequent retention of the material presented.

Graphs should usually be presented as smooth, continuous curves. For instance, the staircase cumulative probability curves should be smoothed out, because the variable plotted (such as net present value) is usually a continuous variable. The process to smooth these graphs is the reverse of the discretization process discussed in Chapter 2.

Decision Analysis Capability Building

Although decision analysis techniques have been used for several decades to treat difficult corporate problems, the analysis itself has often been done on an *ad hoc* basis, often by outside consultants. To an increasing extent, however, the use of these techniques has become part of the problem-solving apparatus and decision-making process in many companies. While it is difficult to generalize, several traits are characteristic of successful decision analysis implementations or decision-making processes within these companies.

- Decision analysis and associated decision-making processes must be accepted, understood, and required by upper level management within the company. More important, decision analysis must have a strong sponsor at this level to thrive. This does not necessarily mean that upper management must understand the techniques; rather, it means the managers accept as a fact of life that uncertainty can and must be addressed in important decisions.

- Middle management also must be aware of, and sympathetic to, the decision analysis process. After all, these are the managers who commission the analyses and support their execution.

- There must be a talented, experienced technical champion of decision analysis. Since he or she will have to deal with often reluctant "clients" within the company, the individual needs skills in managing people, time, and budgets. A viable and attractive career path for this type of person must be created. More than once, a budding decision analysis effort has failed when the key technical person was promoted or left the company.

- A fairly large number of people must have the technical capability to perform the decision analyses and lead the processes. This provides not only stability and continuity in the decision analysis effort, but also contributes to corporate commitment and enthusiasm.

- There must be a mechanism for training new facilitators within the company or for obtaining them from outside the company. A good facilitator requires some form of internship or apprenticeship—not just an academic background in the subject.

- The decision facilitator should be positioned in the company so he or she has access to the decision-maker, is authorized to obtain whatever information is necessary, and is not identified with any particular party or faction within the company.

- Many decision facilitators (and decision analysis groups) have a strong engineering or physical science background or philosophy. Decision analysis uses mathematical tools only insofar as they contribute toward an end. Decision-making processes must also deal with the organizational/people side of the problem. The personality of the facilitator (and group) must be comfortable with this; otherwise, analyses tend to become overly complicated and technical and miss the decision-maker's real needs.

- The first decision analyses within the company should be chosen with care, being neither too simple ("Why spend all this effort on the obvious?") nor too complex. When problems are too complex, there is the danger of spending an inordinate amount of effort on the analysis and frustrating everyone involved.

Decision analysis may seem to be an expensive and time-consuming process. However, time and experience will show this is not so. When the philosophy, framework, process, and methodology have become established, decisions will be made efficiently and economically.

Once the initial effort has been made, most companies have found the investment in decision analysis capability justified. The variety of options considered, the quality of the knowledge employed, and the clear logic used lead to a decision process of high quality.

Summary

Decision-making in the modern corporation almost always involves cross-organizational teams both to analyze the problem and to make the decision. This adds a dimension of organization/people concerns to effective decision-making.

The Dialog Decision Process meets the challenges of implementing the logic of decision analysis in the team environment. A structured series of dialogs between the project team and the decision team provides the direction, reflection, insight, and communication needed to arrive at a decision.

For long-term, effective utilization of decision analysis in corporate environments, the insights of the analysis must be well-communicated and the facilitators themselves must be appropriately positioned and supported. Presentations are the most important in-house means of communicating the results of a decision analysis. Properly positioning and supporting the facilitators includes personnel selection and training, management understanding and support, and appropriate analysis project selection.

Problems and Discussion Topics

8.1   Although the Dialog Decision Process has four distinct meetings, the first two meetings (Framing and Alternatives) are sometimes combined into one short meeting. This often occurs for the evaluation of Research and Development (R&D) projects. Why might this be true? What problems might arise in moving too quickly through these two meetings?

8.2   In high-level corporate strategy decisions, the Framing dialog can be the longest and most complex of the dialogs, and sometimes is broken into two meetings. Why might this be true? Why might the Alternatives dialog be especially important in this situation?

8.3   Consider some personal decision situation, either past or future, which involves several people. Examples of such decisions are a group choosing a restaurant for dinner, a student choosing which college to attend, a couple deciding whether and when to get married, a class deciding on a class outing.

a. Who should be on the project team?

b. Who should be on the decision board?

c. If there are people who will be affected by the decision, but who are not on either team, what type of communication should be set up?

d. How do the answers to a, b, and c lead to decision quality? What potential decision quality problems could occur?

8.4   How much effort that should be devoted to the four parts of the decision process: framing, alternatives, analysis, decision?   Express your answer in percentage of time/work in each part (four numbers adding to 1) for the following decision situations:

a. Choice of a college or graduate school to attend.

b. Choice of a restaurant for a special (e.g., birthday or anniversary) dinner.

c. A life-changing decision situation such as marriage, decision to have children, choice of career, etc.

d. Decision whether to buy a state lottery ticket when the prize has grown enormous because no body has won for several weeks.

e. Decision whether to attend a party on Monday night (e.g., Monday night football) or study for an exam Tuesday afternoon.

f. Choose between a fixed and variable-rate mortgage.

g. Choice between treatment alternatives for some life-threatening medical situation.

8.5   In presenting a decision analysis, you often need to clearly and credibly present results to people who may not be familiar with or understand the methodology used to arrive at the results. In what other kinds of business situations is this also the case?

8.6   List some of the considerations in deciding what level of detail to include in a decision analysis presentation.

8.7   How might you prepare a presentation differently if you were presenting to the operations research staff group as opposed to the vice president of marketing?

8.8   What kinds of changes in procedures for making decisions might occur as a company adopts decision analysis? How would the number and function of people involved in decision-making change?

8.9   Why might decision analysis have been adopted more rapidly in some industries than in others? Can all industries benefit from decision analysis?

8.10 The Lone Star Drilling Company has several prospects in Oklahoma, Texas, and Louisiana. One of these prospects, in the state of Oklahoma, is called Moose Hill. A promising region for natural gas underlies the Moose Hill area at 20,000 feet. Gas discovered at this depth qualifies as "deep gas" and is allowed to sell at a free market price under current regulations. (This is a disguised version of an analysis performed in the late 1970s.) There is little chance of finding oil under Moose Hill.

For gas to be found, there must be a structural trap. Currently available seismic studies indicate 7 chances in 10 there will be a structural trap. Even with a trap, there is a good chance that the water saturation will be too high for a producing gas well. A producing well could yield between 2 and 25 MCF/day the first year (MCF = million cubic feet); yields over 30 MCF/day are unlikely. Over the 10-year life of the well, annual production is expected to decline by 20 to 25 percent per year.

Lone Star is currently drilling a well on the Moosejaw 1 section at Moose Hill. While that well is not expected to reach 20,000 feet for another year, it appears that the cost of drilling a 20,000-foot well will be $6 million to $10 million, plus about $2 million for completing the well if sufficient gas potential is found. Annual operating costs for similar wells run between $15,000 and $25,000.

Property in the area is divided into sections of one square mile. Operators with mineral leases within a given section usually pool together and drill one well per section. However, under Oklahoma's forced-pooling statutes, any mineral leaseholder in a given section can decide to drill and invoke "forced pooling." Holders of the remaining leases in the section must then either join in a drilling operation within 90 days, sharing proportionally in drilling costs and potential gas yield, or offer to sell their rights to the first leaseholder at a price set by the state. The purpose of the statute is to encourage drilling in Oklahoma.

Lone Star holds 99 percent of the mineral rights to Moosejaw 2, a section adjacent to Moosejaw 1. The holder of the other 1 percent of the mineral rights has invoked forced pooling. The state is in the process of setting a "fair" price.

If Lone Star decides to pool and drill on Moosejaw 2, it has the option of negotiating with another exploration company, Delta Resources, for a joint venture—proportional sharing of all future costs and revenues from the property. Delta Resources has expressed an interest in this joint venture opportunity.

Your group is to recommend the best courses of action for the Lone Star Drilling Company. As part of your presentation, include the following.

- What is the minimum amount of compensation Lone Star should accept to sell its current 99 percent share to the owner of the remaining 1 percent, assuming Lone Star must otherwise bear 99 percent of the costs of drilling (no joint venture with Delta Resources)?
- Assuming Lone Star decides to go ahead and drill, what joint venture share should it offer to Delta Resources?
- Assume the state sets $500,000 as the "fair" price for Lone Star's interests in the lease. Calculate the expected value of perfect information on a few crucial uncertainties.

Make sure the presentation will be acceptable to, and understood by, the president of Lone Star, an old-time driller who never graduated from high school, but who has acquired considerable wealth, experience, and expertise over the years.

8.11 Air Wars, Inc., a U.S. manufacturer of fighter planes, is aggressively marketing its popular Galaxy-MX and Scoop-UMi models to several emerging countries of the world. Sales discussions with two such countries, the Democratic Republic of Azultan (which has a reasonably stable government) and Byasfora's new government (which is an uneasy coalition between the Leninist-Marxist wing and the rightist Christian Democrats), are in the final stages in early 1985. Both of these governments are also concurrently negotiating their air force armament needs with Le Mon Corporation, a European manufacturer. The discussions between the Le Mon Corporation and the governments of Azultan and Byasfora are of serious concern to the management of Air Wars, Inc.

Dr. Ian Winthrop, the CEO of Air Wars, Inc., has called an urgent meeting on the coming Saturday to assess Air Wars' position and to develop a clear strategy to make these sales. Dr. Winthrop, in his memo to senior management, reaffirmed the urgency of the situation and called for their input during the weekend meeting. Dr. Winthrop stressed Air Wars' commitment to growth during the coming years. He also brought senior management up to date on the key items in connection with the potential sale of the planes to Azultan and Byasfora.

Air Wars' Washington representative thought the U.S. government favorably regarded the plane sales to both the Azultan and Byasfora governments. However, the future stability of the new government in Byasfora was in question. A change in Byasfora's government was likely to result in a much more extreme left-wing government supported by neo-communists, creating concern about a reversal of the U.S. government's current support of the sale.

Probability of change of government in Byasfora by 1990: .45

The Washington representative also stressed the importance of the 1988 presidential election in relation to the sales to Byasfora. The most likely contender for president, if elected, is expected to consider the seriousness of the reported human rights violations in Byasfora and oppose the sale.

Probability of administration change in 1988: .80

Probability of opposition by new administration to Byasfora sale: .90

The negotiations with the U.S. government on Air Wars' cost structure for the sale of the Galaxy-MX and Scoop-UMi planes are nearing completion. Air Wars' Finance Department projects the following prices in 1985 dollars (contingent upon three possible U.S. government positions on cost structure).

	Unit Price ($ million)		
Probability	.3	.6	.1
Galaxy-MX	$3.9	$4.6	$5.2
Scoop-UMi	$2.65	$2.8	$3.15

Last week, Dr. Winthrop met with the Secretary of State and the National Security Advisor. He was briefed on the current U.S. position with regard to the regional strategic balance of power in the Azultan and Byasfora area. As a result, Dr. Winthrop feels that the current administration is unlikely to approve the sales to both the Azultan and Byasfora governments.

Probability of approving sales to both Azultan and Byasfora during 1987–1988: .01

Recent discussions between Dr. Winthrop and both the Minister of Air Defense of Azultan and the General of Strategic Air Forces of Byasfora resulted in satisfactory agreement on the numbers of planes needed and a shipment schedule for each country:

	1989		1990		1991		1992	
Shipment Schedule								
	Galaxy	Scoop	Galaxy	Scoop	Galaxy	Scoop	Galaxy	Scoop
Azultan	22	9	21	12	8	4	—	—
Byasfora	—	—	18	13	22	8	11	8

In addition, the Azultan agreement calls for a five-year technology assistance contract at the rate of $185 million per year beginning in 1989; the Byasfora agreement calls for a six-year $205 million per year technology assistance contract beginning in 1990. These technology assistance contracts would be terminated if the employees or assets of

Air Wars were threatened by any future catastrophic sociopolitical change in these countries.

Probability of Catastrophic Sociopolitical Situation in early 1990s

Azultan   .10

Byasfora   .45

The Finance Department of Air Wars has completed reports on the credit worthiness of Azultan and Byasfora. The credit worthiness was found to be closely tied to the economic condition of these countries. These countries were also dependent on world economic conditions for a portion of their natural resource base revenues. Based on an analysis of world and domestic economic outlook, the probability of their being unable to finance the necessary portion of the sales amount and honoring the technical assistance contracts is as follows:

Probability of Defaulting on Payments After 1990

Azultan   .30

Byasfora   .25

The option of insuring the credit risk is being considered, and Air Wars is making confidential inquiries to determine the fees for such protection.

Dr. Winthrop wants senior management to come up with a clear strategy for Air Wars and explain why it is the best strategy. In addition, Dr. Winthrop is also interested in trade-offs between price and risks. In view of the Le Mon competition, Dr. Winthrop believes that price flexibility to achieve a competitive price is extremely important for closing the sale. Therefore, an analysis comparing Air Wars' risks in relation to potential sales to Azultan and Byasfora is of significant value to Dr. Winthrop.

Your group is to prepare a presentation for Dr. Winthrop that addresses these concerns and clearly lays out the risks and possibilities inherent in this situation. The information given to you above may be redundant, incomplete, inconsistent, or unbelievable. Your group has to make the best of the situation and present a report. Your report should include:

a. A clear structuring of the uncertainties and their relation to one another and to Air Wars ultimate sales revenues

b. An analysis of the overall risk and the relative risk imposed by the individual uncertainties

c. Values of information for the most crucial uncertainties

d. Recommendations for further study or for possible actions to manage the most serious risks.

9

Decision Quality

Quality in Decision Making _____

In Chapter 3, we made the fundamental distinction between a decision and an outcome—good outcomes are what we desire, whereas good decisions are what we can do to maximize the likelihood of good outcomes. Whether we use the tools and processes outlined in this book or not—whatever the means we use to arrive at our decision—it all comes back to the same question: are we making a good decision?

For the individual decision-maker, it is usually clear when the time comes to make the decision whether the decision is "good," whether he or she is decision-ready. Tools like the value of information and value of control help in making this judgment, but in the end, it is the personal conviction that further work or delay would not be justified.

On the other hand, the multiple decision-maker environment makes it difficult to determine when the organization is decision-ready. First, there must be agreement on the quality of the alternatives, information, and values, the three elements of the decision basis described in Chapter 6. But now there are additional questions that need to be addressed, such as: "Are we all addressing the same problem?" "Can we engage the organization to act?"

In addition, in the structured team environment of the Dialog Decision Process, there is no provision for extensive iteration. If we are to achieve quality at the end of the process, we need to be able to monitor quality during the course of the process in order to design corrective action when problems arise.

To be able to discuss these elements clearly and to judge when the teams are decision-ready, the language of decision quality has been developed.

People Quality and Content Quality

When we speak of quality in a product, we can refer to specific, quantifiable factors such as defect rate, variability, and customer approval. However, when we deal with complex, one-of-a-kind decisions whose outcomes may not be known for years, statistical verification is unrealistic. We can not obtain data regarding the outcomes of our decision until it is too late, and we will never know the outcome of the alternatives we did not choose. And, even if we were to discover the outcomes, we learned at the beginning of Chapter 3 that the quality of a decision involving uncertainty should not be judged by its outcome. How, then, can we assess the quality of such decisions?

In the corporate environment, content quality and people quality should certainly be part of the any definition of decision quality (Figure 9-1).

Content quality: The use of systematic processes and analytical tools leads to a logically correct and defensible decision. Without content quality:

- The choice may be "wrong"—not logically consistent with the company's alternatives, information, and values.
- The choice can not be clearly communicated to the myriad of people responsible for its implementation.
- Later decisions may not be consistent with the original intent.

Figure 9-1

Content and People Quality

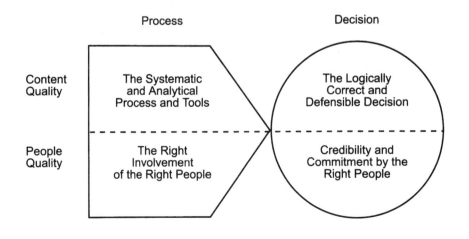

- Bad outcomes may be subject to unwarranted "Monday morning quarterbacking."

People quality: The right involvement of the right people leads to credibility and commitment to the decision by the right people. Without the right people:

- The best alternatives and the best information may not be available to the decision-makers.
- The decision may not be implemented or may languish in the state of perpetual reconsideration.
- The decision may be reluctantly and badly implemented.

The Dialog Decision Process was designed to achieve quality in both of these dimensions. Similarly, the elements used in measuring decision quality have both of these dimensions at their heart.

Elements Used in Measuring Decision Quality _____

Six elements form the basis for measuring the quality of a decision, and each element has its content and people aspects. Decision quality is achieved by achieving quality in all six elements. The "spider diagram" in Figure 9–2 has six spokes radiating from the center, each representing one of the six elements. The outer rim represents 100 percent quality, the point

———————————— Figure 9–2 ————————————

Decision Quality

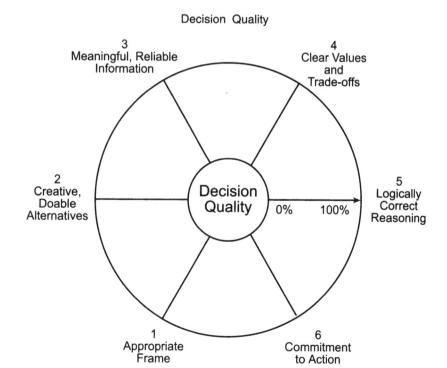

where the cost of improvement exceeds the marginal benefit of the improvement, a concept familiar from the treatment of value of information and value of control in Chapters 3, 4, and 6. The hub represents zero percent. The goal is to get as close to 100 percent in each of the requirements as possible.

What does the spider diagram provide? It provides a language by which the teams can come to agreement on where to focus efforts at successive points in the Decision Dialog Process. At the end of the process, if there is not consensus that adequate quality has been achieved in all six elements, the teams know that their job is not yet finished.

Appropriate Frame

The Framing Dialog typically does not yield 100% framing quality, but is an important step in getting there. Throughout the DDP, framing should be revisited; experience shows that frame shifts are not infrequent and can furnish much of the value of the DDP.

There are three important elements which contribute to framing quality: clear purpose, defined scope, and conscious perspective.

Clear purpose: When a team begins to work on a decision, its members rarely agree on what has to be done. A clear purpose must be established before the group begins to work. Frequently, this purpose is expressed in the form of a project vision or mission statement and a list of deliverables for each stage of the decision process.

Defined scope: What is inside the frame and what is outside the frame? What are the "givens", the policy decisions? The scope of the decision process is the set of decisions that lie between the policies and the tactical decisions, as shown in the decision hierarchy.

Conscious perspective: We all use some (usually unconscious) framing rules to deal with the large amount of data we receive. Irrelevant data is filtered out and relevant data is dealt with. To achieve decision quality, team members must enlarge their perspectives to see the full set of relevant data and to appreciate the issues and concerns of everyone involved.

Failure in developing the appropriate frame can lead to:
- "Frame blindness" when team members do not perceive the limitations of their perspectives
- "Plunging in" without a clear vision of where the team needs to go, resulting in project confusion or in project failure
- Too narrow a scope, so that the true opportunity gets missed
- Too wide a scope, so that the project becomes overly complex and could fail because of project goals that can not be achieved or results that can not be communicated
- Unstated assumptions which, if untrue, could undermine the feasibility or desirability of the decision choice
- Solving the wrong problem.

Measuring decision quality is subjective. This measurement often occurs in the context of a team meeting. The following list provides some descriptions and criteria that can help in starting the conversation that leads to assessments of decision quality in the framing dimension.

 0%—"Plunging in" or "Frame blindness"—no conscious perspective; scope and/or assumptions not stated; decision-makers not identified

 50%—"Lists of issues, but not fully structured"—issues, perspectives, and concerns identified; decision-makers identified

 100%—"Conscious, shared perspective"—clear statements of purpose, scope, perspective, and decisions to be addressed; agreement of decision-makers on frame

Experience has shown that, after initial hesitation, team members readily come up with estimates for the level of quality achieved for each spoke in the decision quality spider diagram. And the estimates are surprisingly consistent among team members.

Creative, Doable Alternatives

The Alternatives Dialog should achieve well over 50% quality in this element. It is important to incorporate high quality alternatives into the process from the beginning—the quality of the decision will be limited by the quality of the alternatives considered. After the first round of analysis, 100% quality can be achieved when the alternatives are refined and, perhaps, a "hybrid" alternative developed.

Six factors define high quality decision alternatives: they must be creative, achievable, significantly different, coherent, compelling, and complete.

Creative: Are the alternatives under consideration truly creative or are they minor variations on doing things as usual?

Achievable: Are time and resources being wasted on considering alternatives that are not achievable?

Significantly different: Do the alternatives span the range of possibilities? The interplay of several significantly different alternatives can lead to insight and the development of new, better alternatives.

Coherent: Do the elements of the alternatives make sense as a whole? A good alternative combines many different elements naturally. For instance, if the choice of new product features, market positioning, and pricing are related, a coherent alternative might be a combination of a high priced product with a full feature set positioned for the high-technology market.

Compelling: The theme and the choices made in each decision area come together in a way that can motivate people and generate a movement toward successful implementation.

Complete: The alternatives should include all the elements needed for beginning a successful implementation.

Failure in developing creative, doable alternatives can lead to:

- Considering only one alternative—a decision is a choice between alternatives, and if there are no alternatives, there is no decision and no point to the project
- Missing a great alternative, resulting in value foregone or even in strategic vulnerability if a competitor finds the great alternative
- Considering impracticable alternatives, resulting in wasted time, money and management attention.

The following list provides some descriptions and criteria that can help in starting the conversation that leads to assessments of decision quality in this element.

0%—"Business as usual"—only one alternative or several similar alternatives; alternatives that are not compelling or not achievable; good/excellent alternatives neglected

50%—"Creative, good alternatives"—alternatives that span the space; feasibility not completely verified; no clear winner, evaluation needed

100%—"Better alternatives created from insights developed"—significantly different and creative alternatives; new alternatives combining best features of original alternatives; implementation issues understood for each alternative

Meaningful, Reliable Information

Developing information quality begins during framing, particularly in problems in which a business assessment is required. It continues during alternative generation, and becomes a major concern during analysis.

Four elements define quality in information: knowing what is important, making sure the information is correct and explicit, using appropriate facts, and including the effect of uncertainty in the analysis.

Know what is important: What do you really have to know to make the decision? Frequently, you will find you need to use available data and to gather new data. If you ascertain your information needs early, you can avoid the pitfalls of needlessly analyzing inappropriate data you already have and of neglecting to gather data you need but do not have.

Make sure the information is correct and explicit: What does the information really say? Do not rely on shortcuts or sloppy conceptualization. Instead of using adjectives (e.g., the effect is "small"), state explicit values (e.g., the value is "approximately 2").

Use appropriate facts: What is the basis for the information? Be sure the underlying data support the conclusion. Trace the ancestry of information—a widely accepted and crucial bit of information may be based on little more than a time-hallowed educated guess.

Include uncertainty in the analysis: One of the important aspects of knowing something is knowing how well you know it. Most important and difficult decisions involve future events which are inherently uncertain.

As a result, it is important to identify and deal explicitly with the effects of uncertainty.

Failure in developing meaningful, reliable information can lead to:

- Ignoring uncertainty, resulting in choices that ignore risk and that can be derailed by challenges of "What if...?" and "Have you considered...?"
- Missing interdependencies between factors, especially when uncertainty is involved, resulting in an incorrect statement of the effect of alternatives or in an under- or overstatement of uncertainty
- Focusing on what we know rather than on what is important, resulting in "near sighted" choices that ignore opportunities and threats, or in "safe" choices that are anything but safe
- Overlooking intangibles, resulting in choices that may ignore the critical element in making the decision.

The following list provides some descriptions and criteria that can help in starting the conversation that leads to assessments of decision quality. Calculations such as value of information and control may help in the assessment.

0%—"Blissful ignorance"—not knowing how much is known or what is important; ignoring uncertainty and/or "intangibles"

50%—"Informed about uncertainty"—knowing information gaps and what is important; uncertainty quantified; interdependencies not explored

100%—"Knowledgeable and ready"—information accurate, explicit, and based on appropriate facts; important knowledge gaps filled and limits of knowledge explored; interdependencies understood and taken into account; sources and rationales well documented

Clear Values and Trade-offs

Decisions are made to achieve something the organization places a value on. Frequently, however, several values can compete for attention in the decision process. Developing quality in this area begins in framing when the decision criterion is identified and is further developed through sensitivity studies and through insights developed during analysis.

To achieve quality in this area, clearly identify the company's decision criteria and establish the extent to which management is willing to trade off among these criteria. Two trade-offs arise in almost every decision problem:

Trade-off between long-term and short-term results: How do we value results today compared with results tomorrow? This trade-off is usually expressed in terms of a corporate discount rate such as the weighted average cost of capital (WACC). As discussed in Chapter 5, it is misleading to adjust this time preference to include risk aversion.

Trade-off between risk and return: How much expected return are we willing to give up to avoid risk? As discussed in Chapter 5, risk aversion can be expressed in terms of a risk attitude. However, it would be an unusual project in which it would be appropriate to introduce this technical topic into the dialog with the decision team. It is usually sufficient to display the probability distribution, thus showing the uncertainty ("risk") in NPV associated with each alternative.

A clear distinction needs to be made between direct values and indirect values. A direct value is one that we seek to maximize in our choices—a decision criterion. An indirect value is one that is useful for management purposes, but is meaningful to the decision only insofar as it relates to the direct value. For instance, market share is often an indirect value, useful in managing a company, but disastrous if used as a decision criterion—one can increase market share by reducing price and profitability.

Failure in developing clear values and trade-offs can lead to:

- Neglecting a key constituency whose values conflict with the decision criterion used in making the decision, resulting in a contentious implementation
- Insufficient clarity in trade-offs, resulting in confusion and misunderstanding among key players
- Neglecting intangibles (e.g., good will on the part of suppliers or customers) which may be essential to successful implementation
- Double-counting the effects of risk, resulting in the choice of "safe" alternatives which may be strategically dangerous.

The following list provides some descriptions and criteria that can help in starting the conversation that leads to assessments of decision quality.

0%—"It's not clear what we want"—preferences not explicit; stakeholders not identified; "intangibles" ignored

50%—"Clear value measures"—stakeholders and criteria identified; direct and indirect values distinguished; trade-offs need work

100%—"Clear trade-offs"—explicit statement of desired results in terms of decision criteria; explicit trade-offs made between criteria; double counting avoided

Logically Correct Reasoning

Clear logic is needed to convert the mass of alternatives, information, and values into a clear choice. Two aspects are important for quality in this area: reasoning clearly and developing the consequences of the alternatives in terms of the decision criterion.

Reasoning clearly: A good measure of quality in reasoning is whether the results can be explained to an intelligent outsider. Most problems do not require complex logic once the problem is well understood.

Developing the consequences of the alternatives in terms of the decision criterion: If the decision criterion is profit, what is the profit associated with each alternative? If it is ethics, what are the ethical ramifications of each alternative?

Failure in developing logically correct reasoning can lead to:
- Use of incorrect logic, resulting in incorrect results or loss of credibility
- Models too cumbersome for sensitivity and probability analysis, resulting in numerical analysis without the insights required for making good decisions
- Reliance on deterministic cases, resulting in inadequate estimates of risk and neglect of risk mitigation choices
- Ignoring the effects of dependencies, resulting in choices that not optimal.

The following list provides some descriptions and criteria that can help in starting the conversation that leads to assessments of decision quality.

0%—"Extinction by instinct"—intuitive evaluation by each decision-maker

50%—"Visibility is still limited"—key sources of value identified; important uncertainties identified; dependencies not accounted for; logic incomplete and/or at insufficient level of detail

100%—"The best choice is clear"—reliable analysis of each alternative; uncertainties, dependencies, and complexities accounted for; analysis is "as simple as possible and no simpler"; clear choice based on frame, alternatives, information, and values

Commitment to Action

The single aspect of quality in this area is the motivation and commitment to action of necessary individuals. A productive way to achieve this is to involve the key implementers in the decision-making process from the beginning, preferably on the decision team or project team. They will then understand the frame, alternatives, information, values, and logic used to arrive at the decision. Their commitment to the process and understanding of the decision will almost always result in enthusiastic implementation.

Failure in developing commitment to action can lead to:
- Poor quality in the other decision quality factors
- Decisions which are never implemented, repeatedly reexamined, or poorly implemented.

The following list provides some descriptions and criteria that can help in starting the conversation that leads to assessments of decision quality.

0%—"Unmotivated"—lack of interest of key decision-makers; insurmountable organizational hurdles; insufficient support

50%—"Active decision board"—active participation by the right people; commitment to achieve decision quality; commitment to "do it right the first time"; buy-in not yet pervasive in the organization

100%—"Take action"—buy-in from project team, decision board, and those affected by the decision; sufficient resources allocated to implement and make the decision stick

Decision Quality and the Smart Organization

The goal of decision analysis is to arrive at a quality decision. There are a lot of elements that go into making a quality decision, and a natural question arises: which elements have successful organizations found most important to identify and promote?

You can turn this question around and ask what an organization can do to most effectively change the culture of an organization? Vince Barabba has drawn on his experience at GM to state, "So if you want cultural change to come about—and to stick—stop fiddling with the organizational chart and start changing the decision-making process."*

It is one thing to know how to use the processes described in this book to make one decision well; it is another thing to have an organization that routinely makes good decisions. There are a surprising number of things, some not obvious, that stand in the way of changing the decision-making process.

Several years ago, two of the authors' colleagues became interested in what practices organizations used to achieve decision quality consistently over the course of many decisions.† R&D organizations appeared to be a good place to look. These organizations make many important decisions and have to live with the consequences. Our colleagues conducted a benchmarking study of practices of hundreds of R&D organizations, and correlated these practices with how "good" the organization was at making R&D decisions. This process identified a list of 45 best practices, which is not of direct interest to us here. What *is* of interest is the key to implementing these best practices.

Examination of the enablers (and barriers) for implementation of the best practices led to the identification of the nine principles of the smart organization (Figure 9–3.) These principles are subtle and work at many levels, influencing the way people think and act. The principles appear to be the world view of "smart" companies—companies that are agile, that are capable of delivering a stream of winning products and services, that make the right decisions at the right time.

---

*Vincent P. Barabba, *Meeting of the Minds: Creating the Market-Based Enterprise*, Boston: Harvard Business School Press, 1995, p. 219.
†See David Matheson and James Matheson, *The Smart Organization: Creating Value Through Strategic R&D*, Boston: Harvard Business School Press, 1998.

Figure 9–3

Nine Principles of a Smart Organization

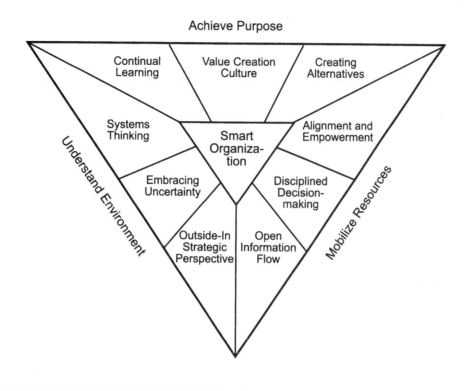

Achieve Purpose

These principles permeate an organization, defining elements of its culture and setting a context for decision making at many levels. When smart principles are in place, behaviors tend to support decision quality. Other principles are often in operation in an organization, and some of them create barriers to achieving decision quality.

All the nine principles directly support the elements of decision quality. In turn, espousing the goal of decision quality can help create the atmosphere in which the nine principles can guide the organization.

Achieve Purpose: Adhering to the principles of Continual Learning, Value Creation Culture, and Creating Alternatives naturally encourages achieving quality in creating an appropriate frame and creative, doable alternatives for all decisions.

Mobilize Resources: Disciplined Decision Making encourages quality in clarity of values and trade-offs and in logically correct reasoning. Alignment and Empowerment encourages quality in commitment to action. Open Information Flow is important for meaningful, reliable information.

Understand Environment: Outside-In Strategic Perspective and Embracing Uncertainty lead to meaningful, reliable information. Systems Thinking encourages logically correct reasoning.

Each of these principles has implications for the philosophy of the organization, the perspective of the people working within the organization, the culture of the organization, and the organization's support systems.

Summary

Decision-making involving cross-organizational teams is difficult to manage. Team members bring different concerns, different perceptions, different values to the decision. How can the team manage this diversity and work toward results that are of high quality? How can the team judge when it is decision ready?

Decision Quality provides a practical framework and language by which teams can measure progress, direct future efforts, and judge when the organization is ready to commit to the choice of an alternative.

Decision quality can be achieved for individual decisions by using the processes and tools described in this book. To achieve decision quality in routine and ongoing decisions, the organization must espouse several important principles, which will have profound consequences within the organization.

Problems and Discussion Topics

9.1   Today's newspaper probably carries several stories relating to decisions announced by a public figure or organization. Choose one of these decisions and describe the tasks that would need to have been done to make this a quality decision. Using your judgment as a member of the public, how would you rate the actual quality of this decision? Note that you do not have to agree with the decision to judge its quality.

9.2   R&D decisions are frequently framed as a basic Go/No Go or Continue/Stop decision for a specific project. What do you think is especially important to achieving quality in an R&D decision?

9.3   Corporate strategy decisions set the direction of the company for the next few years. Acquisitions, divestitures, and shutting down facilities may be part of the strategy. What do you think is especially important to achieving quality in a corporate strategy decision?

9.4   Personal decisions such as choice of college, major, career, or marriage partner are decisions most of us face rarely, but which have great significance in our lives. Pick a personal decision that is (or will be) important to you. What do you think is especially important to achieving quality in this decision?

Part IV

Advanced Topics

10

Probability Theory

Theory Overview

In both business and personal life, we must confront the reality of uncertainty in the world and be able to describe it. As we have emphasized throughout this book, the natural language to describe uncertainty is the language of probability.

The words "probability theory" can induce feelings of apprehension in people who have little experience (or desire to acquire experience) in mathematics. Yet virtually everyone has some familiarity with probability. For example, almost everyone agrees that you win only half the time when calling the outcome of the flip of a fair coin, and most people are even comfortable with more sophisticated statements, such as "There is a 70 percent chance that it will rain today" or "There is only one chance in four that my alma mater will win the football game tomorrow."

The probability theory used in this book does not involve any abstruse concepts or difficult mathematical formalism. The development is as intuitive and simple as possible. This chapter reviews those elements of probability theory that are important for decision analysis. The text of the book does not depend explicitly on the material in this chapter, and, thus, readers already familiar with probability theory can use this as a refresher.

Definition of Events

What is an event? An event is something about which you can say "It happened" or "It did not happen"—if you have sufficient information. This intuitive definition links the "real world" and the formulation of probability theory. The following examples may help to clarify the definition.

- "The spot price of oil was less than $20/barrel at some time during 1986." This is a statement about an event about which you can say "It happened." Note that an event does not necessarily imply some dramatic change in conditions.

- "Our company's net income in 2007 will be greater than $2 million." This statement describes an event which, in 2008, you will be able to characterize as having happened or not. Today, all you can say is that the event may or may not happen.
- "Company Q has developed a new product that will directly compete with our product." You may have heard a rumor to this effect. People at Company Q know whether this event has happened or not. However, your information is insufficient to tell you whether the event has happened or not.

The Venn diagram furnishes a convenient way of representing events. In the Venn diagram, each point represents a different possible world. For instance, one point in the square might represent a world in which the price of oil in 2008 is greater than $300 per barrel, in which the great-great-granddaughter of John F. Kennedy becomes president of the United States, in which Company Q does not come out with its rumored new product, and in which many other events, trivial or important, happen or do not happen. However, only one point in the square represents the world that will be realized as time unfolds.

This rather abstract construct is useful for representing a real problem when the points are arranged into areas in which specific events do or do not happen.

Throughout this chapter, we use the fictitious case of Medequip as a simple example. All Medequip discussions are set in italics.

Medequip manufactures a complete line of medical diagnostic equipment. Medequip's planning department is studying one of the products in this line. The product in question has been a good performer, but competitive pressures have caused unit revenues to decline steadily over the past five years. There is some concern that, even given Medequip's experience in the area, the unit costs will not decline enough over the coming years to keep the product profitable. The planning department has chosen 2007 as a good year to represent the end of the long-term trends. It has defined the following three events in terms of unit costs in that year:

- *C_1—Unit Cost less than $1,000*
- *C_2—Unit Cost between $1,000 and $1,500*
- *C_3—Unit Cost more than $1,500.*

These three events are graphically represented in the Venn diagram (Figure 10–1). The area labeled C_1, for instance, includes all possible worlds in which event C_1 happens.

Distinctions

Thoughts and conversations about *events* are made possible by our capability to make *distinctions*. A distinction is a thought that separates one large thing (or concept) into several smaller things (or concepts.) Distinctions define the lines in Venn diagrams like the diagram in Figure 10–1.

--- Figure 10-1 ---

Venn Diagram Divided into Regions with Different Unit Costs

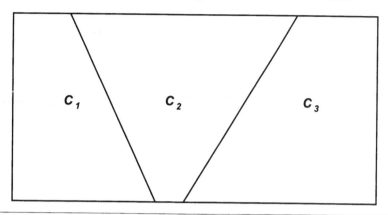

Some familiar distinctions are furnished by the words in italics below:

- Is the unit cost is *less than $1,000/between $1,000 and $1,500/greater than $1,500?*
- Will this R&D project will be *technically successful/unsuccessful?*
- Will this cup of coffee *taste good/bad?*

A high quality distinction needs to be both clear and useful. Both clarity and usefulness are relative terms, and depend on the decision context.

A *clear* distinction is one that passes the clairvoyance test described in Chapter 2. The clairvoyant is a person who can accurately answer any question, even about the future, but who possesses no particular expertise or analytical capability. The clairvoyance test is a mental exercise to determine if the clairvoyant can immediately answer a question or if he needs to know other things first. "Unit cost" is fairly clear, but might need a specification of the product characteristics and the manufacturing conditions before the clairvoyant could answer the question above. "Technical success" would need to be defined before the clairvoyant could answer the question. "Tastes good" is a very personal judgment, and the question could probably never be answered by the clairvoyant.

A *useful* distinction is one that means what we want it to mean, and helps us achieve clarity of action. The mark of an excellent decision facilitator is his or her ability to create distinctions that elegantly cut to the heart of the matter, If we are trying to choose a restaurant for breakfast, the distinction concerning the taste of the coffee could be crucial in achieving clarity in the choice—if only we could create a clear definition! Technical success and unit costs are useful distinctions in arriving at clarity in decisions concerning new product introductions.

Algebra of Events _____

The Algebra of Events is a powerful formalism developed to deal with events and whether they happen or not. We present only a very small portion of this formalism.

Three important operations are used to combine or modify events. If A and B are any two events, then the effect of these operations can be seen graphically in Figure 10–2.

It is convenient to define two special subsets of the possible worlds that can occur. These are the universal set (I) and the null set ($\emptyset$), as defined below.

- I: All possible worlds. Graphically, this is the whole area of the diagram.
- $\emptyset$: No possible worlds. Graphically, this is none of the diagram.

The definition of events and the operations defined above appear in a number of quite different disciplines. Four of these are Algebra of Events, Formal Logic, Boolean Algebra, and Set Theory.

Mutually Exclusive and Collectively Exhaustive Events _____

Probability analysis (and decision analysis) often moves in the direction of dividing up all the possible worlds into finer and finer subsets. This process allows better discrimination among the quantities of interest and better use of the data available. The set of events used to characterize the decomposition or subdivision should be mutually exclusive and collectively exhaustive.

Mutually Exclusive

Let us imagine that we have a set of m events, X_i, with $i = 1, 2, ..., m$. This set of events is mutually exclusive if

$$X_i \text{ and } X_j = \emptyset \tag{10–1}$$

Collectively Exhaustive

The second property desired of a list of events is that it include all possibilities. A set of m events, X_i, with $i = 1, 2, ..., m$ is collectively exhaustive if

$$X_1 \text{ or } X_2 \text{ or } ... \text{ or } X_m = I \tag{10–2}$$

If the set of events is collectively exhaustive, then any point in the Venn diagram is in at least one of the regions X_i. If the set is also mutually exclusive, then any point will be in one (and only one) of the regions X_i.

An example of a set of events that is *neither* mutually exclusive *nor* collectively exhaustive is the set K_1 and K_2 defined below.

- K_1: Company Q introduces an inexpensive new product (priced less than $2,000)
- K_2: Company Q introduces an expensive new product (priced greater than $1,500)

Figure 10–2

Representation of the Operations "And," "Or," and "Not"

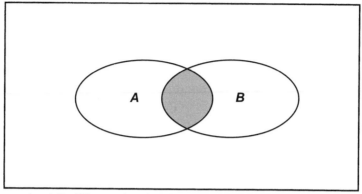

A and *B*: This operation gives the shaded region, where region *A* and
region *B* overlap—worlds in which both *A* and *B* happen.

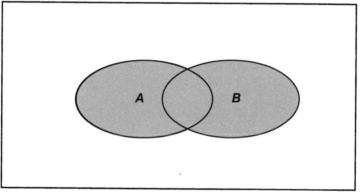

A or *B*: This operation gives the shaded region, the combined area of region *A*
and region *B*—worlds in which either *A* or *B* (or both) happen.

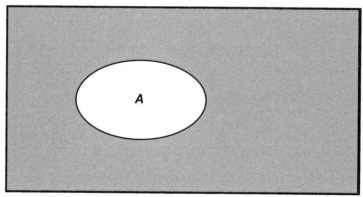

Not *A*: This operation gives the shaded region, the area outside region
A—worlds in which *A* does not happen.

The set in Figure 10–3 is not mutually exclusive because there is some overlap of the regions K_1 and K_2; a price of $1,750 falls in both K_1 and K_2. The set is not collectively exhaustive since there is an area outside the regions K_1 and K_2; the event that Company Q does not come out with its new product falls outside the regions K_1 and K_2.

Medequip was satisfied that its set of events—C_1, C_2, and C_3—was mutually exclusive. However, the planning department found that it is difficult to verify that a list of events is collectively exhaustive. Even in this simple case, there were some problems. For instance, where do the values $1,000/unit and $1,500/unit fall? In event C_2? What of the possibility that the product is not even produced in 2007? Is this represented in event C_3? The planning department refined its definitions as follows:

- C_1—Unit Cost $\leq$ $1,000
- C_2—$1,000 < Unit Cost $\leq$ $1,500
- C_3—$1500 < Unit Cost

The possibility of not manufacturing the product was judged so remote that it could be effectively included in the high-cost scenario, C_3.

In cases of real difficulty, it is possible to define an "all other" event.

$$X_{m+1} = \text{not}(X_1 \text{ or } X_2 \text{ or } \dots \text{ or } X_m) \tag{10–3}$$

This will make the set of events X_i ($i = 1, 2, \dots, m, m+1$) collectively exhaustive. However, this event is useful only as a reminder to keep looking for the (as yet) unknown events needed to completely describe all the possible worlds.

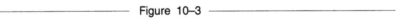

Figure 10–3

Set of Events (K_1 and K_2) That Is Neither Mutually Exclusive nor Collectively Exhaustive

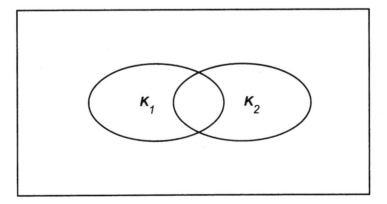

Joint Events

As mentioned above, probability analysis (and decision analysis) often moves in the direction of dividing up all possible worlds into finer and finer subsets. This process is frequently accomplished by combining two different sets of events to give a joint set of events. If A and B are any two events, a joint event is defined as

$$A \text{ and } B \qquad\qquad (10\text{--}4)$$

In addition to being concerned about unit costs, Medequip's planning department was also concerned about unit revenues. For the initial phase of the analysis, they were content to define the following very simple set of mutually exclusive and collectively exhaustive events in terms of unit revenue in 2007 for the product:

- R_1—Unit Revenue ≤ $1,750
- R_2—$1,750 < Unit Revenue

Graphically, this second set could be represented as in Figure 10–4.

These two sets of events combine to give six joint events, M_i, which describe the margin in 2007 (margin equals unit revenue minus unit cost). These six joint events can be represented in the Venn diagram (Figure 10–5).

- M_1—R_1 and C_1
- M_2—R_1 and C_2
- M_3—R_1 and C_3
- M_4—R_2 and C_1
- M_5—R_2 and C_2
- M_6—R_2 and C_3

Note that the operation "and" is often denoted by a comma, as in Figure 10–5.

Tree Representation of Events

Because the tabular definitions and the Venn diagram representation used above become cumbersome for all but the simplest problems, we use tree forms as a simple way to represent even complicated problems. Each set of

——————— Figure 10–4 ———————

Venn Diagram Separated into Regions of Different Unit Revenue

—————————————— Figure 10–5 ——————————————

Venn Diagram Separated into Regions of Different Joint Events

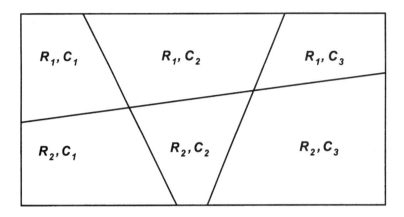

events is represented by a "node" or branching point in the tree. Each branch emanating from a node represents an event. Each path through the tree (moving from left to right) describes one joint event composed of all the events on the path. By convention, the sets of events used at a node are always mutually exclusive and collectively exhaustive.

Figure 10–6 is the tree for the margin for Medequip's product.

—————————————— Figure 10–6 ——————————————

Tree Representation for Different Unit Cost and Revenue Combinations

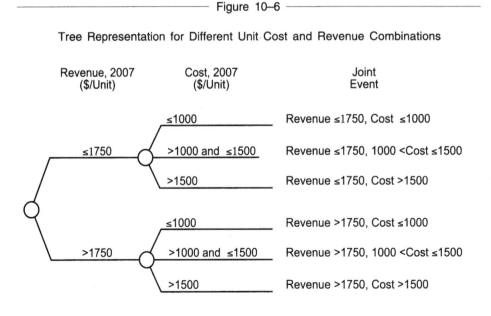

Probability and States of Information

There are some events for which we have sufficient information to say "It happened" or "It did not happen." For instance, most people would agree that the event "Thomas Jefferson became the first president of the United States" did not happen. However, there are other events about which we do not possess enough information to say whether they did or did not happen. We may simply not know what happened in the past. For instance, we may not know whether our competitor had a successful R&D outcome or not. More typically, the event in question is a possible future event. We do not know if our unit cost in 2007 will be less than $1,000. The answer to that question cannot be given until 2008.

While we may not have sufficient information to give a definitive answer to "Did it or will it happen?," we can assign some probability (or likelihood) to whether an event did or will happen. This is something we do informally in everyday business and personal situations.

Let us define

$$p(A \mid S) \tag{10–5}$$

to be the probability we assign that event A did or will happen, given our present state of information, S. While the S is commonly dropped from the notation, if it is dropped there will often be confusion about just what state of information underlies a probability. For instance, someone may judge the probability that event C_1 (unit costs in 2007 less than $1,000) will occur is 1 in 10:

$$p(C_1 \mid S) = .1 \tag{10–6}$$

However, some days later, after learning that a large deposit of a rare and critical raw material has recently been discovered, the person may revise his probability assessment, given the new state of information, S', to 1 in 4:

$$p(C_1 \mid S') = .25 \tag{10–7}$$

If we define the event

D: Large deposit of raw material discovered,

then

$$S' = D \text{ and } S \tag{10–8}$$

As mentioned above, the "and" operation is frequently denoted by a comma in probability notation. We can then write

$$p(C_1 \mid S') = p(C_1 \mid D, S) \tag{10–9}$$

In performing decision analyses, it is often necessary to combine or compare probabilities obtained from different people or from the same person at different times. Explicit reference to the underlying state of information is essential to keeping the calculations consistent and meaningful.

Probability Theory

The theoretical underpinnings of probability theory are really quite simple. There are only three axioms necessary, given our understanding of the events above. If A and B are any two events, then we can state the axioms as follows:

$$p(A \mid S) \geq 0 \tag{10-10}$$

$$p(I \mid S) = 1 \tag{10-11}$$

If A and $B = \emptyset$, then

$$p(A \text{ or } B \mid S) = p(A \mid S) + p(B \mid S) \tag{10-12}$$

If we take the Venn diagram and rearrange and stretch its surface so the areas of each region are proportional to the probability that the event that defines the region happens, then the axioms have the following graphical interpretation:

1. There are no regions of negative area.
2. The area of the total square is unity. This is the definition of the unit of area.
3. If two regions are nonoverlapping (A and $B = \emptyset$) as in Figure 10-7, then the combined region (A or B) as represented by the shaded region has area equal to the sum of the areas of the two component regions.

———————————— Figure 10-7 ————————————

Venn Diagram with A and B Not Overlapping

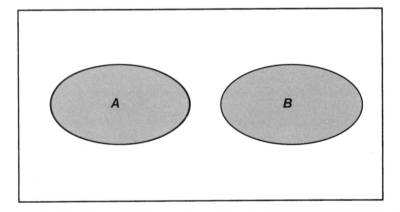

Given these three axioms, we can easily deduce properties commonly associated with probabilities. The following four properties are frequently used. The proof of these properties is left to the problems at the end of this chapter.

1. Probabilities are numbers between zero and one.

$$0 \leq p(A \mid S) \leq 1 \tag{10-13}$$

2. Probabilities sum to one. More precisely, if X_i with $i = 1, 2, ...,$ m is a set of mutually exclusive and collectively exhaustive events, then

$$\sum_{i=1}^{m} p(X_i \mid S) = 1 \qquad (10\text{--}14)$$

3. For A (any event) and X_i with $i = 1, 2, ..., m$ a set of mutually exclusive and collectively exhaustive events,

$$p(A \mid S) = \sum_{i=1}^{m} p(A, X_i \mid S) \qquad (10\text{--}15)$$

This property is often called the Expansion Theorem.

4. For A and B (any two events), then

$$p(A \text{ or } B \mid S) = p(A \mid S) + p(B \mid S) - p(A, B \mid S) \qquad (10\text{--}16)$$

The last term on the right in the above expression compensates for the double counting (if the events are not mutually exclusive) of the overlapping (double shaded) region in Figure 10–8.

Joint, Marginal, and Conditional Probabilities

Rarely is the uncertainty of a problem well described in terms of a single set of mutually exclusive and collectively exhaustive events. More frequent is a description in terms of a set of joint events—several sets of mutually exclusive and collectively exhaustive events are used to subdivide the possible worlds into fine enough detail for the work at hand. The probability of the joint events occurring is called the joint probability. If A and B are any two events, the joint probability for the two events occurring is

$$p(A, B \mid S) \qquad (10\text{--}17)$$

--- Figure 10–8 ---

Venn Diagram with A and B Overlapping

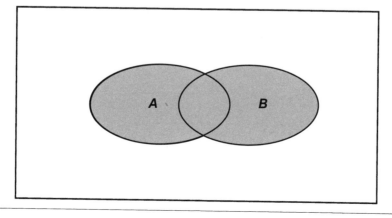

Medequip's planning department used all the information it possessed to estimate the joint probabilities for unit revenue and unit cost. It gathered all the information it could on the principal competitor's process and on his pricing policy. The department studied historical trends on raw material cost and used the judgment of the managers of the production process to estimate future cost trends. All this information was used to estimate the joint probabilities shown in the table below.

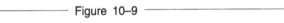

	C_1	C_2	C_3
R_1	.10	.25	.03
R_2	.22	.26	.14

This set of joint probabilities is also displayed in the tree in Figure 10–9.

The marginal probabilities are those placed at the right or bottom edges (margins) of the table of joint probabilities and are obtained by summing probabilities across rows or down columns. This process uses the Expansion Theorem:

$$p(A \mid S) = \sum_{i=1}^{m} p(A, X_i \mid S) \qquad (10\text{–}18)$$

In the above expression, A is any event and X_i ($i = 1, 2, ..., m$) is a set of mutually exclusive and collectively exhaustive events.

Figure 10–9

Display of Joint Probabilities in Tree Form

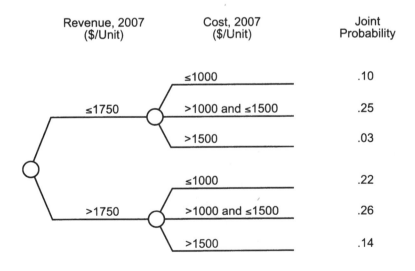

Revenue, 2007 ($/Unit)	Cost, 2007 ($/Unit)	Joint Probability
	≤1000	.10
≤1750	>1000 and ≤1500	.25
	>1500	.03
	≤1000	.22
>1750	>1000 and ≤1500	.26
	>1500	.14

In the Medequip case, the marginal probabilities are easily obtained from the table above. For instance,

$$p(C_1 \mid S) = p(R_1, C_1 \mid S) + p(R_2, C_1 \mid S)$$

$$p(C_1 \mid S) = .10 + .22 = .32 \tag{10-19}$$

The full set of marginal probabilities is presented in the following table.

	$p(R_i, C_j \mid S)$			$p(R_i \mid S)$
	C_1	C_2	C_3	
R_1	.10	.25	.03	.38
R_2	.22	.26	.14	.62
$p(C_j \mid S)$	.32	.51	.17	

Conditional probabilities are defined from the joint and marginal probabilities. If A and B are any two events, then

$$p(A \mid B, S) \tag{10-20}$$

is the conditional probability—the probability that A occurs, given that B occurs and given the state of information S. This conditional probability is obtained from the joint and marginal probabilities by the following definition:

$$p(A \mid B, S) = \frac{p(A, B \mid S)}{p(B \mid S)} \tag{10-21}$$

For the Medequip case, the conditional probabilities are easily obtained from the table above. For instance, the probability of C_1 occurring, given that R_1 occurs is

$$p(C_1 \mid R_1, S) = \frac{p(R_1, C_1 \mid S)}{p(R_1 \mid S)} = \frac{.10}{.38} \tag{10-22}$$

Tables of the values of the conditional probabilities $p(C_j \mid R_i, S)$ and $p(R_i \mid C_j, S)$ are given below.

$$p(C_j \mid R_i, S)$$

	C_1	C_2	C_3
R_1	10/38	25/38	3/38
R_2	22/62	26/62	14/62

$$p(R_i \mid C_j, S)$$

	C_1	C_2	C_3
R_1	10/32	25/51	3/17
R_1	22/32	26/51	14/17

These probabilities show, for instance, that high unit costs are much more likely when unit revenues are high than when unit revenues are low.

In tree form, the probabilities written at the nodes of the tree are, by definition, the probabilities conditional on all the nodes to the left of the node in question. The probabilities of the leftmost node are its marginal probabilities.

For the Medequip case, the tree can be written with the unit revenue node on the left. In the display in Figure 10–10, the values and symbols for the probabilities are both written. The symbols are usually omitted.

Bayes' Rule

Bayes' Rule is a simple rule that relates conditional and marginal probabilities. It is of central importance to decision analysis.

Bayes' Rule solves the following problem: Let X_i $(i = 1, 2, ..., m)$ and Y_j $(j = 1, 2, ..., n)$ be two sets of mutually exclusive and collectively exhaustive events. Given the following marginal and conditional probabilities,

$$p(Y_j \mid S) \tag{10–23}$$

$$p(X_i \mid Y_j, S) \tag{10–24}$$

how do we calculate the other marginal and conditional probabilities? This operation is called for when we reverse the order of nodes in a tree. We can write the joint probability in terms of the given probabilities as follows:

$$p(X_i, Y_j \mid S) = p(X_i \mid Y_j, S)p(Y_j \mid S) \tag{10–25}$$

─────────────────── Figure 10–10 ───────────────────

Tree Representation with Probabilities Displayed at the Nodes

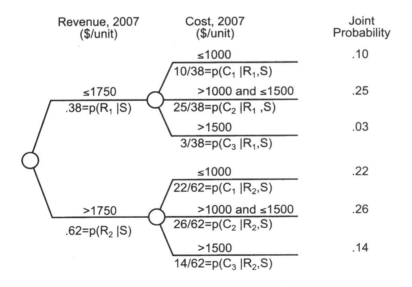

We can just as well write the joint probability in the reversed order, as follows:

$$p(X_i, Y_j \mid S) = p(Y_j \mid X_i, S) p(X_i \mid S) \qquad (10\text{--}26)$$

Equating the right-hand sides of the two equations above enables us to solve for the conditional probability term, as shown below.

$$p(Y_j \mid X_i, S) = \frac{p(X_i \mid Y_j, S) p(Y_j \mid S)}{p(X_i \mid S)} \qquad (10\text{--}27)$$

The only unknown in the right-hand side of this equation is $p(X_i \mid S)$. This can be obtained by using the Expansion Theorem (Equation 10–15) to write this probability in known terms, as illustrated below.

$$p(X_i \mid S) = \sum_{j=1}^{n} p(X_i, Y_j \mid S) \qquad (10\text{--}28)$$

The joint probability on the right-hand side of the above equation can then be written in terms of the known conditional and marginal probabilities. The probabilities we are seeking are then written in terms of known quantities, as follows:

$$p(X_i \mid S) = \sum_{j=1}^{n} p(X_i \mid Y_j, S) p(Y_j \mid S) \qquad (10\text{--}29)$$

$$p(Y_j \mid X_i, S) = \frac{p(X_i \mid Y_j, S) p(Y_j \mid S)}{\displaystyle\sum_{k=1}^{n} p(X_i \mid Y_k, S) p(Y_k \mid S)} \qquad (10\text{--}30)$$

In the Medequip example, assume we know the marginals $p(R_i \mid S)$ and the conditionals, $p(C_j \mid R_i, S)$. This is the information given on the tree at the end of the previous section (Figure 10–10). Then, for example, we could calculate the following probabilities from those given.

$$p(C_2 \mid S) = [p(C_2 \mid R_1, S) p(R_1 \mid S)] + [p(C_2 \mid R_2, S) p(R_2 \mid S)]$$

$$p(C_2 \mid S) = [(25/38) \times .38] + [(26/62) \times .62] = .51 \qquad (10\text{--}31)$$

$$p(R_2 \mid C_1, S) = \frac{p(C_1 \mid R_2, S) p(R_2 \mid S)}{p(C_1 \mid R_1, S) p(R_1 \mid S) + p(C_1 \mid R_2, S) p(R_2 \mid S)}$$

$$p(R_2 \mid C_1, S) = \frac{(22/62) \times .62}{(10/38) \times .38 + (22/62) \times .62} = 22/32 \qquad (10\text{--}32)$$

For Medequip, the tree when reversed is as shown in Figure 10–11.

In this tree, we can see an easy, graphical way of performing the calculations to reverse the order of nodes. First, the joint probabilities are taken from the tree in Figure 10–10 and put at the end of the appropriate branches in the tree in Figure 10–11. The probability for each Cost branch is then obtained by summing the joint probabilities for the Revenue branches following that Cost branch. The individual Revenue probabilities,

—————————————————— Figure 10–11 ——————————————————

Reversing the Tree in Figure 10–10

Cost, 2007 ($/unit)	Revenue, 2007 ($/unit)	Joint Probability

```
                            ≤1750              .10
                    10/32
         ≤1000
    .32         ○    22/32  >1750            .22

                            ≤1750              .25
    .51         25/51
      >1000
      ≤1500  ○  26/51  >1750                .26

                            ≤1750              .03
    .17         3/17
      >1500  ○
                14/17  >1750                .14
```

then, are simply the joint probability divided by the Cost probability (so that the Cost and Revenue probabilities give the right joint probability when multiplied together).

Probabilistic Independence

Sometimes conditional probabilities turn out to be the same regardless of which conditioning event occurs. For instance, prices could be set by a competitor using a process quite different from our own. In this case, the probabilities for prices and for costs might be independent of each other. If there is no correlation among the probabilities, they are said to be probabilistically independent. If A and B are two events, they are probabilistically independent if

$$p(A \mid B,S) = p(A \mid S) \tag{10–33}$$

Multiply or Add Probabilities?

Inevitably, the question arises "When should I multiply probabilities and when should I add them?" For joint ("and") events, conditional probabilities for the component events are multiplied together. For combined ("or") events, probabilities are added (if the events are mutually exclusive).

This is illustrated in terms of the Medequip example. A joint ("and") probability is

$$p(R_2, C_3 \mid S) = p(R_2 \mid S)p(C_3 \mid R_2, S) = .62 \times (14/62) = .14 \qquad (10\text{--}34)$$

A combined ("or") probability is (since the set C_i is mutually exclusive)

$$p(C_1 \text{ or } C_2 \mid S) = p(C_1 \mid S) + p(C_2 \mid S) = .32 + .51 = .83 \qquad (10\text{--}35)$$

Events, Variables, and Values

Many events can be defined by a qualitative description. For instance, "The president of the United States in 2017 will be a Democrat" is a description of a possible event.

In many quantitative situations, however, the event is defined by a variable or parameter taking on a specific value or having a value within a specified range. For instance, in the Medequip example, events have definitions such as "Unit Cost less than or equal to $1,000."

In quantitative situations of this sort, it is convenient to define events by the value the variable takes on—rather than by defining the event by a range of values. Values can be discrete (the variable can take on any one of a finite number of different values) or continuous (the variable can take on any value out of a continuum). Some variables have discrete possible values, such as the marginal income tax rate. Most variables, however, have a continuum of possible values, such as unit cost. Unfortunately, continuous values are difficult to work with, and we will always approximate a continuous set of values by a few discrete values. A good process for making this approximation is discussed in Chapter 2.

To make it clear that an event is defined by a value, we will write the value as a lowercase letter rather than the uppercase letters we have been using for general definitions.

Probabilities and the values associated with them are often referred to as a probability distribution for the variable in question.

Medequip's planning department proceeded to assign a value to represent each of the ranges in the definitions of the events. For unit cost in 2007, they defined the following values:

- c_1—$800
- c_2—$1,250
- c_3—$1,700

For unit revenue in 2007, they defined the following values:

- r_1—$1,500
- r_2—$2,000

This yielded the following set of values for the margin in 2007:

- m_1—$700   = \$1,500 - \$800
- m_2—$250   = \$1,500 - \$1,250
- m_3— -$200   = \$1,500 - \$1,700
- m_4—$1,200   = \$2,000 - \$800
- m_5—$750   = \$2,000 - \$1,250
- m_6—$300   = \$2,000 - \$1,700

Representations of Probabilities for Discrete Values _____

There are a number of ways to represent the probabilities for a set of discrete values. These representations include tabular form, tree form, mass distribution plot, cumulative probability plot, and histogram. We will illustrate each of these representations using the example of the margins from the Medequip case.

Tabular Form

The values and their probabilities are presented in the following simple tabular form:

i	m_i	$p(m_i \mid S)$
1	$700	.10
2	$250	.25
3	–$200	.03
4	$1,200	.22
5	$750	.26
6	$300	.14

Tree Form

These values can be presented in the tree form displayed in Figure 10–12.

Mass Density Plot

Probabilities can be graphed directly against values in what is called, for discrete values, the mass density plot. The plot in Figure 10–13 graphs the probability distribution on margin.

----------------------------------- Figure 10–12 -----------------------------------

Representation of Probabilities and Values in Tree Form

Margin, 2007
($/unit)

.10	700
.25	250
.03	–200
.22	1200
.26	750
.14	300

─────────── Figure 10–13 ───────────

Representation of Probabilities and Values in a Mass Density Plot

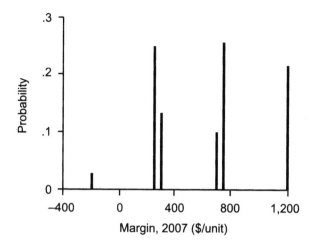

Margin, 2007 ($/unit)

Cumulative Probability Graph

Another graphical representation frequently used is the cumulative probability graph. This graph plots the probability that the value is less than or equal to the value shown on the horizontal axis. Formally, the cumulative probability is defined as

$$P_{\le}(x \mid S) = \sum_i p(x_i \mid S) \tag{10–36}$$

where the sum is over all values of i for which x_i - x. In practice, the outcomes are placed in a table ordered from lowest to highest value; the cumulative probability at each value is calculated as the running sum of the probabilities down to each row. For the margin example, we have the following table:

m_i	$p(m_i \mid S)$	$P_{\le}(m_i \mid S)$
–$200	.03	.03
$250	.25	.28
$300	.14	.42
$700	.10	.52
$750	.26	.78
$1,200	.22	1.00

The cumulative probability is then plotted (Figure 10–14). Note that the curve is flat except at points where the value on the horizontal axis is equal to one of the values in the table.

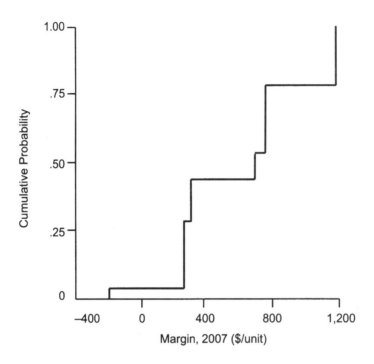

——————————————————— Figure 10–14 ———————————————————
Representation of Probabilities and Values in a Cumulative Probability Plot

Histogram

A final representation is by histogram form. Although this plot is an approximation, it takes the mass density plot and converts it into a form that is more readily interpreted by the eye. The horizontal axis is divided into bins of equal width, and a bar for each bin shows the sum of the probabilities for all the events in that bin. In Figure 10–15, bins of a width of $400 were chosen, with bin edges falling at values that are integer multiples of $400.

Mean, Median, Mode, Variance, and Standard Deviation _____

Another way to represent a set of probabilities is to use a few values to characterize the whole set. A common measure is the mean (or average) of the distribution. In decision analysis, the mean is usually called the expected value. If x_i for i = 1, 2, ..., m is a set of values that define a set of mutually exclusive and collectively exhaustive events, the mean is calculated using the following formula:

$$\text{mean} = \sum_{i=1}^{m} x_i p(x_i \mid S)$$

(10–37)

—————————————————— Figure 10–15 ——————————————————

Representation of Probabilities and Values in a Histogram

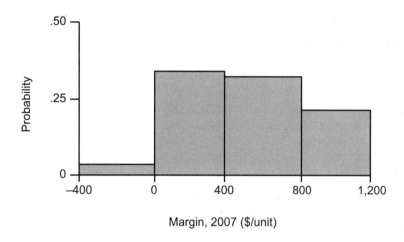

Margin, 2007 ($/unit)

The median is the value at which it is just as probable to be below that value as above it. The mode is the most probable value in the set. The mean, mode, and median are measures that identify the center or most important values in the distribution. Of these measures, though, the mean is most sensitive to the shape of the distribution. The median is often the easiest measure to understand (it is the 50/50 probability point). The mode often works well for describing highly asymmetric distributions (such as the cost). Neither the mode nor the median is very important in applications of probability theory to decision analysis, though they may be important in helping people relate to and understand a probability distribution.

The mean of the probability distribution on Medequip's margin in 2007 is calculated as follows:

$$\text{mean} = (700 \times .10) + (250 \times .25) + (-200 \times .03) + (1200 \times .22) + (750 \times .26) + (300 \times .14)$$

$$\text{mean} = \$628 \tag{10–38}$$

The median is somewhere around $700, since there is a 42 percent chance that the value is less than $700 and a 48 percent chance that the value is greater than $700. (In a set of values this small, there will seldom be a value that is exactly the median.) Finally, the mode of the distribution is $750, since it has the largest probability of any of the values (26 percent).

The variance is a more complicated measure. If the mean measures the average value of the distribution, the variance is a measure of how far off the value might be from this average; it is a measure of how "wide" the distribution is.

$$\text{variance} = \sum_{i=1}^{m} (x_i - \text{mean})^2 \, p(x_i \mid S) \tag{10–39}$$

The standard deviation (written as σ) is the square root of the variance and is a direct measure of the spread or width of the distribution.

The planning department at Medequip calculated the variance in the probability distribution on margin in 2007 as follows. Note that the units of variance here are ($\$)^2$.

$$\text{variance} = .10(700-628)^2 + .25(250-628)^2 + .03(-200-628)^2 + .22(1,200-628)^2$$

$$+ .26(850-628)^2 + .14(300-628)^2$$

$$\text{variance} = 147,719 \qquad (10\text{--}40)$$

The standard deviation is the square root of the variance.

$$\sigma = (147,719)^{1/2} = \$384 \qquad (10\text{--}41)$$

Moments and Cumulants

A more complete and systematic set of parameters to represent a probability distribution is provided by the set of moments. If x_i for $i = 1, 2, ..., m$ is a set of values that define a mutually exclusive and collectively exhaustive set of events, then the moments are defined by the following equation:

$$\mu_n = \sum_{i=1}^{m} x_i^n p(x_i \mid S) \qquad (10\text{--}42)$$

The zeroth moment, μ_0, is 1; this is just the normalization condition that probabilities sum to one. The first moment, μ_1, is the mean of the distribution. These moments are sometimes called the raw moments and provide a complete description of the distribution.

There is a second set of moments that can also be used to describe the distribution—the central moments. For the same values, x_i, the central moments are defined by the following equation:

$$v_n = \sum_{i=1}^{m} (x_i - \mu_1)^n p(x_i \mid S) \qquad (10\text{--}43)$$

The zeroth central moment, v_0, is just 1; again, this is just the normalization condition for probabilities. The first central moment, v_1, is identically zero. The second central moment, v_2, is the *variance*. The third central moment, v_3, is the *skewness*. The fourth central moment, v_4, is the *kurtosis*. The central moments, together with the mean, provide a complete description of the distribution.

Occasionally, it is necessary to transform one representation into the other. In practice, the first five moments are all that are likely to be used in representing a distribution. The mean, μ_1, is common to both representations. The equations transforming raw moments into central moments are:

$$v_2 = \mu_2 - \mu_1^2$$

$$v_3 = \mu_3 - 3\mu_2\mu_1 + 2\mu_1^3$$

$$v_4 = \mu_4 - 4\mu_3\mu_1 + 6\mu_2\mu_1^2 - 3\mu_1^4$$

$$v_5 = \mu_5 - 5\mu_4\mu_1 + 10\mu_3\mu_1^2 - 10\mu_2\mu_1^3 + 4\mu_1^5 \qquad (10\text{--}44)$$

The equations transforming central moments into raw moments are:

$$\mu_2 = v_2 + \mu_1^2$$

$$\mu_3 = v_3 + 3v_2\mu_1 + \mu_1^3$$

$$\mu_4 = v_4 + 4v_3\mu_1 + 6v_2\mu_1^2 + \mu_1^4$$

$$\mu_5 = v_5 + 5v_4\mu_1 + 10v_3\mu_1^2 + 10v_2\mu_1^3 + \mu_1^5 \qquad (10\text{--}45)$$

A third set of parameters used to represent a distribution is provided by the set of cumulants, c_i. The special property of cumulants is that if we wish to add two probabilistically independent distributions, we can simply add the cumulants of each distribution to obtain the cumulants of the sum.*

The first three cumulants are the mean, variance, and skewness, and for many purposes these are sufficient. It would be very unusual to need more than the first five cumulants:

$$c_1 = \mu_1$$

$$c_2 = \mu_2 - \mu_1^2$$

$$c_3 = \mu_3 - 3\mu_2\mu_1 + 2\mu_1^3$$

$$c_4 = \mu_4 - 4\mu_3\mu_1 + 12\mu_2\mu_1^2 - 3\mu_2^2 - 6\mu_1^4$$

$$c_5 = \mu_5 - 5\mu_4\mu_1 - 10\mu_3\mu_2 + 20\mu_3\mu_1^2 - 60\mu_2\mu_1^3 + 30\mu_2^2\mu_1 + 24\mu_1^5 \qquad (10\text{--}46)$$

$$c_2 = v_2$$

$$c_3 = v_3$$

$$c_4 = v_4 - 3v_2^2$$

$$c_5 = v_5 - 10v_3v_2 \qquad (10\text{--}47)$$

In analyzing portfolios, it is often necessary to transform from cumulants to moments. The equations are:

$$\mu_1 = c_1$$

$$\mu_2 = c_2 + c_1^2$$

$$\mu_3 = c_3 + 3c_2c_1 + c_1^3$$

$$\mu_4 = c_4 + 4c_3c_1 + 3c_2^2 + 6c_2c_1^2 + c_1^4$$

$$\mu_5 = c_5 + 5c_4c_1 + 10c_3c_2 + 10c_3c_1^2 + 15c_2^2c_1 + 10c_2c_1^3 + c_1^5 \qquad (10\text{--}48)$$

---

*The theory of moments and cumulants can be found in Alan Stuart and J. Keith Ord, *Kendall's Advanced Theory of Statistics, Volume 1 Distribution Theory*, Sixth Edition, New York-Toronto:Halsted Press, 1994.

$$v_2 = c_2$$

$$v_3 = c_3$$

$$v_4 = c_4 + 3c_2^2$$

$$v_5 = c_5 + 10c_3c_2 \tag{10-49}$$

In analyzing portfolios, it is also often necessary to represent graphically the probability distribution characterized by these moments. See Problem 10-24.

Representations of Probabilities for Continuous Variables _____

Throughout this book, we use discrete approximations instead of continuous values. In the interest of completeness, however, we discuss a few properties and definitions for probability distributions on continuous variables. Continuous probability distributions are usually defined by graphs or by a functional form rather than using an infinite tabular form. For instance, the normal or Gaussian probability distribution is defined by the following equation:

$$p(x \mid \mu_1, v_2, normal) = \frac{1}{\sqrt{2\pi v_2}} e^{-(x-\mu_1)^2 / 2v_2} \tag{10-50}$$

The state of knowledge is completely specified in this case by the value of the mean, μ_1, the value of the variance, v_2, and the knowledge that it is a normal distribution. The value of the function $p(x \mid S)$ is the probability that the value falls in the range between x and $x + dx$. In the graph of the normal probability distribution (Figure 10-16), σ is the standard deviation, the square root of the variance. In Microsoft Excel, the normal distribution is given by NORMDIST(x, μ_1, v_2, k), where if k is TRUE the cumulative probability at x is given, and if FALSE the probability at x is given.

The shaded area equals the probability that x lies within one standard deviation, σ, of the mean, μ_1. For the normal or Gaussian distribution in Figure 10-16, this probability is 68 percent.

The cumulative probability graph is smooth (instead of the staircase found with discrete distributions) and is defined by the following integral:

$$P_\le(x \mid S) = \int_{-\infty}^{x} p(x' \mid S) dx' \tag{10-51}$$

For the normal or Gaussian distribution, the cumulative probability distribution is as shown in Figure 10-17.

Note that for a normal or Gaussian distribution, 84 − 16 = 68 percent of the probability lies within one standard deviation of the mean and 98 − 2 = 96 percent of the probability lies within two standard deviations of the mean. Also, the 10/90 width is 2.56σ for this distribution.

The moments of a probability distribution for a continuous variable are calculated by the equations below.

Figure 10–16

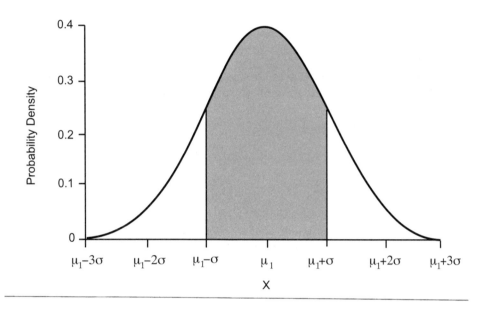

Figure 10–17

Cumulative Probability Graph for the Normal or Gaussian Probability Distribution

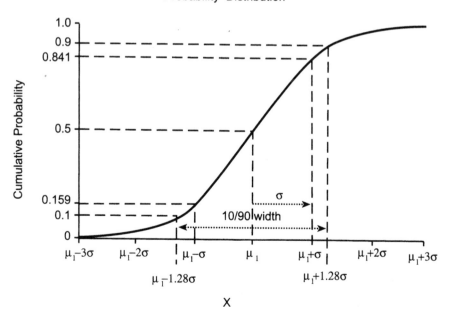

$$\mu_n = \int_{-\infty}^{\infty} x^n p(x \mid S)\,dx \qquad\qquad (10\text{--}52)$$

$$\nu_n = \int_{-\infty}^{\infty} (x - \mu_1)^n p(x \mid S)\,dx \qquad\qquad (10\text{--}53)$$

As you can imagine from the equations above, the use of continuous distributions almost always leads to problems of overwhelming analytical complexity for real situations. For this reason, discrete approximations are almost always used in actual decision analysis applications.

Problems and Discussion Topics _____

10.1   State whether each of the following statements is or is not an event and if not, why not.

  a. The temperature will be greater than 53°F in Bombay tomorrow.

  b. General Motors stock sold for more than $55 per share on the New York Stock Exchange.

  c. The weather is nice today.

  d. The final version of the first printing of this book contains 1,034,246 characters.

  e. Elm trees are taller than oak trees.

10.2   Draw the Venn diagram for the following events: 1,000 – Units Sold < 5,000; Profit Margin per Unit < $2; Profit Margin per Unit ≤ $2. In which region(s) of the Venn diagram do the following events occur? (Profit = Units Sold × Profit Margin.)

  a. Margin = $2 and Profit = $4,000

  b. Margin = $1.50 and Profit = $2,000

  c. Profit < $2,000 and Sales = 500 units

  d. Profit = $15,000

10.3   The New England Patriots and the Cincinnati Bengals both have one game left in the season. They are not playing each other, and each game will go into overtime if necessary to produce a winner.

  a. Draw the Venn diagram for this situation.

  If the Patriots win and the Bengals lose, then the Patriots go to the play-offs. If the Patriots lose and the Bengals win, then the Bengals go to the play-offs. Otherwise, you are not sure who goes to the play-offs.

  b. Show the region on the Venn diagram where you know the Patriots go to the play-offs for certain.

  The Miami Dolphins also have one game left in the season and are playing neither the Patriots nor the Bengals. If

Miami wins and both the Patriots and the Bengals lose, then the Patriots go to the play-offs. If Miami loses and both the Patriots and Bengals win, then the Patriots also go to the play-offs. Otherwise, the Miami game is not relevant.

  c. Redraw the Venn diagram and show the regions where the Bengals go to the play-offs for sure.

10.4 For each of the following events or list of events, complete the list to make it mutually exclusive and collectively exhaustive.

    a. The number of passenger automobiles assembled in the United States in 1985 was at least 20 million and less than 22 million.

    b. The average length of all great white sharks reported caught off the coast of Australia is less than 15 feet.

    c. The variable unit cost for producing the product is $1.75.

    d. The market demand for adipic acid is at least 100 pounds per year and less than 150 million pounds per year. The market demand for adipic acid is greater than 400 million pounds per year.

    e. A competitive product is introduced before our product is introduced.

    f. Our market share is twice that of our nearest competitor.

10.5 A soldier is taking a test in which he is allowed three shots at a target (unmanned) airplane. The probability of his first shot hitting the plane is .4, that of his second shot is .5, and that of his third shot is .7. The probability of the plane's crashing after one shot is .2; after two shots, the probability of crashing is .6; the plane will crash for sure if hit three times. The test is over when the soldier has fired all three shots or when the plane crashes.

    a. Define a set of collectively exhaustive events.

    b. Define a set of mutually exclusive events.

    c. Define a set of mutually exclusive and collectively exhaustive events.

    d. What is the probability of the soldiers shooting down the plane?

    e. What is the mean number of shots required to shoot down the plane?

10.6 Define the joint events for the following two sets of events.

    m_1—Market Share < 5 percent

    m_2—5 percent - Market Share < 10 percent

    m_3—10 percent - Market Share

    d_1—Development Cost - $2 million

d_2—$2 million < Development Cost - $5 million

d_3—$5 million < Development Cost

10.7   For the data in the preceding problem, assume that the events have been approximated by discrete values as follows.

m_1—Market Share = 3 percent

m_2—Market Share = 7 percent

m_3—Market Share = 13 percent

d_1—Development Cost = $1.5 million

d_2—Development Cost = $3 million

d_3—Development Cost = $7 million

a. Define the joint set of events.

b. If Market Size = $100 million and Revenue = (Market Size × Market Share) – Development Cost, calculate the Revenue for each joint event.

c. Calculate the Revenue for each joint event given a Market Size of $60 million.

10.8   On the air route between Chicago and Los Angeles, there is either a head wind or tail wind. Depending on which way the wind is blowing and how fast, flights from Chicago to Los Angeles may be early, on time, or late. We define the following events:

w_1—Head Wind

w_2—Tail Wind

a_1—Arrive Early

a_2—Arrive on Time

a_3—Arrive Late

The joint probabilities are as follows:

w_1 and a_1— .06

w_1 and a_2— .12

w_1 and a_3— .22

w_2 and a_1— .39

w_2 and a_2— .18

w_2 and a_3— .03

a. What is the marginal probability of a head wind?

b. What are the conditional probabilities for arriving early, on time, or late given a tail wind?

c. Given you arrive on time, what is the probability you had a tail wind? If you arrive early? If you arrive late?

10.9   The Surprise Dog man at Fenway Park sells all his hotdogs for the same price, but he does not tell you in advance what you are getting.

You could receive a regular dog or foot-long dog, either of which could be a cheese or chili dog. We define the following events:

l_1—You get a foot-long dog

l_2—You get a regular dog

c_1—You get a cheese dog

c_2—You get a chili dog

The marginal probability of getting a foot-long dog is .25. The probability of getting a foot-long chili dog is .225, and the probability of getting a regular cheese dog is .45.

    a. What is the marginal probability of getting a cheese dog?

    b. What is the probability of getting a regular chili dog?

10.10 A weather forecaster said that San Francisco and Los Angeles have probabilities of .7 and .4, respectively, of having rain during Christmas day. She also said that the probability of their both having rain is .28.

    a. Find the probability of rain in San Francisco on Christmas day given rain in Los Angeles on Christmas day.

    b. Find the probability of rain in Los Angeles on Christmas day given rain in San Francisco on Christmas day.

    c. Find the probability of rain in San Francisco or Los Angeles (or both) on Christmas day.

10.11 Your resident expert on Soviet deployments, Katyusha Caddell, has just given you his opinion on recent Soviet missile developments. The Soviets are building silos that may be of type 1 or type 2 (it is too early to tell), and Katyusha is unsure about which of two possible missile types the Soviets will be deploying in them. He describes the following events:

s_1—Silo of type 1 built

s_2—Silo of type 2 built

m_1—Type 1 missile deployed

m_2—Type 2 missile deployed

Katyusha puts the probability of the silos being type 2 at .6 and figures that type 2 silos mean a .7 probability of type 1 missiles, while type 1 silos mean a .8 probability of type 2 missiles. He further puts the marginal probability of type 2 missile deployment at .6. Do the marginal probabilities agree?

10.12 You and a friend are pondering buying tortilla chips and salsa at a baseball game. Your friend tells you he has made a systematic study of the different varieties of salsa and says the possible types are salsa tomatillo, salsa fresca, and traditional salsa. (The workers at the snack bar do not know what kind it is.) Furthermore, the salsa could be hot (spicy) or not hot. Your friend makes the following predictions:

The chance of hot salsa tomatillo is .08.

The chance of hot salsa fresca is .15.

The chance of not-hot traditional salsa is .18.

The chance of getting salsa fresca is .3 and of getting traditional salsa is .6.

a. What is the probability of getting not-hot salsa tomatillo?

b. What is the conditional probability that the salsa is hot, given that it is salsa tomatillo?

c. What is the marginal probability that the salsa is hot?

d. What is the conditional probability of getting traditional salsa, given that it is not hot?

10.13 Frequently, people use tests to infer knowledge about something. A current (controversial) example is the use of a blood test to see if a person has the AIDS virus or not. The test results reflect current knowledge of the virus' characteristics, and test accuracy may be a matter of concern. How should the information represented by the blood test result be used to update knowledge of the test subject's condition? Bayes' Rule gives the answer to this question.

Suppose a number of people have taken an XYZ virus test with the result shown below. (The numbers are purely illustrative and are not intended to reflect current understanding of the AIDS blood test.)

If a person has taken this test and the result turns out to be positive, what is the probability that he or she does not have the XYZ virus?

(Testing for the AIDS virus involves serious issues of rights to privacy and due process. This problem addresses only the information gained by using a test where the outcome of the test is not a perfect indicator of the underlying condition.)

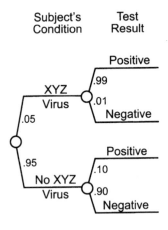

Subject's Condition   Test Result

Positive
.99
XYZ Virus
.01
Negative
.05

.95

Positive
.10
No XYZ Virus
.90
Negative

10.14 Your professor tells you that only 50 percent of the students in her class will do the homework and pass the class; 25 percent will not do the homework and will still pass the class; 8.3 percent will do the homework and study too much (missing sleep) and still pass. The professor figures 30 percent will not do the homework, 60 percent will do the homework, and 10 percent will work too much.

According to the professor, are doing the homework and passing the class probabilistically dependent or independent?

10.15 You suspect that your corns hurt when your mother is about to call you. However, you think that the chance of getting a call from your mother and your corns not hurting is about .5. Your corns hurt about 10 percent of the time.

What is the marginal probability of your mother calling if her calling and your corns hurting are probabilistically independent?

10.16 Use the information from problem 10.7 to perform the following calculations:

    a. Formulate the joint events and calculate the probabilities and revenues for them. Assume probabilities .25, .50, and .25 for m_1, m_2, and m_3 and for d_1, d_2, and d_3, respectively.

    b. Plot the cumulative probability distribution for revenue.

    c. Plot the histogram for revenue. (Choose the bin size to give a good representation of the data.)

    d. Calculate the mean, variance, and standard deviation of the distribution.

10.17 The annual revenues from a new gasoline additive depend on annual U.S. gas consumption and on the average price of gasoline over the next year. It is estimated that 1 bottle of additive will be sold for every 1,000 gallons of gasoline consumed. The price will be set at twice the price for a gallon of gas. Discretized estimates of U.S. gas consumption next year put a .3 chance on consumption being 1 billion gallons, a .6 chance on consumption being 1.5 billion gallons, and a .1 chance on consumption being 2 billion gallons. Similarly, average gas prices have a .25 chance of being $0.50, a .5 chance of being $1.00, and a .25 chance of being $1.25.

    a. Formulate a probability tree for revenue.

    b. Calculate the probabilities and revenues for the joint events.

    c. Plot the cumulative probability distribution for revenue.

    d. Plot the histogram for revenue.

    e. Calculate the mean, variance, and standard deviation of the distribution.

10.18 You are offered an opportunity to engage in a series of three coin flips (.5 probability of winning or losing). For the first flip, you would bet

$1 and either double your money or lose it. For the second flip (if you had won the first flip), you would reinvest your $2 and either double your money or lose it; if you had lost the first flip, you would bet another $1 and double or lose it. The process is repeated for the third coin flip, with having either the money you won on the second flip or a new $1 investment if you lost the second flip.

a. Draw the probability tree for the three coin flips.

b. Calculate your winnings or losses for each joint event and the associated probabilities.

c. Plot the cumulative probability distribution for your proceeds from the flips (wins or losses).

d. Plot the histogram for your proceeds from the flips.

e. Calculate the mean, variance, and standard deviation for your proceeds from the flips.

10.19 Explain graphically why the following relationships are true for the events I and $\emptyset$:

$$I \text{ and } \emptyset = \emptyset$$
$$I \text{ or } \emptyset = I$$

Use these relationships and the probability axioms to prove the following probability:

$$p(\emptyset \mid S) = 0$$

10.20 Let A and B be any two events and let $A' = \text{not } A$. Explain graphically why the following relations are true:

$$A \text{ or } B = A \text{ or } (A' \text{ and } B)$$
$$B = (A \text{ and } B) \text{ or } (A' \text{ and } B)$$
$$A \text{ and } (A' \text{ and } B) = \emptyset$$

Use these relationships, the results of problem 10.19, and the probability axioms to prove the following relationship among probabilities:

$$p(A \text{ or } B \mid S) = p(A \mid S) + p(B \mid S) - p(A \text{ and } B \mid S)$$

10.21 Let A and B be any two events and let $B' = \text{not } B$. Explain graphically why the following relationships are true:

$$A = (A \text{ and } B) \text{ or } (A \text{ and } B')$$
$$\emptyset = (A \text{ and } B) \text{ and } (A \text{ and } B')$$

Use these relationships and the probability axioms to prove the following simple application of the Expansion Theorem:

$$p(A \mid S) = p(A,B \mid S) + p(A,B' \mid S)$$

10.22 Let A and B be any two events. Assume that A is probabilistically independent of B:

$$p(A \mid B,S) = p(A \mid S)$$

Prove that B is probabilistically independent of A.

$$p(B \mid A,S) = p(B \mid S)$$

10.23 Conditional probability is defined as:

$$p(A \mid B,S) = \frac{p(A, B \mid S)}{p(B \mid S)}$$

Show that the definition of conditional probability satisfies the three axioms of probability introduced in Equations 10–10, 10–11, and 10–12.

10.24 Suppose that the moment technique described at the end of Chapter 7 has been used to evaluate a business portfolio. The mean of the distribution is \$230 million, the variance is 18,212 in units of (\$ million)^2, and the skewness is 5,000,000 in units of (\$ million)^3.

a. Large numbers like this are difficult to interpret. More convenient are the standard deviation, σ, and the skewness coefficient, skewness/σ^3. A skewness coefficient outside the range –2 to 2 means the distribution is quite skewed. What is the standard deviation and skewness coefficient for this portfolio?

b. Decision-makers relate better to graphics than to numbers like variance and standard deviation. Use the normal distribution (Equation 10–50) to plot a cumulative probability distribution that has the given mean and variance.

c. Creating a plot that matches mean, variance, and skewness is more difficult. Use the shifted lognormal distribution

$$\frac{1}{\sqrt{2\pi}\, s(x-x_0)} e^{-\frac{1}{2}\left(\frac{\ln(x-x_0)-m}{s}\right)^2}$$

to plot a cumulative probability distribution that matches the given mean, variance, and skewness. (The more familiar, non-shifted lognormal distribution has $x_0 = 0$.)

d. Compare the results of b and c. How different are the distributions? How would the plot differ if skewness were 50,000,000? 500,000?

Hint: Use Microsoft Excel or another spreadsheet program to create the graph. Plot the distribution from (mean – 2σ) to (mean + 2σ).

For the lognormal distribution with $x_0 = 0$, m and s are the mean and standard deviation of $\ln(x)$. The moments of x are given by

$$\mu_1 = e^{m+\frac{1}{2}s^2}$$

$$\mu_k = \mu_1^k e^{\frac{1}{2}k(k-1)s^2} = e^{km+\frac{1}{2}k^2s^2}$$

The following calculations can be used to obtain x_0, m, and s from the moments μ_1 (mean), v_2 (variance), and v_3 (skewness). All that is required to obtain these results is some tedious algebra and solving a cubic equation to determine d. First calculate

$$w = 2v_2^3 / v_3^2$$

$$r = \sqrt{1+2w}$$

$$d = \frac{v_2^2}{v_3} + v_2 \frac{(1+w+r)^{1/3} + (1+w-r)^{1/3}}{(2v_3)^{1/3}}$$

$$A = v_2 + d^2$$

$$B = v_3 + 3dv_2 + d^3$$

These values can then be used to calculate the parameters we need:

$$m = \frac{3}{2}\ln(A) - \frac{2}{3}\ln(B)$$

$$s = \sqrt{\frac{2}{3}\ln(B) - \ln(A)}$$

$$x_0 = \mu_1 - d$$

Note that if the skewness is negative, you need to use the reflected shifted lognormal. To do this, use the absolute value of the mean μ_1 and skewness v_3 in the above calculations, and then substitute $(x_0 - x)$ for $(x - x_0)$ in the equation for the shifted lognormal above.

11

Influence Diagram Theory

The decision facilitator learns early that decision trees grow with amazing rapidity. Add a three-branch node, and the tree becomes three times larger. Add a few more nodes, and you need a wall-size piece of paper to represent the tree. And yet you are discussing only a relatively small number of uncertainties.

Influence diagrams are a means of representing the same decision problem much more compactly. For each chance and decision variable in the tree, there is a single object in the graph. Arrows connecting these objects represent probabilistic and informational relationships.

Influence diagrams are popular and important in the practice of decision analysis for three reasons.

- The influence diagram is compact enough that even the most complex problems can be developed and discussed on a single large sheet of paper. This is a tremendous advantage when structuring the problem, organizing analytical tasks, monitoring problem analysis, and presenting an overview of the problem.
- Influence diagrams appear to be the easiest way to introduce and work with probabilistic dependence, an unfamiliar and difficult concept for many decision-makers.
- An influence diagram is a theoretical construct and an evaluation device with all the power of a decision tree.

In this book, we use the influence diagram for the first and second reasons.

Elements of Influence Diagrams _____

Six basic elements are used in an influence diagram (Figure 11–1).

_____ Figure 11–1 _____

Elements of the Influence Diagram

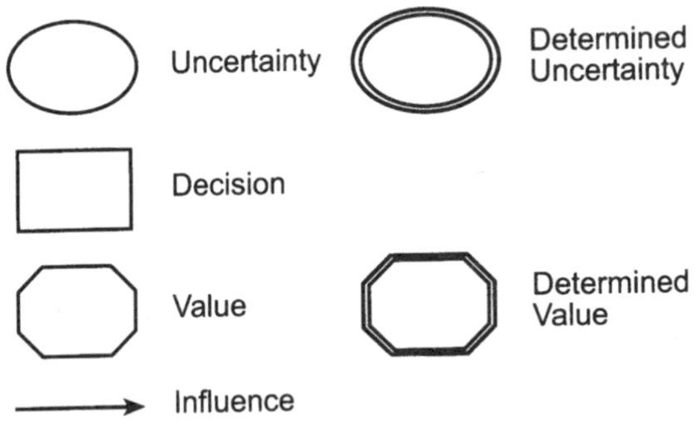

To define each of these elements, we will use the fictitious Medequip example introduced in Chapter 10.

Medequip's planning department continued its study of the product's declining revenues. The planners were considering changing the long-term pricing strategy for the product. Two alternatives suggested themselves. Medequip could choose a Premium Pricing strategy: promote the special characteristics of the product, target specific segments of the market, and set a price 20 percent above the principal competitor's price. Or it could choose a Market Pricing strategy: set price at the competitor's price and compete in all segments of the market.

Critical to the competitive position of Medequip's product was the availability of an essential raw material. It was suggested that a raw material survey could be initiated that could help predict future availability and cost of the raw material. Information like this could help Medequip enter into advantageous long-term supply contracts.

Medequip brought together a number of people from management and planning and created an influence diagram (Figure 11–2) that represented their perception of the problem.

Uncertainty

Uncertainties are represented by ovals. Within the oval is a label that indicates the mutually exclusive and collectively exhaustive set of events among which the node distinguishes. The most desirable label is a variable name, where the value of the variable defines the events. An oval represents a set of possible events and the probabilities assigned to these events.

Figure 11–2

Influence Diagram for Medequip's Decision Problem

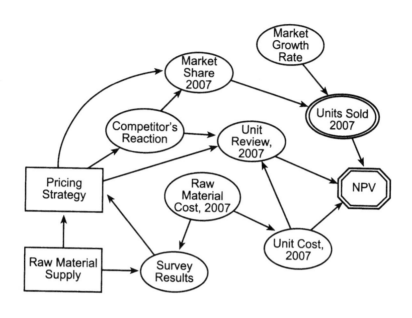

The planning department was uncertain about how rapidly the market for the product would grow. The oval labeled *Market Growth Rate* in the influence diagram represented the uncertainty on the average annual market growth rate during the period until 2007. After the influence diagram had been completed, several of those most knowledgeable about the market assessed the probability distribution represented by the oval. The information contained "inside" the oval is shown in Figure 11–3. This tree representation for the data at a node is called a *distribution tree* and represents a probability distribution on a single set of events.

Decision

Decisions are represented by rectangles. Written in the rectangle is a label for the set of significantly different alternatives being considered.

Representatives from manufacturing were concerned about the cost of the critical raw material used in making the product. It was suggested that a raw material survey would help predict availability and cost of the raw material, and this in turn would have an impact on product unit cost. The rectangle labeled *Raw Material Supply Survey* represents the decision on whether to perform this survey (Figure 11–4).

———————————————————— Figure 11–3 ————————————————————

Distribution Tree for the Data Contained in the Market Growth Rate Node

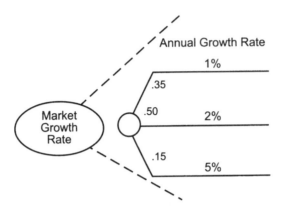

Influence

Influences are indicated by arrows and represent a flow of information and, with decision nodes, a time sequence. As discussed in Chapter 10, all probability assignments are based on the state of knowledge of a particular person at a particular time. Decisions are also made based on a state of knowledge. It is essential that all the probability assignments and decision nodes in an influence diagram share a common state of information, S. The arrow indicates that, in addition to this common state of information, S, there is information concerning the node at the base of the arrow available at the node at the head of the arrow. This concept is made more explicit in the four cases presented below.

———————————————————— Figure 11–4 ————————————————————

Alternatives Represented by the Raw Material Supply Survey Node

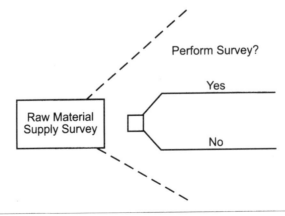

Arrow from Uncertainty Node to Uncertainty Node

If the arrow is between two uncertainty nodes, the probability distribution for the node at the head of the arrow is probabilistically dependent (conditional) on the node at the base of the arrow. If there is an arrow from node A to node B, the diagram is read as "A influences B."* The information flow in this case does not necessarily imply a causal link or a time sequence.

Recently, the term "relevance" has begun to replace the term "influence" (which has a causal connotation) in this context. If there is an arrow from node A to node B, the diagram is read as "A is relevant to B." Influence diagrams that contain only uncertainties are referred to as "relevance diagrams."

Representatives of manufacturing felt much more comfortable assigning probabilities to Unit Cost, 2007 conditional on the cost of raw material around that time. Accordingly, they drew an arrow between the Raw Material Cost, 2007 node and the Unit Cost, 2007 node. If A_i and C_j are a set of mutually exclusive and collectively exhaustive events describing Raw Material Cost and Unit Cost, respectively, and if S is the state of knowledge common to all the nodes in the influence diagram, then the probability distribution represented by the node Unit Cost, 2007 is

$$p(C_j | A_i, S)$$

At a later meeting, the probability assignments (Figure 11–5) were assessed by the representatives of manufacturing.

———————————— Figure 11–5 ————————————

Distribution Tree Representing the Data Contained in the Unit Cost, 2007 Node

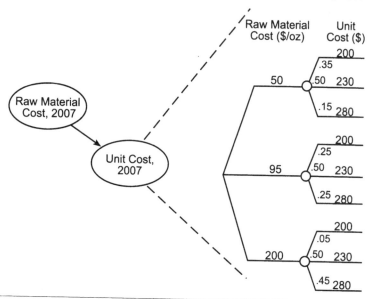

---

* If there are arrows from several nodes to node B, it is this set of nodes (rather than each individual node) that influences node B.

The tree representation for the conditional probability distribution above is a more complex form of distribution tree than the one shown in Figure 11–4. The difference between a distribution tree and a decision tree is that the nodes on the left side of a distribution tree are there only to specify the state of knowledge used in assessing the probabilities for the node on the right. They can be arranged in whatever order helps the assessor assign probabilities. The order of nodes in a distribution tree is not necessarily related to the order of nodes in the decision tree.

Arrow from Decision Node to Uncertainty Node

If the arrow is from a decision node to an uncertainty node, the probability distribution for the node at the head of the arrow is probabilistically dependent (conditional) on the alternative chosen at the node at the base of the arrow. This implies that the decision is made before the uncertainty is resolved and that there is some sort of causal link between the decision and the resolution of the uncertainty.

The representatives of the marketing department were uncertain just how their principal competitor would react to either of the pricing strategy alternatives, but they were sure that the probabilities they assigned would depend on the pricing strategy chosen. For this reason, an arrow was drawn from the Pricing Strategy node to the Competitor's Reaction node. The assessed probability distribution is shown in Figure 11–6.

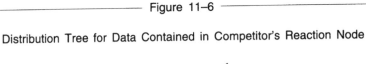

Figure 11–6

Distribution Tree for Data Contained in Competitor's Reaction Node

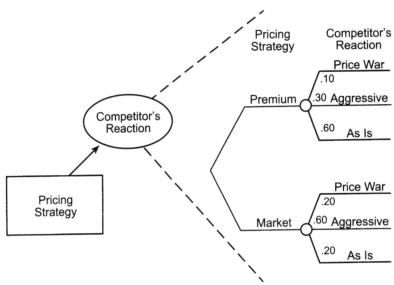

Arrow from Decision Node to Decision Node

An arrow between two decision nodes means that the decision-maker remembers which alternative was chosen at the node at the base of the arrow when he or she comes to make the decision at the node at the head of the arrow. There is a strong chronological assertion here: the decision represented by the node at the base of the arrow will be made before the decision represented by the node at the head of the arrow.

Arrow from Uncertainty Node to Decision Node

If the arrow is from an uncertainty node to a decision node, the uncertainty is resolved before the decision is made and the decision-maker learns what happened before making the decision. Note that, in this case, there is a strong assertion about chronology: the uncertainty is resolved and the information received by the decision-maker before the decision is made.

The Medequip team decided that a decision on whether to perform the raw material supply survey would be made before the pricing strategy decision. Furthermore, it was decided that if a raw material supply survey were decided on, the pricing strategy decision would not be made before the results of the survey were available. The decision-maker would know the survey results when he or she made the decision. An arrow was drawn from the Raw Material Supply Survey node to the Pricing Strategy node and from the Survey Results node to the Pricing Strategy node (Figure 11–7).

_____ Figure 11–7 _____

Tree Representing the Alternatives in the Pricing Strategy Node

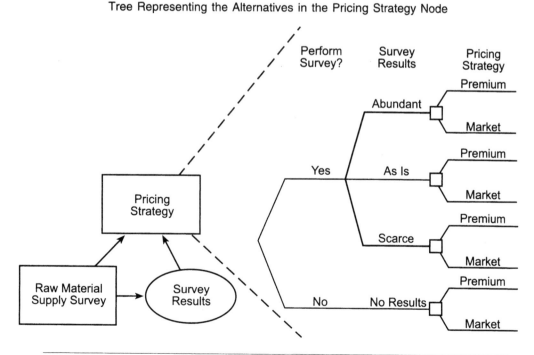

The last example shows one way to represent an asymmetry in an influence diagram. The set of events represented by the node may differ, depending on the event occurring at a node that influences it. In this case, the events represented by the Survey Results node include a single event (no results), which occurs if the survey is not performed.

Determined Uncertainty

As an influence diagram grows and influences (arrows) are added, the uncertainty at a node frequently disappears: once the outcomes are known at all the influencing uncertainty and decision nodes, there is no more uncertainty about the actual event at the influenced node. The node can be left in the diagram, denoted by a double oval. This type of node is usually called a "deterministic node." (The node can also be removed from the diagram, provided you assure the proper information flow by connecting all incoming arrows to all outgoing arrows.)

A deterministic node usually represents either a formula or calculation for which the influencing nodes supply input. Often this calculation is complicated enough that it is made by a computer spreadsheet or other computer program. Occasionally, the deterministic node represents a table of values, one entry for each combination of the events of the nodes that influence it.

One of the first uncertainties the Medequip team identified was the uncertainty represented by the node Units Sold, 2007. As the influence diagram grew, two nodes were created (Market Growth Rate and Market Share, 2007), both of which influenced the node Units Sold, 2007. At this point, there is no uncertainty left at the node Units Sold, 2007: once you know what happened at the influencing nodes, all that remains is a simple calculation (Figure 11–8).

The node Units Sold, 2007 could be removed from the diagram if the arrows coming into it are rerouted to the node that it influences—that is, if arrows are drawn from the Market Growth Rate node to the NPV node and from the Market Share, 2007 node to the NPV node—thus assuring that information flows are maintained.

———————————— Figure 11–8 ————————————

Equation Used at Deterministic Node Units Sold, 2007

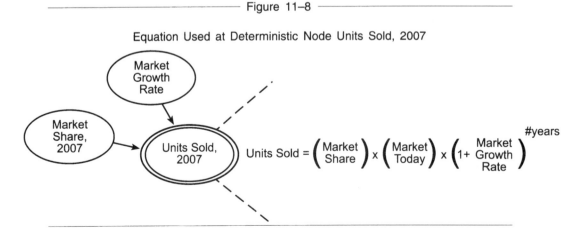

Value and Determined Value

Implicit in an influence diagram is a rule by which decisions are made. As discussed earlier in the text, decisions are made by choosing the alternative that maximizes the certain equivalent of the value measure. In simpler terms, we choose the alternative that gives us the most of what we want.

If there are decision nodes in an influence diagram, there must be one (and only one) node in the influence diagram that represents the value measure used in making the decisions. This value node is always an uncertainty node or a deterministic (determined uncertainty) node. To identify its role, an octagon (double octagon if it is deterministic) is used rather than an oval.

Very early, the Medequip team had chosen NPV of cash flow as the value measure used in making decisions. Given the outcomes of the influencing nodes (Units Sold, 2007; Unit Revenue, 2007; and Unit Cost, 2007), it was felt that most of the uncertainty in NPV would be resolved. For this reason, the node representing NPV was represented by a double octagon (Figure 11-9).

Rules for Constructing Influence Diagrams _____

The following four rules must be obeyed to create meaningful influence diagrams for the type of decision problems dealt with in this book:

    1. *No Loops* —If you follow the arrows from node to node, there must be no path that leads you back to where you started. This is most readily understood in terms of the information flow indicated by the arrows.

Figure 11-9 ――――――

Model Used at Deterministic Node NPV

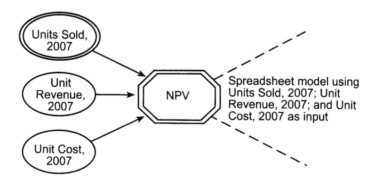

2. *Single Decision-Maker*—There should be just one value measure (octagon), and all decisions should be made to maximize
the same function (expected value or certain equivalent) of this
value.

3. *No Forgetting Previous Decisions*—There should be an arrow
between all pairs of decisions in the diagram. This will establish the order in which the decisions are made and also
indicate that the decision-maker remembers all his or her
previous choices.

4. *No Forgetting Previously Known Information*—If there is an arrow
from an uncertainty node to a decision node, there should be
an arrow from that uncertainty node to all subsequent decision
nodes.

Procedures for Manipulating Influence Diagrams _____

There are two useful procedures for manipulating influence diagrams
without changing the information in the diagram. These procedures are
necessary when solving an influence diagram directly, but may be useful in
restructuring a diagram to facilitate drawing a decision tree.

1. *Adding an Arrow*—An arrow can be added between two uncertainty nodes in an influence diagram, provided it does not
create a loop. The lack of an arrow between two nodes is a
statement that information from one node is not needed to
assess the probabilities at the other. Adding an arrow can be
thought of as making this information available, even though
it does not affect the probabilities assessed.

2. *Reversing an Arrow*—An arrow between two uncertainty nodes
can be reversed if the state of knowledge available at both
nodes is the same. Therefore, to reverse an arrow between two
nodes, all the arrows into both nodes must be the same (except,
of course, the arrow between the two). Once the state of
information is the same, the operation of reversing an arrow
in an influence diagram is the same operation as applying
Bayes' Rule to a probability distribution and "flipping" a probability tree.

*The Medequip team had recognized that the easiest and most reliable means
of assessment was first to have procurement personnel provide probabilities for
raw material cost, then to have manufacturing estimate unit cost (conditional on
raw material cost), and finally to have sales and marketing provide probabilities
for unit revenue conditional on unit cost (Figure 11–10a).*

*There was a desire to see whether assessing the probabilities in a different
order made a difference. First, sales and marketing would estimate unit
revenues, and then manufacturing would estimate unit cost conditional on unit
revenues. (There was some feeling that perhaps cost rose when revenue was
high and was squeezed down when revenue was low.) This assessment entails*

Figure 11–10

Manipulating Influence Diagrams

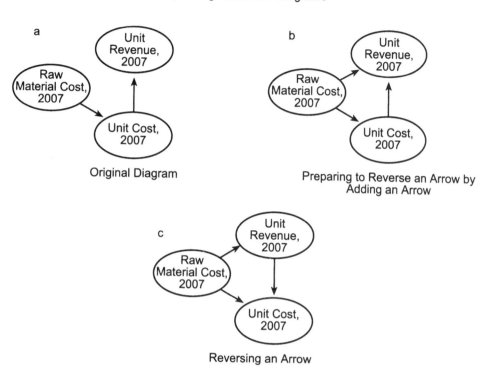

a

Original Diagram

b

Preparing to Reverse an Arrow by
Adding an Arrow

c

Reversing an Arrow

reversing the arrow between Unit Cost, 2007 and Unit Revenue, 2007. Before this
can be done, an arrow from the Raw Material Cost node to the Unit Revenue node
must be added (Figure 11–10b) so that both the Unit Revenue and Unit Cost
nodes share the same state of knowledge. (For this exercise, the arrows from
Pricing Strategy and Competitor's Reaction to Unit Revenue, 2007 were dropped
from the diagram.)

Now the arrow between the Unit Revenue and Unit Cost nodes can be
reversed (Figure 11–10c). At this point, the team realized that the job of the sales
and marketing representatives was harder than they had thought. Unit Revenue
probabilities had to be assessed conditional on Raw Material Cost!

Turning an Influence Diagram into a Decision Tree

The procedure for turning an influence diagram into a decision tree is quite
simple.

    1. Arrange the decision nodes such that all arrows with a
decision node at their base or head point to the right-hand side
of the page. Arrows pointing to or emanating from decision
nodes imply a chronology that must be followed in decision

trees. By convention, the chronology of decisions in a decision tree flows from left to right, and therefore these arrows must point from left to right.

2. Arrange the uncertainty nodes so that no uncertainty node is to the left of a decision node unless there is an arrow from that node to the decision node. In a decision tree, the outcome of a node to the left of a decision node is known to the decision-maker when he or she makes the decision; in an influence diagram, this means there is an arrow from the uncertainty node to the decision node.

3. Arrange, insofar as possible, the uncertainty nodes so that all arrows point to the right. This will cause conditional probabilities to be displayed simply on the tree.

The rules for manipulating influence diagrams can be used to reverse arrows between nodes and make all arrows point to the right. However, at least one decision tree program (Supertree) can accept input in which probabilities at a node depend on nodes that follow it in the tree—that is, for which the arrow to the node points left—and so this last step of arrow reversal is not necessary.

4. Make the deterministic value node a tree endpoint node. This will usually involve calculations to find the value associated with each combination of events at the nodes that influence the value node.

5. If using a program like Supertree, number the nodes, give each node a node name, and input the structure and data.

The Medequip facilitators decided to put the influence diagram into tree form. First, they eliminated the Units Sold, 2007 determined uncertainty node, rerouting the two arrows coming into it to the node it influenced, the NPV node. Following the rules given above, they rearranged the diagram and formed the tree shown in Figure 11–11. Since the tree would be entered in Supertree, they did not need to reverse the arrow from the Raw Material Cost, 2007 node to the Survey Results node because Supertree does this automatically.

The tree is ready to be evaluated. All the information necessary for inputting the nodes is shown except for the probabilities. The probabilistic dependence is shown by the arrows in the influence diagram. For instance, the probabilities of node 9 depend on nodes 3 and 4, and the probabilities for node 2 depend on node 7. The endpoint, node 10, depends on nodes 5, 6, 8, and 9 and will probably be calculated by a spreadsheet. Note the difference in orientation between "influences" and "depends on": if node 3 influences node 9 in the influence diagram, then in the language often used for trees, the probabilities at node 9 depend on node 3.

Particular care should be taken to distinguish the use of the word "successor" between influence diagrams and decision trees. In influence diagrams, it is quite natural to say that a node at the head of an arrow is the successor to the node at the base of the arrow. Thus, in Figure 11–11, the node Survey Results is the successor (direct successor, to be precise) of the node Raw Material Cost, 2007. In decision trees, successor refers only to the

Figure 11-11

Turning the Medequip Influence Diagram into a Decision Tree

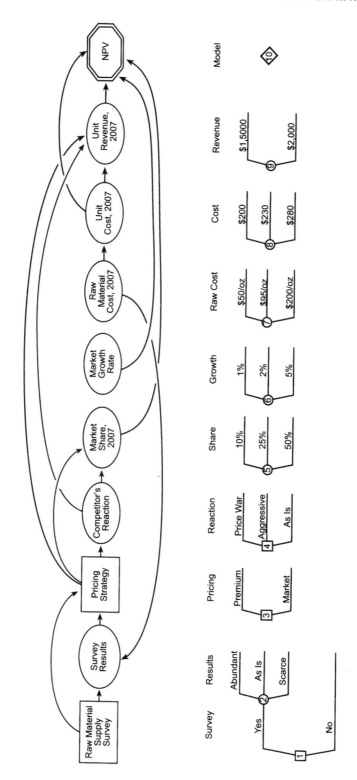

order in the decision tree and does not imply any information flow or dependence between the nodes. Thus, in the tree in Figure 11–11, Market Growth Rate is the successor to Market Share, 2007.

Summary

This example illustrates the power of the influence diagram to represent a problem compactly and to lead people naturally through the complexities of probabilistic dependence. There are 3,888 paths through this tree; at 66 lines per page, the printout of the full tree would be 59 pages long. The dependent probabilities weave a complex pattern through the tree. On the other hand, for the influence diagram we need only one page to draw the diagram and several other pages on which to list the events and probabilities represented by the nodes.

In practice, influence diagrams are currently used mostly in the initial phases of a decision analysis. The process of model construction, data gathering, and sensitivity analysis normally leads to insight and simplification of the structure of the problem and to the natural construction of a simple tree. However, given the rapid evolution of software tools and consulting practice, we can expect to see the unification of these two representations of the problem in a single system.

Problems and Discussion Topics

11.1 How does an influence diagram contribute to making good decisions? (Refer to the elements of a good decision.) What elements of a good decision does an influence diagram not help with and why?

11.2 Describe at least one way that using influence diagrams helps you draw better decision trees and one way that being familiar with decision trees helps you draw better influence diagrams.

11.3 How do you know when an influence diagram has become complicated enough? Relate your answer to the problem of assessing probabilities and to the clairvoyance test.

11.4 Think of a significant decision you have made. Draw the influence diagram for that decision. Were there significant uncertainties? How did you identify and deal with them at the time? Do you have any new insights into the decision? (Relate this last answer to the good decision/good outcome distinction.)

11.5 Draw the influence diagram for the date and time when a specific close relative walks through your front door. Make sure the uncertainty passes the clairvoyance test and try to summon all your information and experience on the factors influencing the uncertainty. Has the exercise changed your understanding of the uncertainty at all? Could you now draw a decision tree and do a meaningful probability assessment? Draw the tree and explain what (if anything) would prevent you from assessing probabilities and calculating the expected date and time that the relative walks through your door.

11.6   Draw an influence diagram for the probability of a major war within the next ten years. Make sure your uncertainties pass the clairvoyance test. How is this problem different from the previous one? Is there anything preventing you from drawing a tree and calculating a probability distribution for this problem?

11.7   Draw the influence diagram for the number of times you eat pizza within the next month. Again, make sure the uncertainty passes the clairvoyance test. Are there any difficulties in completing this problem and, if so, what are they?

11.8   In the influence diagram used to construct the tree in Figure 11–11, there is an arrow pointing to the left.

   a. Reverse this arrow to make the diagram a "decision tree network," one in which the nodes can be arranged so that all the arrows point to the right.

   b. Why is it necessary to reverse this diagram to create a tree? (Hint: How would you display the probabilities at node 2 in the tree?)

11.9   Adding an arrow between an uncertainty and a decision node is related to the value of information calculation described in chapters 2 and 4.

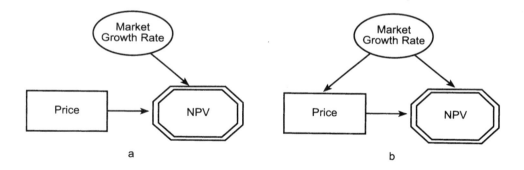

   a. Draw the trees represented by influence diagrams a and b above.

   b. How are influence diagrams a and b related to the value of perfect information on Market Growth Rate?

11.10 In the Howard canonical form of an influence diagram, there are no arrows from a decision node to any uncertainty node aside from the value node. For the purposes of this definition, groups of uncertainty nodes can be amalgamated into a larger uncertainty node (the value node) provided no loops are created.

A company has several different routes it could pursue in developing a new product. The influence diagram representing its problem is shown below.

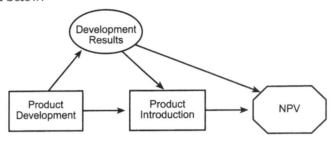

a. Is the influence diagram above in Howard canonical form? The one below?

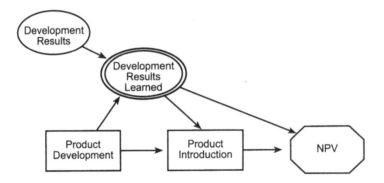

b. Suppose some preliminary work could predict the results of the product development effort before all the necessary development work was done. Which influence diagram could be used to calculate the value of information about development results?

c. Which influence diagram is in Howard canonical form? Draw a tree showing the logic contained in the deterministic node that would make the second diagram equivalent to the one that preceded it.

d. Can the second influence diagram be manipulated to a form from which the value of information about development results can be calculated?

11.11 It is possible to use deterministic nodes to represent asymmetries in the problem in a straightforward way.

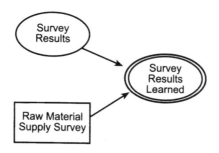

    a. Redraw the influence diagram in Figure 11–11 using the deterministic node defined above. What arrows should be drawn from these nodes to the remainder of the diagram?

    b. What is the logic contained in the deterministic node Survey Results Learned?

    c. Is the tree drawn from the new diagram different from the tree in Figure 11–11?

    d. Make this diagram into a decision tree network. (See problem 11.8 for the definition of a decision tree network.)

    e. Is the influence diagram in Figure 11–11 in Howard canonical form? (See problem 11.10.)

    f. Is the influence diagram drawn as part of this problem in Howard canonical form?

11.12 In Chapter 10, a joint probability distribution was given for the two sets of mutually exclusive and collectively exhaustive events, R_i and C_j.

$$p(R_i C_j | S)$$

	C_1	C_2	C_3
R_1	.10	.25	.03
R_2	.22	.26	.14

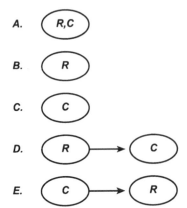

Draw the distribution trees for the nodes in the five influence diagrams above.

11.13 In Figure 11–2, there is no arrow going to the Market Growth Rate node. The lack of arrows is of great significance to the facilitator, since the absence of arrows makes modeling and probability assessment relatively simple.

a. There is no arrow between the nodes Pricing Strategy and Market Growth Rate. What does this indicate about the nature of the market and Medequip's place in the market? Under what circumstances should an arrow be drawn between these two nodes?

b. There is no arrow between the nodes Competitor's Reaction and Market Growth Rate. What does this indicate about the nature of the market and the companies that supply products in this marketplace? Under what circumstances should an arrow be drawn between these two nodes?

c. Under what circumstances should there be an arrow from both the Pricing Strategy and Competitor's Reaction nodes to the Market Growth Rate node?

d. We are not allowed to draw an arrow from Pricing Strategy to Competitor's Reaction, from Competitor's Reaction to Market Growth Rate, and from Market Growth Rate to Pricing Strategy (perhaps to represent a pricing adjustment to changes in market dynamics). Why is this not allowed? How might you represent an adjustment of pricing strategy to market dynamics?

12

Encoding a Probability Distribution

Although most facilitators are familiar with data-gathering methods and problems, decision analysis uses two types of data that require quite different methods to gather data and pose quite different sorts of problems. One type of data is the utility curve. (The methods and conditions for encoding utility curves are discussed in Chapter 5.) The other type of data is the probability distribution, which is used throughout decision analysis. Encoding a probability distribution can be one of the most difficult tasks to perform well in decision analysis. This chapter provides a review of some of the problems encountered in encoding a probability distribution and an outline of the encoding process.

Levels of Detail in Encoding Probability Distributions

Ideally the most important uncertainties in an analysis will be described by probability distributions obtained through the full encoding process: many points for the cumulative probability distribution assessed from some expert. For really important uncertainties, probability distributions may be assessed from several experts.

However, practice over the past decade has shown the importance of obtaining quality in obtaining the 10/50/90 values for uncertain variables. The 10/50/90 values describe the uncertainty in terms of three numbers: a low value (10% chance the true value will turn out to be less than this value), a base value (50% chance the true value will turn out to be less than this value), and a high value (90% chance the true value will turn out to be less than this value, and 10% chance it will turn out to be higher). These values give three points on the cumulative probability curve (see Chapter 2) and are used in the early stages of analyzing the problem (see probabilistic sensitivity analysis in Chapter 6).

There is a temptation to obtain these numbers quickly and carelessly and assume that more care can be spent on encoding the truly important uncertainties later. However, in practice the second encoding session rarely happens. It is well worth a minor investment of time to make sure that, however briefly, all the steps of the encoding session are touched on in assessments of 10/50/90 ranges.

Problems in Encoding Probability Distributions

In Chapter 2, we stated that since probability is used to represent a person's state of knowledge about something, there are no correct or incorrect probabilities. However, two major questions arise in encoding and using probability distributions.

The first question concerns choosing a person to furnish the probability distribution. Does that person have an adequate state of relevant knowledge? Are sufficient and correct experience and data available? Does the person have the training and intelligence to assimilate this experience and data? These questions are familiar to everyone who wonders whom to believe or rely on.

Decision analysis does not offer a new solution to this problem; it simply ensures that the decision-maker considers the person chosen to be knowledgeable or expert in the relevant area. Usually, the facilitator and decision-maker can agree easily on who the appropriate experts are. If there are several possible experts, the facilitator can encode probability distributions from each of them and compare the effect the distributions have on the problem. Different probability distributions may or may not lead to different decisions.

The second question is whether the encoded probability distributions really represent the state of knowledge of the persons involved. A surprising number of biases can sneak in (often at an unconscious level) and make carelessly encoded probability distributions inadequate representations of the subject's state of knowledge. Decision analysis handles this problem by devising methods to deal with the biases that inevitably arise.

Motivational Biases

Motivational biases arise when the encoded probabilities do not reflect the expert's conscious beliefs. The cause of this behavior is usually desire for a reward or fear of punishment, which can be economic, psychological, or physical. An example of this type of bias can occur when a salesman is asked for an estimate of future sales. Sales personnel are often conditioned to respond artificially high (possibly to obtain the rights to sell the product) or artificially low (perhaps to appear good when they exceed their estimates). Another example of motivational bias occurs when people give estimates based on "real, objective data" (which may have limited relevance), rather than take the responsibility to express their own judgment and intuition.

The long-term cure for motivational biases is to align the reward structure to encourage truthful responses. In the short term, however, the facilitator can show the expert the importance to the company of his responses and emphasize that he is recording a state of knowledge—not asking for a prediction or commitment. If the expert has a personal stake in having a particular course of action chosen, the facilitator can divide the quantity being assessed into several subfactors, which brings the assessment down to a level of detail where the expert does not know how to give answers that serve his self-interest. As a last resort, if the above cures do not appear to be working, we can disqualify the expert.

Three forms of behavior can be loosely classified as motivational biases: the manager's bias, the expert's bias, and the facilitator's bias.

The manager's bias is typified by the statement: "If that's what the boss wants, I'll get it done!" In this case, the encoded uncertainty may be very small, while the manager has shifted all the uncertainty to some other unsuspected factor, such as the cost of getting it done.

The expert's bias is typified by the attitude that experts are expected to be certain of things rather than uncertain. Given this attitude, an expert will give a narrow distribution. The obvious errors associated with this sort of reasoning should be discussed with the expert.

The facilitator's bias results from not wanting to appear in disagreement with official company information. It often occurs in an organization with an official in-house forecast. This forecast, which may merely be the result of the latest computer run, is intended primarily to impose consistency on company analyses. Except at top-management levels, it is rare to find anyone who is willing to disagree publicly with this forecast. The encoder must show the expert the origins, limitations, and purpose of the forecast and encourage candid responses. (The in-house forecast can also create a powerful anchor, as discussed below.)

Cognitive Biases

How do people assess the probability of an uncertain event? It turns out there are a limited number of heuristic methods used in this process. (A heuristic involves or serves as an aid to learning, discovery, or problem-solving by experimental, and especially, trial-and-error methods.) In general, these heuristics are quite useful, but sometimes they lead to severe and systematic errors.* Improperly using the cognitive heuristics causes biases and leads to incorrect conclusions.

An example of a heuristic is the use of visual clarity to judge the distance of objects: hazy objects are thought to be distant. An example of an incorrect

---

* There is much literature on the subject. A seminal paper in this area is the excellent and readable article: A. Tversky and D. Kahneman, "Judgment Under Uncertainty: Heuristics and Biases," *Science* 185 (September 27, 1974): 1124-1131. This article is reprinted in *Readings on the Principles and Applications of Decision Analysis*, ed. R.A. Howard and J.E. Matheson, 2 vols. (Menlo Park, California: Strategic Decisions Group, 1984) 2:903-910.

use of this heuristic occurs in the clear air of deserts where distant objects appear to be quite near. Although biases tend to occur at an unconscious level, they are correctable. For example, in a desert, one learns to say "Objects are farther away than they seem!"

Availability Bias

One type of common bias in probability encoding is called the availability bias. In this case, the heuristic is to think of occurrences of an event (or of similar events); the easier it is to think of occurrences, the more likely the event is judged to be. For instance, if eight out of ten small businesses you can think of failed within their first year, you may judge it quite likely that a new small business will fail. This heuristic is quite useful and generally works well. However, a problem occurs because of quirks in the way we store and retrieve information in our minds. For instance, information that is ordered, redundant, dramatic, recent, imaginable, certified, or consistent with our world view is much more likely to be stored and recalled than information that does not have these qualities. As a result, probabilities tend to be unduly weighted by the more available information.

We can counteract this bias in several ways. First, we can check to find out if there are reasons some information is more readily available than other information. If there are, we can discuss and research the less available information. Another cure (which is a powerful cure for other biases as well) is to postulate extreme outcomes and request the expert to give some scenarios that would lead to these outcomes. This technique forces the expert to search his or her mind for little-used information. A final cure (also valuable in confronting other biases) is to have the expert pretend to consider the situation retrospectively from the future. A change of perspective often opens the mind up to new possibilities.

Representativeness Bias

A second type of bias is called the representativeness bias. The heuristic in force here is to look at some evidence and then assign a high probability to the event that makes the evidence most likely. What can go wrong? Studies show that when faced with specific evidence, people often tend to discard (or undervalue) previous experience and general information. For instance, a sharp decrease in a company's net income might lead someone to assign a relatively high probability that the company is in financial trouble. However, mature reflection might reveal that the particular industry has net incomes that tend to vary wildly from year to year and that the latest change has little significance.

Another example of the representativeness bias is the common error of stereotyping: "All people who do X are Y. Therefore, anyone who is Y is very likely to do X." Very few people stop to consider the possibility that there may be many people who are Y and only a few cases of people who do X.

Besides being very common, this bias can be quite subtle and complex, both in its manifestations and in its causes. (For more discussion of this bias, see the article by Tversky and Kahneman.) The cure for this bias is to separate prior or general information from new evidence and to update prior information explicitly using probability theory. (See the treatment of Nature's tree in Chapter 4.)

Adjustment and Anchoring Bias

Adjustment and anchoring give rise to a third common bias. The heuristic is to start from some initial estimate and then adjust the estimate until it seems reasonable. This heuristic is the basis of many engineering or other quantitative estimates. Unfortunately, the adjustment is rarely adequate, and the final estimate tends to be anchored near the initial estimate—no matter how arbitrary the initial estimate was. We see this bias a great deal when encoding probability distributions. For example, people sometimes start by making a best estimate and then attempt to estimate how uncertain the best estimate is, thus arriving at the width of the distribution. What happens is that they get anchored by the best estimate and almost always wind up with too narrow a probability distribution. Other examples of this bias are anchoring on the corporate plan and corporate forecasts—it is difficult to think of futures that are too different. The cure for this bias is to start by discussing extreme outcomes and asking the expert for explanatory scenarios. If the facilitator must start with an initial best estimate, he or she should try to do so in a way that does not commit the expert.

A special case of the anchoring and adjustment bias arises because of conjunctive distortions. We tend to overestimate the probability of success for conjunctive events (where all the individual events must happen for success), because we anchor on the probability of each individual event happening. This bias is particularly important in R&D, where a number of hurdles must be cleared before success is achieved. The obvious cure for this bias is to obtain the probabilities for each event happening and then to multiply them to obtain the probability of success. This type of distortion also occurs when we underestimate the probability of success for disjunctive events (any individual event happening gives success). This bias occurs in research and development when we tend to underestimate the probability of technical success in following parallel but independent research paths.

Implicit Conditioning Bias

Finally, there is the implicit conditioning bias. One form of the heuristic is to tell a story; the more coherent and plausible the story, the more likely we judge the outcome we are trying to explain. The bias is that we can forget to examine the likelihood of the enabling events needed to start the story. Another form of the heuristic occurs when we make certain assumptions to make the assessment process easier. The bias arises when we subsequently forget these assumptions exist. The cures for this type of bias are, first, to postulate extreme outcomes and request explanatory scenarios and, second, to examine probabilities of any enabling events for the scenarios. It also helps to have a checklist of some common assumptions (no fire, strikes, lawsuits, war, competitive breakthrough, etc.). You can also identify hidden assumptions by asking the expert what he or she would like to insure against. One way to verify that the results are now accurate is to ask the expert if he or she would invest personal funds using the probability distribution just encoded.

Probability Encoding Process

After the preceding discussion, it may seem virtually impossible to get a reliable probability distribution. However, the process described below incorporates cures for the common biases. The process has a strong effect—experts usually adjust their answers considerably when it is used and usually in the "right" direction of broader probability distributions. Moreover, we can obtain a high degree of consistency in encoded distributions: points tend to lie along smooth curves, and the degree of repeatability in responses is high. Finally, experts have considerable confidence in the results generated through the process compared with those obtained through other methods. As a result, they typically become strong supporters of the analysis.

The process related here (originally described in the 1972 joint ORSA-TIMS-AIEE national meeting in Atlantic City*† is typically conducted in five stages. While the process may seem long and very detailed, many of the steps take only a few seconds, and the process is natural enough that the details are not obvious.

It is usually best to conduct the encoding in private, so that group pressures do not bias the results. After the initial encoding, however, a group review frequently proves useful in resolving differences and sharing information.

Stage 1: Motivating

The motivating stage establishes the necessary rapport with the subject and explores whether a serious potential for motivational biases exists. After explaining his delegated authority to conduct the interview, the

* Carl S. Spetzler and Carl-Axel S. Staël von Holstein, "Probability Encoding in Decision Analysis," *Management Science*, Vol. 22, No. 3 (November 1975): 340-358. A slightly different version of this article is reprinted in *Readings on the Principles and Applications of Decision Analysis*, ed. R.A. Howard and J.E. Matheson, 2 vols. (Menlo Park, California:Strategic Decisions Group, 1984) 2:601-625.

† Much of the material in this section is drawn from work done with M.W. Merkhofer, "Quantifying Judgmental Uncertainty: Methodology, Experiences, and Insight," *IEEE Transactions on Systems, Man, and Cybernetics*, Vol. SMC-17(Sept.-Oct. 1987):741-752.

encoder explains the decision problem, describes the decision model that has been constructed, and shows how all the uncertain factors will be accounted for in the analysis. This ensures that the subject can clearly focus on the task at hand.

Next, the encoder explains the importance of accurately assessing uncertainty on the quantity and emphasizes that the intent is to measure the expert's knowledge and best judgment—not to predict the value. The importance of emphasizing this distinction depends on how much the encoder detects the possibility of the manager or expert having the biases mentioned above.

Finally, the encoder discusses the expert's personal involvement with the decision and with the variable being encoded to identify any asymmetries in the payoff structure that might encourage the expert to bias his or her estimates high or low. Note-taking by the encoder is useful because it encourages a more balanced presentation of issues.

The conversation covering the motivating stage for encoding product cost for a new product might resemble the following:

As you may know, the VP of marketing has asked us to look into the possibility of developing and marketing the following new product. One of the important considerations in making this decision is product cost, and your boss has asked us to consult you in this area. More specifically, we are looking into the following alternatives for the new product, and here is how product cost fits in to our analysis. [A simplified version of the strategy table and influence diagram can help at this point.] *What we are looking for is an estimate of the uncertainty in what product cost will be over the life of the product; at this point, nobody is asking for predictions or budget commitments. By the way, are you involved in this decision? And are you the right person to supply these estimates?*

Stage 2: Structuring

The structuring stage has two purposes: to structure the variable clearly and to explore how the subject thinks about it. The first step is to precisely define the variable whose uncertainty is to be assessed, using, for example, the clairvoyance test described in Chapter 2. The next step is to explore the possibility of decomposing the variable into more elemental quantities and then to assess those elemental quantities individually. The third step is to elicit and list all assumptions the subject is making in thinking about the variable. To identify hidden assumptions, it is useful to ask the subject what he or she would like to insure against. Finally, the encoder selects an appropriate measuring scale—most importantly one that uses the units most familiar to the expert. (One unit to avoid is a growth rate. Encoding the uncertainty on compound growth rates is difficult, because few people adequately appreciate the effects of compounding over long periods of time. It is better to encode the uncertainty on the actual value of the quantity at the end of the growth period and then calculate the implied growth rate.)

The conversation covering the structuring stage might resemble the following:

The variable we hoped to assess is product variable cost, excluding depreciation, fixed costs, and allocated costs. Is this the way you think of product cost, or are you more familiar with reports of full product cost? How do we factor in things like the possibility of supply interruption or labor difficulties? Do you think in terms of dollars/unit or in terms of raw material/unit; if the latter, from whom should we get raw material costs? What is the best way to think of the evolution of this cost over time: Initial cost declining to some steady state cost? What of inflation?

Stage 3: Conditioning

In the conditioning stage, the expert draws out the expert's relevant knowledge about the uncertain variable. Often, discussion will indicate that the expert is basing his or her judgment on both specific information and general information. Given the problems of the representativeness bias, it may be appropriate to encode probabilities from prior information and to update this prior information with the specific information. (See Chapter 4.) Fortunately, it is usually adequate to educate the expert about the representativeness bias.

The next step is to counteract the anchoring and availability biases, something the encoder can do by eliciting extreme values of the variable from the expert and then asking for scenarios that would explain these outcomes. (At this point, hidden assumptions are often uncovered.) The encoder should also explore for the presence of anchors, such as corporate plans or forecasts.

This step is very important. Working with the subject to explore how extreme scenarios may occur (and perhaps even writing down the reasons why) broadens and unlocks (unbiases) people's thinking in an almost magical way.

Another useful method is to explain or demonstrate what we call the 20/50 rule. In many seminars, we have asked attendees to assign probability distributions to the answers to questions drawn from an almanac. Usually, the specific question is to give a range such that the correct answer has only a 20 percent chance of falling outside that range. In other words, if people correctly perceived their uncertainty about the answer, 20 percent of the time the answers would be expected to fall outside the 10 percent and 90 percent fractiles they defined. Over the 25 years we have been giving this demonstration, we have found that over 50 percent of the answers fall outside this range. People tend to think they know things better than they actually do, and probability distributions tend to be far too narrow.*

---

* Similar experiences are reported in E.C. Capen, "The Difficulty of Assessing Uncertainty," *Journal of Petroleum Technology* (August 1976): 843-850. This article is reprinted in *Readings on the Principles and Applications of Decision Analysis*, ed. R.A. Howard and J.E. Matheson, 2 vols. (Menlo Park, California: Strategic Decisions Group, 1984) 2:591-600.

The conversation covering the conditioning stage might resemble the following:

First, let us deal with the steady state cost, the cost that we get to X years after production starts. Before we get down to serious numbers, we would like to explore the range of possibilities. What is the highest steady state product cost you could imagine? What would need to happen for something like that to occur? Imagine we met in an airport ten years from now and that product cost was 20% higher than even the highest we had estimated; explain to me how this outcome might have happened. How about the lowest steady state cost you could imagine?

Stage 4: Encoding

Having defined the variable, structured it, and established and clarified the information useful for assessing its uncertainty in the first three stages, the encoder quantifies that uncertainty in this stage.

Of the various encoding methods available, we have found a reference method using a probability wheel (Figure 12–1) to be the most effective.

The probability wheel is divided into a blue and an orange sector, the relative sizes of which can be adjusted. To use the wheel, the encoder selects a value for the variable the expert thinks is not too extreme—but not the most likely or central value. The encoder then asks the expert, "Would you rather bet that the variable will be less than this value or that when I spin this wheel the pointer lands in the blue region?" The relative sizes of the blue and orange regions are then adjusted and the question repeated until a setting is found for which the subject is just indifferent. In other

Figure 12–1

Probability Wheel

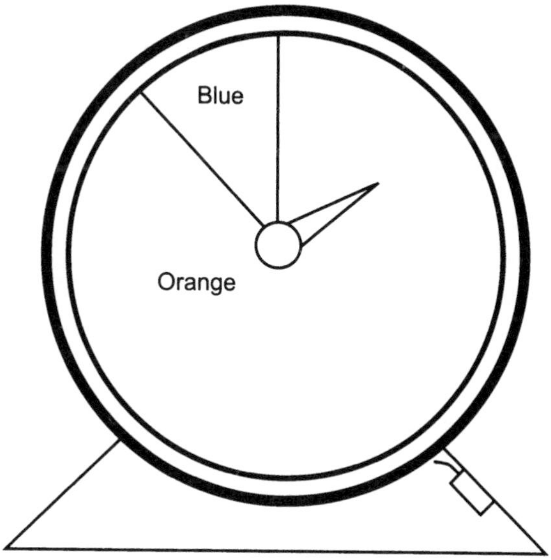

words, the encoder finds the point where the expert believes the probability of the two events (variable less than stated value or pointer landing in blue) are identical. The quick check of reversing the question—"Would you rather bet that the variable would be greater than this value or that the pointer lands in the orange?"—frequently makes the expert rethink the question and adjust the answer. A scale on the back of the wheel gives the probability of the event. This value is then plotted as one point on a cumulative distribution. Repeating this process for different values of the variable leads to a collection of points that may be connected by a smooth curve (Figure 12–2).

In using the probability wheel, the encoder should follow two important rules. First, the encoder must carefully avoid leading the expert to a value the facilitator thinks makes sense or is consistent. A wiser approach is to strive to confound the expert's possible attempts to mislead or impose false consistency in responses by, for example, varying the form of the questions and by skipping back and forth from high to low values so that the expert really has to think about each individual question.

Second, the encoder should plot and number the encoded points out of the expert's view and then look for inconsistencies and odd discontinuities. The encoder should note any changes in the expert's thinking that might be indicated by shifts in the points plotted. Often, he or she will see the curve along which the points lie shift because the subject has suddenly thought of some new piece of information. When this happens, the encoder should discuss the new thought and be prepared to discard all the earlier points if the perspective has been improved.

The conversation covering the encoding stage might resemble the following:

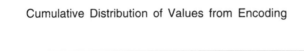

Figure 12–2

Cumulative Distribution of Values from Encoding

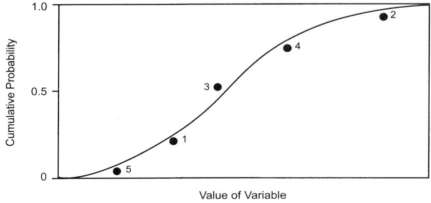

Now it is time to get some specific estimates. What value would you like to put down for a high estimate for steady state product cost. By "high" we mean a value such that there is one chance in ten that the value will be higher, and nine chances in ten that it will be lower. [At this point, it is useful to pull out a probability wheel or similar device to demonstrate what 10% means.] *What value would you like to put down for a low estimate. "Low" means one chance in ten the value will be lower.* [For a full encoding of a probability distribution, many more points would be assessed on the cumulative distribution, probably using the probability wheel.] *Finally, how about a base case value? For "base case" we like a value for which it is equally likely for the true value to turn out to be higher or lower.*

Stage 5: Verification

The last stage of the encoding process is to test the judgments obtained in the encoding stage by explaining the encoded distribution to the subject. It is often useful to convert the cumulative distribution into histogram form and to discuss bimodal shapes or sharp extremes with the expert. To verify the distribution, the encoder can ask whether the expert would willingly invest his or her own money based on the encoded results. The encoder can also form equally likely intervals based on the distribution and see if the expert would have a difficult time choosing which interval to bet on.

The conversation covering the verification stage might resemble the following:

Here are the results we are going to use in the analysis. Does everything look right to you? If you were put in charge of implementing this decision, is there anything else in the product cost area you would be worried about?

Experiences and Insights from Practice

One obvious question is how long the encoding process normally takes. If the encoding session goes smoothly, the process may be completed in as little as half an hour, especially if only 10/50/90 ranges are being encoded. A complete encoding process for a critical uncertainty may require one to three hours. Incidentally, if resources permit, having a second facilitator present at the interview to record the data and to observe will expedite the interview and help in the subsequent review of results.

One point that new facilitators are often skeptical about is whether the probability wheel really works. Furthermore, they worry that the executive or expert will not take seriously questions based on the probability wheel and will not tolerate the exercise for the length of time involved. Our experience is that assuring experts that their superiors have approved and requested their participation in the encoding usually leads to a positive response. In virtually all cases, the expert readily accepts the wheel and adapts quickly to its use.

Probability encoding has gained considerable use by practicing decision facilitators. The process yields results, and experts and facilitators seem to like it.* As with quantitative analysis in general, the real value of probability encoding is determined not so much by whether it does or does not produce the correct bottom line as by the insights and improved clarity it provides decision-makers. And regardless of whether quantitative methods like probability encoding are perfectly accurate, decision-makers must continue to make decisions based on incomplete knowledge. Methods like probability encoding have proven too valuable to be dismissed lightly.

Summary

Obtaining high-quality probability distributions for crucial uncertainties is a vitally important step in every decision analysis. Although common motivational and cognitive biases tend to reduce the quality of a probability assessment, careful attention to the five steps of the assessment process can greatly improve the quality of the assessment.

Problems and Discussion Topics

12.1 Discuss the differences in the processes by which motivational and cognitive biases arise. What implications do these differences have for the methods to overcome them?

12.2 List a bias that commonly arises in an area other than probability assessment. How is the bias recognized and overcome? If it is not overcome, is it because it is not possible to do so or not important enough to do so? Or is it because it is not even recognized?

12.3 You are about to assess the probability distribution on the average growth rate over the next year for the entire energy industry. The expert is a market facilitator who closely follows the stocks of the large oil companies. What biases might you expect to encounter?

12.4 One technique for overcoming several kinds of biases is called the "Rip Van Winkle Technique." To apply it, you would discuss with the subject the highest and lowest possible outcomes of an uncertain variable. You would then say that it is a number of years after the actual outcome of the variable was discovered. The two of you run into each other again. You inform him that the variable turned out to be 10 percent higher than his highest possible estimate years before.

---

* Encoded probabilities have been tracked in the business area. The reported results show that carefully encoded probabilities correspond quite well to the frequencies with which the outcomes actually occur. See the following articles: H.U. Balthasar, R.A.A. Boschi, and M.M. Menke, "Calling the Shots in R&D," *Harvard Business Review* (May–June 1978):151–160; Irwin Kabus, "You Can Bank on Uncertainty," *Harvard Business Review* (May–June 1976): 95–105; and W.E. Sander, "The Validity of Subjective Forecasts by R&D Project Managers," *IEEE Transactions on Engineering Management* (February 1969):35–43.

You ask him to explain how it turned out higher than either of you had thought possible.

Why does this technique work?

12.5 Find a friend to serve as a subject in the following subjective probability experiment. Alternatively, try the experiment on yourself.

a. Tell the subject that a fair coin [$p(\text{head}|S) = .5$; $p(\text{tail}|S) = .5$] will be flipped six times. Assess the subject's cumulative probability distribution on the number of heads that occur in the six flips. Discourage your subject from trying to make any mathematical calculations of the odds. If you ask the questions in the right way, it will be very difficult for him or her to make any such calculations.

b. Now tell your friend that you have three coins (two of which are unfair) with different probability distributions.

1. $p(\text{head}|S) = .25$, $p(\text{tail}|S) = .75$
2. $p(\text{head}|S) = .50$, $p(\text{tail}|S) = .50$
3. $p(\text{head}|S) = .75$, $p(\text{tail}|S) = .25$

Then tell the subject that one of those coins will be randomly selected and flipped six times. Assess his or her subjective cumulative distribution on the total number of heads that result.

c. Calculate the actual distributions for a and b under the given assumptions. Compare these distributions with the assessments from your subject. Also note any difference between the subject's distributions in a and b. What might explain the differences, if any, between the various distributions?

12.6 Break into groups of two or three and encode probability distributions. Role playing by the "expert" and the "facilitator" can help make the exercise more realistic, especially if assumed motivational biases are written down beforehand (but not revealed to the facilitator). The quantity encoded should be a continuous variable for which the uncertainty will be resolved some time after the encoding session. Be sure to spend time describing and structuring the variable and exploring the possibility of biases. You may find it useful to structure a simple influence diagram with the subject before assessing the probability.

Some possible topics for assessment are (make sure the definitions pass the clairvoyance test):

a. The price of a stock two weeks from now

b. The difference in temperature between Stockholm and Rio de Janeiro on a particular day

c. The number of people attending a large undergraduate class on a given day.

12.7 Slippery Company produces, among other things, special types of lubricants for specific mechanical applications. There is one type of lubricant it does not produce. This lubricant is currently produced by several large companies from a feedstock of ethylene. Since ethylene prices are rising along with petroleum prices, the cost to produce this lubricant is rising. (This case is a disguised version of an analysis done in the late 1970s.) Slippery knows that the lubricant can be made from the oil of the "oily bean" at a cost that appears competitive today with the ethylene-based process. Since oily bean oil prices are not rising, Slippery is considering constructing a facility to produce the lubricant from oily bean oil. However, two factors worry Slippery. First, there is a rumor that several other companies are considering the same move, which would saturate the market with cheap lubricant. Second, although oily bean oil prices are fairly constant, droughts make the price jump temporarily every couple of years.

a. Structure the problem and determine your information needs. Be sure to draw an influence diagram.

b. For one of the necessary items of information, designate an expert, motivate the expert, and assess a probability distribution on the item.

Bibliography

The literature on decision analysis is extensive, and there are several quite different areas of investigation discussed in this literature. The following books should help the interested reader delve more deeply into these areas.

Allen, Michael S., *Business Portfolio Management: Valuation, Risk Assessment, and EVA Strategies*, New York: John Wiley & Sons, 2000.

Amran, Martha, and Nalin Kulatilaka, *Real Options: Managing Strategic Investment in an Uncertain World*, Boston: Harvard Business School Press, 1999.

Barabba, Vincent P., *Meeting of the Minds: Creating the Market-Based Enterprise*, Boston: Harvard Business School Press, 1995.

Behn, Robert D., and James W. Vaupel, *Quick Analysis for Busy Decision Makers,* New York: Basic Books, Inc., 1982.

Bodily, S., *Modern Decision Making: A Guide to Modeling with Decision Support Systems,* New York: McGraw-Hill Book Co., 1984.

Brown, Rex V., A. S. Kahn, and C. R. Peterson, *Decision Analysis: An Overview,* New York: Holt, Rinehart, and Winston, 1974.

Bunn, D. W., *Applied Decision Analysis*, New York: McGraw-Hill, 1984.

Clemen, Robert T., *Making Hard Decisions: An Introduction to Decision Analysis*, Duxbury Press, 1996.

Cotovello, Vincent T., and Miley W. Merkhofer, *Risk Assessment Methods: Approaches for Assessing Health and Environmental Risks*, Plenum, 1993.

Golub, Andrew L., *Decision Analysis: An Integrated Approach*, New York: John Wiley & Sons, 1996.

Hammond, John, Ralph L. Keeney, and Howard Raiffa, *Smart Choices: A Practical Guide to Making Better Decisisons*, Boston: Harvard Business School Press, 1998.

Holloway, Charles A., *Decision Making Under Uncertainty: Models and Choices*, Englewood Cliffs, NJ: Prentice-Hall Inc., 1979.

Howard, Ronald A., and James E. Matheson, eds., *Readings on the Principles and Applications of Decision Analysis*, 2 volumes, Menlo Park, California: Strategic Decisions Group, 1984.

Keeney, Ralph L., and Howard Raiffa, *Decisions with Multiple Objectives: Preferences and Value Tradeoffs*, New York, NY: Cambridge University Press, 1993.

Keeney, Ralph L., *Value Focused Thinking: A Path to Creative Decisionmaking*, Boston: Harvard University Press, 1996.

Luenberger, David G., *Investment Science*, Oxford University Press, 1997.

Matheson, David, and James Matheson, *The Smart Organization: Creating Value Through Strategic R&D*, Boston: Harvard Business School Press, 1998.

Merkhofer, M. W., *Decision Science and Social Risk Management,* Boston: Reidel, 1987.

Newendorp, Paul D., *Decision Analysis for Petroleum Exploration*, Planning Press, 1998.

Raiffa, Howard, *Decision Analysis*, McGraw Hill College Division, 1997.

Raiffa, Howard, *Decision Analysis: Introductory Lectures on Choices Under Uncertainty*, New York: Random House, Inc., 1986.

Samson, Danny, *Managerial Decision Analysis,* Homewood, IL: Richard D. Irwin, Inc., 1988.

Schlaifer, Robert, *Analysis of Decisions under Uncertainty*, Melbourne, FL: Robert E. Krieger Publishing Co., Inc., 1978.

Skinner, David C., *Introduction to Decision Analysis*, Probabilistic Press, 1999.

Spurr, William A., and Charles P. Bonini, *Statistical Analysis for Business Decisions*, Homewood, IL: Richard D. Irwin, Inc., 1973.

Thompson, Mark S., *Decision Analysis for Program Evaluation*, Cambridge, MA: Ballinger Publishing Co., 1982.

Tummala, V. M., and Richard C. Henshaw, eds., *Concepts and Applications of Modern Decision Models*, Michigan State University Press, 1976.

von Winterfeldt, Detlov, and Ward Edwards, *Decision Analysis and Behavioral Research*, New York, NY: Cambridge University Press, 1988.

Index

Authors

Peter McNamee

Peter McNamee obtained a Ph.D. in theoretical physics from Stanford University. After ten years of university teaching and physics research, he decided to leave the realm of academia for the practical world of decision analysis. He feels, however, that both vocations have similar purposes: to find the order in seeming chaos and to communicate the insights obtained in the process.

First with SRI International (formerly Stanford Research Institute) and then with Strategic Decisions Group, Peter has worked for companies in many areas, including bidding, energy, consumer goods, oil, telecommunications, chemicals, and insurance.

Peter has lectured on decision analysis both in the United States and abroad. One of his ongoing interests is education, which led to his co-authoring of this book. He feels computer software is essential to making decision analysis more practical. For this reason, he has played a principal role in developing several generations of Supertree software.

Peter is now one of the founders of SmartOrg, a company dedicated to developing systems to help organizations develop superior management decision skills through education and training, and through the development and implementation of advanced decision systems.

John Celona

John Celona has pursued his long-time interest in making difficult decisions and implementing the choice through a number of disciplines and vocations; first with a degree in industrial engineering and engineering management, then as a management consultant for Strategic Decisions Group, then as a lawyer specializing in litigation risk analysis, then as an independent consultant.

Then, things got really interesting as he tried to sit on the other side of the table by being interim CEO of two successive startup companies. This, of course, requires developing and implementing a business strategy for oneself. The first one never got off the ground. The second one is up and running. Meanwhile, John went back to consulting while considering what next.

339

Cmd-shift = remove item from master
Select → Cmd-shift - scales photo content in frame
cmd-shift > makes type bigger
"w" removes + brings backs printer marks

SECOND EDITION

book

no break - select word in Typing, Ctr-T, "no brake"

design

made simple

A step-by-step guide to designing and typesetting
your own book using Adobe® InDesign®

Eyedropper tool - if held down, can chose color theme tool. To remove color theme toolbar press ESC

FIONA RAVEN ♦ GLENNA COLLETT

12 PINES PRESS

VANCOUVER, CANADA ♦ BOSTON, MASSACHUSETTS

Published by 12 Pines Press
Vancouver, Canada
Boston, Massachusetts

E-mail: info@BookDesignMadeSimple.com

www.BookDesignMadeSimple.com

First Printing June 2017
Second Printing January 2020
Printed in the United States of America

ePub conversion by
eBook DesignWorks, June 2017

Library and Archives Canada Cataloguing in Publication

Fiona Raven, author
    Book design made simple : a step-by-step guide to
designing and typesetting your own book using Adobe
InDesign / Fiona Raven, Glenna Collett. — Second edition.

Includes bibliographical references and index.
Issued in print and electronic formats.
ISBN 978-0-9940969-2-0 (softcover)
ISBN 978-0-9940969-1-3 (ebook)

    1. Book design—Handbooks, manuals, etc. 2. Adobe
InDesign (Electronic resource)—Handbooks, manuals, etc.
I. Collett, Glenna, 1950–, author. II. Title.

Z246.R28 2017   686.2'252   C2017-900572-3
                                      C2017-900573-1

Library of Congress Control Number 2017900747

Editing by Joanna Eng
Book design by Fiona Raven
Proofreading by Dania Sheldon
Indexing by Katherine Stimson
Cover photograph by kertlis / iStock

The text in otherwise uncredited sample page designs is from either the first draft of this book or *Alice in Wonderland* by Lewis Carroll.

To my mentor, Richard Bartlett ~

the first person to have faith in me as a designer.

~ Glenna

◆ ◆ ◆

To my mum ~

the first self-publisher I ever knew,
who took a flyer on an inexperienced book designer
and launched my passion for book design.

Thanks, Mum! This one's for you.

~ Fiona

◆ ◆ ◆

And to YOU, our readers,
for inspiring us to write this book!

We hope you'll be equally inspired
to make your own book look its best.

~ Glenna & Fiona

Acknowledgments

In this second edition, we still owe a lot to many people for their help, encouragement, and advice.

We are especially indebted to our reviewers. They have encouraged us tremendously while proposing improvements for this edition.

We are also very much indebted to our readers. Some of you have corresponded with us, asking questions and pointing out topics that needed addressing. This has led to some interesting blog posts, and even to the development of our YouTube channel.

The enormous and excellent contribution of our original production team has stood us in good stead for this edition. We would like to thank them again: Joanna Eng, copy editor; Dania Sheldon, proofreader; and Katherine Stimson, indexer.

Our ebook conversion provider, Mark D'Antoni of eBook DesignWorks, has done a heroic job of converting our second edition to a fixed layout ebook. Thank you, Mark!

We would also like to acknowledge the boost we received simply by being members of various independent publishers' groups: the Independent Book Publishers Association (IBPA), the Independent Publishers of New England (IPNE), and the Association of Publishers for Special Sales (APSS). They have provided knowledge, networking, and industry discounts, and we encourage all of you aspiring publishers to consider joining these groups or similar ones in your area.

We are grateful for the continued support and encouragement of our husbands and families, too, of course.

We couldn't have done it without all of you!

Contents

Introduction

You've found your way to this book, so chances are good that you're a self-publishing author or a small publisher wanting to design and typeset your own book. This book is written specifically for *you*! Welcome!

Self-publishing a book involves a huge learning curve. So do designing and typesetting a book, but now you have *Book Design Made Simple* to guide you through every step of the production process. Think of this book as having two experienced book designers looking over your shoulder, offering suggestions and tips throughout the process. We've got your back!

We're assuming you've never used InDesign before, nor any other page layout software. Most likely you've written your book in Word and now want it to look professional and to compete with other books in the marketplace.

We'll explain how to lease InDesign and how you can expect it to differ from Word in **Part I: Getting Started**. You'll also get a guided tour of InDesign, and step-by-step instructions on how to set up your pages.

In **Part II: Creating Your Styles**, we'll explain what styles are for and why you need them, and lead you step by step through creating them for your book.

In **Part III: Formatting Your Pages**, you'll apply the styles you've created to all the text in your book. And by the end of this section, you'll have created a professional page design. If you're satisfied with the look of your pages, then you can skip the next part and head straight into adding images and/or typesetting your text.

At this stage, however, you may want to customize the design of your pages to suit your material. Perhaps you'd prefer a modern rather than traditional look for your pages, or a funky chapter opening page to suit your genre. In **Part IV: Designing Your Pages**, you'll find lots of design ideas and suggestions for your chapter opening pages, headings, page numbers, and every other element in your text. Have fun adding your own special touches! You'll also learn what to put in your book's front matter and back matter, and how to organize and design it, from title page to index.

Please don't think you'll need to read this entire book. Simply use the sections that'll help you design *your* book and feel free to skip the rest.

Adobe is constantly updating InDesign. So from time to time you may discover a new feature or find a process that works a little differently from what is described in this book. We keep up with the relevant changes and post articles on our blog at BookDesignMadeSimple.com/blog. We also post videos to demonstrate methods when words aren't quite enough, at BookDesignMadeSimple.com/videos.

In **Part V: Adding Shapes & Color**, you'll learn how to create shapes and add colors to them. You might find that you need a shape to place in the background behind your sidebars or chapter numbers. And perhaps you'll decide to use color in your print book or, if not, in your ebook edition.

In **Part VI: Adding Images**, you'll learn how to add images to your pages, vary their size and placement, add captions, and optimize the images so they print looking their best. You'll also learn an easy way to keep your images organized on the computer. And if you don't have images inside your book, just skip this part.

Part VII: Typesetting is a chapter you won't want to skip. Here we explain how to polish your text so that it looks professionally typeset and flawless from start to finish.

Part VIII: Designing Your Cover guides you through the process of making your cover work in the marketplace to sell your book. You'll learn about using a cover image, choosing colors, finding a good arrangement for your title type, and combining all of that into a coherent unit. You'll also find out how to best use the space on your back cover and the flaps of your dust jacket—what elements to put there and how to arrange them for the greatest impact.

 For the most part, ebooks can accommodate anything that goes into a print book, but there are exceptions, and they are noted with this symbol.

And, finally, in **Part IX: Preparing to Publish**, you'll obtain ISBNs and a barcode, and create a high-resolution PDF of your pages and cover to upload to your printer. In this part you'll learn about converting to ebooks, too.

Be sure to use the **Glossary** and **Index** at the back of this book to find what you're looking for. And note the list of InDesign Keyboard Shortcuts and the Self-Publishing Process chart. Please feel free to contact us at info@BookDesignMadeSimple.com if something in this book isn't clear. We're always looking for ways to make *Book Design Made Simple* the best it can possibly be for our readers.

All the best in designing success, and have fun!

Fiona and Glenna

Part I: Getting Started

1

From Word to InDesign

You will soon discover that designing a book is nothing like writing a book, for you'll be more concerned with the way the words look than what they say. In general, InDesign cannot be thought of as any kind of word processing program. It is more like a drawing program in which you make shapes and then pour text into the shapes. And once you've done that, you can control every little thing about the type: the size, the amount of space between lines and between letters, the number of lines on a page, and so on.

If you wrote your book in a program other than Word, don't worry. See instructions on page 44.

Most likely you've written your book in Microsoft Word, and are familiar with how Word works. In Word, you begin at the top of your document and work downward in a linear fashion. Pre-made styles are available for titles and paragraphs, and are applied simply by selecting them.

InDesign allows you much more control over the different elements in your book, both on a large scale (for example, the overall size of your pages), right down to a very small scale (such as the amount of space surrounding a single letter).

How are the decisions you make carried out globally in your book? Well, that's where InDesign really shines!

Any large-scale changes (such as changes to your trim size or margins) are made on a master page that controls all other pages. When you make a large-scale change on a master page, all other pages in your book will change too.

For smaller-level changes, InDesign has a system of styles, including paragraph styles, character styles, object styles, table of contents styles, and so on. Each style includes detailed specifications for the appearance of one element.

Paragraph styles, for example, control the way your paragraphs look, similar to the way styles in Word work. You'll create a unique paragraph style for each different type of paragraph (main narrative, quotes, extracts, and so on), and apply one of those styles to every paragraph in your book. Then, if you subsequently make a change to a paragraph style, it'll globally change every paragraph with that style applied to it.

So *everything* in InDesign is explicitly controlled, not just the visible elements, but even the white space between paragraphs, words, and characters. InDesign works on several levels simultaneously, from the grand to the miniscule.

InDesign also allows you to place photos or drawings anywhere you like at any size—not just inside the margins, as in Word. You can tell the program to run type around the images, too, as you've seen in many print publications. You can run type vertically, at any other angle, or even on a curve if you want to, because InDesign incorporates many features that a drawing program would have. Using this great, comprehensive program, you can make an infinite variety of shapes and fill them with colors or images.

Don't worry; it's not difficult, it's just different! As you progress through *Book Design Made Simple*, you'll be guided through setting up the styles you need for *your* book—from the title page through the index—and applying them to the appropriate text or shapes. Then you'll be sure that everything in your book is consistent and can be changed quickly and easily if needed.

We truly hope that you find enjoyment and satisfaction in making the transition from writer to designer. By the time you finish the next two chapters of this book, you will have Adobe InDesign, Adobe Photoshop, and Adobe Acrobat on your computer. InDesign is the most popular design software in the graphics and publishing fields. Combining InDesign with the other two programs, you will have everything you'll need to complete your book project and get it off to the printer and your ebook conversion provider. And then when you're finished, you can remove the programs from your computer and end your lease agreement.

Let's get started!

Windows vs. Mac

InDesign works exactly the same way whether you are using Windows or a Mac operating system. The only difference is in the names of a few of the keyboard keys:

Windows uses **Control (Ctrl)**, **Alt (Alt)**, **Shift**, and **Enter**

Mac uses **Command (Cmd)**, **Option (Opt)**, **Shift,** and **Return**

In this book, the Windows and Mac abbreviations are combined for brevity. So rather than saying:

> Press Control+Shift+S in Windows and
> press Command+Shift+S on a Mac to "save as"

you'll see:

> Press Ctrl/Cmd+Shift+S to "save as"

The numerous screenshots in this book were taken from both PC and Macintosh computers. They look so similar that most of the time we don't mention it, but when there is a difference, we show both.

Leasing InDesign

InDesign is created by Adobe and is available on their website at adobe.com. Adobe software is available to lease by the month, and you can either lease individual apps (say, InDesign, Acrobat, and/or Photoshop), or simply lease their Creative Cloud package, which includes all their apps (recommended, as it also includes typefaces and off-site storage).

Although it costs a bit more per month to lease the Creative Cloud package, you'll probably find that Creative Cloud (CC) provides everything you need without your having to go out and find other programs, typefaces, or storage on your own.

Make sure your computer has the minimum requirements to run Creative Cloud!

You'll definitely need InDesign (for page layout) and Acrobat (for creating PDFs for printing), and you may also need Photoshop (if you have images in your book). You'll also use the typefaces that come with CC (the service is called Typekit), and you may want to use Adobe's site for off-site backup of your working files.

Be aware that leasing the apps means that you will not own them, and you'll need to connect to the Internet in order to download the apps and try different fonts. When you're ready to lease InDesign or the CC package, go to www.adobe.com and click "For Individuals." Then click "Choose a Plan" and find the plan that is right for you (either Single App for InDesign and Acrobat, or All Apps for the CC package.

Another option is a free 7-day trial of InDesign, but it's not recommended for book design as it doesn't include the fonts you will need. And most likely one week is not enough time.

Here are the steps for setting up CC and Typekit on your computer:

1 Click "Buy Now" and approve the license agreement.
2 Provide credit card or other payment information.
3 Download the desktop CC app, which you'll use to install CC.
4 Run the CC setup application. In the CC window that opens (see page 6), click the first button to install apps. Then choose InDesign, Acrobat, and/or Photoshop. Wait while the apps are synced to your computer. The installations take a while, but do not click anywhere else on the screen while you're waiting. If you lose the screen you are

on, click on the CC icon at the top of your screen (Mac) or find the newly created icon on your desktop (Windows), then click Home (see below).

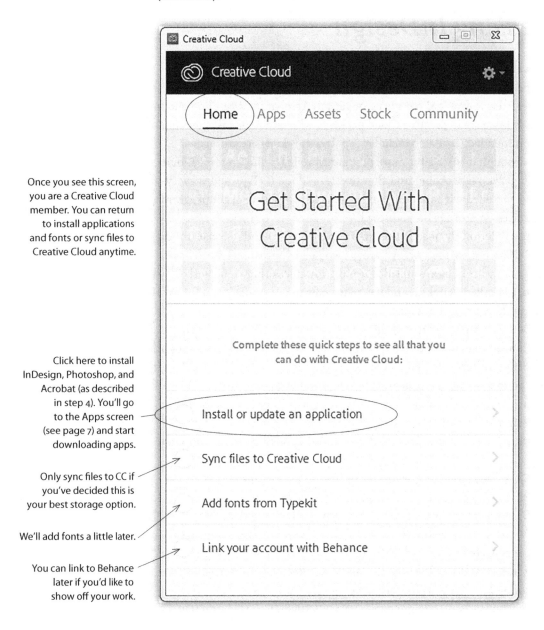

Once you see this screen, you are a Creative Cloud member. You can return to install applications and fonts or sync files to Creative Cloud anytime.

Click here to install InDesign, Photoshop, and Acrobat (as described in step 4). You'll go to the Apps screen (see page 7) and start downloading apps.

Only sync files to CC if you've decided this is your best storage option.

We'll add fonts a little later.

You can link to Behance later if you'd like to show off your work.

5 Once your apps are downloaded, your Apps screen will look similar to the one below. Next explore the CC tabs:

- **Home**: You can install an app, sync files to CC, add fonts from Typekit, and link your account with Behance. The Home screen will later show your activity stream (downloads, updates, and so on).
- **Apps** (see below) lists all the Adobe apps you've installed at the top, and the ones available to you below.

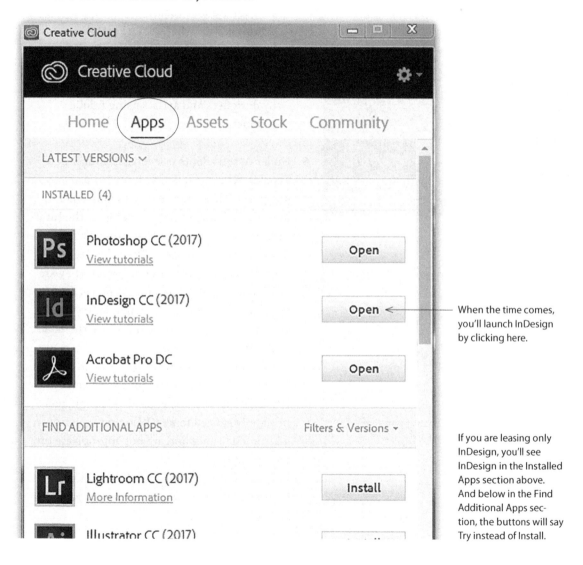

When the time comes, you'll launch InDesign by clicking here.

If you are leasing only InDesign, you'll see InDesign in the Installed Apps section above. And below in the Find Additional Apps section, the buttons will say Try instead of Install.

Creative Cloud app

- **Assets:** Under Files you can sync your files to the cloud and have access to them anywhere. Under Fonts, you'll find Typekit (see step 6). And Market includes content usable by paid CC members, including vectors, icons, patterns, brushes, and more.
- **Stock:** You can purchase images online through Adobe Stock.
- **Community:** Using Adobe Portfolio, you can build a website to showcase your work. Your website will link to your Behance profile. (Behance is an online gallery of work created by designers and artists using Adobe products.)

6 Under Assets>Fonts (see left), is your link to Typekit, where you'll sync fonts for use on your computer. Click Browse Fonts from Typekit, and this will open Adobe Typekit on the Internet. Typekit is a service that provides a number of fonts for CC members. The fonts are not actually *on* your computer, however; they are only synced to it. So any fonts you get from Typekit will no longer be available to you once you uninstall CC; if you want to use them later, you'll need to buy them.

   The fonts you get from Typekit can be used in any Adobe application, plus in Microsoft Office and iWork. For your book design, you need only synced fonts. (Web fonts require an additional license and are not appropriate for your print book.)

   You'll find more information on buying, leasing, and the legal use of fonts on page 132.

7 To sync Typekit fonts to your computer, start by unchecking the "Include web only families" box at the top of your Browse Fonts screen (see below). Now you'll only see font families that are available to sync.

Uncheck this box

8 Typekit's home page will look something like the screen shown below. On the left, Typekit displays a font card for every font that's available to you. On the right are filters you can use to narrow your search results for specific kinds of fonts.

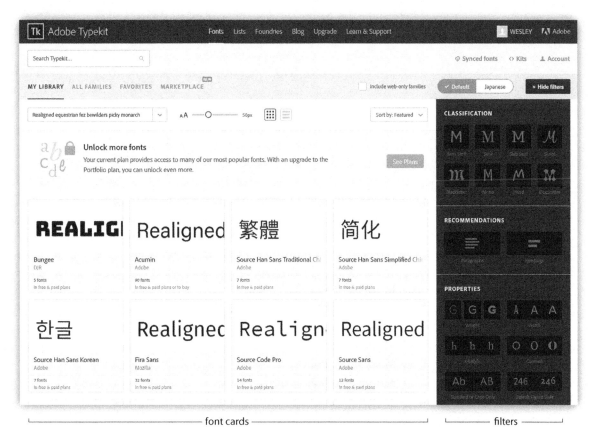

font cards — filters

Open a font by clicking anywhere in a font card. You'll see the whole type family (i.e., regular, italic, bold, etc.), and at the right you'll see whether you can sync that font for free or whether you must purchase it. To sync a font to your computer, simply click Sync, and to purchase one, click the price button.

Skolar Sans Latin Extended Black

Realigned equestrian fez bewilde

Skolar Sans Latin Extended Black Italic

Realigned equestrian fez bewilder

Skolar Sans PE Thin

Realigned equestrian fez bewilders picky m

Skolar Sans PE Thin Italic

Realigned equestrian fez bewilders picky mono

Realigned

Skolar Sans
Rosetta Type Foundry

144 fonts
in paid plans or to buy

font card

9   In *Book Design Made Simple*, you'll be using Minion Pro for your book (at least at first). Type "Minion" in the Search field at the top, then click the Search icon to the right. Click Minion in the search results and the whole font family will appear. Scroll down to see all the fonts that are available, and note that some can be synced and others must be purchased first.

The Minion fonts you'll need for your book can all be synced, so find the following fonts and click Sync for each one:

☐ Minion Pro Regular
☐ Minion Pro Italic
☐ Minion Pro Semibold
☐ Minion Pro Semibold Italic
☐ Minion Pro Bold
☐ Minion Pro Bold Italic

Now you're ready to go!

All the synced fonts will be added to the fonts menu in each Adobe app, alongside all of your already-installed fonts. They will be immediately available in most other programs too, but some (Microsoft Office, for instance) will need to be restarted to add the synced fonts to the menu.

Trying fonts in Typekit

Later on, when you get to the design stage in your book, you can return to Typekit to search for other fonts. To get back there, open your CC app, then click Assets>Fonts>Browse Fonts (step 6 on page 8).

You'll see the filters with the classifications and properties to choose from on the right side of your screen (as shown here). You'll soon understand the classifications and choices, and be able to find what you're looking for quite efficiently.

For example, if you're looking for a suitable typeface for your main narrative, try selecting the filters that are highlighted in the example to the right. As you make your selections, you'll see the available typefaces decrease in number, leaving only font cards that fit your parameters.

Next, click on each font card to check availability and price. Then click the Sync button next to the ones that interest you most.

These filters allow you to search for specific types of fonts. Some of these type classifications and properties are defined in the glossary of this book.

A quick tour of InDesign

Now that you've leased and downloaded InDesign, this chapter will help you get familiar with it and learn the basics:

1 Starting a new document
2 Navigating through your document
3 Learning to use the tools in the Toolbox
4 Using panels
5 Watching the Control panel

Launch InDesign for the first time by double-clicking the program in Creative Cloud under Apps (see page 7). Once it's open, you'll see a screen that looks something like this:

On a Macintosh, this may look different.

Throughout this book, you may see images of screens and dialog boxes that don't look quite like what you're seeing on your own computer, as there are many visual differences between Macintosh OS and Windows. You will find the same information on your screen, but perhaps in a different spot.

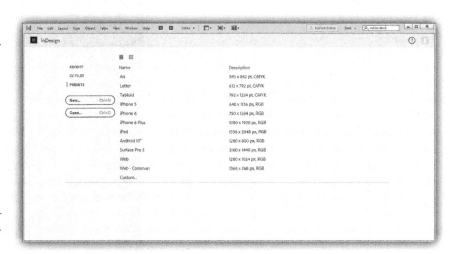

InDesign often changes the look of the opening screen, so don't worry if your screen doesn't look like this. You'll use the menu along the top to get started.

1 Starting a new document

Start a new document by choosing File>New>Document. When the New Document dialog box appears, it will look similar to the one below.

Your measurements might be in millimeters or picas rather than inches. You'll change that later.

In chapter 7 you'll start a new document specifically for *your* book, but for now just make two changes to the dialog box: change the Number of Pages to 3, and check the box next to Facing Pages. This way you'll have a few pages to navigate through in the next example. Then click OK.

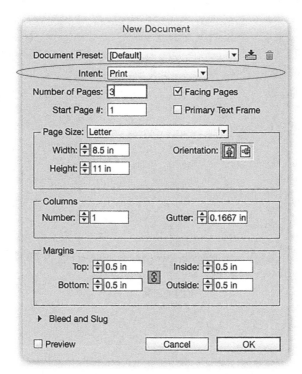

Don't worry if your New Document box doesn't look exactly like this one. It might be darker or have different values in the boxes. Just set the Number of Pages to 3, check the Facing Pages box, click OK, and turn the page to take a tour of InDesign.

One task, many ways to complete it

InDesign provides different ways of completing most tasks. You can use the Control panel across the top, keyboard shortcuts, menus, or various other methods to accomplish the same task. After using the program for a while, you'll find which method works best for you.

For example, to view something larger, you can:
- use the Zoom Tool and click on the page a few times
- drag diagonally over an area with the Zoom Tool
- hold Ctrl/Cmd and press = a few times

Now your screen will look something like this:

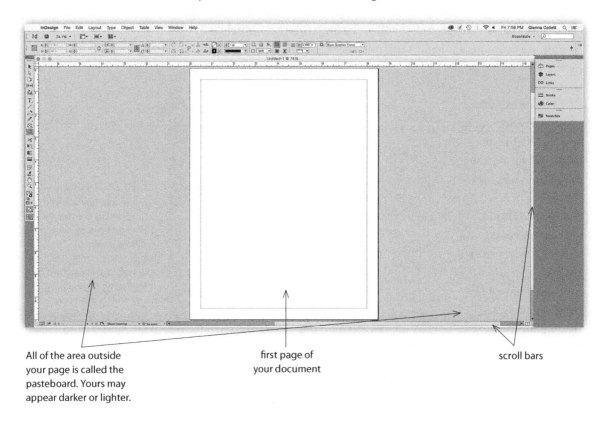

All of the area outside
your page is called the
pasteboard. Yours may
appear darker or lighter.

first page of
your document

scroll bars

2 Navigating through your document

The first page of your document is displayed on the screen. When you
started this document, you checked Facing Pages in the New Document
dialog box, and therefore your pages will be displayed in two-page
spreads, or 2-*up* (except the first page, of course).

There are a few ways of viewing the pages in your document:

When you see a new or
puzzling term, look in the
glossary that begins on
page 470 of this book.

• You can scroll up and down through the pages using the scroll bar on
the right side of your document window, by rolling your mouse wheel
back and forth, or by using the touchpad on your laptop.

- At the bottom left of your screen, you'll see the number 1. Click the downward-facing arrow just to the right and a pop-up menu will show you all the page numbers in your document. Choose any number to go directly to that page. Alternately, you can type Ctrl/Cmd+J and type in the page number you want to jump to, then hit Enter/Return.

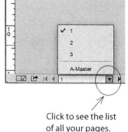

Click to see the list of all your pages.

- Click on the arrows immediately to the left and right of that pop-up menu and you'll proceed to the page before or after the current page, or the first or last page of your document.

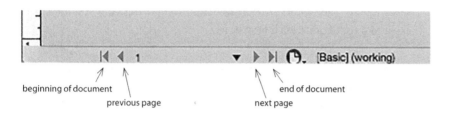

Watch the video "Navigating InDesign" at Book DesignMade Simple.com/videos.

beginning of document

previous page

next page

end of document

- Also in your top menu bar is a drop-down menu that lets you display your pages at different sizes. You may want to see whole pages at a time or zoom in up to 4000% for fine-tuning your text.

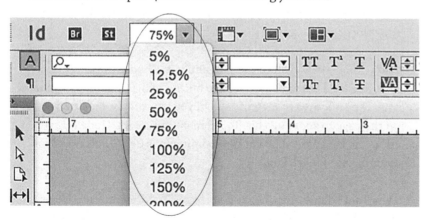

So the top and bottom of your screen have some great tools for navigating through your document.

Selection Tool

Type Tool
(currently
in use)

Hand Tool

Zoom Tool

View Tool

Type W
to toggle
between
Normal and
Preview.

3 Learning to use the tools in the Toolbox

The Toolbox is displayed on the left side of your screen. Each tool in the Toolbox has a different function. Hover over a tool and its function is displayed. When a tool is in use, there's a square behind it. For detailed descriptions of the tools, go to Window>Utilities>Tool Hints.

For now, you'll only be using a few tools:

- **Type Tool** allows you to add text, select text, and make corrections or changes to it. Choose the Type Tool now, and create a text frame by holding down the left mouse button and dragging diagonally down and to the right anywhere on the page. When you release the mouse button, you'll see a cursor flashing. Type something, and you'll have created a text frame with text in it.

- **Selection Tool** allows you to select frames that contain text or images and make adjustments to them. Choose the Selection Tool now, then click on your text frame to select it. Press your up, down, left, and right arrow keys to move it a tiny bit at a time. Press the Delete key to delete it.

- **Hand Tool** allows you to move the page around on your screen. Choose the Hand Tool now, and your mouse pointer will change into a small hand icon. Click anywhere on the page to "grab" the page, then drag the page into any position you choose.

- **Zoom Tool** allows you to zoom in and out. Choose the Zoom Tool now, and hold down the left mouse button while dragging diagonally over a specific area to magnify it. Or, you can simply click anywhere on the page to zoom in a bit. To zoom out, press Alt/Opt while you click. The keyboard shortcut for zooming in is Ctrl/Cmd+ = and for zooming out is Ctrl/Cmd+ -.

- **View Tool** allows you to view your pages in different ways. **Normal** shows all your non-printing guides, such as margins. **Preview** shows your pages without non-printing guides, the way they'll appear in your printed book. Click and hold the View Tool to see the choices.

4 Using panels

Panels provide a quick and easy way to do things in InDesign. Each panel is for a specific group of functions. For example, the Pages panel is for navigating around the pages, the Character panel is for adjusting type characters, and the Paragraph panel is for adjusting paragraphs.

Panels are "docked," or parked, on the right side of your screen, with a few choices on how to display them. Find the drop-down menu for panels at the top right of your screen:

Try several of the menus and see that they each include a different set of default panels. Start with the Typography menu, as it includes all the panels you'll need to get started. You can add other panels later as you need them by clicking the Window menu at the top of your screen, then choosing a panel to open. Once open, simply drag it into the docking area to attach it to the existing dock.

Because panels take up valuable space on your screen, you'll only want to display the panels you're actively using. The panels in your dock just show the name and icon of the panel, to save space. Click on one of the panel icons, and the panel will fly out to the left. Click on a different icon and watch its panel fly out while the first one disappears back into the dock. Notice that the panels are docked in groups of two or three.

Select the double-arrows at the top right of the dock, and the panels will expand to their normal size. However, you'll only see one panel from each group. The others are behind it and are accessed by selecting the tabs along the top of each group or by selecting the appropriate icon.

You may prefer to select the double-arrows again to reduce the panels to just the docked icons. This gives you the maximum screen area to view your document, and you can fly out the panels as you need them.

For designing your book, you'll be using five panels the most: the **Pages**, **Paragraph**, **Paragraph Styles**, **Character**, and **Character Styles** panels.

Do the panels shown below take up too much room on your screen? Simply drag the left edge of them toward the right and they will collapse down to icons.

docked Typography panels

fly-out panel

5 Watching the Control panel

The Control panel across the top of your workspace is loaded with information. Whenever you use the Type Tool, the Control panel displays text mode (top below), and whenever you use the Selection Tool, it displays object mode (bottom below). All of this information is also displayed in your docked panels, so you can choose where to make changes or find information.

Control panel in text mode

Go to Bridge (p. 285) or
Adobe Stock (p. 379)
Current page
view size (p. 15)

View options:
rulers, guides, grids

Current view
mode (p. 16)

Arrange documents in window

Current type fill color
(upper) and outline
color (lower)

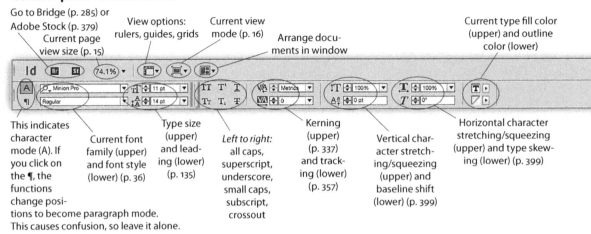

This indicates
character
mode (A). If
you click on
the ¶, the
functions
change positions to become paragraph mode.
This causes confusion, so leave it alone.

Current font
family (upper)
and font style
(lower) (p. 36)

Type size
(upper)
and leading (lower)
(p. 135)

Left to right:
all caps,
superscript,
underscore,
small caps,
subscript,
crossout

Kerning
(upper)
(p. 337)
and tracking (lower)
(p. 357)

Vertical character stretching/squeezing (upper) and
baseline shift
(lower) (p. 399)

Horizontal character
stretching/squeezing
(upper) and type skewing (lower) (p. 399)

Control panel in object mode

Position of
object or cursor in space
relative to the
zero points on
your rulers

Width (upper)
and height
(lower) of
object

Rotate (upper)
or skew (lower)
an object

Rotate 90°
one way or
the other

Select previous object
(upper) or next
object (lower)

Weight (upper)
and style
(lower) of rule
or frame (p. 272)

Apply the most
common text
wrap functions (p. 296)

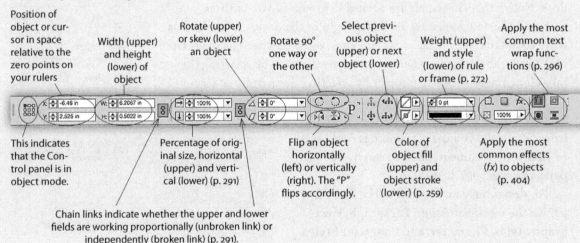

This indicates
that the Control panel is in
object mode.

Percentage of original size, horizontal
(upper) and vertical (lower) (p. 291)

Flip an object
horizontally
(left) or vertically
(right). The "P"
flips accordingly.

Color of
object fill
(upper) and
object stroke
(lower) (p. 259)

Apply the most
common effects
(fx) to objects
(p. 404)

Chain links indicate whether the upper and lower
fields are working proportionally (unbroken link) or
independently (broken link) (p. 291).

In this book, you'll use the panels in your dock for most functions, so don't worry about learning about all the uses for the Control panel. Just be aware that it displays a lot of information, and sometimes you'll find it very handy either to use as a reference or to make a quick change.

Once you're more familiar with the panels in the dock, you'll start to recognize their counterparts in the Control panel.

Publish Online is not covered in this book.

Left indent (upper) and first line indent (lower) (p. 37)

Typography indicates the kinds of panels automatically docked at the right of your screen (p. 17).

Search

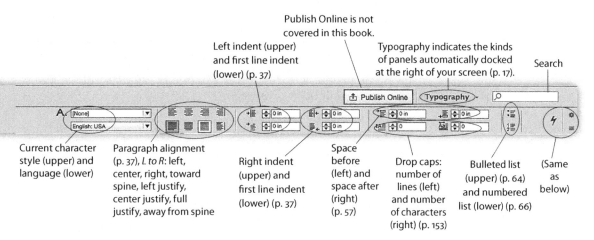

Current character style (upper) and language (lower)

Paragraph alignment (p. 37), *L to R*: left, center, right, toward spine, left justify, center justify, full justify, away from spine

Right indent (upper) and first line indent (lower) (p. 37)

Space before (left) and space after (right) (p. 57)

Drop caps: number of lines (left) and number of characters (right) (p. 153)

Bulleted list (upper) (p. 64) and numbered list (lower) (p. 66)

(Same as below)

Please note that not every icon or function is visible at the same time. Some appear only when you might need them.

Customize the Control panel.

Various ways to fit an image to its frame

Object style (p. 276)

Quick Apply menu

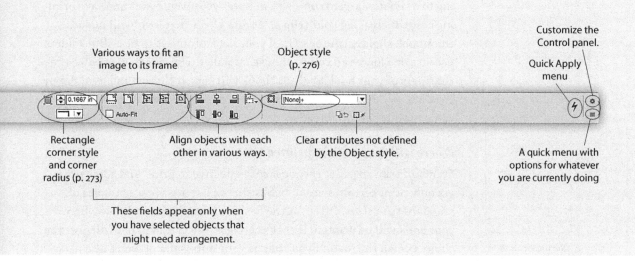

Rectangle corner style and corner radius (p. 273)

Align objects with each other in various ways.

Clear attributes not defined by the Object style.

A quick menu with options for whatever you are currently doing

These fields appear only when you have selected objects that might need arrangement.

5

Choosing your trim size

Trim size is the size of the *pages* of a book, regardless of the type of book cover. A hardcover book will appear larger than a softcover book with the same trim size because the hardcover itself is larger than the pages.

What size should your book be? You'll want to consider three things when choosing your book's trim size:

- What sizes are other books in the same genre?
- Do you want a thinner or thicker book?
- Where will your book be printed?

What sizes are other books in the same genre?

Your book should fit in perfectly with other books in the same genre. Browse your bookstore or library and see what sizes the other books are.

Do you want a thinner or thicker book?

If you have a lot of text and want to keep your printing costs down, moving to a slightly larger trim size can lower your page count and save printing costs. Increasing your trim size from 5″ × 8″ to 6″ × 9″ will make a thick book slightly thinner. Or, if your book promises to be a slim volume because of a low word count, choose a smaller trim size to maximize the thickness of your book. A 5″ × 8″ book will appear thicker and less "floppy" than a 6″ × 9″ book with the same word count and give more perceived value to your potential reader.

Where will your book be printed?

Standard trim sizes are the most cost-effective to print, and some printers only print certain sizes of books. To the left are some examples of standard trim sizes. Often, at the design stage, you won't know where your book will be printed. If that's the case, select a size that will give you choices down the road. If you change your mind later, it won't be a disaster. Chapter 19 offers instructions on how to change your trim size.

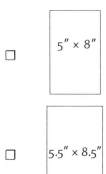

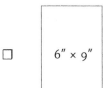

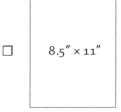

the most common standard trim sizes

Printers' specifications for trim sizes

Printers offer standard trim sizes for cost-effective printing. Below are standard trim sizes from a sampling of printers, just to get you started. This is only a small sampling, so if you have a printer in mind, don't hesitate to contact them directly and ask what book sizes they print. Also, keep in mind that printers' specifications change from time to time, so be sure to double-check these specs when you're ready to begin your book design. See page 22 for an explanation of the different printing methods.

	5″ × 8″	5.5″ × 8.5″	6″ × 9″	7″ × 10″	8.5″ × 11″
Digital printers (for short-run printing)					
Blitzprint blitzprint.com	•	•	•		•
Bookmasters btpubservices.com		•	•	•	•
Bookmobile bookmobile.com	•	•	•		•
DeHART's deharts.com	•	•	•		•
Gorham Printing gorhamprinting.com		•	•		
King Printing kingprinting.com		•	•	•	•
Printorium printoriumbookworks.islandblue.com	•	•	•	•	•
Print-on-demand printers					
Amazon Kindle Direct Publishing kdp.amazon.com	•	•	•	•	•
IngramSpark ingramspark.com	•	•	•	•	•
Lightning Source lightningsource.com	•	•	•	•	•
Traditional printers (offset press)					
Friesens friesens.com	•	•	•	•	•
McNaughton & Gunn mcnaughton-gunn.com		•	•		•
Puritan Capital puritanpress.com	•	•	•		
Sheridan sheridanbooks.com		•	•	•	•

Two methods of printing

	Traditional offset printing	Digital printing
Method	Books have traditionally been printed on a printing press using ink. A full-color book cover is printed with four ink colors (cyan, magenta, yellow, and black, or CMYK). The pages are printed with black ink or CMYK colors on large sheets of paper, which are then folded into signatures (see page 321). Sheet-fed presses use 32-page signatures and are better for printing photographs and color; web presses use 48-page signatures and are more cost-effective for printing text and line art (black line drawings with no grays).	Digital printing technology allows books to be printed on high-quality laser and inkjet printers. The term **short-run printing** refers to digitally printing a small volume of books (say 20 to 1,000). Print-on-demand (POD) refers to printers that use digital printing to print and ship books after they are ordered (often one at a time). A different digital technology is used for long runs. The quality of digital printing varies widely because of the different technologies, ranging from not-so-great (cheaper) to excellent (more expensive).
Cost comparison	Offset printing is very cost-effective in larger quantities: the more copies printed at a time, the less it costs per book. However, you need to print at least 1,000 copies to make your offset printing cost effective because of the cost of setting up the press.	For a small quantity of books, digital printing will result in a lower total cost. However, digitally printed books are more expensive to produce *per book* than those printed on a press, as there is no cost saving for printing in quantity. Each book costs the same, no matter how many or few are printed.
Quality comparison	Offset printing allows you to control the quality of your book and gives you lots of flexibility. You can work with your printer to choose your book size, type of paper, binding, and many other options, to create a quality book exactly the way you want it. Offset printers offer numerous choices of paper, including environmentally friendly papers with recycled content.	Digital printing offers several choices of trim sizes. Paper choices are somewhat limited, as digital printers require certain types and thicknesses of paper. Text and images can sometimes lack the clarity of offset printing; however, many books look just fine within these limitations, and most readers would not know the difference.
Which is better?	Offset printing is better if you're printing in quantity or if you want to choose a certain trim size or paper for your book. Some publishers use digital printing for advance review copies or to test their market and, if the book does well, switch to a larger print run on a press later.	Digital printing is better if you want smaller quantities and if your book is a standard size. Some publishers have already sold a large print run of books and now just want to print small quantities digitally as needed to keep their book in stock.

Planning your pages

6

Before setting up your pages in InDesign, take a few minutes to figure out what you'll need to include in your book pages. Use this chapter to make two checklists: one of the types of pages you'll include in the front and back matter of your book, and the other of the typographic elements you'll need to use throughout your book.

1 Choosing your front and back matter pages

Books can have several pages before and after the main text. As readers, we expect to find at least some of these pages in every book. A simple book, such as a novel, may only include a title page, copyright page, and dedication page at the front of the book. A nonfiction book may include a title page, copyright page, dedication page, table of contents, foreword, preface, and introduction in the front, and perhaps a glossary and index in the back. The material at the front of the book is called front matter, and the material at the back is called back matter.

On pages 24 and 25 you'll see the typical order of pages. All of the pages in the front and back matter are optional except the title page and copyright page. Odd-numbered pages are on the right-hand side of the book (called recto pages), and even-numbered pages are on the left (called verso pages).

Which types of pages will you need for your front and back matter? And is your book divided into parts or sections? Review the next two pages and make a note of which pages you might include in your book.

In a book, every single page is counted whether a page number is showing or not.

verso pages	recto pages
	half title i
blank ii	title iii
copyright © iv	dedication v
blank vi	contents vii
contents 2 or blank viii	acknowledg- ments ix
blank x	introduction xi
introduction 2 or blank xii	

Front matter (includes some or all of these pages)

☐ **half title** includes just the book title

☑ **title page (mandatory)** includes the book title, subtitle, author's name, and (optional) publisher's company, city, and logo

☑ **copyright page (mandatory)**

☐ **dedication**

☐ **quote or epigraph**

☐ **contents** (table of contents)

☐ **list of illustrations**

☐ **foreword** written by someone other than the author

☐ **preface** written by the author

☐ **acknowledgments** (or they can go at the back of the book)

☐ **introduction**

There are only two pages you *must* include in your front matter: a title page and a copyright page. The title page must go on a recto page, and the copyright page must go on the verso page immediately following the title page (in other words, the copyright page is printed on the back of the title page).

All other pages in the front matter are optional. The usual order of the front matter is shown above. It's customary to begin each new item on a recto page (which may cause a few blank verso pages), or you may choose not to start each new item on a recto page, and that's fine too. You may decide that a Contents requiring two pages looks nicer on a spread. You'll see what suits *your* book when the time comes.

Front matter pages are usually numbered with lowercase roman numerals (i, ii, iii, and so on). It is less common, but still acceptable, to number a whole book consecutively starting with number 1. Page numbers are only added to pages following the Contents and never to blank pages. However, your final page count includes all blank pages.

Main text

☐ **page 1** chapter 1 starts here, on a recto page

Or, if your main text is divided into parts:

☐ **page 1** part 1 heading page
☐ **page 2** blank
☐ **page 3** chapter 1 starts here

verso pages	recto pages
	part one 1

| blank

2 | chapter one

3 |

Back matter (includes some or all of these pages)

☐ **acknowledgments** (if not included at the front of the book)

☐ **appendix(es)** usually listed as Appendix A, B, C, etc., or I, II, III, etc.

☐ **endnotes** numbered, sometimes divided into chapters

☐ **abbreviations**

☐ **glossary**

☐ **bibliography or references**

☐ **index(es)**

last page of text or blank \#	appendix \#

appendix 2 or blank \#	endnotes \#

endnotes 2 or blank \#	index \#

index 2 or blank \#

Including back matter in your book is optional. Most nonfiction books include some back matter, perhaps a glossary, bibliography, or index. The order of pages shown above is customary but not mandatory. It's recommended that the index go last.

Back matter pages are numbered continuously with the main text. If your main text ends on page 138, your back matter will start on page 139.

As a self-publisher, you may want to include a few extra pages at the back of your book to advertise other products and services you offer, list your website and social media links, as well as an "About the Author" page with your bio and photo.

2 **Choosing which typographic elements to include**

heading 1 →

no indents →

Every book is different, and before creating your page design you'll need to know which typographic elements to include in your book design. For example, look carefully at this page. It starts with a heading, followed by a few paragraphs of text. Below are bulleted lists with run-in subheads. A running foot and folio (page number) are at the bottom.

main text → with indent

The treatment of these elements was planned in the design stage to make this book easy for readers to follow. Flip through the pages and you'll easily find where each new part begins, the start of each chapter, the main headings, and so on.

The goal of good book design is to guide readers through your book in an unobtrusive way. Do this by providing clear and consistent treatments for each element.

run-in subhead

The two most common elements in a book, and ones you'll find in your manuscript, are:

- **chapter openings** can be as simple as starting a new page, or can include a number, title, and/or opening quote
- **main text** this is your book's narrative

Your manuscript may also include:

bulleted list →

- **no indents** the first paragraph following any heading, including the chapter title, is not indented. This is traditional, and it does look nice and neat.
- **paragraph separators** extra space between paragraphs, sometimes including an ornament or asterisks (∗ ∗ ∗), to denote the passage of time or a change of subject
- **bulleted lists** any list with bullets, like this one
- **numbered lists** same as bulleted lists except with numbers
- **extracts** lengthy quotations within the main text, usually indented or set in slightly smaller type to set them apart
- **sidebars** text expanding on the main text but set apart from it by a different type treatment or background, like the one opposite

running foot

folio

- **run-in subheads** headings that are on the same line as the text they precede, like this one

- **captions** explanatory notes for text or images
- **chapter numbers** can be spelled out (chapter one), a combination of words and digits (chapter 1), or simply digits (1)
- **chapter titles** can vary in length from one word to a phrase requiring multiple lines
- **opening quotes** a short quote at the beginning of each chapter
- **quote attributions** crediting the author of an opening quote
- **headings** if you have more than one level of heading, separate them into Heading 1, Heading 2, Heading 3, and so on. Heading 1 will be the most prominent heading, and each subsequent level will be less prominent so the reader can follow your hierarchy
- **running heads or feet** a repetitive heading above or below the main text. Often the book title goes on the verso page, and either the chapter title or the author's name goes on the recto page
- **folios** page numbers

Look through your manuscript now and make a note of all the typographic elements you'll need to include in your book design.

sidebar

☑ **main text**
- ☑ text
- ☑ no indents
- ☐ paragraph separators
- ☐ bulleted lists
- ☐ numbered lists
- ☐ extracts
- ☐ sidebars
- ☐ run-in subheads

☐ **images**
- ☐ captions

☐ **chapter openings**
- ☐ chapter numbers
- ☐ chapter titles
- ☐ opening quotes
- ☐ quote attributions

☐ **headings**
- ☐ heading 1
- ☐ heading 2
- ☐ heading 3

☐ **page navigation**
- ☐ running heads or feet
- ☐ folios

Creating your document

Next you'll create a document for the pages of your book. All your book pages will be contained in this one document, so it's important to set it up correctly from the start.

This document will ensure that all your pages have consistent margins and spacing. You'll also create a paragraph style for your main text. This style will define the typeface and settings for your main text and, once applied to your paragraphs, they'll all be consistent.

Start by closing the document you experimented with in chapter 4 by clicking File>Close (there's no need to save this document). Next you'll set up a document for *your* book as described in this chapter, and chances are the settings will be just fine for your whole book. If you want to adjust a few things later on, you'll be able to do so easily. Once your document is set up, you'll be able to change your trim size, margins, or any of your paragraphs quickly, easily, and globally, simply by changing a few settings in your styles.

To create your document, the steps you'll take are:

1 Setting your Preferences
2 Starting a new document
3 Setting your Basic Paragraph style
4 Saving your document

InDesign's Book feature

If your book is going to be long and full of images, consider creating a series of documents, each comprising a section or part, or even a single chapter. You can work on each document separately and in any order, and then when you're nearing completion, you can gather them together into a Book using InDesign's Book feature.

For now, though, set up your document as described in this chapter. If you choose to create separate documents for each section of your book, you'll use this first one as a template for subsequent ones. Read more about the Book feature on our blog at BookDesignMadeSimple .com/using-the-book-feature-in-indesign.

1 Setting your Preferences

InDesign comes with a default set of Preferences. Not all of these are optimal for book design (because InDesign is used for many other kinds of design), so while no documents are open, make a few changes to your Preferences, and these will stay in effect for every document you open.

Choose Edit>Preferences>Interface (Windows) or InDesign>Preferences>Interface (Mac). This is one of the few menus in which Windows and Mac OS differ.

The Interface preferences affect the way the windows look on your screen. A light color theme is used for the screenshots in this book, but you may choose any color theme you like.

Once you get used to working in InDesign, you might want to change some of these settings. They will not affect your design or layout in any way.

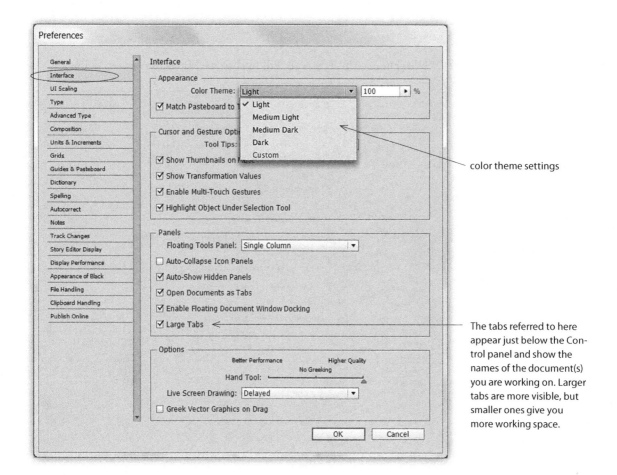

color theme settings

The tabs referred to here appear just below the Control panel and show the names of the document(s) you are working on. Larger tabs are more visible, but smaller ones give you more working space.

Select the UI Scaling tab on the list of Preferences. It deals with scaling the size of the user interface (the size of the type in your panels, for example) on your monitor. In this book we're not concerned with these settings, but if you need to adjust the scaling, feel free to do that.

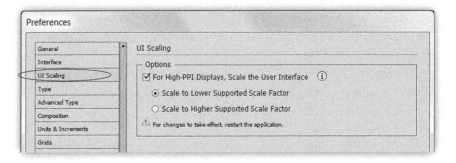

Now choose the Type tab. Fill in the checkboxes as shown below.

Notice this setting. It means that in order to select a single line of type and nothing else above or below it, you will put your cursor in the line of type and then click 3 times.

In order to select a single word, you'll click twice. To select an entire paragraph, you'll click 4 times.

Don't worry—we'll remind you of this again later.

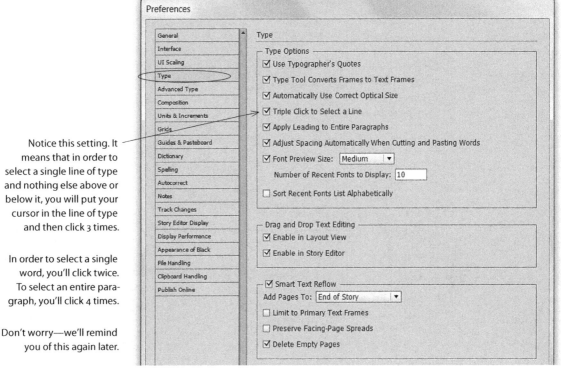

Next you'll check some settings on the Advanced Type tab. Type "67" in the Superscript and Subscript boxes if that is not the default setting, and leave the rest of the dialog box alone.

The Size settings for ^{superscript} and $_{subscript}$ characters determine the percentage of full-size characters that they will be. If they are any less than 60% of full size, they are usually too small to read. Sixty-seven percent is usually a good, readable size.

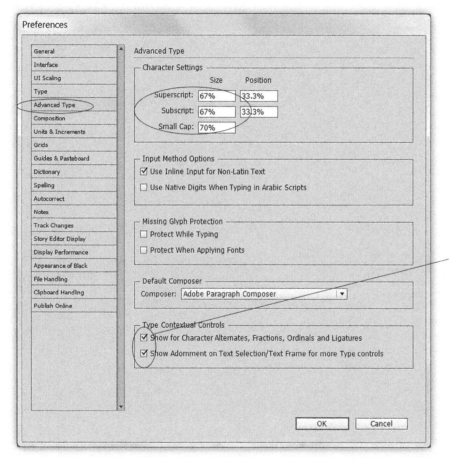

If you check these boxes, a small OpenType "O" icon will pop up near your cursor, offering you alternative characters for the type that is in place. Uncheck the boxes circled here if you're not interested.

You can read more about the Type Contextual Controls at BookDesign MadeSimple.com/adobe-creative-cloud-CC2017.

Next, select the Composition tab on the left and check the boxes as shown below. For now, don't try to understand the meanings of these settings. By the time you've finished with your book design, they will all be perfectly clear. If you're curious, though, the terms are all included in the glossary at the back of this book.

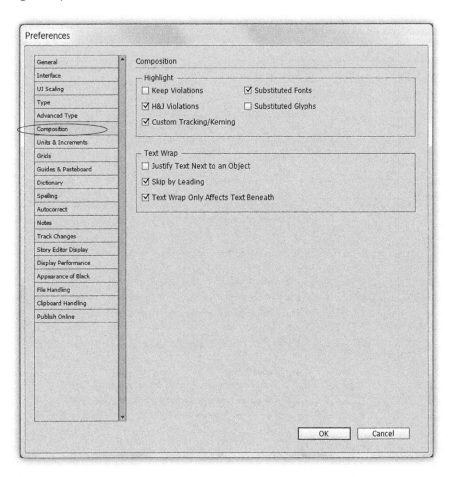

Finally, select the Units & Increments tab on the left, and under Ruler Units, change both Horizontal and Vertical to Inches.

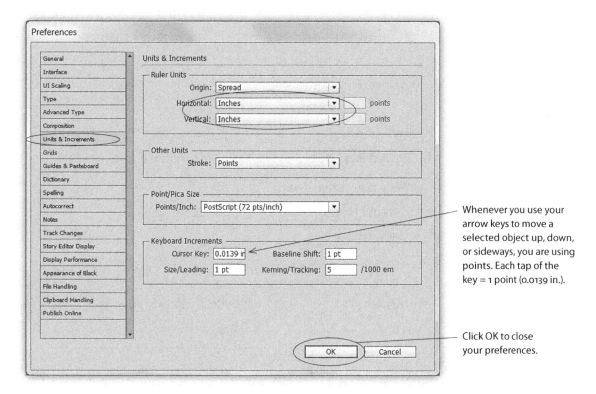

Whenever you use your arrow keys to move a selected object up, down, or sideways, you are using points. Each tap of the key = 1 point (0.0139 in.).

Click OK to close your preferences.

Inches, millimeters, points, or picas?

- Historically, typographers used points and picas (12 points = 1 pica; 72 points or 6 picas = 1 inch. Fonts are based on point sizes, such as 9-point Myriad, used in this sidebar).

- Printers outside North America use millimeters because their paper and book sizes are metric.

- Printers within North America use inches because their paper and book sizes are imperial.

- If your book is set up in inches and goes to a printer that uses metric measurements, it's no problem whatsoever, as long as the trim size is accurate in whatever measurement you've used.

2 Starting a new document

Start a new document by clicking File>New>Document. When the New Document dialog box appears, fill out the dialog box as shown below.

If you already know your book's trim size, feel free to add it into the width and height boxes now. If you're not sure yet, just use the trim size shown, and you can easily change it later on.

The margins shown work well for trim sizes 5″ × 8″, 5.5″ × 8.5″, and 6″ × 9″.

If your book will have a larger trim size, such as 7″ × 10″ or 8.5″ × 11″, use these margins for now. You'll adjust your margins for a larger trim size later on, in chapter 20.

This link should be "broken" to allow all the margins to have different sizes. If, by default, it's not broken, just click once to change it.

If you don't see the Bleed and Slug options at the bottom, click the little triangular button.

New Document

Document Preset: [Custom]	
Intent: Print	
Number of Pages: 3	☑ Facing Pages
Start Page #: 1	☐ Primary Text Frame

Page Size: Letter - Half

Width: 5.5 in   Orientation: 🖼 🖼
Height: 8.5 in

Columns

Number: 1   Gutter: 0.1667 in

Margins

Top: 0.85 in   Inside: 0.75 in
Bottom: 0.75 in   Outside: 0.75 in

Bleed and Slug

	Top	Bottom	Inside	Outside	
Bleed:	0.125 in	0.125 in	0.125 in	0.125 in	🔗
Slug:	0 in	0 in	0 in	0 in	🔗

☐ Preview   Cancel   OK

When you've completed the dialog box, click OK.

3 Setting your Basic Paragraph style

A paragraph style is a group of settings that can be applied to any number of paragraphs to make them all consistent. It specifies the typeface, type size, indents, and any other settings you choose.

The beauty of paragraph styles is that once you've applied them to your text, you can change all the text globally just by changing the paragraph style.

Every InDesign document comes with a default Basic Paragraph style. Open your Paragraph Styles panel and you'll see that your document already includes a paragraph style called Basic Paragraph. The style name is in square brackets because it's a default style and you don't have the option of deleting it. You'll use this style as a basis for all your text and adjust the settings so your type will look great.

Double-click the Basic Paragraph style in your Paragraph Styles panel, and you'll see the Paragraph Style Options dialog box:

Paragraph Styles panel

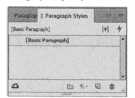

The Basic Paragraph style for *this* book specifies:

• Chaparral type, size 10.5 pt
• leading 14 pt
• left aligned

and so on.

Paragraph Style Options

General
Basic Character Formats
Advanced Character Formats
Indents and Spacing
Tabs
Paragraph Rules
Paragraph Shading
Keep Options
Hyphenation
Justification
Span Columns
Drop Caps and Nested Styles
GREP Style
Bullets and Numbering
Character Color
OpenType Features
Underline Options
Strikethrough Options
Export Tagging

Style Name: [Basic Paragraph]

Location:

General

Based On: [No Paragraph Style]

Next Style: [Same style]

Shortcut:

Style Settings: Reset To Base

[No Paragraph Style] + next: [Same style]

☐ Apply Style to Selection

☐ Preview   Cancel   OK

On the left side of the dialog box are several different categories.

The General category is selected in the example shown here. You needn't worry about all the categories and options. The ones you'll need are explained in this chapter.

General

No need to change any settings in the General category. You'll change these options in future paragraph styles, but the Basic Paragraph style is fine with the defaults.

Basic Character Formats

This is where you'll set the typeface and type size for the main narrative in your book. Select options from the drop-down menus to match what you see below.

The settings shown here are a good starting point for your book. This doesn't mean you're stuck with these settings. You may decide to change them later on, but for now they'll do just fine.

You synced Minion Pro to your computer on page 10. But if you do not see it in your list of available font families, go into the Creative Cloud application and click on Assets>Fonts> Add Fonts from Typekit. Type "Minion Pro" in the Search Typekit box. When you see the fonts displayed, click "+ Use fonts."

Minion is a typeface commonly used for all sorts of books, including fiction and nonfiction. It is easy to read and looks good at both small and large sizes. It includes bold, italics, and small caps, as well as condensed type and special ornaments and figures.

Leading is the space between lines of type. Tracking controls the amount of space between letters.

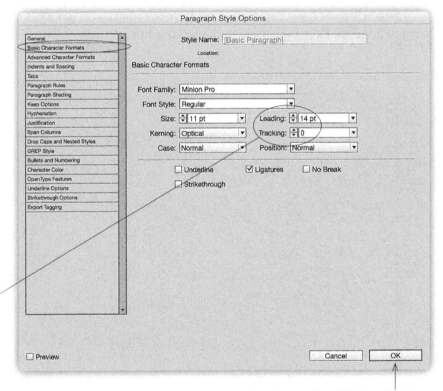

There's no need to click OK until you've made changes in all the tabs in the Paragraph Style Options in this chapter.

Advanced Character Formats

There's no need to change any settings in Advanced Character Formats unless your book is in another language or in a version of English other than U.S. English. If so, select the appropriate language from the drop-down menu.

Indents and Spacing

This category lets you set your indents, as well as spaces before and after paragraphs. The only setting you need to change is the Alignment. Make sure it's set to Left Justify. That way, your text will be left justified (aligned on the left and right, which is standard for books).

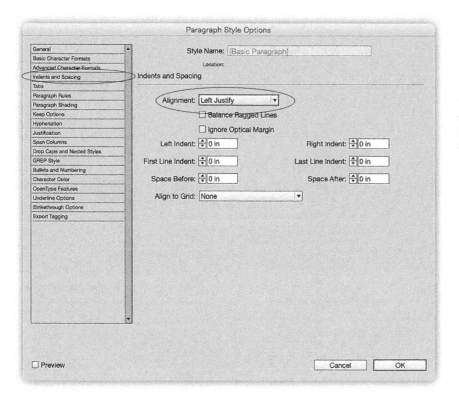

This book is set with unjustified, or ragged right, type. In InDesign, ragged right alignment is called "Left."

Tabs, Paragraph Rules, Paragraph Shading

No need to change any settings in the Tabs, Paragraph Rules, or Paragraph Shading categories.

Keep Options

In book typesetting, it's okay to have the first line of a paragraph be the last line on a page (an orphan) if it's unavoidable. However, it's never okay to have the last line of a paragraph be the first line on a page (a widow). The settings below will ensure that widows never happen.

Orphans are defined differently in various typography books. Some say an orphan is as described here, the first line of a paragraph at the bottom of a page.

Orphans are also defined as the last line of *any* paragraph containing only a very short word or phrase. This leaves a mostly empty linespace between paragraphs.

Generally, any word or line fragments stranded by themselves at the beginning or end of a paragraph are best avoided if possible.

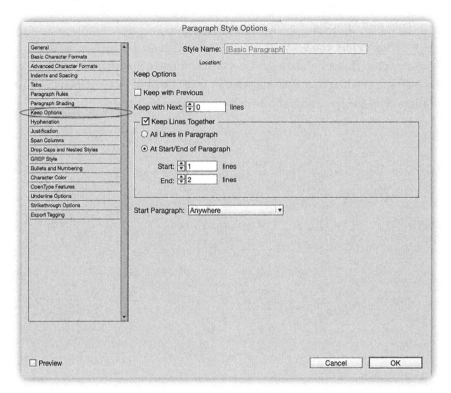

Widows are *never* okay.

A few orphans are okay if kept to a minimum.

Hyphenation

These hyphenation settings are recommended for justified text. They ensure that:

- there aren't too many hyphens in a row
- words don't get broken with just two letters on a line, such as op-era or opi-um
- the last word in a paragraph isn't hyphenated, leaving part of a word alone on the last line

With these settings, you can be confident that most, if not all, of your paragraphs will have even spacing and not too many hyphens.

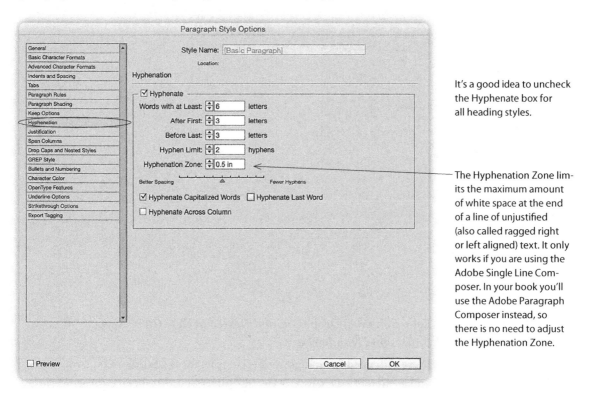

It's a good idea to uncheck the Hyphenate box for all heading styles.

The Hyphenation Zone limits the maximum amount of white space at the end of a line of unjustified (also called ragged right or left aligned) text. It only works if you are using the Adobe Single Line Composer. In your book you'll use the Adobe Paragraph Composer instead, so there is no need to adjust the Hyphenation Zone.

Justification

When text is justified, InDesign must do its best to make your type look as evenly spaced as possible, a difficult task as every line contains a different number of characters. These settings allow InDesign to add or remove space between words (word spacing) and between letters (letter spacing), and even to make the characters slightly wider or narrower (glyph scaling), in order to make your paragraphs look their best.

The Adobe Paragraph Composer adjusts letter spacing and word spacing to achieve the best look for the paragraph as a whole. The Adobe Single Line Composer adjusts spacing for the best look of each line separately.

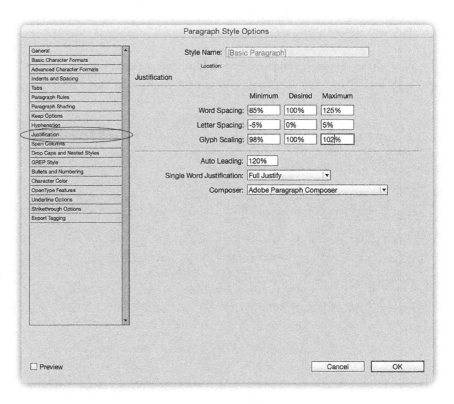

Span Columns, Drop Caps and Nested Styles, GREP Style, Bullets and Numbering

There's no need to change any settings in the Span Columns, Drop Caps and Nested Styles, GREP Style, or Bullets and Numbering categories.

Character Color

This is the color of your text, and it is always set to Black. This is the default color, hence the square brackets. Using the default color ensures that the black color of your text isn't made up of a combination of other colors, so it will print properly with one ink color.

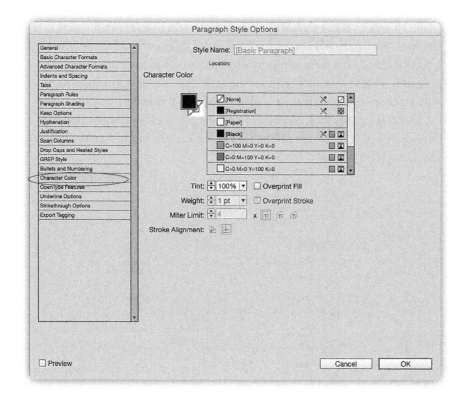

The solid black square (■) signifies the color of the type. The other square (☐) behind it signifies the color of the outline around the type. Since we don't want any outlines around our letters, we make sure that the outline color is None.

You can switch between fill (■) and outline (☐) by clicking on the symbol that's in back to bring it to the front.

You will encounter the fill and outline symbols often when you work with objects and design your cover (see chapter 31).

OpenType Features

Proportional oldstyle:
a1b2c3d4e5f6g7h8i9j10

Proportional lining:
A1B2C3D4E5F6G7H8I9J10

You can choose the way numbers (called figures) are displayed in your book. Oldstyle figures look like this: 1234567890. They are the same size as the lowercase letters in your text. Lining figures look like this: 1234567890. They are the same size as the uppercase or capital letters.

Choose Proportional Oldstyle if your book is a novel or nonfiction book. However, if the numbers in your main text are very important (such as in a math, science, or history book), then choose Proportional Lining instead. The term "proportional" means that the numbers will be spaced so that they look their best visually. For example, the number 8 will get more space than the number 1 because 8 is wider.

Oldstyle figures might be changed to lining figures automatically in an ebook. So if you're producing only an ebook, use proportional lining figures.

Oldstyle figures look nicer than lining figures in regular text because they match in size and therefore aren't emphasized more than the surrounding text.

Later you may choose to create a different style for charts or tables where it's important that the numbers line up in columns. You'll choose Tabular figures in that case (either oldstyle or lining), because Tabular figures are each allocated the same amount of space, so they'll line up properly in columns.

Check Preview.

Underline Options, Strikethrough Options, Export Tagging

No need to change any settings in the Underline Options, Strikethrough Options, or Export Tagging categories.

Once you've set all your options as shown, make sure the Preview box in the bottom left corner is checked, then click OK.

Open your Character panel and you'll see the new settings you created in the Basic Paragraph style. Then open your Paragraph panel and see the new settings there.

Character panel   Paragraph panel

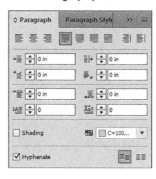

The Basic Paragraph style will be the master or parent style for all the paragraph styles you create for your book in subsequent chapters.

4 Saving your document

Before going any further, be sure to save your document by clicking File>Save As and navigating to an appropriate place to save your document. You may want to name your file with your book title and the date, to keep subsequent versions in order. Here is a sample file name for your document:

BookTitle_Pages_YY-MM-DD.indd

Now you've created an InDesign document for your pages, complete with a Basic Paragraph style for your book. You're ready to add your manuscript!

Placing your manuscript

Now you've set up your document with the appropriate trim size and margins for your book and created a Basic Paragraph style. Your next step is to place your manuscript into the document.

Text is always "placed" into your document in InDesign, rather than copied and pasted. If you copy and paste text from your Word document into InDesign, you risk losing some of the formatting, such as italics. So always *place* your text.

If your Word document includes embedded images, remove the images before placing your manuscript in InDesign. Save a copy of your Word document under a different name (InDesignCopy, for example) and then delete all the images from that copy. That way you'll still have your original manuscript to refer to later when you're placing your images.

The steps you'll take to place your manuscript are:

1 Placing your manuscript in your InDesign document
2 Autoflowing your text to create the pages of your book
3 Saving and backing up your file

InDesign can import files in .doc, .docx, .txt, and .rtf formats. If your book was not written in Word, you will need to convert it to one of these formats before you can proceed.

1 Placing your manuscript into your InDesign document

Open your InDesign document and navigate to page 1. With the Selection Tool, choose File>Place to open the Place dialog box. Browse to find the Word document containing your manuscript. Make sure Show Import Options at the lower left is checked, as shown here, then click Open.

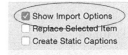

You'll see the Import Options dialog box appear. Check the boxes as shown on page 45, and click OK.

The keyboard shortcut for Place is Ctrl/Cmd+D.

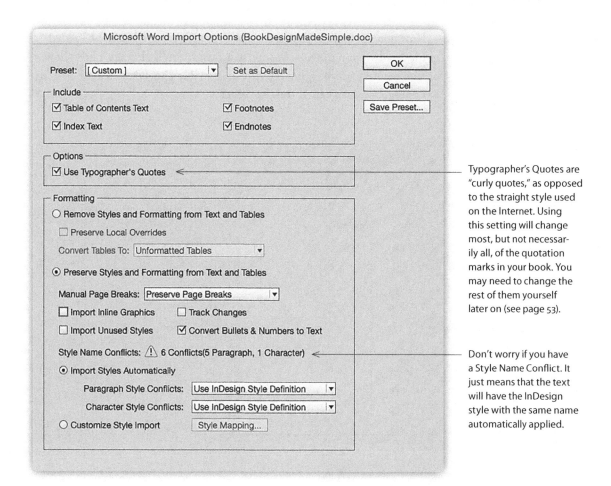

Typographer's Quotes are "curly quotes," as opposed to the straight style used on the Internet. Using this setting will change most, but not necessarily all, of the quotation marks in your book. You may need to change the rest of them yourself later on (see page 53).

Don't worry if you have a Style Name Conflict. It just means that the text will have the InDesign style with the same name automatically applied.

If your word-processing document includes any fonts that aren't available in InDesign, you'll see the Missing Fonts dialog box shown to the right. You'll fix any missing fonts later, so for now just click Close.

Now your pointer will be loaded with text, and you'll see the loaded text icon when you move your mouse around. You'll also see a box showing you where your margins are. The area inside this box is where all your text will go, and it's called the text block.

loaded text icon

margins   text block   outside edges of page

Move your mouse so the loaded text icon is poised at the top left corner of your text block, and then click your left mouse button once. The text will flow onto the page, staying within the margins.

Page 1 will now look something like this:

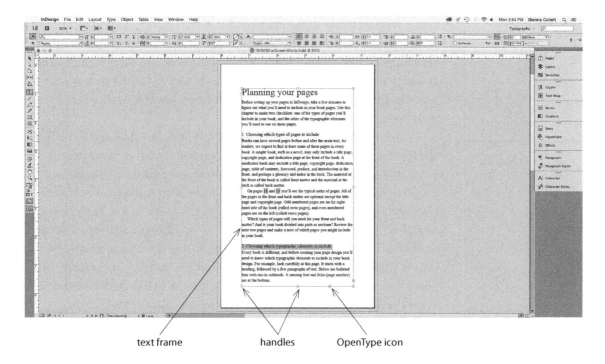

text frame   handles   OpenType icon

You'll see the first page of your manuscript here. When you clicked the loaded text icon inside your margins, InDesign placed your manuscript into the text block. The text is enclosed in a text frame, which has a blue outline, as well as small boxes at each corner and in the center of each side, called handles. You'll also see a small OpenType icon on the bottom of the text frame. Take a moment to check this out. You still have the Selection Tool selected and can see a black arrow wherever you move your mouse. Move the Selection Tool over any of the handles and a small arrow will appear, showing the directions in which you can resize or change the shape of the text frame. Click and drag any of the handles to change the shape of your text frame. Then return the frame back to fit the margins.

You've now placed your manuscript into InDesign. You'll flow your text onto the pages next.

If your margins and text frame aren't visible, change to Normal view using the View Tool (see page 16), or simply press W.

NOTE: If you imported endnotes from your Word document, InDesign will create a text frame containing the endnotes on page 2 of your document.

For now, go to page 2, select the endnotes text frame with your Selection Tool, then drag it onto the pasteboard to the side of page 2.

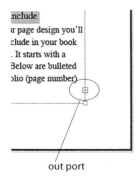

out port

2 Autoflowing your text to create the pages of your book

So far you only have three pages in your book. On the first page is a text frame with your whole manuscript in it.

There's a small red box with a plus sign at the lower right side of the text frame, called the out port. This means there is more text in this text frame than you can see. Your next step is to flow all of the text in your manuscript into your document and see how many pages there are in your book so far.

With the Selection Tool, click on the out port and once again you'll see the loaded text icon. While the loaded text icon is active, you can still navigate to different pages in your document or create new pages.

Go to page 2 of your document, and move your mouse so the loaded text icon is poised at the top left corner of your text frame. Press the Shift key, and notice that the loaded text icon changes. Instead of a text icon, you'll see a curved line with an arrow. This is called autoflow and means that InDesign will create however many pages are necessary to flow all of the text in your manuscript into your InDesign document. Press the Shift key, click the left mouse button, then release both.

Your whole manuscript will flow into your InDesign document. This may take a moment or two. Then open the Pages panel, and see how many pages your book has now.

On rare occasions, a manuscript will stop flowing into InDesign before it gets to the end. If that happens to you, try going back into Word and deleting any page break or extra line spaces before the place where the document stopped flowing. Or you might find a table or image in that spot. Sometimes the problem is caused by some very large type. Simply delete whatever is causing the problem in Word or InDesign and try again.

Pages panel

The Pages panel shows thumbnails of the actual text on each page. At the bottom is the total number of pages, followed by the number of 2-page spreads.

| ◇ Pages | Layers | Swatches | ▶▶ | ▾≡ |

[None]

A-Master

1

2-3

84 Pages in 43 Spreads

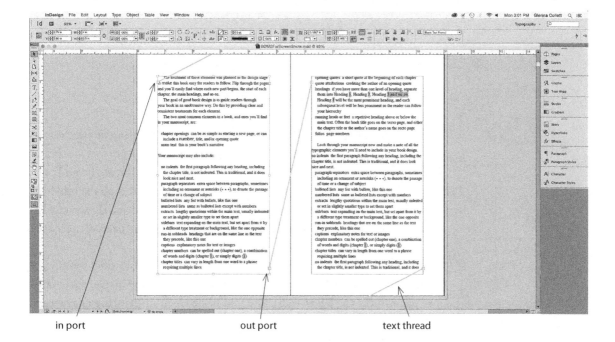

in port   out port   text thread

Notice that each page has a text frame containing text. Each text frame has handles for manipulating the frame, as well as an in port at the top left side and an out port at the bottom right side. If the ports have arrows in them, it means that the text is either continued from the previous page or continues on to the next page. The exceptions are that the very first page won't have an arrow in the in port, and the very last page won't have an arrow in the out port. Those ports will be empty.

Don't worry if your text comes into InDesign looking like a patchwork of typefaces, sizes, and alignments. You'll straighten everything out as you go.

To see how your text frames are linked together, choose View>Extras>Show Text Threads. You won't see these threads until you select a text frame with the Selection Tool. Then you'll see connecting threads between the out ports and in ports.

3 Saving and backing up your file

Now that your book is well underway, be sure to save it under today's date. Also consider saving a copy on a memory stick, external hard drive, or wherever it's convenient for you to keep a backup copy. You may also want to save a copy off site. Adobe Creative Cloud includes backup storage in the Cloud, so that is a good choice for free off-site storage.

Optimizing your text

Manuscripts tend to accumulate a lot of extra non-printing characters, such as tabs, spaces, and end-of-paragraph returns. In a perfect world, your manuscript would have one end-of-paragraph return at the end of each paragraph and one space between words, and paragraphs would be indented using paragraph styles rather than tabs or spaces. However, the odds are excellent that your manuscript isn't completely perfect, at least in the non-printing character department.

First take a look at the non-printing characters in your document by clicking Type>Show Hidden Characters. You must be in the Normal view (see page 16 for the View Tool), and you'll see the non-printing characters in blue.

You'll optimize your text by:

1　Removing extra spaces and end-of-paragraph returns
2　Removing spaces at the beginning and end of paragraphs
3　Removing extra tabs
4　Changing straight quotes to curly quotes
5　Saving your work

1　Removing extra spaces and end-of-paragraph returns

See those tiny blue dots between words? Each tiny dot represents a space. You should only see one dot at a time in your document, never two dots together. Repeat: never two dots together.

Chances are you have dots all over the place. If you're not a regular tab user, you probably used spaces to indent your paragraphs and center your headings. Or you may have used two spaces after periods and colons. There are lots of ways for extra spaces to creep in.

The keyboard shortcut for the Find/Change dialog box is Ctrl/Cmd+F.

Extra spaces are easy to remove using the Find/Change feature in InDesign. Click Edit>Find/Change to display the Find/Change dialog box.

In the Query drop-down menu, choose Multiple Space to Single Space. Click Change All, and all the extra spaces will be eliminated in one step.

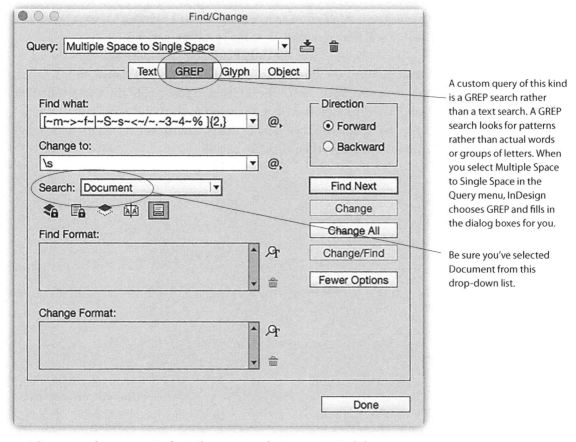

A custom query of this kind is a GREP search rather than a text search. A GREP search looks for patterns rather than actual words or groups of letters. When you select Multiple Space to Single Space in the Query menu, InDesign chooses GREP and fills in the dialog boxes for you.

Be sure you've selected Document from this drop-down list.

If you typed spaces to indent the paragraphs in your Word document, there will still be one space at the beginning of each paragraph. You'll remove these on page 52.

End-of-paragraph returns look like this: ¶. Manuscripts often have two end-of-paragraph returns after each paragraph to create extra space for editing and proofreading. In InDesign, you'll be controlling the amount of space between paragraphs using paragraph styles rather than extra end-of-paragraph returns, so any extras need to be removed.

In the Query drop-down menu, choose Multiple Return to Single Return. Click Change All to remove all extra end-of-paragraph returns.

2 Removing spaces at the beginning and end of paragraphs

Two more useful searches are for spaces stranded at the beginning and ends of a paragraph. If you used spaces to indent paragraphs in your manuscript or left extra spaces at the ends of paragraphs, your previous search will have removed all of the spaces except one.

To remove spaces at the end of paragraphs, choose Remove Trailing Whitespace in the Query drop-down box, and click Change All.

To remove spaces at the beginnings of paragraphs, first select the Text tab, then type ^p followed by one space in the "Find what" box, and type ^p in the "Change to" box. Make sure Document is selected in the Search drop-down menu, then click Change All.

The space that you typed after "^p" is invisible.

The ^p symbol represents the end-of-paragraph return. To type it, first type the caret symbol (^) by pressing Shift+6. Then type the letter P, which can be upper- or lowercase.

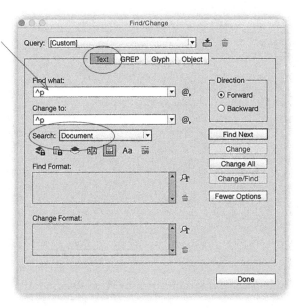

When you're finished with the Find/Change dialog box, click Done or the X (Windows) or button (Mac) at the top to close the box.

3 Removing extra tabs

If you've used tabs to indent the paragraphs in your manuscript, these tabs will need to be removed. But first be aware of whether or not you used tabs elsewhere in your manuscript. Lists and charts also use tabs, and you'll want to keep those tabs intact.

If you used tabs in your manuscript only to indent your paragraphs, first select the Text tab in the Find/Change dialog box, then type ^t in the Find what box, and make sure the Change to box is completely empty by selecting and deleting anything in there. That way, you'll be finding all the tabs and replacing them with nothing (in other words, deleting them). In the Search drop-down menu, choose Document. Then click Change All. InDesign will tell you when the search is completed and how many replacements were made.

If your manuscript includes a number of tabs that you want to keep (in lists and charts, for example), then you'll remove the tabs selectively. Fill in the Find/Change dialog box as described above, but instead of clicking Change All, click Find Next. You'll jump to the first tab and can either click Change to remove it (i.e., change it to nothing) or click Find Next to go to the next tab without making a change. When you've jumped to every tab in the document, a dialog box will appear saying "Search is completed."

When you're finished, click Done to close the Find/Change dialog box, and save your file.

4 Changing straight quotes to curly quotes

If you notice any straight quotation marks (" or ') in your text, find and change them all to typographer's quotes ("" or ''). Select the Text tab, then look in the Query drop-down list and select Straight Double (or Straight Single) to Typographers Quote.

The Query drop-down list in Find/Change might be full of possibilities for you.

5 Saving your work

Always remember to save your document after making substantial changes. Here is a suggested workflow for saving:

1   The first time you save your document each day, click File>Save As (or Ctrl/Cmd+Shift+S) and save a new document with today's date.
2   Every time you complete a substantial change, click File>Save (or Ctrl/Cmd+S) to update your current work in the same file.
3   At the end of each day, save a copy of your latest file onto a memory stick or external hard drive, or upload it to an off-site storage space such as Creative Cloud.

Congratulations on learning how to navigate around InDesign, setting your Preferences and Basic Paragraph style, and placing and optimizing your text!

You're well underway now, and in Part II: Creating Your Styles you'll take another huge step and create all the styles you'll need for your book.

Part II: Creating Your Styles

Creating your paragraph styles

Paragraph styles are an essential component of InDesign. They control every paragraph in your book, that is, every bit of text that finishes with an end-of-paragraph return, including titles, headings, page numbers, and so on. *All* the text in your book will ultimately have a paragraph style applied to it.

What is a paragraph style?

A paragraph style is a group of settings that make a paragraph appear a certain way.

For example, *this* paragraph has the Text style applied to it. The Text style specifies that the type is set in the typeface Chaparral Pro Regular at point size 10.5. It also specifies that the first line of the paragraph is indented 0.2″. The Text style is applied to all of the main narrative in this book, and therefore all the paragraphs with this style applied look the same.

Besides keeping paragraphs looking consistent, using paragraph styles makes it easy to implement global changes to paragraphs. You can change all the text in your main narrative to a different typeface, for example, just by changing that setting in your Text paragraph style. Or you can increase or decrease the type size. Any changes you make to a paragraph style will change *all* the paragraphs in your book with that style applied to them.

Using paragraph styles

There are two steps involved in using paragraph styles: 1) *creating* the styles and 2) *applying* the styles. In this chapter you'll *create* a standard set of paragraph styles for your book, and in chapter 14 you'll *apply* them to your text.

A set of paragraph styles for your book

On page 27 you completed a checklist of all the typographic elements you'll need to include in your book, such as chapter titles, headings, and so on. You'll create a separate paragraph style for each of these elements, using the design specifications provided in this chapter.

You may be satisfied with the way your pages look using these design specifications, or you may decide to make changes to some of your paragraph styles. When the time comes, you'll be able to make changes globally simply by changing the settings in a paragraph style rather than by changing each instance of that element individually. That's the beauty of paragraph styles!

Paragraph styles control more than just text

Besides controlling the way your text looks, paragraph styles also control:

- **white space** you can specify the amount of white space before and after a paragraph
- **rules** you can specify the size, weight, and type of a horizontal line (solid, dotted, dashed, and so on) above and below a paragraph

Creating new paragraph styles down the road

The paragraph styles you'll create in this chapter are for all the main typographic elements in your book. However, you'll need to add a few new styles later on.

Remember that *every* paragraph in your book needs to have a paragraph style applied to it. As you start applying paragraph styles to your text (in chapter 14), you'll find there are instances where you don't yet have a suitable paragraph style for that particular text. Perhaps you need a style with more white space after it, or a new style for, say, footnotes.

In chapter 14 you'll learn some easy ways to create new paragraph styles as needed.

Understanding the paragraph styles family tree

On page 59 you'll see the paragraph styles family tree that you'll be using for *your* book. At the top is the Basic Paragraph style. You've already set up your Basic Paragraph style (on page 35). All of the subsequent paragraph styles you create will be based on your Basic Paragraph style. It's the matriarch in your family of paragraph styles!

Creating subsequent paragraph styles *based on* the Basic Paragraph style sets up a parent-child relationship between the styles. The child inherits all the characteristics of the parent but also has unique characteristics of its own.

For example, look at the paragraph styles in Column A in the flowchart on page 59. The Text style is identical to Basic Paragraph, *except* it includes a first line indent (like this paragraph).

When a change is made to a parent style, that change will in turn be made to its children and to all subsequent generations. If you change the typeface in your Basic Paragraph style, for example, the typeface will change in all styles based on that style and in subsequent generations. The only exception is if that particular setting was modified earlier in one of those styles (say, you previously changed the typeface in the Captions style to Myriad), in which case InDesign will respect that prior change.

Your family of paragraph styles

Take a moment to refer back to page 27 and see the checklist you made of all the typographic elements you'll need for your book. Using that information, check all the paragraph styles you'll need in the paragraph styles family tree on page 59.

Now you can create your paragraph styles using the style settings provided in this chapter. You'll be guided step by step through setting up each style, and by the end of the chapter you'll have a set of styles ready to apply to your text.

Paragraph styles family tree

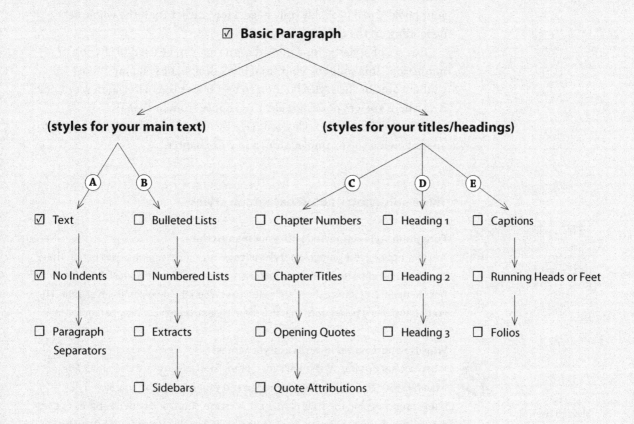

☑ **Basic Paragraph**

(styles for your main text)   **(styles for your titles/headings)**

Ⓐ   Ⓑ   Ⓒ   Ⓓ   Ⓔ

☑ Text   ☐ Bulleted Lists   ☐ Chapter Numbers   ☐ Heading 1   ☐ Captions

☑ No Indents   ☐ Numbered Lists   ☐ Chapter Titles   ☐ Heading 2   ☐ Running Heads or Feet

☐ Paragraph Separators   ☐ Extracts   ☐ Opening Quotes   ☐ Heading 3   ☐ Folios

☐ Sidebars   ☐ Quote Attributions

Ⓐ styles for main narrative

Ⓑ all these styles have indents

Ⓒ styles for chapter opening pages

Ⓓ styles for headings

Ⓔ much smaller type

Above is a family tree of typical styles for a book. Refer back to the list on page 27 and check which of these styles you'll need to create for *your* book. Each style is grouped with other styles requiring similar attributes. That way, a minimum number of changes are required from the parent style to the child, to keep it simple.

Creating the paragraph styles you need

Creating paragraph styles sounds complicated, but it really isn't. Over the next several pages you'll find a set of paragraph styles designed to use for your book. You'll probably only need a few, rather than the whole set, depending on the elements in your book.

This set of styles is for a book design that can be used for fiction or nonfiction. This could be your final book design, or you may choose to change some of the styles later on to better suit the material in *your* book. If so, there are lots of design ideas to choose from in Part IV.

For now, create the styles you need by using the eight steps on page 61 and following the examples shown in this chapter.

Three quick notes about paragraph styles

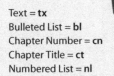

Paragraph styles imported with your manuscript

You may notice a few paragraph styles already in your Paragraph Styles panel. These are styles that imported with your manuscript. Some will have a small download icon next to them. Just ignore these styles for now. When the time comes (in chapter 14), you'll transfer any paragraphs that use these styles over to your new paragraph styles.

Why use abbreviated lowercase style names?

When you set up your styles, you'll use abbreviated lowercase style names. For example, your Text style will be named **tx** and your Paragraph Separator style named **sep**. Keeping the style names in lowercase, short, and with no spaces or commas aids in ebook conversion by keeping the file size down and complying with ebook specifications.

Text = **tx**
Bulleted List = **bl**
Chapter Number = **cn**
Chapter Title = **ct**
Numbered List = **nl**

The new Creative Cloud Library feature

When you create your new styles following the steps in this chapter, you'll notice a checkbox with the option to save each style to a CC Library. If you plan to use more than one device to work on your book design, and/or if you are working on it with a group, then you'll find this dynamic new feature to be useful and should refer to a CC tutorial for information on using it. Otherwise, uncheck this box.

Create a new paragraph style in 8 steps

1 With the Selection Tool, click anywhere outside the text frames to make sure no text or frames are selected.

2 Open the Paragraph Styles panel.

3 Click once on the *parent style* of the style you are creating, to select it.

4 Open the Paragraph Styles fly-out menu by clicking the four horizontal lines at the top right of the panel (see example, above right), then click New Paragraph Style. This will open a New Paragraph Style dialog box with the General category selected on the left. It'll look familiar, as it has the same categories and options you went through in chapter 7.

5 In the General category, type the name of your new paragraph style in the Style Name box.

6 In the Based On box, use the drop-down menu to find the parent style.

7 Using the other tabs in the dialog box, make the appropriate changes to your new style (the things that make it different from its parent style).

8 Click OK, and your new style will appear in the Paragraph Styles panel.

Click here to open the Paragraph Styles fly-out menu.

Check or uncheck this box—it's up to you (see page 60).

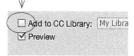

If you happen to be *writing* your book in InDesign, as we did with this book, use the Next box in the General category to indicate which style will normally follow the one you're setting up. (For instance, all heading styles are always followed by the No Indent [**tx1**] style.) That way, when you're typing, the correct style will begin automatically when you start a new paragraph.

If you're not writing your book in InDesign, just ignore the Next box.

Creating the paragraph styles in Column A

Column **A** (see page 59) includes three styles: Text, No Indents, and Paragraph Separators. You'll definitely need the Text and No Indents styles. You'll use the Text style for your main narrative and the No Indents style for paragraphs following a chapter title or heading (such as this paragraph). Whether or not you need the Paragraph Separators style depends on whether there are breaks in the main narrative in your book.

Follow the eight steps listed on page 61 to create all the paragraph styles you need for *your* book. Use the settings shown for each paragraph style, and just skip the ones you don't need.

☑ **Text [tx]**
General:

Changes from the [Basic Paragraph] style:
Indents and Spacing:

Parent = [Basic Paragraph]
Style Name = **tx**
Based On = [Basic Paragraph]

First Line Indent = 0.2 in

☑ **No Indents [tx1]**
General:

Changes from the [Basic Paragraph] style:
None

Parent = [Basic Paragraph]
Style Name = **tx1**
Based On = [Basic Paragraph]

☐ **Paragraph Separators [sep]**
General:

Changes from the No Indent style:
Indents and Spacing:

Parent = **tx1**
Style Name = **sep**
Based On = **tx1**

Alignment = Center
Space Before = 14 pt *or* 0.1944 in
Space After = 14 pt *or* 0.1944 in

from a bottle marked 'poison,' it is almost certain to disagree with you, sooner or later.¶

However, this bottle was *not* marked 'poison,' so Alice ventured to taste it, and finding it very nice, (it had, in fact, a sort of mixed flavour of cherry-tart, custard, pine-apple, roast turkey, toffee, and hot buttered toast,) she very soon finished it off.¶

*　—　*　—　*¶

'What a curious feeling!' said Alice; 'I must be shutting up like a telescope.' And so it was indeed: she was now only ten inches high, and her face brightened up at the thought that she was now the right size for going through the little door into that lovely garden. First, however, she waited for a few minutes to see if she was going to shrink any further: she felt a little nervous about this; 'for it might end, you know,' said Alice to herself, 'in my going out altogether, like a candle. I wonder what I should be like then?' And she tried to fancy what the flame of a candle is like after the candle is blown out, for she could not remember ever having seen such a thing.¶

After a while, finding that nothing more happened, she decided on going into the garden at once; but, alas for poor Alice! when she got to the door, she found she had forgotten the little golden key, and when she went back to the table for it, she found she could not possibly reach it: she could see it quite plainly through the glass, and she tried her best to climb up one of the legs of the table, but it was too slippery; and when she had tired herself out with trying, the poor little thing sat down and cried.¶

'Come, there's no use in crying like that!' said Alice to herself, rather sharply; 'I advise you to leave off this minute!' She generally gave herself very good advice, (though she very seldom followed it), and sometimes she scolded herself so severely as to bring tears into her eyes; and once she remembered trying to box her own ears for having cheated herself in a game of croquet she was playing against herself, for this curious child was very fond of pretending to be two people. 'But it's no use now,' thought poor Alice, 'to pretend to be

tx Text style

sep Paragraph Separator style using three asterisks (Shift+8) with em spaces between them (Ctr/Cmd+Shift+M)

tx1 No Indents style

tx Text style

The Basic Paragraph style is never actually applied to any paragraph in your book. It is simply used as a base for all the other styles.

Creating the paragraph styles in Column B

Column B includes four paragraph styles: Bulleted Lists, Numbered Lists, Extracts, and Sidebars. All of these styles have indentations.

In order to typeset indented paragraphs nicely, it's easiest to create three different paragraph styles for each type of indented paragraph. This is because there is often an extra linespace before and after the indented paragraphs but not always *between* them.

If you have **bulleted lists** in your book, set up the three paragraph styles below for bulleted lists.

☐ **Bulleted Lists, First [bl1]**   Parent = [Basic Paragraph]
General: Style Name = **bl1**
                                                Based On = [Basic Paragraph]

Changes from the [Basic Paragraph] style:
Indents and Spacing: Left Indent = 0.2 in
                                                First Line Indent = −0.15 in
                                                Space Before = 14 pt *or* 0.1944 in
Bullets and Numbering: List Type = Bullets

☐ **Bulleted Lists, Middle [bl2]**   Parent = **bl1**
General: Style Name = **bl2**
                                                Based On = **bl1**

Changes from the Bulleted Lists, First style:
Indents and Spacing: Space Before = 0

☐ **Bulleted Lists, Last [bl3]**   Parent = **bl2**
General: Style Name = **bl3**
                                                Based On = **bl2**

Changes from the Bulleted Lists, Middle style:
Indents and Spacing: Space After = 14 pt *or* 0.1944 in

It may seem onerous to create three paragraph styles for each type of indented paragraph, but it will greatly simplify your typesetting later on. You'll apply the appropriate styles and everything will fall into place.

Geography. London is the capital of Paris, and Paris is the capital of Rome, and Rome—no, *that's* all wrong, I'm certain! I must have been changed for Mabel! I'll try and say "How doth the little—"' and she crossed her hands on her lap as if she were saying lessons, and began to repeat it, but her voice sounded hoarse and strange, and the words did not come the same as they used to do:¶

- 'How doth the little crocodile¶ ←
- Improve his shining tail,¶
- And pour the waters of the Nile¶ ←
- On every golden scale!¶
- 'How cheerfully he seems to grin,¶
- How neatly spread his claws,¶
- And welcome little fishes in¶
- With gently smiling jaws!'¶ ←

'I'm sure those are not the right words,' said poor Alice, and her eyes filled with tears again as she went on, 'I must be Mabel after all, and I shall have to go and live in that poky little house, and have next to no toys to play with, and oh! ever so many lessons to learn! No, I've made up my mind about it; if I'm Mabel, I'll stay down here! It'll be no use their putting their heads down and saying "Come up again, dear!" I shall only look up and say "Who am I then? Tell

bl1 This style sets the amount of space *before* the first item in the list (in this list there is one linespace before the first item).

bl2 This style sets the amount of space *between* the items (in this list there are no linespaces between the items).

bl3 This style sets the amount of space *after* the last item in the list (in this list, there is one line-space after the last item).

Hanging Indents

Bulleted and numbered lists have *hanging indents*. In other words, the whole paragraph is indented from the left, *except* the first line. This is done by giving the whole paragraph a left indent but then giving the first line a negative number for its indent.

Hanging first line indent is −0.2"
Left indent is 0.2"

1. Here is an example of a numbered list. You'll see that the whole paragraph is indented 0.2" on the left.
2. The first line, however, is indented −0.2", causing the whole first line to start flush at the left margin.

Numbered lists are the same as bulleted lists, with two exceptions. First, the hanging indent for the first line is slightly larger in numbered lists, as numbers and periods need more space. Second, the numbering is set up so that each new numbered list begins with the number 1.

If you have **numbered lists** in your book, set up the three paragraph styles below for numbered lists.

☐ **Numbered Lists, First [nl1]**
General:

Parent = [Basic Paragraph]
Style Name = **nl1**
Based On = [Basic Paragraph]

Changes from the [Basic Paragraph] style:
Indents and Spacing:

Left Indent = 0.2 in
First Line Indent = −0.2 in
Space Before = 14 pt *or* 0.1944 in

Bullets and Numbering:

List Type = Numbers
Number = ^#.^t
Mode = Start At 1

^# is code for a digit and ^t is code for a tab.

☐ **Numbered Lists, Middle [nl2]**
General:

Parent = **nl1**
Style Name = **nl2**
Based On = **nl1**

Changes from the Numbered Lists, First style:
Indents and Spacing:
Bullets and Numbering:

Space Before = 0 in
Mode = Continue from Previous Number

☐ **Numbered Lists, Last [nl3]**
General:

Parent = **nl2**
Style Name = **nl3**
Based On = **nl2**

Changes from the Numbered Lists, Middle style:
Indents and Spacing:

Space After = 14 pt *or* 0.1944 in

of Rome, and Rome—no, *that's* all wrong, I'm certain! I must have been changed for Mabel! I'll try and say "How doth the little—"' and she crossed her hands on her lap as if she were saying lessons, and began to repeat it, but her voice sounded hoarse and strange, and the words did not come the same as they used to do:¶

1. » 'How doth the little crocodile¶
2. » Improve his shining tail,¶
3. » And pour the waters of the Nile¶
4. » On every golden scale!¶
5. » 'How cheerfully he seems to grin,¶
6. » How neatly spread his claws,¶
7. » And welcome little fishes in¶
8. » With gently smiling jaws!'¶

'I'm sure those are not the right words,' said poor Alice, and her eyes filled with tears again as she went on, 'I must be Mabel after all, and I shall have to go and live in that poky little house, and have next to no toys to play with, and oh! ever so many lessons to learn! No, I've made up my mind about it: if I'm Mabel, I'll stay down here!

nl1 This style sets the amount of space *before* the first item in the list (in this list there is one linespace before the first item). It also starts the numbering at 1.

nl2 This style sets the amount of space *between* the items (in this list there are no linespaces between the items).

nl3 This style sets the amount of space *after* the last item in the list (in this list, there is one linespace after the last item).

Keyboard shortcuts

You may have noticed the option to create a shortcut in the General section of the Paragraph Styles Options box. Shortcuts can be very handy, and some people prefer them to using the mouse or trackpad to apply styles when typesetting.

To create a shortcut, double-click a paragraph style name in the Paragraph Styles panel to open the Paragraph Styles Options box. In the General section, click your cursor in the Shortcut box, and choose any combination of Control and Shift (Windows), or Command, Option, and Shift

(Mac), plus a number. For example, you might use Shift+1 for your Text style.

To use the shortcut to format your text (see chapter 14 of this book), place your cursor anywhere in a paragraph of text and type the shortcut. The paragraph style will be applied to the paragraph you've chosen.

Read more about keyboard shortcuts at Book DesignMadeSimple.com/indesign-keyboard-shortcuts.

Extracts are longer indented quotations, separated from the main text by indenting and a smaller type size. If you have extracts in your book, set up the four paragraph styles below for extracts.

☐ **Extracts, First [ext1]**
General:

Changes from the [Basic Paragraph] style:
Basic Character Formats:
Indents and Spacing:

Parent = [Basic Paragraph]
Style Name = **ext1**
Based On = [Basic Paragraph]

Size = 10 pt
Left Indent = 0.2 in
Right Indent = 0.2 in
Space Before = 14 pt *or* 0.1944 in

☐ **Extracts, Middle [ext2]**
General:

Changes from the Extracts, First style:
Indents and Spacing:

Parent = **ext1**
Style Name = **ext2**
Based On = **ext1**

First Line Indent = 0.2 in
Space Before = 0

☐ **Extracts, Last [ext3]**
General:

Changes from the Extracts, Middle style:
Indents and Spacing:

Parent = **ext2**
Style Name = **ext3**
Based On = **ext2**

Space After = 14 pt *or* 0.1944 in

☐ **Extracts, Only [ext0]**
General:

Changes from the Extracts, First style:
Indents and Spacing:

Parent = **ext1**
Style Name = **ext0**
Based On = **ext1**

Space After = 14 pt *or* 0.1944 in

measure herself by it, and found that, as nearly as she could guess, she was now about two feet high, and was going on shrinking rapidly: she soon found out that the cause of this was the fan she was holding, and she dropped it hastily, just in time to avoid shrinking away altogether.¶

'That *was* a narrow escape!' said Alice, a good deal frightened at the sudden change, but very glad to find herself still in existence; 'and now for the garden!'¶

As she said these words her foot slipped, and in another moment, splash! she was up to her chin in salt water. Her first idea was that she had somehow fallen into the sea, 'and in that case I can go back by railway,' she said to herself.¶

(Alice had been to the seaside once in her life, and had come to the general conclusion, that wherever you go to on the English coast you find a number of bathing machines in the sea, some children digging in the sand with wooden spades, then a row of lodging houses, and behind them a railway station.)¶

However, she soon made out that she was in the pool of tears which she had wept when she was nine feet high.¶

'I wish I hadn't cried so much!' said Alice, as she swam about, trying to find her way out. 'I shall be punished for it now, I suppose, by being drowned in my own tears! That *will* be a queer thing, to be sure! However, everything is queer to-day.'¶

Just then she heard something splashing about in the pool a little way off, and she swam nearer to make out what it was: at first she thought it must be a walrus or hippopotamus, but then she remembered how small she was now, and she soon made out that it was only a mouse that had slipped in like herself.¶

'Would it be of any use, now,' thought Alice, 'to speak to this mouse? Everything is so out-of-the-way down here, that I should think very likely it can talk: at any rate, there's no harm in trying.'

ext1 This style sets the amount of space *before* the first paragraph in the extract (in this extract there is one linespace before the first paragraph).

ext2 This style sets the amount of space *between* the paragraphs (in this extract there are no linespaces between the paragraphs).

ext3 This style sets the amount of space *after* the last paragraph in the extract (in this extract, there is one linespace after the last paragraph).

ext0 This style sets the amount of space *before* and *after* this single-paragraph extract.

Sidebars are usually set in italics or a different typeface and separated from the main text by indents or by placing them in a separate box. If you have sidebars in your book, set up the four paragraph styles below.

☐ **Sidebars, First [sb1]**
General:

Changes from the [Basic Paragraph] style:
Basic Character Formats:
Indents and Spacing:

Parent = [Basic Paragraph]
Style Name = **sb1**
Based On = [Basic Paragraph]

Font Style = Italic
Left Indent = 0.2 in
Right Indent = 0.2 in
Space Before = 14 pt *or* 0.1944 in

☐ **Sidebars, Middle [sb2]**
General:

Changes from the Sidebars, First style:
Indents and Spacing:

Parent = **sb1**
Style Name = **sb2**
Based On = **sb1**

First Line Indent = 0.2 in
Space Before = 0

☐ **Sidebars, Last [sb3]**
General:

Changes from the Sidebars, Middle style:
Indents and Spacing:

Parent = **sb2**
Style Name = **sb3**
Based On = **sb2**

Space After = 14 pt or 0.1944 in

☐ **Sidebars, Title [sbt]**
General:

Changes from the Sidebars, Middle style:
Basic Character Formats:

Parent = **sb1**
Style Name = **sbt**
Based On = **sb1**

Font Style = Bold

So she began: 'O Mouse, do you know the way out of this pool? I am very tired of swimming about here, O Mouse!' (Alice thought this must be the right way of speaking to a mouse: she had never done such a thing before, but she remembered having seen in her brother's Latin Grammar, 'A mouse—of a mouse—to a mouse—a mouse—O mouse!') The Mouse looked at her rather inquisitively, and seemed to her to wink with one of its little eyes, but it said nothing.¶

Sidebar Example¶

'Perhaps it doesn't understand English,' thought Alice; 'I daresay it's a French mouse, come over with William the Conqueror.'¶

(For, with all her knowledge of history, Alice had no very clear notion how long ago anything had happened.) So she began again: 'Ou est ma chatte?' which was the first sentence in her French lesson-book.¶

The Mouse gave a sudden leap out of the water, and seemed to quiver all over with fright. 'Oh, I beg your pardon!' cried Alice hastily, afraid that she had hurt the poor animal's feelings. 'I quite forgot you didn't like cats.'¶

'Not like cats!' cried the Mouse, in a shrill, passionate voice. 'Would *you* like cats if you were me?'¶

'Well, perhaps not,' said Alice in a soothing tone: 'don't be angry about it. And yet I wish I could show you our cat Dinah: I think you'd take a fancy to cats if you could only see her. She is such a dear quiet thing,' Alice went on, half to herself, as she swam lazily about in the pool, 'and she sits purring so nicely by the fire, licking her paws and washing her face—and she is such a nice soft thing to nurse—and she's such a capital one for catching mice—oh, I beg your pardon!' cried Alice again, for this time the Mouse was bristling all over, and she felt certain it must be really offended. 'We won't talk about her any more if you'd rather not.'¶

sbt This style sets the amount of space *before* the sidebar title.

sb1 This style sets the amount of space *before* the first paragraph in the sidebar (in this sidebar there is one linespace before the first paragraph).

sb2 This style sets the amount of space *between* the paragraphs (in this sidebar there are no spaces between the paragraphs). It also gives the paragraphs a first line indent.

sb3 This style sets the amount of space *after* the last paragraph in the sidebar (in this sidebar, there is one linespace after the last paragraph).

Creating the paragraph styles in Column C

Column C includes all the paragraph styles needed for your chapter opening pages. You may only need **chapter numbers** for your novel, or you may need all four paragraph styles for the chapter opening pages in your nonfiction book. Set up the paragraphs styles you need as shown.

☐ **Chapter Numbers [cn]**

	Parent = [Basic Paragraph]
General:	Style Name = **cn**
	Based On = [Basic Paragraph]

Changes from the [Basic Paragraph] style:

Basic Character Formats:	Size = 14 pt
Indents and Spacing:	Alignment = Center
	Space Before = 28 pt *or* 0.3889 in
	Space After = 56 pt *or* 0.7778 in
	(If your book includes Chapter Titles, set Space After at 28 pt or 0.3889 in instead)
OpenType Features:	Figure Style = Proportional Lining

☐ **Chapter Titles [ct]**

	Parent = [Basic Paragraph]
General:	Style Name = **ct**
	Based On = [Basic Paragraph]

Changes from the [Basic Paragraph] style:

Basic Character Formats:	Size = 14 pt
	Leading = 28 pt
Indents and Spacing:	Alignment = Center
	Space After = 56 pt *or* 0.7778 in
	(If your book includes Opening Quotes, set Space After at 28 pt or 0.3889 in instead)
Hyphenation:	Hyphenate = Unchecked

¶

3¶

A Caucus-Race and a Long Tale¶

They were indeed a queer-looking party that assembled on the bank—the birds with draggled feathers, the animals with their fur clinging close to them, and all dripping wet, cross, and uncomfortable.¶

The first question of course was, how to get dry again: they had a consultation about this, and after a few minutes it seemed quite natural to Alice to find herself talking familiarly with them, as if she had known them all her life. Indeed, she had quite a long argument with the Lory, who at last turned sulky, and would only say, 'I am older than you, and must know better'; and this Alice would not allow without knowing how old it was, and, as the Lory positively refused to tell its age, there was no more to be said.¶

At last the Mouse, who seemed to be a person of authority among them, called out, 'Sit down, all of you, and listen to me! I'LL soon make you dry enough!' They all sat down at once, in a large ring, with the Mouse in the middle. Alice kept her eyes anxiously fixed on it, for she felt sure she would catch a bad cold if she did not get dry very soon.¶

'Ahem!' said the Mouse with an important air, 'are you all ready? This is the driest thing I know. Silence all round, if you please! "William the Conqueror, whose cause was favoured by the pope, was soon submitted to by the English, who wanted leaders, and

tx Text

cn Chapter Numbers style

ct Chapter Titles style

Chapter titles are usually larger than headings, and it's important that the Chapter Titles style works equally well for different lengths of titles. For example, a short title like "Styles" should look just as good in the chapter opening as a longer title like "Impact of Paragraph Styles on Chapter Titles." Most books have a variety of title and heading lengths, some perhaps occupying two lines rather than one.

Chapter opening quotes require two paragraph styles: one for the opening quote itself and the other for the quote author's name (also called the attribution). If your book has opening quotes, then create these two styles. If not, just skip them.

☐ **Opening Quotes [quo]**

General:

Parent = [Basic Paragraph]

Style Name = **quo**

Based On = [Basic Paragraph]

Changes from the [Basic Paragraph] style:

Basic Character Formats:

Font Style = Italic

Indents and Spacing:

Alignment = Center

Left Indent = 0.5 in

Right Indent = 0.5 in

☐ **Quote Attributions [quoattr]**

General:

Parent = **quo**

Style Name = **quoattr**

Based On = **quo**

Changes from the Opening Quotes style:

Basic Character Formats:

Font Style = Regular

Size = 9 pt

Advanced Character Formats:

Baseline Shift = –5 pt

Indents and Spacing:

Space After = 56 pt *or* 0.7778 in

3¶

A Caucus-Race and a Long Tale¶

A book can look good using almost any typeface;¬
it just depends on how the type is set.¶

—Fiona Raven, book designer¶

quo Opening Quotes

quoattr Quote Attributions

They were indeed a queer-looking party that assembled on the bank—the birds with draggled feathers, the animals with their fur clinging close to them, and all dripping wet, cross, and uncomfortable.¶

The first question of course was, how to get dry again: they had a consultation about this, and after a few minutes it seemed quite natural to Alice to find herself talking familiarly with them, as if she had known them all her life. Indeed, she had quite a long argument with the Lory, who at last turned sulky, and would only say, 'I am older than you, and must know better'; and this Alice would not allow without knowing how old it was, and, as the Lory positively refused to tell its age, there was no more to be said.¶

At last the Mouse, who seemed to be a person of authority among them, called out, 'Sit down, all of you, and listen to me! I'LL soon make you dry enough!' They all sat down at once, in a large ring, with the Mouse in the middle. Alice kept her eyes anxiously fixed on it, for she felt sure she would catch a bad cold if she did not get dry very soon. 'Ahem!' said the Mouse with an important air, 'are you all ready? This is the driest thing I know. Silence all round, if

These paragraph styles are for clean and simple chapter opening pages. If you'd like to embellish these styles, or add a feature to the first paragraph such as a drop cap or the first few words in small caps, see chapter 24.

Creating the paragraph styles in Column D

Create the levels of **headings** you need using the styles shown.

☐ **Heading 1 [h1]**   Parent = [Basic Paragraph]
  General: Style Name = **h1**
      Based On = [Basic Paragraph]

  Changes from the [Basic Paragraph] style:
  Basic Character Formats: Size = 14.5 pt
  Indents and Spacing: Alignment = Center
      Space Before = 28 pt *or* 0.3889 in
      Space After = 14 pt *or* 0.1944 in

  Keep Options: Keep with next 2 lines
  Hyphenation: Hyphenate = Unchecked

☐ **Heading 2 [h2]**   Parent = **h1**
  General: Style Name = **h2**
      Based On = **h1**

  Changes from the Heading 1 style:
  Basic Character Formats: Font Style = Semibold
      Size = 12 pt
      Case = OpenType All Small Caps
      Tracking = 50
  Advanced Character Formats: Baseline Shift = 2 pt
  Indents and Spacing: Alignment = Left
      Space Before = 14 pt *or* 0.1944 in
      Space After = 0 in

☐ **Heading 3 [h3]**   Parent = **h2**
  General: Style Name = **h3**
      Based On = **h2**

  Changes from the Heading 2 style:
  Basic Character Formats: Font Style = Semibold Italic
      Size = 11 pt
      Case = Normal
      Tracking = 10

"Edwin and Morcar, the earls of Mercia and Northumbria, declared for him: and even Stigand, the patriotic archbishop of Canterbury, found it advisable—"¶

'Found *what*?' said the Duck¶

'Found *it*,' the Mouse replied rather crossly: 'of course you know what "it" means.¶

In books where bolder headings are required, often the headings are set in a different typeface from the main text. You can experiment with alternate typefaces later (chapter 25).

Heading 1 Sample¶

h1 Heading 1 style

'I know what "it" means well enough, when I find a thing,' said the Duck: 'it's generally a frog or a worm. The question is, what did the archbishop find?'¶

The Mouse did not notice this question, but hurriedly went on, '—found it advisable to go with Edgar Atheling to meet William and offer him the crown. William's conduct at first was moderate. But the insolence of his Normans—" How are you getting on now, my dear?' it continued, turning to Alice as it spoke¶

HEADING 2 SAMPLE¶

h2 Heading 2 style

'As wet as ever,' said Alice in a melancholy tone: 'it doesn't seem to dry me at all.'¶

'In that case,' said the Dodo solemnly, rising to its feet, 'I move that the meeting adjourn, for the immediate adoption of more energetic remedies—'¶

Heading 3 Sample¶

h3 Heading 3 style

'Speak English!' said the Eaglet. 'I don't know the meaning of half those long words, and, what's more, I don't believe you do either!' And the Eaglet bent down its head to hide a smile: some of the other birds tittered audibly¶

'What I was going to say,' said the Dodo in an offended tone, 'was, that the best thing to get us dry would be a Caucus-race.'¶

'What IS a Caucus-race?' said Alice; not that she wanted much to know, but the Dodo had paused as if it thought that somebody

Most nonfiction books have three levels of headings at most, as any more tend to confuse the reader.

Creating the paragraph styles in Column E

The **Captions**, **Running Heads or Feet**, and **Folios** paragraph styles all use type in sizes quite a bit smaller than the main text. Create the styles you'll need for your book using the settings below.

☐ **Captions [cap]**
General:

Parent = [Basic Paragraph]
Style Name = **cap**
Based On = [Basic Paragraph]

Changes from the [Basic Paragraph] style:
Basic Character Formats:

Font Style = Italic
Font Size = 10 pt

Indents and Spacing:

Align to Grid: First Line Only

Running heads go at the top of pages and running feet go at the bottom. Choose **rh** or **rf**, whichever you prefer.

☐ **Running Heads or Feet** [rh *or* rf]
General:

Parent = [Basic Paragraph]
Style Name = **rh** *or* **rf**
Based On = [Basic Paragraph]

Changes from the [Basic Paragraph] style:
Basic Character Formats:

Size = 9 pt
Case = OpenType All Small Caps
Tracking = 50

Indents and Spacing:

Alignment = Center

☐ **Folios [fol]**
General:

Parent = **rh** *or* **rf**
Style Name = **fol**
Based On = **rh** *or* **rf**

Changes from the Running Heads or Feet style:
Indents and Spacing:

Alignment = Away From Spine

Congratulations! You've finished creating all the paragraph styles you'll need for your book. Click on the fly-out menu at the top right of the Paragraph Styles panel, and select Sort By Name. This will put all your paragraph styles into alphabetical order. Then save your document.

rh Running Head style

fol Folio style

could not think of anything to say, she simply bowed, and took the thimble, looking as solemn as she could.¶

The next thing was to eat the comfits: this caused some noise and confusion, as the large birds complained that they could not taste theirs, and the small ones choked and had to be patted on the back. However, it was over at last, and they sat down again in a ring, and begged the Mouse to tell them something more.¶

'You promised to tell me your history, you know,' said Alice, 'and why it is you hate—C and D,' she added in a whisper, half afraid that it would be offended again.¶

'Mine is a long and a sad tale!' said the Mouse, turning to Alice, and sighing.¶

'It IS a long tail, certainly,' said Alice, looking down with wonder at the Mouse's tail; 'but why do you call it sad?' And she kept on puzzling about it while the Mouse was speaking, so that her idea of the tale was something like this:—¶

'Fury said to a mouse, That he met in the house, "Let us both go to law: I will prosecute *you.*—Come, I'll take no denial; We must

This is the caption that explains the image.

cap Caption style

Creating your character styles

Character styles are similar to paragraph styles in that they are applied to text. The difference is that paragraph styles are applied to entire paragraphs, whereas character styles are applied to individual characters or words within a paragraph.

When are character styles needed?

Character styles are needed when some characters in a paragraph need to be different from the rest of the paragraph. Here are some examples:

- **italics** Chances are your book includes a number of italicized words. Italics are used for emphasis, for specifying foreign words, for terms listed in a glossary, for book titles, and for many other reasons.

- **bold** If all the bold characters in your manuscript are in your titles and headings, then there's no need for a character style for bold, as bold is included in your headings paragraph styles. But if you've used bold for emphasis elsewhere in your manuscript, then you'll need a character style for bold.

- **digits** Digits look their best when they have extra spacing between them. It's a good typesetting practice to add more generous spacing to digits, using the Tracking feature in a character style.

- **run-in subheads** These are subheadings set into the beginning of a paragraph or list entry, such as this one.

- **small caps** Small caps are used for acronyms (e.g., CIA or UNHCR) and abbreviations (e.g., A.M. or BCE). Depending on your book design, the first few words in each chapter or after a paragraph separator might be set in small caps, and sometimes running heads or feet are set in small caps as well (as in this book).

• **reference numbers for notes** The numbers that appear in the text, referring to footnotes or endnotes, are normally set as superscripts.

Using character styles

As with paragraph styles, there are two steps involved in using character styles: *creating* the styles and *applying* the styles. In this chapter you'll *create* a set of character styles for your book, and in chapter 13 you'll *apply* them to your text.

A set of character styles for your book

Take a moment now to look through your manuscript and see which character styles you'll need. Are there italicized words? Is bold used for emphasis? Does your text include lots of acronyms and/or numbers? Do you use run-in subheads? Check off the character styles below that you'll need to create for your book.

☐ Italics   ☐ Run-In Subheads

☐ Bold   ☐ Small Caps

☐ Digits   ☐ Reference Numbers for Notes

Now you can create your character styles using the style settings provided in this chapter. You'll be guided step by step through setting up each style, and by the end of the chapter you'll have a set of styles ready to apply to your text.

If you intend to create an ebook version of your print book, character styles are essential.

Click here to open the Character Styles fly-out menu.

Check or uncheck this box—it's up to you (see page 60).

You may use keyboard shortcuts for character styles if you like. See page 67.

Create a new character style in 8 steps

1 With the Selection Tool, click anywhere outside the text frames to make sure no text or frames are selected.

2 Open the Character Styles panel.

3 Click once on the [None] style to select it.

4 Open the Character Styles fly-out menu by clicking the four horizontal lines at the top right of the panel, then click New Character Style. This will open a New Character Style dialog box with the General category selected on the left. It'll look familiar, as it has some of the categories and options you've seen when setting up your paragraph styles.

5 In the General category, type the name of your new character style in the Style Name box.

6 In the Based On box, the parent style will default to [None].

7 Using the other category tabs on the left, make the appropriate changes to your new style (the things that make it different from its parent style).

8 Click OK, and your new style will appear in the Character Styles panel.

Create a character style for italics

Create the **Italics** character style by following the eight steps shown on page 82 and using the settings below.

☐ **Italics [ital]**
General:

        Parent = [None]
        Style Name = **ital**
        Based On = [None]

Changes from the [None] character style:
Basic Character Formats:

        Font Style = Italic

Create a character style for bold

Create the **Bold** character style by following the eight steps shown on page 82 and using the settings below.

☐ **Bold [bold]**
General:

        Parent = [None]
        Style Name = **bold**
        Based On = [None]

Changes from the [None] character style:
Basic Character Formats:

        Font Style = Bold

Create a character style for digits

Create the **Digits** character style by following the eight steps shown on page 82 and using the settings below.

Tracking is a means of adding or subtracting space between characters. It is measured in thousandths of an em. So a tracking value of 50 is 5%. (An em is a value that is equal to the type size.)

☐ **Digits [digits]**

General:

Changes from the [None] character style:
Basic Character Formats:

Parent = [None]
Style Name = **digits**
Based On = [None]

Tracking = 50

Create a character style for run-in subheads

Create the **Run-In Subheads** character style by following the eight steps shown on page 82 and using the settings below.

☐ **Run-In Subheads [ris]**

General:

Changes from the [None] character style:
Basic Character Formats:

Parent = [None]
Style Name = **ris**
Based On = [None]

Font Style = Bold

You may wonder why the Run-In Subheads character style is exactly the same as the Bold character style. You're creating separate character styles for these elements because you may decide down the road to change your run-in subheads to, say, semibold. It'll be an easy change then, since your run-in subheads will have a separate character style applied to them.

Create a character style for small caps

Create the **Small Caps** character style by following the eight steps shown on page 82 and using the settings below.

☐ **Small Caps [smcap]**	Parent = [None]
General:	Style Name = **smcap**
	Based On = [None]
Changes from the [None] character style:	
Basic Character Formats:	Case = OpenType All Small Caps
	Tracking = 25

Create a character style for reference numbers for notes

Create the **References** character style for the superscript numbers that refer to footnotes or endnotes. Follow the eight steps shown on page 82 and use the settings below.

☐ **Reference Numbers for Notes [ref]**	Parent = [None]
General:	Style Name = **ref**
	Based On = [None]
Changes from the [None] character style:	
Basic Character Formats:	Tracking = 20
	Position = Superscript

When you're finished working with a character style, be sure to go back into your Character Styles panel and select [None] by clicking it once. Otherwise, you'll start typing something down the road and wonder why everything is showing up in the wrong style.

Great! You've finished creating all the character styles you'll need for your book. Click on the fly-out menu at the top right of the Character Styles panel, and select Sort By Name. This will put all your character styles into alphabetical order. Then save your document.

Reversing or undoing mistakes

It's never too early to learn how to reverse or undo mistakes. As soon as you begin typesetting your book, you'll find yourself in "oops" situations from time to time. Here are three ways to reverse or undo mistakes:

1 **Undo the last few things you did** You can undo something you just did by choosing Edit>Undo or simply pressing Ctrl/Cmd+Z. Undo once, and you'll undo the most recent step you took. Or, you can undo several times and go back several steps. If you undo too many steps by mistake, you can redo those steps by pressing Ctrl/Cmd+Shift+Z (or choosing Edit>Redo). This also comes in handy for seeing whether you prefer a change you made, or whether it was better the way it was.

2 **Reverting to your last save** Suppose you open your document, start working on it, and suddenly you've lost some text or things have gone horribly wrong. You can revert back to how your document was the last time you saved it, by choosing File>Revert. InDesign will ask you if you're sure you want to do that, as you'll lose any changes you've made since the last save. Usually you don't want to keep those changes, so click OK and start fresh from your last save.

3 **Going back to an earlier version** It's always useful to save your document under a different date each day you work on it. That way, earlier versions are always available to you. If your current document gets messed up for any reason, you can always close it and open an earlier version. Or, you may change your mind and decide to include a chapter you've deleted, and can then copy it from an earlier version and paste it into your current document.

It's inevitable that you'll make mistakes. Now you know how to fix them quickly and easily.

Part III: Formatting Your Pages

13

Applying your character styles

Now that you've set up your document, placed your manuscript, and created paragraph and character styles for the different elements in your book, your next step is to format *all* your text.

In chapter 14, you'll apply paragraph styles to every paragraph in your whole book. But before doing that, it's important to apply your character styles first. Why? Because when you apply a paragraph style to a paragraph, it makes the whole paragraph comply to the settings you've specified in that style. So, for example, if you've specified Regular or Roman type in your Text paragraph style, it will convert the *whole* paragraph to Regular or Roman text, including any words or characters you may have italicized or bolded in the original manuscript. However, if you apply those character styles first, they will remain in place when your paragraph styles are applied.

You'll definitely want to apply the Italics character style to your text. Whether you choose to apply the Bold, Digits, and Small Caps character styles at this stage depends on whether you have those elements in your book. And sometimes it's simpler to apply them as you're formatting your pages (in chapter 14).

Start by applying the Italics character style, then read the explanations for the other character styles, and decide whether you need to apply them and, if so, now or later. Either way is fine.

Any character styles that imported with your Word document will show a download icon at the right (see below). If any of these styles are duplicating ones you've created (e.g., emphasis is the same as **ital**), drag them onto the trash can at the bottom right. A Delete Style dialog box will appear, and you can replace that style with the one you created in chapter 11.

Character styles imported with your Word document

Look in your Character Styles panel to see whether any character styles were imported with your Word document. Delete these files one at a time, as explained to the left, and replace them with the styles you created in chapter 11. If you can't tell what a style is for by its description, double-click it to open it and see what settings are specified. Many imported Word styles have no settings specified, and these can be deleted outright.

You may find some character styles created by Word for footnotes. If so, just leave these for the time being, and you'll adjust those on pages 348–349.

Applying the Italics character style

You'll apply the Italics character style using the Find/Change feature in InDesign. Open Find/Change by clicking Edit>Find/Change or using the keyboard shortcut Ctrl/Cmd+F, then take the following steps:

The keyboard shortcut for Find/Change is Ctrl/Cmd+F.

1   Select the Text tab, then select and delete anything appearing in the Find What and Change To boxes. In the Search drop-down menu, choose Document.

2   Click once inside the empty Find Format box to open the Find Format Settings dialog box. Select Basic Character Formats from the list on the left, and in the Font Style drop-down box, select Italic and click OK.

3   Click once inside the empty Change Format box to open the Change Format Settings dialog box. Select Style Options from the list on the left, and in the Character Styles drop-down box, select Italics [**ital**] and click OK.

4   Now you'll see that the Find Format and Change Format boxes are filled in as shown to the right. Now click the Change All button and InDesign will give all your italic type the Italics [**ital**] character style.

Click your Type Tool in any italicized word, and you'll see that the Italics [**ital**] character style is applied to it. Now save your document.

Delete anything here from before

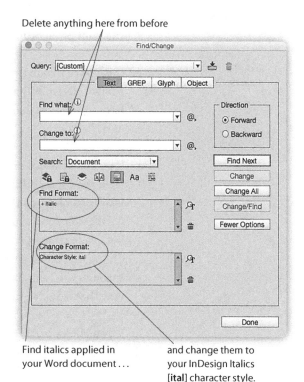

Find italics applied in your Word document . . .

and change them to your InDesign Italics [ital] character style.

Applying the Bold character style

If all the bold characters in your manuscript are in your headings, then there's no need to use a Bold character style, as bold is included in your paragraph styles for headings. But if you've used bold for emphasis elsewhere in your manuscript, then you'll want to apply the Bold character style to any bolded text that is not a heading. To apply the Bold character style to your bolded text, follow these steps:

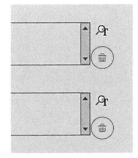

Click the trash cans to clear the Find Format and Change Format boxes.

1   In the Find/Change dialog box, click on the little trash cans next to the Find Format box and the Change Format box to delete the styles you added earlier. This deletes the styles so you can start fresh.

2   While still in Find/Change, select the Text tab, and click once inside the empty Find Format box to open the Find Format Settings dialog box. Select Basic Character Formats from the list on the left, and in the Font Style drop-down box, select Bold and click OK.

3   Click once inside the empty Change Format box to open the Change Format Settings dialog box. Select Style Options from the list on the left, and in the Character Styles drop-down box, select Bold [**bold**] and click OK.

4   If you used styles in Word when typing your headings, you may now click the Change All button and InDesign will give all your non-heading bold type the Bold [**bold**] character style. If, however, you used bold type in your headings in Word by applying the Bold attribute each time, it will be best to click the Find button and then Change each instance individually, skipping the headings as you go through the text and only applying the Bold [**bold**] character style to text that is not in headings.

If you click your Type Tool in any bold word, you'll see that the Bold [**bold**] character style is applied to it. Now save your document.

Applying the Digits character style

Digits look their best when they have extra spacing between them. It's a good typesetting practice to add more generous spacing to digits using the Tracking feature.

Applying the Digits character style uses a similar method to what you did for italics and bold type, but it involves a GREP search. Here's what you do:

A GREP search looks for patterns or attributes rather than actual characters or digits.

1 Open Find/Change and clear the Find Format and Change Format boxes if necessary by clicking on the little trash cans next to the boxes (see step 1 on page 90).

2 Select the GREP tab. To the right of the Find what box, click the little @ symbol, scroll down to Wildcards, then select Any Digit. Or you can type \d in the box.

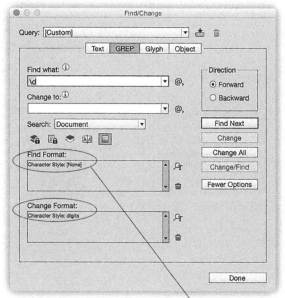

3 Click once in the Find Format box to open the Find Format Settings dialog box. Select Style Options from the list on the left, and in the Character Styles drop-down box, select [None] and click OK. Then click once in the Change Format box to open the Change Format Settings dialog box. Select Style Options from the list on the left, and in the Character Styles drop-down box, select Digits [**digits**] and click OK.

4 Click the Change All button and InDesign will apply the Digits [**digits**] character style to all your digits.

The character style [None] is included here so that your Digits [**digits**] character style doesn't get applied to digits that are already set in italics.

Now select any digit with your Type Tool, and you'll see that the Digits [**digits**] character style has been applied.

Change to Normal view (see page 16, or switch to your Selection Tool and press W), and you'll see that your digits are now highlighted with light blue. This is because they have a tracking value applied to them.

Applying the Small Caps character style

Small caps are used for acronyms (e.g., NASA or UNHCR) and abbreviatons (e.g., A.M. or BCE). Depending on the book design, the first few words in each chapter or after a paragraph separator might be set in small caps, and sometimes running heads or feet are set in small caps as well.

You may decide that it's simpler to change the appropriate type to small caps as you format your pages (chapter 14), and that is perfectly fine. But if you want to change them all at once, follow the steps below.

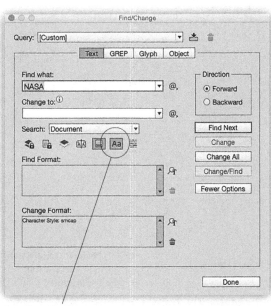

Ebooks do not recognize small caps consistently. If you use them, be sure to type them all in lower-case as noted above.

1   In the Find/Change dialog box, under the Text tab, first clear out any old searches. Click on the little trash cans next to the Find Format and Change Format boxes to start fresh.

2   In the Find What box, type the specific acronym in uppercase letters (in this example, NASA).

Case Sensitive icon

3   Click the Case Sensitive icon (Aa) to turn it on. This is important! You might search for an abbreviation such as AM, and without the Case Sensitive icon turned on, all instances of am will be changed, including in words like amnesty, cream, and so on.

4   Click once inside the empty Change Format box to open the Change Format Settings dialog box. Select Style Options from the list on the left, and in the Character Styles drop-down box, select Small Caps [**smcap**] and click OK. Then click Change All.

If your acronyms don't change to small caps using this method, it's probably because the typeface you're using doesn't support the OpenType All Small Caps feature. In addition to the steps above, type each acronym in lowercase in the Change to box.

If you'd prefer to change *all* your acronyms at the same time in one big search, do this:

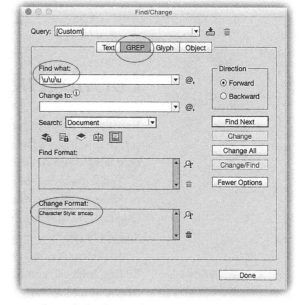

1 In Find/Change, first clear out any old searches. Then click on the GREP tab. Type \u\u\u in the Find What box. This sets up a search for any three uppercase letters in a row, which should catch all your acronyms, even if they have four or more letters.

2 Click once inside the empty Change Format box to open the Change Format Settings dialog box. Select Style Options from the list on the left, and in the Character Styles list, select Small Caps [**smcap**] and click OK.

3 Click Find Next, stop and change the first instance, then click Change/Find, and change the next. Go through the entire document this way, changing each acronym as you go.

Applying the References character style

It's important that your reference numbers be readable and consistent. To change all your current superscripts to the **ref** style, follow these steps:

1 In the Find/Change dialog box, clear out any old Text searches.

2 Click inside the empty Find Format box, go to Basic Character Formats in the list on the left, then in the Position field, scroll down to Superscript, select it, and click OK.

3 Click inside the empty Change Format box. Then in the Character Style list, choose **ref**, and click OK.

4 With your cursor in the text, click Find Next, then Change. Check to see if the replacement was done correctly, then click Change All.

A GREP search for \u\u\u will catch any group of three uppercase letters in a row. Since almost all acronyms are at least three characters long, this will catch them all.

Always set reference numbers after punctuation except for a dash:

text,[86] *not* text[86],

text[86]— *not* text—[86]

Reference numbers are the same for footnotes and endnotes. You can adjust the appearance of your reference numbers in the **ref** character style, making them slightly larger or smaller (size), higher or lower (baseline shift), or bolder (font style).

14

Formatting your pages

Now you're ready to format your pages. You have two goals in this chapter: to rough in all the pages of your book, and to apply paragraph and character styles to every bit of text on every page.

You'll make two or three passes through your book, depending on whether your book has sidebars and images. In the first pass (in this chapter), you'll rough in your front and back matter, set up your chapters, and apply your paragraph and character styles to all the text.

In your second pass (see Part V: Adding Shapes & Color and Part VI: Adding Images), you'll add all the sidebars, images, and captions you need. (If you don't have any sidebars or images, you'll skip this pass.)

In your final pass (in Part VII: Typesetting), you'll refine your typesetting and put finishing touches on all your pages.

Why not do everything in one pass? Because after your first pass you may want to make some changes to your page design, such as modifying your chapter openings or typeface, to suit the material in *your* book. After your first pass, you'll be able to make whatever adjustments you choose by following the instructions in Part IV: Designing Your Pages.

When you're satisfied with the way your pages look, you'll do a second pass, adding shapes (such as boxes behind sidebars, see Part V: Adding Shapes & Color) and images and captions (see Part VI: Adding Images).

Changing your page design and adding shapes and images will change the flow of text in your book, and that's the reason your final typesetting refinements will be done when you're satisfied with the look of all the elements in your book, have added all your sidebars and images, and won't be making any further changes to your page design and layout. That's when you'll make the final pass through your book.

Ready to start your first pass? Applying styles to your text can be the most time-consuming stage of your book's production, so be prepared to spend some time doing it. Navigate to page 1 of your document, and start formatting your pages.

Click Type>Show Hidden Characters to display all the characters in your document that don't show up in print, such as spaces, end-of-paragraph returns, and so on. These characters will show in blue when you view your document in Normal view.

If you created an index in your manuscript in Word, you'll notice blue insertion points throughout your text wherever an index entry was added (when you are in Normal view with visible hidden characters). Be careful not to delete any of these while you're formatting your text. You'll typeset your index in chapter 54.

Roughing in your front matter

On pages 24–25 of this book you made a list of all the pages to include in your front matter. Now you'll set up those pages. Your front matter text may already be in your InDesign document if it was included in your manuscript, or you may not have it ready yet. Either way is fine. For the time being, you'll just rough in the pages.

Start with page 1. This is your title page, or your half title page if you choose to include one. If you already have your title or half title page text on page 1, then just make sure there is a page break after the appropriate text. A page break will force everything following it onto the next page. To insert a page break, use the Type Tool and click to place your cursor where you want the break to occur. Then press Enter/Return on your *numeric* keypad, or choose Type>Insert Break Character>Page Break.

Then move on to page 2. If you have a half title page on page 1, then page 2 will be blank. Just insert another page break to move everything following over to page 3. If your title page is on page 1, then page 2 will be your copyright page. Go to the bottom of your copyright page text (whatever you have there), and insert a page break. As you work through your front matter, inserting page breaks at the end of each item, you'll find your front matter starting to materialize.

If you don't have any front matter yet, you can still create your front matter pages using placeholders. For example, at the top of page 1 in front of your main text, insert the cursor with your Type Tool and simply type "Title Page," then insert a page break. On page 2, type "Copyright Page," then insert a page break. Carry on creating a new page for each item in your front matter until you've created all the necessary pages.

You may want to force a blank page. Suppose your front matter ends on a recto page. Chapter 1 or Part 1 always starts on a recto page, so you may need to add one blank page at the end of your front matter. To do so, place the cursor at the top of the page you want to be blank, and insert a page break.

When you've finished roughing in your front matter, not only will you see how many pages it will require, but you'll have added the actual pages to your book. Whether or not your front matter text is finalized isn't important at this stage. You simply want to allocate the pages for now, and you can fill them in later.

Applying paragraph and character styles to your main text

Now that you've roughed in your front matter, your goal is to go through every page in your book and apply paragraph styles to every bit of text.

Why is it important that *all* your text has paragraph styles applied to it? There are two reasons:

1 **Every single paragraph needs a style for ebooks** There is a limited amount of formatting that ereaders recognize. They do not recognize more than one end-of-paragraph return at a time or more than one space at a time. So the amount of space after paragraphs cannot be controlled by adding several end-of-paragraph returns; rather, it must be controlled by adding space within the paragraph style settings. Same with using multiple spaces to indent paragraphs—ereaders won't recognize more than one space at a time. If your spacing is controlled exclusively by paragraph styles, then your ebook will look as expected. *Only one space and end-of-paragraph return at a time (really!).*

2 **Future design changes are easy** Suppose after your first pass you decide your type size needs to be a bit bigger. With paragraph styles applied to all your text, you can simply change the type size in your Basic Paragraph style, and just about all the type in your book will change accordingly. *And*, because you've controlled the space after paragraphs using your paragraph styles, you won't find any extra end-of-paragraph returns showing up in awkward places, such as at the top of your pages, because your text has reflowed.

Get ready to apply your styles by dragging your Paragraph Styles and Character Styles panels out of the dock so they are visible all the time. You may find it handy to assign keyboard shortcuts to the paragraph styles you are using frequently. For example, you might assign Shift+1 to your Text [**tx**] style, Shift+2 to your No Indents [**tx1**] style, and so on (see page 67).

Roll up your sleeves and get ready to go! Navigate to page 1 of your book, select your Type Tool, and get started.

Applying paragraph styles to your front matter

You'll be designing your front matter after you've finalized the design of your pages, so for the time being simply apply your Text [**tx**] style to *all* of your front matter. The box below explains several easy ways of selecting text in order to apply a paragraph style to it.

Easy ways to select text

Select one word Double-click on the word.

Select one line Triple-click anywhere in the line.

Select one paragraph Quadruple-click anywhere in the paragraph.

Select several paragraphs at a time on the same page Drag your mouse from the beginning of the first paragraph to the end of the last paragraph.

Select several pages of text Select a few words at the beginning of the first paragraph, scroll down to the page with the last paragraph, press Shift, and click at the end of the last paragraph.

Select all the text in linked text frames Put your cursor anywhere in the text and click Edit>Select All or press Ctrl/Cmd+A. This will select all text that is connected by text threads (referred to as a Story), but not any text in text frames that are separate.

Place your cursor at the very beginning of page 1, then scroll down through the pages until you reach the end of your front matter. Press Shift and click at the end of your front matter to select all the text. Then apply your Text [**tx**] paragraph style to the text by clicking the Text [**tx**] style once in your Paragraph Styles panel.

You'll notice that if there was any italicized or bolded text in your front matter, it remains unchanged despite applying the Text [**tx**] paragraph style. Any text with a character style applied will remain constant as you apply your paragraph styles to the text.

This is where you can begin using keyboard shortcuts if you wish. Refer back to page 67 to see how to set them up.

Read more about keyboard shortcuts at BookDesign MadeSimple.com/indesign-keyboard-shortcuts.

Now you'll be at the beginning of chapter 1 (or Part 1, if your book is divided into parts), starting on a recto page. If your book is divided into parts, create a page for your Part I divider by typing "Part I" and the part title, if any, at the top of your recto page, followed by two page breaks. That way, the verso page following your Part I divider will be blank, and you'll be starting your first chapter on the next recto page. You'll create paragraph styles for your part dividers later on, but for now apply your Text [**tx**] paragraph style to them.

Applying paragraph styles to your chapter openings

Start each chapter with an end-of-paragraph return at the top of the page (see facing page) by inserting your cursor just before your chapter opening and pressing Enter/Return. Then select the end-of-paragraph return and apply the Text [**tx**] style to it by clicking that style in the Paragraph Styles panel. Do this at the beginning of every chapter.

You need an end-of-paragraph return at the beginning of each new chapter so you can control how far down the page your chapter openings start. Without that, InDesign will automatically put your first element right at the top of the text frame.

You've already created all the paragraph styles you need for your chapter openings, so now you can apply them by inserting your cursor in the text and selecting the appropriate paragraph style in the Paragraph Styles panel.

Start with your chapter number. Make sure your chapter number is separate from your chapter title. You may need to insert an end-of-paragraph return after it to separate it. Then insert your cursor anywhere in the chapter number and apply your Chapter Number [**cn**] paragraph style by selecting that paragraph style in the Paragraph Styles panel. You'll see your chapter number change to the new style. If you're using the style suggested in this book, you'll want to use digits for your chapter numbers and remove the word "chapter."

Next, click on your chapter title and apply the Chapter Titles [**ct**] paragraph style to it. Do the same with your opening quote and quote attribution. You'll see the text change to the new styles.

Don't worry if the text in these styles flows onto two or more lines. You'll fine-tune these styles and choose exactly where the lines will break when you make your third pass (see chapters 50 and 51).

¶

3¶

A Caucus-Race and a Long Tale¶

A book can look good using almost any typeface;¬
it just depends on how the type is set.¶

—Fiona Raven, book designer¶

They were indeed a queer-looking party that assembled on the bank—
the birds with draggled feathers, the animals with their fur clinging
close to them, and all dripping wet, cross, and uncomfortable.¶

The first question of course was, how to get dry again: they had
a consultation about this, and after a few minutes it seemed quite
natural to Alice to find herself talking familiarly with them, as if she
had known them all her life. Indeed, she had quite a long argument
with the Lory, who at last turned sulky, and would only say, 'I am
older than you, and must know better'; and this Alice would not
allow without knowing how old it was, and, as the Lory positively
refused to tell its age, there was no more to be said.¶

At last the Mouse, who seemed to be a person of authority among
them, called out, 'Sit down, all of you, and listen to me! I'LL soon
make you dry enough!' They all sat down at once, in a large ring,
with the Mouse in the middle. Alice kept her eyes anxiously fixed
on it, for she felt sure she would catch a bad cold if she did not get
dry very soon. 'Ahem!' said the Mouse with an important air, 'are
you all ready? This is the driest thing I know. Silence all round, if

An end-of-paragraph return (text [**tx**] style) at the top of every chapter opening allows InDesign to recognize the "space before" specification in your Chapter Numbers paragraph style.

Chapter Numbers [**cn**] paragraph style

Chapter Titles [**ct**] paragraph style

Opening Quotes [**quo**] paragraph style

Quote Attributions [**quo-attr**] paragraph style

No Indents [**tx1**] paragraph style is always applied to the first paragraph following a chapter opening or a heading.

Text [**tx**] style is applied to all the paragraphs in your main narrative.

Now that your first chapter opening has paragraph styles applied to it, carry on applying styles through the rest of the chapter.

Paragraph styles imported with Word

As you go through each paragraph in your first chapter, you may notice that some paragraphs already have a style applied to them. Styles imported from Word will display a download icon to the right, and they'll remain applied to your paragraphs. This can save you some time!

Simply delete the Word paragraph styles one at a time and replace them with the paragraph styles you created in chapter 10.

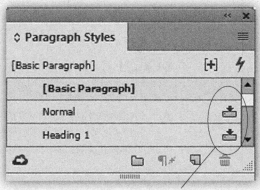

Styles imported from Word

Start with the Normal style. Delete it by dragging it onto the Trash icon at the bottom right. The Delete Paragraph Style box will open, and you'll replace the Normal paragraph style with your Text [**tx**] style by selecting it from the drop-down menu, then click OK.

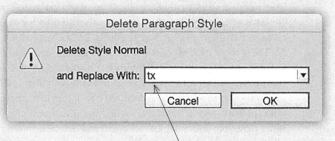

Replace with the style *you* created

Do this with every paragraph style that imported from Word. First figure out which paragraphs the style is applied to, then delete the style and replace it with a style you created in chapter 10.

Then, as you go through your chapters, you'll see that some of your styles are already applied.

Click in each paragraph (or select several similar paragraphs at a time) and look for a plus sign (+) next to the style name (see page 101). That will tell you whether the style applied properly. If it didn't, use the steps on page 101 to properly apply the style.

Applying paragraph styles to your chapters

The first paragraph following your chapter opening is not indented, so apply the No Indents [**tx1**] paragraph style to it. Then check each paragraph within your first chapter and apply the appropriate paragraph style to each one.

Main text

Apply the Text [**tx**] style to your main text even though it appears to be the same as the Basic Paragraph style. Apply the No Indents [**tx1**] style at the beginning of chapters and after any heading or paragraph separator.

    You may notice a blank linespace at the bottom of a page. This is because your Text [**tx**] style is not allowing any widows, and rather than leave the last line of the paragraph stranded alone at the top of the next page, InDesign has moved a line from the bottom of the previous page over to join it. For now, this is fine. You'll fine-tune the number of lines per page during your third pass, in chapter 51.

Some lines of text may be highlighted with yellow That's because the spacing in that line is slightly tighter or looser than optimum, despite InDesign's best efforts. You'll find this information useful in chapter 51.

If paragraph styles don't apply properly

Sometimes you'll apply a paragraph style, but the text won't change properly. You'll notice the typeface didn't change, or the spacing is wrong. There'll be a plus sign (+) next to the style name in the Paragraph Styles panel. This means that something in that paragraph was changed manually, probably in your Word document, and InDesign is respecting the prior formatting.

To clear the overrides in a paragraph, place your cursor anywhere in the paragraph, then click Clear Overrides. The text will comply with the style you've applied to it. If this doesn't work, click on the paragraph 4 times, then click Clear Overrides.

Style Override Highlighter

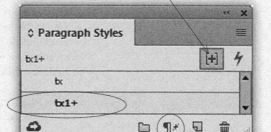

Clear Overrides

An easy way to spot text that doesn't conform to a paragraph style is to turn on the Style Override Highlighter by clicking the button shown above. Then all non-conforming text will be highlighted in blue.

Choosing Your Book's Trim Size

Trim size is the size of the *pages* of a book, regardless of the type of book cover. A hardcover book will appear larger than a softcover book with the same trim size because the hardcover itself is larger than the pages.

What size should your book be? You'll want to consider three things when choosing your book's trim size:

- What sizes are other books in the same genre?
- Do you want a thinner or thicker book?
- Where will your book be printed?

WHAT SIZES ARE OTHER BOOKS IN THE SAME GENRE?

Your book should fit in with other books in the same genre. Browse your bookstore or library, and see what sizes the other books are. Take a ruler with you, and measure in inches.

WHERE WILL YOUR BOOK BE PRINTED?

Standard sizes are the most cost-effective to print, and some printers and POD publishers only print certain sizes of books. To the left are some examples of standard trim sizes. Often at the design stage, you won't know where your book will be printed or published. If that's the case, select a size that will give you choices down the road.

> With all the InDesign type effects available to the self-publisher and anyone who is designing a book, it may be hard to believe that the basic guiding principle remains that a good book design goes unnoticed by the reader. Temptations abound! But reserve InDesign's showier elements for your book marketing.

Of course, you can choose any trim size for your book, but be aware that some sizes are more expensive to print and may require special binding, packaging, and shipping. Standard book sizes fit into standard shipping boxes, envelopes, and bookracks, and are

If you have a lot of text and want to keep your printing costs down, moving to a slightly larger trim size can lower your page count and save printing costs.

Inches, millimeters, points, or picas?

Historically typographers used points and picas (12 points = 1 pica, 72 points or 6 picas = 1 inch. Fonts are based on point sizes, such as 11-point Minion Italic, used in this sidebar.

Printers outside North America use millimeters because their standard paper and book sizes are metric.

If your book is set up in inches and goes to a printer that uses metric measurements, it's no problem, as long as the trim size is accurate in whatever measurement you've used.

This is sidebar text with a head. For now, keep it with the rest of the text. This example uses all four sidebar paragraph styles [**sbt, sb1, sb2, sb3**].

If you've just leased InDesign and need to familiarize yourself with the software, this chapter will help you get started. Your first task in InDesign is to learn the basics:

1. starting a new document
2. navigating through your document
3. learning to use the tools in the toolbox
4. using panels

Numbered Lists, First, Middle, and Last styles [**nl1, nl2, nl3**]

In chapter 3 you'll start a new document specifically for your book, but for now just make two changes to the dialog box.

Headings
Paragraph styles for headings include specifications for space before and after the heading. There is always more space before than after a heading.

Heading 3 [**h3**] followed by No Indent [**tx1**] style

This is a caption for an illustration.

Captions [**cap**] style. Keep captions in the same text frame with the book text for now as a reminder of where the illustration will go when you work on the second pass.

Delete any extra end-of-paragraph returns before and after each heading. The paragraph following a heading should have the

As you go through your chapters applying your styles, you'll probably come to some text that you haven't created an appropriate style for yet. Chances are good that you'll need to create some styles of your own to suit the material in *your* book. Remember, if you need extra white space after a paragraph, use Space After in your paragraph styles. There are easy ways of creating new styles, set out on page 108.

Paragraph separators

These are used to indicate the passage of time or a change of place within the narrative. Apply the Paragraph Separators [**sep**] style to whatever symbols you've used, and they will be centered with a linespace before and after them.

Asterisks (*) separated by em or en spaces (Ctrl/Cmd+Shift+M or N) are most commonly used for paragraph separators; however, you may prefer to use an ornament (see page 105).

Some authors use two types of paragraph separators: a single blank linespace for a short break in the narrative, and a paragraph separator with an ornament for a substantial break in time or place. If you choose to use a single blank linespace as a paragraph separator, don't just add an extra end-of-paragraph return! You'll need to create a new paragraph style for your main text that includes one blank linespace after it. Use the settings below for the new style.

Use asterisks (* * *) for separators if you plan to convert to an ebook. The spaces between the asterisks should be either em or en spaces (Type>Insert White Space>Em Space or En Space or Ctrl/Cmd+Shift+M or N), rather than multiple word spaces, because ebooks don't respect more than one word space in a row.

☐ **Text with Space After [txspaft]**   Parent = **tx**
General: Style Name = **txspaft**
                                                                 Based On = **tx**

Changes from the [Basic Paragraph] style:
Indents and Spacing: Space After = 14 pt

Whichever type of paragraph separator you choose to use, the first paragraph following the break is not indented, so apply your No Indent [**tx1**] paragraph style to paragraphs following the breaks in the narrative.

Several of the typefaces that come with InDesign include some ornaments. To open your Glyphs panel, choose Window>Type & Tables>Glyphs, or Type>Glyphs. In the Show drop-down menu, select Ornaments. Then double-click on any ornament to insert it at the cursor in your text.	Shift+8, any typeface, with em spaces (Ctrl/Cmd+Shift+M) between characters ⟶ * * *
	Alt/Opt+8, any typeface, with em spaces (Ctrl/Cmd+Shift+M) between characters ⟶ • • •
	Minion Pro ornament ⟶
If you decide to use an ornament from a different typeface from your Text [**tx**] style, be sure to change the Font Family in your Paragraph Separators [**sep**] paragraph style to that typeface.	Minion Pro ornament ⟶ ~
	Chaparral Pro ornament ⟶
	Adobe Garamond Pro ornament ⟶

Headings

Paragraph styles for headings include specifications for space before and after the heading. There is always more space before than after a heading, so that the heading connects visually to the paragraph following it. Delete any extra end-of-paragraph returns before and after each heading. The paragraph following a heading should have the No Indent [**tx1**] paragraph style applied to it.

Headings should always be followed by a minimum of two or three lines of text. You may find that InDesign has left a space at the bottom of a page to keep a heading and its following lines together at the top of the next page. Don't worry if this looks awkward; you'll resolve these issues in your second pass.

Bulleted lists

The Bulleted Lists [**bl**] paragraph styles specify automatically adding bullets to your paragraphs. This ensures that the bullets are the same typeface and size as your bulleted lists (rather than a different typeface, such

You may need to delete any tabs that imported with your Word document bullets, as they're not needed with InDesign bullets.

as Wingdings, that may have been used in your Word document). If the original bullets imported into InDesign, you'll now see two bullets at the start of each paragraph. Simply delete one. Use all three Bulleted Lists paragraph styles to get the correct spacing before and after your lists.

Numbered lists

The Numbered Lists [**nl**] paragraph styles specify automatic numbering. The numbering from your Word document may or may not have imported into InDesign. If it did, you'll now see two sets of numbers. Simply delete the second set. Use all three Numbered Lists paragraph styles to get the correct spacing before and after your lists.

3. » This Numbered Lists paragraph begins with a number, followed by a period and a tab. The tab ensures that the first line is aligned with the rest of the paragraph.

Extracts

Use the appropriate Extracts [**ext**] paragraph styles to get the spacing right before and after your extracts.

Images and captions

If you have images to go in your book, just leave them out on your first pass. If the captions for the images are included in your main text, then apply the Captions [**cap**] paragraph style to them, but leave them in with your main text for the time being. You'll place your images and add the captions to them in chapters 43 and 44.

Sidebars: separate or linked?

The sidebars (this one, for example) in this book have been completely separated from the main text and placed on a gray (10% black) background. They are no longer linked with the main text and will stay in their current position on the page regardless of what changes are made to the main text.

During the first pass through your chapters, it's best to leave your sidebars as part of the main text, simply applying the Sidebars paragraph styles to them. Later, when your book design is finalized and during your second pass, you'll separate your sidebars and add graphic treatments to them.

Starting chapters on recto or verso pages

When you come to the end of each chapter, remember to add a page break, forcing all the remaining text onto the following page.

Traditionally chapters always began on recto pages. Nowadays it's acceptable to begin chapters on recto pages, verso pages, or a combination of both (as in this book). Sometimes the chapters themselves will dictate this for you. For example, suppose you begin all your chapters on recto pages, then discover your book has a dozen blank verso pages as a result. Today there is a higher priority on keeping both printing costs and ecological footprints to a minimum, rather than following any recto-page rules. Of course, if you have a low page count and want to expand your book as much as possible, then beginning all your chapters on recto pages is a good way to increase your page count unobtrusively.

During your first pass, let your chapters begin on recto or verso pages. In chapter 24 you'll decide whether to start them on recto pages only.

Applying character styles

You probably applied your character styles by using Find/Change in chapter 13. But as you go through your book one page at a time, you'll probably find places where you still need to apply a character style.

Run-in subheads

You'll apply the Run-In Subheads [**ris**] character style to your run-in subheads as you go through your book. Simply select the word or phrase (see page 97 for easy ways to select text), then click the character style once to apply it.

Acronyms and abbreviations

You also might find an acronym or abbreviation that needs to be changed to small caps. Follow the steps on pages 92 and 93 to search for all instances of the acronym or abbreviation, and apply the Small Caps [**smcap**] character style to them.

Easy ways to create new paragraph and character styles as needed

Sometimes, as you're formatting your text, you suddenly find that you need a new paragraph style. A simple way to create a new style is to first make the changes directly to the paragraph you're working in and then name the style you've just created. Follow the steps below.

1. Select all the text in the paragraph by quadruple-clicking, then make changes to it using the Paragraph (not Paragraph Styles) and/or Character (not Character Styles) panels, or the Control panel at the top of your screen. You may add space before and/or after, change the typeface, the size or leading, the alignment, the indents, the color, etc.

2. When you've found a look that you like, keep your cursor in that paragraph and open the Paragraph Styles panel.

3. Click on the fly-out menu at the upper right corner of the panel and select New Paragraph Style. In the General area, give the new style a name. If you only made a couple of small changes from the style you were originally using (keeping your styles family tree in mind), scroll to that style name in the Based On list. If your new style is completely different, select [No Paragraph Style] from the list.

4. Go through the other areas of the Paragraph Styles panel and look at the settings. You'll find that your new style has adopted all the settings of the selected paragraph. Think about whether you should perhaps add space above or below this new style, whether it should be hyphenated or not, and anything else that might improve it. Be sure that you've checked Apply Style to Selection in the General area of the Paragraph Styles panel. Then, any changes you make to the settings will affect the current paragraph as well as any future paragraphs that use this new style.

To create a new character style, follow the same procedure. Make changes to your selected text using either the Character (not Character Styles) panel or the Control panel. Then open the Character Styles panel, create a new style, give it a name, check the settings, and make any changes that you think will improve the style.

Even if you think you'll only use this new style once in the entire book, give it a name anyway. If you're planning an ebook, you *must* do this. Every single paragraph in an ebook needs a paragraph style! Every single character not conforming to a paragraph style in an ebook needs a character style, too!

Roughing in your back matter

Many books don't contain any back matter and, if that's the case with your book, simply skip this section. Make sure your book ends on a verso page (i.e., has an even number of pages). If it ends on a recto page, just add a blank page at the end.

If your book includes appendixes, endnotes, references, a bibliography, a glossary, resources lists, an index, or any other back matter, then you'll need to allocate some pages for them.

If you need to, return to page 25 to see the normal order for back matter elements.

Rough in your back matter the same way you did your front matter. The first back matter item always begins on a recto page, so you may need to insert an extra page break at the end of your chapters to start your back matter on a recto page.

Now go through your back matter and insert page breaks at the end of each item in the back matter to rough in the pages. If you don't have any back matter yet, you can still create your back matter pages using place-holders. For example, type "Glossary" at the top of a page, then insert one page break for each page your glossary will require. Do the same for each item in your back matter until all the pages you'll need are roughed in.

You'll create separate paragraph styles for your back matter in chapter 29. For the time being, select all the text in your back matter and apply the Text [**tx**] paragraph style to it.

You've finished the first pass through your whole book, roughing in all your pages and applying your paragraph and character styles to absolutely everything. Way to go!

15

Adding folios and running heads

Folios and running heads are your book's navigation tools. They usually go at the tops of your pages, with the chapter title on the left and the author's name or chapter title on the right.

The folios and running heads are always placed on master pages. Master pages can be described as a style for the overall look of pages, much the way paragraph styles are used to control the overall look of paragraphs. Each master page is set up with a particular format, which can then be applied to pages within your book. And each master page is based on its parent page, the A-Master.

At present you have one master page in your document: A-Master. Look at the top portion of your Pages panel, and you'll see A-Master there. Below A-Master are thumbnails of all your pages, and they all have the letter A at the top outer corners. This means that A-Master is applied to these pages.

Double-click on A-Master in your Pages panel, and the A-Master two-page spread will open. These pages are the same trim size as your whole document, and they have the margins that you specified when you set up your document.

A-Master is the master template for your whole document. This is important! This means that from now on, every time you make a change that needs to affect all the pages in your document, you'll make that change on A-Master.

Pages panel with A-Master at the top and pages with A-Master applied to them below.

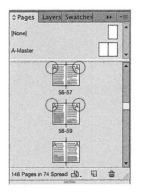

Adding folios to A-Master

Open A-Master by double-clicking it in your Pages panel. Using your Selection Tool, select Normal view in the Toolbox (or press W) so you can see the margins on A-Master. Click View>Show Rulers or press Ctrl/Cmd+R to display rulers along the top and down the left of your screen.

Most printers require a minimum of 0.5″ clearance from the top edge of the page, so your running heads and folios must be below that mark. Drag a guide to the 0.5″ mark by clicking inside the top ruler, dragging a guide down to the 0.5″ mark on the left ruler, and releasing the mouse button.

Switch to the Type Tool, and drag a new text frame anywhere in the top margin on, say, the verso page. In the Paragraph Styles panel, click the Folio [**fol**] paragraph style once to select it. Instead of typing a page number in the text frame, you'll add a Current Page Number marker by clicking Type>Insert Special Character>Markers>Current Page Number or pressing Ctrl/Cmd+Shift+Alt/Opt+N. On A-Master, the marker will appear as a capital A; however, on any page in your book with A-Master applied, the actual page number will show.

With the Selection Tool, drag the text frame into position. Align the left side with the outside margin and the top with the guide, and the bottom with the top margin; the right side can go anywhere you like.

Now you'll add a folio to the recto page. Select the folio text frame on the verso page with the Selection Tool and press Alt/Opt+Shift (to duplicate the text frame *and* keep it in the same horizontal plane as its original), while dragging the copy across to the recto page, positioning the right edge against the outside margin.

Voilà! Now go back to your Pages panel and double-click any page or two-page spread in your book. You'll see that all your pages now have page numbers.

While you are dragging a guide down, hold the Ctrl/Cmd key to make the guide extend across both pages and the pasteboard. If the guide only extends across one page, select it with your Selection Tool and press Ctrl/Cmd to extend it.

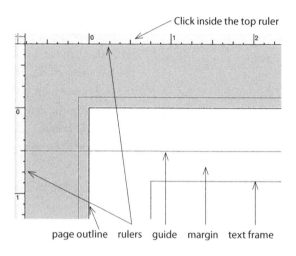

Click inside the top ruler

page outline · rulers · guide · margin · text frame

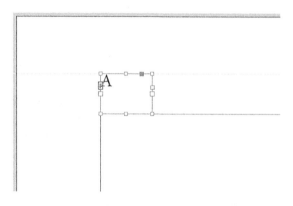

The Current Page Number Marker will appear in the top outside corner of your text frame, as the Folio [**fol**] character style applied to it specifies alignment away from the spine.

Adding running heads to A-Master

To switch from the Selection Tool to the Type Tool, press T. To switch from the Type Tool to the Selection Tool, press Esc (Windows) or V (Mac OS). Make sure no type or object is selected when you do this.

Open your A-Master page and, using the Type Tool, drag a new text frame anywhere across the top margin on the verso page. In the Paragraph Styles panel, click the Running Heads [**rh**] paragraph style once to select it, and type your book's title in the text frame.

With the Selection Tool, drag the text frame into position. Align the left side with the outside margin (yes, overlapping with the folio) and the top with the guide. Then adjust the other edges of the text frame so that the bottom is a bit below the text and the right side is aligned with the inside margin. Note that the folio's text frame is taller than the running head's text frame so that each is easy to select in the future and not stuck behind the other one.

Pressing Alt/Opt while dragging a frame with the Selection Tool will create a duplicate of the frame and its contents (whether text or an image).

Pressing the Shift key while dragging a frame will keep the frame in the same position either vertically or horizontally on the page.

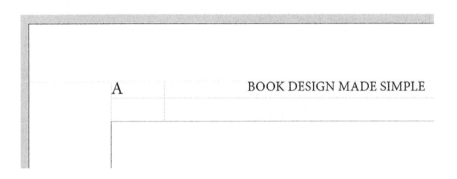

 When you convert to a reflowable ebook, all your folios and running heads will be deleted.

Now add a running head to the recto page. Select the running head text frame on the verso page with the Selection Tool, press Alt/Opt+Shift, and drag the copy across to the recto page, positioning the right edge against the outside margin. Switch to the Type Tool and replace the book title with the author's name or chapter title.

Return to any two-page spread in your book by going back to your Pages panel and double-clicking any page or two-page spread. You'll see that all your pages now have folios *and* running heads. Don't worry if every recto page has the same chapter title on it. You'll put the correct chapter titles in the running heads later on, in chapter 52. It doesn't pay to use the specific chapter titles at this stage, because your chapters are probably going to shift forward and backward a bit before settling into place.

Printing pages

16

InDesign gives you a lot of control over how your pages print. You can print spreads (two facing pages on one sheet), scale your pages to fit standard paper sizes, and so on.

In this chapter, you'll:

1 Set up your printer to print book pages
2 Save your print settings as a preset
3 Print some pages, trim to size, and see what they look like

Open your Print dialog box by choosing File>Print or by pressing Ctrl/Cmd+P. The Print dialog box will open with the General category selected on the left.

1 Setting up your printer
General

Choose your printer from the Printer drop-down menu if it didn't automatically appear in the Printer box. Next, in the Pages: Range box, type the page numbers you want to print. To print consecutive pages, type the first and last page numbers, separated by a hyphen (e.g., 7-9). To print non-consecutive pages, type the page numbers, separated by commas (e.g., 7,9,12). Or, you can print a combination of both (e.g., 7-9,12). Note that there are no spaces between the numbers, just a hyphen or comma.

Under Options, check Print Blank Pages.

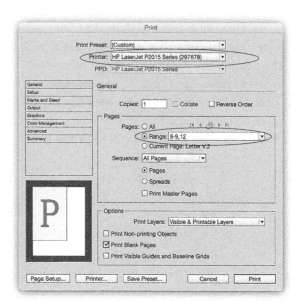

Setup

Click the Setup category on the left. Under Paper Size, the size of paper available in your printer should show there (usually US Letter or 8.5″ × 11″ in the Americas, and A4 or 8.27″ × 11.69″ elsewhere). The Orientation is Portrait.

Under Options, keep the Scale at 100%, but change Page Position to centered. You'll see the thumbnail with the letter P in it at the left change when you change the Page Position.

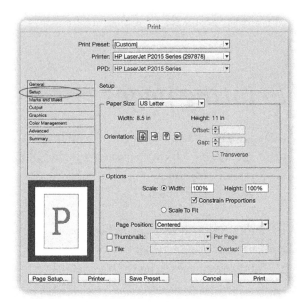

Marks and Bleed

Under Marks, check Crop Marks and Page Information. That way, when you print your pages, the crop marks will show the trim size of your pages, and the page information will print the name of the document, page number, and date and time of printing.

In the Bleed and Slug box, check Use Document Bleed Settings. That way anything that extends into the bleed area will be printed.

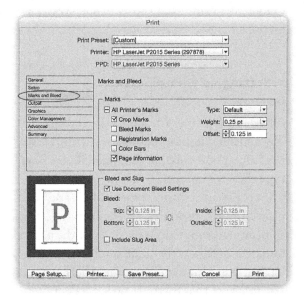

Output

This category lets you set your color parameters. For now, if you are printing on a color printer, leave the default color setting at Composite RGB. If you are printing with black ink only, change the Color to Composite Gray.

Graphics, Color Management, Advanced, Summary

No need to change any settings in the Graphics, Color Management, Advanced, or Summary categories.

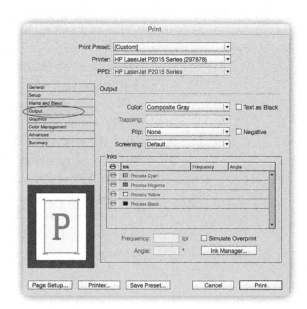

2 Saving your preset

Now that you've adjusted the settings in your Print dialog box, be sure to save them as a preset. That way, every time you print from InDesign, your settings will automatically appear.

Click the Save Preset button at the bottom left of the Print dialog box, and the Save Preset dialog box appears. Type in a name for your preset, then click OK. Now your preset will show in the Print Preset drop-down menu at the top of the Print dialog box.

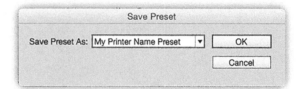

3 Printing your pages

To print pages or a whole document using these settings, simply open your Print dialog box, select your preset, choose the page numbers you want to print, and click Print.

Another way to choose the pages you want to print is by selecting them in the Pages panel. Holding the Ctrl/Cmd key, click on various thumbnails. Hover over a selected page in the Pages panel, then right-click and select Print Pages. The Range field will be filled in automatically.

The next section in this book explains how to customize the design of your book's pages at every level, starting from your book's overall trim size and going right down to the smallest details in your paragraph and character styles.

If you're satisfied with the way your book looks now, feel free to skip Part IV: Designing Your Pages and go straight to Part V: Adding Shapes & Color. If you don't need any shapes or color in your pages, then skip to Part VI: Adding Images. If you don't have any images inside your book, you'll still want to follow the instructions in chapter 23 to set up a baseline grid for your pages.

Chances are good that, even if you don't have shapes or images in your book, you'll refer back to Parts V and VI when you begin designing your book cover.

Part IV:
Designing Your Pages

17

Changing your page design

Now that you've applied your paragraph and character styles to all the text on your pages, look through your pages in InDesign or print them, and see if you're satisfied with the design you created following the instructions in this book. Even if you're pleased with the way your book looks (its trim size, the layout of the pages, the typeface and type size of all your text, and so on), be sure to read chapter 23 on setting up your baseline grid. Then feel free to skip the rest of Part IV: Designing Your Pages.

However, if you'd like to change some aspects of your page design to better suit your book, then Part IV is written for you! You'll be guided through changing the design of every aspect of your pages.

Part IV is set up so that the first changes you make, if you wish, are ones that affect the book and pages as a whole. These are large-scale changes that will affect the flow of text on all pages, and these changes are made globally on the A-Master page (see chapters 18–20).

Once your page size and margins are established, you'll make any changes you choose to the typeface and type size for your main text, and for other text in your book as needed. These are mid-scale changes that affect all the text in your book, and these changes are made globally to your Basic Paragraph and other paragraph styles (see chapters 21–23).

Then you'll be guided through making changes to your chapter opening pages, headings, folios and running heads, and all the other elements you set up paragraph styles for in Part II (see chapters 24–27).

And, finally, you'll design all the text and pages in your front and back matter based on the final design of your chapter pages (see chapters 28 and 29).

Now that the hard work of creating and applying your paragraph styles is done, enjoy the creative process of experimenting with changes to your book design. Have fun!

If you are working with separate documents for each chapter or section of your book, you can change the styles in just one document and then synchronize all the others with it when you gather the files into a Book using InDesign's Book feature. See the blog post with step-by-step instructions at BookDesignMadeSimple .com/using-the-book-feature-in-InDesign.

Using master pages

Master pages are used to make global changes to pages, much the way paragraph styles are used to make global changes to paragraphs. Each master page is set up with a particular format, which can then be applied to pages within your book.

At present you have one master page in your document: A-Master. This is the master page you added your folios and running heads to in chapter 15. Double-click on A-Master in your Pages panel to open it. Note that these pages are the same trim size as your whole document, and they have the same margins that you specified when you set up your document.

A-Master is the master template for your whole document. This is important. This means that from now on, every time you make a change that needs to affect *all* the pages in your document, you'll make that change on A-Master. For example, if you decide to change your margins, you'll change them on A-Master. That way, *all* your pages will be changed and get exactly the same margins at the same time.

In a typical book, A-Master controls the margins, running heads/feet, and folios. So if you decide to move your running heads/feet or folios to a different position on the page, you'll make that change on A-Master.

All of the items on A-Master will be visible on the pages to which A-Master is applied. However, you won't be able to select them using the Selection or Type tools on any pages except A-Master without specifically overriding them.

It's possible that a book with a simple layout (say, a novel) could have just one master page—A-Master. With the running heads set with the book's title on the left page and the author's name on the right page, all the pages in the book could have the same master page. You would simply delete the folios and running heads from any pages that didn't require them (such as front matter or chapter opening pages).

Pages panel with A-Master at the top and pages with A-Master applied to them below.

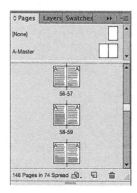

If, for some reason, you need to move, delete, or change any master page item while you're working on a book page, you can select it by holding down Ctrl/Cmd+Shift while you click on the item with any tool.

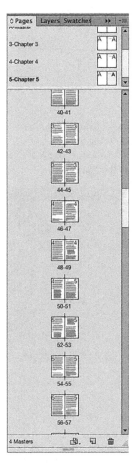

However, most books have more than one master page, usually one for each chapter (with the chapter title in the running head) and a few for the front and back matter, with all master pages being based on A-Master.

For example, this book has 75 master pages that are all based on A-Master. A-Master contains the margins, running feet, and folios, as well as columns (see page 128), guides (see page 127), and a baseline grid (see chapter 23). There is a separate master for each chapter because the chapter title in the running feet at the bottom right is different for each chapter. So it's easiest to create a new master for each chapter, *based on A-Master*, with just the chapter title changed. You'll learn how to do this in chapter 52.

For now, the important thing to remember is that any changes you make to your margins, running heads/feet, or folios will be made on A-Master.

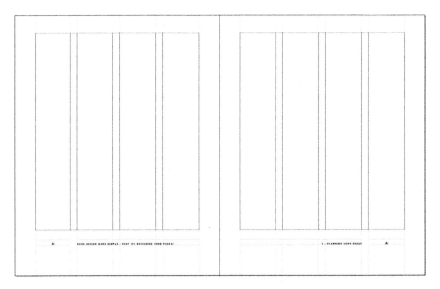

The A-Master pages for *this* book include margins, running feet, folios, columns, guides, and a baseline grid.

Changing your trim size

There are lots of reasons why you might want to change your book's trim size. For starters, it's an easy way to gain or lose several pages if you'd prefer a thicker or thinner book. Or, you may want your pages to look more or less spacious than they do now. Or, perhaps you've simply changed your mind since choosing a trim size in chapter 5.

Before changing your trim size, be sure to enable your Layout Adjustment. When Layout Adjustment is enabled, InDesign adjusts all your text frames and margins every time you make a change.

Let's say you change your trim size from 5.5″ × 8.5″ to 6″ × 9″. InDesign will move your margins so that now they are the specified distance from the new edges of your pages. InDesign will also resize all your text frames so they fit within the margins and will reflow all the text within those frames. This saves you from changing the size of every text frame manually.

You don't need to open A-Master to change your trim size; it can be done from anywhere in your document.

Enabling Layout Adjustment

Click Layout>Margins and Columns and then check the Enable Layout Adjustment box. Click OK.

If you plan to print your book on a traditional offset press (as opposed to a digital press), now is the time to start thinking about your final page count. On an offset press, books are printed in groups of pages on one large sheet of paper, so the number of pages in the book must be divisible by the number of pages that fit on one sheet. Your printer will tell you this number (called a "printing number"). See more in chapter 48 about offset printing and what you need to do to plan your final page count.

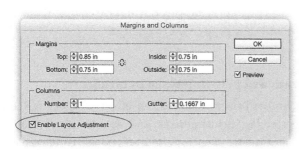

Changing your book's trim size

Click File>Document Setup to open the Document Setup dialog box. Choose your new trim size by changing the numbers in the Width and Height boxes, then click OK.

Click the down arrow to show the Bleed and Slug settings if you don't see them.

Check Preview to see your changes as you make them.

Document Setup

Intent: Print

Number of Pages: 146 ☑ Facing Pages

Start Page #: 1 ☐ Primary Text Frame

Page Size: [Custom]

Width: 6 in   Orientation:

Height: 9 in

Bleed and Slug

	Top	Bottom	Inside	Outside
Bleed:	0.125 in	0.125 in	0.125 in	0.125 in
Slug:	0 in	0 in	0 in	0 in

☑ Preview   Cancel   OK

You'll see that your pages now have the new trim size, but the margins are the same distance from the edges of the pages as they were before. The size of your text frames, however, will have changed, causing your text to reflow and your page count to change.

Keeping standard printing sizes in mind

Remember, standard sizes are more cost-effective to print. Refer to pages 20 and 21 for standard printing sizes, and also check printers' websites for other available standard sizes for children's books, coffee table books, and other larger-sized books.

Changing your margins

Increasing or decreasing your margins affects both the look of your pages *and* your page count. Any changes made to your margins are always made on A-Master.

Design considerations when adjusting your margins

White space is good

It never hurts to be generous with white space. Think about your experience with reading books. If the text is too close to the spine, it's uncomfortable to read. Your hand gets sore trying to keep the book open enough to easily read all the text.

Same with the text towards the outsides and bottom of the pages. These areas are known as "thumb space." Do you have to keep moving your thumbs to read the text at the outsides or bottoms of the pages? Lack of white space in these areas makes it frustrating to read.

Margins increase as leading increases

As a general rule, type set with lots of leading looks odd with very narrow margins (left below). Conversely, type set with very little leading looks odd with generous margins (right below). If the type and leading are generous, the margins should be generous too, and vice versa.

 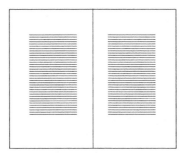

Quick notes on margin settings

Inside margin

The standard size of the inside margin is 0.75″. Most books with trim sizes of 5″ × 8″, 5.5″ × 8.5″, and 6″ × 9″ have an inside margin of 0.75″. That allows enough space for binding the book.

When a book gets to a certain thickness (usually around 400 pages), the inside margin can be a bit bigger, say 0.875″ or 1″. Books with sewn binding (more expensive) will lie open flatter, and the inside margin will be less of a issue. But books with perfect binding (glued) will need a bit more room on the inside margin if they are over 400 pages.

Top margin

Remember that your running heads and folios appear above the top margin, so they are not counted in the margin measurements.

Most books have running heads rather than running feet. If you are planning to have running heads, the top margin needs to be large enough to accommodate them.

A standard top margin in a book with running heads is 0.825″ to 0.875″. In books without running heads, the minimum margin is 0.5″, as some printers have a minimum clearance from the edges of pages of 0.5″.

Outside margin

The outside margin is often the same size as the inside margin, yet the outside margin still *appears* larger because part of the inside margin is hidden in the binding.

Bottom margin

Remember that if you're using running feet and drop folios, they appear below the bottom margin.

Having an ample bottom margin is never a bad thing, and ideally it should be your largest margin. Also keep in mind that when a book is printed and bound, everything always looks lower on the page (really!). So don't be tempted to narrow your bottom margin too much (say a minimum of 0.75″).

One last thing to remember: generous leading calls for generous margins, and narrower leading calls for narrower margins.

Adjusting your margins

Open A-Master to get started. You'll want to see your changes as you make them. An easy way to do so is to copy and paste a 2-page spread onto A-Master. Find any 2-page spread where the text fills both pages, then select both text frames by holding Shift and clicking them with the Selection Tool. Copy the text frames by clicking Edit>Copy, then double-click A-Master to open it. Paste the text frames into A-Master in the exact place they were on your 2-page spread by clicking Edit>Paste in Place. Now you're ready to adjust your margins.

Click Layout>Margins and Columns to open the Margins and Columns dialog box. If you've set your margins following the guidelines on page 34, your Margins and Columns dialog box will look something like this:

The keyboard shortcut for Copy is Ctrl/Cmd+C.

The keyboard shortcut for Paste is Ctrl/Cmd+V.

The keyboard shortcut for Paste in Place is Ctrl/Cmd+Shift+Alt/Opt+V.

This link is broken since not all the margins are the same size.

Enable Layout Adjustment should be checked. You may need to check it every time.

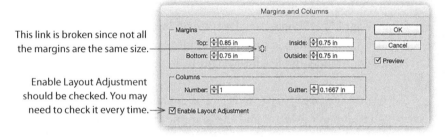

Select both A-Master pages in the Pages panel to make changes on both pages at once.

If you change your margins and columns at the same time, it's possible that your text frames won't adjust automatically. If so, try doing this operation in two separate steps: First change the margins and click OK. Then go back and change the columns.

Make sure the Preview box is checked. Try changing the top margin by clicking the up and down arrows next to it. You'll see that the margin shifts each time you click it. This may take a moment or two, depending on how many pages are in your book, as InDesign will be changing all your pages at the same time.

Review the design considerations and margin settings on pages 123 and 124, and then start making your adjustments on A-Master. When you're finished, use the Selection Tool to delete the two text frames of type that you pasted into A-Master.

How wide can your margins be? That depends on your typeface and type size. Your text frame should accommodate a minimum of 27 characters per line, around 40 is optimal, and 70 is the maximum. To see how many characters fit on one line in *your* book, type a line of numbers:

The main text frame on *this* page is 64 characters wide. If the type size and leading were smaller, these lines would seem too long to be comfortably read. But at a type and size of Chaparral 10.5 pt and with generous leading of 14 pt, a line length of 64 characters is comfortable to read.

1234567890123456789012345678901234567890123456789012345678901234

Using margins and columns to change your page layout

Most books are designed with one column containing the main text frame. However, some books are designed with a wider format to accommodate images, sidebars, or text in multiple columns. Examples are coffee table books, cookbooks, and how-to books, like this one.

For a larger-format book, it's often helpful to create a grid of columns rather than just, say, two. You might think the layout grid for this book is two columns (one large column toward the spine for the main narrative and a smaller column on the outside for captions), but actually it has four columns. This way, the main text occupies three columns and the captions one column, but there is also the choice of setting type or images in two equal columns side by side. Read more about using columns in larger-format or more complex books on our blog:

- BookDesignMadeSimple.com/layout-grid-book-design
- BookDesignMadeSimple.com/design-coffee-table-book
- BookDesignMadeSimple.com/designing-a-cookbook

Since you have already checked the box enabling Layout Adjustment (see page 125), open A-Master and the Margins and Columns dialog box again. Under Columns, enter the number of columns you want and the gutter between them. Just make sure that Enable Layout Adjustment is checked, and click OK.

Look at any 2-page spread in your book and you'll see that InDesign has reflowed your text into columns on each page, with individual text frames for each column. If you've created a two-column format, the text will have reflowed perfectly into two columns on each page with two linked text frames, and you are good to go.

But what if you don't want the text to flow into every column? Suppose you want your main text frame to be three columns wide with no text frame in the fourth column, as in this book. You simply need to trick InDesign slightly by pretending you want four columns and then switching to one column at the end. See the next page for instructions.

The page layout of *Book Design Made Simple* is based on a 4-column grid with a 0.25" gutter between them, as indicated by the light gray lines on this page.

For recipes, you might want a narrow column on the left for ingredients and a wider one on the right for instructions, but the proportions mentioned on this page will probably not work. To find the best column widths, experiment with your longest recipe until it fits well on the page, and then base all your other recipes on that layout by making a master page spread. For more cookbook tips, see our blog post at Book DesignMadeSimple.com/ designing-a-cookbook.

captions =
← 1 column wide →

← main text frame = 3 columns wide →

By following the steps below, you will get pages that will look more like the gray outlines shown on *this* page. Make sure you're on your A-Master page and in the Normal view mode.

1   If you want to start over, undo the columns you made earlier.

Undo your most recent change by clicking Edit>Undo or by using the keyboard short-cut of Ctrl/Cmd+Z.

2   Return to Layout>Margins and Columns and uncheck the Enable Lay-out Adjustment box. Select the number of columns you want to base your grid on and the gutter between them, and click OK. On A-Master, drag vertical guides to the left and right edge of each column that you made. (Put your pointer in the ruler on the left edge of the screen and drag to the right to make the guides.) For a four-column page like this one, you should end up with eight vertical guides. Repeat this on the other page of the A-Master spread. See figure A on the next page.

vertical guides

3   Using the Measure tool (⌗), put your pointer ('⌗) at the outside trim edge of one of the pages, then hold down Shift as you drag horizon-tally to the outside of the main text area that you want to create; on *this* page it would be the third guide from the outside trim (as in fig-ure A on the next page). When the Info panel pops up automatically, make a note of the width (W) of the line. Close the Info panel. The mark made by the Measure tool will disappear as soon as you click on another tool.

The Measure tool might be hiding behind the Eyedropper or the Color Theme tool.

outside edge of text frame

4   Go to Layout>Liquid Layout and in the fly-out menu click Layout Adjustment. Uncheck Allow Ruler Guides to Move, then click OK. Go to Layout>Margins and Columns and first check Enable Layout Adjustment, then change the number of columns to 1. Next, change the outside margin to the width of the line you measured in step 3. Click OK, and InDesign will reflow all your text into the new single column that you made. Your page will have an enormous outside mar-gin, with two vertical guides showing you where your outside column is, and the other vertical guides indicating the rest of your grid. Figure B on the next page shows the result.

captions = 1 column wide

←———————— main text frame = 3 columns wide ————————→   ←—— 1 column wide ——→

A

Drag vertical guides (see page 111) to the left and right edges of each column.

The light gray area represents the 4-column text frame that you created in the Margins and Columns dialog box in step 2 on page 127.

B

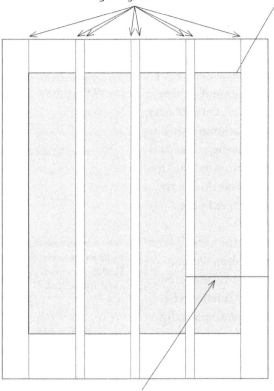

outside margin

Use the Measure tool to find out the distance from the out-side trim to the outside of the area that you want for your main text frame. Look in the Info panel for the value.

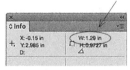

This is how a recto page will look. (A verso page will be a mirror image of it.) The text frame (light gray) is only 1 col-umn, but it's 3 columns wide. The outer column is 1 column wide. When you want to use the outer column, simply draw a text frame between the outer guides. All of the vertical guides are there when you need them to show you where to place captions or 2-column-wide text and images.

You can watch this pro-cedure in the video called "Using columns to change your layout" at BookDesignMade Simple.com/videos.

Because Layout Adjustment is turned on, InDesign automatically fills exactly the area that you want to use on each page for your main text and leaves the rest free for captions, images, and so on.

A three-column or five (or more)-column grid might work better for your book. It all depends on the page dimensions and the sizes and shapes of your images and materials.

Changing your main typeface

21

The single most important part of book design is ensuring that your main text is easy to read. This means you'll use a typeface suitable for long documents. Take a quick look through the books on your shelf. You'll see that most books use serif typefaces for the main text, because they are the easiest to read for long, continuous blocks of text.

Three categories of typefaces

Serif	Sans Serif	Display

Minion Pro	Myriad Pro	Brush Script Std

Serif typefaces have strokes, mostly either horizontal or oblique, added to the basic letterform. They are the easiest to read at smaller sizes, especially for long blocks of text.

Sans serif typefaces don't have any additions to the basic letterform and are more difficult to read in continuous text. They are used for headings, running heads/feet, folios, and sidebars.

Display typefaces are not suitable for continuous text. They are used for design elements such as chapter numbers, chapter titles, or drop caps at the beginning of chapters.

Adobe Creative Cloud has many typefaces that are suitable for books. You can search the Recommended for Paragraphs category in Typekit to find one that you like. Each typeface has different characteristics that will determine whether it is the perfect choice for *your* book.

Comparing four popular serif typefaces

Caslon Pro

This paragraph is set in Adobe Caslon Pro. This typeface is classic, and the letters look a bit old fashioned and flowery. The letters appear slightly bigger than in the typefaces below, even though the type size is the same (11/14). Caslon is ideal for historical novels, nonfiction books, and poetry.

One great thing about Caslon is its ornaments: ⌛ ✤ ❦ ❉ ✿ ✄ ❀

Chaparral Pro

This paragraph is set in Chaparral Pro (as is the main text in this book). This typeface is modern, and the letters are a bit industrial-looking. See how this typeface is slightly bolder and darker on the page than the others. Chaparral is ideal for fiction, science fiction, how-to books, and friendly nonfiction.

One great thing about Chaparral is that its **bold is very BOLD.**

Garamond Pro

This paragraph is set in Adobe Garamond Pro. This typeface is classic and very easy to read at small sizes. See how much less crowded Garamond looks because of the smaller lowercase letters? Garamond is ideal for any book and is one of the most often-used typefaces for books.

One great thing about Garamond is its BEAUTIFUL SMALL CAPS.

Minion Pro

This paragraph is set in Minion Pro. This typeface is modern and clean. See how the letters are straightforward and direct. Minion is ideal for business books, nonfiction, and fiction, and it pairs well with the sans serif Myriad for titles and subheadings.

One great thing about Minion is its *gorgeous italics.*

What to look for in a font family

A font family is comprised of several related typefaces, all designed to be used together. For your book, you'll want to choose a font family that includes all the faces you'll need.

Example: Minion Pro font family

Regular (used for your main text)
lowercase: abcdefghijklmnopqrstuvwxyz !@#$%^&*()+
uppercase: ABCDEFGHIJKLMNOPQRSTUVWXYZ
oldstyle figures: 1234567890   lining figures: 1234567890

Some fonts use the term Roman for regular type—it's the traditional term for neither italic nor bold.

Italic (used for emphasis, headings, book titles, etc.)
lowercase: *abcdefghijklmnopqrstuvwxyz !@#$%^&*()+*
uppercase: *ABCDEFGHIJKLMNOPQRSTUVWXYZ*
oldstyle figures: *1234567890*   lining figures: *1234567890*

Small capitals (good for subheadings and acronyms)
regular: ABCDEFGHIJKLMNOPQRSTUVWXYZ !@#$%^&*()+
italic: *ABCDEFGHIJKLMNOPQRSTUVWXYZ*
oldstyle figures: 1234567890   lining figures: 1234567890

Semibold or Medium (good for headings)
lowercase: abcdefghijklmnopqrstuvwxyz !@#$%^&*()+
uppercase: ABCDEFGHIJKLMNOPQRSTUVWXYZ
oldstyle figures: 1234567890   lining figures: 1234567890

Semibold Italic or Medium Italic (good for headings)
lowercase: *abcdefghijklmnopqrstuvwxyz !@#$%^&*()+*
uppercase: *ABCDEFGHIJKLMNOPQRSTUVWXYZ*
oldstyle figures: *1234567890*   lining figures: *1234567890*

Bold (good for headings but not used for emphasis in main text)
lowercase: **abcdefghijklmnopqrstuvwxyz !@#$%^&*()+**
uppercase: **ABCDEFGHIJKLMNOPQRSTUVWXYZ**
oldstyle figures: **1234567890**   lining figures: **1234567890**

Bold Italic (good for headings but not used for emphasis in main text)
lowercase: ***abcdefghijklmnopqrstuvwxyz !@#$%^&*()+***
uppercase: ***ABCDEFGHIJKLMNOPQRSTUVWXYZ***
oldstyle figures: ***1234567890***   lining figures: ***1234567890***

Fonts: Using them legally

Most people give no thought to the legal use of fonts. But those in the publishing industry (that's you!) need to be aware of legitimate font use at all times. Luckily, Adobe Creative Cloud has simplified the issue by allowing you to use Typekit fonts without restriction—as long as you stick with Desktop use and don't stray into Web use. Web fonts have a separate license.

You may legally use the CC fonts for printing your book, making an ebook file (but see the Typekit Services Agreement for a few restrictions), and creating any kind of printed advertising or products, such as T-shirts, bookmarks, postcards, or business cards. You may also make PDFs to distribute as you like. Do not use the fonts as HTML type on your website without first signing up for Web font service.

When you uninstall the Creative Cloud package, you lose all the fonts because they were never really yours to begin with; they are just synced to your computer while you are signed up for the service.

If you would like to use some of the fonts in the future outside of CC, you will need to purchase them.

"Typeface" vs. "Font"

What's the difference? A typeface is the design that makes Caslon look different from Helvetica, for instance. A font is the delivery system for the typeface, whether it be a computer file or a set of metal type.

Fonts: How and what to buy

There are a great many websites that sell fonts. At BookDesignMadeSimple.com/resources, we keep an updated list of the more commonly used sites, but you may discover others. Here are a few:

- myfonts.com
- fonts.com
- fontshop.com

Always buy OpenType fonts. When you browse for fonts online, look for the OpenType symbol (a two-color, italic "O") or the word "OpenType" in the product description. OpenType fonts are produced through a collaboration between Microsoft and Adobe, and both companies, and others, have brought their older font products into the OpenType format. That is why you might see various additional phrases that describe font software, such as "Type 1 OpenType," "TrueType flavor," "PostScript flavor," or "OpenTypeCFF." All of these are fine to use.

One great thing about OpenType fonts is that they work on both Windows and Macintosh computers. Another is all the special features that come with them, such as the various kinds of figure styles, the ability to build fractions easily, and everything else you can see in the OpenType Features dialog box in your Paragraph Styles and Character Styles panels.

Once you purchase and download the product, you'll receive a folder or file with installation instructions.

Choosing a typeface for your main text

The easiest way to choose a typeface for your main text is to experiment with some typefaces you can sync with Creative Cloud's Typekit. That way you can see what *your* words look like in different typefaces.

All the changes you make to your type at the design stage will be done within your paragraph styles. Find a 2-page spread in your document with a lot of type on it. Using your Selection Tool, click anywhere outside your document to make sure nothing is selected, then switch to Preview mode using the View Tool or by pressing W.

Double-click your Basic Paragraph style in the Paragraph Styles panel, and select Basic Character Formats on the left. Make sure the Preview box at the bottom left is checked. All the typefaces installed on your computer are contained in the drop-down menu called Font Family. At present, you'll see Minion Pro in the Font Family drop-down menu. Choose a different typeface from the menu, and you'll see all the type on your pages change to that typeface.

While your cursor is in the Font Family drop-down menu, you can use your up and down arrow keys to try every typeface on your computer. Of course, most of the typefaces won't be suitable for your main text, but it's interesting to see how different your type looks in different typefaces. Make a list of the typefaces you think have potential for your book.

These typeface changes you are viewing are only temporary while Paragraph Style Options is open. To close Paragraph Style Options without making any changes, simply click Cancel. To change your Text [**tx**] style to a different typeface, choose the typeface from the Font Family drop-down menu, and click OK.

You'll need to print several 2-page spreads while you're designing your pages. Whenever you adjust your typeface, type size, leading, or margins, the overall look of your pages will change. The easiest way to check that the changes are improving your design is to print two pages, trim them to size, and tape them together in a 2-page spread. Then insert the pages into a similarly sized book and see what they will look like when your book is printed and bound.

To sync a new font to use in InDesign, go into the Creative Cloud app and click on Assets>Fonts>Browse Fonts. Then follow the instructions on page 11 to find and sync suitable fonts to try.

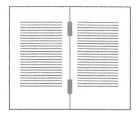

Looking more closely at type

Now that you've been looking at and thinking about typefaces for a while, you may have become curious about typographic design. How is it that the typefaces look similar but also different?

ascenders

descenders

Many books have been written about the history and design of type. But to make a very long story extremely short, the design of type began in the Western world as soon as Johannes Gutenberg typeset and printed copies of the Bible in the 1450s. He based the shapes of his metal letters on the standard German handwriting of the time. As the centuries advanced and the technology spread, different typesetters developed their own styles, each time expanding the collection of typefaces. Many fonts are named after their designers, such as Garamond, Jenson, Bodoni, Caslon, and even Zapf Dingbats.

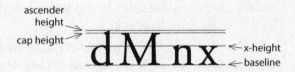

ascender height

cap height

x-height

baseline

Nowadays we have access to just about every type design that has come before, and more are being introduced all the time. It's almost overwhelming (though fascinating) to browse through a font vendor's website. You can usually read a brief history of any font you choose, and often you'll discover that you can tell the difference between a very old typeface and a contemporary one at a glance. To be very untechnical about it, somehow the letters just give off a vibe from their century of origin.

serifs

stems

arms

crossbars

To the right you'll see the names of some letter parts. Every typeface applies the shapes of these parts in a very consistent way, and the combinations of shapes and proportions are what give a typeface its look.

axes

bowls

counters

link
ear
loop

Setting type size and leading

Once you've chosen a typeface for your main text, you'll want to experiment with its size and leading (rhymes with heading). A type size of 11 pt is very common for books, and the leading is usually set two or three points above the type size. If your type size and leading are set at 11 pt and 14 pt respectively, then it's written like this: 11/14 (say 11 on 14).

You'll want to change your type size and leading if your book needs a larger type size (for example, for a younger or older readership), or if the main typeface you chose looks a bit small or crowded at 11/14.

What is the best type size and leading for your book? This will depend on marketplace standards and personal preferences. Look at several other published books in your genre and see what type sizes are used. Most type for fiction and nonfiction books is set in the 10 pt to 12 pt range. Large-print and children's books are often set in the 12 pt to 16 pt range. Find a book you like with an appropriate type size for your book, and use it as a starting point.

Try copying and pasting a paragraph from your book into a new page or document. Paste it again several times, then apply various type sizes and leading combinations in each paragraph. Print out the page and place it next to some text in another book in your genre.

Setting your type size

To set the type size for your main text, double-click the Basic Paragraph style in your Paragraph Styles panel to open the Paragraph Style Options. Make sure the Preview box at the bottom is checked so you can see changes on the fly. Select the Basic Character Formats category on the left, then change the Size drop-down menu to your new type size. You can either type in a size or select a standard size from the drop-down menu. Fractional sizes are also available, such as 11.5 pt or 10.75 pt.

When you've set your new type size, click OK to make the change throughout your main text. Print a page (see chapter 16) to see how the type looks in print. You'll see that your type size has changed but the leading is still the same, so if your type is bigger it will look more crowded, and if your type is smaller it will look more spacious.

Finding the ideal leading for your type

Leading is usually set two or three points larger than the type size. For example, if your type size is 11 pt, then your leading could be 13 or 14 pt. Leading set two points larger is the minimum you want for your book, as less will look crowded and be harder to read. Adding leading to your type is a way to create a more spacious feel for your book and make your paragraphs easier to read.

Look at the samples on page 137 to see how changing the amount of leading changes the look and feel of the type, and the color of the page as a whole. If the leading is too tight, the words look crowded. If it's too spacious, the lines begin to appear unconnected. So find a happy medium for your type—not too crowded and not too spacious. If you're in doubt, go through other books in your genre and see what looks best to you.

The main text in this book is set in Chaparral Pro at 10.5/14.

Experiment with the amount of leading in your main text by going back into your Paragraph Style Options for the Basic Paragraph style. Select the Basic Character Formats category on the left, then change the Leading drop-down menu to a size that is two or three points larger than your type size. You can either type in the size or select a standard size from the drop-down menu. Fractional sizes are also available, such as 13.5 pt or 12.75 pt.

The margin captions in this book (such as this one) are set in Myriad Pro at 8/10.5.

When you've set your new leading size, click OK to make the change throughout your main text. Print a 2-page spread to see how the type looks in print. Change the amount of leading a few times and print a 2-page spread each time. Then compare the spreads to see which type and leading combination works the best for your book.

Keep in mind that increasing your leading means there could be one fewer line per page, and decreasing it could add a line to each page.

Type size and leading examples

Below are samples of type set in Adobe Garamond Pro (on the left) and Adobe Minion Pro (on the right). The lines in these columns are narrower than the lines in your book will be, but they'll give you a good idea of how type size and leading interact.

The first paragraph in each column is set in 11/14, the second in 11/13, and the third in 11/12. Notice how the different leadings affect the look of the paragraphs even though the type is all the same size. Also note that Minion requires more lines than Garamond.

This paragraph is set in Adobe Garamond Pro 11/14. The type looks spacious and is easy to read. This is a standard size of type and leading for fiction and nonfiction books. Generous leading can reduce the number of lines per page.

This paragraph is set in Adobe Minion Pro 11/14. The type looks spacious and is easy to read. This is a standard size of type and leading for fiction and nonfiction books. Generous leading can reduce the number of lines per page.

This paragraph is set in Adobe Garamond Pro 11/13. This paragraph looks slightly darker on the page than the paragraph above because of less leading, but it is still easy to read. The reduced leading may allow one extra line on every page.

This paragraph is set in Adobe Minion Pro 11/13. This paragraph looks slightly darker on the page than the paragraph above because of less leading, but it is still easy to read. The reduced leading may allow one extra line on every page.

This paragraph is set in Adobe Garamond Pro 11/12. The type is now looking a bit crowded, and it's harder for readers to find the beginning of the next line, particularly when the lines go across the whole page rather than a narrow column, such as this one.

This paragraph is set in Adobe Minion Pro 11/12. The type is now looking a bit crowded, and it's harder for readers to find the beginning of the next line, particularly when the lines go across the whole page rather than a narrow column, such as this one.

23 *Setting up your baseline grid*

Baseline grids are horizontal guide lines that keep lines of text consistent from page to page. Hold up a book and look at one of the pages against a lit background. The lines of type on both sides of the page should line up.

Baseline grids are always set to the size of the leading. If your main text has 14 pt leading, then your baseline grid is set to 14 pt. Sometimes if a book has very complex headings, subheadings, bulleted lists, etc., the baseline grid may be set to one half of the leading (say, 7 pt instead of 14 pt). This allows half-linespaces between headings and lists and can save space while still adhering to a baseline grid. But in most books, the baseline grid is simply set to the same point size as the leading.

All the text and images in your book will be aligned to your margins, column(s), and baseline grid.

Setting up your baseline grid

Open your Grid Preferences by clicking Edit>Preferences>Grids (Windows) or InDesign> Preferences>Grids (Mac). You set some of your preferences earlier, in chapter 7.

In the Baseline Grid box, choose a light color from the Color dropdown menu (Light Gray is a good choice). See the settings on page 139.

In the Start box, type "0 in," and in the Relative To box, select Top of Page. This Start box setting is perfect for books with running feet (such as this book); however, if your book has running heads, you'll change your Start box setting (see page 139).

In the Increment Every box, type the size of your leading (i.e., 14 pt). Leave everything else in this dialog box with the InDesign defaults.

Click OK, and a baseline grid will appear on your A-Master. If the grid doesn't appear automatically, you may need to show it by clicking View>Grids & Guides>Show Baseline Grid and switching to Normal view. Now you'll see horizontal lines 14 pts apart across your 2-page spread from top to bottom.

Your baseline grid will only be visible in Normal view, not in Preview. Press W to switch views while the Selection Tool is in use and nothing is selected.

Running heads and/or folios are placed two baselines above the main text. Running feet and/or folios are placed two or three baselines below the main text.

The keyboard shortcut to show or hide the baseline grid is Ctrl/Cmd+Alt/Opt+'.

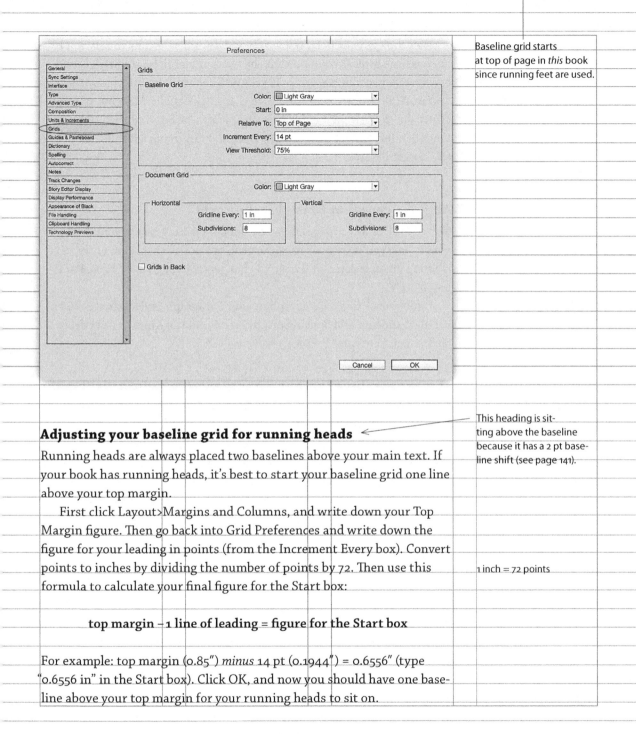

Preferences

Baseline grid starts at top of page in *this* book since running feet are used.

Adjusting your baseline grid for running heads

This heading is sitting above the baseline because it has a 2 pt baseline shift (see page 141).

Running heads are always placed two baselines above your main text. If your book has running heads, it's best to start your baseline grid one line above your top margin.

First click Layout>Margins and Columns, and write down your Top Margin figure. Then go back into Grid Preferences and write down the figure for your leading in points (from the Increment Every box). Convert points to inches by dividing the number of points by 72. Then use this formula to calculate your final figure for the Start box:

1 inch = 72 points

top margin − 1 line of leading = figure for the Start box

For example: top margin (0.85″) *minus* 14 pt (0.1944″) = 0.6556″ (type "0.6556 in" in the Start box). Click OK, and now you should have one baseline above your top margin for your running heads to sit on.

Now look at your bottom margin and see where it falls in relation to the baseline grid. If you find that the bottom margin is slightly *above* a baseline, adjust the margin so it's slightly below instead. Otherwise your text won't flow onto that line. To do this, click Layout>Margins and Columns, check both the Enable Layout Adjustment box and the Preview box, then increase or decrease the Bottom Margin until it falls just below the closest baseline. Click OK.

Return to any 2-page spread by double-clicking the page icon in your Pages panel.

Aligning your text to the baseline grid

Switch back to any 2-page spread by double-clicking one in your Pages panel. Now you'll *see* your baseline grid, but notice that none of the text is lining up on it yet. You'll need to change a setting in your Basic Paragraph style.

Double-click Basic Paragraph in your Paragraph Styles panel to open it. Select Indents and Spacing on the left. From the Align to Grid drop-down menu, choose All Lines, then click OK.

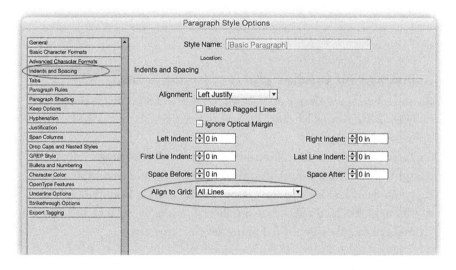

All your text *based on* the Basic Paragraph style (remember your paragraph styles family tree on page 59) will now align with the baseline grid. In other words, all the text in every paragraph style in your book should now align with your baseline grid.

Look through your pages and see how they look aligned to the baseline grid. Your main text should look fine, as will all text set with the same leading value as your baseline grid. However, not all of your text will look fine with that leading value. This includes text with smaller leading values (such as your copyright page, endnotes, index, and so on), as well as text with larger leading values (for example, titles and headings).

If you notice some text that shouldn't be aligned to the baseline grid, you can open the relevant paragraph style and, under Indents and Spacing, change Align to Grid: to None.

If you have just a bit of text that you want to take off the grid, simply remove it by selecting the Do Not Align to Grid icon in your Paragraph panel (see example on page 295).

Occasions to lift off from the baseline grid

You might notice in your own book, and in this one, that the type in the Heading 2 style does not actually align with the baseline grid. There is more space than usual below the heading. That is because of the baseline shift applied to the style (see page 76). Baseline shift raises or lowers characters from their normal position but does not affect any type before or after it. To apply it, highlight all the letters that you want to move up or down, find the Baseline Shift icon (pictured at right) in the Control panel or Character panel, then type in the number of points (or even hundredths of points) that you want the type to shift. Remember to make character styles for type that uses baseline shift. You could name a style with 6 pts of baseline shift "tx+6," for instance.

To typeset complex mathematics or scientific formulas, you might need to leave the principal line of the equation on the grid but allow the rest to shift up or down. Manipulating the baseline grid for fractions is a very useful tool. Here is an example:

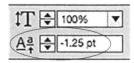

Baseline shift increments can be as small as hundredths of a point.

To learn more about typesetting math, see pages 350–351, and read our blog post at BookDesignMade Simple.com/typesetting-math-in-indesign.

$$\frac{(x-3)^2}{4} + \frac{(y-2)^2}{3} = 1$$

Baseline shift for type in the numerator: 6 points

No baseline shift for "+" or "= 1"

Baseline shift for type in the denominator (set on the next line): 8 points

The main line of this equation (the "+" and the "= 1") remains on the grid, but everything else is set with a baseline shift. After the math, the type goes back to aligning with the grid.

24 Designing chapter and part openings

Chapter openings are a major part of the look and style of your book. The type sizes of chapter numbers and titles are generally larger than the main text, allowing more freedom in choosing typefaces. Decorative elements can also be used. Because they set the tone of your book, chapter openings should be appropriate for your subject and genre.

What type of book do you expect to read when you see the chapter openings below?

3 The City

They were indeed a queer-looking party that assembled on the bank—the birds with draggled feathers, the animals with their fur clinging close to them, and all dripping wet, cross, and uncomfortable.

The first question of course was, how to get dry again: they had a consultation about this, and after a few minutes it seemed quite natural to Alice to find herself talking familiarly with them, as if she had known them all her life. Indeed, she had quite a long argument with the Lory, who at last turned sulky, and would only say, 'I am older than you, and must know better'; and this Alice would not allow without knowing how old it was, and, as the Lory positively refused to tell its age, there was no more to be said.

At last the Mouse, who seemed to be a person of authority among them, called out, 'Sit down, all of you, and listen to me! I'LL soon make you dry enough!' They all sat down at once, in a large ring, with the Mouse in the middle. Alice kept her eyes anxiously fixed on it, for she felt sure she would catch a bad cold if she did not get dry very soon.

'Ahem!' said the Mouse with an important air, 'are you all ready? This is the driest thing I know. Silence all round, if you please!

{ CHAPTER THREE }

the City

They were indeed a queer-looking party that assembled on the bank—the birds with draggled feathers, the animals with their fur clinging close to them, and all dripping wet, cross, and uncomfortable.

The first question of course was, how to get dry again: they had a consultation about this, and after a few minutes it seemed quite natural to Alice to find herself talking familiarly with them, as if she had known them all her life. Indeed, she had quite a long argument with the Lory, who at last turned sulky, and would only say, 'I am older than you, and must know better'; and this Alice would not allow without knowing how old it was, and, as the Lory positively refused to tell its age, there was no more to be said.

At last the Mouse, who seemed to be a person of authority among them, called out, 'Sit down, all of you, and listen to me! I'LL soon make you dry enough!' They all sat down at once, in a large ring, with the Mouse in the middle. Alice kept her eyes anxiously fixed on it, for she felt sure she would catch a bad cold if she did not get dry very soon.

'Ahem!' said the Mouse with an important air, 'are you all ready? This is the driest thing I know. Silence all round, if you please!

In this chapter you'll:

1   Learn basic principles of good page design
2   Choose a look for your chapter openings
3   Try the chapter opening designs in this chapter
4   Try the part opening designs in this chapter
5   Consider some variations

1 Basic principles of good design

Three basic principles of good design are:

REPEAT ELEMENTS   RULE OF THREE   WHITE SPACE

Repeat elements

Books look professional when they have a consistent and cohesive look throughout. An easy way to accomplish this is to choose a few elements and repeat them throughout your book. Here are some options to consider:

- **alignment** Choose one method of alignment and stick to it throughout your whole book. If you like to center things, then center *everything* (except your main text, of course). Or, if you prefer aligning things to the left or to the outside margins, then make that your rule and follow it throughout your book.

- **typefaces** Choose a typeface for your main text and use that same typeface throughout your book. Try using italics or caps (large or small) as a repeating theme in your chapter openings, headings, running heads, and folios. You may want to use a second typeface for some things, such as titles and/or headings. It's fine to use two typefaces in the same book, as long as they look nice together. Try to avoid using more than two typefaces.

- **graphic elements** Repeating a graphic element throughout your book can be very effective. Something as simple as bullet points can be used in your chapter opening (say, a bullet point on either side of the chapter number), as well as in running heads/feet (see the bottom of this page), and perhaps as a simple paragraph divider as well (three bullet points separated by en spaces). There are lots of graphic elements available in every typeface, such as: ~ * >> } and —. Some typefaces come with ornaments. As long as the same element is repeated (and not too loudly or too often), it can enhance your design.

Rule of three

Visual elements look best in groups of three. If a page has too many visual elements, they compete with each other and the reader doesn't know where to look first.

To find out which graphic elements or ornaments a typeface includes, open the Glyphs panel (or go to Type>Glyphs) and in the Show drop-down list choose Entire Font.

The three visual elements on a regular page of text are the folio, the running head, and the text block. On a chapter opening page, they are the chapter opening, the text block, and the drop folio.

You'll apply the drop folio in chapter 52.

Notice that the chapter opening in the image on page 144 includes a number of visual elements: the chapter number spelled out, fancy brackets, and the chapter title. Although comprised of different elements, your chapter opening should function as one cohesive visual unit rather than a number of separate ones.

Don't be tempted to use every book design element you've ever seen. If you want to start each chapter with a drop cap, fine. If you want to start each chapter with an image or a graphic element, fine. But don't use absolutely everything at the same time. Keep it simple.

White space

You've already learned that generous margins add valuable white space to pages, giving the main text block some breathing room and allowing thumb space for your readers.

The same goes for your chapter openings. Be generous with white space. The chapter opening occupies the top portion of the page, and its length will depend on how many elements are in your chapter opening. Novels often just include a chapter number or title, whereas some nonfiction books may include a chapter number, chapter title, opening quote with attribution, and so on.

Be aware that the amount of white space in your chapter opening will affect your page count.

2 Choosing a look for your chapter and part openings

There are unlimited variations of chapter and part openings, but they can be loosely categorized as follows:

- **Classic** Use the same typeface for everything throughout your book. The type size and style will vary for different design elements. Small and all caps are used for headings. Ornaments or flourishes are used, and most elements are centered. This look works equally well for nonfiction and fiction books.

- **Modern** Use a serif typeface for main text and a sans serif for titles and headings. Sans serif type gives both novels and business books a modern edge. Modern designs are often asymmetrical, with geometric graphics such as rules and rectangles to add clean lines.

- **Characteristic** Some books need openings with character. If your story is a Western, you may want to add a touch of Mesquite or Giddyup typefaces to your chapter openings. A romance calls for a flourishy script. The key here is to add *a touch* of character, as a little goes a very long way.

Readers shouldn't be distracted by a showy design. Rather, they should be led straight into your words. Good page design is invisible.

3 Trying the chapter opening designs in this chapter

All the designs that follow are based on the paragraph styles you've created up to this point. So be sure to save a copy of your book before proceeding, just in case you want to revert back to them in the future.

The designs that follow include all the specs you need for the paragraph and character styles in your chapter openings. Find a design that suits *your* book, then change your paragraph styles accordingly.

Go to one of your chapter opening pages, then open the first paragraph style that needs changing. Make sure the Preview box is checked so you can see the changes as you're making them.

Most chapter openings only include four or five paragraph styles at most—Chapter Numbers, Chapter Titles, Opening Quotes, Quote Attributions, and possibly an ornament—so it doesn't take long to adjust the settings. If you don't like the way the changes look, simply click Cancel instead of OK, and none of the changes will be made.

The only typefaces used in the sample designs are Minion (a serif), Myriad (a sans serif), and a few display types in the Characteristic designs. Most of these typefaces are included with InDesign and demonstrate the variety of designs available to you using just those typefaces. Feel free to substitute any serif or sans serif in *your* design, and experiment with the typefaces you have available to you.

Also be sure to look at other books for inspiration. If you find a chapter opening you particularly admire, try using a similar typeface and spacing for *your* chapter openings.

Chapter title considerations

Chapter titles are all different lengths, and single-word titles must look just as good as long titles. After changing your Chapter Titles paragraph style, make sure *all* your chapter titles look equally good.

If the type size of your chapter titles is large or your titles are long, some titles may require two or more lines. If so, you can control where the lines break by adding a soft return, which forces a new line but keeps it within the same paragraph for spacing purposes. Insert the cursor where you want the line to break, then press Shift+Enter/Return. If you have chosen to show your hidden characters (Type>Show Hidden Characters), you'll notice that the soft return symbol looks like this: ¬

A chapter title should never, ever be hyphenated.

Keyboard shortcuts for ornaments commonly used in chapter openings:

asterisks (*)
Shift+8

bullets (•)
Alt/Opt+8

en dashes (–)
Alt/Opt+ -

em dashes (—)
Alt/Opt+Shift+ -

Chapter number considerations

Chapter numbers can be set in many different ways. In each case, you could set them in all caps, caps and lowercase, all small caps, or all lowercase:

Chapter One (chapter and number spelled out)
Chapter 1 (chapter spelled out, number is a digit)
One (just the number spelled out)
1 or 1   (just the digit, as an oldstyle or lining figure)
* 1 * or – 1 – or • 1 • or { 1 }   (digit with an ornament on either side)
I   (roman numeral)

Consider a few factors when choosing the numerals for a chapter number style.

- How many chapters are in your book? Would spelled-out numbers get longer and longer (and thus more and more difficult to read)?
- Is the typeface readable?
- Do you want the reader to pay attention to the number or just barely notice it?

Experiment with the paragraph rule to move it up or down, make it heavier, or change its color. Keep the Preview box checked.

The chapter number and chapter title are centered, with plenty of white space above, below, and between them. This gives a classic and very comfortable and familiar look to the chapter opening page.

Notice that the drop folio is centered, too. You may choose to include drop folios on all your pages or just on your chapter opening pages. You'll apply the drop folio in chapter 52 using master pages.

CHAPTER ONE

CHAPTER OPENINGS

They were indeed a queer-looking party that assembled on the bank—the birds with draggled feathers, the animals with their fur clinging close to them, and all dripping wet, cross, and uncomfortable.

The first question of course was, how to get dry again: they had a consultation about this, and after a few minutes it seemed quite natural to Alice to find herself talking familiarly with them, as if she had known them all her life. Indeed, she had quite a long argument with the Lory, who at last turned sulky, and would only say, 'I am older than you, and must know better'; and this Alice would not allow without knowing how old it was, and, as the Lory positively refused to tell its age, there was no more to be said.

At last the Mouse, who seemed to be a person of authority among them, called out, 'Sit down, all of you, and listen to me! I'LL soon make you dry enough!' They all sat down at once, in a large ring, with the Mouse in the middle. Alice kept her eyes anxiously fixed on it, for she felt sure she would catch a bad cold if she did not get dry very soon.

'Ahem!' said the Mouse with an important air, 'are you all ready? This is the driest thing I know. Silence all round, if you please!

1

DESIGN 1: Classic with a paragraph rule, *continued*

This classic design uses the same typeface for all the elements in the design (Minion). However, other serif typefaces will work just as well. You may like to try Caslon, Chaparral, Garamond, or any other serifs you have available to you, to see which suits your book the best.

See page 176 for a part opening design that matches this chapter opener.

☐ **Chapter Numbers [cn]**

Changes from the Chapter Numbers style (see page 72):

Basic Character Formats:	Size = 11 pt
	Case = OpenType All Small Caps
	Tracking = 50
Indents and Spacing:	Space After = 42 pt *or* 0.5833 in
Paragraph Rules:	Rule Below = Rule On
	(Fill in as shown below)
OpenType Features:	Figure Style = Proportional Oldstyle

Note that the paragraph style at the beginning of the chapter opening includes a Space Before *and* a Space After, but subsequent paragraph styles just include a Space After.

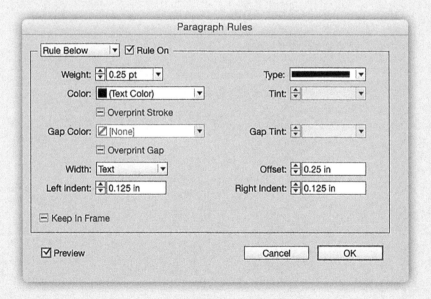

Paragraph rules affect everything in the paragraph and are not for single words on a line. For that, go to Character>Underline Options.

☐ **Chapter Titles [ct]**

Changes from the Chapter Titles style (see page 72):

Basic Character Formats:	Size = 13 pt
	Case = All Caps
	Tracking = 50
Indents and Spacing:	Space After = 84 pt *or* 1.1667 in

· · [1] · ·

CHAPTER OPENINGS

*A book can look good using almost any typeface;
it just depends on how the type is set.*

FIONA RAVEN, book designer

Tʜᴇʏ ᴡᴇʀᴇ ɪɴᴅᴇᴇᴅ a queer-looking party that assembled on the bank—the birds with draggled feathers, the animals with their fur clinging close to them, and all dripping wet, cross, and uncomfortable.

The first question of course was, how to get dry again: they had a consultation about this, and after a few minutes it seemed quite natural to Alice to find herself talking familiarly with them, as if she had known them all her life. Indeed, she had quite a long argument with the Lory, who at last turned sulky, and would only say, 'I am older than you, and must know better'; and this Alice would not allow without knowing how old it was, and, as the Lory positively refused to tell its age, there was no more to be said.

At last the Mouse, who seemed to be a person of authority among them, called out, 'Sit down, all of you, and listen to me! I'LL soon make you dry enough!' They all sat down at once, in a large ring, with the Mouse in the middle. Alice kept her eyes anxiously fixed

· 1 ·

The chapter number is centered between square brackets and middle dots (these are smaller than bullets and available in the Glyphs panel), and all are separated by en spaces (Ctrl/Cmd+Shift+N).

The [**chtx1**] paragraph style is applied to the first paragraph, giving it the 2-line drop cap, and then the Small Caps [**smcap**] character style (see page 85) is applied to the first few words.

Before you decide to use a drop cap in this way, check the first paragraph of each chapter to make sure there are enough lines of type to accommodate the drop cap.

The drop folio is centered between two middle dots. En spaces separate the dots from the folio.

DESIGN 2: Classic with a two-line drop cap, *continued*

A drop cap is an attractive feature on a chapter opening page. It helps draw the reader's eye down to the beginning of the narrative. The settings are shown in the First Paragraph style.

☐ **Chapter Numbers [cn]**
Changes from the Chapter Numbers style (see page 72):
Basic Character Formats: Tracking = 25

☐ **Chapter Titles [ct]**
Changes from the Chapter Titles style (see page 72):
Basic Character Formats: Font Style = Bold
                                                                              Size = 13 pt
                                                                              Case = All Caps
                                                                              Tracking = 100

☐ **Opening Quotes [quo]**
Changes from the Opening Quotes style (see page 74):
Basic Character Formats: Size = 10 pt
                                                                              Tracking = 10

Use soft returns to control where the lines in your opening quotes break (Shift+Enter/Return).

Indents and Spacing: Space After = 14 pt *or* 0.1944 in
Hyphenation: Hyphenate = Unchecked

☐ **Quote Attributions [quoattr]**
Changes from the Quote Attributions style (see page 74):
Advanced Character Formats: Baseline Shift = 0
Indents and Spacing: Space After = 70 pt *or* 0.9722 in

DESIGN 2: Classic with a two-line drop cap, *continued*

Create a new paragraph style called First Paragraph [**chtx1**] for the first paragraph in every chapter.

☐ **First Paragraph [chtx1]**   Parent = **tx1**

   General: Style Name = **chtx1**

                                               Based On = **tx1**

   Changes from the No Indents style (see page 62):

   Drop Caps and Nested Styles: Lines = 2

                                              Characters = 1

After you create this new paragraph style, be sure to select the first paragraph in your chapter and apply it. Then you'll see the drop cap appear.

Sometimes it's necessary to adjust the space to the right of the drop cap to improve the appearance. Place the cursor before the first letter following the drop cap, then try various positive or negative values in the kerning box in the Control panel. See page 337 for more on kerning.

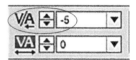

You may find that the first character in a chapter is a quotation mark. Here is an easy way to deal with this situation:

1 Delete the opening quotation mark. Now the first character in your paragraph is the drop cap.
2 Create a new text frame in the inside margin by dragging your cursor, and add an opening quotation mark (Alt/Opt+[). Apply the No Indent [**tx1**] paragraph style to it. In the Paragraph panel, choose Align Right.
3 Using your Selection Tool, drag the text frame so the opening quotation mark is next to the drop cap. Choose a position that looks pleasing and is close to the top of the drop cap.

It's best to deal with opening quotation marks after you've finalized your chapter opening design and page layout. Otherwise, the text frame with your opening quotation mark may get separated from the drop cap.

Move the quotation mark left to right to find the best position next to a letter.

In this chapter opening, the ornaments frame the title. They are glyphs in a typeface (rather than images) and so have an Ornaments [**orn**] character style applied to them.

Note that the drop folio is set in italics this time.

1

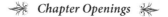 *Chapter Openings*

They were indeed a queer-looking party that assembled on the bank— the birds with draggled feathers, the animals with their fur clinging close to them, and all dripping wet, cross, and uncomfortable.

The first question of course was, how to get dry again: they had a consultation about this, and after a few minutes it seemed quite natural to Alice to find herself talking familiarly with them, as if she had known them all her life. Indeed, she had quite a long argument with the Lory, who at last turned sulky, and would only say, 'I am older than you, and must know better'; and this Alice would not allow without knowing how old it was, and, as the Lory positively refused to tell its age, there was no more to be said.

At last the Mouse, who seemed to be a person of authority among them, called out, 'Sit down, all of you, and listen to me! I'LL soon make you dry enough!' They all sat down at once, in a large ring, with the Mouse in the middle. Alice kept her eyes anxiously fixed on it, for she felt sure she would catch a bad cold if she did not get dry very soon.

'Ahem!' said the Mouse with an important air, 'are you all ready? This is the driest thing I know. Silence all round, if you please! "William the Conqueror, whose cause was favoured by the pope, was soon submitted to by the English, who wanted leaders, and

1

DESIGN 3: Classic with ornaments, *continued*

This classic design includes ornaments on either side of the chapter title. These particular ornaments are from the typeface Arno, one of several typefaces available from Typekit that come with ornaments. Open the Glyphs panel and select Ornaments from the Show drop-down menu to see them.

For this design you'll need to create a new character style called Ornaments [**orn**] and apply it to the ornaments.

☐ **Chapter Numbers [cn]**

Changes from the Chapter Numbers style (see page 72):

Basic Character Formats: Tracking = 50

☐ **Chapter Titles [ct]**

Changes from the Chapter Titles style (see page 72):

Basic Character Formats: Font Style = Semibold italic

                                                                           Size = 12 pt

Indents and Spacing: Space After = 70 pt *or* 0.9722 in

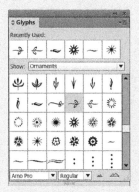

☐ **Ornament [orn]** *character* **style**   Parent = **[None]**

General: Style Name = orn

                                                                    Based On = [None]

Changes from [None] character style :

Basic Character Formats: Font Family = Arno Pro

                                                                     Font Style = Regular

                                                                     Size = 18 pt

Advanced Character Formats: Baseline Shift = –1 pt

Once you've created a new character style for your ornaments, insert your cursor where an ornament is to go. Select the [orn] character style, then double-click the ornament you want in the Glyphs panel. Then add an en space between the ornament and chapter title by pressing Ctrl/Cmd+Shift+N.

DESIGN 4
Modern
chapter opening
– with –
number and title
on same line

The opening quote goes on the top line, so there is no need for an end-of-paragraph return before it (see page 99).

When the chapter number and title are on the same line, the Chapter Title paragraph style is applied, and a new Chapter Number *character* style is applied just to the number.

This style of chapter title looks best with short titles that fit on one line.

When you design your chapter opening pages, consider whether there are appendixes in your book. If so, think now about where you will place the word "Appendix." If you needed to put "Appendix" and a letter on this chapter opener page, where would they go? For suggestions, see pages 247 and 248.

Note that there is no drop folio on the opener page in this design.

A book can look good using almost any typeface;
it just depends on how the type is set.

—FIONA RAVEN
book designer

1 Chapter Openings

They were indeed a queer-looking party that assembled on the bank—the birds with draggled feathers, the animals with their fur clinging close to them, and all dripping wet, cross, and uncomfortable.

The first question of course was, how to get dry again: they had a consultation about this, and after a few minutes it seemed quite natural to Alice to find herself talking familiarly with them, as if she had known them all her life. Indeed, she had quite a long argument with the Lory, who at last turned sulky, and would only say, 'I am older than you, and must know better'; and this Alice would not allow without knowing how old it was, and, as the Lory positively refused to tell its age, there was no more to be said.

At last the Mouse, who seemed to be a person of authority among them, called out, 'Sit down, all of you, and listen to me! I'LL soon make you dry enough!' They all sat down at once, in a large ring, with the Mouse in the middle. Alice kept her eyes anxiously fixed

DESIGN 4: Modern with number and title on same line, *continued*

This modern design uses Myriad for all the elements set in a sans serif typeface (titles and headings). However, other sans serif typefaces will work just as well. Try any other sans serifs you have available to you, and see which one suits your book the best.

See page 178 for a part opening design that matches this chapter opener.

☐ **Opening Quotes [quo]**

Changes from the Opening Quotes style (see page 74):

Basic Character Formats:	Size = 10 pt
	Tracking = 10
Indents and Spacing:	Alignment = Right
	Space After = 14 pt *or* 0.1944 in
Hyphenation:	Hyphenate = Unchecked

To move the opening quote and attribution to the top of the page, select both (including their end-of-paragraph returns—and switch to Normal view if you don't see them). Cut the text by clicking Edit>Cut or pressing Ctrl/Cmd+X, then paste it at the top of the page by inserting your cursor at the top and clicking Edit>Paste or pressing Ctrl/Cmd+C.

☐ **Quote Attributions [quoattr]**

Changes from the Quote Attributions style (see page 74):

Advanced Character Formats:	Baseline Shift = 0
Indents and Spacing:	Space After = 84 pt *or* 1.1667 in

☐ **Chapter Titles [ct]**

Changes from the Chapter Titles style (see page 72):

Basic Character Formats:	Font Family = Myriad Pro
	Font Style = Light Condensed
	Size = 30 pt
	Tracking = 50
Indents and Spacing:	Alignment = Left
	Space After = 70 pt *or* 0.9722 in

DESIGN 4: Modern with number and title on same line,
continued

Create a new *character* style called Chapter Number [**cn**] as shown below. Then insert your cursor in front of your chapter title and type your chapter number followed by an en space (Ctrl/Cmd+Shift+N). Apply the [**cn**] character style to the chapter number.

☐ **Chapter Number [cn]** *character* **style**   Parent = [None]
General: Style Name = **cn**
                                                         Based On = [None]

Changes from [None] character style:
Basic Character Formats: Font Style = Semibold Cond
OpenType Features: Figure Style = Proportional Lining

Consider trying a few variations of the chapter number and title:

The first example is the one used in Design 4. You may want your title to be bolder than the number, or to change the alignment from left to right. Experiment.

1 Chapter Openings

In these examples, the chapter number is separated from the title with an en space (Ctrl/Cmd+Shift+N).

1 / **Chapter Openings**

A variation using Bold and Condensed type.

1 Chapter Openings

DESIGN 5
Modern
chapter opening
– with –
drop cap in a
different font

CHAPTER ONE

Chapter Openings

THEY WERE INDEED a queer-looking party that assembled on the bank—the birds with draggled feathers, the animals with their fur clinging close to them, and all dripping wet, cross, and uncomfortable.

The first question of course was, how to get dry again: they had a consultation about this, and after a few minutes it seemed quite natural to Alice to find herself talking familiarly with them, as if she had known them all her life. Indeed, she had quite a long argument with the Lory, who at last turned sulky, and would only say, 'I am older than you, and must know better'; and this Alice would not allow without knowing how old it was, and, as the Lory positively refused to tell its age, there was no more to be said.

At last the Mouse, who seemed to be a person of authority among them, called out, 'Sit down, all of you, and listen to me! I'LL soon

1

This is a 3-line drop cap set in a sans serif font to match the chapter title. Start the first line of type one line below the top of the drop cap simply by adding a soft return (Shift+Enter/Return) right after the drop cap.

The drop folio is aligned away from the spine in this modern, asymmetrical design.

DESIGN 5: Modern with drop cap in a different font, *continued*

The large three-line drop cap is included in a nested style in your First Paragraph style. This means that *within* that paragraph style, a character style is assigned to the drop cap. Create a new paragraph style called First Paragraph [**chtx1**] for the first paragraph in every chapter.

☐ **Chapter Numbers [cn]**
Changes from the Chapter Numbers style (see page 72):
Basic Character Formats: Size = 12 pt
                                           Case = OpenType All Small Caps
                                           Tracking = 50
Indents and Spacing: Alignment = Left
                                           Space Before = 140 pt *or* 1.9444 in
                                           Space After = 14 pt *or* 0.1944 in

☐ **Chapter Titles [ct]**
Changes from the Chapter Titles style (see page 72):
Basic Character Formats: Font Family = Myriad Pro
                                           Font Style = Semibold Condensed
                                           Size = 24 pt
Indents and Spacing: Alignment = Left
                                           Space After = 70 pt *or* 0.9722 in

☐ **First Paragraph [chtx1]**   **Parent = tx1**
General: Style Name = **chtx1**
                                           Based On = **tx1**
Changes from the No Indents style (see page 62):
Drop Caps and Nested Styles: Lines = 3
                                           Characters = 1
                                           Character Style = New
                                               Character Style . . .
                                               (see next page)

DESIGN 5: Modern with drop cap in a different font, *continued*

When you selected "New Character Style …" from the Character Style drop-down menu (see bottom of page 160), a new dialog box appeared called New Character Style. You'll be familiar with this from setting up your original character styles (see pages 80–82). Create a character style for your drop cap as shown below, then click OK.

☐ **Drop Cap [dc]** *character* **style**
General:

Changes from [None] character style:
Basic Character Formats:

Parent = **[None]**
Style Name = **dc**
Based On = [None]

Font Family = Myriad Pro
Font Style = Condensed

After you've created the new First Paragraph [**chtx1**] style with this nested Drop Cap [**dc**] character style, be sure to select the first paragraph in your chapter and apply it. Then you'll see the drop cap appear.

Your last steps are:

• Place your cursor just to the right of the drop cap, and insert a soft return (Shift+Enter/Return). This moves the top line of text down so that the text begins in the middle of the drop cap.
• Select the first few words following the drop cap, and apply the Small Caps [**smcap**] character style to them (see page 85).

The shaded graphic behind the chapter number is created using the Paragraph Rule feature.

1

CHAPTER OPENINGS

*A book can look good using almost any typeface;
it just depends on how the type is set.*
FIONA RAVEN, book designer

They were indeed a queer-looking party that assembled on the bank—the birds with draggled feathers, the animals with their fur clinging close to them, and all dripping wet, cross, and uncomfortable.

The first question of course was, how to get dry again: they had a consultation about this, and after a few minutes it seemed quite natural to Alice to find herself talking familiarly with them, as if she had known them all her life. Indeed, she had quite a long argument with the Lory, who at last turned sulky, and would only say, 'I am older than you, and must know better'; and this Alice would not allow without knowing how old it was, and, as the Lory positively refused to tell its age, there was no more to be said.

At last the Mouse, who seemed to be a person of authority among them, called out, 'Sit down, all of you, and listen to me! I'LL soon make you dry enough!' They all sat down at once, in a large ring, with the Mouse in the middle. Alice kept her eyes anxiously fixed

The folio is aligned away from the spine and indented 0.2″ to complement this asymmetrical design.

1

DESIGN 6: Modern with shaded graphic, *continued*

You can add lines and shapes to your chapter opening pages manually (by creating the line or shape then copying and pasting it onto each chapter opening page); however, it's simpler if the graphic is part of a paragraph style. That way, it won't get misplaced as a result of style adjustments.

☐ **Chapter Numbers [cn]**

Changes from the Chapter Numbers style (see page 72):

Basic Character Formats:	Font Family = Myriad Pro
	Font Style = Bold
	Leading = 28 pt
	Tracking = 50
Indents and Spacing:	Alignment = Right
	Space After = 126 pt *or* 1.75 in
Paragraph Rules:	Rule Below = Rule On
	(Fill in as shown below)
Character Color:	[Paper]

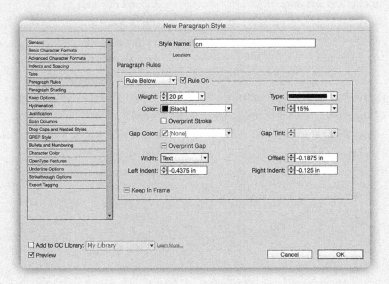

DESIGN 6: Modern with shaded graphic, *continued*

Here are the rest of the paragraph styles for Design 6.

☐ **Chapter Titles [ct]**

Changes from the Chapter Titles style (see page 72):

Basic Character Formats:	Font Family = Myriad Pro
	Font Style = Black
	Size = 12 pt
	Case = All Caps
	Tracking = 200
Indents and Spacing:	Alignment = Left

☐ **Opening Quotes [quo]**

Changes from the Opening Quotes style (see page 74):

Basic Character Formats:	Size = 10 pt
	Tracking = 10
Indents and Spacing:	Alignment = Left
	Left Indent = 0
	Right Indent = 0
Hyphenation:	Hyphenate = Unchecked

☐ **Quote Attributions [quoattr]**

Changes from the Quote Attributions style (see page 74):

Advanced Character Formats:	Baseline Shift = 0
Indents and Spacing:	Alignment = Left
	Space After = 28 pt *or* 0.3889 in

DESIGN 7
Characteristic
chapter opening
– with –
paragraph rules
above and below
and initial cap

CHAPTER OPENINGS

This chapter is unnumbered. Anthologies and collections of essays are often not meant to be read in any particular order, so there's no need for a numbering system.

THEY WERE INDEED a queer-looking party that assembled on the bank—the birds with draggled feathers, the animals with their fur clinging close to them, and all dripping wet, cross, and uncomfortable.

The first paragraph has a larger indent and begins with an initial cap followed by the first few words in small caps.

The first question of course was, how to get dry again: they had a consultation about this, and after a few minutes it seemed quite natural to Alice to find herself talking familiarly with them, as if she had known them all her life. Indeed, she had quite a long argument with the Lory, who at last turned sulky, and would only say, 'I am older than you, and must know better'; and this Alice would not allow without knowing how old it was, and, as the Lory positively refused to tell its age, there was no more to be said.

At last the Mouse, who seemed to be a person of authority among them, called out, 'Sit down, all of you, and listen to me! I'LL soon make you dry enough!' They all sat down at once, in a large ring, with the Mouse in the middle. Alice kept her eyes anxiously fixed on it, for she felt sure she would catch a bad cold if she did not get dry very soon.

'Ahem!' said the Mouse with an important air, 'are you all ready? This is the driest thing I know. Silence all round, if you please!

1

This drop folio is centered and set in italics.

DESIGN 7: Characteristic with paragraph rules above and below and initial cap, *continued*

For this design you'll need rules both above and below the chapter title. Use the settings below, or experiment with your own. Be sure to check the Preview box so you can see your changes instantly.

☐ **Chapter Titles [ct]**
Changes from the Chapter Titles style (see page 72):

Basic Character Formats:	Font Family = Myriad Pro
	Font Style = Semibold Condensed
	Case = All Caps
	Leading = 28 pt
	Tracking = 200
Indents and Spacing:	Space Before = 56 pt *or* 0.7778 in
	Space After = 112 pt *or* 1.5556 in
Paragraph Rules:	Rule Above = Rule On
	Rule Below = Rule On
	(Fill in as shown on page 167)

In the Paragraph Rules dialog boxes, here is what the terms mean:

- **Width** "Text" means *the width of the type* on the line, and "Column" means *the width of the text frame* or column you're in.
- **Indents** These are indents from the left and right edges of either the text or the column. If you want the type to extend a bit beyond the type or column, set negative indents by clicking the down arrows.
- **Offset** This is vertical distance. Instead of typing values in the box, it's easiest to click the up or down arrows.

DESIGN 7: Characteristic with paragraph rules above and below and initial cap, *continued*

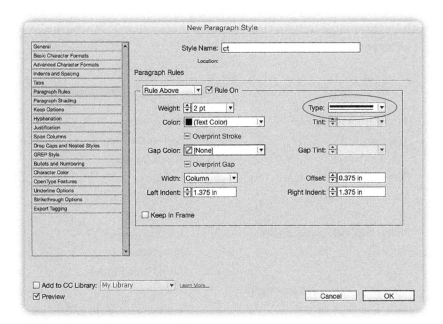

In the Type drop-down menu, choose Thick-Thin for the rule above.

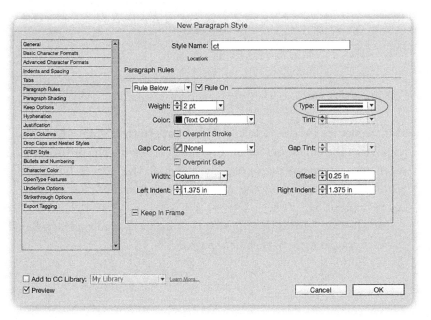

In the Type drop-down menu, choose Thin-Thick for the rule below.

DESIGN 7: Characteristic with paragraph rules above and below and initial cap, *continued*

To set up the first paragraph in this design, you'll create a paragraph style with an extra-large first line indent, and a character style for the initial cap in a sans serif typeface.

After you've created the new First Paragraph [chtx1] style, be sure to apply it to the first paragraph in your chapter.

Then when you've created the Initial Cap [ic] character style, apply it to the first character in the first paragraph.

☐ **First Paragraph [chtx1]**   Parent = **tx1**
   General: Style Name = **chtx1**
                                         Based On = **tx1**

   Changes from the No Indents style (see page 62):
   Indents and Spacing: First Line Indent: 0.375 in

☐ **Initial Cap [ic]** *character* **style**   Parent = [None]
   General: Style Name = **ic**
                                        Based On = [None]

   Changes from [None] character style:
   Basic Character Formats: Font Family = Myriad Pro
                                        Font Style = Light
                                        Size = 36 pt

Your last steps are:

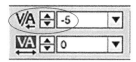

- Sometimes it's necessary to adjust the space to the right of the initial cap. Place the cursor before the first letter following the initial cap, then try various positive or negative values in the kerning box in the Control panel by clicking the up and down arrows. See page 337 for more on kerning.
- Select the first few words following the initial cap, and apply the Small Caps character style to them (see page 85).

One ∽

They were indeed a queer-looking party that assembled on the bank—the birds with draggled feathers, the animals with their fur clinging close to them, and all dripping wet, cross, and uncomfortable.

The first question of course was, how to get dry again: they had a consultation about this, and after a few minutes it seemed quite natural to Alice to find herself talking familiarly with them, as if she had known them all her life. Indeed, she had quite a long argument with the Lory, who at last turned sulky, and would only say, 'I am older than you, and must know better'; and this Alice would not allow without knowing how old it was, and, as the Lory positively refused to tell its age, there was no more to be said.

At last the Mouse, who seemed to be a person of authority among them, called out, 'Sit down, all of you, and listen to me! I'LL soon make you dry enough!' They all sat down at once, in a large ring, with the Mouse in the middle. Alice kept her eyes anxiously fixed on it, for she felt sure she would catch a bad cold if she did not get dry very soon.

'Ahem!' said the Mouse with an important air, 'are you all ready? This is the driest thing I know. Silence all round, if you please! "William the Conqueror, whose cause was favoured by the pope, was soon submitted to by the English, who wanted leaders, and

1

This chapter has a number and no title, as is often the case in novels. Spelling out the chapter number uses more space than a digit, but be aware that if you have lots of chapters, the spelled out numbers will get longer and longer (and thus more difficult to read).

The ornament is a small graphic (or image) created from a glyph and then rotated sideways. See page 170 to learn how to do this.

This drop folio is aligned away from the spine and set in semibold italics to match the chapter number. It creates a nice diagonal from the chapter number down to the folio.

DESIGN 8: Characteristic with rotated ornament, *continued*

This design requires a Chapter Number paragraph style, then the ornament is copied and pasted as an inline graphic.

☐ **Chapter Numbers [cn]**	Based On = **cn**
Changes from the Chapter Numbers style (see page 72):	
Basic Character Formats:	Font Style = Semibold Italic
	Size = 22 pt
Indents and Spacing:	Alignment = Left
	Space After = 126 pt *or* 1.75 in

Never use Vertical scale or Horizontal scale on text type! But when you're creating a swash or ornament from a glyph, feel free to try any effect you like.

To make the ornament in this design, draw a new text frame and choose Minion Pro Regular 27 pt from the Control panel. Go to the Glyphs panel, choose the Greek category, and double-click the Greek small letter XI (ξ), then manipulate it in this way:

1. Highlight the character, then set the Vertical Scale (T) in the Control panel to 145% and the Horizontal Scale (T) to 80%.
2. Switch to the Selection Tool and use the Control panel to rotate the text frame counterclockwise.
3. Make the text frame smaller to fit the character closely by pressing Ctrl/Cmd+Alt/Opt+C.
4. To anchor the object in the text, select the text frame with the Selection Tool and cut it by pressing Ctrl/Cmd+X.
5. Switch to the Type Tool by pressing T, then put your cursor at the end of the chapter title and insert an en space (Ctrl/Cmd+Shift+N). Then go to Edit>Paste (Ctrl/Cmd+V), and your newly invented swash will appear next to the chapter number.

Now wasn't that fun?

They were indeed a queer-looking party that assembled on the bank—the birds with draggled feathers, the animals with their fur clinging close to them, and all dripping wet, cross, and uncomfortable.

The first question of course was, how to get dry again: they had a consultation about this, and after a few minutes it seemed quite natural to Alice to find herself talking familiarly with them, as if she had known them all her life. Indeed, she had quite a long argument with the Lory, who at last turned sulky, and would only say, 'I am older than you, and must know better'; and this Alice would not allow without knowing how old it was, and, as the Lory positively refused to tell its age, there was no more to be said.

At last the Mouse, who seemed to be a person of authority among them, called out, 'Sit down, all of you, and listen to me! I'LL soon make you dry enough!' They all sat down at once, in a large ring, with the Mouse in the middle. Alice kept her eyes anxiously fixed on it, for she felt sure she would catch a bad cold if she did not get dry very soon.

'Ahem!' said the Mouse with an important air, 'are you all ready? This is the driest thing I know. Silence all round, if you please!

{ 1 }

DESIGN 9
Characteristic
chapter opening
– with –
display type

Often in script fonts the type size looks smaller than you'd expect, and leading that is less than the type size works just fine as long as the ascenders and descenders do not crash. The example below is set in 14/12 point Brush Script.

An example
on two lines

Notice above that the *p* in the first line and the *l* in the second line come close to touching each other. If they did touch ("crash"), you'd change the leading, the alignment (to left, perhaps), or the tracking.

This drop folio is enclosed in fancy brackets. You might consider putting just this folio at the top center of your recto pages, with just the chapter title at the top of the verso pages. Not every page has to have a page number.

DESIGN 9: Characteristic with display type, *continued*

Display type is very helpful in creating a mood or look for a book. There are cowboy fonts, script fonts, whimsical fonts, grunge fonts, scary or bleeding fonts, and any other kind of font you can imagine. Many display fonts are free on the Internet.

Having said that, a very little goes a long way when it comes to display fonts. Used sparingly, they can add character and charm to your book.

☐ **Chapter Titles [ct]**
   Changes from the Chapter Numbers style (see page 72):

Basic Character Formats:	Font Family = Bickham Script Pro
	Font Style = Regular
	Size = 43 pt
Indents and Spacing:	Space Before = 70 pt *or* 0.9722 in
	Space After = 70 pt *or* 0.9722 in

Script typefaces often come with alternate letters, such as swash caps and swooshy tails. Open your Glyphs panel and choose Alternates for Selection from the Show drop-down menu. Then select any character in your chapter title and see what alternates are available. To select an alternate, simply double-click it.

Often the letters in a script typeface don't have perfect joins between the letters and need kerning a bit. Place your cursor between two letters that don't join properly, and click the up and down arrows in the Kern box until they line up properly. See page 337 for more on kerning. You may want to zoom in quite closely to kern the letters. To do so, hold down the Ctrl/Cmd key and hit = a few times. To zoom out, hold down the Ctrl/Cmd key and hit - a few times.

DESIGN 9
**Characteristic
chapter opening
– with –
display type,**
continued

Chapter Openings

They were indeed a queer-looking party that assembled on the bank—the birds with draggled feathers, the animals with their fur clinging close to them, and all dripping wet, cross, and uncomfortable.

The first question of course was, how to get dry again: they had a consultation about this, and after a few minutes it seemed quite natural to Alice to find herself talking familiarly with them, as if she had known them all her life. Indeed, she had quite a long argument with the Lory, who at last turned sulky, and would only say, 'I am older than you, and must know better'; and this Alice would not allow without knowing how old it was, and, as the Lory positively refused to tell its age, there was no more to be said.

At last the Mouse, who seemed to be a person of authority among them, called out, 'Sit down, all of you, and listen to me! I'LL soon make you dry enough!' They all sat down at once, in a large ring, with the Mouse in the middle. Alice kept her

This is a fun chapter title set in AR HERMANN 28 pt type. It's suitable for a children's chapter book.

Note that the main text is larger for a children's chapter book (12/17 in this design).

DESIGN 9
Characteristic
chapter opening
– with –
display type,
continued

Mesquite Regular with 100 tracking at 24 pt all caps.

No matter how badly you want to use a typeface, be sure it's appropriate for your book's subject matter.

To see a matching part opener, go to page 180.

Try your chapter title in different display type-faces in Typekit and/or on font websites online.

CHAPTER OPENINGS

They were indeed a queer-looking party that assembled on the bank—the birds with draggled feathers, the animals with their fur clinging close to them, and all dripping wet, cross, and uncomfortable.

The first question of course was, how to get dry again: they had a consultation about this, and after a few minutes it seemed quite natural to Alice to find herself talking familiarly with them, as if she had known them all her life. Indeed, she had quite a long argument with the Lory, who at last turned sulky, and would only say, 'I am older than you, and must know better'; and this Alice would not allow without knowing how old it was, and, as the Lory positively refused to tell its age, there was no more to be said.

At last the Mouse, who seemed to be a person of authority among them, called out, 'Sit down, all of you, and listen to me! I'LL soon make you dry enough!' They all sat down at once, in a large ring, with the Mouse in the middle. Alice kept her eyes anxiously fixed on it, for she felt sure she would catch a bad cold if she did not get dry very soon.

'Ahem!' said the Mouse with an important air, 'are you all ready? This is the driest thing I know. Silence all round, if you please!

4 Trying the part opener designs in this chapter

Part openings always appear on recto pages, usually followed by a blank verso page. Sometimes, however, the verso page is used to list the chapters to come or to offer a short introduction. In *this* book, we simply used that verso page to carry on with the text, and that is fine, too, though more unusual.

By this time, you can probably predict what we are going to say about the design of your part openers: that they should be consistent with what you've done throughout your book. If you used a classic chapter opener, stick with a classic look for the part opener, and so on. In this section you'll see some selected part opening designs, each one closely related to one of the chapter openers shown in the previous pages.

The numbering system for your parts should be different from the one you used for your chapters, to avoid confusion. For instance, if you used arabic numerals for your chapters, either use roman numerals or spell out the numbers for your parts.

Part opening pages are a good place to show photos or other images at a large size, if it's appropriate for your book. Does your book use any bleeds in the design? If so, you might as well take advantage of bleeds for the part opening pages, too. Anything that bleeds off the page is visible from the outside edge of the book, which makes that page easier to find.

Check with your printer to find out whether bleeds will cause your printing costs to rise (see chapter 37 about adding a bleed).

Perhaps the idea of designing a page with very little on it is a bit intimidating. But don't panic; simply remember the basic principles of good page design:

REPEAT ELEMENTS   RULE OF THREE   WHITE SPACE

One group of elements on the page (circled above) is more pleasing to the eye than two groups would be.

First, you'll **repeat** the ideas from your chapter openings. Though you might not have as many as **three elements** on the page, simply try to consolidate everything into a single group (because odd numbers are better than even ones). As for **white space**, you'll have plenty of that.

You could begin by setting the part number using the Chapter Number [**cn**] style and part title in the Chapter Title [**ct**] style, and then make them both a bit larger. Perhaps that will be all you need. Study the designs on the next few pages to find ideas for *your* part opening pages.

Because "PART I" is such a short line, the paragraph rule settings used in the Chapter Number [**cn**] style for Design 1 (page 148) don't work here. This rule is instead set to a negative indent value, making it longer than the text.

PART I

PART OPENINGS

Notice that there is no folio on the part opener. That makes the page look more important, helps keep the number of visual elements to an odd number (one), and prevents unnecessary distraction.

DESIGN 1: Classic with paragraph rule, *continued*

This design is based on the chapter opening design shown on page 148. Both the part number and the part title are related to their chapter opening counterparts but are a bit larger, to make them more important and so they are not lost in all that white space.

☐ **Part Numbers [pn]**   Based On = **cn**

Changes from the Chapter Numbers style in Design 1 (see pages 72 and 149):

Basic Character Formats: Size = 14 pt

Paragraph Rules: (Fill in as shown below)

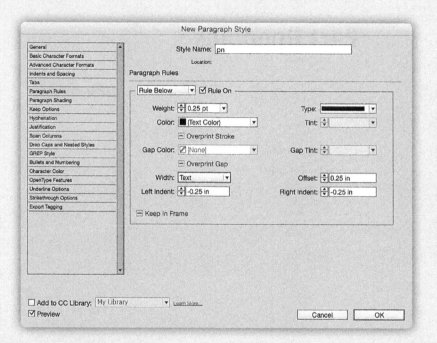

After you've created the new Part Numbers [**pn**] and Part Titles [**pt**] paragraph styles, be sure to apply them to your part numbers and part titles.

Also make sure there is an end-of-paragraph return at the top of each part opening page, before the part number, with the Text [**tx**] paragraph style applied to it (see example on page 99).

☐ **Part Titles [pt]**   Based On = **ct**

Changes from the Chapter Titles style (see pages 72 and 150):

Basic Character Formats: Size = 20 pt

                                             Case = OpenType All Small Caps

**DESIGN 4
Modern
part opening
– with –
mini table of
contents**

Reflecting the Design 4 chapter opening (see page 156), this page has three major visual elements: an element at the upper right, another at left center, and some text below it.

The part number is centered on the chapter opening quotation in Design 4. The part title aligns with the chapter title, and the start of the mini table of contents aligns with the first text line of any chapter.

Set a tab *before* each chapter title and an em plus an en space *after* each one. Using this fixed amount of space after the title keeps the page numbers nearby and eliminates the need to look from left to right on the page. Also, it conveniently helps to keep the number of visual elements on the page to three.

Part One

Part Openings

DESIGN 4: Modern with mini table of contents, *continued*

This part opener is used to help the reader grasp the organization of the book at a glance with a mini table of contents, just as in *Book Design Made Simple*. Create the following new paragraph and character styles:

☐ **Part Numbers [pn]**   Based On = **cn**

Changes from the Chapter Numbers style (see pages 72 and 158):

Basic Character Formats: Font Family = Myriad Pro

Font Style = Light Condensed

Size = 22 pt

Tracking = 20

Indents and Spacing: Alignment = Right

Space After = 2 in

☐ **Part Titles [pt]**   Based On = **ct**

Changes from the Chapter Titles style (see pages 72 and 157):

Basic Character Formats: Font Style = Bold Condensed

Indents and Spacing: Space After = 1 in

☐ **Part Contents [ptoc]**   Based On = **tx1**

Changes from the No Indents style (see page 62):

Indents and Spacing: Alignment = Left

Left Indent = 18 pt *or* 0.25 in

First Line Indent = –18 pt *or* –0.25 in

Space After = 4 pt *or* 0.0556 in

Align to Grid = None

☐ **Part Contents Chapter Number [ptoc-cn]** *character* **style**

Based On = [None]

Changes from [None]:

Basic Character Formats: Font Style = Bold

After you've created the new Part Numbers [pn], Part Titles [pt], and Part Contents [ptoc] paragraph styles, be sure to apply them to the text on your part opening page.

Also make sure there is an end-of-paragraph return at the top of each part opening page, before the part number, with the Text [tx] paragraph style applied to it (see example on page 99).

And, finally, select each chapter number in your part contents and apply the Part Contents Chapter Number [ptoc-cn] character style to them.

Chances are that if your book's chapters aren't numbered, you won't want to number the parts, either. This part title is exactly the same as the chapter title shown on page 174. A 10% black, full-bleed background is added to help the reader find this important divider.

Before adding a bleed to any of your design elements, check with your printer to see whether adding a bleed to your design will increase your printing costs. Then see chapter 37 to add a bleed to your page design.

PART OPENINGS

Display type examples

When thinking about using a display typeface, consider several factors before settling on one. 1) How appropriate is the type to your subject matter? 2) Did you (or will you) use one of these for your cover? If so, it would be smart to include it in the interior of your book instead of introducing another one. 3) Is the type readable? 4) Does it include both uppercase and lowercase characters?

Be aware that any of the typefaces below are suitable for display, but the only one suitable for book text is Myriad (for titles, headings, sidebars, and so on).

The samples below are some of the ones included when you lease InDesign, but thousands more are available online.

Sans Serif Display

Letter Gothic
1 2 3 4 5 6 7

LITHOS
1 2 3 4 5 6 7 8 9 0

Myriad
1 2 3 4 5 6 7 8 9 0

ORATOR
1 2 3 4 5 6 7 8

Poplar
1 2 3 4 5 6 7 8 9 0

Tekton
1 2 3 4 5 6 7 8 9 0

Serif Display

Birch
1 2 3 4 5 6 7 8 9 0

Blackoak
1 2 3 4 5 6

MESQUITE
1 2 3 4 5 6 7 8 9 0

Nueva Condensed
1 2 3 4 5 6 7 8 9 0

ROSEWOOD
1 2 3 4 5 6 7 8 9 0

STENCIL
1 2 3 4 5 6 7 8 9

TRAJAN
1 2 3 4 5 6 7 8 9 0

Script

Brush Script
1 2 3 4 5 6 7 8 9 0

Giddyup
1 2 3 4 5 6 7 8 9 0

Display number examples

Consider a few factors when choosing the numerals for a chapter number style.

- How many chapters are in your book? Would spelled-out numbers get longer and longer (and thus more and more difficult to read)?
- Is the typeface readable?

- Do you want the reader to pay attention to the number or just barely notice it?

In the examples below, both short and long numbers are shown in several display typefaces (see page 181 for more). Some interesting features but also several difficulties are immediately evident.

Myriad	**FOUR**	**TWENTY-SEVEN**	Rosewood	IV	XXVII
Brush Script	*FOUR*	*TWENTY-SEVEN*	Prestige Elite	IV	XXVII
Giddyup	FOUR	TWENTY-SEVEN	Brush Script	*IV*	*XXVII*
Lithos	FOUR	TWENTY-SEVEN	Trajan	IV	XXVII
Brush Script	*Four*	*Twenty-Seven*	Nueva	· 4 ·	· 27 ·
Giddyup	Four	Twenty-Seven	Letter Gothic	· 4 ·	· 27 ·
Tekton	**Four**	**Twenty-Seven**	Blackoak	▪ 4 ▪	▪ 27 ▪
Nueva	**Four**	**Twenty-Seven**	Giddyup	· 4 ·	· 27 ·
Brush Script	*4*	*27*	Brush Script	*four*	*twenty-seven*
Poplar	**4**	**27**	Prestige Elite	four	twenty-seven
Stencil	**4**	**27**	Birch	four	twenty-seven
Prestige Elite	4	27	Trajan	FOUR	TWENTY-SEVEN

5 Consider some variations

Aside from the samples and tips in this chapter, there are many more things you can do to change your chapter and part openers. You might want to try a couple of the ideas below, but, again, don't overdo it. When in doubt, leave it out.

- If you are already using a bleed somewhere else in the book, you might bring a panel of color (or gray) down from the top and put the chapter or part number in it, or from the outside and put the chapter title in it.

- How about putting the number inside a circle or other shape that's relevant to your subject matter? Keep it minimal so as not to distract the reader.

- Add a different photo for each chapter or part in a nonfiction book. Size and place it the same each time.

- If you've decided to use rules, try some different styles offered in the Paragraph Rules dialog box (Paragraph Styles>Paragraph Rules>Rule Above or Rule Below checked>Type). It's tempting, once you've discovered the possibilities, to use one of each. But don't—it's a sure sign that an inexperienced designer is at work. Stick with one style throughout the book whenever you need to use a rule.

- When choosing a display typeface or graphic for your chapter or part opener, always consider whether there is some way to use something from one of these pages on the cover.

25

Designing headings

There are a few factors to consider when designing a set of headings. Common sense will tell you that if there's only one level of heading, it doesn't need to be very big or bold to be noticed, but if there are multiple levels of headings, the most important ones should be bumped up a bit and given more white space so they will be more visible than the others. In this section you'll learn four ways to set up three levels of headings.

Books with one level of heading

If your book has only one kind of heading, you are lucky because you won't need to come up with a scheme to differentiate among the levels of heads. Look at the heading designs on the next several pages, and simply pick one of the Heading 1 [**h1**] or Heading 2 [**h2**] styles from the design that is closest to the one you're developing for your book.

Books with two levels of headings

Designing two heading levels is fairly uncomplicated. But even with this simple arrangement, you must still work to make the hierarchy clear. It's easy for an author to get carried away and lose track of the structure that the headings are supposed to mark for the reader. If you're confused by your own headings, try making an outline list out of them to see whether your structure is logical.

Go through the designs in this chapter and pick styles to suit the look of your book so far.

Books with three levels of headings

Now things start to get a bit complicated. But don't worry; you already set up three heading styles for your book, and at this point you just want to find a look that you like. The two options for Heading 3 styles are a stand-alone style (heading on its own line, using Heading 3 [**h3**]) or a run-in style (heading on the same line as the start of the first paragraph, using the Run-in Subheads [**ris**] character style). A stand-alone style is easier in most cases, but a run-in style will save space, and many people prefer the way it looks. Study your book to see which will work best for you.

If you decide to use a run-in style, you'll have to make two decisions: how to separate it from the text that follows and what case to use.

There are four basic choices of separators:

- A period plus an em space (**Heading here.**   Text starts here)
- No period with an em space (**Heading here**   Text starts here)
- A period plus an en space (**Heading here.** Text starts here)
- No period with an en space (**Heading here** Text starts here)

To set an em space, go to Type>Insert White Space>Em Space or type Ctrl/Cmd+Shift+M. To set an en space, go to Type>Insert White Space>En Space or type Ctrl/Cmd+Shift+N.

As for the case, you should first coordinate with your Heading 1 and Heading 2 styles; don't start a new capitalization scheme at this point. Your options are:

- Capitalize the First Letter of Major Words (Sometimes Called Title Case)
- Capitalize only the first letter of the head (called initial cap/lowercase)
- USE SMALL CAPS THROUGHOUT

Initial cap/lowercase is sometimes called sentence case.

When you study the designs on the next pages, keep these options in mind. You can easily customize one of the suggested designs to suit your needs.

Stacking heads

Sometimes one head directly follows another one, resulting in an undesirably large gap between the heads. If this happens, honor the normal space *below the first head*, and then go into the Paragraph panel or the Control panel to delete any extra space above the second head. With your cursor still in the second head, use the Paragraph Styles panel to create a new style for this heading; for instance, if a Heading 2 directly follows a Heading 1, you could call it "h2-belowh1" or "h2-nospaceabove."

Classic centered headings

Baseline shift = a quarter of a line of space

The semibold Heading 2 is different enough from the bold all-caps Heading 1 style so that nobody will be confused by them.

If your book has only one level of heading, take your pick from the **h1** or the **h2** style shown here.

For the run-in Heading 3, apply the [**h3**] paragraph style to the paragraph, and then apply the Run-in Subheads [**ris**] character style to the actual heading.

Alice was beginning to get very tired of sitting by her sister on the bank, and of having nothing to do: once or twice she had peeped into the book her sister was reading, but it had no pictures or conversations in it, 'and what is the use of a book,' thought Alice 'without pictures or conversation?'

HEADING LEVEL 1

So she was considering in her own mind (as well as she could, for the hot day made her feel very sleepy and stupid), whether the pleasure of making a daisy-chain would be worth the trouble of getting up and picking the daisies, when suddenly a White Rabbit with pink eyes ran close by her.

Heading Level 2

There was nothing so VERY remarkable in that; nor did Alice think it so VERY much out of the way to hear the Rabbit say to itself, 'Oh dear! Oh dear! I shall be late!' (when she thought it over afterwards, it occurred to her that she ought to have wondered at this, but at the time it all seemed quite natural); but when the Rabbit actually took a watch out of its waistcoat-pocket and looked at it, and then hurried on, Alice started to her feet, for it flashed across her mind that she had never before seen a rabbit with either a waistcoat-pocket, or a watch to take out of it, and burning with curiosity, she ran across the field after it, and fortunately was just in time to see it pop down a large rabbit-hole under the hedge.

Heading Level 3. In another moment down went Alice after it, never once considering how in the world she was to get out again. The rabbit-hole went straight on like a tunnel for some way, and then dipped suddenly down, so suddenly that Alice had not a moment to think about stopping herself before she found herself falling down a very deep well.

Either the well was very deep, or she fell very slowly, for she had plenty of time as she went down to look about her and to wonder

42

Classic centered headings, *continued*

These headings work well with chapter opening designs 1 or 2, shown on pages 148 and 151. Stick with the one font used throughout the book and the theme of centered elements.

☐ **Heading 1 [h1]**

Changes from the Heading 1 style (see page 76):

Basic Character Formats:	Font Style = Bold
	Size = 12 pt
	Case = All Caps
	Tracking = 50
Advanced Character Formats:	Baseline Shift = 3.5 pt ←———————
Indents and Spacing:	Space After = 0

If you've changed the leading of *your* book text, you could also change the Baseline Shift shown here to 1/4 of a line of space.

☐ **Heading 2 [h2]**

Changes from the Heading 2 style (see page 76):

Basic Character Formats:	Size = 11.5 pt
	Case = Normal
	Tracking = 20
Advanced Character Formats:	Baseline Shift = 0
Indents and Spacing:	Alignment = Center

Be sure to change the Based On setting in the General tab from **h2** to **tx1**.

☐ **Heading 3 [h3]** Based On = **tx1** ←———————

Changes from the No Indents style (see page 62):

Basic Character Formats:	Font Style = Regular
	Tracking = 0
Indents and Spacing:	Space Before = 14 pt *or* 0.1944 in

Your last steps are to apply the Run-In Subheads [**ris**] character style (see page 84) to the actual Heading 3, then choose how to separate it from the rest of the paragraph. In this design, Heading 3 has a period and an en space after it. Feel free to do it differently in *your* book (see page 185).

Alice was beginning to get very tired of sitting by her sister on the bank, and of having nothing to do: once or twice she had peeped into the book her sister was reading, but it had no pictures or conversations in it, 'and what is the use of a book,' thought Alice 'without pictures or conversation?'

Following the chapter opening style on page 156, this Heading 1 style is set in Myriad Pro Semibold with extra tracking. The paragraph rule below it helps to differentiate Heading 1 from Heading 2.

Heading Level 1

So she was considering in her own mind (as well as she could, for the hot day made her feel very sleepy and stupid), whether the pleasure of making a daisy-chain would be worth the trouble of getting up and picking the daisies, when suddenly a White Rabbit with pink eyes ran close by her.

Heading Level 2

There was nothing so VERY remarkable in that; nor did Alice think it so VERY much out of the way to hear the Rabbit say to itself, 'Oh dear! Oh dear! I shall be late!' (when she thought it over afterwards, it occurred to her that she ought to have wondered at this, but at the time it all seemed quite natural); but when the Rabbit actually took a watch out of its waistcoat-pocket and looked at it, and then hurried on, Alice started to her feet, for it flashed across her mind that she had never before seen a rabbit with either a waistcoat-pocket, or a watch to take out of it, and burning with curiosity, she ran across the field after it, and fortunately was just in time to see it pop down a large rabbit-hole under the hedge.

Heading Level 3

In another moment down went Alice after it, never once considering how in the world she was to get out again. The rabbit-hole went straight on like a tunnel for some way, and then dipped suddenly down, so suddenly that Alice had not a moment to think about stopping herself before she found herself falling down a very deep well.

Either the well was very deep, or she fell very slowly, for she had plenty of time as she went down to look about her and to wonder

Modern headings with paragraph rule, *continued*

This set of sleek, modern-looking headings coordinates with chapter opening design 4, shown on page 156. If you only need one kind of heading, simply pick one of the larger ones in this design. Remember to use the leading from *your* book if you've changed it for your main text.

☐ **Heading 1 [h1]**

Changes from the Heading 1 style (see page 76):

Basic Character Formats:
Font = Myriad Pro

Font Style = Semibold Condensed

Size = 15 pt

Tracking = 40

Indents and Spacing:
Alignment = Left

Paragraph Rules:
Rule Below = Rule On

(Fill in as shown to the right)

OpenType Features:
Proportional Lining

Style Name:	h1
Location:	

Paragraph Rules

Rule Below ▾ ☑ Rule On

Weight: 0.5 pt ▾   Type: ▬▬▬ ▾
Color: ■ (Text Color) ▾   Tint: ▾
☐ Overprint Stroke
Gap Color: ▨ [None] ▾   Gap Tint: ▾
☐ Overprint Gap
Width: Text ▾   Offset: 0.0625 in
Left Indent: -0.125 in   ght Indent: 0 in

☐ Keep In Frame

When you add a paragraph rule to **h1**, it will also appear in the styles based on **h1**. That's why you need to turn it off in **h2**.

☐ **Heading 2 [h2]**

Changes from the Heading 2 style (see page 76):

Basic Character Formats:
Font Style = Semibold Condensed

Size = 12.5 pt

Case = Normal

Tracking = 40

Paragraph Rules:
Rule Below = Uncheck Rule On

If you don't see Myriad Pro in your font list, go into the Creative Cloud application and click on Assets>Fonts> Add Fonts from Typekit. Type "Myriad Pro" in the Search Typekit box. When you see the fonts displayed, click Sync beside the ones you want to use.

☐ **Heading 3 [h3]**

Changes from the Heading 3 style (see page 76):

Basic Character Formats:
Font Style = Condensed

Size = 11.5 pt

Modern headings
– with –
two typefaces

This heading is set in 16 pt type with 14 pts of leading. It will only work if all of the headings are one line long, because the type crashes when there are more lines.

If your book has longer headings, simply reduce the size of the Heading 1 style to 14.5 pt and the size of the Heading 2 style to 12 pt.

Alice was beginning to get very tired of sitting by her sister on the bank, and of having nothing to do: once or twice she had peeped into the book her sister was reading, but it had no pictures or conversations in it, 'and what is the use of a book,' thought Alice 'without pictures or conversation?'

Heading Level 1

So she was considering in her own mind (as well as she could, for the hot day made her feel very sleepy and stupid), whether the pleasure of making a daisy-chain would be worth the trouble of getting up and picking the daisies, when suddenly a White Rabbit with pink eyes ran close by her.

Heading Level 2

There was nothing so VERY remarkable in that; nor did Alice think it so VERY much out of the way to hear the Rabbit say to itself, 'Oh dear! Oh dear! I shall be late!' (when she thought it over afterwards, it occurred to her that she ought to have wondered at this, but at the time it all seemed quite natural); but when the Rabbit actually took a watch out of its waistcoat-pocket and looked at it, and then hurried on, Alice started to her feet, for it flashed across her mind that she had never before seen a rabbit with either a waistcoat-pocket, or a watch to take out of it, and burning with curiosity, she ran across the field after it, and fortunately was just in time to see it pop down a large rabbit-hole under the hedge.

HEADING LEVEL 3   In another moment down went Alice after it, never once considering how in the world she was to get out again. The rabbit-hole went straight on like a tunnel for some way, and then dipped suddenly down, so suddenly that Alice had not a moment to think about stopping herself before she found herself falling down a very deep well.

Either the well was very deep, or she fell very slowly, for she had plenty of time as she went down to look about her and to wonder

Modern headings with two typefaces, *continued*

In chapter opening design 5 (page 159), small caps and two different fonts are used, so you can take advantage of the variety of choices. Remember, as always, that all of the Space Before and Space After settings in the examples are based on Text [**tx**] style with 14 pts of leading. If your leading is different, change the settings to match.

☐ **Heading 1 [h1]**
Changes from the Heading 1 style (see page 76):

Basic Character Formats:	Font = Myriad Pro
	Font Style = Semibold Condensed
	Size = 16 pt
Indents and Spacing:	Alignment = Left
OpenType Features:	Proportional Lining

☐ **Heading 2 [h2]**
Changes from the Heading 2 style (see page 76):

Basic Character Formats:	Font Style = Semibold Condensed
	Size = 12.5 pt
	Tracking = 20

☐ **Heading 3 [h3]**   Based On = **tx1** ⟵ Be sure to change the Based On setting in the General tab from **h2** to **tx1**.

Changes from the No Indents style (see page 62):

Basic Character Formats:	Font Style = Regular
	Tracking = 0
Indents and Spacing:	Space Before = 14 pt *or* 0.1944 in

☐ **Run-In Subheads [ris]** *character* style
Changes from the Run-In Subheads character style (see page 84):

Basic Character Formats:	Font Style = Regular
	Case = OpenType All Small Caps
	Tracking = 40

Your last steps are to apply the Run-In Subheads [**ris**] character style to the actual Heading 3, then choose how to separate it from the rest of the paragraph. In this design, Heading 3 has an em space after it. Feel free to do it differently in *your* book (see page 185).

Modern headings
– with –
shaded graphic

Alice was beginning to get very tired of sitting by her sister on the bank, and of having nothing to do: once or twice she had peeped into the book her sister was reading, but it had no pictures or conversations in it, 'and what is the use of a book,' thought Alice 'without pictures or conversation?'

HEADING LEVEL 1

So she was considering in her own mind (as well as she could, for the hot day made her feel very sleepy and stupid), whether the pleasure of making a daisy-chain would be worth the trouble of getting up and picking the daisies, when suddenly a White Rabbit with pink eyes ran close by her.

Heading Level 2

There was nothing so VERY remarkable in that; nor did Alice think it so VERY much out of the way to hear the Rabbit say to itself, 'Oh dear! Oh dear! I shall be late!' (when she thought it over afterwards, it occurred to her that she ought to have wondered at this, but at the time it all seemed quite natural); but when the Rabbit actually took a watch out of its waistcoat-pocket and looked at it, and then hurried on, Alice started to her feet, for it flashed across her mind that she had never before seen a rabbit with either a waistcoat-pocket, or a watch to take out of it, and burning with curiosity, she ran across the field after it, and fortunately was just in time to see it pop down a large rabbit-hole under the hedge.

Heading Level 3

In another moment down went Alice after it, never once considering how in the world she was to get out again. The rabbit-hole went straight on like a tunnel for some way, and then dipped suddenly down, so suddenly that Alice had not a moment to think about stopping herself before she found herself falling down a very deep well.

Either the well was very deep, or she fell very slowly, for she had plenty of time as she went down to look about her and to wonder

In a font family with many weights, it's best to skip a weight when you want the difference between two styles to be noticeable. In this case, the h1 and h2 are set in Black and the h3 is set in Semibold. The Bold weight in between them was skipped.

Modern headings with shaded graphic, *continued*

Chapter opening design 6 (page 162) features a light gray box (actually a paragraph rule) behind the chapter number. Here we repeat that idea in the Heading 1 design.

☐ **Heading 1 [h1]**

Changes from the Heading 1 style (see page 76):

Basic Character Formats:	Font = Myriad Pro
	Font Style = Black
	Size = 12 pt
	Case = All Caps
	Tracking = 150
Indents and Spacing:	Alignment = Left
	Space After = 0
Paragraph Rules:	Rule Below = On
	(Fill in as shown
	to the right.)
OpenType Features:	Proportional Lining

When you add a paragraph rule to **h1**, it will also appear in the styles based on **h1**. That's why you need to turn it off in **h2**.

☐ **Heading 2 [h2]**

Changes from the Heading 2 style (see page 76):

Basic Character Formats:	Font Style = Black
	Size = 11 pt
	Case = Normal
	Tracking = 40
Paragraph Rules:	Rule Below = Uncheck Rule On

☐ **Heading 3 [h3]**

Changes from the Heading 3 style (see page 76):

Basic Character Formats:	Font Style = Semibold
	Tracking = 0

26 *Designing other elements*

In this chapter you'll learn how to design some of the more complicated elements that might appear in your book. Simply skip this chapter if your book has none of the following:

- Extracts
- Display material
- Lists of all sorts
- Sidebars

Your book may have other elements, such as poetry, math, tables (charts), or footnotes. If so, you'll find solutions to typesetting that material in chapter 50.

Designing extracts

Poems (and song lyrics) that are extracts are covered in chapter 50.

You designed your extracts along with your other paragraph styles in Part II, and those extract styles should work well for most books. In this section, though, you can explore some alternatives. General rules for setting extracts are:

- Set extracts 1 point size smaller than your book text.
- Indent them the same amount as your paragraph indent, on both left and right. (An alternative is to indent them only on the left.)
- Leave one line of space above and below.
- Do not indent the first line of the extract. Extracts that are longer than one paragraph should use paragraph indents for the following paragraphs. Or, leave a full or half line of space between extract paragraphs and don't use any first line indents at all.

If you'd like to make extracts more visible on the page (and save a little space), you can use less leading than in your book text. So, if your main book text is set at 11/14, your extract could be set at 10/13 or 10/12. This extract should not sit on the baseline grid (Paragraph Style Options>Indents and Spacing>Align to Grid: None).

Quotation marks

Do not use quotation marks with extracts or chapter opening quotes. The layout and spacing of these elements signify that the text is a quotation; quotation marks would be redundant.

The Paragraph styles for the example below and the one on page 197 are laid out for you. Perhaps one of these styles (or a hybrid of your own choosing) will work for *your* extracts.

had never before seen a rabbit with either a waistcoat-pocket, or a watch to take out of it, and burning with curiosity, she ran across the field after it, and fortunately was just in time to see it pop down a large rabbit-hole under the hedge.

Extract Heading

In another moment down went Alice after it, never once considering how in the world she was to get out again. The rabbit-hole went straight on like a tunnel for some way, and then dipped suddenly down, so suddenly that Alice had not a moment to think about stopping herself before she found herself falling down a very deep well.

Either the well was very deep, or she fell very slowly, for she had plenty of time as she went down to look about her and to wonder what was going to happen next. First, she tried to look down and make out what she was coming to, but it was too dark to see anything; then she looked at the sides of the well, and noticed that they were filled with cupboards and book-shelves; here and there she saw maps and pictures hung upon pegs.

—Lewis Carroll, *Alice in Wonderland*

She took down a jar from one of the shelves as she passed; it was labelled 'ORANGE MARMALADE', but to her great disappointment it was empty: she did not like to drop the jar for fear of

ragged right text (Alignment = Left)

This extract text is one point size smaller than the main text but uses the same leading.

one linespace between paragraphs

This is one way to show the attribution. (Not all extracts have attributions, of course.)

Here are the paragraph styles for the extract shown on the previous page. You may not need all of them.

☐ **Extracts, First [ext1]**
Changes from the Extracts, First style (page 68):
Indents and Spacing: Alignment = Left
                                               Space After = 14 pt *or* 0.1944 in

☐ **Extracts, Middle [ext2]**
Changes from the Extracts, Middle style (page 68):
Indents and Spacing: First Line Indent = 0

☐ **Extracts, Last [ext3]**
Changes from the Extracts, Last style (page 68): No Changes

☐ **Extracts, Only [ext0]**
Changes from the Extracts, Only style (page 68): No Changes

The Extracts, Only style is for an extract that is only one paragraph long.

☐ **Extracts, Head [exth]**   Based On = **ext1**
Changes from Extracts, First style:
Basic Character Formats: Style = Bold
Advanced Character Formats: Baseline Shift = 3 pt
Indents and Spacing: Space After = 0

Create the **[exth]** and **[ext1-ffhead]** paragraph styles if your extracts have headings. Then apply the styles to your extract headings and the first paragraph following them.

☐ **Extracts, First after Head [ext1-ffhead]**   Based On = **ext1**
Changes from Extracts, First style:
Indents and Spacing: Space Before = 0

If there's an attribution after the last paragraph, create the **[ext3attr]** paragraph style and apply it to the last paragraph instead of **ext3** so there will be no space after.

☐ **Extracts, Last with Attribution [ext3attr]** Based On = **ext3**
Changes from Extracts, Last style:
Indents and Spacing: Space After = 0

Attributions can be set in small caps, italics, or roman (regular). Pick a character style that will work with the rest of your design.

☐ **Extracts, Attribution [extattr]**   Based On = **ext3**
Changes from Extracts, Last style:
Indents and Spacing: Alignment = Right

In the extract sample below, the type is set at 10/12, justified, with a half-linespace between paragraphs and before and after the entire block of type. Notice that even though the type is the same size as in the previous example, the first paragraph uses five lines instead of six. This is due to the justified type. So this sample saves space in three ways: leading, justification, and spacing.

the field after it, and fortunately was just in time to see it pop down a large rabbit-hole under the hedge.

Extract Heading

In another moment down went Alice after it, never once considering how in the world she was to get out again. The rabbit-hole went straight on like a tunnel for some way, and then dipped suddenly down, so suddenly that Alice had not a moment to think about stopping herself before she found herself falling down a very deep well.

Either the well was very deep, or she fell very slowly, for she had plenty of time as she went down to look about her and to wonder what was going to happen next. First, she tried to look down and make out what she was coming to, but it was too dark to see anything; then she looked at the sides of the well, and noticed that they were filled with cupboards and book-shelves; here and there she saw maps and pictures hung upon pegs.

LEWIS CARROLL, *Alice in Wonderland*

She took down a jar from one of the shelves as she passed; it was labelled 'ORANGE MARMALADE', but to her great disappointment it was empty: she did not like to drop the jar for fear of

one half-linespace before and after the entire extract

justified text (Alignment = Left Justify)

one half-linespace between paragraphs

You may find a larger space here because the paragraph following is aligned to the baseline grid.

☐ **Extracts, First [ext1]**

Changes from the Extracts, First style (page 68):

Basic Character Formats:	Leading = 12 pt
Indents and Spacing:	Space Before = 7 pt *or* 0.0972 in
	Align to Grid = None

☐ **Extracts, Middle [ext2]**

Changes from the Extracts, Middle style (page 68):

| Indents and Spacing: | First Line Indent = 0 |
| | Space Before = 7 pt *or* 0.0972 in |

(continued on page 198)

☐ **Extracts, Last [ext3]**
Changes from the Extracts, Last style (page 68):
Indents and Spacing: Space After = 7 pt *or* 0.0972 in

☐ **Extracts, Only [exto]**
Changes from the Extracts, Only style (page 68):
Indents and Spacing: Space After = 7 pt *or* 0.0972 in

The Extracts, Only style is for an extract that is only one paragraph long.

☐ **Extracts Head [exth]**   Based On = **ext1**
Changes from Extracts, First style:
Basic Character Formats   Style = Bold

Create the **[exth]** and **[ext1-ffhead]** paragraph styles if your extracts have headings. Then apply the styles to your extract headings and the first paragraph following them.

☐ **Extracts, First after Head [ext1-ffhead]**   Based On = **ext1**
Changes from Extracts, First style:
Indents and Spacing   Space Before = 0

Attributions can be set in small caps, italics, or roman (regular). Pick a character style that will work with the rest of your design.

☐ **Extract Attribution [extattr]**   Based On = **ext3**
Changes from Extracts, Last style:
Indents and Spacing: Alignment = Right

Dealing with display material

Display text comes in many forms. It can be a mathematical or scientific expression, an important declaration (such as a rule or the moral of a story), or the reproduction of a storefront sign, for instance. Despite the diversity of material, there is one basic way to treat all of it (except complex math; see page 141): Set the type the same as your book text, but center it. Leave a full line of space above and below. Examples:

For math display text, see page 141.

$$E = mc^2$$

The pen is mightier than the sword.

BRAKE FOR MOOSE

For simple display text like this, make a paragraph style called Display **[disp]** based on **tx1** except with 1) centered alignment and 2) one line of space before and after.

Using tabs

You can master tabs with some practice. To see the Tabs panel, go to Type> Tabs or type Ctrl/Cmd+Shift+T. Here's how each tab aligns list items:

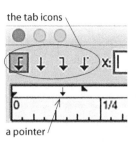

the tab icons

a pointer

left aligned ↓	center aligned ↓	right aligned ↓	decimal aligned ↓
oranges	oranges	oranges	1234.5
178	178	178	6
3	3	3	7.890

To add a tab, first make sure that all of your list copy is left aligned. Next put your cursor before the word or number where you want a tab, then hit the Tab key. (For now, the location of the tabs is not important, so even if some of your text items jump to the right or down to the next line, don't worry.) Repeat for all the items in your list, then highlight them all. In the Tabs panel, select the correct tab icon for your first tabbed column. Type a value in the "X" box, or click and drag the pointer (↓) in the white area just above the ruler. If you want to set a tab farther to the right than what shows on the ruler, hover your cursor over the ruler and a hand icon will appear. Use the hand to drag the ruler left or right. Repeat for each column in your list.

Leave the Leader box empty unless you want to fill the space before the tabbed item with something, such as a series of dots.

The "Align On" box can help you align list items on a specific character of your choice, such as an equals sign. Use the decimal tab to get access to this function, then type the character in the Align On field.

Notice that the numerals in the last column (above left) are Tabular Lining figures. Assigning Tabular figures (whether Lining or Oldstyle) assures that they line up with each other vertically.

 Tabs are very useful in printed books. However, EPUB format does not recognize them. We recommend using tabs in your printed book and then reformatting the tabbed material as a table with invisible (no color ▱) strokes for your ebook.

Designing lists

There are many kinds of lists! A well-planned book should have only a few types of lists in it, though. Aside from more details about numbered and bulleted lists, in this section you'll also find guidelines and settings for numbered paragraph, unnumbered, multicolumn, and sublists.

If your book has too many kinds of lists, reorganize or rethink.

Numbered lists

Why do we need to talk about numbered lists again if your styles are already set up? Because the list styles you have now only work for single-digit lists. If you have 10 or more entries, they will look sloppy.

9. List
10. List

en space

The display to the left shows the ideal alignment of numbers and periods for numbered lists. The *a* value is the width of the widest number in the list plus the period. A right-aligning tab is set to the right of the period. The *b* value is where the list entries start, one en space beyond the period. The list's hanging indent is set for this location. The settings for a two-digit list in 11/14 Minion are shown below; if you're using a different font or size, continue reading.

Sometimes ragged right (Alignment = Left) works better for numbered lists. See how yours look before you decide.

☐ **2-Digit Numbered Lists, First [nl1-00]** Based On = **tx1**
Changes from the No Indents style (see page 62):
Indents and Spacing: Left Indent = 0.2571 in
First Line Indent = −0.2571 in
Space Before = 14 pt *or* 0.1944 in
Tabs: (Fill in as shown to the left)
OpenType Features: Tabular Oldstyle

☐ **2-Digit Numbered Lists, Middle [nl2-00]** Based On = **nl1-00**
Changes from the 2-Digit Numbered Lists, First style:
Indents and Spacing: Space Before = 0

Remember to insert tabs before and after each paragraph number as shown on page 201.

☐ **2-Digit Numbered Lists, Last [nl3-00]** Based On = **nl2-00**
Changes from the 2-Digit Numbered Lists, Middle style:
Indents and Spacing: Space After = 14 pt *or* 0.1944 in

For a detailed explanation of how tabs work, see page 199.

Most of the time the Info panel is too distracting to have in front of you. Once you're finished using it, click the X to make it disappear.

Here's how to find the values for *your* two-digit numbered lists:

1 Make a new text frame on the pasteboard and, using the No Indents style [**tx1**], type the widest numeral in your lists, plus a period. Then set an en space (Ctrl/Cmd+Shift+N) and type "List." Highlight the number and give it the Digits character style for your book.

2 Open the Info panel (Window>Info). This panel shows you the exact location of your cursor at any time. Place your cursor to the right of the period, and write down the X value. This corresponds to the *a* value in the demo above.

3 Place your cursor to the left of "List" and write down the X value. This is your *b* value from the demo.

4 Open the Paragraph Styles panel and start a new style called 2-Digit Numbered Lists, First [**nl1-00**], based on your No Indents [**tx1**] style. In Indents and Spacing, add one line of space before it.

5 Also in Indents and Spacing, use *b* for the Left Indent and –*b* for the First Line Indent. This will give you the hanging indent you need.

6 In the Tabs section, select the right-aligning tab icon (↓), then type the value of *a* in the X: box. Then click OK.

7 Now set up a 2-Digit Numbered Lists, Middle [**nl2-00**] style with zero space before, and a 2-Digit Numbered Lists, Last [**nl3-00**] style with one line of space after, based on **nl2-00**.

When you are formatting the lists, you must type a tab before the number and another one before the list entry, as shown at right. Also, remember to apply your Digits character style, if you're using one.

What if there's a mixture of one- and two-digit lists in your book? The best bet for most books is simply to treat them all like two-digit lists. This makes them all consistent, and you don't have to worry about misalignment of two different lists on the same page.

And three-digit lists? If you have any of these, make a separate style for them using the method above, and only use that style for the rare occasions when you need it. Then stick with the two-digit style for all the rest.

Numbered paragraphs

Also called paragraph lists, numbered paragraphs are easy to typeset because they are almost identical to your Text style. Simply apply your **Bold** character style to the number and period at the beginning of the paragraph, then set an en space (Ctrl/Cmd+Shift+N), and continue on with the text. Whether you want a line of space between entries is up to you. Styles for numbered paragraphs are shown on page 202.

Unnumbered (or unordered) lists

Unnumbered lists look quite simple on a page but do take some thought to set up. Look at the unnumbered lists in your book. Are they short or

X value

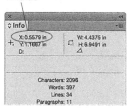

You can set up your single-digit lists to align on the periods, too. Use the *a* value for the tab, but for the hanging indent simply use your normal paragraph indent measurement.

After reading this section, you might have noticed that in *this* book we have ignored our own instructions regarding numbered lists. This is a case of rules being made to be broken! We're striving for a minimalist look throughout, and this is just one of our design tricks. For 99% of our readers, the instructions given above will be the best method.

numbered paragraphs

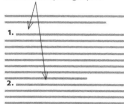

☐ **Numbered Paragraphs, First [np1]** Based On = **tx**
Changes from the Text style (see page 62):
Indents and Spacing: Space Before = 14 pt *or* 0.1944 in

☐ **Numbered Paragraphs, Middle [np2]** Based On = **np1**
Changes from the Numbered Paragraphs, First style:
Indents and Spacing: Space Before = 0 *or* no change

☐ **Numbered Paragraphs, Last [np3]** Based On = **np2**
Changes from the Numbered Paragraphs, Middle style:
Indents and Spacing: Space After = 14 pt *or* 0.1944 in

long? Are the entries short or long or a mixture? Would extra space between entries make them easier to read? Do you think they would look better in multiple columns? Do you need to save space throughout your book? Keep all of these factors in mind as you read this and the multi-column lists section that follows. Styles are shown on page 203.

Multicolumn lists

These lists can be set up in two different ways. An *anchored list* is a little easier to typeset but could cause paging headaches if it appears at the bottom of a page and needs to flow to the next. A *tabbed list* is more work to typeset but will flow to the next page with no trouble. Because of the way each is set up, the two kinds of lists are read in different ways, as shown below. This may influence which kind you choose.

anchored list

tabbed list

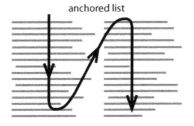
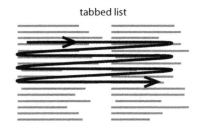

Sometimes a complicated multicolumn list works better as a table. See pages 342–347.

☐ **Unnumbered Lists, First [unl1]**   Based On = **tx1**
Changes from the No Indents style (see page 62):
Indents and Spacing: Alignment = Left
                                                    Left Indent = 0.4 in
                                                    First Line Indent = –0.2 in
                                                    Space Before = 14 pt or 0.1944 in

☐ **Unnumbered Lists, Middle [unl2]**   Based On = **unl1**
Changes from the Unnumbered Lists, First style:
Indents and Spacing: Space Before = 0 ←

If your lists are a bit hard to read, consider adding 1/4 to 1/2 of a linespace between entries. If you add extra space, change your Align to Grid setting to None under Indents and Spacing.

☐ **Unnumbered Lists, Last [unl3]**   Based On = **unl2**
Changes from the Unnumbered Lists, Middle style:
Indents and Spacing: Space After = 14 pt *or* 0.1944 in

Anchored list   To typeset an unnumbered anchored list, set up the styles shown on page 204. The good news about an anchored list is that you need only the Middle style [**mcl2**] and perhaps the Column Head style [**mcl-colh**]. (The others are for tabbed lists.) Now complete these steps:

If your anchored multi-column list is bulleted or numbered, simply use the Middle styles you already have set up for those kinds of lists.

1 Make a new text frame the same width as your basic text frame, then go to Object>Text Frame Options and specify the number of columns and width of the gutters (the space between the columns). A gutter measurement that usually works well is 0.25″.

2 Highlight the list text that is on your page(s), copy it, place your cursor at the top left of the text frame you just made, and paste it. The text should flow into the columns.

3 Make the columns equal length, more or less, by dragging the center bottom handle of the text frame up or down. In any multicolumn list, it's desirable to make the left column(s) longer than the right one(s) if they cannot all be the same length. To force copy into the next column, type a soft return (Shift+Enter/Return).

4 Anchor the list to the book text this way: With the Selection Tool, select then cut the text frame containing your list (Ctrl/Cmd+X). With

the Type Tool, place your cursor at the end of the text line above where you want the list to go, press Enter/Return to make several extra lines of space, apply your **tx1** style to those lines, and then paste the list in the last blank line (Ctrl/Cmd+V). The text frame should appear just where you expected it, but if not, you may need to press Enter/Return once or twice more, or perhaps delete some of the blank lines. If you need to, you can resize the anchored text frame at any time.

The main problem with an anchored list is that if it doesn't all fit on the page and needs to flow to the next page, the entire thing moves as a

You'll need to point this list out to your ebook conversion service so they can anchor it in place without using the extra linespaces.

☐ **Multicolumn Lists, First [mcl1]**   Based On = **tx1**
Changes from the No Indents style (see page 62):
Indents and Spacing: Alignment = Left
                                     Left Indent = 0.2 in
                                     First Line Indent = –0.2 in
                                     Space Before = 14 pt *or* 0.1944 in
Tabs: Add tabs for tabbed list only

For a tabbed list, add tabs. A sample tab setup for 3 columns is shown on the next page.

☐ **Multicolumn Lists, Middle [mcl2]**   Based On = **mcl1**
Changes from the Multicolumn Lists, First style:
Indents and Spacing: Space Before = 0

For an anchored list without column heads, you only need the Middle style.

☐ **Multicolumn Lists, Last [mcl3]**   Based On = **mcl2**
Changes from the Multicolumn Lists, Middle style:
Indents and Spacing: Space After = 14 pt or 0.1944 in

☐ **Multicolumn Lists, Column Head [mcl-colh]**   Based On = **mcl1**
Changes from the Multicolumn Lists, First style:
Basic Character Formats: Style = Bold *or* Italics

The Column Head style can double as a head for the entire list.

☐ **Multicolumn Lists, First after Head [mcl1-ffh]**   Based On = **mcl1**
Changes from the Multicolumn Lists, First style:
Indents and Spacing: Space Before = 0

unit. One way out of this awkward layout situation is to give the list a title (use the **mcl-colh** style provided on the previous page) and then place the entire list at the top or bottom of the same page or a nearby one, on the same spread if possible. Then in the text, refer to the list by its title, rather than by saying "the list below."

Another way out of the situation is to make a tabbed list instead.

Tabbed list This method is definitely more laborious, but it's also more flexible, as it will flow from one page to the next without any problem. First, set up the multicolumn list paragraph styles shown on the previous page. To typeset the list, use left-aligning tabs (↓) to set up a number of columns of equal width. Be sure to include all the tabs in the **mcl1** paragraph style. A sample tab panel for a two-column list is shown below. Yours will probably be different.

To typeset the list, go *across* the page rather than down, like this:

This is entry one, and it is »more than one line long.　　»　　This is entry two, and it turns over¶
　　　　　　　　　　　　　　　　　»　　» onto a second line.¶
This is entry three, and it is »longer than one line.　　　　»　　This is entry four, and it's short.¶

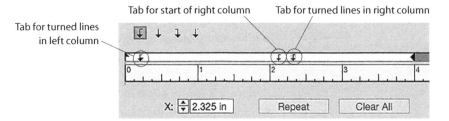

Tab for start of right column　　　Tab for turned lines in right column

Tab for turned lines in left column

For a detailed explanation of how tabs work, see page 199.

X: 2.325 in　　Repeat　　Clear All

Bulleted lists

You set up bulleted list styles in chapter 10, and most likely you can keep them just as they are. But if for some reason you don't like the bullet that comes with your book text font, simply change it. Here's how:

1 Open your **bl1** paragraph style in the Paragraph Styles panel and select Bullets and Numbering from the list on the left. In the List Type menu, make sure it says "Bullets."

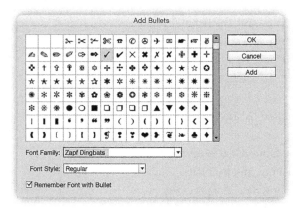

2 In the Bullet Character area, click on Add. The Add Bullets dialog box pops up, and you can browse through various typefaces. Start with your Text typeface. If that doesn't satisfy, try looking in Zapf Dingbats (shown to the left) or Wingdings, and choose a character you like.

3 If your new bullet is part of a different font family from your book text, check the "Remember Font With Bullet" box. Click Add, then OK.

4 Return to the Bullet Character chart in the Paragraph Style Options dialog box for **bl1**, and click on the new bullet to highlight it. This character will now appear in all your bulleted lists.

5 To change the color or size of your new bullet, make a character style for it while you're still in the Bullets and Numbering dialog box. Select New Character Style from the Character Style drop-down list. Name the style simply "bullet." This style should include *only the differences* from your **bl1** style, such as the font for the bullet, the new size, the baseline shift, the new color or tint of black, etc. There's no need to fill in every blank in the dialog box. Click OK to close the dialog box, then OK to finish.

Choose New Character Style from the list and name it "bullet."

Sure, it's fun to experiment with bullet characters, but don't get carried away. Unless bulleted lists are a major feature in your book, they shouldn't stick out like a sore thumb.

Sublists

Sometimes a list entry has subentries below it—bullets below numbers, letters below bullets. The number of variations is huge. You've learned how to set up lists, so a few suggestions should be all you need at this stage to create good-looking sublists. The marker (bullet, number, or letter) for any sublist entry should align with the main entry (not the marker) above it, and then the subentry should indent more: add the same amount of indent that you used in the main list. The example to the right shows the alignments. Here are a couple of general rules:

- Lowercase or uppercase letters align *at left* with each other.
- Roman numerals align *on the periods*, as for numbered lists.

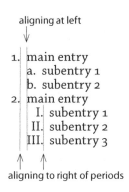

aligning at left

1. main entry
   a. subentry 1
   b. subentry 2
2. main entry
    I. subentry 1
   II. subentry 2
   III. subentry 3

aligning to right of periods

Designing sidebars

Along with chapter numbers and titles, sidebars are often the most noticeable design feature in a book. Indeed, if readers find your sidebars to be especially entertaining or instructive, they will often seek them out before reading the rest of the text.

You set up your original **sb** styles on page 70.

In the next several pages you'll find some basic sidebar designs and the style settings for each. A few of these designs require making shapes and using layers and colors (even if your book is going to be printed in black ink only). Part V: Adding Shapes & Color will show you how.

And in every one of these designs, your first step will be to cut the sidebar copy from your main text and paste it into a new text frame.

In addition to the designs shown on the next several pages, you'll find a few more suggestions in the list below. Mix and match some of the ideas to find the best look for *your* book.

- Bleed a background box across a 2-page spread.
- Use a drop cap to start the sidebar text.
- Design a heading area for the sidebar title.
- If your book text is justified, set sidebars ragged right (Alignment = Left).
- Run the title vertically if the same title repeats with each sidebar.
- Set the first few lines the full width and the rest in two or three columns.
- Place a vertical rule to the left of the sidebar text.

Whatever design you use should work for *all* of your sidebars. Go through each one and think about its features—the amount of copy, lengths of headings, and kinds of lists—before making a final decision.

**Classic
two-column
sidebar
– in –
one-column text**

Alice was beginning to get very tired of sitting by her sister on the bank, and of having nothing to do: once or twice she had peeped into the book her sister was reading, but it had no pictures or conversations in it, 'and what is the use of a book,' thought Alice 'without pictures or conversation?

So she was considering in her own mind (as well as she could, for the hot day made her feel very sleepy and stupid), whether the pleasure of making a daisy-chain would be worth the trouble of getting up and picking the daisies, when suddenly a White Rabbit with pink eyes ran close by her.

There was nothing so VERY remarkable in that; nor did Alice think it so VERY much out of the way to hear the Rabbit say to itself, 'Oh dear! Oh dear! I shall be late!' (when she thought it over afterwards, it occurred to her that she ought to have wondered at this, but at the time it all seemed quite natural); but when the Rabbit actually took a watch out of its waistcoat-pocket and looked

Leave 2–3 lines of white space between the text and the sidebar.

SIDEBAR TITLE

For a minute or two she stood looking at the house, and wondering what to do next, when suddenly a footman in livery came running out of the wood—(she considered him to be a footman because he was in livery: otherwise, judging by his face only, she would have called him a fish)—and rapped loudly at the door with his knuckles.

It was opened by another footman in livery, with a round face, and large eyes like a frog; and both footmen, Alice noticed, had powdered hair that curled all over their heads. She felt very curious to know what it was all about, and crept a little way out of the wood to listen. The Fish-Footman began by producing from under his arm a great letter, nearly as large as himself, and this he handed over to the other, saying, in a solemn tone, 'For the Duchess. An invitation from the Queen to play croquet.' The Frog-Footman repeated, in the same solemn tone, only changing the order of the words a little, 'From the Queen. An invitation for the Duchess to play croquet.' Then they both bowed low, and their curls got entangled together.

If your sidebar has a title, make a separate text frame for it. Place it so the base of the title is 2 baselines above the base of the first line of sidebar text.

Sidebar text is 1 pt size smaller than the text, with 2 pts less leading.

This style of sidebar should always appear at the top or bottom of the text page— never in the middle.

42

Classic two-column sidebar in one-column text, *continued*

First, make room for the sidebar by moving the top or bottom of the main text frame up or down. Then cut the sidebar text (Ctrl/Cmd+X) from the main text frame and paste it (Ctrl/Cmd+V) into a new text frame. Go to Object>Text Frame Options and specify two columns with a 0.25″ gutter between them. Then equalize the column lengths by moving the bottom center text frame handle up or down. You can force type into the next column by typing a soft return (Shift+Enter/Return) where you want the break. Type styles for this sidebar are shown below.

In multicolumn text it is always more desirable for the left column to be longer than the right one if they cannot be equal in length.

☐ **Sidebars, First** [sb1]

Changes from the Sidebars, First style (see page 70):

Basic Character Formats:	Font Style = Regular
	Font Size = 10 pt
	Leading = 12 pt
Indents and Spacing:	Left Indent = 0
	Right Indent = 0
	Space Before = 0
	Align to Grid = None
Drop Caps and Nested Styles:	Drop Caps Lines = 2
	Drop Caps Characters = 1

See page 153 for how to deal with a drop cap that has a quotation mark before it.

☐ **Sidebars, Middle** [sb2]

Changes from the Sidebars, Middle style (see page 70):

Indents and Spacing:	First Line Indent = 12 pts *or* 0.1667 in
Drop Caps and Nested Styles:	Drop Caps Lines = 0

☐ **Sidebars, Last** [sb3]

Changes from the Sidebars, Last style (see page 70): No changes

☐ **Sidebars, title** [sbt]

Changes from Sidebars, Title style style (see page 70):

Basic Character Formats:	Case = OpenType All Small Caps
Indents and Spacing:	Alignment = Center
Drop Caps and Nested Styles:	Drop Caps Lines = 0

Modern sidebar
– with –
text wrap and a
bleed background

The type in this sidebar is on the baseline grid, looking nice and neat next to the main text. Also note that the sidebar text aligns at left with the folio.

1. Format the sidebar type in its own text frame.
2. Give the new text frame a text wrap.
3. Position the top and bottom of the text frame on the closest available baselines. Then position the outside edge to align with the folio below. Move the inside edge to the center of the page (you'll see a guide appear when you reach the center line).

If the sidebar text were any wider the letter spacing and word spacing in the main text would probably look very poor—either too tight or too loose.

Alice was beginning to get very tired of sitting by her sister on the bank, and of having nothing to do: once or twice she had peeped into the book her sister was reading, but it had no pictures or conversations in it, 'and what is the use of a book,' thought Alice 'without pictures or conversation?

So she was considering in her own mind (as well as she could, for the hot day made her feel very sleepy and stupid), whether the pleasure of making a daisy-chain would be worth the trouble of getting up and picking the daisies, when suddenly a White Rabbit with pink eyes ran close by her.

There was nothing so VERY remarkable in that; nor did Alice think it so VERY much out of the way to hear the Rabbit say to itself, 'Oh dear! Oh dear! I shall be late!' (when she thought it over afterwards, it occurred to her that she ought to have wondered at this, but at the time it all seemed quite natural); but when the Rabbit actually took a watch out of its waistcoat-pocket and looked at it, and then hurried on, Alice started to her feet, for it flashed across her mind that she had never before seen a rabbit with either a waistcoat-pocket, or a watch to take out of it, and burning with curiosity, she ran across the field after it, and fortunately was just in time to see it pop down a large rabbit-hole under the hedge. In another moment down went Alice after it, never once considering how in the world she was to get out again. The rabbit-hole went straight on like a tunnel for some way, and then dipped suddenly down, so suddenly that Alice had not a moment to think about stopping herself before she found herself falling down a very deep well. Either the well was very deep, or she fell very slowly, for she had plenty of time as she went down

SIDEBAR TITLE

For a minute or two she stood looking at the house, and wondering what to do next, when suddenly a footman in livery came running out of the wood— (she considered him to be a footman because he was in livery: otherwise, judging by his face only, she would have called him a fish)—and rapped loudly at the door with his knuckles.

It was opened by another footman in livery, with a round face, and large eyes like a frog; and both footmen, Alice noticed, had powdered hair that curled all over their heads. She felt very curious to know what it was all about, and crept a little way out of the wood to listen.

Modern with text wrap and a bleed background, *continued*

To make this sidebar, first cut the sidebar text (Ctrl/Cmd+X) from the main text frame, paste it (Ctrl/Cmd+V) into a new text frame, then place it next to the main text. Give the sidebar text frame a text wrap (in your panels at the right of your screen or Window>Text Wrap) with the settings shown to the right. Finally, position your sidebar as described on page 210.

Text wrap settings for sidebar text frame

☐ **Sidebars, First** [sb1]

Changes from the Sidebars, First style (see page 70):

Basic Character Formats:	Font Family = Myriad Pro
	Font Style = Condensed
	Font Size = 10 pt
Indents and Spacing:	Left Indent = 0
	Right Indent = 0
	Space Before = 0
Paragraph Shading:	Shading = On
	(Fill in as shown
	to the right.)

☐ **Sidebars, Middle** [sb2]

Changes from the Sidebars, Middle style (see page 70):

Indents and Spacing:	First Line Indent =
	12 pt *or* 0.1667 in

☐ **Sidebars, Last** [sb3]

Changes from the Sidebars, Last style (see page 70): No changes

☐ **Sidebars, Title** [sbt]

Changes from Sidebars, Title style (see page 70):

Basic Character Formats:	Font Style = Bold Condensed
	Case = All Caps
Indents and Spacing:	Alignment = Left

Adjust the Left value to extend to the outside edge of the bleed in *your* book (outside margin + 0.125").

For sidebars on recto pages, create a second set of identical paragraph styles except reverse the Left and Right values.

Modern sidebar
– with –
graphic and title

The title aligns with the fourth line of text.

In this design the graphic icon and the title always appear in the outer margin area, aligning toward the spine. So on a recto page the icon and title are on the right, aligning left.

The sidebar's text frame is the same width as the main text frame, minus 0.125″ so that the type doesn't touch the inside edge of the background box.

It would be smart to construct an empty sidebar—complete with graphic (if any), title text frame, and background box—for a verso page and another for a recto page and then put them both into a library. Then whenever you need a sidebar you can drag one or the other out of the library, all ready to use. See chapter 39 for more about libraries.

SIDEBAR TITLE

For a minute or two she stood looking at the house, and wondering what to do next, when suddenly a footman in livery came running out of the wood—(she considered him to be a footman because he was in livery: otherwise, judging by his face only, she would have called him a fish)—and rapped loudly at the door with his knuckles.

It was opened by another footman in livery, with a round face, and large eyes like a frog; and both footmen, Alice noticed, had powdered hair that curled all over their heads. She felt very curious to know what it was all about, and

crept a little way out of the wood to listen.

The Fish-Footman began by producing from under his arm a great letter, nearly as large as himself, and this he handed over to the other, saying, in a solemn tone, 'For the Duchess. An invitation from the Queen to play croquet.' The Frog-Footman repeated, in the same solemn tone, only changing the order of the words a little, 'From the Queen. An invitation for the Duchess to play croquet.' Then they both bowed low, and their curls got entangled together.

Alice was beginning to get very tired of sitting by her sister on the bank, and of having nothing to do: once or twice she had peeped into the book her sister was reading, but it had no pictures or conversations in it, 'and what is the use of a book,' thought Alice 'without pictures or conversation?'

So she was considering in her own mind (as well as she could, for the hot day made her feel very sleepy and stupid), whether the pleasure of making a daisy-chain would be worth the trouble of getting up and picking the daisies, when suddenly a White Rabbit with pink eyes ran close by her.

There was nothing so VERY remarkable in that; nor did Alice think it so VERY much out of the way to hear the Rabbit say to itself, 'Oh dear! Oh dear! I shall be late!' (when she thought it over afterwards, it occurred to her that she ought to have wondered at this, but at the time it all seemed quite natural); but when the Rabbit actually took a watch out of its waistcoat-pocket and looked at it, and then hurried on, Alice started to her feet, for it flashed across her mind that she had never before seen a rabbit with either a waistcoat-pocket, or a watch to take out of it, and burning with curiosity, she ran across the field after it, and fortunately was just in time to see it pop down a large rabbit-hole under the hedge. In another moment down went Alice after it, never once considering

This design works in any trim size that is wide enough to allow for an outer column. You could try any number of variations on what you see above. The background box could bleed left and/or right. The sidebar text could be set in one column. The title could appear above the text instead of next to it. The icon could be removed and the title moved up. You could set the first few words in small caps. Look again at the list on page 207 for other variations that would suit *your* book design.

Modern with graphic and title, *continued*

To make this sidebar, first format the sidebar text in its own two-column text frame that is 0.125″ narrower than the main text frame. Place the title in a different text frame. Make a 10% black background box that is the full width of the type area and 0.2917″ taller than the sidebar text. Place the top of the background box 0.125″ (9 pts) above the top of the text and either behind it (Object>Arrange>Send to Back) or on its own layer.

For a detailed explanation of how to set up a two-column text frame for a sidebar, see the top of page 209. See chapters 31 and 33 for how to make shapes and apply colors.

☐ **Sidebars, First [sb1]**
Changes from the Sidebars, First style (see page 70):

Basic Character Formats:	Font Family = Myriad Pro
	Font Style = Regular
	Font Size = 10 pt
	Leading = 12 pt
Indents and Spacing:	Alignment = Left
	Left Indent = 0
	Right Indent = 0
	Space Before = 0
	Align to Grid = None

☐ **Sidebars, Middle [sb2]**
Changes from the Sidebars, Middle style (see page 70):

Indents and Spacing:	First Line Indent = 12 pts *or* 0.1667 in

☐ **Sidebars, Last [sb3]**
Changes from the Sidebars, Last style (see page 70):   No changes

☐ **Sidebars, Title [sbt]**
Changes from Sidebars, Title style (see page 70):

Basic Character Formats:	Font Style = Bold Condensed
	Font Size = 12 pt
	Case = All Caps
	Tracking = 25
Indents and Spacing:	Alignment = Towards Spine

Modern sidebar
– with –
rounded corners

This design could also work with a narrower trim size, as in the design on page 208.

The background box for the title is 60% black, which contrasts well with the white type.

See page 215 for instructions on how to make these boxes with some square corners and some rounded corners.

Alice was beginning to get very tired of sitting by her sister on the bank, and of having nothing to do: once or twice she had peeped into the book her sister was reading, but it had no pictures or conversations in it, 'and what is the use of a book,' thought Alice 'without pictures or conversation?

So she was considering in her own mind (as well as she could, for the hot day made her feel very sleepy and stupid), whether the pleasure of making a daisy-chain would be worth the trouble of getting up and picking the daisies, when suddenly a White Rabbit with pink eyes ran close by her.

There was nothing so VERY remarkable in that; nor did Alice think it so VERY much out of the way to hear the Rabbit say to itself, 'Oh dear! Oh dear! I shall be late!' (when she thought it over afterwards, it occurred to her that she ought to have wondered at this, but at the time it all seemed quite natural); but when the Rabbit actually took a watch out of its waistcoat-pocket and looked at it, and then hurried on, Alice started to her feet, for it flashed across her mind that she had never before seen a rabbit with either a waistcoat-pocket, or a watch to take out of it, and burning with curiosity, she ran across the field after it, and fortunately was just in time to see it pop down a large rabbit-hole under the hedge.In another moment down went Alice after it, never once considering how in the world she was to get out again. The rabbit-hole went

SIDEBAR TITLE

For a minute or two she stood looking at the house, and wondering what to do next, when suddenly a footman in livery came running out of the wood—(she considered him to be a footman because he was in livery: otherwise, judging by his face only, she would have called him a fish)—and rapped loudly at the door with his knuckles.

It was opened by another footman in livery, with a round face, and large eyes like a frog; and both footmen, Alice noticed, had powdered hair that curled all over their heads. She felt very curious to know what it was all about, and crept a little way out of the wood to listen.

The Fish-Footman began by producing from under his arm a great letter, nearly as large as himself, and this he handed over to the other, saying, in a solemn tone, 'For the Duchess. An invitation from the Queen to play croquet.' The Frog-Footman repeated, in the same solemn tone, only changing the order of the words a little, 'From the Queen. An invitation for the Duchess to play croquet.' Then they both bowed low, and their curls got entangled together.

42 RUNNING FOOT

In this design the text frames *are* the background boxes. This is a useful technique to learn (and could be used for the sidebar design on page 210, too). Once you've made the text frames, you can either use object styles for them (chapter 38) or put them into a library (chapter 39). Either method will remember and store your work for future use.

Modern with rounded corners, *continued*

To make the text frame for the sidebar text as its own background box:

1. Make a text frame the full width of the type area in your design.
2. Select the box with the Selection Tool, go to Object>Text Frame Options, fill in the dialog box as shown to the right, and click OK.
3. With the text frame still selected, open the Corner Options dialog box (Object>Corner Options) and fill it in as shown below.
4. With the text frame still selected, open the Swatches panel, and specify 10% black for the fill and None for the stroke. (See chapter 31 to learn how to apply colors.)

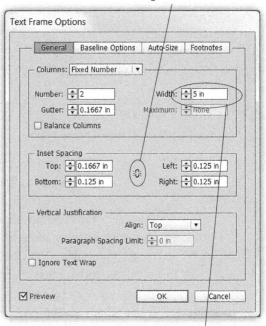

Unlinked chain symbol allows each setting to be different.

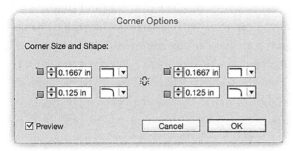

These widths will be the width of your text frame.

To make the text frame for the sidebar title as its own background box:

1. Make a text frame the full width of the type area in your design and one baseline high.
2. Using the Selection Tool, click on the box. Then go to Text Frame Options (Object>Text Frame Options), fill in the dialog box as shown to the right, and click OK.
3. With the text frame still selected, open the Corner Options dialog box and fill it in as shown on page 216, and click OK.

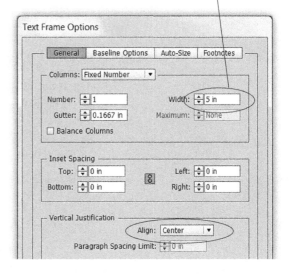

Modern with rounded corners, *continued*

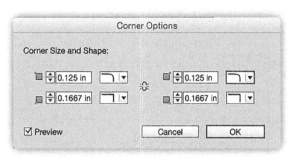

Corner options for the sidebar title text frame

4 With the text frame still selected, open your Swatches panel, and specify 60% black for the fill and None for the stroke.

5 Apply the paragraph styles shown below and on page 217 to your sidebar text and title, then cut the sidebar text (Ctrl/Cmd+X) from the main text frame and paste it (Ctrl/Cmd+V) into your new text frame. Do the same with your sidebar title.

After all of your sidebar text is flowed into its text box and formatted, use the Selection Tool to drag the center bottom handle up (or down) just enough so that the last lines of type do not disappear.

Your final job is to place the title box above the text box and group them together. Select the text box with the Selection Tool and enlarge your view (Ctrl/Cmd+=) so you can work with precision. Drag the title box so its base just touches the top of the text box and the square corners line up. Now select both boxes at once, and group them (Object>Group or Ctrl/Cmd+G). This will ensure that the whole sidebar will stay together even if you move it. If you ever need to do more work on the box, simply ungroup it first (Ctrl/Cmd+Shift+G).

☐ **Sidebars, First [sb1]**
Changes from the Sidebars, First style (see page 70):

Basic Character Formats:	Font Family = Myriad Pro
	Font Style = Regular
	Font Size = 10 pt
	Leading = 12 pt
Indents and Spacing:	Left Indent = 0
	Right Indent = 0
	Space Before = 0
	Align to Grid = None

Modern with rounded corners, *continued*

☐ **Sidebars, Middle [sb2]**
Changes from the Sidebars, Middle style (see page 70):

Indents and Spacing:	First Line Indent = 12 pt *or* 0.1667 in

☐ **Sidebars, Last [sb3]**
Changes from the Sidebars, Last style (see page 70):   No changes

☐ **Sidebars, Title [sbt]**
Changes from Sidebars, Title style (see page 70):

Basic Character Formats:	Font Style = Black
	Font Size = 11 pt
	Case = All Caps
	Tracking = 50
Indents and Spacing:	Alignment = Center
Character Color:	[Paper]

By now you've become a real designer, and you're probably coming up with better ideas as you progress. This is a good time to stop and look closely at your book as a whole to see whether all of your design elements still hang together. If not, which elements please you the most? Is there a way to take something from them and replace something that you did earlier that no longer fits with the rest? On the other hand, you might find a way to use your favorite parts of the design in your running heads and folios, which you will read about in the next chapter. Remember that consistency, with two or three distinctive visual elements throughout, is the key to a successful book design.

27 *Designing folios and running heads*

Folios and running heads (or feet) are your book's navigation tools, so they need to be very clear and simple. There are many ways you can position them, and this will depend on your book's design and your personal preferences. Running heads are more common than running feet and are recommended for fiction and nonfiction because the layout is more forgiving. For example, if some of your pages are one line shorter or longer for typesetting reasons, it's not so obvious. In this chapter, you'll learn:

Your folios and running heads are on A-Master. Refer back to chapters 15 and 18 if you need to.

1 Where to place your folios and running heads
2 What text to include: book title and . . . ?
3 Alignment: centered or away from spine?
4 How to choose typefaces and sizes
5 Fine-tuning folios and running heads

1 Where to place your folios and running heads

Folios and running heads are placed at the top of pages, two baselines above the main text. In other words, there is one blank linespace between the running heads/folios and the main text.

When you convert to an ebook, you'll delete all your folios and running heads or feet.

Running feet are placed at the bottom of pages, two or three baselines below the main text so there are one or two blank linespaces between the main text and the running feet and folios.

On the first page of each chapter, the running heads are removed, and usually the folio is moved from the top of the page to the bottom (called a *drop folio*) or eliminated altogether.

Running foot aligned away from spine 3 lines below main text block

Folio centered in outside column

And, of course, rules are made to be broken. This book has running feet on the first page of each chapter. Some books have folios on recto pages only, and perhaps the book title only on verso pages. There are many variations. Choose a configuration that looks good and gives readers everything they need to navigate your book.

2 What text to include: book title and . . . ?

In a novel, the book title usually goes on the left and the author's name on the right. In nonfiction books, the book title usually goes on the left and the chapter title on the right. These are just guidelines, and you can put whatever you like in the running heads. Look at several books and you'll see a variety of options.

When choosing text to include in your running heads, always consider your readers first. How will they make their way through your book? In novels, often there are no chapter titles or table of contents, so the book title and author's name is sufficient. In nonfiction, readers navigate from the table of contents or index, so it's helpful to see chapter titles in the running heads. In *this* book, the book title and part title are on the left and the chapter number and title are on the right. Choose running heads that will be most helpful for readers navigating your book.

3 Alignment: centered or away from spine?

Folios are most often aligned to the outside margins, and running heads are either centered or left/right aligned a short distance away from the folios. But again, there are many possible variations.

A good rule of thumb is to keep everything consistent. If your chapter title and headings are centered, center your running heads too. If your chapter title and headings are left or right aligned, then align your running heads away from the spine. See the examples to the right and on the next page.

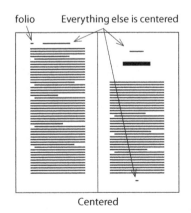

folio — Everything else is centered   folio — All left or right aligned

Centered   Aligned away from spine

240   SHLOMIT KRIGER

backgrounds: black and white, Asian and Hispanic, those from lands touched by the Holocaust, and those in the rest of world whose ancestors barely knew what was happening.

    Survivors have been surprised by the way in which they have been received in American classrooms, as well as in Europe and Israel. Their

MARKING HUMANITY   241

for their age. Representatives of the past who often trace their roots back to places that had barely entered the twentieth century, they are respected by those who grew up in the age of computers, digital music players, the Internet, and instant messaging—not because they are of the here and now, but because they lived then and there. The encounter is remarkable

Consider saving space by putting folios and running heads in the outer column—if they won't interfere with your book's content.

chapter number and title on verso, current heading 1 on recto

178
CHAPTER 7
Children and
Numeracy

they had some incredible teachers who introduced them to interesting authors and poets, and I observed the joy they got out of reading. The one constant in our family was reading. To this day, we still trade books and authors and talk about what we have read.

    I am not suggesting that everyone should educate their children

Unfortunately, with the introduction of new gadgets and technology, effective reading instruction has taken a backseat in many schools. Too many children cannot read at their grade level. Too many children are pushed through school without being able to read at all. With reading comes thinking, and with thinking comes the curiosity

179
How Children Absorb
Information about
Numbers

Gray-to-white gradient bleeds top.

part number and title
(separated by a dingbat) on verso

chapter number and title (separated by a dingbat) on recto

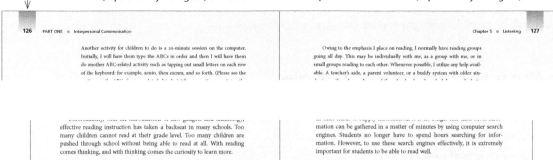

126   PART ONE ▪ Interpersonal Communication

Another activity for children to do is a 20-minute session on the computer. Initially, I will have them type the ABCs in order and then I will have them do another ABC-related activity such as tapping out small letters on each row of the keyboard: for example, aeuio, then zxcnm, and so forth. (Please see the

Chapter 5 ▪ Listening   127

Owing to the emphasis I place on reading, I normally have reading groups going all day. This may be individually with me, as a group with me, or in small groups reading to each other. Whenever possible, I utilize any help available. A teacher's aide, a parent volunteer, or a buddy system with older stu-

effective reading instruction has taken a backseat in many schools. Too many children cannot read at their grade level. Too many children are pushed through school without being able to read at all. With reading comes thinking, and with thinking comes the curiosity to learn more.

10   READING METHODS THAT WORK

mation can be gathered in a matter of minutes by using computer search engines. Students no longer have to spend hours searching for information. However, to use these search engines effectively, it is extremely important for students to be able to read well.

Introduction   11

book title in small caps, centered   chapter title in upper and lowercase italics, centered

unnumbered part title on verso   unnumbered chapter title on recto

den elsewhere in the value chain. Profits continue to stagnate or fall.

    In working with scores of companies since the 1980s, we've studied how complexity infects a company's entire value chain and identified the most common culprits for its spread: bad economic data, overoptimistic sales expectations,

"The High Price of Service Complexity.")

    What makes the problem particularly damaging is that it tends to be invisible to management. Look at what happened when one automaker started offering tinted windshields as an option. On the surface, the move looked like a clear

140 | Operational Excellence   Innovation Versus Complexity | 141

Vertical rules bleed bottom and separate folios from running feet.
Folios appear outside the normal text area.

4 How to choose typefaces and sizes

Folios

If your design uses any sans serif type for sidebars, tables, captions, or display, use that type for your folios. Sans serif numerals are just a bit easier to read at a glance. If you're using oldstyle numbers throughout, stick with them for folios. On the other hand, if you have a lot of numbers in the text, you're probably using lining figures, so use them for folios, too. Folios can be the same size as the text or a bit smaller—or, if your book makes major use of an index (such as in a reference book or cookbook), bigger.

Now set up a **Folio** paragraph style (see page 78), and remember that in Indents and Spacing you can set the alignment to Towards Spine, Away From Spine, or Centered to make this style simple to use.

Running heads

Design your running heads to match either your text style (probably a serif typeface) or your folio style (possibly a sans serif). Since you've already determined that the two typefaces match each other nicely, it is fine to mix them here.

Running heads can be the same size as the folios or a bit smaller. Study the examples on the previous page to see whether any of these general ideas would work in your book. The main thing is to be sure that your entire navigation system is readable at a glance.

Set up a **Running Head** paragraph style (see page 78). Under Indents and Spacing, choose Towards Spine, Away From Spine, or Centered. In the Align to Grid drop-down menu, choose All Lines.

5 Fine-tuning folios and running heads

Look at several of your 2-page spreads and see whether your folios and running heads look okay. You may want to apply Small Caps or Italics character styles to your running heads/feet, or change your folios to lining figures. Sometimes it helps to look at other books to see how they've handled folios and running feet.

There are no hard and fast rules here, so go with what you think looks best. Print a few 2-page spreads to be sure.

28

Designing your front matter

You've done a lot of work and are perhaps getting a bit weary at this point, hoping that now you can simply stick the front matter at the front of the book and be done with it. But this chapter and and the next (Designing your back matter) are actually very important, so take care with them.

On page 24 you learned all the elements that might go into your front matter, with only the title page and copyright page being absolutely required. You've also roughed in the pages (chapter 14). In this section we'll discuss all the common front matter items in more detail, and you'll create and apply paragraph styles throughout your front matter. You'll also set up a page numbering system, as the front matter is numbered separately from the rest of the pages, in lowercase roman numerals.

Title page

The title page is supremely important. Your goal is to give the reader a positive and accurate first impression by integrating design elements from the interior and the cover of the book. If your design is a classical one with centered headings and conservative chapter openings, don't switch to left or right alignments or jazzy typefaces on this page. Stick with your own look.

Pages in the front matter coming before the Contents do not have visible page numbers.

At the end of this chapter, on page 245, you'll assign lowercase roman numerals to your front matter pages. For now, arabic numerals are fine.

The title page will appear either on page i or—if you are going to use a half title page—on page iii. You should place the elements on the title page more or less as shown on the next page, with the title first and the publisher at the bottom. As you move them around, reduce the page size on the screen and squint at them to see which elements form groups. The title, subtitle, and edition (if any) should be in a group. The author's name should be somewhat close to the title but not quite in the same group. The publisher (and possibly the city) should always be by itself, flush bottom on the page. Move the title group up and down a bit and see what looks balanced, then carefully place the author. And remember the basic principles of good design: repeat elements, the rule of three, and white space.

Try aligning elements much the way you have in the rest of the book. If headings are generally flush left, try placing type flush left on this page, too. If you use a particular type ornament or other graphic throughout the book, see whether it works here, too. If you're in love with the image on your front cover, you may repeat all or part of it on this page, as long as the typeset information remains very readable. Study other books to find out how they have used the space on their title pages, and be creative within the design you've already established.

The title page contains much of the official information about the book—in other words, whatever is on the title page will be entered into a library's database, plus that of the Library of Congress or Library and Archives Canada. Do not include quotations or any other copy (although artwork is fine).

You don't need to use the baseline grid on the title page.

See chapter 59 for ways to isolate a section of your cover image, or to fade it back.

A title page includes:
Title [ttl]
Subtitle [subttl]
Edition (2nd edition +) [ed]
Author(s) [au]
Author Affiliation(s) [auaffil]
Publisher [pub]
Publisher's Location [city]

Design your title page (*left*) first, then base the half title page on the title page.

Sun Showers
on a Sunday

a memoir by
Felicity Menendez

Felicity's Press
Whitehorse

Sun Showers
on a Sunday

Half title page

If you're going to use a half title page (sometimes called a bastard title), base it on the title page. Here you will set only the book title—no author, no subtitle, no ornaments. You might use the same typeface you used for the title on the title page or, if you used a display face on the title page, use a more conservative one here. If the title page title is on two or more lines, you could set it that way on the half title page, too. The type size should be smaller than on the title page, and in most books, the half title is centered. Consider placing it at the same height on the page as the title on the title page so that the reader's eye doesn't have to jump up or down when turning the page.

Sometimes a half title page is used again on the recto page just before the start of the main text. If you want to do this, use the Selection Tool to select the type on your first half title page, copy it, and paste it in place (Edit>Copy, then Edit>Paste in Place) on the second half title page so that this page is an exact copy of the first one.

Family names

Over the centuries of bookmaking, some interesting jargon has developed.

A **widow** is the last line of a paragraph, stranded by itself at the top of a new page. Widows are simply not allowed.

An **orphan** is defined in a couple of different ways: a very short final line of a paragraph, or the opening line of a paragraph, placed as the last line on a page. Orphans of both kinds are to be avoided whenever possible.

A **bastard** is another name for a half title page.

In InDesign, you've used **parent and child** styles when setting up your style sheets. These family terms are newer ones.

How did these references to family members (and nonmembers) come about? Good question! But if you remember the typesetter's socially outdated rule that a widow has no future and an orphan has no past, it will help you remember at least those two terms.

Copyright page

Another mandatory front matter element, the copyright page always appears on the verso after the title page.

Many new authors find the copyright page confusing and intimidating. Below is an explanation of each item and how to get the information you need. Be sure not to leave any of it for the last minute.

- **Publisher's address** A URL or email address is passable, but these do change, perhaps more often than a physical address. You need to include an address of some kind so that someone can contact you if they want to quote from your book later on.

- **Copyright notice** Include a minimum of the © symbol, year, and the name of the copyright owner. Canadian authors have automatic copyright protection, so they may simply write a copyright notice of their choosing. Authors in the U.S. have three options:
  1. Obtain an official copyright from the Library of Congress. This may be done before publication or up to three months after publication. At this writing, the cost is $35.
  2. Invent a copyright notice of your own, or copy one from another book, without the backing of the Library of Congress.
  3. Protect yourself by doing the following: Make two hard copies of the manuscript and put them both into mailing envelopes addressed to yourself. Write a statement saying "I __[your name]__ am putting this manuscript in an envelope on __[add date]__." Make two copies of the statement and have them notarized separately. Mail each manuscript and its notarized statement to yourself separately, using certified mail with a return receipt for each, and keep the tracking numbers, then track the package online and print out the tracking information. When you receive the packages, *do not open them*. This process will show that you were in possession of the written material on a certain date; therefore, if someone steals your words later on, you will have proof of this to show to your attorney. You'll have a witness (the notary public), evidence (the package), and a date and time (the tracking information). The second package will remain unopened as untampered evidence to use in court.

A complete, annotated copyright page is shown on page 226.

Read more about copyright page elements at BookDesignMadeSimple.com/copyright-page-end-the-confusion.

When should you complete your copyright page? A complete schedule of the self-publishing process is laid out on pages 478–479.

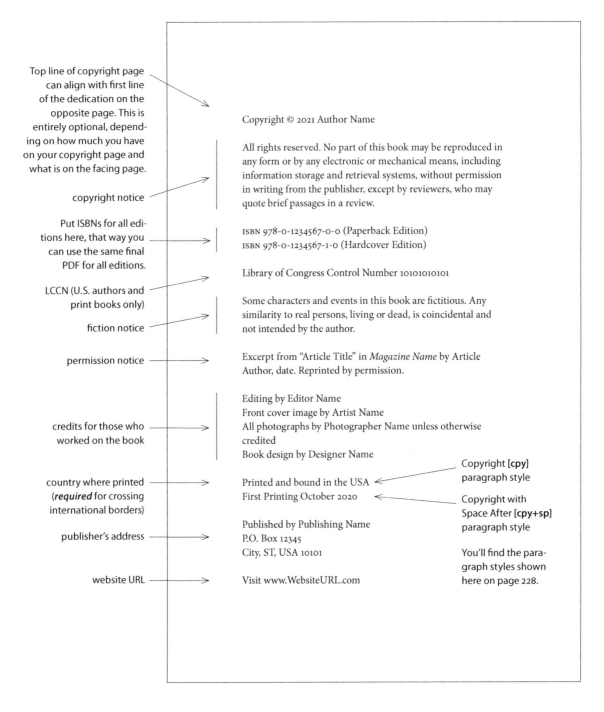

Top line of copyright page can align with first line of the dedication on the opposite page. This is entirely optional, depending on how much you have on your copyright page and what is on the facing page.

copyright notice

Put ISBNs for all editions here, that way you can use the same final PDF for all editions.

LCCN (U.S. authors and print books only)

fiction notice

permission notice

credits for those who worked on the book

country where printed (*required* for crossing international borders)

publisher's address

website URL

Copyright © 2021 Author Name

All rights reserved. No part of this book may be reproduced in any form or by any electronic or mechanical means, including information storage and retrieval systems, without permission in writing from the publisher, except by reviewers, who may quote brief passages in a review.

ISBN 978-0-1234567-0-0 (Paperback Edition)
ISBN 978-0-1234567-1-0 (Hardcover Edition)

Library of Congress Control Number 10101010101

Some characters and events in this book are fictitious. Any similarity to real persons, living or dead, is coincidental and not intended by the author.

Excerpt from "Article Title" in *Magazine Name* by Article Author, date. Reprinted by permission.

Editing by Editor Name
Front cover image by Artist Name
All photographs by Photographer Name unless otherwise credited
Book design by Designer Name

Printed and bound in the USA
First Printing October 2020

Published by Publishing Name
P.O. Box 12345
City, ST, USA 10101

Visit www.WebsiteURL.com

Copyright **[cpy]** paragraph style

Copyright with Space After **[cpy+sp]** paragraph style

You'll find the paragraph styles shown here on page 228.

- **Copyright date** This can be a bit tricky. If you get your copyright from the U.S. Library of Congress on a certain date, use that year for your copyright date. Otherwise, use the year of publication. If you print the book near the end of the calendar year, though, use the following year for your copyright date. The more recent the date, the happier potential readers will be, especially for non-fiction and how-to books.

- **Edition number** Include this only if the book is in its second or higher edition. A second printing is *not* a new edition. If you make slight changes for a second or subsequent printing—perhaps adding some new book reviews or a new foreword—that's not a new edition, either. A new edition must be substantially changed from the previous one, with new information, rearranged and rewritten chapters, etc.

- **ISBN (International Standard Book Number)** All books need a number if they are to be sold. Obtain ISBN(s) in your own country so you can sell books worldwide. See the URLs listed in the sidebar above, and see chapter 68 for more details on where to purchase ISBNs, how many to buy, and how to assign them to different editions of your book.

- **CIP (Cataloguing-in-Publication) data and LCCN (Library of Congress Control Numbers)** Library and Archives Canada and the U.S. Library of Congress provide CIP data, but only to large publishers— and that's not you (yet). You can get CIP data from a private source.

    In the U.S., you also need to ask the Library of Congress for the all-important LCCN (at no charge). This number shows that the Library of Congress has registered your book (and you will send them a copy as soon as you publish). It also will help local librarians process your book more quickly.

Front matter resources

U.S. copyright
United States Copyright Office
   www.copyright.gov

ISBN (International Standard Book Number)
Within Canada: Library and Archives Canada
   www.bac-lac.gc.ca/eng/services/isbn-
   canada/Pages/isbn-canada.aspx
Within USA: R. R. Bowker LLC
   www.myidentifiers.com

LCCN (Library of Congress Control Number)
Within USA: United States Library of Congress
   loc.gov/publish/pcn/

Learn why you need CIP data and how to get it at BookDesignMadeSimple .com/your-book-needs-cip-data.

See chapter 41 for much more on permissions.

- **Credits for artwork and permissions** For copyrighted quotes, song lyrics, and artwork, you need written permission (an email message is acceptable). Write for permission as soon as you decide to use the material, because it can take months to track down the copyright owner and come to an agreement. You may have to pay to use the material. Have a backup plan in case you don't receive permission in time or it's denied altogether. Often the permission will come with specific wording that the owner wants to see in your book. Be prepared to send a free copy of your book to the copyright owner.

- **Credits to those who helped you** Some authors like to list some or all of their paid assistants: editors, proofreaders, printer, etc. This is not the place for acknowledgments, though—simply a list.

You may have noticed that on *our* copyright page (see page iv) we have Canadian Cataloguing in Publication (CIP) data *and* a U.S. LCCN number. Normally just the library information from your own country appears here, however in our case one author is American and the other is Canadian, so we are able to have both.

- **Country of printing** This is mandatory for customs reasons. Simply state "Printed in the United States of America," "Printed in Canada," or the appropriate country.

Study copyright pages in other books and the example on page 226 to see how others have dealt with all of this information. Set up the two paragraph styles below for your copyright page. Feel free to change the suggested type size and leading so that all the material will fit properly on *your* copyright page.

☐ **Copyright [cpy]**   Based On = **tx1**
Changes from the No Indents style (see page 62):
Basic Character Formats: Font Size = 9 pt
                                                             Leading = 11 pt
Indents and Spacing: Alignment = Left
                                                             Align to Grid = None

☐ **Copyright with Space After [cpy+sp]**   Based On = **cpy**
Changes from the Copyright style:
Indents and Spacing: Space After = 11 pt *or* 0.1528 in

Dedication page

The dedication almost always appears on the recto that faces the copyright page. Keep it simple. There is no need for a heading or to say "Dedicated to" here, as everyone knows what this page is for. Place the dedication about one-third of the way down the page, on the baseline grid. It's customary, although not mandatory, to set it in italics and center each line. Use the same typeface and size as your Text style.

    If you are trying to keep your page count to a minimum, place the dedication at the top of the copyright page instead of on a separate page.

Drag the top of the text frame down to position your dedication vertically on the page.

For my sisters and brothers
with love

Be careful how you break the lines in the dedication.

For my sisters
and brothers with love

means something different from

For my sisters and brothers
with love

    Set up your Dedication using the paragraph style shown below. Feel free to change the indents to suit your copy. Be thoughtful about the line breaks, and use hard returns between the lines.

☐ **Dedication [ded]**	Based On = **tx1**	
Changes from the No Indents style (see page 62):		
Basic Character Formats:	Font Style = Italic	
	Tracking = 10	
Indents and Spacing:	Alignment = Center	
	Left Indent = 0.75 in	
	Right Indent = 0.75 in	
Hyphenation:	Hyphenate = Unchecked	

Epigraph

Place this on the next recto after the dedication page, with a blank verso page in between. Using the same typeface and size as your Text style, start the quotation on the same baseline as the dedication, and indent it left and right equally, so that it's a compact block of type. Set the attribution on the next line.

Drag the top of the text frame down to position your epigraph vertically on the page.

If your epigraph is poetry, see pages 352–355 for how to align the lines properly.

> History would be an excellent thing
> if only it were true.
>
> —Leo Tolstoy

From *Crimson Snow* by David Shone

An epigraph can be set in italics or roman. Each line can be centered, or left aligned with the text block centered. The attribution, as you saw on pages 151 and 156, can be centered or right aligned. The paragraph styles offered below are for the epigraph on this page. If your indents result in a lopsided page, simply increase or decrease the indents until everything is centered and the attribution aligns at right with the longest epigraph line.

☐ **Epigraph [epi]**   Based On = **tx1**
Changes from the No Indents style (see page 62):
Basic Character Formats: Tracking = 10
Indents and Spacing: Alignment = Left
                                                                          Left Indent = 0.87 in
                                                                          Right Indent = 0.87 in
                                                                          Align to Grid = None

☐ **Epigraph Attribution [epiattr]**   Based On = **epi**
Changes from the Epigraph style:
Indents and Spacing: Alignment = Right
                                                                          Space Before = 7 pt *or* 0.0972 in

Front and back matter titles

You'll design a paragraph style for the titles of your front and back matter sections—"Contents," "Preface," "Glossary," "References," and so on. Sample paragraph styles are offered in the next few pages. Base your front and back matter titles on your Chapter Title [ct] paragraph style, but use less space before and after them. For example, if your chapter titles are a quarter of the way down the page, put your front and back matter titles at the top. This distinguishes them from chapter titles and saves space.

First create a paragraph style for your front and back matter titles (see the Front and Back Matter Title [fbt] paragraph style samples on pages 233 and 236), then apply the style to your front and back matter titles.

Contents

Begin the table of contents (TOC) on the next recto after the epigraph and a blank verso. Or, if your Contents are going to fill only two pages, you might want to place this section on a spread instead—pages iv–v, for instance. Don't leave a blank recto page before a Contents spread, though.

Novels almost never include a table of contents.

Before you start designing the Contents, you'll need to make two basic decisions:

1 How many levels of headings do you want to show? If you have plenty of space to fill, you might include headings 1–3; on the other hand, if you are squeezed for space, you might only include chapter numbers and titles. Consider your reader in this decision, too. If your chapters are quite long, will the reader be able to find everything he or she needs if you list only chapter titles? Also think about the potential buyer, who might very well use the Contents to decide whether to buy, either in a store or online.

2 Where do you want to put the page numbers? If you place them flush right in the text block, will they be so far from the titles that they are hard for the reader to figure out? Should you perhaps place them a set distance from the titles or headings themselves, not lining up flush right at all (as in *this* book)? Study examples in other books and the ones on the following pages to get ideas for your Contents.

If you have a very simple TOC with just a few entries, you might consider just applying the paragraph and character styles you create to your typed TOC. However, there are two benefits to using an automatic TOC: 1) it'll update page numbers automatically, and 2) it'll generate a navigation system when converted to an ebook.

Once you have set up the paragraph styles for your Contents, you'll learn how to generate an automatic TOC (see pages 240–244), which "types" the entire list, including page numbers, for you.

 An automatic table of contents is especially useful in an ebook, where it becomes a navigation chart.

DESIGN A
Classic contents
– with –
part and
chapter titles

These sections are part of the front matter but appear *after* the Contents in the book. Their paragraph style in the TOC is **toc-fbt**.

TOC Part Title **[toc-pt]** with TOC Part Number character style **[toc-pn]** applied to the part number.

TOC Chapter Title **[toc-ct]** with TOC Chapter Number character style **[toc-cn]** applied to the chapter number.

Tabular Oldstyle figures are used in all the TOC styles so that the numbers line up neatly below each other.

Folio but no running head or foot

CONTENTS

· v ·

From *Sassy Gal's How to Lose the Last Damn 10 Pounds* by Sharon Helbert

Classic contents with part and chapter titles, *continued*

This Contents design is related to the classic chapter opening with two-line drop cap (Design 2) on pages 151–153. Page numbers are flush right in the text frame because the chapter titles in this example are long enough so that it's easy to locate the correct page number for each. If your chapter titles are short, consider putting the page numbers one em space after each title (see page 238) or adding a dot leader to the tab (see below). Use the following style settings to set up the table of contents on page 232.

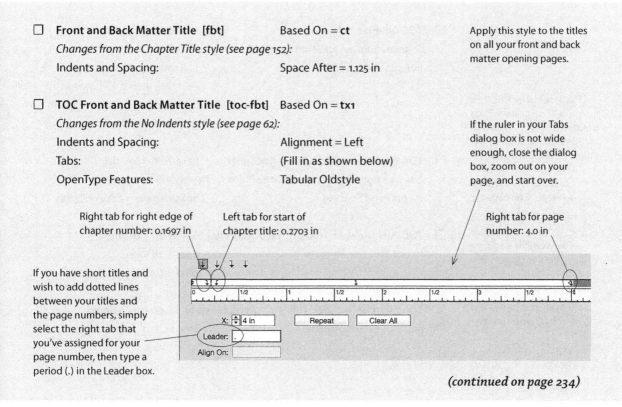

□ **Front and Back Matter Title [fbt]**   Based On = **ct**   Apply this style to the titles on all your front and back matter opening pages.
Changes from the Chapter Title style (see page 152):
Indents and Spacing: Space After = 1.125 in

□ **TOC Front and Back Matter Title [toc-fbt]**   Based On = **tx1**   If the ruler in your Tabs dialog box is not wide enough, close the dialog box, zoom out on your page, and start over.
Changes from the No Indents style (see page 62):
Indents and Spacing: Alignment = Left
Tabs: (Fill in as shown below)
OpenType Features: Tabular Oldstyle

Right tab for right edge of chapter number: 0.1697 in

Left tab for start of chapter title: 0.2703 in

Right tab for page number: 4.0 in

If you have short titles and wish to add dotted lines between your titles and the page numbers, simply select the right tab that you've assigned for your page number, then type a period (.) in the Leader box.

X: 4 in   Repeat   Clear All
Leader: .
Align On:

(continued on page 234)

The tabs above should work for your book if you have changed neither the trim size of 5.5″ × 8.5″ nor the margins from the original settings in chapter 7. If you have changed trim size or margins, you'll need to move the rightmost tab to the right edge of your text frame.

Classic contents with part and chapter titles, *continued*

Set up the rest of your paragraph and character styles as shown below.

☐ **TOC Part Title [toc-pt]**   Based On = **toc-fbt**

Changes from the TOC Front and Back Matter Title style (see page 233):

Basic Character Formats: Font Style = Semibold

Indents and Spacing: Space Before = 14 pt *or* 0.1944 in

                                                                      Align to Grid = None

☐ **TOC Chapter Title [toc-ct]**   Based On = **toc-fbt**

Changes from the TOC Front and Back Matter Title style (see page 233):

Indents and Spacing: Left Indent = 0.2703 in

                                                                      First Line Indent = −0.2703 in

The Back Matter Title, First
is self-explanatory. Extra
space is needed before this
title to distance it from the
last chapter. Use the **toc-fbt**
style for any subsequent
back matter heads. See
an example on page 238.

                                                                      Space Before = 4 pt *or* 0.0556 in

                                                                      Align to Grid = None

☐ **TOC Back Matter Title, First [toc-bmt1]**   Based On = **toc-fbt**

Changes from the TOC Front and Back Matter Title style (see page 233):

Indents and Spacing: Space Before = 28 pt *or* 0.3889 in

Insert an em space
between the part num-
ber and the part title.

☐ **TOC Part Number [toc-pn]** *character* style Based On = **[None]**

Basic Character Formats: Case = All Caps

                                                                      Tracking = 50

Type a tab before and
after the chapter number.

☐ **TOC Chapter Number [toc-cn]** *character* style Based On = **[None]**

Basic Character Formats: Font Style = Semibold

                                                                      Size = 14 pt

Now generate an automatic TOC for Design A by following the example on pages 240–242). Then add your part numbers, followed by an em space, and apply the **toc-pn** character style to them. Add your chapter numbers, with a tab before and after, and apply the **toc-cn** character style to them. Apply the **toc-bmt1** style to the first back matter entry, and make any other adjustments needed.

Notice that the heading
for the table of contents is
always simply "Contents."

Contents

toc-h2   Level 2 headings grouped together with no page numbers. Because the sections are short, often more than one Heading 2 appears on the same page in the book, so it would be easy for the reader to find them without being given a page number. Also, this method saves space.

From *Storytelling in Words and Pictures* by Janet Stone

Modern contents with headings run together, *continued*

This table of contents design is compact and easy to read, with the second-level headings grouped together without page numbers. It corresponds with Design 4, Modern chapter opening with number and title on same line, pages 156–158. The paragraph and character styles for this design are:

Apply this style to the titles on all your front and back matter opening pages.

Front and Back Matter Title [fbt]   Based On = **ct**
Changes from the Chapter Title style (see page 157):
Indents and Spacing: Space Before = 9 pt *or* 0.125 in
                                                         Space After = 45 pt *or* 0.625 in

TOC Front and Back Matter Title [toc-fbt]   Based On = **tx1**
Changes from the No Indents style (see page 62):

Sometimes you can't see the entire ruler in the Tabs dialog box. If that is the case, click and hold down the mouse on the main part of the ruler and you'll see a hand. Drag the hand to the left to expose the right end of the ruler.

Basic Character Formats: Font Family = Myriad Pro
                                                         Font Style = Light Condensed
                                                         Tracking = 40
Indents and Spacing: Alignment = Left
Tabs: Set a right tab at 4 in
                                                            (see example on page 233)
OpenType Features: Figure Style = Tabular Lining

TOC Chapter Title [toc-ct]   Based On = **toc-fbt**
Changes from the TOC Front and Back Matter Title style:
Basic Character Formats: Size = 13 pt
Indents and Spacing: Left Indent = 0.2 in
                                                         First Line Indent = −0.2 in
                                                         Space Before = 22.5 pt *or* 0.3125 in
                                                         Align to Grid = None

TOC Back Matter Title, First [toc-bmt1]   Based On = **toc-fbt**
Changes from the TOC Front and Back Matter Title style:
Indents and Spacing: Space Before = 28 pt *or* 0.3889 in

☐ **TOC Heading 1 [toc-h1]**   Based On = **tx1**
Changes from the No Indents style (see page 62):
Indents and Spacing: Alignment = Left
                                                Left Indent = 0.3 in
                                                First Line Indent = –0.1 in
Tabs: Set a right tab at 4 in
                                                    (see example on page 233)
Hyphenation: Hyphenate = Unchecked
OpenType Features: Figure Style = Tabular Lining

☐ **TOC Heading 2 [toc-h2]**   Based On = **toc-h1**
Changes from the TOC Heading 1 style:
Indents and Spacing: Left Indent = 0.4 in
                                                Right Indent = 0.5 in
                                                First Line Indent = 0
Tabs: No tabs ←——————————————   To delete the tab set at
                                                           4", simply drag it down-
                                                           ward and it'll disappear.

☐ **TOC Chapter Number [toc-cn]** *character* style Based On = [None]
Basic Character Formats: Font Style = Semibold Condensed
                                                Size = 13 pt
OpenType Features: Figure Style = Tabular Lining

Now generate an automatic TOC for Design B by following the examples on pages 240 and 243. Then you'll need to check that the page numbers are lining up on your right margin. If not, open the **toc-fbt** paragraph style, and drag the right tab into position (you'll see the page numbers shift as you do this). Do the same tab adjustment in the **toc-h1** paragraph style. Next, run the level 2 headings together by deleting the hard return after each one (except the last in each group). Set an en space, a solidus (/), and another en space between entries (or choose another character, such as a bullet). Use soft returns between lines (if needed), and never begin a line with a solidus. Add your chapter numbers, followed by a tab, and apply the **toc-cn** character style to them. Finally, apply the **toc-bmt1** style to the first back matter entry (see page 238).

It helps in this operation if you can see the hidden characters. If you're not seeing them, go to Type>Show Hidden Characters.

On the next page you'll see the TOC from the same book laid out in a different way.

DESIGN C
Modern contents
– with –
headings stacked

one em space

In this example the amount of space between each heading and its page numbers is one em space (Ctrl/Cmd+Shift+M).

The first back matter head **[toc-bmt1]** has its own style with space above.

Use the Front and Back Matter Title **[toc-fbt]** style for the rest of the back matter headings.

vii

From *Storytelling in Words and Pictures* by Janet Stone

This is the same table of contents as in Design B, but the level 2 heads are typed in a list instead of being run together. Most of the headings are very short and the page numbers are placed a uniform distance after each, making them easy to find.

Most of the paragraph styles are identical to those shown for Design B on pages 236–237 except for the one shown below. What makes this design different is that the page numbers are separated from the titles and headings by an em space rather than a tab. In this design the figures look better as Proportional Oldstyle, and this is the only difference between the following paragraph style and the one on page 237.

☐ **TOC Heading 1 [toc-h1]**   Based On = **tx1**
Changes from the No Indents style (see page 62):

Indents and Spacing:	Alignment = Left
	Left Indent = 0.3 in
	First Line Indent = –0.1 in
Tabs:	Set a right tab at 4 in
	(see example on page 233)
Hyphenation:	Hyphenate = Unchecked

In this style the figures (page numbers) remain Proportional Oldstyle, as in the **tx1** style. So they are not mentioned here; compare with the almost identical style on page 237.

If you like, naturally you can type your own TOC. Simply use one of the suggested designs or make up your own, then apply the paragraph and character styles to everything. The following pages of instructions, though, are for those who want to take advantage of InDesign's full power, ensure accuracy, and automate the system for easy updating.

Now that you've set up your styles, you'll learn how to generate an automatic table of contents. It may seem complicated at first, but it's worth the effort to learn, because any changes that you make in the book can be updated in the TOC with just a couple of clicks. Also, in an ebook, all of the items in the TOC will be hyperlinked to the content.

Generating an automatic table of contents

Begin by going to Layout>Table of Contents. Your dialog box will look something like the one below. Click the More Options button at the right if you don't see all the choices shown.

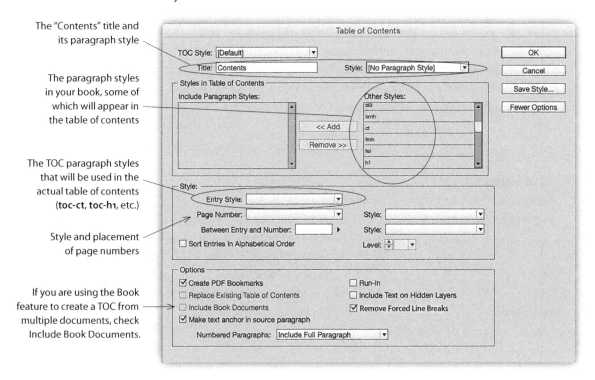

The "Contents" title and its paragraph style

The paragraph styles in your book, some of which will appear in the table of contents

The TOC paragraph styles that will be used in the actual table of contents (**toc-ct**, **toc-h1**, etc.)

Style and placement of page numbers

If you are using the Book feature to create a TOC from multiple documents, check Include Book Documents.

How it works

The only difference in generating an automatic TOC using the Book feature is that you'll check the Include Book Documents box (see above). Refer to the blog post with step-by-step instructions at BookDesignMadeSimple .com/using-the-book-feature-in-InDesign.

The Table of Contents dialog box allows you to control every aspect of your TOC. First you'll assign a paragraph style to the title that reads "Contents." Then you'll choose which paragraph styles you want to include in your TOC (part titles and chapter titles, for example) from the box on the right and add them to the box on the left. For each one, you'll assign an entry style, which is the TOC paragraph style you just set up on the preceding pages. After that, you'll instruct InDesign where to place the page number and what character style to use for it. And finally, you'll save your settings as a TOC style. Let's go through the process step by step for designs A, B, and C next.

Automatic table of contents for Design A

To generate an automatic TOC for Design A (page 232), fill out the Table of Contents dialog box as shown below.

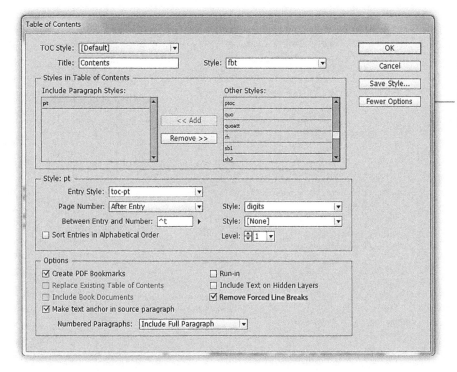

If you don't see all the options in the Style and Options sections, click the More Options button to display them.

1   To the right of "Title: Contents," choose the **fbt** style from the drop-down list. This will give the title "Contents" the style you want.

2   Select the **pt** style in the Other Styles column, click the Add button, and the **pt** style will move to the Include Paragraph Styles column.

3   In the Entry Style drop-down list, choose **toc-pt**, the style you set up for your TOC part titles. Don't worry about the part number character style for now; you'll apply that later.

4   Between Entry and Number (meaning page number) you want a tab, so leave "^t" as it is. In the upper Style box, enter the **digits** character style. Ignore the lower Style box. Assign Level 1 to every entry.

Now repeat these steps for your chapter titles (entry style = **toc-ct**) and your front and back matter titles (entry style = **toc-fbt**).

It doesn't matter what order the paragraph styles are listed in. InDesign will create your TOC in the order of appearance.

Select each style in the Include Paragraph Styles column after adding it, and then make changes.

Next, save your work by clicking on Save Style and naming your TOC style. When you're finished, your dialog box should look more or less like this:

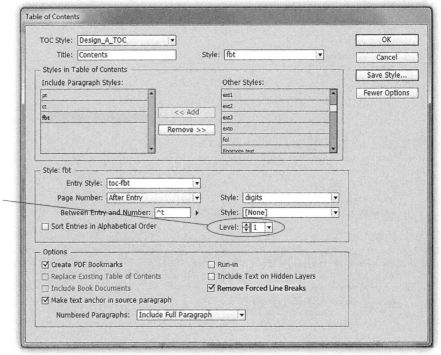

If you had not made different paragraph styles for each of your title levels, you could use the Level numbers to indent the titles for you, but the results would be rather crude.

Be sure to flow your automatic TOC into a text frame that isn't linked to the text in your book. It needs to be separate in order to update properly.

Now click OK. This closes the dialog box and loads your cursor with the TOC text, so go to the page you set up for your Contents, then click to flow it into a new text frame. The result may not come out exactly as you planned, but it'll be close enough that you only need to adjust a few things on your page, such as applying the character styles to your part and chapter numbers. Follow the instructions on page 234 to finalize your TOC. You can also change your TOC paragraph styles now, if you want, and see the changes take place on your TOC page just as you would on any other page.

Automatic table of contents for Design B

Design B on page 235 has the level 2 headings run together without page numbers, and the rest of the headings with page numbers flush right. You'll use the Table of Contents dialog box as explained for Design A (pages 241–242), with one exception: For the **h2** paragraph style, you'll indicate No Page Number, as shown below:

Design B doesn't include part titles, so you'll add your **fbt**, **ct**, **h1**, and **h2** styles to the automatic TOC.

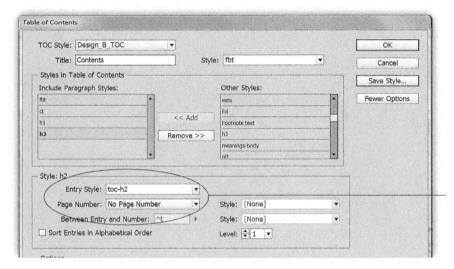

No Page Number is selected for the **toc-h2** style.

Now click Save Style and give the style a name, then click OK. Go to the page you set up for your Contents (see page 235), then click to flow it into a new text frame. You'll notice the level 2 headings are not run together the way you planned, and you'll also need to apply your character style [**toc-cn**] to each chapter number. Follow the instructions on page 237 to finalize your TOC.

If you subsequently make any changes to your book, such as adding pages or moving text, simply go to Layout>Update Table of Contents. You'll be notified that your Contents has been updated. Then look at the TOC and you'll see that the page numbers have changed accordingly.

Whenever you go into the Table of Contents style dialog box to make a change to your TOC structure—adding a new level of heading, for instance—you must click on Save Style. Then click OK to generate the newly designed TOC.

Automatic table of contents for Design C

In Design C (page 238), each heading has its page number a set space after the entry. You'll use the Table of Contents dialog box as explained for Design B (page 243), with one exception: You'll select Em Space from the Between Entry and Number drop-down list, as below. Repeat this for each TOC paragraph style.

First select and delete anything in this box, then use the drop-down list to find Em Space, and InDesign fills in the field for you.

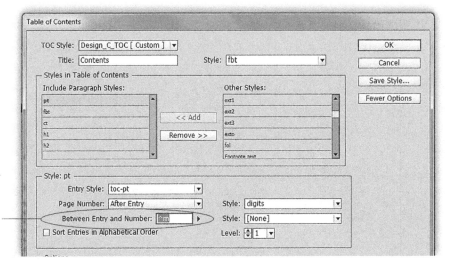

Now click Save Style, give the style a name, then click OK. Go to the page you set up for your Contents, then click to flow it into a new text frame. The only adjustment you need to make now is to apply your character style [**toc-cn**] to each chapter number.

Chances are that *your* table of contents will not quite resemble any of the samples we've shown on these pages, as your titles, headings, and page numbers will differ. But the principles remain the same no matter how many levels of titles and headings you have. Pick and choose from what you see in the samples, or find a more appealing style in another book. Once you understand how the TOC paragraph styles and the Table of Contents dialog box work, you'll be able to design and generate just the right TOC for your book.

Preface, Foreword, and Introduction

If your book has these sections, you probably already have all the paragraph styles you'll need for them. For the titles, apply the Front and Back Matter Title paragraph style [**fbt**] that you set up for your Contents. For the text, apply your regular text styles.

Note the correct spelling of Foreword (not Forward!).

Controlling your page numbering system

Your front matter will have a separate page numbering system from the rest of your book, using lowercase roman numerals. To make your page numbering system work this way, follow the instructions below.

If you are using the Book feature to control page numbering over multiple documents, see the step-by-step instructions on our blog at BookDesignMade Simple.com/using-the-book-feature-in-indesign.

Go to the Pages panel, click on the thumbnail image of the first page of the book to highlight it, then find Numbering & Section Options in the Pages fly-out menu. Select Start Page Numbering at 1, and the lowercase roman numeral style, as shown to the right. Click OK, and all the pages will now be numbered with lowercase roman numerals.

Next, in the Pages panel, click on the thumbnail of the first page of chapter 1 (a recto page). On the other hand, if your first chapter begins with a 2-page spread, make the page before that spread be page 1 by inserting a half title page. If your book is divided into parts, then the recto page for Part I will be page 1.

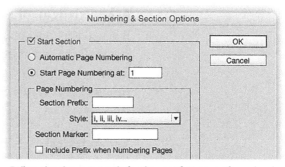

Follow the above example for the very first page of your book.

Then find Numbering & Section Options in the Pages fly-out menu. Check the Start Section box, then select Start Page Numbering at 1, and the arabic numeral style. Click OK, and this page will be numbered 1 with all the pages after it continuing in order, with arabic numerals.

Notice that on the Pages panel, the first page of each page numbering section is marked with a small triangle above it.

If you delete or add pages at any time in the future, the new pages will tuck neatly into the numbering scheme you have just set up.

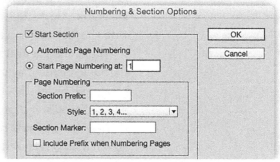

Follow this example for the first page of the main part of your book.

29

Designing your back matter

In chapter 14 you roughed in your back matter pages. All of these sections should match the style of the rest of your book, but each has its own conventions. The most common back matter sections are reviewed below.

Back matter titles follow the same style as front matter titles (see page 233). Simply apply your **fbt** paragraph style to the title of each back matter section, and the page numbers will continue on from the chapters. The first page of the back matter always starts on a recto page.

Acknowledgments

If you did not put your Acknowledgments in the front matter, put them just after the end of the text. Set this section just as you did the Preface, Foreword, and/or Introduction (see page 245), using your **fbt** style for the title, and your regular styles for the text.

Appendix(es)

If you have more than one appendix, you may treat the opening pages the same as your chapter openers, but set "APPENDIX A" (or "B," "C," etc.) in place of the chapter number (see example on page 247). If there's only one appendix, you could simply run the word "APPENDIX" and a colon in with the rest of the main title.

Appendix text and headings may be treated the same as in the rest of the book, or you may use smaller type and less leading, requiring new paragraph styles. If you decide to use a different column arrangement, make new master pages for appendixes (see index example on page 369).

Because appendix copy may come in the form of tables, narrative, lists, legal language, scientific or mathematical formulas, and so on, we are not offering paragraph styles. However, you'll see appendix opener samples on the next two pages.

APPENDIX A

———

APPENDIX TITLE

Alice was beginning to get very tired of sitting by her sister on the bank, and of having nothing to do: once or twice she had peeped into the book her sister was reading, but it had no pictures or conversations in it, 'and what is the use of a book,' thought Alice 'without pictures or conversation?'

So she was considering in her own mind (as well as she could, for the hot day made her feel very sleepy and stupid), whether the

A drop cap at the beginning of a chapter or section is usually used with narrative. Even if an appendix consists of narrative, it does not normally begin with a drop cap.

The appendix opener above is based on chapter opening Design 1 (page 148), with the "number" and title the same size as in the chapter opener, but notice that they are closer together and placed at the top of the page.

Use the paragraph settings below for this design.

☐ **Appendix Letters [appl]**   Based On = **cn**
Changes from the Chapter Numbers style (see page 149):
Indents and Spacing: Space Before = 0
                                        Space After = 0.0625 in
Paragraph Rules: Rule Below = Rule On
                                        Offset = 0.125 in

☐ **Appendix Titles [appt]**   Based On = **ct**
Changes from the Chapter Titles style (see page 150):
Indents and Spacing: Space After = 0.56 in
                                        Aligned to Grid = None

There is a line of space (**tx** style) above the appendix number, just as for most of the chapter opener examples in this book.

Appendix A

Appendix Title

If you were to place the related chapter opening page and this appendix opening page next to each other, you'd see that the beginning of the appendix text lines up with the chapter title.

Alice was beginning to get very tired of sitting by her sister on the bank, and of having nothing to do: once or twice she had peeped

Here you see an opening page that is based on both the chapter opening Design 4 on page 156 and the part opening Design 4 on page 178. Paragraph styles for this design are shown below.

☐ **Appendix Letter [appl]**   Based On = **pn**
Changes from the Part Numbers style (see page 179):
Basic Character Formats: Size = 18 pt
Indents and Spacing: Space Before = 9 pt *or* 0.125 in
                    Space After = 9 pt *or* 0.125 in

☐ **Appendix Titles [appt]**   Based On = **pt**
Changes from the Part Titles style (see page 179):
Indents and Spacing: Space After = 1.125 in

Endnotes

Endnotes became live in InDesign CC 2018. This means you can now add or delete endnotes anywhere in your document, and the numbering system will automatically update.

Visit BookDesignMadeSimple.com/indesign-endnotes-go-live-cc2018 for details on how to place and manage live endnotes. Be sure to read the comments as several issues are discussed there, such as placing endnotes at the end of chapters rather than in the back matter.

Endnotes take the form of a numbered list. In the sample below are two different styles: left justified type with indented paragraphs in the left column, and ragged right (Alignment = Left) type with hanging indents in the right column. Paragraph styles for both can be found on the next page. Try both one- and two-column formats; you might be surprised by which will save more space.

The paragraph styles shown on the next page are simply suggestions to get you started on designing your endnotes pages. If you decide to use more than one column, make a new master page (use one you previously set up for your appendix, or see index example on page 369).

If you imported your endnotes from Word with your manuscript, the text frame containing your endnotes will be on the pasteboard of page 2. Simply cut and paste it into your back matter for formatting.

Endnotes placed in your back matter are entitled "Notes" rather than "Endnotes."

To format endnote reference numbers (the superscript numbers within your main narrative), see pages 85 and 93.

---

and then put both into a library. Then whenever you need a sidebar you can drag one or the other out of the library, all ready to use. See p. 123 for more about libraries.

14. The inside edge of the sidebar is at the center of the page. If the sidebar text were any wider, the letter spacing and word spacing in the main text would probably look very poor—either too tight or too loose.

15. This shows corner options for the sidebar title text frame.

CHAPTER 14

16. When you convert to an ebook, you'll delete all your folios and running heads or feet.

17. Pages in the front matter coming before the Contents do not have visible page numbers.

18. Shone, David. *Champagne Haze.* Kettering, OH: Hour Glass Books, 2009.

19. Some of the online publishing services offer a free ISBN. You may use theirs if you like, but we believe it's best to own and control your own ISBNs. Also, the numbers you receive in a bunch will be more or less sequential and thus better organized.

20. Wray, David. *The Secret Roots of Christianity: Decoding Religious History with Symbols on Ancient Coins.* Needham, MA: Numismatics and History, 2012.

Left justified with indented paragraphs

whenever you need a sidebar you can drag one or the other out of the library, all ready to use. See p. 123 for more about libraries.

14. The inside edge of the sidebar is at the center of the page. If the sidebar text were any wider, the letter spacing and word spacing in the main text would probably look very poor—either too tight or too loose.

15. This shows corner options for the sidebar title text frame.

CHAPTER 14

16. When you convert to an ebook, you'll delete all your folios and running heads or feet.

17. Pages in the front matter coming before the Contents do not have visible page numbers.

18. Shone, David. *Champagne Haze.* Kettering, OH: Hour Glass Books, 2009.

19. Some of the online publishing services offer a free ISBN. You may use theirs if you like, but we believe it's best to own and control your own ISBNs. Also, the numbers you receive in a bunch will be more or less sequential and thus better organized.

20. Wray, David. *The Secret Roots of Christianity: Decoding Religious History with Symbols on Ancient Coins.* Needham, MA: Numismatics and History, 2012.

Left aligned with hanging indents

Styles for the justified example in the left column, page 249:

Notice that the list numbers in this design are set in **bold** character style. Set an en space after each number and period.

☐ **Endnotes Text [end]**   Based On = **tx1**
　Basic Character Formats: Size = 9 pt
　　　　　　　　　　　　　　　　　　Leading = 11 pt
　　　　　　　　　　　　　　　　　　Tracking = –5

　Indents and Spacing: First Line Indent = 11 pt *or* 0.1528 in
　　　　　　　　　　　　　　　　　　Align to Grid = None

The type and leading sizes shown here are just suggestions; quite possibly you'll find that different sizes work better for you.

☐ **Endnotes Chapter Numbers [end-cn]**   Based On = **end**
　Changes from the Endnotes Text style above:
　Basic Character Formats: Font Style = Semibold
　　　　　　　　　　　　　　　　　　Case = OpenType All Small Caps
　　　　　　　　　　　　　　　　　　Tracking = 0

　Indents and Spacing: Alignment = Center
　　　　　　　　　　　　　　　　　　Space Before = 11 pt *or* 0.1528 in

Styles for the ragged right example in the right column, page 249:

☐ **Endnotes Text [end]**   Based On = **tx1**
　Basic Character Formats: Size = 9 pt
　　　　　　　　　　　　　　　　　　Leading = 11 pt

　Indents and Spacing: Alignment = Left
　　　　　　　　　　　　　　　　　　Left Indent = 14 pt *or* 0.1944 in
　　　　　　　　　　　　　　　　　　First Line Indent = –14 pt *or* –0.1944 in
　　　　　　　　　　　　　　　　　　Align to Grid = None

Type a tab before each number and another tab before each entry.

　Tabs: Set a right tab at 0.145 in

☐ **Endnotes Chapter Numbers [end-cn]**   Based On = **end**
　Changes from the Endnotes Text style above:
　Basic Character Formats: Font Family = Myriad Pro
　　　　　　　　　　　　　　　　　　Font Style = Semibold Condensed
　　　　　　　　　　　　　　　　　　Case = All Caps
　　　　　　　　　　　　　　　　　　Tracking = 20

　Indents and Spacing: Space Before = 11 pt *or* 0.1528 in
　OpenType Features: Figure Style = Proportional Lining

Glossary

Readers may refer to the glossary often, so use larger type than you did for the endnotes. If you have enough space, simply use the same size and leading as your text style.

A hanging indent usually works well. Or don't use any indents but add space between entries. Set the glossary term in semibold or bold, then set an en or em space before the definition. You can also add the book page where the term first appears, as shown below. Put this number in parentheses and perhaps set the number (but not the parentheses) in italic.

The Find function (Edit> Find/Change) is very helpful for locating the first use of your glossary terms.

signatures (*3*) Groups of book pages that are printed on the same sheet and folded. The number of pages in a signature varies according to the size of the paper and the size of the book pages. Common numbers of pages in a signature are 16 and 32, but 24 and 48 are also used.

small caps (*69*) Capital letters that are the same size as the lower-case letters in a font. Commonly used for acronyms and terms such as A.M., P.M., B.C., and A.D.

soft return (*128*) A line return that forces a new line but keeps it within the same paragraph. Place the cursor where you want the break, then press Shift + Enter. See also hard return.

softcover (*240*) Commonly called a paperback, but soft covers can also be made of a

blind stamping, the design is pressed into the cover with no ink or foil.

swatch (*260*) A small sample of a color. The Swatches panel lists all the named colors in the document.

tabular lining or oldstyle figures (*18*) Numerals, either lining or oldstyle, that are spaced evenly so that they can be aligned in columns.

text block (*34*) The area on a page in which the main body of text is placed. The text block does not include the running head (or foot) or the folio, or any material in a side column.

text frame (*16*) A box in which type is placed

text wrap (*208*) The method for allowing type to run around the edges of a graphic shape or image rather than flowing across it

In addition to the paragraph style below, you might want to create a character style for the glossary terms. You could add tracking, set the terms in your sans serif font, use semibold rather than bold, and so on.

You'll find another glossary example on page 252.

☐ **Glossary Text [gloss]**   Based On = **tx1**
Changes from the No Indents style (see page 62):
Indents and Spacing: Left Indent = 14 pt *or* 0.1944 in
                                        First Line Indent = –14 pt *or* –0.1944 in

In your book, a one-column glossary might work better. The design below uses a half-linespace between entries, and so the type is taken off the baseline grid.

> **signatures**   Groups of book pages that are printed on the same sheet and folded. The number of pages in a signature varies according to the size of the paper and the size of the book pages. Common numbers of pages in a signature are 16 and 32, but 24 and 48 are also used.
>
> **small caps**   Capital letters that are the same size as the lower-case letters in a font. Commonly used for acronyms and terms such as A.M., P.M., B.C., and A.D.
>
> **soft return**   A line return that forces a new line but keeps it within the same paragraph. Place the cursor where you want the break, then press Shift + Enter. See also hard return.
>
> **softcover**   Commonly called a paperback, but soft covers can also be made of a plastic material.
>
> **spiral**   A type of binding that uses one continuous metal wire (plastic coated or not), curled into a spiral, to hold the pages together.

In this example, an em space is set after each term (Ctrl/Cmd+Shift+M).

☐ **Glossary Text [gloss]**   Based On = **tx1**
Changes from the No Indents style (see page 62):
Indents and Spacing: Space After = 7 pt *or* 0.0972 in
                                                              Align to Grid = None

☐ **Glossary Term [glossterm]** *Character* **Style**   Based On = [None]
Basic Character Formats: Font Family = Myriad Pro
                                                              Font Style = Semibold

As with the endnotes designs (pages 249–250), these glossary samples are meant to show you options so that you can design the best glossary for *your* book. Change or combine the given features as much as you need to for the best results.

Bibliography or References

Treat this section much the same as the endnotes (pages 249–250), with smaller type and less leading than your Text style. Add space between entries, or use a hanging indent. Use one or two columns. If you divide the list into sections with headings, design the headings the same as those in your endnotes, to match your overall design.

Garabedian-Weber, Dawn. *Become Aware: A New Life Has Begun.* Worcester, MA, 2008.

Hager, Margaret Henderson. *Farewell, Samsara: Selected Poems.* Philadelphia, 2014.

Helbert, Sharon. *Sassy Gal's How to Lose the Last Damn 10 Pounds or 15, 20, 25 . . .* Boston: Alegcris Press, 2014.

CHAPTER 2

Kriger, Shlomit, ed. *Marking Humanity: Stories, Poems, & Essays by Holocaust Survivors.* Toronto, ON: Soul Inscriptions Press, 2010.

Muñoz-Jordan, Ana S. *How Turtle Became a Dolphin: A Story about Adapting to Life's Changes.* Jupiter, FL: Tortuphina Press, 2009.

Poole, Scott. *The Sliding Glass Door.* Spokane: Colonus

Garabedian-Weber, Dawn. *Become Aware: A New Life Has Begun.* Worcester, MA, 2008.

Hager, Margaret Henderson. *Farewell, Samsara: Selected Poems.* Philadelphia, 2014.

Helbert, Sharon. *Sassy Gal's How to Lose the Last Damn 10 Pounds or 15, 20, 25 . . .* Boston: Alegcris Press, 2014.

CHAPTER 2

Kriger, Shlomit, ed. *Marking Humanity: Stories, Poems, & Essays by Holocaust Survivors.* Toronto, ON: Soul Inscriptions Press, 2010.

Muñoz-Jordan, Ana S. *How Turtle Became a Dolphin: A Story about Adapting to Life's Changes.* Jupiter, FL: Tortuphina Press, 2009.

Poole, Scott. *The Sliding Glass Door.* Spokane: Colonus Publishing, 2011.

Sarich, Angie. *Leaving Parma.* Spokane: Colonus House,

Left justified with space between   Left aligned with hanging indents

Styles for the justified example in the left column above:

☐ **References Text [ref]**   Based On = **tx1**
  Basic Character Formats: Size = 9 pt
                                              Leading = 11 pt
  Indents and Spacing: Space After = 4 pt *or* 0.0556 in
                                              Align to Grid = None

☐ **References Chapter Numbers [ref-cn]**   Based On = **ref**
  Changes from the References Text style above:
  Basic Character Formats: Font Style = Semibold
                                              Case = OpenType All Small Caps
  Indents and Spacing: Alignment = Center
                                              Space Before = 7 pt *or* 0.0972 in   *(continued on page 254)*

Styles for the ragged right example in the right column, page 253:

☐ **References Text [ref]**   Based On = **tx1**
　Basic Character Formats: Size = 9 pt
　　　　　　　　　　　　　　　　　　　　　　Leading = 11 pt
　Indents and Spacing: Alignment = Left
　　　　　　　　　　　　　　　　　　　　　　Left Indent = 14 pt *or* 0.1944 in
　　　　　　　　　　　　　　　　　　　　　　First Line Indent = –14 pt *or* –0.1944 in
　　　　　　　　　　　　　　　　　　　　　　Align to Grid = None

☐ **References Chapter Numbers [ref-cn]**   Based On = **ref**
　Changes from the References Text style above:
　Basic Character Formats: Font Family = Myriad Pro
　　　　　　　　　　　　　　　　　　　　　　Font Style = Semibold Condensed
　　　　　　　　　　　　　　　　　　　　　　Case = All Caps
　　　　　　　　　　　　　　　　　　　　　　Tracking = 20
　Indents and Spacing: Space Before = 11 pt *or* 0.1528 in
　OpenType Features: Figure Style = Proportional Lining

Index

The index is complex and deserves a section of its own (see chapter 54).

　　Congratulations! You've successfully designed every element in your book's pages, and applied appropriate paragraph and character styles to every bit of text in your book. Well done!

　　Next, in Parts V and VI, you'll add shapes, images, and captions to your book, if needed. This will constitute the second pass through your book. If you don't have any shapes, images, or captions inside your book, skip to Part VII: Typesetting, and that's where you'll do your final pass through your pages.

Part V:
Adding Shapes & Color

30

Working with shapes

In Parts V and VI, you'll add shapes, colors, images, and captions to your book, which will constitute the second pass through your pages. If your book pages don't require shapes or color, then feel free to skip to Part VI: Adding Images for the time being (you'll refer back to Part V when you design your book cover).

Shapes are used for lots of reasons: to make sidebars stand out, to draw your reader's attention to something, to create an illustration or diagram, or to simply add color. And they're fun to create!

Before getting started with shapes and color, make sure you've already set up a baseline grid (see chapter 23), as you'll use the grid to easily align shapes on your pages.

Adding shapes and images during your second pass may increase the number of pages. If you'll be printing on an offset press, refer to chapter 48 for ways to control your page count.

Using shapes in conjunction with text

There are two ways to combine text with shapes:

The text in *this* box has been cut from the main narrative and pasted into this rectangle shape.

1   Leave the text where it is in the main narrative and create a shape behind it, as in *this* box.

2   Cut the text out of the main narrative and paste it into a separate text frame (as in the example to the left).

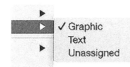

Every shape that you make has an assigned purpose: graphic or text (or unassigned, meaning neither one). If you mistakenly use the Type Tool to draw a shape to place behind your sidebar text, your shape will be a text frame. You can easily change that by selecting it with the Selection Tool, going to Object>Content, and choosing Graphic.

If you think about this, you'll realize that you could use a circle or polygon as a text frame. Go ahead—try it! Draw a circle or polygon, change its content to Text, and type something in there.

Working with color

There are three types of color available in InDesign: CMYK, RGB, and spot colors. Most likely you'll be using CMYK colors for your printed pages and book cover. For an ebook, you'll use RGB color. Here is a brief overview of the three types:

CMYK is an acronym for the four ink colors used on a printing press—Cyan, Magenta, Yellow, and blacK. Believe it or not, all the beautiful full-color books and magazines you see are usually printed with just four ink colors. This is the type of color you'll be using for your book cover and pages. Your book pages will use CMYK color if they'll be printed in color, but if they are printed with black ink only, you'll use the default [Black] for text, and shades of the CMYK black (percentages of the K) for gray.

RGB refers to the three colors of light displayed on all monitors and screens—red, green, and blue. When you take a photo with your digital camera or phone, or scan an image with your scanner, the image will have RGB color. When you import a Word document into InDesign, if there were any colors specified in Word, they'll be RGB, too. RGB color usually needs to be converted to CMYK for printing.

RGB images are now accepted by some POD and digital printers, such as Amazon KDP.

SPOT colors are ink colors that are premixed by companies such as Pantone. Premixing inks allows a greater color range than is possible by just using the four CMYK ink colors. Spot colors are often more brilliant and include neon and metallic colors. Company logos often use spot colors. If you use a spot color in your book, it will be more expensive to print, requiring an extra ink color on the press. Also, the spot color will need to be separated from the other colors in your digital files when you package them for the printer. This is beyond the scope of this book.

Spot colors are only available in offset printing.

Two-color printing is another option. It uses black (usually) and one other color. Learn about it at BookDesignMadeSimple .com/2-color-printing.

Organizing the colors in your Swatches panel

Start by opening and getting familiar with the Swatches panel (to open it, click Windows>Color>Swatches). Your Swatches panel will look something like this:

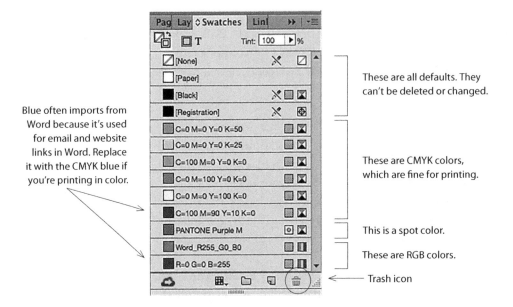

Blue often imports from Word because it's used for email and website links in Word. Replace it with the CMYK blue if you're printing in color.

These are all defaults. They can't be deleted or changed.

These are CMYK colors, which are fine for printing.

This is a spot color.

These are RGB colors.

Trash icon

It's a good idea to keep the colors in your Swatches panel organized by deleting any RGB and spot colors. To delete a color, drag it onto the trash icon at the bottom right to open the Delete Swatch dialog box. If you're printing with black ink only (like most book pages), simply replace the swatch with the default [Black] as shown below. If you're printing with color, replace the swatch with a similar CMYK color.

See page 260 for how to create a new defined swatch.

Applying colors to your shapes and type

You'll apply up to two colors to every shape you create: one for the fill (the inside of the shape) and one for the stroke (the outline of the shape). The two boxes at the top left of your Swatches panel control the color of the fill and stroke.

Click the Fill box (upper left) or Stroke box (lower right) to bring it to the front.

Click the curved arrow to swap the colors. In this example, the fill becomes black and the stroke gray.

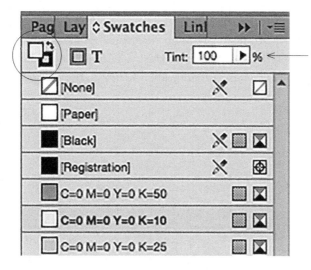

Use of Tint (less than 100% of a color) not recommended (see note at bottom of page 261).

The upper left box controls the fill (the inside) of your shape. To fill a shape with a color, bring the Fill box to the front by clicking it. Then click one of the colors in the Swatches panel to apply it to the fill of your shape.

The lower right box controls the stroke (the outline) of your shape. To add a stroke, bring the Stroke box to the front by clicking it. Then click one of the colors in the Swatches panel to apply it to the stroke of your shape. (See page 272 to set the attributes of the stroke.)

The same principles apply if you want to add color to type. Select the type with the Type Tool, then pick a color fill from the Swatches panel. You could also add a stroke to the type, but that would only be appropriate in a large heading or on your cover. The stroke will be 1 pt in weight by default, but you can change the weight (thickness) in the Weight field of the Stroke panel. Any weight less than 0.25 pt will not print reliably, however. See chapter 35 for more details.

Stroke = 100% black
Fill = 10% black

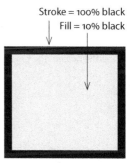

To add a color to a paragraph or character style, specify it in the Character Color section of the appropriate paragraph or character style.

Changing or adding color swatches

There's a good chance the colors in your Swatches panel are not the exact colors you'll need for your book. It's easy to either change an existing color or add a new one.

To change an existing color, double-click the color in the Swatches panel to open the Swatch Options box. Simply move the sliders to change the color, then click OK.

To add a new color, click the Swatches Panel fly-out menu and select New Color Swatch. In the New Color Swatch dialog box, move the sliders to get the color you want, click Add, then click Done.

For help in coming up with a good set of colors, see our blog post at BookDesignMadeSimple .com/devising-a-color-palette-for-your-book.

If you like, you can name your swatch—call it "side-bar," for instance. In this example the swatch is named with its color values.

You can change an exist-ing RGB color to a CMYK color simply by chang-ing the Color Mode.

To change an existing color or create a new color, move the sliders, or type color values in the percentage boxes.

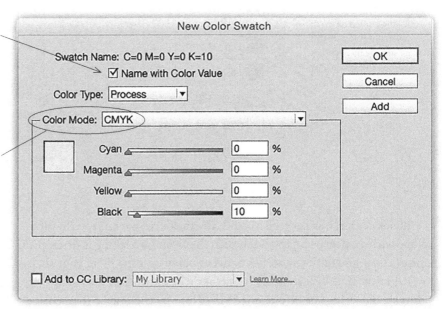

How do you know you've chosen a "good" color?

For information about Pantone colors, go to colorguides.net.

You don't! But there are a couple of ways you can check. You can refer to Pantone Process color samples or other printed samples that show the CMYK values of the printed colors. Or, you can simply get some pages or your cover printed at your local copy store on their color printer and see how they look.

Creating a color for shapes behind sidebars and text

Most shapes placed behind text are a light gray color. Light gray is a good color choice because 1) the text remains easy to read, 2) gray is a neutral color (plays nicely with other colors), and 3) gray is available for pages that are printed with black ink only.

The most common light gray color used is 10% black. To create a 10% black color, add a new color as explained and shown on page 260, and move the Black slider to 10%. Done! Now you'll be able to create shapes and apply your 10% black color (or any other color you choose) to a shape's fill. Usually the color applied to the stroke is None; in other words, the shape doesn't have a stroke.

10% black

Many printers will insist that no percentage below 5% be used in a solid block of color because it will not print reliably.

A quick word about the Tint feature

You can enter a percentage into the Tint box to fade the color of a fill or stroke. For example, you could select the default [Black] color and then choose a Tint of 10% to fade the color from black to gray.

That works fine for the shape currently selected. However, if you are using a tint in more than one place (for example, in all the sidebar boxes in your book), it's better to create a swatch specifically for that tint. That way, if you want to change the tint globally from, say, 10% to 15%, you can simply move the slider(s) on that color.

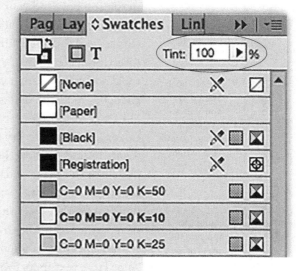

The sidebar boxes in *this* book have a color value of C=0 M=0 Y=0 K=10 (see the swatches to the right). They are not the default [Black] with a 10% tint applied.

linear
gradient

radial
gradient

short drag

long drag

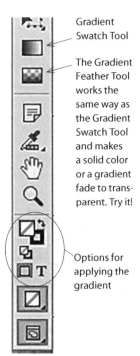

Gradient
Swatch Tool

The Gradient
Feather Tool
works the
same way as
the Gradient
Swatch Tool
and makes
a solid color
or a gradient
fade to trans-
parent. Try it!

Options for
applying the
gradient

radient

Making and using gradients

A gradient is a smooth-looking transition between or among colors or tints. The two types available in InDesign are shown to the left. The strategic use of gradients can boost a design nicely, but don't overuse them.

Applying a gradient

Before creating your own gradient, you need to understand how gradients work and how to apply them. First, locate the Gradient panel either at the right of your screen or by going to Window>Color>Gradient. Draw a shape (see chapter 33), select it with the Selection Tool, make sure that Fill is in front in the Swatches or Toolbox, then open the Gradient panel and choose either Linear or Radial from the Type drop-down list. Your shape will be filled with the default gradient that's shown in the panel. Try clicking on the little arrows to reverse the direction of the gradient, and entering positive or negative values in the Angle field to see the effects.

Now, with your shape selected, click on the Gradient Swatch Tool (▣) in the Toolbox, and your cursor will become a small crosshair. Click anywhere inside or even outside your shape and drag in any direction. Repeat this several times, clicking and dragging from various points in different directions each time. If you drag a short distance, the change of color is rapid and condensed; if you drag beyond the edges of the shape, the change is more gradual (see examples above left). If you hold down the Shift key while dragging, the direction will be strictly horizontal or vertical, or at a 45° angle. Try these techniques with both linear and radial gradients to find out how they work. With a radial gradient, start in the middle of the shape and drag outward. Once you've tried that, start in other spots and drag in other directions to see the various effects. And don't forget that you can reverse the colors anytime by clicking on the Reverse arrows in the Gradient panel.

You can apply gradients to type as well as shapes. To do this, first type some large text in its own text frame. Next click on your type frame with the Selection Tool, then the Gradient Swatch Tool, and lastly on the "T" near the bottom of the Toolbox. Now choose Linear or Radial in the Gradient panel. Your type will take on the selected gradient. You can then use the Gradient Swatch Tool crosshairs to change the angle and length of the gradient just as with a shape.

Gradients look smooth, but they are actually made up of a series of shades between the colors. You can avoid obvious visible banding (see example to the right) if you follow these guidelines:

- Lighter colors work better than darker ones.
- Stick with similar colors; a drastic change between colors (e.g., green to orange) can result in banding.

- If you're using two shades of the same color, a higher percentage of color change (10% to 70%, for instance) will work better because there will be a greater number of smaller steps between the ends of the gradient.
- Use gradients in relatively small areas rather than across an entire page.

banding

Creating a gradient

Now that you're familiar with how gradients work, you can make your own by following these steps:

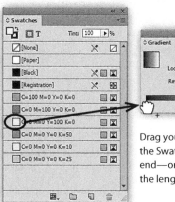

1 In the Swatches panel, make a swatch (see page 260) for each end of the gradient.

2 Drag the Swatches panel out from the dock, and open the Gradient panel. This way you can work with both at once.

3 Choose Linear or Radial in the Type list. Drag one of your new swatches to the left end of the gradient display in the Gradient panel. When a hand with a plus sign appears, you have hit the target and can let go of the swatch with the mouse or trackpad. Repeat this at the other end of the gradient with the second color. Your gradient should now show the two colors you intend to use. If you like, you can add a third color to the gradient by making another swatch and dragging it somewhere between the ends of the current gradient in the Gradient panel. You can also slide any of the colors left or right.

4 You may now drag the thumbnail of the new gradient from the Gradient panel over to the Swatches panel if you like, so you'll have the gradient handy if you want to reuse it. Double-click on "New Gradient Swatch," then type in a new name for the swatch.

Drag your swatch from the Swatches panel to one end—or anywhere along the length of the gradient.

Return the Swatches panel back to the dock when you're finished.

Adobe offers a good tutorial on using and creating gradients if you want more details and tricks.

32

Using layers for shapes

Using the Layers panel will help you keep all the elements on your pages or cover organized. You can easily arrange elements so that some are in front of others (such as text being in front of a shape). You can also lock layers to keep some things in place while you move others around. And you can turn layers on and off to control what you see and/or print.

The layer itself is transparent; the objects on the layer are not. You can shuffle the stack of layers anytime, and you can move objects from one layer to another.

It's useful to have two layers for your pages if you're adding shapes: one for text and one for shapes. The Shapes layer includes all your elements that are *behind* everything else. And the Text layer is *in front* of all other layers, and includes all your text frames.

To set up your layers, open your Layers panel at the right of your screen or by clicking Window>Layers. You'll see there is one layer, called Layer 1. Select any text frame with your Selection Tool and its outline will be the same color as shown for Layer 1. To change the name of Layer 1 to "Text," double-click Layer 1 to open your Layer Options dialog box, change the name to Text, then click OK.

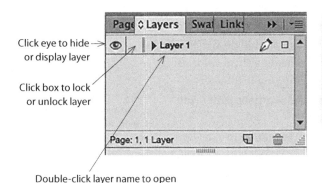

Shape on lower layer, type on upper layer

Shape on upper layer, type on lower layer

Go to BookDesignMade Simple.com/videos to watch a short lesson on using layers.

Click eye to hide or display layer

Click box to lock or unlock layer

Double-click layer name to open Layer Options dialog box

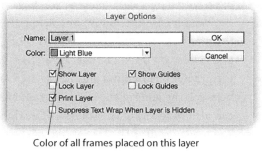

Color of all frames placed on this layer

Add a new layer by clicking the Create New Layer icon on the Layers panel (see example below). A new layer called Layer 2 will appear above your Text layer. The color for this layer is probably red. Double-click Layer 2, change its name to Shapes, and click OK. Then, because everything on the Text layer should be in front of or *above* everything on the Shapes layer, drag the Shapes layer down so it appears *below* the Text layer.

The layer at the top of the list is in front. The layer at the bottom of the list is behind. You can change their order anytime by dragging layers up or down the list.

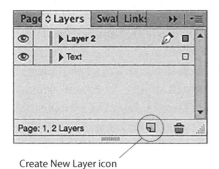

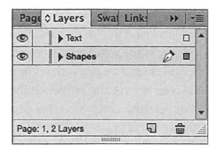

Another way to create a new layer or access the Layer Options dialog box is by clicking the fly-out menu on the Layers panel and choosing those options there.

Create New Layer icon

Now, whenever you add a shape to your pages, first select the Shapes layer in your Layers panel so that your shape will be added to that layer and appear on the page *behind* your text. While adding shapes, you may find it easier to lock your Text layer (click once in the Lock box to turn the lock on or off) so you don't select a text frame by mistake. You can also turn a layer on or off by clicking once in the Visibility box (the eye icon).

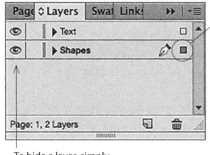

Select a frame and you'll see which layer it's on by the color of the box in the Layers panel and the color of the frame. Drag this box to another layer to move the frame. The box and frame will change color to match the new layer.

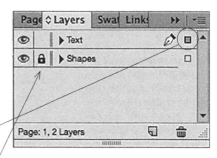

To hide a layer, simply click once in the Visibility box.

To lock a layer, simply click once in the Lock box.

33

Using the shape tools

Three shape tools are in your Toolbox—Rectangle, Ellipse, and Polygon (click and hold the visible one to see the others). Take a moment to check this out. Select any shape tool, then drag to create that shape. Hold the Shift key while you drag to keep the width and height equal (the Rectangle Tool creates a square, the Ellipse Tool creates a circle, and the Polygon Tool creates a regular polygon). The shape will acquire the fill and stroke colors selected in the Swatches panel (you learned about the Swatches panel in chapter 31). You can delete your experimental shapes by simply selecting the shape with the Selection Tool and pressing the Delete key.

Rectangle Tool	M
Ellipse Tool	L
Polygon Tool	

Creating rectangles to go behind text in the main narrative

The most common shapes used in book pages are rectangles placed behind text to make it stand out from the main narrative. Here are the steps you'll take when creating these shapes:

Line up your rectangle with your baseline grid and margins or column(s).

If you have trouble moving the handles precisely, your guides might be the problem. Go to View>Grids & Guides and check or uncheck Snap to Guides. Keep this in mind anytime you move an object.

1. Open your Layers panel and select the Shapes layer (see chapter 32). Lock your Text layer to make it easier to work with the shapes you'll draw on the Shapes layer (otherwise the text frame above the shape will get selected by default because the Text layer is above the Shapes layer).
2. Select the Rectangle Tool and draw a shape by clicking and dragging.
3. Switch to your Selection Tool and drag the edges of the frame to make it the right size and shape. Switch to Normal view by pressing W and line up the edges of the rectangle with your baseline grid, margins, and column(s), as shown with *this* box.

BOOK DESIGN MADE SIMPLE · PART V: ADDING SHAPES & COLOR

4 Select appropriate fill and stroke colors for your shape (see chapter 31 about working with color and the Swatches panel).

5 Add a corner option to your rectangle, if you wish (see page 273 about adding corner options).

6 Create an object style for your sidebar boxes. Thought you were finished with styles? Not just yet. Object styles make it easy to create lots of shapes with the same characteristics (for example, same color, corner options, fill, and stroke). See chapter 38 about object styles.

This rectangle has rounded corners, one of the Corner Options available (see page 273).

NOTE: Remember that during your second pass you'll add your shapes and images *at the same time* as you progress through your pages. Adding shapes and images will change the flow of your text, so you'll finalize the layout of each page as you go.

In addition to creating rectangles with the Rectangle Tool, you can also use the Ellipse Tool to create ovals and circles, and the Polygon Tool to create starbursts. Any of these tools can be used to add a shape to your pages or cover.

Also in your Toolbox, you'll notice Rectangle, Ellipse, and Polygon *Frame* Tools. These look the same as the Rectangle, Ellipse, and Polygon Tools except they have an X across them. They are used for placeholders. For example, you might add a rectangle frame where you intend to add type or an image later. The X in the frame will make it easier to see in Normal view, while it's still empty (see below).

Using the Polygon Tool

The Polygon Tool is a bit different from the Rectangle and Ellipse Tools, in that you can choose the number of sides and the optional star inset.

Double-click the Polygon Tool in the Toolbox to open Polygon Settings and choose the number of sides and inset of the points. Then click OK.

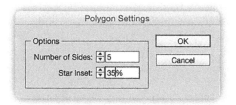

5 sides, 35% star inset
1 pt solid stroke, color fill

25 sides, 50% star inset
No stroke, color fill

7 sides, 0% star inset
1 pt solid stroke, color fill

Watch a demonstration of the Polygon Tool, if you like, at BookDesign MadeSimple.com/videos.

34

Using the drawing tools

There are three drawing tools in your Toolbox—the Line, Pen, and Pencil tools. These can be used to create any kind of line or shape. Use the Line Tool for single straight lines; the Pen Tool for straight lines, curves, and shapes; and the Pencil Tool for drawing freehand lines and shapes.

Any time you use a drawing tool, the line or shape you draw will include the stroke and fill colors selected in your Swatches panel (see chapter 31).

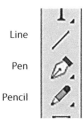

Line

Pen

Pencil

Using the Line Tool

With the Line Tool selected, it's easy to create a straight line. Simply click and drag a line anywhere on your page. If you want the line to be horizontal, vertical, or at a 45° angle, press the Shift key while you drag. Once you've created a line, use the Selection Tool to move it or change its length, or the Free Transform Tool (, see page 289) to rotate it.

Once your line is positioned where you want it, choose a stroke color in the Swatches panel (see page 259), and use the Stroke panel to choose the weight (thickness) and type of stroke (see page 272).

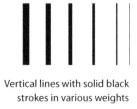

Vertical lines with solid black
strokes in various weights

Using the Pen Tool

Watch the Pen and
Pencil Tools in action at
BookDesignMade
Simple.com/videos.

The Pen Tool is very versatile and allows you to create both straight and curved lines that can be adjusted at will. Anchor points are created wherever you click the Pen Tool, connected by straight or curved lines, and together they form adjustable paths.

Drawing shapes with straight lines

The simplest use of the Pen Tool is to create a shape using straight lines. Click (don't drag) the Pen Tool anywhere to get started, and you'll see a small solid square appear (your first anchor point). Click again (don't

First anchor point

drag) in another spot, and a second anchor point will appear with a connecting line. Note that this anchor point is solid, and now the first anchor
point is hollow. Keep clicking, and you'll create more anchor points connected with lines.

To complete your path, you can:

1   Close it by returning to your first anchor point (you'll see a small cir-
    cle next to the Pen Tool: ✎₀) and clicking on the first anchor point; or
2   Leave it open by pressing Ctrl/Cmd and clicking anywhere outside an
    object, or by pressing Enter/Return and switching to a different tool.

Once your path is complete, you can select stroke and fill colors in the
Swatches panel (see page 259) and use the Stroke panel to choose the
weight and type of stroke (see page 272).

To move any of the anchor points after the path is complete, drag the
anchor point using the Direct Selection Tool (the white pointer in your
Toolbox).

Drawing shapes with curved lines

Curved lines are drawn a bit differently from straight lines. When you set
a new anchor point for a curved line, you'll drag instead of clicking. Dragging creates an anchor point with handles that allow you to control the
amount and direction of the curve. Here's an example:

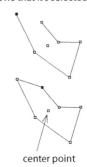

A solid anchor point
shows that it's selected.

center point

▷ Direct Selection Tool

If you click or drag in the
wrong place by mistake,
undo the anchor point
by pressing Ctrl/Cmd+Z
or clicking Edit>Undo.

Set the first anchor point by clicking
and dragging in the direction you want
the curve to go in. Drag about 1/3 of
the distance to the next anchor point.

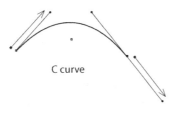

C curve

Set your second anchor point by
clicking and dragging in any direction. As you drag, you'll see the curve
developing. Stop dragging when
the curve is where you want it.

It is worth the
effort to practice this
method until you get
a smooth movement
going, because the
resulting curves are
very graceful.

S curve

Drag your second anchor point
in a different direction to create a
C curve (top) or in the same direction to create an S curve (bottom).

You can create curved lines that consist of a combination of C and S curves by changing the direction in which you drag after clicking anchor points.

Anchor points are *between* the curves, not at the peaks or troughs.

S curve   C curve   C curve   C curve   handles

To complete your path, you can:

1   Close it by returning to your first anchor point (you'll see a small circle next to the Pen Tool:), clicking on the first anchor point, and dragging; or
2   Leave it open by pressing Ctrl/Cmd and clicking anywhere outside an object, or by pressing Enter/Return and switching to a different tool.

Once your path is complete, you can easily adjust it using the Direct Selection Tool. Move any of the anchor points by selecting and dragging them, or change the curve between anchor points by selecting the curve, then dragging the handles.

Add color to your path by choosing stroke and fill colors in the Swatches panel (see page 259), and use the Stroke panel to select the weight and type of stroke (see page 272).

This curved line is shown in the example above right but has been rotated 90° and has a 2 pt black dotted stroke applied with a barbed arrow at the end.

Using the Pencil Tool

The Pencil Tool is for freehand drawing. Simply grab the tool ( ), position the pointer where you want to start, and begin to draw with your mouse or on your keypad. You'll find that the resulting shape will have many more anchor points than something you'd draw with the Pen Tool, and you might want to smooth out some of your lines. As an example, we'll improve the flower sketch to the left. Your drawing will be different, of course, so you may not need all of the options listed on the next page.

The original flower with dozens of anchor points. The starting and ending points are not connected.

- To fill in the little gap near the center of the shape, zoom in, get the Direct Selection Tool, and drag a small rectangle around the first and last anchor points to select them both. Then go to Object>Paths>Close Path *or* Join. An alternative is to use the Direct Selection Tool to drag the last anchor point so it overlaps the first anchor point. If you're drawing a curved line like the one at the top of the previous page, you don't need a closed path.

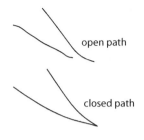

open path

closed path

- To smooth out the path, get the Smooth Tool (, in the same group as the Pencil Tool), and draw on or near the sections of the path that need smoothing. This will delete some of the anchor points and smooth out the lines somewhat. If you double-click the Smooth Tool in the Toolbox, you'll see a dialog box similar to the one below. Move the slider to achieve a smoother line, click OK, and try smoothing again.

After using the Smooth Tool

- You can also move, delete, and add anchor points. To move one, select it with the Direct Selection Tool and drag it to a new position. To delete a point, use the Delete Anchor Point Tool (, in the Pen Tool group) to click on the point. To add a point, get the Add Anchor Point Tool ( ) and click on the existing line where you want the new point to appear.

After dragging the handles at two anchor points

- You can manipulate the handles that emanate from the anchor points. This action changes the direction and size of the curves between the anchor points. To access the handles, click between two anchor points, or directly on one anchor point, with the Direct Selection Tool.

To achieve smooth curves right from the start, you can set the Pencil Tool preferences before you begin to draw. Double-click on the Pencil Tool, and a dialog box like the one below will appear. Use the Smoothness slider and experiment. The flower to the right was drawn using the settings shown here.

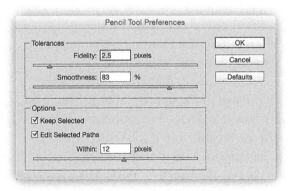

Pencil Tool Preferences

Tolerances

Fidelity: 2.5 pixels

Smoothness: 83 %

OK

Cancel

Defaults

Options

☑ Keep Selected

☑ Edit Selected Paths

Within: 12 pixels

A new flower with Smoothness set at 83%. The Smoothness setting for the original flower was zero.

There are many more tricks for using all of the drawing tools. Refer to BookDesign MadeSimple.com/resources for links to tutorials.

35

Using the Stroke panel

As you saw on page 259, the *color* of a stroke is selected in the Swatches panel. However, the Stroke panel is where you'll choose the weight and type of stroke. Open your Stroke panel at the right of your screen or by clicking Window>Stroke, and it'll look something like this:

The thinnest line acceptable to offset printers is 0.25 pt. So don't use the "hairline" option unless you're sure you won't be printing offset.

To add a stroke to text, select the text with your Type Tool, then use the Stroke panel to apply a stroke.

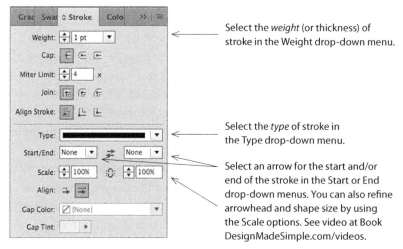

Select the *weight* (or thickness) of stroke in the Weight drop-down menu.

Select the *type* of stroke in the Type drop-down menu.

Select an arrow for the start and/or end of the stroke in the Start or End drop-down menus. You can also refine arrowhead and shape size by using the Scale options. See video at Book DesignMadeSimple.com/videos.

A few stroke types

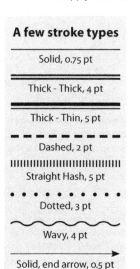

Solid, 0.75 pt

Thick - Thick, 4 pt

Thick - Thin, 5 pt

Dashed, 2 pt

Straight Hash, 5 pt

Dotted, 3 pt

Wavy, 4 pt

Solid, end arrow, 0.5 pt

Strokes can be applied to shapes created with shape tools (see chapter 33), to lines created with the Line Tool, Pen Tool, or Pencil Tool (see chapter 34), and even to text and image frames.

Select your shape, line, or frame using your Selection Tool, then select the type and weight of the stroke in the Stroke panel.

You can specify the size of start and end arrowheads and shapes by scaling them independently. Link the start and end sizes by clicking the link icon if you want them to stay proportionate as they are scaled.

Adding corner options to rectangles and polygons

There are five different corner options you can add to rectangles and polygons, shown to the right.

To add corner options to a shape, first either create a rectangle using the Rectangle Tool or a polygon using the Polygon Tool, or select an existing shape using your Selection Tool. Click Object>Corner Options to open the Corner Options dialog box (shown below).

The default corner options are for four square corners. You can change all four corners at the same time by leaving the link icon in the middle locked. Click one of the drop-down menus to see the five corner options and try a few to see how they look (with Preview checked, you can see the options as you try them). Make the corner option larger or smaller by clicking the up and down arrows next to the size. You can change any corner independently by clicking the link icon to unlock it.

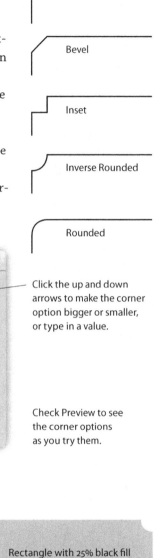

Fancy

Bevel

Inset

Inverse Rounded

Rounded

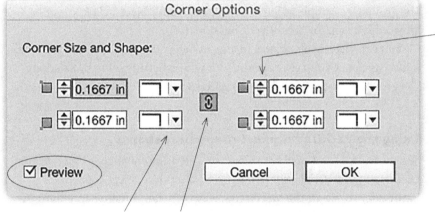

Corner Options

Corner Size and Shape:

0.1667 in   0.1667 in

0.1667 in   0.1667 in

☑ Preview   Cancel   OK

Click the up and down arrows to make the corner option bigger or smaller, or type in a value.

Check Preview to see the corner options as you try them.

Click the drop-down menu to try different corner options.

Click the link icon to unlock it and set each corner option independently.

Rectangle with 1 pt black stroke
No corner options added at top
0.125" rounded corners at bottom

9-sided polygon
with 40% star inset
10% black fill
0.1" bevel corners

Rectangle with 25% black fill

0.125" inverse rounded corners

36 *Putting objects into groups*

There are many instances where you may want to group two or more objects together so they don't get separated. For example, in *this* book, there are lots of diagrams with images, circles, arrows, and text, all meant to stay together (for example, the two diagrams opposite). You can select multiple objects by clicking on them individually while holding the Shift key. To deselect any object from the ones you've already selected, hold the Shift key while clicking on it.

How do you make sure various objects stay together? Using the Selection Tool, drag to select all the objects you want to stay together, then click Object>Group (or press Ctrl/Cmd+G). You'll see a dotted line around the group (see sample at left). To ungroup your objects, click Object>Ungroup (or press Ctrl/Cmd+Shift+G).

You can also group objects in stages. Say you group a few objects, then add a caption. Group the caption with your existing group by selecting the group and caption and pressing Ctrl/Cmd+G.

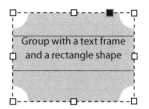

Group with a text frame and a rectangle shape

You can change text in an existing group by selecting it with the Type Tool. To change a shape or image, select it with the Direct Selection Tool (below).

Using the Pathfinder panel to combine shapes

Shapes can be combined to create new and different shapes by grouping them using the Pathfinder panel. Go to Window>Object & Layout> Pathfinder to see all the interesting ways you can combine and manipulate shapes and lines. Below are two examples of how you can combine a square and ellipse by either adding them together or subtracting one from the other. Have fun experimenting!

You can watch a demonstration of the Pathfinder at BookDesignMade Simple.com/videos.

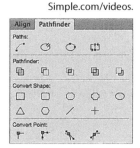

Pathfinder panel

two separate shapes

ellipse in front of square, Object>Pathfinder>Add

ellipse in front of square, Object>Pathfinder>Subtract

Adding a document bleed

37

Bleed is a printing term referring to anything printed beyond the edge of the page. When a shape, color, or image goes to the edge of a page or cover, it actually must print *past* the edge because trimming the paper after printing is imprecise. If a shape, color, or image ends right where the paper will be trimmed, there's a chance that a strip of unprinted paper will be left showing. To avoid this problem, all shapes, colors, and images that you want to go to the edge of your page or cover will actually have to extend ⅛" or 0.125" *past* the edge of the paper.

You probably included a bleed when you originally set up your document (see page 34), but if not, adding a bleed area to your document in InDesign is easy and can be done anytime from anywhere in your document (see below). Click File>Document Setup, then the triangle next to Bleed and Slug, to open the full Document Setup dialog box. In the Bleed area at the bottom, make sure the link icon at the far right is unbroken, then type 0.125 in the box at the left and press Tab. The same setting will fill in all the boxes. Click OK.

Switch to Normal view and you'll see that InDesign has added a red line 0.125" *outside* the edges of all your pages or cover. Now whenever you add a shape, color, or image to your pages or cover that goes right to the edge, make sure it extends to the edge of the bleed rather than the edge of the page.

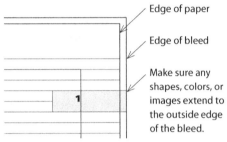

Edge of paper

Edge of bleed

Make sure any shapes, colors, or images extend to the outside edge of the bleed.

First make sure the link is unbroken.

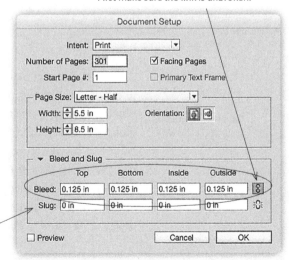

Ignore the Slug settings.

Using object styles

An object style contains a group of settings that makes an object (a shape, line, or frame) appear a certain way. Object styles control objects in a way similar to how paragraph styles control paragraphs.

Object styles are super-handy for making sure any text frames, shapes, and images you use frequently throughout your book are consistent. If you'll be constantly drawing arrows or circling things to point out features or applying text wraps to your images, it's quick and easy to set up an object style and apply it as you go. Consider creating an object style for image frames with text wraps, arrows, shapes, sidebar boxes, and even text frames for captions (see chapter 44).

Below are two examples of object styles used throughout *this* book:

This is the Screenshot object style, with rounded corners and a drop shadow.

The arrow shown above is used throughout this book. The Arrow object style is set for a 0.4 pt solid stroke with a simple arrow at the end.

See how Object Styles might help you at BookDesignMade Simple.com/videos.

Object styles control settings for fill and stroke, corner options, paragraph styles, text wrap, drop shadows, and much more. Besides keeping objects looking consistent, object styles make it easy to change objects globally. For example, you can change *all* your sidebar boxes to a different color just by changing that setting in your Sidebar object style. Or you can change its corner options. Any changes you make to an object style will change *all* the objects in your book with that style applied.

There are two steps involved in using object styles: 1) *creating* the object styles, and 2) *applying* the object styles.

Creating object styles

To create an object style, first select a shape, line, text frame, or image frame that is already set up the way you want it, then create a new object style for it. Here are the steps:

1 Open your Object Styles panel by clicking Window>Styles>Object Styles.
2 Using your Selection Tool, select a shape, line, or frame.
3 Click the fly-out menu in the Object Styles panel, then select New Object Style. Fill in the dialog box as shown below, then click OK.

Add a name here.

Later you can change any of the Style Settings by opening the appropriate setting and adjusting it as needed.

Make sure the Apply Style to Selection and Preview boxes are checked.

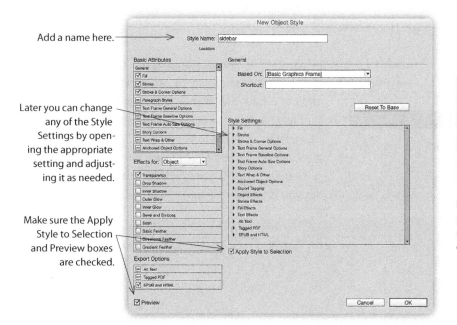

Object Styles panel fly-out menu

Drag your Object Styles panel into the dock at the right of your screen for easy access next time.

Applying object styles

Now that you've created an object style, it's easy to apply it to your objects. Using your Selection Tool, select the object you want to apply the object style to, then click that style in the Object Styles panel. Voilà!

As you add shapes, lines, text frames, or image frames to your pages, apply the appropriate object style to each one.

You might need to click the Clear Overrides icon (▢✸) at the base of the Object Styles panel to force the object to accept the style.

39

Using a library

The library function in InDesign is a very handy tool and easy to use. You simply set up a library (formally called an Object Library) for anything out of the ordinary that you use repeatedly in the book, such as graphics, inline art, fractions, foreign phrases, and so on. Whenever you want to use one of the items, you can simply open the library, which appears as a panel similar to any of your other panels, and drag the item onto the page. Here's how:

To see how an InDesign library works, and to compare it with object styles, watch the video at BookDesignMade Simple.com/videos.

1 Choose File>New>Library, and the CC libraries box might appear (see below). If it does, click No, then name your new library and save it to the same folder with your InDesign file. Note that it will have an .indl extension and that you will see it as an independent file in your folder.

2 In order to make the library always ready to use, dock it with the other panels on the right side of your screen. If you choose not to dock it, you can let it float

A Creative Cloud Library is an asset-sharing tool used among Adobe applications, devices, and users. You might find it useful, but it's not what we are discussing here.

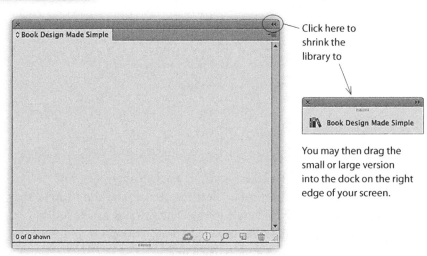

Click here to shrink the library to

You may then drag the small or large version into the dock on the right edge of your screen.

Book Design Made Simple.indl

in front of the document, or you can close it for now and then open it again anytime (File>Open).

3 With the library open, find an object that you want to add to it and use the Selection Tool to drag the object onto the Library panel. If it's type that you want to add, copy the type into its own text frame first, then drag the whole frame.

4 Double-click the object in the library, and name it in the space below the box in the library that it's now sitting in. The objects will arrange themselves alphabetically.

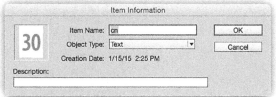

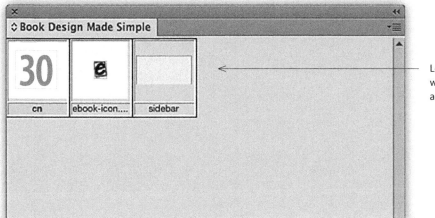

Left to right: a text frame with type in it, an image, and a graphic shape

5 When you want to use a library object, simply open the library and use the Selection Tool to grab the object and drag it onto your page or pasteboard. It will appear at full size, ready to use, while leaving the library object in place.

To change or replace a library object, drag it to the trash icon and answer Yes to the dialog box that appears (right). Then drag your new object into the libary and name it. This action does not affect any library objects that you've already placed.

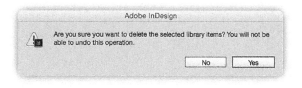

Please note that when it comes time to package your files (chapter 71), your library will not be included in the package (though the objects in the library will). If you want to include your library for future use, simply locate it on your computer and add it to the packaged folder.

Now that you've learned how to add shapes to your book and apply color and object styles to them, your next step is to learn how to add images and optimize them for printing (see Part VI: Adding Images).

Adding shapes and images to your pages usually affects the flow of text, and that's why it's important to add both to your pages at the same time. This constitutes the second pass through your pages, and you're almost there!

Part VI: Adding Images

40 *Preparing to add images*

If you're including images in your book, Part VI: Adding Images is for you! You'll have already set up your baseline grid in chapter 23 (which will help you to align your images nicely within margins and/or columns), and you'll also have learned about creating and applying object styles in Part V: Adding Shapes & Color (which will be useful for applying consistent text wraps to your images and captions).

If you don't have any images inside your book, feel free to skip to Part VII: Typesetting, where you'll do your final pass through all your pages. If you skip Part VI: Adding Images now, you'll come back to it when you design your book cover, to learn about getting permission to use images, as well as placing, sizing, and optimizing them for print.

In Part VI: Adding Images, you'll be using what you learned in previous chapters of this book about baseline grids, using a bleed, and using object styles. You'll also learn to use Adobe Bridge—a useful and labor-saving tool for organizing your images.

Adding images and captions will increase your page count. If you'll be printing on an offset press, you'll want your page count to fit into signatures. See chapter 48 for ways to adjust it to fit.

You may want to read through chapters 41 to 44 in this section while working on the first image in your book. That way, you'll be able to add a text wrap, caption, credit, and/or bleed to it right away and decide on its final size. All these things will affect the flow of text for the remainder of your chapter, so it's good to resolve each image, in order, as you progress through your pages.

So read on, or if there are no images in your pages, skip Part VI for now and come back to it later when you need it.

Getting permission to use images

41

Chances are you'll use at least one image in your book—the author photo! And commonly, you'll have front and back cover images and some photos, drawings, and/or illustrations on some of your pages.

Requesting permission is not only the law but also a common courtesy. Imagine how you'd feel if you found that someone used the material in *your* book without asking. So, when do you need to get permission? Simply put, if any of the images you're using were photographed, drawn, or created by someone else, you need to get permission.

Make a list of all the images used in your book, exactly where you got them, and who created them. Here are some of the possibilities.

- **online image bank** If you searched for your image in one of the many online stock photo providers, first read the fine print about licensing. When you begin your search, you can restrict the listing to royalty-free images, which are the best choice in most cases. A *royalty-free* image can generally be used for any purpose as often as you like— once you purchase it, of course. On the other hand, a *rights-managed* image or a *licensed* image will have restrictions, and you will pay only for the one intended purpose. You might find yourself using one of these if you want famous images or images of famous people. Start with a royalty-free search, then move on to rights-managed or licensed images if you can't find what you want.

- **elsewhere on the Internet** If you found an image somewhere else on the Internet, make sure you have permission to use it. You might assume that photos on sites such as Wikimedia Commons or Google Images are copyright-free, but that is not always the case. Read the fine print, and copy and paste the exact wording of the credit line into your list of permissions. If you need permission, get it.

- **a museum** Most museums charge a fee for use of their images, and they all have strict rules about how they can be used, so follow them

Visit BookDesignMade Simple.com/resources or look on page 379 of this book for a listing of some of the many image banks.

Even if you found your image on the Adobe Stock website, you must purchase a license to use it in your book.

Always use the exact credit or permissions wording you are given by any image provider.

If all your images are created by the same person, with the exception of a few, add a credit to the copyright page like this:

All photos by Glenna Collett unless otherwise credited.

and then add a credit to specific photos by adding to the end of the caption:

Photo credit: Fiona Raven

If your images don't have captions, add the credit underneath or up the side of the photo (see pages 295–297). The credit can be in very small type.

to the letter. Before the institution grants permission, they will want to know how large the image will be on the page, whether it will be printed in color or black and white, and the topic under discussion. You'll need additional written permission if you want to crop. Allow plenty of time (months, in many cases) for the permissions process.

- **historical photos**   These may be copyright-free, but they are often owned by an organization, such as a historical society. Ownership will be noted somewhere on the site you're visiting. Ask for permission.
- **public domain**   This term simply means works that have run out of their copyright and are now owned by the public—for instance, music by Beethoven. With images, this is a bit tricky, because although the object itself may be in the public domain, an image of it may not. An example would be a photo of a painting of an early American president. Think twice before assuming anything is in the public domain.
- **a photographer you've hired**   If you've hired someone to take any photo in your book—and this goes for illustrators too, of course—find out what wording they want for their credit line and follow it exactly.

How to write for permission

Search using the term "permission to use image" + the name of the institution.

You can sometimes find a permissions request form for a specific institution on the Internet. If there's no form, write a letter (email is fine) respectfully asking to use the image and telling the title of your book, the chapter title, and the topic of discussion. Tell the size at which you want to use the image and whether it will be black and white or color. Ask about fees and their preferred credit verbiage. Keep a record of all correspondence.

Where to list credits and permissions in your book

If you have only a very few, put them on the copyright page. If you have a great many, list them in your back matter under the heading "Photo [or Image or Illustration] Credits." You might list them in groups by creator or in numerical order by page number.

Another option is to place a credit line in small type next to each image (see page 297) or include it at the end of the image caption. There are many ways to deal with credits, so look in other books to see how they have handled them.

Organizing your images

Keeping your images well organized is one of those tasks you'll be glad you took the time to do. Here is a simple method: Give each image a number that shows what chapter it's in and its position. For instance, "03-06" would be the sixth image in chapter 3. (If you've already assigned numbers to your images and captions, simply follow your own numbering system.) Feel free to use descriptive information in the file name, but put the numbering scheme first so the files will always be in the correct order when listed (e.g., "03-06_orange_cat" would be followed by "03-07_brown_cow"). If it helps you, make a different folder for each chapter or part in your book.

It is a good idea to use short file names for ebook conversions.

Using Adobe Bridge

If you have a large number of images in your book, consider using Adobe Bridge as an efficient way to keep track of them. In Bridge, images are displayed at any size you like, from thumbnails to rather large, and you can place an image by simply dragging its thumbnail onto your page. If you are visually oriented, you might find this method more logical than using the Place command, which requires you to remember a file name—see page 288.

Adobe Bridge comes with any of the apps you lease through Creative Cloud.

Br Bridge icon

To use Bridge, you first need to install it. Open the Creative Cloud app, go to Apps, choose Bridge, and click Install. Once the download is complete, open Bridge. When the panel first opens, make sure it says Essentials at the top of the screen. Then use the navigation area at the left of the panel or at the top to locate the folder with your image files in it. Double-click that folder and your images will appear as thumbnails in the main panel. You can then size the entire screen to your liking, and the image thumbnail size with the slider at the bottom of the panel.

See an illustration of the Bridge screen on page 286.

Bridge is a very robust application that allows you to organize your images in any way you like. While viewing them all in one location, you

Navigate to the folder containing your images by double-clicking in the list on the left or at the top.

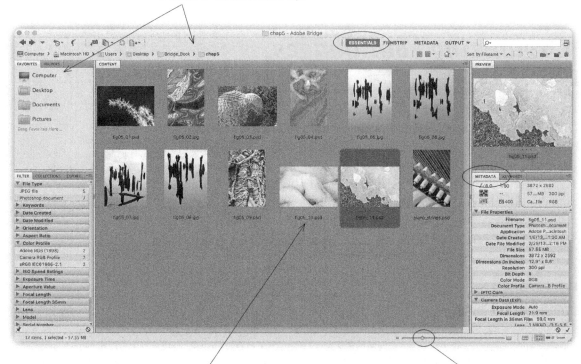

On the main panel, you can rename the image files. Also take this opportunity to look at them all simultaneously to discover any redundancies or other overall problems. Check the Metadata panel to see the resolution and color space of each image.

Use the slider to adjust the size of the images.

can compare and rate them, rename them, get information (metadata) about them, and even make contact sheets of them to share with others. View an Adobe or lynda.com tutorial to find out all the ways that Bridge can help you to work more efficiently.

To add an image to your book page, first you might want to make the Bridge screen a bit smaller, so that you can see your InDesign screen behind it. Then simply click on your image in Bridge, drag it off the Bridge screen and onto your InDesign screen, and you'll see your mouse loaded with the image. Click on your InDesign screen to activate it, then click to drop the photo onto your page or pasteboard.

Placing and positioning images

A picture is worth a thousand words, right? So your book's pictures need to be as high quality as you can possibly make them, and they must be well and intelligently placed. Before you learn the details of preparing your images for printing, you'll lay them out in your pages and make decisions about sizing and cropping.

First and most important: *Every image in your book must be a free-standing file.* In other words, each image will be saved on your computer with its own file name, as a specific file type (such as PSD, TIF, JPG, PNG, GIF, BMP, AI, EPS, and so on).

If some or all of your images are in your Word document, you'll need to extract them before proceeding. If not, go to page 288.

Extracting images from a Word document

In Word you may have inserted some images, but once they were embedded they became unusable by InDesign or Photoshop. This is why you deleted them before placing your manuscript in InDesign (see page 44). In doing that, though, you should have kept a copy of the original image files and can use them in your book. If not, here is how to extract images from a Word document:

1   Open the Word document with your images in it.
2   Save the document in Web Page (.htm) format. The result will be a folder containing an HTM file and a list of image files called "image001," "image002," and so on.
3   Select (single-click) each image in this folder (many of them will be listed two or more times). Find the highest-quality file for each image—almost always the largest file—and put it in a separate folder, ready to be used in your book. Don't worry about file format at this stage.

Placing images on the page

Images are always *placed* in InDesign, never copied and pasted. Why? Because if you copy and paste an image onto a page, it becomes embedded in your InDesign document, bloating your document's file size and making it impossible to optimize the image in Photoshop.

Conversely, when you *place* an image in InDesign, a link is created between the original image file and your InDesign document. The image exists as a separate file that can be sized, cropped, and optimized, and it still remains linked to your page in InDesign. You'll have control over your linked images through the Links panel. To open your Links panel, first look in your docked panels; if it's not there, click Window>Links.

Links panel before any images are placed

Placing images using the Place command

Using your Selection Tool, first click outside of any frames to make sure nothing is selected. Then click File>Place (or press Ctrl/Cmd+D) to open the Place dialog box. Browse for the file you want to place, then click Open. You'll see a miniature version of the image attached to your mouse pointer. Click once anywhere on your page or pasteboard, and the image will be placed in your document.

You can place multiple images at a time by selecting multiple images from a folder (hold Ctrl/Cmd while selecting images), then clicking Open. Your mouse pointer will be loaded with all the images you selected, and you'll place one each time you click on the page or pasteboard.

Placing images using Bridge

If you have a large number of images, you may want to organize them in Bridge, an application that is included in the Adobe CC package (see page 285). You can place an image from Bridge by first clicking on the image icon in Bridge to select it, dragging it onto your page, and then clicking anywhere on the page or pasteboard to place the image. Review chapter 42 for details on using Bridge.

If your placed image is much larger than your page or even the pasteboard, simply zoom out (Ctrl/Cmd+-) until you can see the entire image frame. Using the Free Transform tool ( ), click on one corner of the frame, hold down the Shift key, and drag inward to resize it.

Sizing and cropping images

After you've placed an image on a page, there are two easy ways to size and crop it: using the Free Transform Tool and using the Selection Tool. You'll probably find using a combination of both is easiest, perhaps starting with the Free Transform Tool and fine-tuning with the Selection Tool.

1   **Using the Free Transform Tool ()** The Free Transform Tool is best for making large adjustments to an image, such as reducing its size and rotating it. To change the size of your image, press and hold the Shift key, then click and drag on any corner of the image's frame. (Pressing the Shift key prevents the image from becoming distorted.) Feel free to reduce the size of the image as much as you like, but only enlarge it a bit, as images become blurry and pixelated if they are enlarged too much from their original size.

    Position your image on your page by dragging it. You'll want to align the image with your baseline grid, margins, columns, and text.

    Rotate your image by hovering anywhere outside the image frame and you'll see a curved arrow. Drag vertically or horizontally and you'll see your image rotating. You can also see your changes (amount of rotation) in the Control panel.

2   **Using the Selection Tool ()** The Selection Tool is best for fine-tuning the size of your image frame and cropping the image. Click on an image with your Selection Tool, and you'll see the frame around it (also called the bounding box). Drag your image into its final position on the page, then drag each side of the frame or bounding box as needed to fit the image exactly within a specific space.

    If you want to keep the frame or bounding box at a certain size but crop the image within it, first hover over the image with the Selection Tool until a doughnut appears in the center (called the content grabber). Hover directly over the doughnut and a grabber hand appears. Click once on the doughnut, and you'll see a frame with a different color appear around the image. You can now resize, rotate, and move the *contents* of the frame (i.e., the image) independently of the bounding box until you're satisfied. This is one way you can crop your image in InDesign.

Switch from the Selection Tool to the Free Transform Tool by pressing E. Switch from the Free Transform Tool to the Selection Tool by pressing V.

Use the Free Transform Tool for sizing and rotating images.

In positioning images, try to be as precise as possible. If you are having trouble with this, your guides might be the cause. Go to View>Grids & Guides and check or uncheck Snap to Guides. Keep this in mind anytime you move an object.

You can move an object a tiny amount with the Selection Tool and an arrow key. Every time you hit the key, the object moves one point.

link OK symbol   frame

handles

content grabber

The image frame or bounding box defines the edges of the *visible* image. Select it with the Selection Tool.

Use the content grabber to select the *contents* of a frame (i.e., the entire image).

Alternatively, you can use the Direct Selection Tool ( ) to select the contents.

Commonly in InDesign, a file that you place will look very rough on the page. But before you panic, print out that page, and likely you'll discover that the image is fine. This is simply something you'll have to get used to; you can trust the way the file looks in Photoshop.

Cropping is a powerful tool. If you chose to cut a sibling out of a family portrait, for instance, it would send a strong message to your family. In less extreme cases you can still affect how your readers interpret what you're showing. So be as thoughtful when working with photos as you were when writing your manuscript, for this is visual editing.

Experiment with your images to see how they look best. Move the image around in its frame using the content grabber to find the best position and size for the main focus of the image. Crop anything distracting in the background, and feature the most important part of your image prominently.

In this image, the water is uninteresting, the muddy shoreline is unattractive, and the second bird and the log are distracting.

The focus is now on the important part of the image.

If you look at all of your images together (try using Adobe Bridge, see page 285), you might be able to come up with a conscious cropping style. Perhaps you'd like all the portraits to show only the face. Or you might want all the photos of buildings to show the surrounding area as well—trees, neighboring buildings, and the like.

Try to crop and size your images so they fit within your baseline grid and also your vertical guides, the invisible grid you may have set up when constructing your A-Master page (see page 120). This will keep your pages neat and allow the first line of your captions (when you add them) to start on the baseline grid.

another possible photo width

older than you, and must know better'; and this Alice would not allow without knowing how old it was, and, as the Lory positively refused to tell its age, there was no more to be said.

At last the Mouse, who seemed to be a person of authority among them, called out, 'Sit down, all of you, and listen to me! I'LL soon make you dry enough!' They all sat down at once, in a large ring, with the Mouse in the middle. Alice kept her eyes anxiously fixed on it, for she felt sure she would catch a bad cold if she did not get

First line of caption is sitting on the baseline grid.

← Top of photo aligns with the top of a line of type.
Bottom of photo is on the baseline grid.

You can watch demonstrations of placing an image in a shape and in type at BookDesignMadeSimple .com/videos.

You might also consider framing an image inside a non-rectangular shape. To do so, first create the desired shape with the Ellipse or Polygon Frame Tool (see chapter 33). Make sure the shape's fill color is None. Then select the shape with the Direct Selection Tool and place (File>Place) your image file in it. The image will appear at full size inside the shape, and you can size and crop it using the Direct Selection Tool or content grabber.

Whenever you size and crop an object—in this case, an image—your Control panel displays what you're doing. After you've finished making your photo look good, check to make sure the image is still proportional in size to the original. Both width and height scale percentages should match, as shown below. If they don't, type the correct value in one of the scale percentages boxes, make sure that the chain symbol is unbroken, and press Enter/Return. This will result in a proportional image.

When enlarging or shrinking your image, hold the Shift key to keep its width and height proportional.

Width and height
of image or bounding box. If you want to change the size by typing in a new value (but also keeping it proportional to its original size), make sure the chain symbol is unbroken.

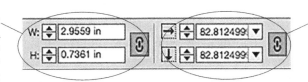

Scale percentages
of the image itself. These values will be the same if your image was sized proportionately.

Positioning images on your pages

Generally it's best to position images at the top or bottom of the page, although naturally there are exceptions. For instance, if you have an outer column, you can place images anywhere north-south in the column, wherever they are the most useful (such as in *this* book). Just be sure not to leave only a few lines of type stranded at the top or bottom of a page above or below an image, as readers will not notice them.

Unless you're required to use entire, uncropped photos (which is usually the case when you're reproducing museum pieces), you have the opportunity to interpret the meaning and importance of each image in your book. It probably seems obvious that a full-page image is more important than a postage-stamp sized one. This is the time to decide which images need to be emphasized over others. Make a list of all images for each chapter and give each one a rating of A, B, or C to signify its importance. This will help you solidify your thoughts about them and set up your layout scheme for the chapter.

If you notice that all the most significant images are bunched together in one part of the chapter, consider rearranging your copy a bit. Showing all the largest illustrations close to each other not only will unbalance the chapter but also will create some difficult layout problems.

Generally it's best to size your images no larger than the type area on the page, unless you want to use a bleed (see below). You'll find that if you use the type column width for photos as often as possible, they will look neater than if you use random widths. (On the other hand, if you have a side column like the one in this book, use that width as often as you can.) When you're sizing photos, leave room for captions, whether they'll appear below or to the side.

If you decide to use a bleed for your image, be sure to extend it the full amount of the bleed, which is usually ⅛″ (0.125″). Your bleed area should appear in red around the edges of your pages in Normal view—see page 275 to set this up if you haven't already. Of course, you must make sure that the most important part of your image is not going to bleed off the page or fall into the gutter between pages, and beware of cutting images of people awkwardly. Also, remember that your printer is not going to trim your book's pages precisely the same for each book; the trimming can vary as much as ⅛″.

If you want your image to bleed off the page, make sure to align the edge(s) with the red bleed lines that are 0.125″ outside the edge of your page.

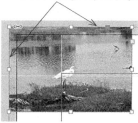

It's also possible to place an image across the gutter or spine of a 2-page spread. Whenever an image, shape, or line is placed across two adjoining pages, it's called a crossover. Images can look very attractive placed across a 2-page spread. Just make sure that the portion of the image that disappears into the spine or binding of the book isn't an important part of your image (such as a face).

The rectangle at the top of this 2-page spread has a 0.125" bleed off the top of both pages, and it also forms a crossover, being placed across the gutter (or spine) of two adjoining pages.

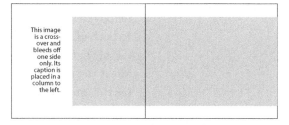

This image is a cross-over and bleeds off one side only. Its caption is placed in a column to the left.

This image is a crossover and bleeds on all four sides. Its caption could be placed on the previous or following page.

This image is a crossover and bleeds off one side only. Its caption is placed in a column to the left.

If you're pairing images of dissimilar shapes on a page, try to make them both the same height (next to each other), both the same width (one above the other), or overlapping (see right). This way, they look like a matched pair and not just two images that happen to be sitting near each other. When you're satisfied with your pairing, you'll find the images easier to move if you group them first by selecting both images, then pressing Ctrl/Cmd+G. (Later, if you want to ungroup the images, select the group and press Ctrl/Cmd+Shift+G.)

As you work with your images, check each one in the Links panel (toggle the arrow in the lower left corner to reveal the Link Info section) to make sure its effective resolution is at least 300 ppi. If the value is below 300 ppi at your image's current size, try using the image at a smaller size on the page. You can see the effective ppi changing in the Links panel as you change the size of your image. (If you really want to use the image at a size where its effective resolution is less than 300 dpi, you'll need to resample the image in Photoshop as described on page 304).

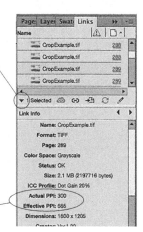

Ideally, your image's Effective PPI should be a minimum of 300.

44

Adding captions and text wraps

Once you've placed an image on your page and positioned it approximately in its final position, you'll want to add its caption and a text wrap to both of them (so the text runs around the image and caption, not on top of them). That way you'll be able to see how the image and caption affect the flow of text on your pages, then adjust their size and placement for the most pleasing layout.

Adding captions

If all of your captions are going to be the same width, consider putting an empty caption text frame into a library (chapter 39) to save time. With your cursor inside the caption text frame, select the **cap** paragraph style (but don't add any type), then put the text frame into the library. Now all of your captions will automatically take on the **cap** style when you insert them into the frame.

Chances are your captions are still within your main narrative and have the Caption [**cap**] paragraph style applied to them. To extract a caption from the main narrative, select the whole caption by quadruple-clicking it with the Type Tool, then cut it from the main narrative by clicking Edit>Cut or pressing Ctrl/Cmd+X.

Next, create a new text frame for the caption by dragging the Type Tool. Paste the caption in the new text frame by clicking Edit>Paste or pressing Ctrl/Cmd+V. Now that your caption is in its own frame, use your Selection Tool to position the frame below or beside the image.

If your captions are not already within your main narrative, simply create a new text frame by dragging your Type Tool, then type the caption in it and apply the Caption [**cap**] paragraph style to it (see page 78).

Placement considerations for captions

The most common types of captions are summarized below, but note that these ideas are very general. Work out a good style and method for your book and stick with it as much as possible.

1 **Put captions below the images** in books that have a single column of type. Set them in the italics of your book text or in a contrasting

typeface, about 1 pt smaller, to differentiate them from the narrative. Align them at left with the image.

Your Caption paragraph style (see page 78) includes aligning the first line of your caption to the baseline grid. This creates a consistent amount of space between the bottom of your image and the top of the caption (see top right).

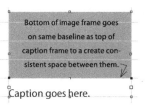

Bottom of image frame goes on same baseline as top of caption frame to a create consistent space between them.

Caption goes here.

If an illustration appears at the bottom of a page, place the last line of the caption flush with the last line of type. To do this, you must stop the first line of your caption from aligning to the grid. Place your cursor anywhere in the caption, then select the Do Not Align to Baseline Grid icon in your Paragraph panel (see right).

Do Not Align to Baseline Grid icon

2. **Put captions beside the images** if you have a column for that purpose (as in *this* book). Use a different typeface, possibly a sans serif if your book text uses a serif font, or use the italic font of your book text. Make the captions smaller than the book text but still readable. The type can be set to align toward the image, and usually side captions are placed to the outside of the image (i.e., away from the spine).

3. **Captions in art books** get a different treatment. Often each image is numbered, so give the label and number (e.g., "Plate 12.4") its own style and color (create a character style with small caps and a different color, for example). For a full-page illustration, the caption can appear on the facing (or even the previous) page, perhaps with a directional note ("left," "opposite page," "overleaf") in italics at the beginning of the caption text. Consider using arrows or triangles as pointers if you think they will help (e.g., ▶ ▷). You can find them in the Glyphs panel (Type>Glyphs). If the typeface for your captions doesn't include an appropriate symbol, try a dingbat or symbol typeface. Examples: Zapf Dingbats, Webdings, Wingdings, and Symbol. Create a new character style for the pointer, specifying its typeface, color, and size.

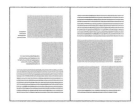

Images toward the spine (above) are preferable to images away from the spine—notice the big empty hole in the middle of the spread below.

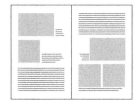

4. **Place captions *above* charts and tables.** Your readers will go through the material in a linear fashion, left to right and top to bottom, so it's best to give them the general explanation of the table in the caption before they start.

Adding a text wrap

Since the advent of desktop publishing, we often see photos sticking into the text with the text running around them. That's because this is now a very simple procedure called Text Wrap. Start by opening your Text Wrap panel (click Window>Text Wrap), and dock it with your other panels.

The following explains a simple way to add a text wrap to an image and the caption placed below it. If your captions are positioned below your images, then this method is for you! If not, page 298 explains all the ways that text wrap can be used for your images and captions.

Adding text wrap to an image

Make sure your image is in *front* of the type you want to wrap around it (text wrap only affects text *behind* it). To put one frame in front of another, select the frame, then click Object>Arrange and choose Bring to Front, or press Ctrl/Cmd+Shift+].

Select an image frame using your Selection Tool, then choose the Text Wrap options shown below left. Note there is no space *below* the image. That's because your caption will be placed below the image. Then create a new object style called **images**, following the instructions on page 277, and apply the **images** object style to every subsequent image you place.

Adding text wrap to a caption

If you prefer, you can use a library instead of object styles to achieve the same goal.

Select a caption frame using your Selection Tool, then choose the Text Wrap options shown below right. Note there is no space *above* the caption. That's because your image will be placed above the caption. Then create a new object style called **captions** and apply the **captions** object style to every subsequent caption you place.

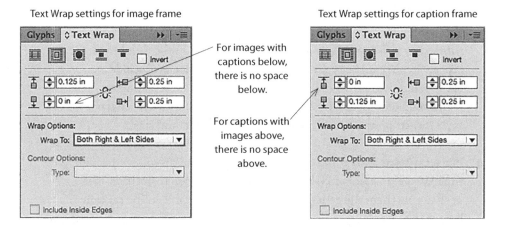

Text Wrap settings for image frame

For images with captions below, there is no space below.

For captions with images above, there is no space above.

Text Wrap settings for caption frame

Adding a credit to the side of an image

If you're planning to place credits up the side of your images, you'll need to create a new object style for credits, specifying the amount of space between the top of the credit text frame and the credit text. That way, all your credits will be an equal distance away from the edge of your images.

Create a new text frame by dragging your Type Tool, and type in the image credit text. Add an inset space to the top of your credit text frame by clicking Object>Text Frame Options and making the selections shown to the right and click OK. Then switch to the Selection Tool and create a new object style called **credits**, following the instructions on page 277, and apply the **credits** object style to this and all subsequent credit text frames.

Finally, rotate the credit text frame by clicking the Rotate 90° Counter-clockwise icon in the Control Panel (⟳). Place the credit frame alongside your image, and align the top of its frame flush with the right side of your image.

Because the text wrap applied to your image only affects text *beneath* it, the text in your credit text frame shouldn't be affected by the text wrap around the image. If the text wrap *is* affecting it, then bring the credit text frame to the front by selecting it with your Selection Tool, then clicking Object>Arrange and choosing Bring to Front, or pressing Ctrl/Cmd+Shift+].

With your credit text frame selected, click the lock icon to unlock it, then set your Top Inset Spacing to suit.

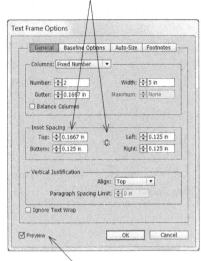

Check the Preview box so you can see the changes as you make them.

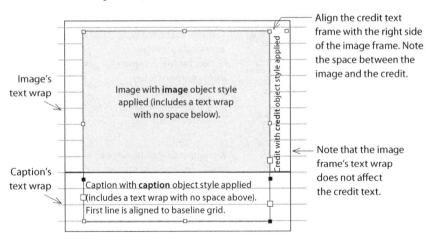

Image's text wrap

Image with **image** object style applied (includes a text wrap with no space below).

Credit with credit object style applied

Caption's text wrap

Caption with **caption** object style applied (includes a text wrap with no space above). First line is aligned to baseline grid.

Align the credit text frame with the right side of the image frame. Note the space between the image and the credit.

Note that the image frame's text wrap does not affect the credit text.

Create a new paragraph style for your credits based on **tx1**, but with small type (6 or 7 pt, depending on the typeface you're using).

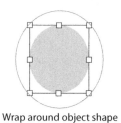

bounding box

text wrap

Wrap around bounding box

Wrap around object shape

Different options for using a text wrap

There are lots of ways you can use the text wrap features in InDesign. Click on any image or text frame, then hover over the top row of options in the Text Wrap panel. From left to right, they are:

- **No text wrap** means that the text runs right over the image. If you want this effect, don't use the text wrap feature at all, and simply place the image behind the type (Object>Arrange>Send to Back).
- **Wrap around bounding box** is most likely the option you'll use. The bounding box is the frame around your image or caption.
- **Wrap around object shape** is best for when the object has an interesting shape (see left, or the two rubber duckies on page 299). Use sparingly, for special effect.
- Use **Jump object** if you've put an image in the middle of the page and want the text to jump right over the image and continue.
- **Jump to next column** makes the text stop just above the image and then start up again at the top of the next column or page.

Once you've chosen an appropriate text wrap option, you'll need to set up your inset (white space) measurements. As you've done before, click on the chain link in the middle of the panel to make all the values either the same (link closed) or independent of each other (link open). Experiment with measurements until you are happy with the amount of space between the frame and the type.

General text wrap options, left to right: No text wrap, Wrap around bounding box, Wrap around object shape, Jump object, and Jump to next column

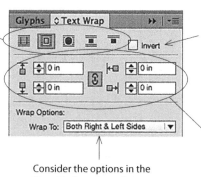

Combined with the Wrap around object shape option, the Invert feature places type *inside* the shape instead of wrapping type around it, as shown to the right.

Combined with the Wrap around object shape option, the Invert feature places type *inside* the shape instead of wrapping type around it.

Amount of white space above, below, to left, and to right of image

Consider the options in the Wrap To drop-down list, too.

The text wrap options shown on the previous page are easy to implement—just select your image and choose one of the icons at the top of the Text Wrap panel. But suppose you want to create a custom shape for your text wrap?

bounding box

text wrap

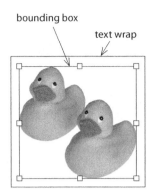

The image to the right shows two rubber ducks on a white background inside a rectangular frame or bounding box. Applying a regular text wrap will form a rectangle around the bounding box, but a text wrap that follows the shape of the ducks (like the one to the left) is more interesting. When you have shapes like this isolated on a white or transparent background, InDesign can detect the shape in the image. Choose the options shown in the Text Wrap panel to the right.

Alternatively, you may want the text wrap to create a completely different shape. In chapter 34 you learned how to create and edit shapes using the Pen Tool and the Direct Selection Tool. These same tools can be used to change the shape of the text wrap.

First select the image and apply any text wrap other than No Text Wrap. Switch to the Pen Tool (or press P).

Create a new anchor point by clicking anywhere between anchor points, and delete an anchor point by clicking directly on it (you'll see a small plus or minus sign next to the Pen Tool). Switch to the Direct Selection Tool temporarily by pressing Ctrl/Cmd to move anchor points or drag handles (as described in chapter 34). Have fun creating custom shapes for your text wrap!

There are other, more complicated, ways to use text wrap, but chances are you won't need them for your book. If you're interested, refer to an InDesign tutorial for instructions.

When you've placed all your shapes and images, added captions to them, and added text wraps where needed, you're ready to package all your linked images into a folder. This is explained in chapter 45.

Packaging your book

Once you've placed all your images, you're ready to package your book. Packaging saves a *copy* of your latest InDesign document and all the images used in your book into a new folder. The images will be linked to your InDesign document. If you choose to optimize any of your images (see chapter 46), you'll make changes to the images in your new folder, while your original images remain intact in their current locations.

Click File>Package to open the Package dialog box. You'll see it's divided into sections on the left for Fonts, Links and Images, and so on. You may see some warnings, but just ignore these for the time being, as you'll make any necessary repairs in chapter 46. Then click Package.

The next dialog box you'll see is for Printing Instructions, so just click Continue for now. Next you'll see a Create Package Folder dialog box like the one at the lower left. Check the boxes at the bottom as shown, navigate to the place where you'll save your new folder, and type a name into the Save As box. Then click Package.

Now your InDesign document, image files, and document fonts are all together in one folder. You'll be using this set of linked images from here on, but you still have your originals in case you need them at any point down the road.

If you are using the Book feature to package, see our blog at BookDesignMade Simple.com/using-the-book-feature-in-indesign.

NOTE: Close the InDesign document you are working on *right now* before proceeding any further. Open the new document in the new folder you just created, and proceed with that one. Also, if you've been using a library (chapter 39), move or copy it into your newly packaged folder.

BOOK DESIGN MADE SIMPLE · PART VI: ADDING IMAGES

Optimizing your images

Now that you've placed all your images, applied text wrap to them, added captions and/or credits, and packaged them into a new folder, it's time to decide whether or not you need to optimize your images.

What, exactly, *is* optimizing? It's improving an image by adjusting its colors or contrast, making it look sharper, increasing its resolution, and making any other changes so the image looks better *in print*.

To optimize or not to optimize?

If your book will be printed with a POD printer such as Amazon KDP or IngramSpark, you probably don't need to optimize your images. When you create a PDF to upload to the printer (see chapter 71), Acrobat will automatically do a number of things to optimize your images: reduce any higher-resolution images to 300 dpi, convert the colors in your images if needed, and crop them to their frames. Simple, right?

Of course you'll want to first check any PDF you'll be uploading to your printer, to make sure all the images look fine. If any happen to need extra attention, you can spend some time improving them, using this chapter as your guide.

If you have some images with effective resolutions *below* 300 dpi, or if any colors are looking dull or lacking contrast in the PDF, you may want to optimize those images individually. This chapter will guide you through a number of steps to help your images look their best.

For a quick way to figure out if your image is high enough resolution for print, see our blog post at BookDesignMadeSimple .com/is-image-high-resolution-for-print.

At what stage should images be optimized?

The best time to optimize your images is when the design and layout of your cover and pages are finished. That way, you'll be sure there are no further changes to the size, placement, and cropping of your images, and you'll optimize them just before creating your final PDF for the printer.

If you choose to optimize any images individually, you'll be taking the following steps:

1 Checking the image in the Links panel
2 Making sure its effective resolution is at least 300 ppi, and cropping the image if needed
3 Converting the colors to a color profile
4 Improving colors and/or contrast
5 Saving the updated image in an appropriate format for printing
6 Relinking the updated image to your InDesign file

You'll use Photoshop to optimize your photographs and Illustrator to optimize any vector images you may have. In this chapter you'll learn the simplest methods to accomplish the essentials of what you may need. If you prefer, you can ask your printer's prepress department to do this for you (for a fee, of course). To execute more complex changes to your images, you may need to take an online tutorial from Adobe, sign up for lynda.com lessons, go through the steps in a how-to book, or take a class. See BookDesignMadeSimple.com/resources for links.

1 Checking your images in the Links panel

The Links panel displays a wealth of information about each image (look in your docked panels or click Window>Links to open it). In the upper section of the panel you'll see a list of your images with their page numbers to the right. You'll also see any alerts for missing or outdated links. (See the example opposite.)

In the upper left corner of any image on your page you'll see a link OK symbol (⊜), a modified file symbol (⚠), or a missing file symbol (❓). The latter two symbols have the same meanings as in the Links panel.

Click on any image with your Selection Tool. You'll see the image's file name highlighted in the upper section, and in the lower section all the information for it is shown. If you don't see the lower section called "Link Info" at the bottom of the list of images, click the arrow at the bottom left of the panel, and it will appear.

The only items on this long list of specifications that are important to you right now are: **Actual PPI**, **Effective PPI**, **Color Space**, and **Format**. Later in this chapter you'll optimize these aspects of your images, but for now here is a simple summary of these items:

- **Actual ppi** is the number of pixels per inch in your original image file. **Effective ppi** is the number of pixels per inch in the image *at the size it is used* in your book. (If there is no actual or effective ppi showing in your Links panel, that means it's a vector image and you don't need to worry about resolution.) If effective ppi is less than 300, that means either the actual ppi is too low, or you have enlarged the image too much on your page and thereby reduced its ppi. Either way, the image will look fuzzy when printed. If this is the case, you have four choices:

1 obtain a higher-resolution image from your image source,
2 use the image at a smaller size so that it will be printed at 300 ppi,
3 resample the image in Photoshop (see page 306), or
4 pay the printer's prepress department to fix this problem for you.

- **Color space** must be either CMYK, Grayscale, or Bitmap. RGB, the color mode used by digital cameras, scanners, computer monitors, and ebooks, is not used in printed books unless your printer specifically states that it is okay. (At the time of writing, Amazon KDP accepts images in RGB format.) You'll convert your images to CMYK or grayscale in either Photoshop (see pages 308–310) or Illustrator (see pages 311–312), or alternatively pay your printer's prepress department to do it for you. Remember that if your book is going to be printed with black ink only, *all* of the images used on your pages must be in either grayscale or bitmap format.

- **Format** This should say PSD (Photoshop), TIFF (or TIF), JPG, PNG, BMP, AI, or EPS. If you come across a different file extension, check under **Creator** and see whether the file was created in Photoshop or Illustrator, as you may still be able to work with it. After you've optimized your images, you'll save them as PSD or JPG files in Photoshop, or as AI files in Illustrator (see pages 314–316).

Get started by checking your first image in the Links panel. Look at the settings for Actual PPI, Effective PPI, Color Space, and Format, to see whether any need optimizing for print. If so, make the necessary adjustments by following the instructions in this chapter.

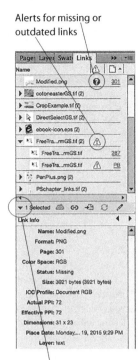

Alerts for missing or outdated links

Click the arrow in the Links menu to see the information about each file.

You'll optimize PSD, TIFF (or TIF), JPG, and PNG files in Photoshop, and AI and EPS files in Illustrator.

If you have not already downloaded Illustrator or Photoshop, simply go back to Creative Cloud and do that now. See page 7.

2 Sizing, cropping, and resolving ppi issues in Photoshop

You don't need to worry about sizing or resolution in images created in Illustrator. They are vector images, made up of lines and curves that are defined with mathematics, and the math stays the same no matter the size.

If you're new to Photoshop, you'll find it similar to InDesign in a number of ways. For starters, both have a Control panel across the top, a Toolbox down the left, and panels docked on the right. Open Photoshop and InDesign at the same time and, if possible, size their screens so you can see both at once, side by side. If not, just jump back and forth between programs as you proceed.

You've already selected an image in InDesign and checked its actual and effective ppi in the Links panel. If its effective ppi is *close to or greater than 300 ppi,* you only need to size and crop the image in Photoshop. However, if the effective ppi of your image is *much smaller than 300 ppi* (say, 280 ppi or less), you'll need to resample the image in Photoshop.

Sizing and cropping an image

Optimize the images in the new packaged folder you created in chapter 45 (all the linked images will be in the Links folder).

Open your image in Photoshop by clicking File>Open, browse for your image, then click Open. You'll adjust the size and resolution of your image and crop it to size all at the same time using the Crop Tool in Photoshop.

First find the exact size of your image's frame or bounding box in InDesign. Switch to InDesign, select your image with the Selection Tool, then look for the width and height displayed in the Control Panel at the top. Write down the dimensions and also note how the image is cropped.

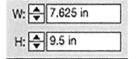

Width and height shown in the Control panel.

Switch back to Photoshop and click on the Crop Tool (⊓) in your Toolbox on the left. The crop menu will appear at the top of your screen. Make the selections as shown below, and type in your image dimensions (followed by "in" for inches). You'll see a crop frame in front of your image, changing size and shape as you do this.

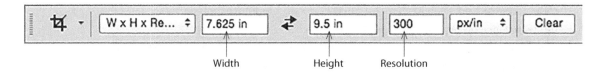

Width   Height   Resolution

Cropping in Photoshop gets rid of unneeded data and keeps your book's file size down.

Drag any handle on the crop frame and the frame will get proportionately larger or smaller. Use this frame to crop your image to the way it looks in InDesign. When you're satisfied, press Enter/Return. Now your image is 300 ppi at the exact size it's placed in InDesign. Voilà!

An easy workflow for optimizing your images

There are so many instructions and options in this chapter! To help you make sense of it all, this sidebar offers a summary of the steps to optimize an image and then put your improved image on your book page in place of the old one. These are the most important procedures, gathered into one place. Here's what you do:

To optimize PSD, TIF, JPG, or PNG files

1   Open Photoshop and InDesign at the same time. In InDesign, select an image with the Selection Tool. Find the width and height of the image in the Control panel. Write down the dimensions, noting how the image is cropped.

2   In Photoshop, if the effective resolution is 300 ppi or higher, size and crop the image. Using the Crop Tool (⧉), fill in the width and height and 300 px/in in the top menu, adjust the frame around the image until it matches the visible parts on your book page, then press Enter/Return (see page 304); *or*, if the effective ppi is too low, resample the image (see page 306).

3   Convert the image to the correct color mode: CMYK, Grayscale, or Bitmap. To convert to CMYK or Grayscale, click Edit>Convert to Profile, then choose the appropriate color profile from the Pro-file drop-down menu under Destination Space (see pages 307–309). To convert to Bitmap, see page 310.

4   If you need to improve the colors and/or contrast in your image, complete the steps on page 313.

5   Flatten the layers (if you choose to do so) by click-ing Layer>Flatten Image (see page 314).

6   Save the image as a PSD file by clicking File>Save As and choosing PSD (see page 315).

7   Return to InDesign and relink the image. Select the image frame with your Selection Tool, then open your Links panel, click on Relink (⊖), and find your new optimized file (see page 317).

To optimize AI or EPS files

1   Open Illustrator and InDesign at the same time.

2   In Illustrator, convert the image to the correct color mode, CMYK or Grayscale. To convert to CMYK, click Edit>Assign Profile, then choose the appropriate color profile from the Profile drop-down menu (see page 311). To convert to grayscale, select the entire image by dragging over it from outside the top left corner to beyond the bottom right corner. Click Edit>Edit Colors>Convert to Grayscale (see page 312).

3   Convert any type in the image to outlines. Select the type with your Selection Tool, then click Type>Create Outlines (see page 312).

4   Save the image as an AI file by clicking File>Save As and choosing AI (see page 316).

5   Return to InDesign and relink the image. Select the image frame with your Selection Tool, then open your Links panel, click on Relink (⊖), and find your new optimized file (see page 317).

Remember that you packaged your links in chapter 45. So your original images are still in their old locations, and you're now going to optimize the images in the Links folder of your new package. You can name your optimized files with the same file names as the originals (although they may have new file extensions) without worrying about mixing them up or losing your original image files in case you need them later.

Resolving too-low ppi issues by resampling

Read the blog post at Book DesignMadeSimple.com/is-image-high-resolution-for-print to learn the quick formula to determine whether an image is high enough resolution.

Let's say you're using an image in your book that you've found on the Internet (with permission, of course). When you check the actual ppi of the image in your Links panel in InDesign, it's 72 ppi (the standard resolution of images intended for viewing onscreen).

In addition to this, you may have enlarged and/or cropped the image when you placed it in InDesign, so its effective ppi is now even lower. Yikes! You could simply change the resolution of your image to 300 ppi in Photoshop, but you'll likely end up with a very blurry image, one that isn't good enough quality to print in your book.

Make a good effort to find a higher resolution version of your image before using this method.

If you want to use an image at a much larger size than its current resolution allows, you'll need to resample the image by enlarging it to an enormous size, sharpening it, then reducing it back to the size you want. Use this type of drastic resampling as a last resort, only if you really can't find a better or higher-resolution version of the image. The results are almost never as sharp as you'd like.

Here are the steps:

A special method for preparing a computer screen shot for print is spelled out at BookDesignMade Simple.com/preparing-a-screenshot-for-print.

• First you'll enlarge your image. In Photoshop, open your Image Size dialog box by clicking Image>Image Size. Fill in the dialog box as shown below. Experiment with other setting in the Resample box while looking at the preview. Then click OK, and Photoshop will do its best to make the resulting huge image look good.

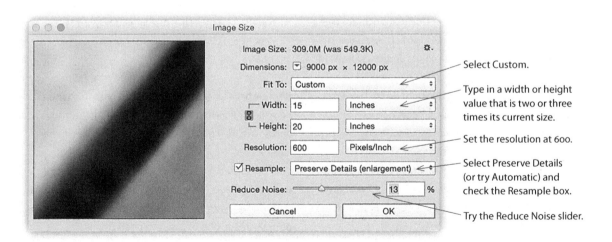

Image Size

Image Size: 309.0M (was 549.3K)

Dimensions: 9000 px × 12000 px

Fit To: Custom — Select Custom.

Width: 15 Inches — Type in a width or height value that is two or three times its current size.

Height: 20 Inches

Resolution: 600 Pixels/Inch — Set the resolution at 600.

☑ Resample: Preserve Details (enlargement) — Select Preserve Details (or try Automatic) and check the Resample box.

Reduce Noise: 13 %

Cancel   OK — Try the Reduce Noise slider.

- Now your image will be huge—in fact, it probably won't fit on your screen. Reduce its display size so you can see the whole image on your screen by pressing Ctrl/Cmd+- (hyphen) as many times as you need to.

- Next, you'll sharpen your image. Open the Unsharp Mask dialog box by clicking Filter>Sharpen>Unsharp Mask. With the Preview box checked, you'll be looking at a small sample of your image. Hover over the sample with your mouse and you'll see a hand tool you can use to move around within your image. Or you can click anywhere in the image itself to see a sample of that area to view the most important parts of the image as you work. Move the three sliders left and right until you get the best possible effect. At this size, no image is going to look great, so use the little zoom tools to see smaller and larger views. You can always undo your work with Ctrl/Cmd+Z, or Edit>Undo, or Edit>Step Backward. If you need more fine-tuning, try the Filter>Noise>Reduce Noise sliders.

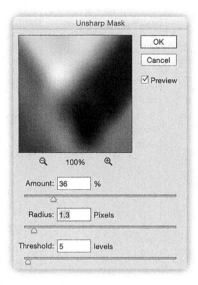

- Finally, you'll size and crop your image to the exact size it's placed at in InDesign. To do this, follow the instructions under Sizing and Cropping an Image on page 304.

3   Converting your images to a color profile

Your images will most likely be printed with black ink only (for book pages) or with CMYK ink colors (for color pages and your book cover). Before you optimize any of the colors in an image or change the level of contrast, you'll want to see how that image will look when it's printed. Converting an image to a suitable color profile will show you that.

Images coming from cameras and scanners are in RGB color. There is a much larger range (or gamut) of colors available in RGB than in CMYK. An image may look fabulous onscreen, with lots of light, bright greens and glowing oranges, but you may find those lustrous colors can't be printed using the four CMYK ink colors. That's why color profiles are helpful.

If you already know where your book will be printed, find out from your printer what color profile you should use. POD printers, such as IngramSpark and Amazon KDP, don't provide color profiles, but Photoshop comes with lots of generic color profiles to choose from.

See page 257 for an explanation of RGB and CMYK colors.

If your printer provides you with a color profile, it'll be a file with the extension .icc. Unzip it if necessary, and save the file to your desktop. To install it in Windows, right-click the file and select Install Profile. To install it on a Mac, copy the file to Computer\Macintosh HD\Library\ColorSync\Profiles. Once it's installed, you can select the profile in Photoshop and Illustrator.

Converting RGB images to CMYK in Photoshop

You've checked the color space of your images in the Links panel in InDesign, and chances are you have at least a few RGB images to convert to CMYK. So open your image in Photoshop, then open the Convert to Profile dialog box by clicking Edit>Convert to Profile.

Below you'll see the Convert to Profile dialog box. The Source Space shows which profile your image is in right now. It probably says Adobe RGB (1998) or another RGB profile.

You'll choose a CMYK color profile for your Destination Space. Read the options below, then choose a profile for your Destination Space:

- **Amazon KDP, IngramSpark, and other POD printers** POD printers don't specify color profiles; however, their PDF instructions include exporting to the default "Working CMYK - U.S. Web Coated (SWOP) v2" color profile, so you'll be fine choosing that one.
- **Offset printer** Find out which color profile your printer uses from their website and download it, or ask them to provide it to you.
- **Not sure?** If you're in doubt, choose U.S. Sheetfed Coated v2 for color images on your cover and color pages.

For a book with lots of images, you can accomplish this task in batches! See BookDesignMadeSimple.com/converting-multiple-images-to-cmyk-in-photoshop.

This is your image's current color profile.

Choose a suitable color profile from this drop-down menu.

Choose these options from the Engine and Intent drop-down menus, and be sure to check the two boxes at the bottom as shown.

Check the Preview box.

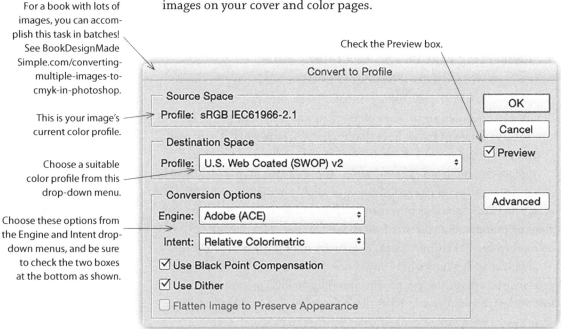

Converting color images to grayscale in Photoshop

If your pages will be printed with black ink only, then you'll need to convert any color *photographs* to grayscale. If you have any images that are black and white only (with *no* shades of gray), those images are considered "line art" and will be treated differently (see below).

  To convert a color image to grayscale, open your image in Photoshop, then open the Convert to Profile dialog box by clicking Edit>Convert to Profile. In the Destination Space drop-down menu, choose the Gray Gamma 2.2 profile. You'll see your image change to grayscale right away. Select the options shown below, and click OK.

Grayscale means that, in addition to black and white, your image contains many shades of gray (such as in a photograph).

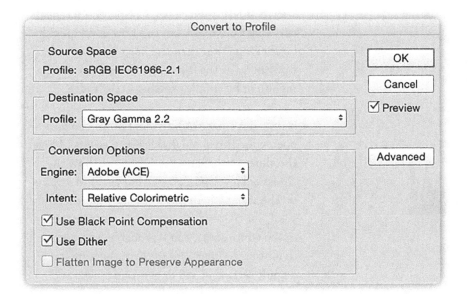

Converting black and white images to bitmap in Photoshop

If you have an image that's black and white (with *no* shades of gray), you'll convert it to a bitmap (unless it's an EPS or AI file, in which case you'll convert the color in Illustrator; see page 312).

  Line art differs from photographs because it needs to be saved at a much higher resolution (1200 ppi) so it doesn't look blurry. The bitmap format (BMP) saves high-resolution images at a very small file size because it only saves black pixels (white areas become transparent in InDesign).

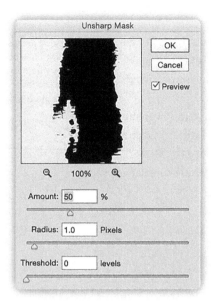

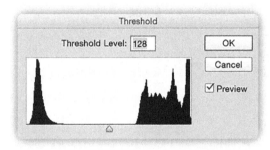

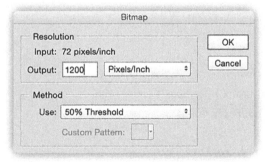

50% Threshold means that any shade of black higher than 50% will become black, and anything less will become white.

Here are the four steps to creating bitmaps:

- First add some contrast to your image using Image>Adjustments>Brightness/Contrast.

- Then you'll use Unsharp Mask to sharpen the edges of your image. This creates a sharp difference between the black and white, to help differentiate them as much as possible. So click Filter>Sharpen>Unsharp Mask to open the Unsharp Mask dialog box. Adjust the settings as shown at left, then click OK. Now you'll repeat this step once more, but can now do so quickly by clicking Filter then Unsharp Mask (which now shows at the top of the Filter drop-down menu), or by simply pressing Ctrl/Cmd+F.

- Next, click Image>Adjustments>Threshold to open your Threshold dialog box (see left). Move the slider to the left and right to see how the threshold level affects your image. Find a place on the slider where the blacks in your image are solid, yet there aren't any black spots or specks in the white areas. You'll probably find you need to move the slider a bit to the right from its default setting of 128 to get solid blacks and clear whites. Then click OK.

- Finally, convert your image to a bitmap by clicking Image>Mode>Grayscale. You'll get a message asking whether it's okay to discard color information, so click Discard. Then click Image>Mode>Bitmap to open your Bitmap dialog box. Set Output to 1200 ppi and choose 50% Threshold, as shown at left. Then save as a PSD file (see page 315).

Converting RGB images to CMYK in Illustrator

Start by opening your image in Illustrator. If the image was created in a previous version of Illustrator, you might get a warning screen that says "This file contains text that was created in a previous version of Illustrator. This legacy text must be updated before you can edit it." Click Update.

To find out the current color space of the image, look at the tab at the top of your screen, where the file name is shown. If it says RGB, then open the Assign Profile dialog box by clicking Edit>Assign Profile.

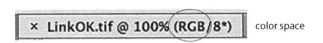 color space

Aside from the color space, the tab also shows the current zoom level (100% in this example).

Below you'll see the Assign Profile dialog box. Read the menu options, then choose a CMYK profile for your image:

- **Amazon KDP, Ingram Spark, and other POD printers** POD printers don't specify color profiles, however their PDF instructions include exporting to the default "Working CMYK - U.S. Web Coated (SWOP) v2" color profile, so you should be fine choosing that one.

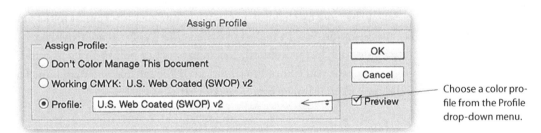

Choose a color profile from the Profile drop-down menu.

- **Offset printer** On your printer's website, find out which color profile your printer uses and download it, or ask them to provide it to you. If you receive one, it will be a file with the extension .icc. Unzip it if necessary, and save the file to your desktop. To install it in Windows, right-click the file and select Install Profile. To install it on a Mac, copy the file to Computer\Macintosh HD\Library\ColorSync\Profiles.
- **Not sure?** If you're in doubt, choose U.S. Sheetfed Coated v2 for color images on your cover and color pages.

These are the same instructions given on page 307. If you already have the profile, there's no need to install it again.

Converting color images to grayscale in Illustrator

Open your image in Illustrator. If the image was created in a previous version of Illustrator, you might get the same warning screen as described on page 311. If so, click Update.

Using your Selection Tool (it looks just like the Selection Tool in InDesign), select the entire image by dragging over it from outside the top left corner to beyond the bottom right corner. Click Edit>Edit Colors>Convert to Grayscale. All the artwork in your image will turn to black and shades of gray.

Converting type to outlines in Illustrator

If your image has any type in it, and especially if the illustration was drawn by someone else, you should convert all of the type to outlines. (If someone else drew the illustrations, instruct them to do this before they send the art to you.) This action converts the letters to shapes so they'll always print properly, regardless of whether or not you have the exact typeface installed on your computer. After the type is converted to outlines, the words can no longer be edited. So before you work with this file, be sure to save it as a copy (File>Save a Copy) or give it a new file name so you can go back to the original later if necessary.

Anchor points in Illustrator are like the ones you see when you draw a shape in InDesign. Each point is movable (see page 268) with the Direct Selection Tool.

Select the type by clicking on it with your Selection Tool (it looks just like the Selection Tool in InDesign), then click Type>Create Outlines. Notice that each letter suddenly has many anchor points and you could alter its shape if you wanted to (but don't). Repeat this operation until all of the type in your image has been converted to outlines.

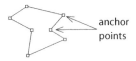

anchor points

Select some type and you'll see a line under it. →

After the type is converted to outlines, it'll have anchor points just like shapes in InDesign.

You might find it interesting to note that you can create type outlines in an InDesign file, too, using this same method. In that way, you can insert an image inside a letter, using the letter shape as the image frame.

You can watch a demonstration at BookDesign MadeSimple.com/videos.

4   Improving the colors and/or contrast in your images

In this section you'll try to make your images look better in just a few quick and easy steps in Photoshop. Save different versions of the image so you can easily get back to earlier ones if you like them more.

Use these suggestions for color or grayscale photographs (but not for bitmaps, EPS, or AI files).

- **Basic levels** Open your photo. Click Image>Adjustments>Levels and, with the Preview box checked, click Auto (right). If you think the photo is improved, click OK. If not, click Cancel.

- **Brightening** You can enhance what you did in the previous step with the Brightness/Contrast feature. Click Image>Adjustments> Brightness/Contrast. Use the sliders to change whatever you like (see below). Have fun playing with the effects, but it's best to be conservative. A good rule of thumb is to make changes of less than 20% to keep your photos looking realistic.

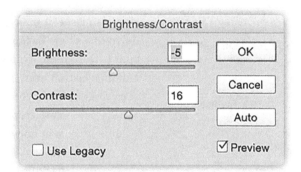

- **Sharpening** If you'd like to sharpen or soften your photo a bit, click Filter>Sharpen>Unsharp Mask. With the Preview box checked, you will be looking at a small sample of the photo, and if you hover over the sample with your mouse you'll see a hand tool that you can use to move around to view the most important part of the photo as you work. Now move the three sliders left and right until you get the effect that you want (see top of page 310).

- **Beyond the basics** Since the entire reason for Photoshop's existence is to improve the way photos look, there are dozens of other things you can do to your images. Feel free to explore and experiment, but don't forget to save, save, save!

5 Saving your image files

Now that you've optimized your images, in either Photoshop or Illustrator, be sure to save your files. When you packaged your InDesign file (in chapter 45), copies of all your original image files were saved in a new folder together with your InDesign file. That is the folder you're working in now, so all your original image files are still intact in their original locations. That's good, as you may want to go back to one of those uncropped RGB images down the road.

You'll want to use your RGB images in your ebook.

Image file size is an especially important issue in an ebook.

All of your updated images will be saved in your new packaged folder under the same names, although some will have different file extensions. So there's no need to worry about overwriting your original images or losing any original image files.

Flattening layers in Photoshop—yes or no?

Photoshop and Illustrator files include layers, just as InDesign files do. You may have purposely created layers in your image file, or your camera or scanner might have automatically saved your image onto a layer. Open your Layers panel by clicking Window>Layers to see whether you have any layers aside from the default Background layer.

Saving an image with layers in Illustrator does not affect its file size, so there's no need to flatten any images in Illustrator.

Saving an image with layers in Photoshop adds to its file size, so if file size is an issue, it makes sense to flatten the layers (i.e., reduce the layers down to a single Background layer) before saving the image for use in your InDesign file. One larger file size isn't a big deal, but if you have several images that aren't flattened, you'll notice a difference. Look at the status bar at the bottom left of your screen and you'll see your flattened/unflattened file sizes (see example at left). Base your decision on whether or not to flatten the file on the difference in file size. Also be aware that flattening an image adds a white background to any transparent areas within the image, so if your image has transparent areas, don't flatten it.

Doc: 27.2M/52.4M

Flattened file size on the left and unflattened file size on the right.

Default Background layer

If you decide to use your layered file in InDesign, save it as a PSD file (see page 315) and place it in your InDesign document. To get back to it quickly for editing while you're working in InDesign, open the Links panel, select the image, go to the flyout menu, choose Edit With, and then choose your version of Photoshop from the list.

If you choose to flatten an image, first save the PSD file *with* its layers intact, in case you want to re-edit the image in the future. Once saved, flatten the layers by clicking Layer>Flatten Image. Click File>Save As to save a flattened copy, and add FLAT to the file name so you'll know it's the flattened file. Then relink it to your InDesign document (see page 317).

Create a separate folder for archiving your layered PSD files. That way they'll be available down the road.

Saving files in Photoshop

Save your optimized images in Photoshop in PSD, TIFF, JPG, or PNG format (in order of preference). PSD is favored for a number of reasons: 1) it saves *all* the image data, unlike the JPG format, which discards much of it to keep the file size small, 2) PSD files can contain more than one layer (although saving with layers will increase the file size), 3) PSDs can be saved with areas that remain transparent when placed in InDesign (see page 403), and 4) PSDs can be edited from within InDesign (see page 314).

Save your file by clicking File>Save As and choosing a format from the Save as type (PC) or Format (Mac) drop-down menu (below left). Photoshop should default to saving this new file in the same location as the previous one (in the Links folder, where you packaged your InDesign file). If not, browse for the correct folder.

Every time a JPG file is saved, more data is stripped away to reduce the file size. If you want to use this format, work on the image in Photoshop (PSD) format, then save to JPG when you are completely finished with it.

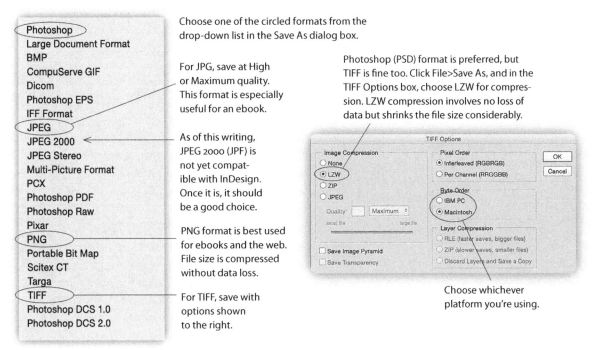

Choose one of the circled formats from the drop-down list in the Save As dialog box.

Photoshop
Large Document Format
BMP
CompuServe GIF
Dicom
Photoshop EPS
IFF Format
JPEG
JPEG 2000
JPEG Stereo
Multi-Picture Format
PCX
Photoshop PDF
Photoshop Raw
Pixar
PNG
Portable Bit Map
Scitex CT
Targa
TIFF
Photoshop DCS 1.0
Photoshop DCS 2.0

For JPG, save at High or Maximum quality. This format is especially useful for an ebook.

As of this writing, JPEG 2000 (JPF) is not yet compatible with InDesign. Once it is, it should be a good choice.

PNG format is best used for ebooks and the web. File size is compressed without data loss.

For TIFF, save with options shown to the right.

Photoshop (PSD) format is preferred, but TIFF is fine too. Click File>Save As, and in the TIFF Options box, choose LZW for compression. LZW compression involves no loss of data but shrinks the file size considerably.

TIFF Options

Image Compression
○ None
⦿ LZW
○ ZIP
○ JPEG
Quality: [ ] Maximum
small file   large file

☐ Save Image Pyramid
☐ Save Transparency

Pixel Order
⦿ Interleaved (RGBRGB)
○ Per Channel (RRGGBB)

Byte Order
○ IBM PC
⦿ Macintosh

Layer Compression
○ RLE (faster saves, bigger files)
○ ZIP (slower saves, smaller files)
○ Discard Layers and Save a Copy

OK
Cancel

Choose whichever platform you're using.

Saving files in Illustrator

Save your optimized image in Illustrator by clicking File>Save As and choosing AI from the Save as type (PC) or Format (Mac) drop-down menu (see top and left below). It should default to saving this new file in the same location as the previous one (in the Links folder, where you packaged your InDesign file). Then click Save and you'll see the Illustrator Options dialog box appear with the default settings as shown at the bottom right. Click OK to save your image.

Choose AI as your file type.

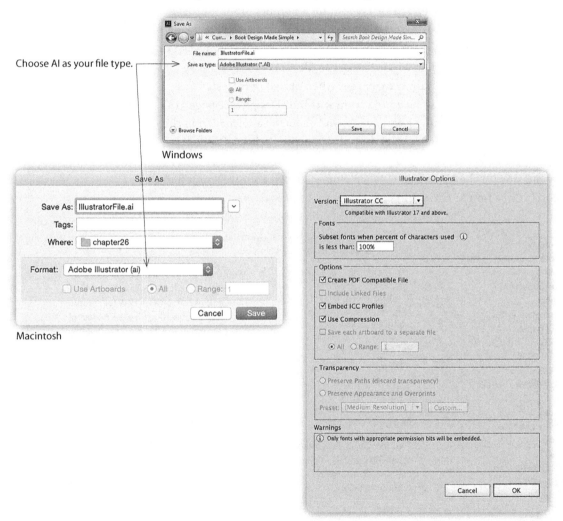

Windows

Macintosh

6   Relinking your images to the InDesign file

When you've finished optimizing and saving an image, you'll need to relink it in your InDesign file. Go back to your InDesign file and select the image using your Selection Tool. You'll see that the image file name is highlighted in the Links panel (the old, pre-optimized file name, possibly with a file extension that you have since changed).

To link your selected image with its newly optimized file, click the Relink icon (⊖), browse for your optimized file, then click Open. If you resized the image in Photoshop, it might not be positioned in the frame exactly the way you had it before. If so, press Ctrl/Cmd+Alt/Opt+E to refit the image to the frame.

If you optimized an image without changing its file name, you'll see an exclamation point symbol next to the image file name in the Links panel. Select the file name and click the Update Link icon, and the linked file will be updated. Again, if the image isn't positioned in the frame exactly the way you had it before, press Ctrl/Cmd+Alt/Opt+E to refit it.

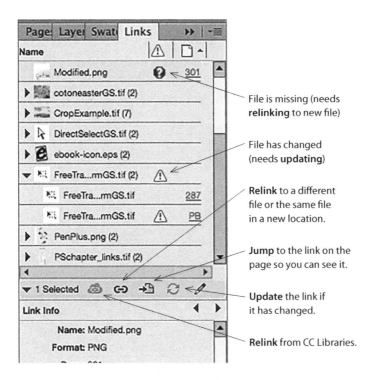

File is missing (needs **relinking** to new file)

File has changed (needs **updating**)

Relink to a different file or the same file in a new location.

Jump to the link on the page so you can see it.

Update the link if it has changed.

Relink from CC Libraries.

In Part VI: Adding Images, you set up your baseline grid and added all your images and captions to your pages. This changed the flow of text on your pages and probably created more pages than you had before.

And now that you've designed all the elements on your pages and applied paragraph, character, and object styles to them, your text and images are pretty much in their final places.

That's a huge accomplishment!

You're ready to do your third and final pass through your book. In Part VII: Typesetting, you'll fine-tune your text, paragraphs, and pages so that every 2-page spread looks perfectly professional.

You're nearly there!

Part VII: Typesetting

Planning your final pass

Your book pages are now substantially complete. You've added styles to all your text and placed your images and captions. You're ready for your final pass through all the pages.

Why do another pass? You've probably noticed that even though you've added styles to all your text, some of the text still requires some polishing. When you placed your images, your type probably moved around a good deal. And, if you intend to print more than 1,000 copies of your book, you'll probably use an offset press, so you'll want to review chapter 48 and adjust the page count in your book for the most cost effective printing.

Once you've finalized all your pages, you'll create a separate master page for each chapter in your book (unless it's a novel) and apply the appropriate one to each of your chapters. At this stage, your book will be ready for proofreading and, after you've made the proofreading corrections to your pages, it'll be ready for indexing (if you intend to include an index). Adding and typesetting the index is the last thing you'll need to do.

So get started on your final pass. If you'll be using a print-on-demand printer or digital printing, skip chapter 48 about page count, and carry on with chapter 49.

Page count for offset printing

If your book will be printed digitally, there's no need to worry about page count, because your book can have any even number of pages.

However, if your book will be printed on a press, you'll need to consider your page count. Because large sheets of paper are used on presses, several pages of your book will be printed on one sheet of paper, then folded and trimmed. Depending on the printer's sheet size and the trim size of your book, each sheet usually holds 8, 16, 32, or 48 pages. The folded sheets are called signatures, and the signatures are bound together to form a book.

Reminder: In a book, every single page is counted, whether a page number is showing or not.

Example of an 8-page signature

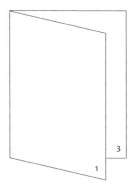

Take a sheet of paper and fold it in half. You'll have 4 pages.

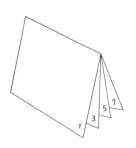

Fold it in half again, and you'll have 8 pages.

Number the pages as if they are pages in a book, then unfold your sheet of paper. The two sides of your paper will look like this:

1	8
4	5

7	2
6	3

The way the pages are positioned on each side of the sheet is called imposition, and your printer will do this for you. One sheet of paper with 8 pages printed on it is an 8-page signature.

Why page count is important for offset printing
Signatures

Ask your printer for the number of pages per signature for *your* book.

Books printed on a press need to have their pages fit into signatures. It is most cost-effective to print in 32-page signatures for a sheet-fed press or 48-page signatures for a web press (explained on page 22).

Perceived value

If you have a slim volume, consider increasing your page count to give potential readers a greater perceived value and to command a higher price for your book. For example, you may want your novel to be over 200 pages so it will be a similar size to other novels selling for the same price.

Minimizing production costs

If you have a tight budget, you can reduce your page count to keep your production costs lower. With a lower page count, your proofreading, indexing, printing, and shipping costs will all be lower.

How close is your current page count to signatures?

Check the chart below. What is the closest page count you can work toward? If your book currently has, say, 232 pages, you can work toward 224 or 256 pages (32s) or 240 pages (48s).

	32-page signatures (for an offset sheet-fed press; best if you have top-quality images for coffee-table or children's books)	48-page signatures (for an offset web press; cheaper if you have b&w images only and don't need top-quality images)
1	32	48
2	64	96
3	96	144
4	128	192
5	160	240
6	192	288
7	224	336
8	256	384
9	288	432
10	320	480
11	352	528
12	384	576
	etc.	etc.

If your page count lands between two signatures, then consider including a half-signature. This usually costs very slightly more but is often well worth it.

Some printers allow quarter-signatures. Again, the cost is slightly more, but may be worth it to you.

Easy ways to increase your page count

See which ideas will work the best for *your* book. It's easiest to implement these changes before adding shapes and images as the text will reflow.

1   **Add blank pages at the back** Easy, right? Simply add blank pages at the back of your book if you're a few pages short of your optimum page count. No one will notice. Two blank pages actually become only one blank sheet of paper, so even if you have six or eight blank pages at the back, there will only be three or four blank sheets.

2   **Add testimonials at the front** Add two new pages at the very front of your book and put testimonials or reviews there. If you have a lot of these, you may need to add several pages, but always add an even number so your title page or half title page starts on a recto page.

3   **Spread out your front matter** Add a half title page followed by a blank page, so that your title page is now on page iii. That will add two pages to your front matter. Sometimes the Contents can be spread over two pages rather than one full page. Consider adding an epigraph on a recto page, followed by a blank page, thereby adding two more pages. If your front matter is fairly lengthy (more than, say, six pages), consider adding two pages at the end of it, just before chapter 1, with a second half title page on the recto side and a blank page following it. Having spacious front matter is a good way to create extra pages without having to change any of your chapters.

4   **Start each chapter on a recto page** Add a blank verso page to the end of every chapter that ends on a recto page. It's an easy way to add a few extra blank pages without being obvious. However, if this creates way too many blank pages, then reconsider. You don't want your book to look padded.

5   **Start each chapter farther down the page** Add more space before your Chapter Number (**cn**) and Chapter Title (**ct**) paragraph styles. They don't have to be at the top of the page. This can give some chapters an extra page, thereby adding to your overall page count.

6 Create new parts Divide your book into parts. Add two new pages at the beginning of each part. On the recto page, put the part number and title (see chapter 24), and leave the verso page following it blank.

7 Increase your margins Generous margins look attractive. The margins in your current document (as set up in chapter 7) are very conservative to keep your page count and production costs as low as possible. However, if you want to create more pages, then increasing your margins is a good way to do so (see chapter 20).

8 Increase your type size and/or leading Even a slight increase—from, say, 11/14 to 11.5/14.5—can create extra pages (see chapter 22). Remember to change your baseline grid to match the new leading.

9 Change your trim size It sounds drastic but can be a simple fix. If your trim size is 6″ × 9″, changing it to 5.5″ × 8.5″ or 5″ × 8″ can make a difference of several pages (see chapter 19).

10 Use drop folios Books often have running heads and folios in the top margin. Moving the folios to the bottom of the page requires a larger bottom margin, thereby reducing the number of text lines per page.

Decorative rules allow this page to be 4 lines shorter.

11 Add a decorative rule to the top and bottom of each page, between the text block and the running head and folio This is a great way to reduce the number of text lines on each page by two or four without being obvious. The top and bottom margins will be even bigger, to allow a horizontal line to separate the running heads at the top and folios at the bottom from the text block.

12 Spread out your back matter Redesign your back matter headings so they occupy more space at the top of the page. Increase the type size and leading (but never make these larger than your main text type). Decrease the number of columns in your endnotes and index. Add a recto page inviting readers to visit your website, followed by a blank page. Add a page about the author, with a photo and bio.

Easy ways to decrease your page count

1 **Remove all unnecessary blank pages** Your title page, chapter 1, and the first section of your back matter must all begin on recto pages, but everything else can just follow on.

2 **Condense your front matter** Don't include a half title page. Use a smaller type size on the copyright page and include the acknowledgments and/or dedication on the copyright page.

3 **Condense your chapter openings** Start each chapter at or close to the top of the page. Consider placing your chapter number and title on the same line to save space (see page 158).

4 **Running chapter titles** To save even more space, start each chapter immediately below the previous chapter (see example at right). Create a two- to four-line Space Before in the Chapter Title (**ct**) paragraph style to make the chapter openings obvious so your readers can easily identify them.

5 **Create new parts by adding a part number and/or title just before the chapter title that follows it** Instead of using two whole pages for a part divider, add a heading at the top of a new page (Part II—Title, for example), followed immediately by the next chapter title.

6 **Decrease your margins** Reducing your margins can make a difference to your page count, as long as your pages don't look cramped (see chapter 20). Most printers require a minimum of 0.5″ on all margins, except 0.75″ for the inside margin.

a running chapter title

ALICE IN WONDERLAND

two people! Why, there's hardly enough of me left to make ONE respectable person!'

Soon her eye fell on a little glass box that was lying under the table: she opened it, and found in it a very small cake, on which the words 'EAT ME' were beautifully marked in currants. 'Well, I'll eat it,' said Alice, 'and if it makes me grow larger, I can reach the key; and if it makes me grow smaller, I can creep under the door; so either way I'll get into the garden, and I don't care which happens!'

She ate a little bit, and said anxiously to herself, 'Which way? Which way?', holding her hand on the top of her head to feel which way it was growing, and she was quite surprised to find that she remained the same size: to be sure, this generally happens when one eats cake, but Alice had got so much into the way of expecting nothing but out-of-the-way things to happen, that it seemed quite dull and stupid for life to go on in the common way.

So she set to work, and very soon finished off the cake.

THE POOL OF TEARS

'Curiouser and curiouser!' cried Alice (she was so much surprised, that for the moment she quite forgot how to speak good English); 'now I'm opening out like the largest telescope that ever was! Good-bye, feet!' (for when she looked down at her feet, they seemed to be almost out of sight, they were getting so far off). 'Oh, my poor little feet, I wonder who will put on your shoes and stockings for you now, dears? I'm sure _I_ shan't be able! I shall be a great deal too far off to trouble myself about you: you must manage the best way you can;—but I must be kind to them,' thought Alice, 'or perhaps they won't walk the way I want to go! Let me see: I'll give them a new pair of boots every Christmas.' And she went on planning to herself how she would manage it. 'They must go by the carrier,' she

28

If you find that InDesign is adding pages at the end of the book every time you decrease your page count, turn off Smart Text Reflow by going to Preferences (InDesign>Preferences on a Mac)>Type and unchecking the Smart Text Reflow box.

7 **Decrease your type size and/or leading** Even a slight decrease—from, say, 11/14 to 10.5/13.5—can reduce the number of pages (see chapter 22).

8 **Change your trim size** If your trim size is 5″ × 8″, changing it to 5.5″ × 8.5″ or 6″ × 9″ can make a difference of several pages (see chapter 19).

9 **Decrease the type size and/or leading in your back matter** Back matter is often set one or two points smaller than the main text, particularly for bibliographies, references, glossaries, and indexes. Increase the number of columns in your endnotes and index. (Sometimes, though, adding a column produces the opposite effect and actually adds pages!)

As you can see, there are many ways to increase or decrease your page count. Some are easy, and some are a bit more complicated, requiring changes to paragraph styles.

During your final pass, keep in mind your goal of increasing or decreasing your page count. You may find ways of adding a page to or removing a page from every chapter.

Adding, deleting, and moving text, pages, and styles

As you go through your final pass, you may find places where you want to add or remove pages, or perhaps move some pages to a different place in your book (say, move your Acknowledgments from the front matter to the back matter). You can even move pages to a different book! You might want to do this if you're planning two different editions or a series.

This chapter explains how to:

- Link and unlink text frames
- Add new pages
- Remove pages
- Move pages within the same document or to a new document
- Transfer styles from one InDesign document to another

InDesign has some ways of handling text flow that aren't immediately apparent. For example, if you delete a page using the Pages panel, you'll find that the text is still there within your linked text frames, and InDesign has simply added a new page to the end of your book so that no text is hidden (remember Smart Text Reflow was enabled in your Preferences, on page 30).

Linking and unlinking text frames

Before you decide to move pages in your book, think about whether linking or unlinking text frames might accomplish your objective. It's important to understand how text threads work so you can change them if necessary. Make sure you can see your text threads before you begin (View>Extras>Show Text Threads), then follow the steps on the next pages for the variations on linking and unlinking text frames.

Linking a new empty text frame

In InDesign you can easily insert a new, empty text frame into a chain of already linked frames. Here's how:

If you draw a frame with the Selection Tool or a shape tool, you can convert it to a text frame in one click by going to Object>Content and choosing Text, or by clicking inside it with the Text Tool.

1   Draw a new text frame with the Type Tool.
2   Using the Selection Tool, click on the out port of the frame you want to appear *before* the new frame.
3   Click the loaded text icon inside the new text frame and the text from the previous frame will flow into the new one. Text that follows will also be threaded from the new frame.

Linking a full text frame

If you have a text frame that already has text in it, you can link it to the beginning of a series of full, threaded frames, or to the end, but not to the middle of the series. To add a full frame to the *beginning* of a series, follow these two steps:

Anytime you're in the middle of an operation, with a loaded text icon to place, and you change your mind, simply go to the Toolbox and click on any tool. Your original operation will be cancelled and you can start over.

1   Click on the out port of the new full frame.
2   Click the loaded text icon at the upper left of the frame you want to link to. Your text will flow together.

To add an already full frame to the *end* of a series:

1   Click on the out port of the last full frame in the series.
2   Click the loaded text icon at the upper left of the frame you want to add. The text will flow together.

To link text in the *middle* of a series of threaded frames, you'll copy and paste instead:

1   Use the Type Tool to copy (Ctrl/Cmd+C) or cut (Ctrl/Cmd+X) the text you want to add.
2   Put your cursor in the text where you want the copy to appear and paste (Ctrl/Cmd+V) the copy.
3   Using the Selection Tool, delete the text frame that it came from.

Unlinking text frames

This operation is simple. In order to unlink text frames, do the following:

1   Using the Selection Tool, double-click on the out port of the frame you want to keep. The type disappears from the second frame.
2   The first frame will have the red overset text symbol (⊞) at the out port. Either extend the text frame to fit the overset text, or make a new text frame, click on the out port, and then click again inside the new text frame. The overset text will flow into the new frame.

Perhaps you simply want to delete one text frame from a series. All you have to do is to delete it using the Selection Tool, and the copy that was in it will flow to the next frame.

Adding, deleting, and moving pages

Before you add, delete, or move any pages, look at your Pages panel. Go to the fly-out menu, and make sure that Allow Document Pages to Shuffle and Allow Selected Spread to Shuffle are checked. "Shuffling" in InDesign means that if you add one page, the one after it will move down to the next spread, and all pages after it will move forward too. Without checking these two shuffle options, you could end up with more than two pages in your spread, as in the example to the right.

You also have the option of disabling Smart Text Reflow by going to Preferences (InDesign>Preferences on a Mac)>Type and unchecking the Smart Text Reflow box. This will prevent InDesign from adding new pages at the end of your book every time you make a change. If you've finished adding images to your book, you'll find this especially helpful.

Oops! If this happens to you, undo your work (Ctrl/Cmd+Z), check the Allow Document Pages to Shuffle option in the Pages menu, and start over.

Adding new pages

Maybe you have overset text at the end of your book, or you simply need to add a page in the middle. There are two basic ways to do this. Review both methods that follow before you decide which will work better for your circumstance.

Insert a page break

Insert a page break by pressing Enter/Return on your *numeric* keypad, or choosing Type>Insert Break Character>Page Break.

The first method is to simply insert a page break somewhere in your text. A blank page will appear where your cursor is. If Smart Text Reflow is on, all your text will move forward, and a new page will be added at the end of the book.

This might not be the effect you wanted, though, especially if you've already added images to your book, because the images will stay where they were but the text will move forward. If this is the case, try the next method instead.

Use the Pages panel

Open the Pages panel, highlight the page before the one(s) to be inserted, then go to the fly-out menu and select Insert Pages. The dialog box will look something like this:

If your layout has elements that need to remain on either verso or recto pages (recto-only chapter openers, for instance), it's best to add an even number of pages.

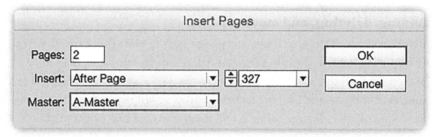

Type in the number of pages you want to add, which existing page they should follow (Insert: After Page) or precede (Insert: Before Page), and which master page should be applied to the new page(s). Most of the time, A-Master is the correct choice here. If you want a completely blank page, choose [None].

The new pages will be blank, except for folios and running heads. To flow your text onto the new pages, use the Selection Tool to click the out port on the page you want text to flow from, place the loaded cursor at the top of the new page, and click. The text will flow onto the page. Repeat this for all the new pages where you want text to appear. If you look at your text threads now (View>Extras>Show Text Threads), you'll see that the new text frames are joined with the rest. Your new pages will be numbered in sequence (pages 328 and 329 in the example above), and the original pages in this example will be renumbered, starting with 330.

Removing pages

If you delete a page in InDesign, your threaded text does not disappear along with the page; it simply flows forward. To remove pages, go to the Pages panel, select the page(s) you want to delete, and click on the trash can at the bottom of the panel. The following warning will pop up:

If you've disabled Smart Text Reflow, or if your page contains unthreaded material, such as images, you'll only see the upper part of this warning.

You can see from the warning that you'll be adding another page at the end of your book unless you go back and uncheck Smart Text Reflow. If the material on the page is not part of your text flow (some images or a table, for instance), you'll get the same warning but without mention of Smart Text Reflow. If you click OK, any unlinked objects will disappear.

Maybe you want to get rid of a page of copy and also the page itself. To do that, cut (and perhaps paste it somewhere else) or delete the text itself using the Type Tool. You'll see other text flowing onto the page, but that is okay. Next, go to the Pages panel, select the page you want to delete, click on the trash can, and when you see the warning shown above, click OK.

Moving pages in the same document

At any time you can change your mind about where things should go in your book. You might want to move a full-page sidebar somewhere else, or transfer your Acknowledgments from the front matter to the back matter. Because all the text frames in your main narrative are linked, moving pages requires some thought so that your text will still flow properly in your text frames. Choose the best approach for moving *your* pages.

Using the Move Pages feature to move pages with no linked text

In the Pages panel, highlight the page(s) you want to move. Then in the Pages fly-out menu, select Move Pages, and a dialog box will pop up, similar to the one shown below.

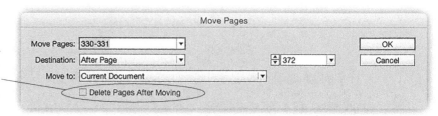

The correct pages should appear in the Move Pages area, so just type in where they should move to, and click OK. The only problem with this method is that any existing text threads move with the pages. This can result in a terrible tangle, with links jumping from page 329 to page 373, 374, and then back to page 330, in this example. Even a small jump in the text threads can be very confusing, so if you have linked text consider using one of the methods listed below, depending on your situation.

Moving pages with linked text

1 Using the Type Tool, select all the text on the pages you want to move, then cut it by pressing Ctrl/Cmd+X (the linked text frames will reflow).
2 Go to the new location and insert your cursor at the top of the page. Paste the text there by pressing Ctrl/Cmd+V, and the text will flow in.

Moving pages with linked text, images and captions

If you are moving pages with different types of frames (some linked and some not), then use this method. In InDesign, you can't simultaneously select frames that are on different spreads, so if you're moving pages on different spreads, you'll have to repeat steps 1–4 as many times as necessary.

1 Add one or two new blank pages in the new location (see page 330).
2 Using the Selection Tool, drag across a whole page or 2-page spread to select all the frames, then press Ctrl/Cmd+X to cut them.

3   In the Pages panel, double-click the page(s) you just added to go there.

4   Still using the Selection Tool, go to Edit>Paste in Place, and the frame(s) will appear on the new page(s). If they were previously threaded together on a spread, they will still be threaded *to each other* on the new pages, but the threads to other pages will now be broken.

5   Go back to the original location, and look at the page immediately following. You'll see that InDesign didn't delete the text in the frames you cut, but just moved it into the next text frame. Select the text you moved using the Type Tool, and delete it by pressing the Delete key.

6   Go to the new location and rethread the text frame(s) to your main narrative (see page 328) if need be.

7   In the Pages panel, select the page(s) you want to delete, and click on the trash can at the bottom of the panel.

Moving pages from one document to another

When you move pages from one document to another, several things move along with them: the paragraph, character, and object styles that are in use on the pages; and the master pages in use.

To move pages from Document A to Document B, go to the Pages panel in Document A and highlight the thumbnails of the pages you want to move. Then in the Pages fly-out menu, select Move Pages. You'll see the dialog box pictured on page 332. Select Document B from the Move to drop-down list and decide whether you want to delete them from Document A or not.

Any document that is open will appear in the Move to drop-down list, so make sure that Document B is open.

Now check Document B's Pages menu and locate your new pages to make sure they are in the right place. Check your Paragraph Styles and Character Styles panels to make sure that the styles imported along with the copy.

Transferring styles from one InDesign document to another

Being able to transfer styles between documents can save you a lot of work if you start a new project. Use the method described on the next page to transfer paragraph, character, and object styles. Paragraph styles are used as an example, but the steps are the same for all.

The same process can be used to transfer color swatches, too. See chapter 31 for more about color.

1   Open the document you want to transfer paragraph styles *into*. Go to the Paragraph Styles fly-out menu and choose Load Paragraph Styles (or Load All Text Styles if you want to deal with your character styles at the same time). In the dialog box, find the document you want to get the styles from, and click Open.

2   You'll see a dialog box like the one below.

If you choose Load All Text Styles, you will see both paragraph styles (¶) and character styles (A) in the same list.

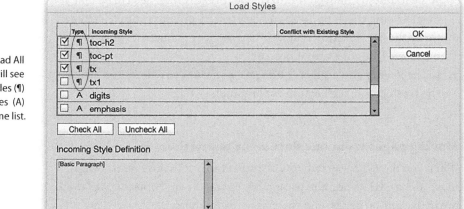

3   If you want to import all the styles, click on the Check All button. If you only want to select a few styles, click the Uncheck All button, then choose the individual styles you want. If you need a reminder of the settings for any particular style, look at the Incoming Style Definition area, where the settings are described. Then click OK.

4   The styles you want will now appear among your new document's paragraph styles.

You will discover a conflict in style names if you've named your styles the same in both documents. You could rename your styles in one of the documents, or you could use one of the methods described below to deal with this situation:

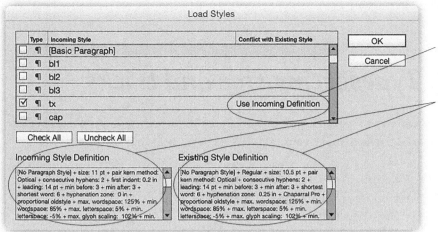

When you highlight a style that has a name conflict, you're given a choice of Use Incoming Style Definition or Auto-Rename. Both the new and the existing styles are defined in the lower part of the dialog box to help you make the decision.

- **To replace the existing style with the new one** If there's a conflict, your Load Styles dialog box will look something like the one above. When you highlight the style that has a conflict, you'll be presented with a menu of choices in the Conflict with Existing Style column. Both style definitions are shown so that you can figure out whether or not to overwrite the existing style with the new style. If you decide to do so, choose Use Incoming Style Definition. Your existing style will disappear.

- **To keep both styles** Highlight the style with the conflict, and choose Auto-Rename in the Conflict with Existing Style column. This will simply import the new style and add "copy" to the end of the style name. You can decide later which style you want to keep, or you can rename or repurpose one of the styles.

You can now see that there are many ways to rearrange your text and pages both within your current document and between documents. We hope these procedures have made it easier for you to avoid confusion while putting everything in your book into the proper order. Once you've accomplished this, save your file with a new file name.

50

Typesetting tips and tricks

Different types of text require different treatments, and you'll learn tips and tricks to make your text look its best, including:

- Kerning for better-looking headings
- Finding and using special characters
- OpenType features
- Typesetting punctuation
- Typesetting charts and tables
- Typesetting footnotes
- Adjusting in-line art
- Typesetting math and fractions
- Typesetting poetry

Before you begin, tidy up your Paragraph Styles and Character Styles panels to remove any unused styles. Click on the fly-out menu in each panel, choose Select All Unused, then click the trash can at the bottom. The Delete Paragraph Style dialog box will pop up, and you can replace the styles in question with Basic Paragraph. Check the Apply to All box at the bottom, and click OK.

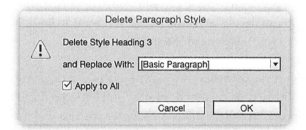

Now sort your styles into alphabetical order. Click on the fly-out menu in each panel, choose Sort by Name, and your styles will be reordered alphabetically.

Kerning for better-looking headings

To kern is to change the amount of space between two characters. You set up your Basic Paragraph style to use optical kerning, and usually it works quite well, but sometimes adjustments are needed. To kern manually, insert your cursor between two characters. Then either type a number in the kerning box in the Control panel, or use the arrows to fix the space as needed. As with tracking, kerning is measured in thousandths of an em.

In chapter titles and other headings where the type is large, use kerning between letter pairs that look poorly spaced. In general, two letters with straight strokes look better when they are separated a bit, and two letters with curves look better closer together. But every typeface is a bit different, and every pair of letters is a new situation. It's easier to see how the type looks if you're in Preview mode, as InDesign will highlight the kerned letters. (You specified that in Preferences>Composition on page 32. If you find the highlighting distracting or annoying, go to Preferences> Composition and uncheck Custom Tracking/Kerning.)

Check each of your chapter titles and chapter numbers (whether spelled out or arabic numerals), and kern them so that all the characters look evenly spaced. Note that if you kern between some characters and then use tracking in that same paragraph, the kerning values are not affected by the tracking.

What, exactly, is the difference between kerning and tracking? Kerning adjusts the space between two characters, making them farther apart or closer together. Tracking stretches or shrinks the spacing between all the characters and spaces selected (usually several lines or a paragraph) for the purpose of improving the look of the whole paragraph or page.

Finding and using special characters

You may sometimes find yourself trying (and failing) to find a special character on your keyboard. Are you searching for a multiplication sign? A foreign language accent? You'll probably find whatever you need in the Glyphs panel (Type>Glyphs). Make sure you are looking at the correct font, then select the kind of character you need from the Show drop-down list, or look at the entire font. When you move your pointer over the glyphs, their Unicode values and names pop up.

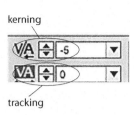

kerning

tracking

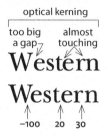

optical kerning

too big a gap   almost touching

Western

Western

−100   20   30

With manual kerning, the spacing within the word looks more even.

The footnote references in your main text may be hard to read, especially if they directly follow quotation marks. Use Find/Change to locate each reference number (**ref** style), then manually add space between the quotation mark and the number, as shown below.

optical kerning

quote."123

quote."123

kern value = 40

If you need to create your own special character, see page 350 for how to add it into your line of type.

Put the cursor where you want the glyph to appear in your text, then scroll down in the Glyphs panel until you find the character, and double-click it. It will then appear in your text. If you need the same glyph more than once, chances are you'll see it in the Recently Used area at the top of the panel, and you won't have to search for it again. (If you don't see a Recently Used area at the top, click on the up-and-down arrows icon just to the left of the word "Glyphs" in the panel.)

You can learn a lot from studying the Glyphs panel for your typeface. Try comparing oldstyle and lining figures, or discover which ligatures, if any, your font comes with. You might learn some new currency symbols, such as the various signs for the euro and the yen, or the sign for the old Spanish currency, the peseta (₧), that you see highlighted below. And the next time you need an oddball character, you'll know exactly where to start your search.

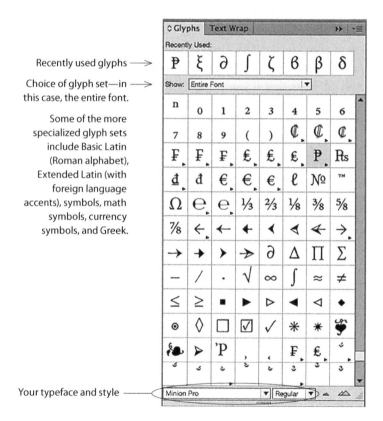

Recently used glyphs ⟶

Choice of glyph set—in ⟶
this case, the entire font.

Some of the more
specialized glyph sets
include Basic Latin
(Roman alphabet),
Extended Latin (with
foreign language
accents), symbols, math
symbols, currency
symbols, and Greek.

Your typeface and style ⟶

OpenType features

Click on the OpenType symbol at the bottom of any text frame using your Selection Tool, and a list of features for your typeface will pop up. Try each one and, if you like any, add them to the OpenType options in your paragraph style.

Typesetting punctuation
Ellipses

Ellipses (also called ellipsis points) are the series of three or four dots or periods that indicate the omission of words in a quotation, or sometimes a pause. For most written material, they work this way:

- **Use three dots in the middle of a quoted sentence** The dots should have space between them. Don't use the ellipsis character (...) that comes with Word and with InDesign, as *it isn't correct for typesetting.* Instead, set the three dots like this: nonbreaking space, period, non-breaking space, period, nonbreaking space, period, space. This will force all the dots to appear on the same line. To set a nonbreaking space, go to Type>Insert White Space>Nonbreaking Space, or press Ctrl/Cmd+Alt/Opt+X. It's fine to end a line with the three-dot ellipsis.

- **Add a period if needed** If the ellipsis appears after the end of a sentence, add a normal period for the sentence, then set the space-dot-space-dot-space-dot-space ellipsis, using nonbreaking spaces as before. The period can be on the first line, with the ellipsis following on the next line if necessary.

- **Add other punctuation** If the omission in the quotation occurs just *before* other punctuation, such as a question mark or semicolon, set the ellipsis first, then a space, and the other punctuation. If the omission occurs just *after* other punctuation, set the punctuation, then a space, then the ellipsis.

Very often, the situation is more complicated than in these examples. Ask your editor if you're confused, or consult *The Chicago Manual of Style,* which has the definitive answers for all things relating to ellipsis points.

OpenType symbol

The Chicago Manual of Style explains the whys and wherefores of ellipses, hyphens, dashes, and punctuation in great detail. This book is every typesetter's friend.

This sentence is interrupted . . . and then continues.

The first quoted sentence ends. . . . Something is omitted, and the quotation continues.

This demonstrates how to use an ellipsis with other punctuation marks . . . ; the semicolon appears *after* some words that were omitted.

This demonstrates how to use an ellipsis with other punctuation marks; . . . the semicolon appears as part of the first phrase, *before* the omitted words.

Hyphens and dashes

Here's what you need to know about hyphens and dashes:

If InDesign hyphenates a word in an awkward place, insert your cursor where you'd prefer to hyphen-ate the word and press Ctrl/Cmd+Shift+hyphen. This will insert a "soft hyphen" which lets InDesign know where to split the word, if needed.

There is an actual minus sign glyph, and it is slightly different, so you should use that if you have seri-ous math in your book. See pages 350–351.

• **Use a hyphen** (-) in hyphenated words and in phone numbers. Most of the time, hyphens will be set automatically by InDesign at the ends of lines, but if you need a hyphen to stay in place even if it's not at the end of a line, just hit the hyphen key.

• **Use an en dash** (–) between numbers, but not in phone numbers. Type Alt/Opt+hyphen. There is no space before or after an en dash. Never begin a line with an en dash. Note that an en dash can also be used as a minus sign, in which case, *do* set a word space both before and after it in an equation.

   In some countries (such as the UK and Australia), en dashes are used in place of em dashes, with a space before and after them. The best way to set en dashes in books with this style specified is to use a nonbreaking space (Ctrl/Cmd+Alt/Opt+X), then the en dash, followed by a regular word space. That way, the en dash never lands at the beginning of a line of type.

• **Use an em dash** (—) to indicate a sudden break or change of topic within a sentence. Type Alt/Opt+Shift+hyphen. In North America, do not set a space before or after the dash. In some European languages, a thin space (Type>Insert White Space>Thin Space) is used before and after it. Never start a line with an em dash that is used in this way. You may have noticed that many people use a space, en dash, and another space instead of the method just described; this is normal usage in the UK and Australia, but not in North America (see en dashes, above). Never use more than two em dashes in the same sen-tence—one before the extra phrase and one after it, as in this sen-tence—otherwise the reader will not understand where you are going with it.

   Another use for an em dash is at the beginning of an epigraph or extract attribution (discussed in chapter 26). Do not set a space between the dash and the writer's name.

Punctuation: roman or italic?

Should punctuation be set in the same style (roman or italic) as the text it follows? Word often makes this decision correctly for you, but you should know the basic rules:

- **Commas** May be set in the same style as the phrase the comma follows (this is more traditional). Or you may set commas always in roman (this is more current). Discuss this issue with your editor, then pick a style and stick with it.

- **Colons, semicolons, question marks,** and **exclamation points** Should almost always be set in the style of the main text surrounding them. But if they are in the middle of a book title or a heading, like the one at the top of this page, set them in the same style as that element.

- **Parentheses ( ) and square brackets [ ]** Are almost always set the same as the surrounding text rather than the text that's enclosed (e.g., [*apparently*]). If an entire italicized parenthetical phrase is sitting on a line by itself, though, set the whole thing in italics. Example:

  (continued on the next page)

  You might notice that the final letter of the italicized type sometimes crashes with the parentheses or brackets (e.g., the final letter in *all*). You should kern (page 337) or set a thin space (Type>Insert White Space>Thin Space) to eliminate this.

- **Periods** Never worry about periods being set in italics, because they look the same both ways.

Punctuation: roman or bold?

For the most part, italics rather than bold type should be used for emphasis. However, if you've used bold type you need to know how to handle the punctuation that accompanies the words. In each instance you should decide whether the punctuation belongs with the bold type or not. See the examples to the right.

Either way is fine.

You may have three, *and only three,* wishes granted. italic

You may have three, *and only three,* wishes granted. roman

What? Only *three*? roman

Maybe you should read *Is This Genie for Real?* italic

Not only is he *real*; he is a genuine genie genius. roman

bold
Hey! What are you doing there?

Didn't you read the sign saying **Keep Out**? roman

Typesetting charts and tables

The table-making function in InDesign is impressively robust, offering more options than you'll find in a word processor. You can import Word tables and Excel spreadsheets, or create them from scratch in InDesign.

Before you jump into this, though, you might want to explore the available options for your table and learn to use the table selection functions by setting up an experimental table. Make a new text frame on the pasteboard, go to Table>Insert Table, and set up some rows and columns. Hover over the upper left corner of the table with the Type Tool cursor, and an arrow (↘) will appear. Click to select the entire table, then open the Table panel (Window>Type & Tables>Table) to see the range of choices. Once you are familiar with this and how to select rows, columns, and the entire table, you may proceed. But you'll find it helpful to keep your experimental table on the pasteboard so you can try various effects.

Adobe provides video tutorials explaining the many effects you can create, and how to insert graphics and even other tables within the table.

Importing tables

When you imported your Word document, chances are that your tables came in with the rest of the text. And chances are also that they don't fit on your page or something has happened to them in the transition. It's probably best to cut and paste each table into its own new text frame, possibly reimporting them from Word, as described below.

Here are some tricks to try if your imported tables are a real mess:

1   Take the table out of your original Word document and put it in a new Word file.
2   Make a new text frame that's the correct width for your book page. Put your cursor in it, then go to File>Place. Select Show Import Options at the bottom of the panel. Find your Word table file, select it, and click Open.
3   When the Import Options panel appears, in the Formatting area, choose Remove Styles and Formatting from Text and Tables, and "Convert Tables To: Unformatted Tables," unless you *really* need to keep specific layout details of your original table intact.

Once you import an Excel spreadsheet, it becomes an InDesign *table*.

Though it may be counter-intuitive, remember to use the Type Tool to select both type and cells in a table. The Selection Tool won't help at all.

Importing from Excel is a bit different from importing from Word. For a full explanation, see our blog post at BookDesignMade Simple.com/import-from-Excel-into-InDesign.

Once your table is imported, continue with these steps:

1 Hold the text cursor over the edge of the table or its columns, and it becomes an arrow (↓, →, ↔, etc.). You'll find that you can stretch or shrink the table and individual columns to fit your space. Note, though, that any table cell with a red dot in the lower right corner has overset text, so resize with caution. You don't need to fix the problem right away, as it might be solved by changing your Table Body paragraph style or your cell inset settings (page 346).

2 Click the type cursor to the left or right of the table, and it becomes the same height as the table (you may need to insert the cursor above or below the table and use the arrow keys to get there). You can then align the table left, right, or center in the text frame by clicking on the appropriate alignment symbol in the Control panel (≣ = left, ≣ = centered, and ≣ = right).

3 To fine-tune the table, select the whole table by clicking your Type Tool at the top left corner, then use the Table>Table Options tools to control the number of rows and columns, add color and rules (called "strokes"), and more. Go to Table>Cell Options to control the appearance of the text in the cells, add strokes and fills, and more.

4 If you have more than one table in your book, save your table style in the Table Styles panel (Window>Styles>Table Styles). Changing the style later will affect all your tables accordingly.

5 Create paragraph styles for your table text using the styles on page 344. If you need more styles—such as numbered or bulleted lists—within your tables, adapt them from others in your book, naming them **tbnl** or **tbbl**, for instance. Styling details for various kinds of table entries are shown on page 345.

6 For a multipage table, you might want to use a footer saying "*(continued on next page)*" in italics at the bottom right of each page (or only on the recto page). The footer looks best if it appears below the table and not as part of the table.

Tables are not easy! But if you've learned how to work with a table that you typed in Word, you can also work with it in InDesign.

For tips on making your table look good, see our blog post at BookDesign MadeSimple.com/ making-tables-look-good-in-indesign.

Unless your table is very short, you should go to Table>Table Options>Table Setup and specify one or more header rows. This will ensure that if your table flows to another page, the header row(s) will repeat at the top of the subsequent page(s).

Create the styles for text in the tables as paragraph styles. Create styles for other features of the table, such as rule weights, insets, and background colors as table styles, using the Table Styles panel. See page 344.

Even if you don't want or need to save a table style, saving cell styles might cut down on your work within the same table (Window>Styles>Cell Styles).

Use Tabular Lining figure style if your tables have numbers that need to line up; otherwise use Proportional Oldstyle.

☐ **Table Body [tb]**   Based On = **tx1**
Changes from the No Indents style (see page 62):
Basic Character Formats: Size = 10 pt
                                                         Leading = 11 pt
Indents and Spacing: Align to Grid = None
OpenType Features: Figure Style = Tabular Lining

☐ **Table Column Heads [tch]**   Based On = **tb**
Changes from the Table Body style:
Basic Character Formats: Style = Bold
                                                         Case = Small Caps
Indents and Spacing: Alignment = Center

☐ **Table Footnotes [tbftn]**   Based On = **tb**
Changes from the Table Body style:
Basic Character Formats: Size = 8.5 pt
                                                         Leading = 10 pt

The Table menu in the Control panel offers more options than this Table panel, but the panel is sometimes quicker to use, and it's the place to store your table and cell styles. When you're not using it, dock it under the Paragraph Styles panel.

Number of rows →
Number of columns
Minimum width of columns
Minimum height of rows
Align type at top, middle, bottom, or evenly spaced in cells
Orientation of type

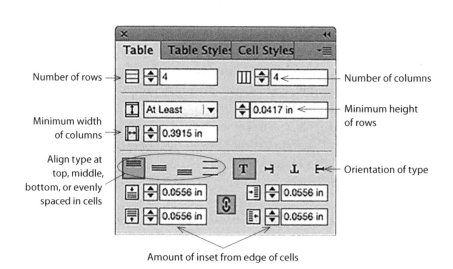

Amount of inset from edge of cells

Numerals are set up in the Table Body **[tb]** paragraph style as Tabular Lining so they will line up neatly in columns.

Use a decimal tab (↓·) to align whole numbers at right with each other.

Align column heads at the bottom of the cell.

STUB HEAD[2]	TABLE TEXT	TABLE CURRENCY	TABLE DECIMALS	TABLE WHOLE NUMBERS	TABLE DATES
		SPANNER HEAD FOR FOUR COLUMNS[1]			
First category	Description of first category	$1234.59[3]	89.572	764	Jan. 17, 1950
	Another description of first category	467.92	3.4	12	Dec. 17, 1960
Second category	Description of second category	13	9425.467	1,456	July 7, 2012
	Description of this category	3693.21	15.246	468	Mar. 7, 2004
	With a horizontally split cell	32.01			
Fourth category	Second and fourth categories have a 10% black background.	145.67	468.34		

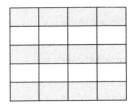

1 A spanner head relates to more than one column head and is centered over those columns. Always merge columns (select the relevant cells, then go to Table>Merge Cells) for a spanner head.

2 The first column head is sometimes referred to as the *stub head*. It can be centered over the column, or flush left over the column even if the other column heads are centered.

3 When setting up tabs for numbers in a table, simply select the whole column, then use the tabs panel (Type>Tabs) to place a decimal tab. The numbers in the column will automatically align on the tab; don't press the Tab key.

To fill a cell with an image, put your cursor in the cell and go to Table>Cell Options>Graphic. Set all cell insets to 0, check Clip Contents to Cell, and click OK. Then File>Place the image. Move and resize the image inside the cell with the Direct Selection Tool if necessary.

Use a decimal tab (↓·) to align decimals and numerals in a column. Slide the tab left or right until the longest number in the column is centered. Whole numbers also align as if they had a decimal.

Table text can be centered vertically in the cell or aligned at the top or bottom (Cell Options>Text).

Use Cell Options to make diagonal lines.

To make the strokes disappear between footnotes, go to Cell Options and make the stroke weight 0.

Alternating rows of a background color can make a table much easier to understand if you want readers to read left to right. If you want them to read down instead, you can make alternating columns.

To the right are the settings for the alternating rows in the simple table on the left (Table>Table Options>Alternating Fills).

Table Setup | Row Strokes | Column Strokes | **Fills** | Headers and Footers

Alternating Pattern: Every Other Row ▼

Alternating

First: ⬍ 1 Rows   Next: ⬍ 1 Rows

Color: ■ [Black] ▼   Color: ☑ [None] ▼

Tint: ⬍ 10% ☐ Overprint   Tint: ⬍ 100% ☐ Overprint

Skip First: ⬍ 0 Rows   Skip Last: ⬍ 0 Rows

☐ Preserve Local Formatting

Building tables in InDesign

InDesign offers so many options that it's sometimes difficult to decide what to choose. Look for tables in other books and figure out what options were used there. Choose a style you like, and if it fits in with the rest of your book design, imitate it.

You can rearrange columns and rows after your table is made. See the Adobe tutorial on that topic.

Naturally, you can also typeset your tables right in InDesign. The principle is the same as for importing tables, but you need to do a bit of prep work before you can start typing your data. Study the example on the previous page. Also, if you haven't done so already, open your Tables panel (Window>Type & Tables>Table). Its functions are shown on page 344.

1   Draw a text frame for the table, or put your cursor at the insertion point in your text (on a new line). Go to Table>Insert Table. Type in the number of columns and rows, and how many of the rows are for headers (column heads, which can be repeated on each page if you so specify) and footers. Include a row for each table footnote that you anticipate having. Then click OK.

2   Type your column heads and data in the cells. Merge or split cells as needed using the options in the fly-out menu on your Table panel.

3   Add paragraph styles (page 344) to all the heads and data.

4   Resize columns and rows using the pointer arrows (↓, →, ↔, etc.), which you access by hovering with the Type Tool. Using these arrows, you can also add and delete columns and rows by first selecting a column or row, then choosing Table>Insert [or Delete]>Row [or Column]. Another option is to make columns equal widths by selecting some adjacent columns and going to Table>Distribute Columns Evenly. Similarly, you can make all adjacent rows equal in height by selecting them and going to Table>Distribute Rows Evenly.

5   Highlight a column of text or numbers, then set up a decimal tab to make them align properly (see examples on page 345). You do *not* need to hit the Tab key to get the text or numbers to line up. Alternatively, you can specify the inset from the left or right side of a column (or an individual cell). Highlight the text in the relevant cells, then go to Table>Cell Options>Text and adjust the Left and Right insets by clicking on the up or down arrows until the material looks centered.

To control strokes and fills, highlight the relevant cells, then go to Table>Cell Options>Strokes and Fills. You'll see a box like the one below with blue outlines representing the sides of the cells. The stroke settings you choose will affect all the blue outlines of the cells. If you don't want a stroke applied to a side, click on that blue side to *deselect* it, then specify the stroke for just the selected sides.

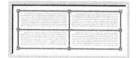

6   Apply stroke and fill styles as needed, including alternating background colors for rows or columns. You can make a table without any visible strokes by specifying "0 pt" as the weight for all strokes in Table Setup, Table Options, and Cell Options. If you want a bit of blank space between columns or rows, insert an empty column or row.

Fitting tables on the page

You might find that your table simply doesn't fit on the book page as well as it did in your Word document. Here are some basic ways to deal with a table that's too wide:

- Squeeze the column widths by dragging the sides
- Reduce the type size by adjusting the paragraph styles
- Use a turned table; in other words, turn it 90° counterclockwise on the page. So you can work on a turned table, go to the Pages panel and select your current page. Then click to get the flyout menu, and select Page Attributes>Rotate Spread View>90° CW. Now you can squeeze or stretch the table to fit the page dimensions, and then edit it and apply styles as needed. If the turned table is smaller than the width of the upright page, place it so the top (on a verso page) or bottom (on a recto page) of the table is touching the outside margin. To rotate the page(s) back to normal, return to Page Attributes>Rotate Spread View, and select Clear Rotation.
- Set the table across a 2-page spread. You can accomplish this within one table by creating a very wide column in the center, equal to the total width of your two inside margins, or 1″ wide at the very least. If necessary, make a white box (see page 256 and 259) to cover visible elements in that middle column so that it appears to be blank space.

To rotate a table 90 degrees, it'll need to be in its own text frame. To separate a table from the main narrative, select the whole table by hovering the Type Tool over the top left corner to get a diagonal arrow, then clicking once. Cut the table (Ctrl/Cmd+X), drag a new text frame on your page or pasteboard, and paste the table in it (Ctrl/Cmd+V).

If the table is two pages, it's always best to place it on a spread so it will all be visible at once.

This is all one table. The empty column that is in the gutter is covered with a solid white rectangle. See Part V to make shapes.

If your table is too tall, continue it onto another page. Your column heads will automatically repeat at the top of each new page (see step 1 in the instructions on page 346). If the table doesn't completely fill the two pages, it might look better if both pages are of equal length. This is easier said than done, however, so don't waste too much time over it if it's just not working out.

Almost any question you might still have about tables will be answered by a Creative Cloud tutorial. Go to the CC icon on your screen (or open Creative Cloud) and under the Apps tab, click on View Tutorials under InDesign.

Typesetting footnotes

Footnotes in InDesign work much the same way as in Word. If you inserted footnotes in your manuscript, they'll appear at the bottom of the appropriate pages in your book.

If, on the other hand, you want to type or import the footnotes as you go along, put your cursor in the position on the page where the note reference (the asterisk or superscript number) will appear, go to Type>Insert Footnote, then start typing (or copy and paste from another document) the footnote text. It will automatically appear at the bottom of the page or column, with the proper number in both the reference location and at the start of the note. See the illustration on page 349 for your options.

Create a paragraph style for your footnotes using the specifications below. Notice that both the type size and the leading are two points smaller than in your Text [**tx**] style.

To fine-tune the footnote layout, open the Footnote Options dialog box by clicking Type>Document Footnote Options. Under the Numbering and Formatting tab, fill in the boxes as shown on page 349. These settings are fine for most books. If you have only a few footnotes, choose the asterisk numbering style, but if you have more than four per chapter, choose arabic numerals.

The Formatting area of the Document Footnote Options refers to the footnote references in the text, so choose "Apply Superscript" next to "Position" if you are using numbers (but not if you are using asterisks). Your Character Style should be None. Under Footnote Formatting, scroll down and select the Footnotes paragraph style [**ftn**] that you just created. The Separator is the space between the footnote number and the footnote

To create the **ref** character style for your footnote reference numbers, see page 85.

Footnote references that are not numbered use a specific set of symbols, in this order:

*, †, ‡, §, **, ††, ‡‡, etc.

In each chapter, start over with *.

If the footnote references in your main text are crashing with quotation marks, kern as shown on page 337.

☐ **Footnotes [ftn]**   Based On = **tx**
Changes from the Text style (see page 62):
Basic Character Formats: Size = 9 pt
                                                            Leading = 12 pt
Indents and Spacing: First Line Indent = 12 pt *or* 0.1667 in
                                                            Align to Grid = None

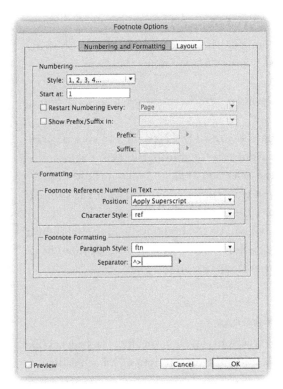

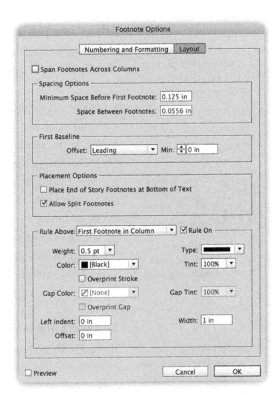

text. Use the drop-down list to go to En Space, which appears as "^>" in the dialog box. If other symbols show up in the box, simply delete them.

Moving on to the Layout tab (above right), set the minimum space before the first footnote at 0.125 in. This will provide at least one line of white space between the text and the first footnote. If you want more space, type in a higher value. Set the Space Between Footnotes at 0.0556 in (4 pts).

Under Placement Options, selecting Place End of Story Footnotes at Bottom of Text means that you want to use endnotes instead of footnotes; this was discussed on pages 249–250. Allow Split Footnotes means that when a note is too long it will continue onto the next column or page. This is a perfectly standard practice, so check this box.

If you want a short rule to appear above the first footnote in the column or page, choose this option from the drop-down list, and check Rule On. Change the weight to 0.5 pt, and leave the rest of the options as they appear in the illustration.

Choose all the footnote settings carefully, keeping in mind the requirements of *your* book.

In the Numbering and Formatting tab, you might want to restart the numbering in every section. See page 245 to learn how to make page numbering sections.

In the Layout tab, you can choose to have your footnotes span all columns by checking the Span Footnotes Across Columns box at the top. So in a 3-column layout, each footnote would be 3 columns wide.

Adjusting inline art (anchored objects)

To see this method in action, watch "Anchored Objects" at BookDesign MadeSimple.com/videos.

Sometimes words alone just don't do the trick, and you need to show a small piece of art in your text. Here's how you make that happen:

1. Make your symbol in InDesign or another program (e.g., ⬡). You can even use a photo file.
2. Place the symbol on the pasteboard (File>Place) next to your page in InDesign and make it the right size for your line of type (◯).
3. Select the symbol using the Selection Tool, and copy it (Edit>Copy).
4. Switch to the Type Tool, put your cursor where you want the symbol to go in the text, then paste the symbol (Edit>Paste).
5. Chances are that the symbol will be too high on the line. Highlight it with the Type Tool, then use the baseline shift arrows (or input box) in the Control panel to lower it into its proper place.

Baseline shift increments can be as small as hundredths of a point.

Typesetting math and fractions

For a detailed explanation on typesetting math equations, see our blog post at BookDesignMade Simple.com/typesetting-math-in-indesign.

There are three basic kinds of fractions: level, or on-line, fractions (1/2); case fractions (usually ½, or ⅔); and built-up fractions ($\frac{1}{2}$). Each is discussed below.

Use **level fractions** if you're not discussing math but need to insert an occasional fraction or mathematical expression, such as $(a + b)/c$ or $(12 + 9)/3$, in line with the rest of your text. Oldstyle numerals are distracting in math, so use lining figures. (Highlight your numerals, then go into the Character panel fly-out menu and select OpenType>Tabular Lining, or create a new character style as shown below.) For the slash in the fraction, simply use the one on the keyboard, which is also called a solidus. Also note that in $(a + b)/c$, only the letters are in italic—not the parentheses or the solidus. In $(12 + 9)/3$, nothing is set in italic.

If you are typesetting a cookbook, experiment with the various kinds of fractions to find the most readable format, and increase the leading if necessary. Ingredient lists need to be very clear and easy to read.

☐ **Lining Figures [lfig]** *character* **style**   Based On = **[None]**
OpenType Features: Figure Style = Tabular Lining

A few commonly used **case fractions** are probably provided with your font; look in the Glyphs panel. If you need to set fractions not included with your font, you can construct your own. There are three options:

- Type the numbers separated by a slash, highlight them, go to the fly-out menu in the Character panel, and choose OpenType>Fractions. Bingo! InDesign even converts the solidus to a fraction slash for you. Examples: ½, ⁵⁄₁₆, and ³⁵⁄₄₂ were all set using this method; note that they are identical to the fractions in the next option.

- You'll find both numerators and denominators for each numeral in the Glyphs panel (read the labels that appear as you hover over the glyphs), as well as a "fraction slash." Simply set the numbers and fraction slash (put your cursor in place on the page, then double-click each glyph), and you'll probably discover that no kerning is needed. Examples: ½, ⁵⁄₁₆, and ³⁵⁄₄₂ were all set using glyphs from the panel.

- If you're using a font that doesn't come with numerators and denominators, you can use superscripts and subscripts for the numerals, but you will have to use kerning and baseline shift to make them look good. If a fraction slash is not provided, try typing a regular slash and setting it in italic.

If you do discuss a good deal of math in your book, you should use **built-up fractions** with full-size numerals. Be sure to use Tabular Lining figures, and remember to take numerators and denominators off the baseline grid (Paragraph panel> ☰☰). See page 141 for an example of how to use baseline shift to place the numbers properly. You might also want to use underline options to make the horizontal bar. To do this, highlight the characters that need the underscore, then go to Underline Options in the Character panel fly-out menu. Here you can select a line weight and move the bar up or down for best appearance. While you're at it, create a character style for future use.

In most cases you should treat these full-size built-up fractions as display material. Set the math on its own line(s), not running in with other text. You may either center each set of math expressions or indent them all equally from the left—usually a paragraph indent.

If you're not using an OpenType font, the Open-Type features aren't available to you, but read on to learn how to build fractions by hand.

keyboard slash (solidus)

fraction slash

Math plug-ins are available for use with InDesign. See BookDesignMade Simple.com/resources to find the latest. Another alternative is to hire a math typesetting service.

In the Glyphs panel you will find a minus sign:

en dash

minus sign

It's common to align several lines of math on the equals signs. (This may or may not be appropriate for your book.) Review the section on using tabs, on page 199, for instructions.

Typesetting poetry
Occasional poems

Treat poems that show up occasionally in your book as Extracts and create the paragraph styles shown below. Use the Extracts, Poetry, First style at the beginning of each stanza, as this will add a linespace between stanzas. If the poem has an attribution, treat it the same way as a quotation attribution (see pages 194–198). For the extra indents seen in many poems, set one or a series of em spaces (Type>Insert White Space>Em Space, *or* Ctrl/Cmd+Shift+M). See the next page for an example of a simple poetry extract.

You must use em spaces rather than word spaces for extra indents if you want to make an ebook. Neither ebooks nor websites can recognize more than one word space in a row.

Use this style for the first line of the poem and the first line of a new stanza, too.

☐ **Extracts, Poetry, First [extpo1]**
Changes from the Extracts, First style (see page 68):
Indents and Spacing:

Based On = **ext1**

Left Indent = 0.4 in
First Line Indent = −0.2 in

☐ **Extracts, Poetry, Middle [extpo2]**
Changes from the Extracts, Poetry, First style:
Indents and Spacing:

Based On = **extpo1**

Space Before = 0

Use this style for the very last line of the poem, but only if it has no attribution.

☐ **Extracts, Poetry, Last [extpo3]**
Changes from the Extracts, Poetry, Middle style:
Indents and Spacing:

Based On = **extpo2**

Space After = 14 pt *or* 0.1944 in

If your attribution sticks out to the right a lot more than the longest line of the poem, change the settings to give the attribution a larger right indent.

☐ **Extract Attribution [extpoattr]**
Changes from Extracts, Last style:
Indents and Spacing:

Based On = **extpo3**

Alignment = Right

☐ **Extracts, Poetry, Title [extpot]**
Changes from the Extracts, Poetry, First style:
Basic Character Formats:

Based On = **expo1**

Bold

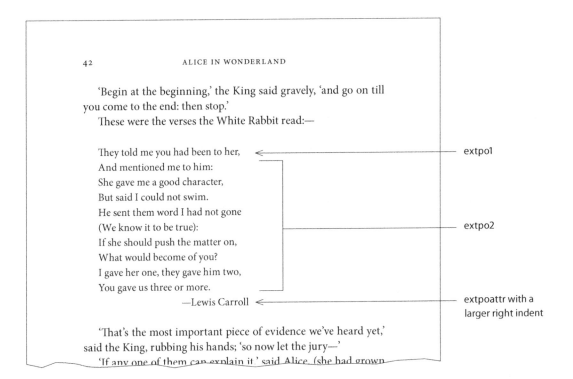

'Begin at the beginning,' the King said gravely, 'and go on till you come to the end: then stop.'

These were the verses the White Rabbit read:—

They told me you had been to her,   ←——————————— extpo1
And mentioned me to him:
She gave me a good character,
But said I could not swim.
He sent them word I had not gone
(We know it to be true):   ————————————————— extpo2
If she should push the matter on,
What would become of you?
I gave her one, they gave him two,
You gave us three or more.
            —Lewis Carroll ←——————————— extpoattr with a
                                           larger right indent

'That's the most important piece of evidence we've heard yet,' said the King, rubbing his hands; 'so now let the jury—'

'If any one of them can explain it,' said Alice, (she had grown

A book of poetry

For an entire book of poetry, you'll need a different approach. The idea is to set all the lines with left alignment and then center each poem left-to-right (called *east-west*) on its own page.

Begin by setting up the Poems paragraph styles on page 355.

Next, go to your A-Master page and draw a rectangle on one of the pages, making it the full width of the type area. With the rectangle selected, drag a vertical guideline to the middle of the rectangle. Repeat this process on the other page of the spread. Now delete both of the rectangles that you drew. Return to your text pages and notice the vertical guide in the center of every page in the book. You will use these to center your poems later.

Now format each poem using the styles given on page 355. Begin each poem at the top of a new page. Add space between stanzas or verses by using the Poem with Space After [**pospaft**] style. If a poem is a few lines too long for the page, just end it on the next page, but try to have *at least*

Watch two videos about typesetting poetry at BookDesignMadeSimple .com/videos. One is called "Typesetting a poetry book," and the other "Centering poems in text."

Each poem should begin at the top of a text page. Even if it is very short, don't be tempted to move it down to center it north-south on the page. If *all* of your poems are short, use an extra-large top margin.

Note that the running head is a bit smaller than usual, with extra space below it (a large top margin, see page 125 to increase the top margin) so as not to interfere with the poem titles.

The poem title is at the top of the text area, centered.

The poem is also centered east-west in the text frame, using the method described on page 355.

The Evidence

They told me you had been to her,
And mentioned me to him:
She gave me a good character,
But said I could not swim.
He sent them word I had not gone
(We know it to be true):
If she should push the matter on,
What would become of you?
I gave her one, they gave him two,
You gave us three or more;
They all returned from him to you,
Though they were mine before.
If I or she should chance to be
Involved in this affair,
He trusts to you to set them free,
Exactly as we were.
My notion was that you had been
(Before she had this fit)
An obstacle that came between
Him, and ourselves, and it.
Don't let him know she liked them best,
For this must ever be
A secret, kept from all the rest,
Between yourself and me.

Centered drop folios (see page 362 for style) emphasize the centeredness of the page.

43

☐ **Poems [po]**   Based On = **tx1**

Changes from the No Indents style (see page 62):

Indents and Spacing: Left Indent = 11 pt *or* 0.1528 in

                                      First Line Indent = –11 pt *or* –0.1528 in

☐ **Poems with Space After [pospaft]**   Based On = **po**   Use the Poems with Space After style for the last line of each stanza or verse.

Changes from the Poems style:

Indents and Spacing: Space After = 14 pt *or* 0.1944 in

☐ **Poem Titles [pot]**   Based On = **po**

Changes from the Poems style:

Basic Character Formats: Bold

Indents and Spacing: Alignment = Center

                                      First Line Indent = 0 (change this setting before changing Left Indent)

                                      Left Indent = 0

                                      Space Before = 14 pt *or* 0.1944 in

                                      Space After = 14 pt *or* 0.1944 in

four lines on the continuing page. Breaking between stanzas is always preferred. Running the first page a couple of lines short is better than having the continuing page with fewer than four lines on it. And never leave a single line of a stanza by itself at the top or bottom of a page.

The next steps will give your poems the finishing touch. On each page, do the following:

There are many variations on poetry book layouts. Look at other books for something that will work in *your* book.

1 Select the text frame with the Selection Tool, then grab the center right handle of the frame and move it to the left until it almost touches the longest line of the poem, being careful not to cause any type to bump over to the next line.

Watch "Typesetting a poetry book" at Book DesignMadeSimple .com/videos.

2 With the text frame still selected, move the whole frame to the right until it is centered on the vertical center guide on the page. Both the poem and its title should now be centered east-west on the page.

Remember that you can drag an object straight in one direction by holding the Shift key as you drag.

Repeat these steps on each page. Yes, it's laborious, but entirely worth the effort to achieve a professional look.

51

Improving your page layout

You've fine-tuned all the parts of your text that needed special typesetting, so now you're ready to look critically at the pages in your book, fixing any problems as you go.

You'll go through each chapter as a separate unit, making sure all your facing pages align at the top and bottom, and there are no instances of awkward hyphenation, widows or orphans, and other page layout no-nos.

Some of these typesetting rules have been mentioned already in this book, but seeing them in one place should help you put them all together now. All of the book layout rules below are interconnected, so it might be helpful to first read through the chapter before you get started.

Pages and spreads should align at top and bottom

Always, always begin your pages at the top margin. Even your chapter and part opening pages start at the top margin, with an end-of-paragraph return set in your Text [**tx**] paragraph style. The only exception is on pages that have an illustration that extends above the top margin.

Ideally, the only pages that won't line up with your closest baseline above the bottom margin are the last pages in each chapter and a few of the pages in your front matter (your title page, copyright page, Contents, and epigraph, if you have one).

As you go through your book, look at each 2-page spread to make sure the two pages align with each other at the bottom margin. There may be several instances where they don't. This is because the Basic Paragraph style (Keep Options) is set up so that the last line of a paragraph cannot be alone at the top of a page (a widow). InDesign will pull the penultimate line of that paragraph to the top of the page as well, to remove the widow. As a result, the previous page will be left one line short.

What can you do when this occurs? Try the following adjustments, which are shown in order of preference:

- Reword some text to make it longer or shorter.
- Resize an illustration.
- Use tracking to gain or lose lines (see below).
- Shorten the two page frames so they are both one line short. Spreads that run one line long are discouraged—especially if your book uses running feet—but can be tolerated if you have run out of other options. Be sure your *next* spread is normal length.
- Add or delete extra space above (but never below) headings. Adjust the space the same amount above all equal headings on the 2-page spread. In order for this to work, you may have to take the text off the baseline grid on this page.

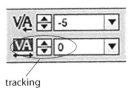

tracking

Using tracking to balance the number of lines on facing pages

So you start going through your pages and notice that several pages are one line short. Ack! What to do?

Start with the first instance of a short page in your chapter. Make sure you're in Normal view so you can see your baseline grid and end-of-paragraph returns. On that short page, do you see any paragraphs that end very close to either the beginning or end of a line? If you can't reword, you might be able to make those paragraphs one line shorter or longer using tracking.

Select the paragraph in question by quadruple-clicking it with your Type Tool. Using Tracking in the Control panel (see above), first try –10 or +10 to see whether you can shrink or expand the paragraph to lose or gain

a line. If so, great! Focus on that paragraph, and try to get the Tracking value as small as possible, otherwise the paragraph could look squished or stretched.

If you can't find a paragraph on that page to shrink or stretch, look at the previous page. Any possibilities?

If you absolutely can't find any way of making the two pages the same length, then drag the bottoms of the text frames up so that *both* pages are one line shorter.

Don't apply tracking to whole pages, or both pages of a 2-page spread. Instead try to minimize the amount of tracking within a paragraph, so the reader won't notice that it's been squeezed or stretched.

For ideas for cookbook page designs, see the blog post at BookDesign MadeSimple.com/ designing-a-cookbook.

There are exceptions to the page balancing rule. Some books, such as cookbooks, workbooks, and teachers' manuals, present a different topic or issue on each page. In these books, pages should still align at the top, but a "ragged bottom" look is fine. The same goes for poetry books. In fiction and most nonfiction books, however, page balancing is a must.

One other interesting exception is children's picture books and art books, which are laid out to make each 2-page spread look balanced and attractive.

Widows and orphans

Orphans are discouraged in headings, too, by the way.

We have discussed widows and orphans dozens of times already, but we bring them up here again to emphasize just how interlocked all the typesetting and layout conventions are. When you fix one problem, another one can arise. Just do your best! And read on.

Letter spacing and word spacing

Look at a single paragraph in your book. Do you see lots of white space between letters or words on some lines? On the other hand, do any of the lines look crammed in? This can be caused by several factors, such as columns—or lines wrapped around an illustration—that are too narrow, your hyphenation settings, or possibly your justification settings.

kerning (see page 337)

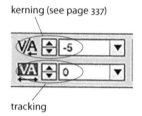

tracking

Tracking is usually the best way to adjust spacing in any block of type—see the sidebar on page 357. Tracking values are measured in thousandths of an em, so if you type 10, it's a 1% increase in spacing. As a general rule, it's best not to use values lower than –10 or higher than 10 in regular book text.

Your text becomes highlighted in green after it's tracked or kerned so you can easily see (in Normal view) which paragraphs have been affected. If it annoys you, go to Preferences (InDesign>Preferences on a Mac)>Composition and uncheck Custom Tracking/Kerning.

Check the justification settings for your Text [**tx**] style and compare them to those on page 40. If your settings are okay but you're still having a problem with a specific paragraph, you can change the justification for that one paragraph by clicking the fly-out menu on the Paragraph panel, choosing Justification, and changing some settings there.

The next three sections in this chapter address similar issues that affect spacing. Read them before you decide which action to take in each situation.

Fine-tuning hyphenation and word breaks

You may find some instances where InDesign has hyphenated a word in a very awkward or unusual place. You specified the hyphenation settings for your Basic Paragraph style on page 39, but occasionally you may need to change the settings for a single paragraph.

First, try adding a soft hyphen to break the word in your preferred place. Insert your cursor where you'd prefer the word to break, then press Ctrl/Cmd+Shift+hyphen. A soft hyphen is inserted, which means that InDesign will break the word there if a hyphen is needed, but if not, no hyphen will show. For example, if you end up adding tracking or new copy to that paragraph down the road, and the word no longer needs to be hyphenated, you won't be stuck with an unwanted hyphen in the middle of your word.

If that doesn't work, insert your cursor in the problem paragraph, then open the Hyphenation dialog box by clicking the fly-out menu in the Paragraph panel and choosing Hyphenation. Check the Preview box, then try changing different settings to see what helps improve your paragraph. Move the Spacing slider left and right, perhaps try reducing the number of letters from 3 to 2, and check and uncheck the boxes at the bottom. Remember, you're just changing the settings for this one paragraph. After you've changed the settings, look at the paragraph style name for that paragraph in the Paragraph Styles panel. You'll see a plus sign next to the style name, reminding you that some settings have been changed.

Awkward page or line breaks confuse the reader

Check the last line of each recto page. Has the text broken in the middle of a phrase that should be kept together? Here are some word groups to avoid breaking between pages, and even between lines:

- dates (e.g., 25 / B.C., or May / 13)
- names (e.g., John / Allen Lerner, John Allen / Lerner, J.A. / Lerner)
- hyphenated words with an extra hyphen (e.g., self-sus- / taining)
- phone numbers, or two numbers separated by an en dash
- addresses (e.g., 38250 / Willow Street)
- prefixes (e.g., Mr., Ms., or Dr., separated from the surname)
- page or chapter numbers (e.g., page / 24, or chapter / 2)

Using a soft hyphen instead of a hard one will also prevent the word from being hyphenated in the middle of a line in your ebook. Every ebook reader will show the type in a different size and style, after all.

You may be tempted to use soft returns to control the line endings in a problem paragraph, however they will mess up the flow of text in your ebook. Instead, use non-breaking spaces (Ctrl/Cmd+Alt/Opt+X) between words to control the line endings.

Any yellow highlighting that appears in your text indicates lines in which the Adobe Paragraph Composer has not been able to achieve perfect spacing. The darker the yellow, the worse the problem. To fix it, you might have to use tracking, adjust your hyphenation, or reword. But many times you'll find you can just leave the type as is.

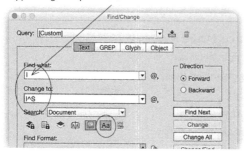

Use these settings in the Find/Change box to keep the word "I" with the word that follows it. If your book is written in first person, several instances of "I" can become stranded on your right margin.

ladder

This little paragraph demonstrates three things discussed in this section. **Ladders** are three or more hyphens in a row. A **stack** appears when your text is appropriately full of words approved by your editor that unfortunately don't work well on the page. A **river** shows up when the spacing is difficult; perhaps the column is too narrow (like this one).

stack   river

InDesign can help you prevent such breaks. Select the text you want to keep together, then either 1) open the Character panel and select No Break from the fly-out menu or 2) select No Break from the drop-down list at the far right of the Control panel.

A great way of keeping two words together is to use a nonbreaking space between them (Ctrl/Cmd+Alt/Opt+X). Use the Find/Change feature (Ctrl/Cmd+F) to search for the words, and change the space to a nonbreaking space.

Here are some examples showing the nonbreaking space character inserted to keep words together:

Ms.ˆCollett   Chapterˆ4
1234ˆMy Street   Augustˆ7

Avoiding ladders, stacks, and rivers

A **ladder** is a series of three or more hyphens in a row at the ends of lines. In your paragraph styles, you set up your hyphenation options to avoid ladders (see page 39), but it's still a good idea to look through your book just in case some snuck in where you typed hard returns.

A **stack** is the appearance of the same series of characters at the start or end of three or more consecutive lines. These become very obvious once you start looking for them, and they can attract the reader's eye unnecessarily. The words don't even have to be the same each time; if you stacked "ate," "create," and "obliterate" above each other, it would look like a stack of *ate*'s just the same. Use tracking or soft hyphens to fix the problem.

A **river** is an unfortunate arrangement of white spaces that happen to line up in such a way as to look like white worms or a meandering stream of water on the page. They can appear everywhere once you start looking, but don't worry about minor ones. If there are really obvious rivers, reword slightly, or use tracking or soft hyphens, to make these disappear. A soft, or discretionary, hyphen is invisible unless needed to break a word. Put your cursor in the word and go to Type>Insert Special Character>Hyphens and Dashes>Discretionary Hyphen, or press Ctrl/Cmd+Shift+hyphen.

No blank recto pages

The heading says it all. Never, ever leave a recto page blank unless it's at the very end of your book. A blank right-hand page signals THE END to the reader.

No really short pages

Very short pages usually show up only at the end of a chapter. Not only do they look silly, but they also might make some readers think that the typesetter is either inexperienced or is deliberately trying to pad the book. A good rule of thumb is to have a minimum of six typeset lines on a page.

As you apply these layout and typesetting rules to your pages, you'll find that you can use one layout rule to help you resolve a problem with another rule. This takes practice, so take it slowly at first. Go through one chapter at a time and scan for trouble spots; sometimes it helps to highlight the problem by temporarily changing the color of the type in the trouble spot using the Swatches panel. Then start over in the chapter and remedy each problem in turn. Very often you'll discover that when you've fixed one, you've also solved one on the next page in the process. Or you may have even caused trouble for yourself on the next page. This can be frustrating, but remember that at this point you're doing the real work of page layout, and you will get better at it as you go along. We hope you'll come to enjoy the problem solving and start to think of your book as one big, challenging, and enjoyable puzzle.

Remember to return all your type to black after fixing each chapter.

Congratulations once again! Your chapters are now in fine shape, and you have only a few remaining steps before you can send your book to the printer. You'll finalize your running heads or feet, deal with proofreading corrections, and add your index.

52

Creating and applying chapter master pages

Now that your pages are finalized, you'll create and apply master pages.

Creating B-Master for chapter opening pages

Chapter opening pages usually differ from regular chapter pages in that they don't have running heads/feet and usually have a drop folio (a page number at the bottom). It's easy to create a separate master for chapter opening pages and, once applied, this makes it easy to see where new chapters start in your Pages panel.

In your Pages panel, open A-Master by double-clicking it, then click the fly-out menu and select New Master. Fill in the New Master dialog box as shown below, and click OK.

Fill in *your* book's trim size here.

You'll see that you can't select any of the text frames on the B-Master, as they're based on the A-Master page, and so are locked in place. To unlock a frame, press Ctrl/Cmd+Shift and click on it with any tool. Unlock and delete the running head/feet frames, and move the folio frames down to two or three baselines below the bottom margin. Decide whether you want the drop folios to be centered on the page or on the outside.

Apply this paragraph style to the two drop folios on your B-Master page.

☐ **Drop Folios [dfol]**
Changes from the Folio style:
Indents and Spacing:

Based On = **fol**

Alignment = Center

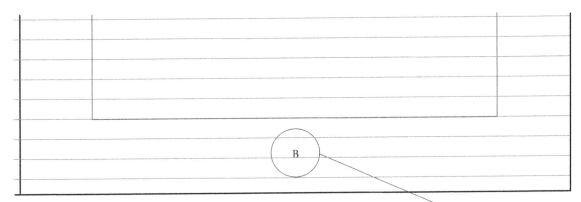

Note that the Current Page Number marker says "B" on B-Master.

If your Folio paragraph style is aligned Away From Spine, but you want your drop folios centered, you need to create a new paragraph style:

Creating a separate master page for each chapter

One possible way to make your life easier is to create a separate master page for each chapter or part of your book. But this only helps if both of the following are true:

- The running heads change with each chapter or part
- Most of your chapters are more than a couple of pages long

To create a new master page for each chapter or part, open the Pages panel and select New Master from the fly-out menu. In the Prefix box type the chapter number—even if you're not using numbers—so that the chapters will be listed in the correct order (you can use 0 for your front matter). In the Name box type in the chapter title or an abbreviated version of it. In the Based On Master area, select A-Master. Then select 2 for the number of pages, and click OK. You'll now see the master page you've just created.

The only thing you'll want to change on this new master page is the number and chapter title in the running head. To make the running head text frame on your new master page editable, hold down Ctrl/Cmd+Shift, then click on the text frame. Select the copy you need to change, then type the correct words there. You don't need to touch the folios.

InDesign offers a way to automate running heads using text variables. Read our instructions at Book DesignMadeSimple.com/ text-variables-in-indesign.

Is one of your chapters only a couple of pages long, so that the chapter title running head only appears on one recto page? If so, you might simply apply the previous chapter master page to it and override that running head. To select it, press Ctrl/Cmd+Alt/Opt and click on the running head. Then change the chapter title.

Repeat this process for every chapter or part in your book, including each section of your back matter. When you're finished, you'll have a separate master page for each one. (See page 369 for creating columns on the master page for your index.)

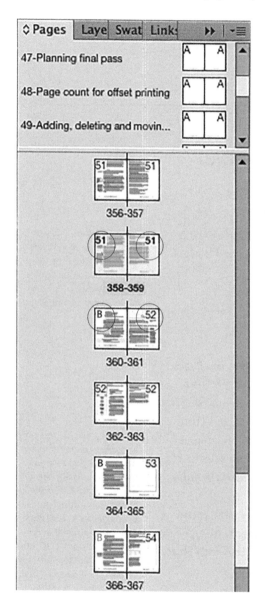

Applying your master pages

Print your Contents or make a list so you have all the page numbers handy for each chapter, then apply the correct master pages to all the pages in your book. Start with your front matter:

- Open your Pages panel fly-out menu
- Choose Apply Master to Pages
- Select 0–Front Matter from the Apply Master drop-down menu
- Add the page range separated by a hyphen (e.g., i–xvi)
- Click OK

Now scroll down your Pages panel and make sure all your front matter pages have the 0–Front Matter master page applied.

Next apply B-Master to the chapter opening page for chapter 1. You can use the method above, but it's simpler to just drag the B-Master icon onto the appropriate page thumbnail. You'll see a B displayed in the corner of that page thumbnail when it's applied.

Repeat the steps above for every chapter, first applying B-Master to the chapter opening page, then applying the chapter master to the rest of the chapter pages using Apply Master.

When you're finished, every page in your book will have a master page applied to it, and every page thumbnail in your Pages panel will display a letter or number in its out-side corner (see example to the left).

If you change the titles of any chapters later on, simply change the running head on its master page, and all the running heads in the chapter will automatically change too.

Removing running heads and folios from certain pages

Now that you've applied master pages to every page in your book, they'll all display running heads and folios except the chapter opening pages, which will only display drop folios.

There are certain pages that never display running heads or folios:

- All the front matter before the Contents
- All blank pages

So you'll need to take one more quick trip through all your pages, and remove the running heads and folios from the pages listed above.

Navigate to page i, hold Ctrl/Cmd+Shift (to override the master page), and click the running head text frame to select it. Press Delete. Do the same for the folio text frame. Or, you can drag to select both frames at the same time (if they're near each other), then press Delete. Be sure not to delete any other content from your pages!

Go through all your chapters, deleting the running heads and folios from any blank pages.

If a page you deleted the text frames from ends up having text or images on it later on, simply go into the Pages panel and drag the master page icon back onto the page thumbnail to reapply the master page elements.

Final proofreading corrections

A proofreader is someone who reads proofs. This means that he or she never sees your pages until *after* they have been laid out. The proofreader should be a different person from the editor because a fresh set of eyes will see many things that you and even your editor never noticed. Also, the proofreader will check your running heads, hyphenation, and other issues that may have arisen during the layout process. It is always worthwhile to hire a good proofreader.

The proofreader's corrections might come to you in PDF format. Or they might come handwritten on a hard copy. If you receive a PDF, the corrections will probably have been made using the Comments feature. In Acrobat, click View>Tools>Comment>Open—or simply click on "Comment" in the toolbar to the right of the workspace—to see a list of comments docked at the right of your screen. You'll be able to click each comment in the list to see it displayed on the appropriate page.

If you receive handwritten corrections, however, the proofreader may have used many markings that are new to you. A chart of proofreading symbols appears on the opposite page.

You'll no doubt have lots of corrections to make, so be sure to save your InDesign file with a new name or date, and get started.

Once you've entered and double-checked all the corrections, go back and review one last time for spacing, hyphenation, tracking, page alignment, and all the other issues you took care of earlier (chapters 48–51).

Once your final proofreading corrections are finished, you'll forward your pages to your indexer for indexing. Or, if your book won't include an index, feel free to skip to Part IX: Preparing to Publish, where you'll create a high-resolution PDF of your pages for printing.

Congratulations on a job well done.

Symbol	Meaning
ℓ	Delete
⊂	Close up; delete space
stet	Let it stand as it was originally
#	This is the symbol for space. You might see −# or +#
eq#	Make space between words (or between lines) equal
¶	Begin new paragraph
□	Add one em space (the amount equal to the type size measured in points)
⊠	Add one en space (half the size of an em space)
⅂	Move right
⊏	Move left
⅂⊏	Center
⊓	Move up
⊔	Move down
fl	Flush left
fr	Flush right
‖	Align vertically
tr	Transpose
bb	Bad break, as in a word hyphenated wrong at the end of a line
sp	Spell out

Symbol	Meaning
ital	Set in italic
rom	Set in roman
bf	Set in boldface
lc	Set in lowercase
caps	Set in caps (CAPITAL letters)
sc	Set in small caps, like this: SMALL CAPS
wf	Wrong font; set in correct type
×	Check type for a blemish
∧	Insert something here
∧	Insert comma
∨ ∨	Insert apostrophe or single quotation marks
∨ ∨	Insert quotation marks
⊙	Insert period
;	Insert semicolon
∧∨	Insert colon
=	Insert hyphen
⊥/m	Insert em dash (a dash that is equal in length to the type size)
⊥/n	Insert en dash (a dash that is half as long as an em dash); these are used almost exclusively between two numbers
( )	Insert parentheses

Common proofreader's marks on hard copy

54

Adding your index

You create your index (or finalize it, if you built it in Word) after your book has been proofread and all the corrections entered. That way, you'll be sure that none of your text will reflow on your pages, and the page numbers in your index won't change.

Most authors choose to have a professional indexer create their index. A professional indexer will sort out the important from the unimportant and organize the index to make it easier for readers to find the information they're looking for. A good index not only helps the reader but also is a sign of a well-made book.

Did you already add index entries to your manuscript in Word? If so, your index imported into InDesign with your Word document. You'll see blue insertion points ($\wedge$) dotted throughout your text when you're in Normal view.

Before working with an indexer, it's a good idea to study indexes in other books on your topic. Read the main entries and see what subentries are listed under them. Try looking up an obscure term to see whether it's listed; if so, is it in a logical place in the index? Can this index serve as a model for your own? Use it as a starting point and discuss its pros and cons with your indexer. Also discuss your audience and the number of pages you want the index to fill. That way, your indexer will be able to produce a helpful and appropriate guide for your readers. When your index is ready, your indexer will supply your index in Word.

Setting up the first page of your index

If you haven't already done so, add a new page (see page 329) at the back of your book for the index, and apply to it the master page you created for your index on page 363.

If you created your index in Word, your index entries may have flowed in at the back of your manuscript and already appear in your text. If so,

If you don't see your index markers in Normal view, click Type>Show Hidden Characters.

If you are printing your book on an offset press, make sure your index will fit into an optimum page count for signatures (see chapter 48).

select the index heading and all the entries and delete them (really!). That index was static, so you'll generate a new one using InDesign's Index feature that will update automatically.

So now you have a blank page at the back of your book with the index master page applied to it.

Adding columns to your index master page

Open your index master page by double-clicking its icon in the top section of your Pages panel. The 2-page spread should look the same as all your other master pages, except the running head says Index.

To add columns, click Layout>Margins and Columns. In the Margins and Columns dialog box, fill out the Columns section as shown below to create two columns. (The Margins area will show the measurements for *your* book.)

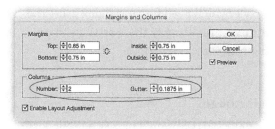

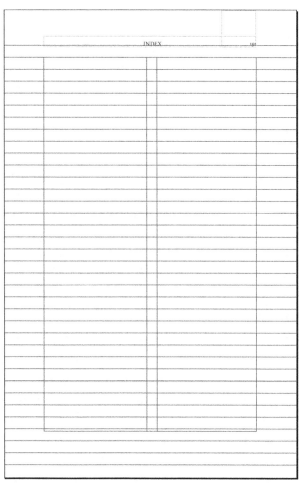

If your book has wider pages, or your index entries are very short, you may prefer a three-column index. You'll be able to change the number of columns easily using the Margins and Columns dialog box. Make sure the Preview and Enable Layout Adjustment boxes are both checked, and that way you can change the number of columns even after your index text is placed.

Creating paragraph styles for your index

Take a look through your index, and see what type of indentation scheme your indexer (or you) have used. It's very important to preserve the hierarchy that has been set up. Notice how many levels of entries there are.

Indexes with two or three levels of entries are the most common. Here is an example of an index with three levels:

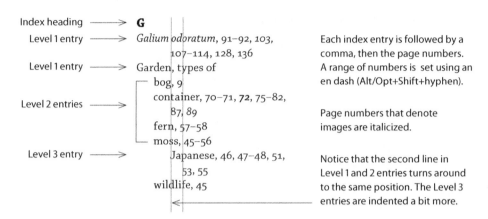

Now create the paragraph styles you'll need for your index using the settings shown on the opposite page. You'll apply these settings to your index text after you've flowed it into your index pages.

Placing your index Word document

If your book has been professionally indexed, you'll receive a Word document containing your index. (If you created your own index with your original manuscript in Word, then skip this section and follow the instructions in the next one instead.)

First navigate to your first index page. You'll see a blank page with two columns like the example on page 369. Place your Word document in the left column. If necessary, add one more index page, then click in the out port and hold down the Shift key to autoflow the text to the second index page. InDesign will create as many new pages as needed to flow all the text in your index into columns.

Now skip to "Applying your index paragraph styles" on page 373.

☐ **Index Level 1 [ind1]**   Based On = **tx1**
Changes from the No Indents style (see page 62):
Basic Character Formats: Size = 9 pt
                                               Leading = 11 pt
Indents and Spacing: Alignment = Left
                                               Left Indent = 27 pt *or* 0.375 in
                                               First Line Indent = –27 pt *or* –0.375 in
                                               Align to Grid = None

☐ **Index Level 2 [ind2]**   Based On = **ind1**
Changes from the Index Level 1 style:
Indents and Spacing: First Line Indent = –13.5 pt *or* –0.1875 in

☐ **Index Level 3 [ind3]**   Based On = **ind2**
Changes from the Index Level 2 style:
Indents and Spacing: Left Indent = 36 pt *or* 0.5 in
                                               First Line Indent = –9 pt *or* –0.125 in

☐ **Index Heading [indh]**   Based On = **ind1**
Changes from the Index Level 1 style:
Basic Character Formats: Font Style = Bold
                                               Size = 10 pt
Indents and Spacing: Space Before = 11 pt *or* 0.1528 in

Generating your manuscript index in InDesign

If you are using the Book feature to generate an index from multiple documents, check the Book box.

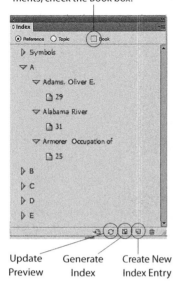

Update Preview Generate Index Create New Index Entry

If you created your own index in your manuscript, your next step is to generate your index using InDesign's automated index feature.

Open the Index panel by clicking Window>Type & Tables>Index. You'll see your index entries sorted alphabetically. You can examine individual entries by clicking the arrows next to the letters to reveal the entries. If you click the arrow next to the entry, you'll see the page number(s) displayed (see example to the left).

To generate your index, first navigate to your index page. You'll see a blank page with two columns like the example on page 369. Click the Generate Index icon at the bottom of your Index panel, and then fill in the Generate Index dialog box as shown below.

Click OK, and your cursor will be loaded with the index text. Place your cursor in the left column and hold down the Shift key to autoflow the text. Your index text will flow into the two columns on your index page, and InDesign will create as many new pages as needed to flow all the text in your index into columns.

Using the Index panel, you'll be able to add new index entries using the Create New Index Entry icon.

If you make any changes to your index, either by adding or removing material from your pages or by adding or changing entries, first open this dialog box, check Replace Existing Index, and click OK. You'll see a box with confirmation that your index has been updated. Then in future simply click the Update Preview icon at the bottom of your Index panel.

If you are using the Book feature to generate an index from multiple documents, check the Include Book Documents box.

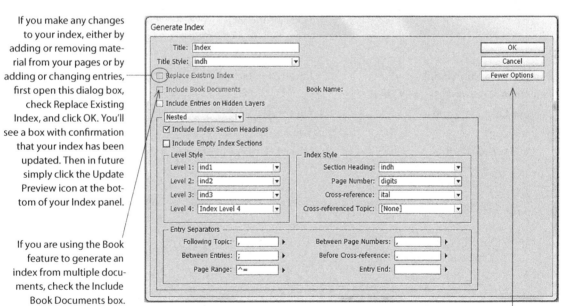

If you don't see the lower options, click the More Options button.

Applying your index paragraph styles

Now that your index text is placed in columns, you'll apply your new paragraph styles to the text.

First check to see whether the entries already have paragraph styles applied to them. They probably do, as indexers and the automatic InDesign Index feature both supply text with styles attached.

Follow the instructions on page 100 to delete the imported styles and substitute them with the styles you just created. That will save a lot of time. If no styles were imported, simply apply them manually.

If you get an error message "index entries contain invalid characters" when generating your Word index, don't panic. Read BookDesignMadeSimple .com/error-importing-word-index-indesign.

Typesetting your index

Don't apply your B-Master Chapter Opening page to the first page of your index, as B-Master has a single-column format. Instead you'll mimic the chapter opening page on the first page of your index. Drag down the tops of the text frames to make some space, and create a new single-column text frame at the top that extends right across the columns. Add your usual chapter opening for your back matter [**fbt**], using the title Index.

Then delete the running head and folio from the top of this page by pressing Ctrl/Cmd+Shift and selecting them, then pressing the Delete key. Add a drop folio to the bottom of the page by opening B-Master, copying the drop folio (select the text frame with the Selection Tool and press Ctrl/Cmd+C), then going back to the first page of your index and pasting it in place (Ctrl/Cmd+Shift+Alt/Opt+V).

Now drag the tops of the two index text frames to the same baseline where all the other material in your back matter begins.

Look through your index pages and see how the entries have flowed. Ideally, each column begins with an entry (rather than a line of just page numbers) and ends just above your bottom margin. Keep in mind that these entries aren't aligned to your baseline grid.

Starting on the first page, make sure the second column doesn't start with a line of page numbers, and that the columns have the same number of lines. You may need to apply tracking or soft returns to some entries to balance the number of lines in the columns (see page 357). It's acceptable to make all the columns on a 2-page spread one line shorter, if that helps to balance the columns.

In your index, always set "*See*" and "*See also*" (referring readers to other index entries) in italics. Use Find/ Change to help you.

The only hard and fast rule for index layout is: Never begin a column with a page number.

Once you've laid out your columns, you'll probably notice that some subentries continue onto the next page. It will help your reader if you add a "continued" line at the top of any verso page where this occurs so they will see what entry they are looking at. For instance, if your main entry is "colors" and its subentries continue from the bottom of a recto page onto the top of a verso page, add a line saying "colors (*continued*)." This might throw off your careful layout, but every effort on your part to improve your reader's experience is worth it.

For examples of "continued" lines, see pages 482, 488, and 496 in *this* book.

If your index is too long (needs to fit within fewer pages), consider: 1) deleting the alphabetical headings and simply adding one blank line between sections and/or 2) increasing the number of columns on your index master page (see page 369).

If your index is too short, consider: 1) changing the settings in your Index Heading [**indh**] paragraph style to increase the amount of space before (from 11 pt to, say, 22 pt) and/or 2) increasing the type size and leading in your Index Level 1 [**ind1**] paragraph style to, say, 10/12 (this will increase the size in all your other index paragraph styles, too).

Now you must go back and move or change any "continued" lines that you've added and then balance the columns again. An index is very fussy to work on but it's vital to get it just right.

Finally, make the columns on the last page of your index the same length. If this is not possible, make the left one longer than the other(s). And you're done!

Now that you've finished working through Part VII: Typesetting, your book pages should be completely finished. What a huge accomplishment!

In Part VIII: Designing Your Book Cover, you'll learn how to set up your book cover template in InDesign and then get started with your cover design.

Or, you can skip straight to Part IX: Preparing to Publish and generate a high-resolution PDF of your book pages to upload to your printer.

Part VIII: Designing Your Cover

Researching your target market

The first step in designing a compelling book cover is learning about your target market. Who is likely to buy your book? What group of people did you have in mind when you wrote your book?

Before you wrote your book, you were perhaps not very concerned with other books that would compete with yours in the marketplace. Or, it's possible that you wrote your book specifically to improve on or challenge others that were already out there. Either way, you'll want to research your target market, and here's why.

Your book needs to have a look and feel that is similar (but not *too* similar) to the others in the same category so that potential readers are not thrown off by it at first glance. When they browse in a bookstore or library, they have certain expectations—whether they are aware of them or not—about the kind of book they are looking for. These people are your target market, and you'll be catering specifically to them. Planning early to make your book the right size and to grab your reader's attention will help you hit the bullseye.

In this chapter you'll be:

- Defining your target market
- Comparing your book with others
- Planning your front cover to appeal to your market

Defining your target market

Chances are that your book is not going to appeal to every single person on this earth, so just what kind of person did you have in mind as you were writing your book? Think about those people now. Where do they live? Are they a certain age? What kind of clothing do they wear? What is their income level? Where do they shop? More specifically, where are they most likely to shop for books?

What kinds of images came to mind while you were picturing your audience? Did you visualize any colors? Bright and loud ones? Muted tones? Do you have a mental picture of stripes in primary colors? Tweed jackets? Fragrant flowers? Make a nice long list of any impressions you have about these readers of yours.

Now define the category your book fits into. Perhaps it fits into more than one (e.g., nonfiction + history + Civil War + collectibles), and if so, list them all, and then look at the list. See whether you can trim it down to two or at most three categories that are the most closely related to the main point of your story, and thus the most realistic for selling your book.

If your book is nonfiction, try going to some online bookstores. What keywords work best for finding books like yours? These words should help you define *your* category, too. If you plan to sell your book online, start listing your own keywords for that purpose now.

On Amazon.com, there are specific categories already set up for you. To find them, simply start a search for your general topic, and a list of categories will appear on your screen (on the left on a desktop computer). Click on a category and subcategories will appear. Continue doing this until you find the best match for your book.

Comparing your book with others

Next, make a trip to your local bookstore or library. Take a notebook and ruler with you (for measuring in inches), and do some market research.

Once you've found the section of the store or library where your book will be displayed, study the other books. Use your ruler to measure their pages (horizontal × vertical inches) and note which size is the most prevalent. Notice whether the books have hard or soft covers. You want your book to fit in nicely with the others on the shelf. If you were to decide to make yours oversized, for whatever reason, it would probably have to be stored on a different shelf—not very good for sales!

If you've already designed your book's pages, you made your trim size decisions earlier, and this is just a refresher.

While you're at it, write down the prices of these books and see whether they have fewer or more pages, illustrations, or information than yours. Are the pages printed in color or black ink? Try to determine objectively whether each book's perceived value matches its price, and begin to figure out where your book should fit within the range of prices.

Now start over, and examine their front covers. Do certain colors predominate? Does almost every cover feature a photograph, do they show illustrations, or do they simply use type? Which ones are the most eye-catching, which of them appeals to you the most, and why? Make notes about your impressions.

Once again, start over, and read their back covers. You'll probably notice that they all have pretty much the same kinds of information on them. You are going to put very similar information on the back cover of your book, too.

Planning your front cover to appeal to your market

Here's where your thinking about the target market comes in. Get out that list you made of your impressions of your future readers. Which of the listed items still really resonate with you? Now that you've studied some competing books, which of the listed items did you see reflected in those books? Do your ideas seem to jibe with what other people think about the same audience?

Start a new list now. Write down descriptive words for the kind of feeling you want readers to get the instant they pick up your book. Remember that the front cover grabs, and the back cover sells. So on the front, you want potential customers to get the intended feeling right away. Some possible items on your list might be: active, exciting, calm, feminine, masculine, fun, serious, techie, conservative, mysterious, etc.

Now that you've pinpointed your target market's demographic and researched other competing books in the marketplace, you're ready to start designing your front cover.

Perhaps you are a bit nervous about your abilities as a cover designer. If so (or even if not), you can and should get ideas from other books. Learn to use a critical way of seeing—everyone can. If you haven't looked with a critical eye lately, check out our blog post at BookDesignMade Simple.com/developing-an-eye-for-good-design. And then observe a cover design coming together in small steps at BookDesignMadeSimple .com/the-evolution-of-a-book-cover.

Starting your front cover design

Most front covers have the same basic format as the cover on *this* book: a title, subtitle (optional), author's name, and graphic elements (images or simply color). Your goal is to find a combination of type and image(s) that will appeal to your target market and look professional.

In this chapter you'll be:

- Finding images to experiment with
- Creating a cover design file in InDesign
- Placing your images on the pages
- Experimenting with title layouts
- Combining type with images

Finding images to experiment with

There are lots of places you can find images to use on your front cover:

- Use an image from inside your book
- Use a photograph taken by yourself or someone else
- Use a piece of art or illustration created by yourself or someone else
- Purchase an image from an online image bank

If you don't have any images to try, browse through images at an online image bank for inspiration. It's a great way to get ideas and see what kinds of images appeal to you. Find your notes from your target market research and get started. Here are a few image banks to try:

- Adobe Stock (part of CC)
- istockphoto.com
- dreamstime.com
- bigstockphoto.com

- 123rf.com
- morguefile.com (free photos)
- imagezoo.com (for illustrations)
- pixabay (free photos and illustrations)

If you've got a group of related books to design, advance planning is key. Read BookDesignMade Simple.com/designing-a-book-series.

Start by searching for some words or a phrase and see what comes up in the results. You'll most likely get several pages of results and can scroll through thumbnails. If one appeals to you, click on it to see a larger version of the image, together with the prices.

Some of the image banks offer a Lightbox feature, where you can store thumbnails of your favorites as you continue to search.

Right-click on a larger image and save a copy to use in your design. This image will be low resolution and have the image bank's watermark on it, but it'll be fine to use for experimenting with your cover designs. When you've settled on an image for your cover you'll purchase the high-resolution image, but for now just gather ideas.

Use as many search terms as you can think of. Try keywords from your book's title. Try phrases from your chapter titles. Try concepts. When you find an image with potential, look to see what search terms have been used for that image. You can click on those search terms to find similar images, and you can view other images by the same person.

Creating a cover design file in InDesign

It's easiest to experiment with cover designs in an InDesign file set up for that purpose. So start a new document using the dimensions of your front cover, like this:

Start a new document by clicking File>New>Document or pressing Ctrl/Cmd+N.

Naturally you should use the dimensions of your own book in the Width and Height fields.

A few pages to experiment on

Printers don't allow important info within 0.25" of the trimmed edges.

Your image will extend into the bleed area.

New Document

Document Preset: [Custom]

Intent: Print

Number of Pages: 3   ☐ Facing Pages

Start Page #: 1   ☐ Primary Text Frame

Page Size: Letter - Half

Width: 5.5 in   Orientation:

Height: 8.5 in

Columns

Number: 1   Gutter: 0.1667 in

Margins

Top: 0.25 in   Left: 0.25 in

Bottom: 0.25 in   Right: 0.25 in

Bleed and Slug

	Top	Bottom	Left	Right
Bleed:	0.125 in	0.125 in	0.125 in	0.125 in
Slug:	0 in	0 in	0 in	0 in

☐ Preview   Cancel   OK

Placing your images on the pages

Images are always *placed* in InDesign, rather than copied and pasted, so that a link is created to the image's file on your hard drive.

To place an image, choose the Selection Tool and click File>Place (or Ctrl/Cmd+D), then browse through the Place dialog box to find the image you want to place. Select an image and click Open. Your cursor will now be loaded with the image. Click anywhere on page 1 and the image will be placed at its actual size. Move the image around the page by selecting and dragging it with the Selection Tool. Enlarge or shrink it by pressing Shift (to keep the proportions the same) and using the Free Transform Tool.

Each page in your document will be a sample cover design, so place all the images you gathered onto separate pages. Add more pages to your document (see page 329) if you need them.

If you've already placed images inside your book, some of this material will be a review. Just skim through until you get to something new.

Switch from the Selection Tool to the Free Transform Tool by pressing E. Switch back again by pressing V.

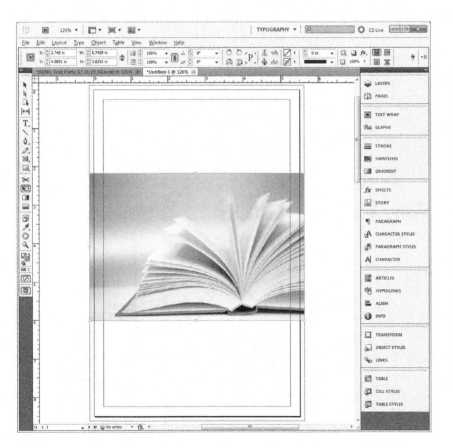

When you're browsing the Place dialog box for images to place, you can load the pointer with several images at once by holding Ctrl/Cmd and clicking several images. They'll all load onto the pointer at the same time.

Then click on a page to add the first image at actual size, or drag to add the image at the size of your choice.

To place subsequent images loaded on your pointer, go to the next location and click or drag. You'll "unload" the pointer one image at a time.

Starting with page 1, find the most pleasing placement of your image. You're just experimenting at this stage, so have fun! Try these ideas:

Flip the image horizontally or vertically by clicking Object>Transform>Flip Horizontal/Vertical, or by clicking one of the Flip icons in the Control panel.

To enlarge or shrink an image, click and drag any corner box with the Free Transform Tool (press E to switch to that tool). To keep the proportions of the image, hold down the Shift key while you're resizing it.

Free Transform Tool

To rotate an image, hover anywhere outside the image with the Free Transform Tool. You'll see a curved arrow and can rotate the image by simply clicking and dragging. Or click one of the Rotate 90° icons in the Control panel.

Experimenting with title layouts

Using the Type Tool, drag a text frame across the full width of your front cover and type in your title. It's easiest to experiment with the type using the Paragraph Style dialog box, so create a new paragraph style (see page 56) for your title and name it, say, **title1**. Now open the paragraph style and try some different typefaces and sizes for your title (see page 384).

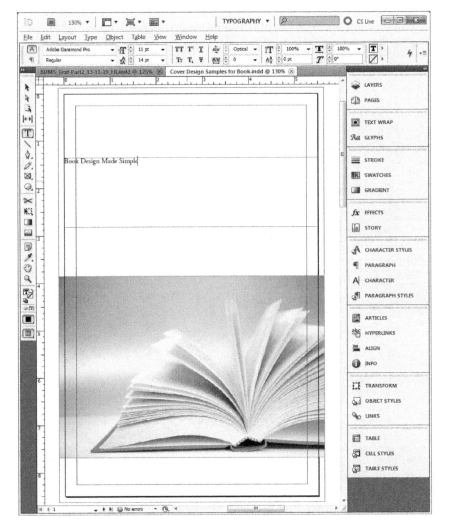

Set up your Basic Paragraph style to the same specifications you used for the main narrative in your pages (see chapter 7). That way, when the time comes to add your back cover, you can use the same typeface for your back-cover copy.

Choosing appropriate typefaces

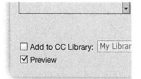

Open the paragraph style you created for your title by double-clicking it in the Paragraph Styles panel, and make sure the Preview box at the bottom left is checked (see left). Now any changes you make in the paragraph style will immediately show in your title. Position your page and Paragraph Styles panel so you can see your title while you're changing the paragraph style settings.

Start by centering your title (Indents and Spacing tab) and making its size bigger (Basic Character Formats tab). Still in the Basic Character Formats tab, click the Font Family drop-down menu, scroll up to the top of the list of typefaces, and select the first one. Using your down arrow key, go down through the list and see how your title looks in each typeface.

In your Font Family drop-down menu, select the typeface at the top of your list. You'll see your title change to that typeface.

Then use the down arrow on your keyboard to see how your title looks in every font available to you in InDesign.

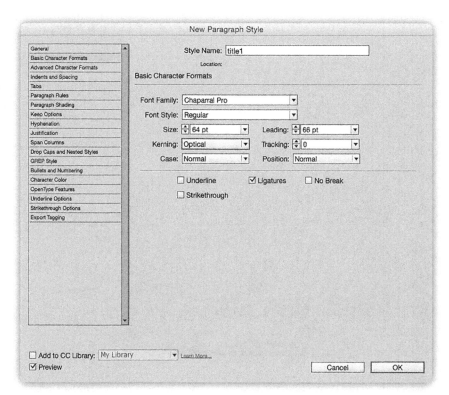

Write down the typefaces your title looks good in. As with shopping for clothes, not everything you try will be the right fit or style. Review the list of descriptive words you made in the previous chapter when thinking about your target market. Which typefaces best suit your subject matter? If you've written a business book, do the typefaces you've chosen look businesslike? If you've written a romance, does your title look romantic?

Now try your title in all caps (select All Caps from the Case dropdown menu) and go through the list of typefaces again.

Make a list of finalists. These are the typefaces you'll experiment with in your front cover designs.

Try new typefaces! In Adobe Typekit, type your book's title in the Choose Sample Text field and try any font that appeals to you before syncing it.

Book Design Made Simple

AbsaraHeadOT 29 pt

Book Design Made Simple

Chaparral Semibold 29 pt

Book Design Made Simple

Corinthian Regular 42 pt

Book Design Made Simple

Arno Regular 31 pt

BOOK DESIGN MADE SIMPLE

Myriad Regular 26 pt

Finding interesting title layouts

Take a moment to study the words in your title. If your title contains just one word, then it can go straight across the cover. Or, if your title lends itself to being broken into two or more lines, you can split the words up. Remember, if your book is sold online you'll want the title to be readable at thumbnail size. Try splitting your title into sections. Is it better or worse that way?

Part of your title could be set in a different type style or typeface, to give it more prominence. Some words can be larger and some smaller. Try setting part of your title in italics or all caps. Try all lowercase letters, a mix of upper- and lowercase, and small caps. Keep experimenting.

If the author is well known, you may want the author's name to be more prominent on the cover than the book's title. If this is the case, focus on creating an interesting type treatment for the author's name that could be used on several books.

AbsaraHeadOT 38 and 31 pt. Looks good centered on 2 lines. See how the g and l connect nicely? However, the k looks strange with the missing serif on the bottom.

Book Design
Made Simple

Chaparral Bold 36 pt and Semibold Italic 30 pt. Emphasizes first two words; looks better left-aligned, all letters lowercase.

book design
made simple

Corinthian Regular 72 pt, all lowercase, and Myriad Semiextended 15 pt, all caps. Second line centered between left edge and swoosh of g.

book design
MADE SIMPLE

Look at other books to get ideas. Every book on your bookshelf holds potential inspiration for your title. Round up some books and try the same title treatments with your title without judging in advance how it'll look. You may be surprised!

You might find it easier to split the words or phrases into separate text frames. That way you can move the frames around on the page with your Selection Tool to find the best juxtaposition of the words.

If you find a layout that's interesting but isn't working with a particular typeface, try the same layout with a different typeface. There might be a letter or word in your title that looks great in one typeface and is too difficult to read in another.

If your final title is comprised of more than one text frame, you can group them together. Select all the frames by dragging the Selection Tool, then group them together by pressing Ctrl/Cmd+G. To ungroup them, press Ctrl/Cmd+Shift+G.

Arno Regular 50 and 33 pt. Arno's k is a better choice than AbsaraHeadOT's. Taking the connecting g and l further, the first phrase is split onto two lines, and the o and d are connected. Lowercase letters connect more easily.

BOOK DESIGN MADE SIMPLE

Myriad Regular 42 pt and Light 18 pt. (The Corinthian script was too flowery.) Myriad is used inside the book for captions, so could be a good choice for the title, although it looks a bit cold and formal.

Setting up your design document

Now that you've experimented with some suitable images and possible treatments for your title, it's time to experiment with some front cover designs using those elements.

If you have a great testimonial from a well-known person, consider adding the best part of it to the front cover for impact (see page 428 on typesetting testimonials).

Choose a title treatment and add it to a page in your design document. Then add any other text you need, such as the subtitle, author's name, or testimonial, by creating a text frame and typing in the words. Leave all the text black for the time being. Add an image if you intend to use one.

Using layers to organize your cover elements

It's a good idea to place your front cover elements onto layers at this stage. Using layers separates your text frames from your images and makes it easier to lock some elements in place while you move others around.

Refer to chapter 32 to set up layers for your book cover. It's useful to create three layers for your book cover: Text, Graphics, and Background. The Text layer is in *front* of all other layers and includes all your text frames. The Graphics layer is *behind* the Text layer and in *front* of the Background layer, and it includes images (later on you'll add your publishing logo and barcode to the spine and back cover). And the Background layer includes all your elements that are *behind* everything else, such as a solid background color or image.

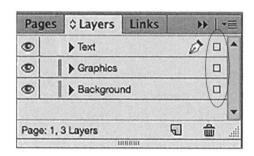

Select any frame with your Selection Tool, and its frame will match the color of the layer it is on. Move it to a different layer by dragging its color square (shown at right) onto the appropriate layer.

Take a moment now to create the layers you'll need, and place your text and image frames onto the appropriate layers.

Experiment with some different designs at the same time

Once you've set up a page with your front cover text and image on the appropriate layers, it's easy to duplicate that page and create some already-set-up pages to experiment with.

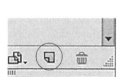

Create New Page icon

Simply open your Pages panel and drag the page you've set up onto the Create New Page icon at the bottom to create identical new pages. Now you can experiment with some variations in the same document.

A *few design principles*

You can probably recognize good or bad design when you see it, but you may not be aware of *why* one design is more successful than another.

Following are a few design principles that will help you create a more effective book cover. Keep these in mind while you're experimenting with your cover designs in chapter 59.

Keeping it simple

Keeping it simple is important for any kind of design, but it's especially important for the front cover of your book. It's tempting to try to capture every single thing about your book on the front cover—every plot twist, every character, or every concept. Don't do it!

Potential customers and readers will often be looking at a very small image of your front cover, probably a thumbnail on the Internet or in a catalog (perhaps even printed in black and white). Make sure your cover is easy to understand at a small size.

Try zooming out to a mini view so you can see what elements disappear at a small size, what elements might need to be enlarged, or which ones overwhelm the rest.

As you design your front cover, keep asking yourself which elements are *really* necessary and whether they can be simplified. Keep your type as simple as possible, without strokes or drop shadows unless absolutely necessary. Just because lots of effects are available in InDesign doesn't mean they should all be used.

TITLE TITLE

Which is easier to read, the plain word or the one with the embossing, stroke, and drop shadow?

Choose one or two typefaces at most. Simplify an image by cropping or removing it from its background. Use a limited color palette.

You'll find lots of ideas in this chapter, so be selective, and just use the ideas that make *your* book cover more compelling.

Never typeset a script or other fancy font in all caps. It will be *UNREADABLE*.

Creating a focal point

Busy covers with lots of competing elements are confusing. Everything is vying for attention, so where do you look first?

Make it easy for your audience by creating a hierarchy of elements on your cover. Your focal point will be dominant, and the surrounding elements will support the focal point without competing with it. Your focal point could be your title or a portion of it, an image or a portion of it, or the author's name. What will *your* hierarchy be?

There are many ways to draw your reader's eye to a specific element on your cover. Here are some ideas:

On *this* book's cover, the title is the focal point (using size and color to make it dominant), followed by the image, then the authors' names, and finally the subtitle.

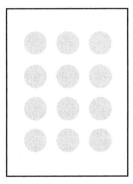

All elements are identical. There is no focal point.

Use a different **color** to create a focal point.

Use a different **shape** to create a focal point.

Use **white space** to create a focal point.

Use placement or **position** to create a focal point.

Use a larger **size** to create a focal point.

Using type as a visual element

Part of keeping your cover design simple is using type in a clean and uncluttered way. There are lots of ways to create visual interest with your type using size, contrast, and color. Here are some ideas:

Use size extremes
(Arno Pro, 105/13 pt).

Use contrasting typefaces
(Corinthian Pro/Myriad Pro).

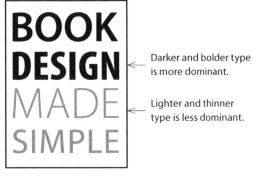

Darker and bolder type is more dominant.

Lighter and thinner type is less dominant.

Use color and weight
(Myriad Pro, 100/50% black).

When designing your title treatment, keep in mind the typefaces you've used inside your book. Perhaps the same typeface(s) can be used on the cover, too, if not for the title then for other text, such as the author's name, endorsements, or back-cover copy.

Just because the other text on your front cover isn't your focal point doesn't mean it should be boring. Here are a couple of ideas for treatment of authors' names:

F I O N A   R A V E N • G L E N N A   C O L L E T T

Add lots of tracking to all caps (Myriad Pro Black with 500 tracking).

FIONA **RAVEN**
GLENNA **COLLETT**

Myriad Pro Light/Bold adds contrast, and the alignment adds interest.

Using repetition and alignment to create a unified look

Repetition and alignment help to tie different elements together to create a unified look for your cover.

Repetition means repeating colors, shapes, lines, and textures:

  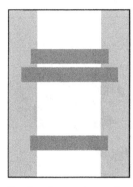

Repeating color blocks adds symmetry and focus.

A **predictable shape** allows a focus on the words.

Overlapping creates tension, but symmetry relieves it.

In symmetrical designs, elements are aligned consistently, and colors and weights can be repeated. In asymmetrical designs, there is a visual relationship that unifies but also often creates a path for the eye to follow. Asymmetry can create interesting tensions between elements.

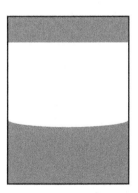  

The **weight** of this cover is at the bottom.

Lines of type are **off center** but still **balanced.**

Overlaps, bleeds, and differing **shapes** create interest.

Using white or negative space

White space is the breathing space around type and images, and it doesn't have to be white. Also known as negative space, it's the areas on your cover that *don't* include information. These areas are just as important as the areas that do include information.

Let's say you have a busy background image to use on your cover. As you'll see in the example below, a busy background is difficult to set type over, and it also reduces the significance of both the image and the type. Try removing part of the image and replacing it with a color to create a clean area for type with an uneven edge. Adds interest, right?

See page 403 to learn how to hide part of your image.

A busy background image adds clutter and makes type harder to read.

Removing part of your image adds focus, clarity, and interest to your cover.

Making an image small can magnify its importance and create a focal point.

Sometimes making an image quite small makes it seem more important. It's like a little treasure. You have to look a bit closer, perhaps actually pick up the book in a bookstore. It draws people in.

One design corner you might get backed into is when all your elements are rectangular. This can easily happen when using photographs and all caps. Even the border around the cover creates a rectangle.

Try taking images out of boxes and putting them on a plain background with perhaps a drop shadow. And try changing type from all caps to upper- and lowercase. Free yourself from the rectangle!

Rectangular shapes abound in photos and all caps.

There are no rectangles here, just various shapes.

Creating a color palette

How do you choose suitable colors for your type and other elements? And how will you know which colors go well together?

An easy way to create a color palette for your book cover is to use the colors within an image. If you're using an image on your front cover, you can pick colors from that image. If not, find something that has a color palette you like, such as a postcard, a surface (like brick or marble), a piece of fabric, a china pattern, a scarf, or anything that can be scanned or photographed to create a digital image.

Creating a color palette from images

Color Theme Tool
(it may be behind the
Eyedropper Tool or
the Measure Tool)

You can use the Color Theme Tool to create color palettes right from any image placed in InDesign. Select the Color Theme Tool, then hover over any image or frame. You'll see a larger border appear around any frames that can be sampled for colors. Click on any image and a palette with five colors appears (see below). If you want to clear that palette and sample something else, press Esc and try again. You can sample a part of an image by dragging the Color Theme Tool over a specific area, or even sample several images at a time by dragging across all of them.

Click arrow to see all five color themes

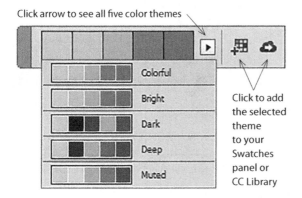

Click to add
the selected
theme
to your
Swatches
panel or
CC Library

Click on the arrow in the color palette and up to five color themes appear. Each theme is named and includes five colors.

Converting your Color Theme Tool to CMYK

Since you're creating a file for print, you'll want any colors you select to be CMYK colors (see page 257). Double-click on the Color Theme Tool in the Toolbox to open the Color Theme Options dialog box. Choose Convert to CMYK in the drop-down menu, and click OK.

Color Theme Options
☐ Ignore opacity and other applied effects while picking colors   **OK**
When applying colors: [Convert to CMYK ▼]   **Cancel**

Adding colors to your text, shapes, and images

It's easy to add any of the colors in your color theme to text, shapes, and images. Click on the theme of your choice, then on one of the colors in that theme and you'll see the eye dropper change direction; now it points to the right and has a color square next to it.

Hover over text and a small T appears, then click on the text to apply the color to it. Hover over the edge of any frame and the color square will show an outline, then click to apply a color stroke to the frame. Hover inside a frame and click to apply a color fill to the frame.

You can add any of these color themes to your Swatches panel by selecting one and clicking the Swatches icon (⊞) on the Color Theme palette. The colors are added to a theme folder in your Swatches panel. If you want to change the name of the folder, double-click it and type a new name. To experiment with or expand the theme—or any of the colors in the theme—first select the theme, then click on Add this theme to my current CC library (☁). Now continue on to the next page.

Pay attention to the names of the color themes because one or more of them might correspond to the feeling you are aiming to convey. But if you planned for a bold, bright cover and are currently leaning toward more muted colors, it might be appropriate to rethink the goals you set up in chapter 55.

You only need to choose Convert to CMYK once. All subsequent color themes will be in CMYK color.

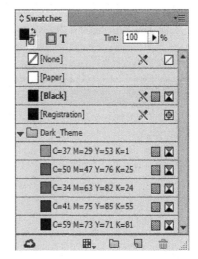

When you add a color theme to your Swatches panel, the colors are in a folder with the name of the theme you chose.

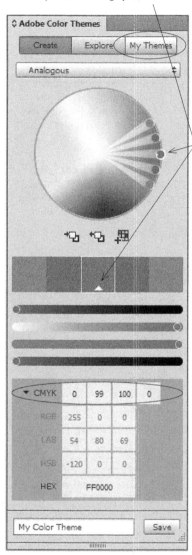

Expanding your color palette

The colors in the color themes you got from your image will obviously go nicely with it. But chances are good that you'll want a wider range of suitable colors in your palette, including an accent color or one that will really stand out.

Expanding your color palette is easy using the InDesign color wheel. Click Window>Color>Adobe Color Themes to open your Adobe Color Themes panel (see left). Click CMYK in the bottom section so all the colors you choose will be CMYK.

Click the My Themes button at the top right and look for a theme you just added (see bottom of page 395). Under your theme, click on Actions>Edit This Theme. Now you'll see the color wheel with your theme displayed below. Pick one of the colors to become the one you'll base your experiments on by clicking the small triangle that appears at the bottom of the color (it says Set as Base Color when you hover over it). This color will stay the same as you try new colors to go with it. Try different settings from the drop-down menu just above the color wheel: Analogous, Triad, and so on. Each setting will show you different colors that go nicely with your base color.

If you want to make changes to your base color, drag the circles in the color wheel around. Dragging a color toward the center of the wheel makes it lighter or grayer, and dragging it toward the outside makes it darker or more intense. To fine-tune a color even further, use the sliders below the theme. If you just want to get back to your original color, start over in My Themes and choose your theme again.

To make a theme from one of your other swatch colors, type the CMYK values of the swatch in the area below the wheel.

When all the colors in the theme are exactly as you want them, click Save at the bottom right. Choose whether you want to save it as a new theme (Save a Copy) or to replace your original one (Save Changes), and your color theme will be saved in the My Themes section. To save this theme to your Swatches panel, return to My Themes, click Actions (under the theme), then click Add to Swatches.

Polishing your front cover

You've set up your InDesign document to experiment with some front cover designs and added some great colors to your Swatches panel, but your cover doesn't look remotely professional yet! Don't panic . . . book covers normally go through a stage where they look just terrible. Every book cover and its designer endures this stage in the creative process before the cover evolves into its final form.

Now you'll focus on fine-tuning and polishing the elements on your cover to make it look just right. This is when the disparate parts come together to form a cohesive whole. You'll experiment with type treatments, images, color, balance, and proportion (all the while keeping your list of descriptive words from chapter 55 in mind), and hopefully enjoy the design process!

Lots of ideas follow in this chapter, so be sure to try any you think could be suitable for *your* cover.

Fine-tuning the type on your front cover

Now that you've placed your text on the front cover and positioned it appropriately, you'll want to make more improvements. Here are a few tricks to upgrade your type.

Adding color to your type

Add color to your type in InDesign by 1) selecting it with the Type Tool, then using the Swatches panel to apply a stroke or fill, the same way you apply colors to a shape (see page 259), or 2) select a color with your Color Theme Tool and drag over your text to change its color (see page 395).

Start with your title (or the type you want to be the most prominent), and try all the colors in your color palette. Lighter colors generally display better over darker backgrounds, and vice versa. See page 391 for examples of possible type treatments for your cover.

If you find a particular color you want to use for your title, but it's too loud or quiet, make the type smaller or larger until you find the right balance of color and size. Large type with a quieter color will seem equally prominent as small type with a louder color.

book

Here are a few more tips when adding color to your type:

BOOK DESIGN

Add a solid fill and/or stroke by selecting the type and assigning fill and stroke colors (see page 259).

BOOK DESIGN

Complementary colors, such as blue and orange, can make text pop in a bad way. Try darkening or lightening them a bit.

BOOK DESIGN

Try printing your cover in b&w to check the type contrast, in case it's featured in a b&w catalog or publication.

BOOK DESIGN

If your type doesn't stand out sufficiently against your background, consider adding a drop shadow (see page 405).

Consider using different colors for words in your title or author's name, to give one more prominence.

book design

Feel free to let type flow outside of the edges of any background shapes, as it adds interest!

Stretching type to fit a specific space

Let's say you want your title or author's name to fit across the width of your cover or to fill a specific space. One way to stretch or shrink type is by using the Vertical and Horizontal Scales in your Character panel (below), but this can create distorted-looking type. There are several other ways to stretch or shrink your type's width and/or height using a combination of tracking and condensed or expanded typefaces.

Use the up and down arrows in the Character panel's Vertical and Horizontal Scales to stretch and shrink your type.

BOOK DESIGN

Stretch your title's width by applying tracking and a bolder typeface (Myriad Pro Black 18 pt with 300 tracking).

BOOK DESIGN

Increase your title's width and height by increasing the type size (Myriad Pro Bold 28 pt with 50 tracking).

BOOK DESIGN

Use a condensed typeface to increase the height of the title (Myriad Pro Bold Condensed 37 pt with 50 tracking).

BOOK DESIGN MADE SIMPLE

To create a consistent-looking block of text using different sizes of words, choose a typeface with several weights (from light to bold) as well as Condensed or Expanded instances. Set each line of type in a size and instance to fill the space. (Myriad Pro: BOOK = Bold SemiExtended 61/40+50Tracking, DESIGN = Condensed 87/76, MADE = Light SemiExtended 44/46+510Tracking, SIMPLE = Semibold 56/54+50Tracking.)

Kern → Kern

If your type doesn't have consistent spacing *between* the characters, you can kern them (see page 337).

Combining type and images on your cover

Finding the right combination of type and images for your cover is important. You'll want the type to be easily readable and your images interesting but not overwhelming your type.

Successfully combining type and images depends on what kind of images you're using. If an image fills your cover, you'll be looking for ways to make your type stand out on top of it. In this case, you might add a drop shadow or a color bar behind your text. Or, if your image won't fill your front cover, then you'll be looking for interesting juxtapositions between your image and type.

Using horizontal images on vertical covers

Most fiction and nonfiction books are taller than they are wide, so they lend themselves nicely to using an image with a vertical orientation that fills the cover. But suppose the image you want to use on your vertical cover has a horizontal orientation? Or it's just not the right shape?

There are a few ways of getting around this dilemma that you'll recognize from other book covers you've seen. You can add a color bar across the top and/or bottom to fill the white space or add a color background behind the image (see chapter 33). If you have the skills in Photoshop, you can make your image the right size and shape to fill your cover.

If you're using an image with a shadow and type with a shadow, make sure that all the shadows go in the same direction, unless you are trying for a specific surreal effect. (In the Drop Shadow dialog box, the number of degrees in Angle should be the same.)

Create a color bar above and/or below the image.

Add a color background that blends with the image.

Change the image in Photoshop so that it fits the cover.

Or use a combination of these ideas to suit *your* cover.

Matching a color background to the image on your cover

Suppose you're creating a color background for your front cover, and you want the color to match a specific color in your cover image. How do you find out what that color is? That's what the Eyedropper Tool is for.

The Eyedropper Tool 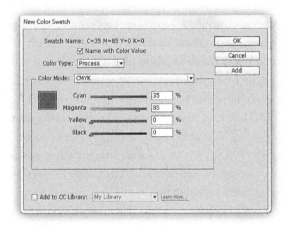 may be behind the Measure Tool or Color Theme Tool.

Select the Eyedropper Tool, and you'll be able to move it around with your mouse. It'll be pointing down from the right, just like in the Toolbox icon. Click the eyedropper on any color on your cover to "pick" the color and load it into the Eyedropper Tool. When it's loaded, the Tool will look half full and shift its position to the left.

Click the eyedropper on any shape you've made to fill it with the color you picked. Or, select type with the eyedropper to color the type. (To remove this color from the eyedropper, simply click again on the Eyedropper Tool in the Toolbox.)

Using the Eyedropper Tool is a simple way to pick just one color—it doesn't involve making a palette of colors the way the Color Theme Tool does.

The color you picked will appear in the Swatches panel as the current fill or stroke color (whichever is in front in the upper left corner of your Swatches panel). To add it to your swatches so you can use it again, select New Color Swatch from the Swatches fly-out menu and your new color will appear. Make sure that the Color Type is Process and the Color Mode is CMYK. Next, click Add, then Done.

If your cover has a black background, use a rich black (combination of ink colors) rather than just 100% black ink. A nice, rich black is 60% cyan and 100% black.

NOTE: Offset printers will not accept colors that contain more than 300% ink colors. In other words, a color with 100% cyan, 100% magenta, 100% yellow, and 20% black contains too much ink—it will saturate the paper beyond what it can absorb.

This is known as ink density, or total area coverage (TAC).

Unbox your images and set them free!

Removing an image from its box can change its shape from a square or rectangle to a more dynamic shape. It can also create new white space (space without information) in which to place your type.

To remove the background from your image, open it in Photoshop. Open your Layers panel by clicking Window>Layers. You'll see that your image is on a layer called Background. This layer is automatically locked, so create a new unlocked layer by following the steps below.

Drag the Background layer onto the New Layer icon to create a copy of that layer.

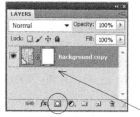

Now drag the Background layer onto the Trash icon to delete that layer.

To add a layer mask to your new unlocked layer, click the Add Layer Mask icon.

A layer mask allows you to hide parts of your image without actually deleting those parts. That way, you can add them back if you change your mind later.

Click the curved arrows once to switch the background color to the foreground.

Foreground and background colors are set to black and white when you're working in your layer mask.

Pressing the \ key will give you a pink checkered background, which might help you better see what you're drawing.

Now you have a layer with your image and a layer mask. In the Layers panel, you'll see two thumbnails on your layer: one of your image on the left, and the Layer Mask Thumbnail box (currently white) on the right. Click once in the Layer Mask Thumbnail box to make sure it's selected.

Now look at the foreground and background colors at the bottom of your Toolbox (they'll be black and white when you're working in your layer mask). With black as your foreground color, select your Pencil Tool (✏️) or Brush Tool (🖌️), which can be found by hovering on the Pencil Tool, and drag anywhere directly on your image. When black is selected, that part of your image becomes masked (invisible!)—and you'll see a checkered background revealed behind it. That area is now transparent.

When you draw in black, the areas you cover become hidden. You'll see black showing on the layer mask thumbnail in the Layers panel. When you draw in white, those areas are revealed again. The Pencil Tool makes a sharp edge, and the Brush Tool makes a soft edge. Select the hardness of the brush or pencil using the Brush Preset Picker just above the Toolbox. You can also select degrees of transparency (Opacity: 100% or less).

Keep in mind:

- Black hides and white reveals. Switch by clicking the curved arrows.
- To change the size of your Pencil or Brush Tool, press [to make it smaller and] to make it larger.
- To zoom in or out of your image, press Ctrl/Cmd and the equals (=) or minus (-) signs.
- If you mistakenly do the wrong thing, press Ctrl/Cmd+Z to undo it.

It's easiest to first zoom in on the edge of the image you want to isolate. Next choose the Pencil or Brush Tool and adjust the size of the Tool so it's easy to see. Then start drawing around the edge of your image. To create a smooth edge, click the Tool at your starting point, then hold the Shift key and click farther along the edge. Holding the Shift key fills in the area between clicks and creates a smooth line (see below).

Original image, full size.

Once you've isolated the edge of your image, "erase" the rest of your background image by enlarging the Pencil Tool and drawing with black over the rest of the background.

When you're done, save your image as a PSD (or a TIF with the settings shown at the right). Finally, place your image in InDesign, and its background will be transparent.

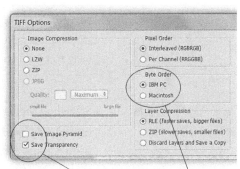

Choose your platform here.

Be sure to check the Save Transparency box.

First zoom in to your image and trace around the edge with a small tool (use the Pencil Tool for a crisp edge or the Brush Tool for a soft edge).

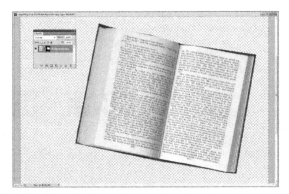

Then switch to a large Pencil Tool and "erase" the whole background. You'll see the area you've hidden shown in black in the layer mask thumbnail in the Layers panel.

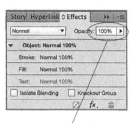

Move the Opacity slider to make your image more or less transparent.

Image at 100% opacity before screening to 10%, enlarging, and placing behind the main narrative to the right.

Text of different opacities require separate frames. In the two examples to the right, the screened text is in one frame and the 100% black text in another.

Screening images, shapes, and text

You may want some type or an image to be screened—in other words, to make it partially transparent.

To screen an image or text, click Window>Effects to open the Effects panel in InDesign. Select your image or text frame with the Selection Tool, and you'll see its opacity is 100% in the Effects panel. To change the opacity, simply click on 100% and move the slider to the left until the image is at the desired opacity.

Screening images

An image used in the background of your cover or pages can be screened to, say, 10 or 15% to give the effect of a watermark (like the large background image on this page). If the image is screened back enough, it's easy to read type placed on top of it, even small type like in this paragraph.

Screening shapes

It might be hard to read your title because of the background image. Adding a screened shape (like a rectangle or oval) between the title and image makes the title easier to read. In the example below, the rectangle is screened from solid white to 65% opacity.

Screening text

Making type partially transparent can produce interesting effects on your book cover, as shown below.

Making type stand out using drop shadows or outlines

A sure sign that a book is self-published is extensive use of default drop shadows and strokes, so don't use them on your cover unless they're absolutely necessary to make your type more visible against a background image. Before resorting to a drop shadow or stroke, try making your type bigger, bolder, or brighter first.

One circumstance where a drop shadow and/or stroke will help your title to pop out of the background is when you have a light-colored title against a darker, busy background. Below you'll see how a drop shadow can create more contrast without being obvious.

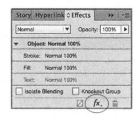

In the Effects panel, click *fx* and select Drop Shadow from the fly-out menu.

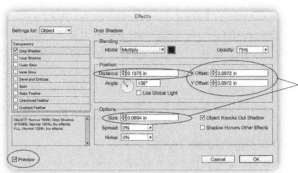

Reducing these numbers brings the drop shadow closer to your text.

The default Drop Shadow settings are applied here. See that the K in BOOK is not properly visible because the shadow is too far below the text. To optimize your drop shadow, check the Preview box at the bottom left of the Effects panel, then experiment with your settings.

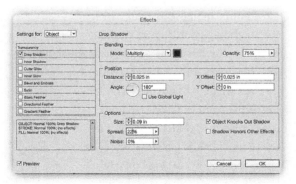

Try adding a stroke around the type (see page 272) using a dark background color.

In this example, the Distance and Offset are smaller, bringing the shadow right up behind the text rather than below it. The Size and Spread are larger, filling in more space behind the characters. You can drag the Angle around to experiment with what angle suits you best.

Finishing your front cover

Getting proofs printed

When you have one (or a few) front cover designs coming together, it's often helpful to get prints made. Simply export your InDesign file to PDF (see chapter 71) and email or upload the PDF to your local copy store. Ask them to print the cover(s) on glossy cardstock (80 lb or thicker) on a high-quality color laser printer. Then trim the cover(s) to size on a paper trimmer using the crop marks.

These prints come in handy. Stand them up on a table or shelf and live with them for a while. Take them to your local bookstore and stand them on a bookshelf with other books in your genre. How do they compare? Get feedback from people whose opinions you value, but keep in mind you won't please everyone, nor will you follow every suggestion given.

You'll undoubtedly make a few adjustments after seeing printed proofs, perhaps fine-tuning colors or adjusting sizes of type and images.

When you're satisfied with your front cover, you'll want to save it in a folder together with its fonts and images using the Package feature.

Packaging your front cover

To package your front cover, first save it with a current name (perhaps including today's date in the file name). Then follow the instructions in chapter 45 to package your file. The only difference in packaging your front cover is that your images may be in RGB color and will therefore show an error message. No need to worry about that now.

The settings shown to the right will produce a JPG file at 72 ppi and the same dimensions as the trim size of your book (for example, 5.5" × 8.5" or 396 × 612 pixels).

If you're using your front cover for an ebook, your images can stay in RGB color. Save your cover as a JPG for uploading to ebook vendors by clicking File>Export then choosing JPEG from the Save as type (PC) or Format (Mac) drop-down menu and click Save. Next you'll see the Export JPEG dialog box (right). Use the settings shown and click Export. The resulting JPG is suitable for uploading to ebook vendors.

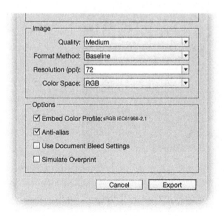

Choosing your book's binding

There are many types of book bindings available. Which is best suited for *your* book? (If you're publishing an ebook and not a print edition, then skip to the next chapter, as ebooks only require a digital front cover.)

Types of book bindings

Trade paperbacks

Trade books are what you see in a bookstore. They are aimed at the general public. Bookstores are filled with trade paperbacks of all shapes and sizes in every category. Is *your* book a trade paperback? Most likely, the answer is yes, but if not, you have other options.

Trade paperback with flaps

Some trade paperbacks have flaps on their covers, much like the flaps on dust jackets. The cover on a paperback with flaps is a little sturdier because of the double layer of cover stock when it's folded over. You might choose this binding if your front and back covers are filled with large, significant images that you don't want overprinted with type, or you might have a great deal of important information that simply must be on the cover somewhere. On the other hand, you might just want your book to stand out a little from the rest.

Hardcover with dust jacket

Traditionally, most books started out as hardcover books and then, if they proved popular, came out in paperback form. These days, the vast majority of books start life as paperbacks and stay that way. But a hard cover still makes a book seem more important than a soft cover does.

If you decide to use a hard cover, you'll need to make design decisions about the cover itself as well as the dust jacket that protects it. Hard covers and dust jackets cost more than paperbacks to produce.

Perfect binding is a method of binding both hardcover and softcover books whereby the pages are glued along the spine edge, and then the cover is glued to the spine.

Smyth-sewn binding is a stronger (and more expensive) method of binding whereby the signatures are sewn together along the spine edge, and the pages are held to the spine with some cloth and the endsheets. Books lie open flatter with sewn binding, and libraries prefer it because of its durability.

Most hardcovers are wrapped with colored paper or cloth, foil-stamped on the spine with the book title and author's name, then wrapped with a dust jacket. Children's books and picture books are often hardcovers wrapped with printed paper, and the dust jacket is optional.

The dust jacket includes information and images that would appear on a paperback cover, and you will use the jacket flaps as well. The front flap usually gives information about the content of the book, sometimes continuing onto the back flap. The back flap often has the author's photo and bio, and credits for the jacket design and artwork. This leaves the back of the jacket for your marketing blurbs and reviews.

Less common binding styles to consider

There are plenty of other kinds of bindings that might fit *your* book better than the more common hard and soft covers. Here are some ideas:

- **Saddle stitch** Used for very short books that consist of only one signature (see pages 321–322). The signature is stapled two or three times at the fold.
- **Spiral** Like a spiral notebook, with metal or plastic-coated wires.
- **GBC binding** Also called Cerlox®, it holds the pages together with a cylindrical plastic comb. It requires rectangular holes to be punched near the inside edges of your pages. You can choose from many colors and sizes, and the binding can be printed on with your spine information. Consider using this for cookbooks or technical books.
- **Wire-O® binding** Similar to spiral, but the wires are parallel to each other and in pairs. Used sometimes for technical or reference material.
- **Concealed Wire-O** Like Wire-O, but the front-cover material continues across to the back (as in a hardcover book) and conceals the wires so the spine can be printed on.

In most of the bindings listed above, the inside margin on your pages must be wide enough to allow for the holes that need to be punched for the binding (usually 0.5"). Ask your printer for their requirements.

Your book will lie open flat with all of these types of binding.

Paperback (with flaps)

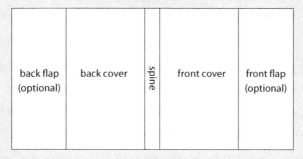

Casebound hardcover

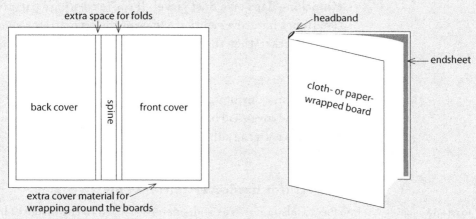

Dust jacket

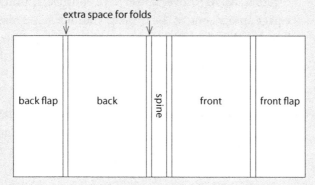

Inside covers

Printing on the inside covers will add to the cost of printing, and most print-on-demand and digital printers don't offer this option.

However, if your printer supports this option, you may choose to use the extra space on the inside covers for:

- **Advertising** Showcasing other books you've written or adding testimonials.
- **Maps and diagrams** If your readers are going to have to refer repeatedly to references such as maps, charts, diagrams, or lists, consider putting them on the inside cover.
- **Decorative** The inside cover can be printed with a color wash, to add impact to the overall book design.
- **Mimicking flaps on a dust jacket** If you're creating a paperback edition from a hardcover edition and want the cover to look similar to the dust jacket, then the material from the flaps can be printed on the inside cover.

Note that most printers do not allow anything to be printed in the area where the cover will be glued to the spine of the book, because the ink interferes with the adherence of the glue in the binding process.

Endsheets (for hardcover editions only)

To set up a template for your endsheets, see page 443.

Endsheets (also known as endpapers) are glued to the inside of hardcover books and are partially responsible for holding the cover and pages together. All hardcover books have endsheets. Think of the them as a 2-page spread, one at the front of your book and one at the back. They can be printed (using either the same material for the front and back or different material), or you can simply use plain colored paper to lend a little color to the inside of the book.

Once you've decided which type of binding is appropriate for your book, your next step is to download or create a template in InDesign for your whole book cover. The following two chapters will help you do that.

Using a printer's cover template

If you're printing your book with a POD printer such as Amazon KDP or IngramSpark, you can generate a template for your book cover on their website. Just fill in the specs for your book (trim size, page count, and so on), and request the template. Either you'll download it or it'll be sent to your email address, depending on the printer.

Cover templates come in a variety of formats, but they fall into two categories: an InDesign file or a file that can be placed into an InDesign file (such as PDF, PNG, and EPS). Choose the format you feel most comfortable working with based on the processes explained below.

POD printers' templates are often set up on a large sheet of paper, with specific placement of the book cover on that sheet.

Using an InDesign cover template

If you choose "InDesign CS3 and newer" for your template, you'll get an InDesign file that is already set up on the correct sheet size, and it'll include guides to show you where to place all the elements on your cover.

Open the template in InDesign and save it with a new file name. Note that there are two layers in the file, Guides (a locked layer) and Layer 1. Click the eye icons at the left of each layer to show and hide them so you can see what they include. Usually the bottom layer has colored areas showing you where to place your images and text, and the top layer has non-printing guides, written specs, and possibly a barcode.

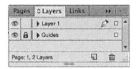

The typical layers included in a printer's cover template.

Next you'll copy and paste the front cover you've already created into layers that are *between* the two existing layers. So go ahead and create new layers between the two existing layers with the same names you used in your front cover InDesign file (see page 388). Then open your front cover InDesign file and select everything on one layer (lock the other layers to make that easier). Copy everything on the layer by clicking Edit>Copy, then paste it into the new layer on your new template by selecting that layer and clicking Edit>Paste. Finally, drag the text and images into the appropriate place on your template.

The keyboard shortcut for Copy is Ctrl/Cmd+C.

The keyboard shortcut for Paste is Ctrl/Cmd+V.

Using a PDF, PNG, or EPS cover template

If you choose a file format other than InDesign for your cover template, you'll incorporate that file into your existing InDesign front-cover file by placing it onto a separate layer. Here are the steps:

Click in this column
to hide a layer.

Click in this column
to lock a layer.

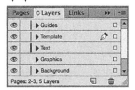

Two new layers at the top
for guides and template.

For a more detailed
explanation on adding
guides, see page 421.

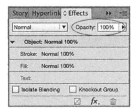

Move Opacity slider to 50%.

1 Open the file by double-clicking it and look for the Document Size or Sheet Size (usually 17″ × 11″ or 15″ × 12″ or something similar).

2 Open your front-cover InDesign file and change the width and height of your document (click File>Document Setup) to match the Document Size or Sheet Size in your template.

3 Create two new layers *above* your existing layers (see page 388) and call them Template and Guides.

4 Select the Template layer and place your template on it by clicking File>Place (or pressing Ctrl/Cmd+D), selecting the file, and clicking Open. Line up the edges of the template with the edges of your document (not the bleed). Don't resize the template.

5 Select the Guides layer and add vertical guides to the left and right edges of your cover (line them up on the trim marks), and to the left and right edges of your spine (line them up with the fold marks), by dragging guides from the ruler at the left. (If your rulers aren't showing, click View>Show Rulers or press Ctrl/Cmd+R.) Add horizontal guides to the top and bottom edges of your cover (line them up on the trim marks), by dragging guides down from the ruler at the top.

6 Now make the template transparent so you can see your cover through it. Open your Effects panel by clicking Window>Effects. Select your template using the Selection Tool, then move the Opacity slider in the Effects panel to 50% so your template is transparent.

7 Lock the Template and Guides layers by clicking in the Lock Layer box (see above left), then drag to select all your front cover elements and move them into position, lining them up with the template and guides.

8 Finally, hide the Template layer by clicking the eye icon (see above left). Now you'll be able to build your spine and back cover using the guides, and any time you need to refer to your template, simply show the Template layer (click the eye icon again), and change the opacity back to 100%.

Creating your own cover template

If you haven't decided yet where you'll be printing your book, you can still create a cover template based on your trim size and type of binding. Estimate the spine width for the time being, and adjust it at the last minute when you've chosen a printer and learned the thickness of their paper.

Here are the steps you'll take:

1   Calculate your cover's approximate dimensions
2   Set up your template in InDesign
3   Add guides to show fold and spine allowances (if needed)

You'll notice that the whole book cover—front, spine, and back—is printed on one sheet of paper, with the back on the left and the front on the right. If you're designing a dust jacket, it will also include the back flap on the left and the front flap on the right.

1 Calculate your cover's approximate dimensions

To calculate the size of your cover template, you'll need the trim size of your pages (for example, 5.5″ × 8.5″, 6″ × 9″, etc.), and for now you'll just estimate the width of the spine as a starting point. You'll request the exact dimensions of the cover from your printer later on, after you've chosen a printer and established your exact page count. But for now, it's easy to get started using an approximate spine width.

On the following pages are examples of different types of book covers, showing their dimensions. Find the appropriate cover and binding for *your* book, and use the example shown to calculate the dimensions for your cover template.

You'll see that the size of the bleed is not included in the calculations, as you'll add the bleed to the *outside* of your cover template using the bleed feature in InDesign.

The spine width will be finalized at the last minute, when your page count is final and when you know the thickness of the paper your printer will be using.

Softcover

When a softcover book is bound, the cover is wrapped around the *book block* (the block of printed pages) and glued down the spine, then the bleed is trimmed off the outside edges. The final spine width provided by your printer allows for the fold at the edges of the spine.

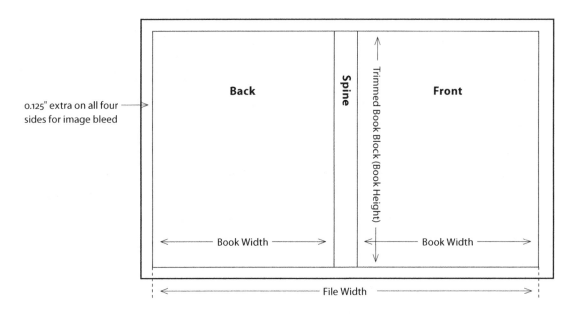

File Width Formula: Book Width × 2, plus Spine Width
File Height Formula: Book Height

Let's say your trim size is 5.5″ × 8.5″ and you have approximately 200 pages. Your book width is 5.5″, your book height is 8.5″, and you can estimate your spine width for the time being at, say, 0.5″. Therefore your file width is 11.5″.

$$5.5 × 2 = 11 + 0.5 = 11.5″$$

Softcover with flaps

When a softcover book with flaps is bound, first the bleed is trimmed off the left and right edges and the flaps folded in. Then the cover is wrapped around the book block and glued down the spine, and the bleed is trimmed off the top and bottom. The final spine width provided by your printer allows for the fold at the edges of the spine; however, you'll need to add a small amount to the width to allow for the flaps to fold into the book.

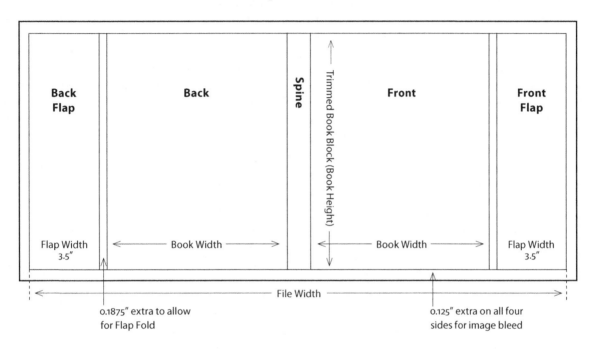

Width Formula: Flap Width × 2, plus Flap Fold × 2, plus Book Width × 2, plus Spine Width
Height Formula: Book Height

Let's say your trim size is 5.5″ × 8.5″ and you have approximately 200 pages. Your book width is 5.5″, your book height is 8.5″, say your flap width is the standard 3.5″, and say your flap fold is 0.1875″. You can estimate your spine width for the time being at, say, 0.5″. Therefore your file width is 18.875″.

$$(3.5 \times 2) + (0.1875 \times 2) + (5.5 \times 2) = 18.375 + 0.5 = 18.875″$$

Printed hardcover wrap

When a hardcover book is bound, the cover is glued to the *book boards* (the three cardboard pieces—front, spine, and back—that form the hard-cover), and the large bleed wraps around to the inside of the boards. The spine width is larger than for softcover books to allow for the width of the boards, and extra allowance is given for the spine fold.

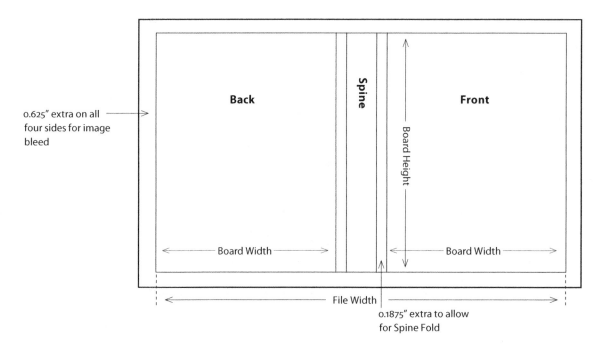

Width Formula: Board Width × 2, plus Spine Fold × 2, plus Spine Width
Height Formula: Board Height

The Board Width is usually about 0.1875″ less than your trim size, and the Board Height is usually about 0.25″ more than your trim size. So calculate those two numbers first. Let's say your trim size is 5.5″ × 8.5″ and you have approximately 200 pages. Your board width is, say, 5.3125″, your board height is, say, 8.75″. You can estimate your spine folds at 0.1875″ each and the spine width for the time being at, say, 0.75″. Therefore your file width is 11.75″.

$$(5.3125 \times 2) + (0.1875 \times 2) = 11 + 0.75 = 11.75''$$

Dust jacket

The dust jacket (DJ) will be trimmed on all four sides after it's printed, then wrapped around a hardcover book. The spine width is larger than for softcover books to allow for the width of the hardcover boards, and extra allowance is given for the flaps to fold around the boards.

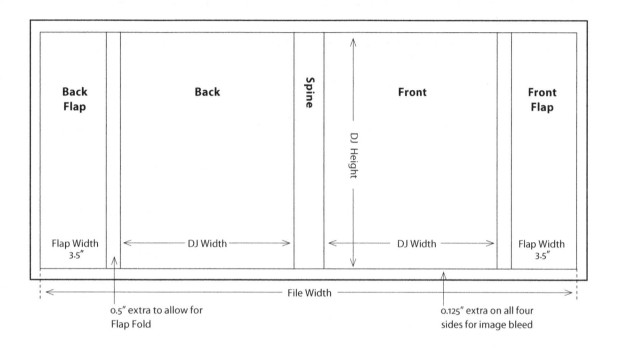

Width Formula: Flap Width × 2, plus Flap Fold × 2, plus DJ Width × 2, plus Spine Width
Height Formula: DJ Height

The DJ Width is usually about 0.1875" more than your trim size, and the DJ Height is usually about 0.25" more than your trim size. So calculate those two numbers first. Let's say your trim size is 5.5" × 8.5" and you have approximately 200 pages. Your DJ width is, say, 5.6875" and your DJ height is, say, 8.75". You can estimate your flap folds at 0.5" each and the spine width for the time being at, say, 0.5". Therefore your file width is 19.875".

$$(3.5 \times 2) + (0.5 \times 2) + (5.6875 \times 2) = 19.375 + 0.5 = 19.875''$$

2 Set up your template in InDesign

There are two ways to set up your template: by creating a new InDesign cover template, or by changing your existing front cover InDesign file to include the cover template. If you've already designed your front cover in InDesign, it will be easier to change your existing document (see page 420).

Creating a new InDesign document for your cover template

Start a new document in InDesign by selecting File>New>Document (Ctrl+N). Fill in the boxes using the calculations you made earlier in this chapter, then click OK. (In the example below, the dust jacket calculations from page 417 were used.)

Fill in the Width and Height you calculated earlier in this chapter.

The Number of columns is 2, and the Gutter between the two columns is your estimated spine width.

If your book cover includes flaps, add left and right margins to act as guides for the flaps at 3.5". Otherwise, leave all the margins at zero. Click the "link" button to enter different numbers in the boxes.

If you don't see the Bleed and Slug options at the bottom, press the triangle here.

Fill in the amount of bleed for your book cover here. All four numbers are the same. Use 0.125" for all covers except a printed hardcover, which has a bleed of 0.625".

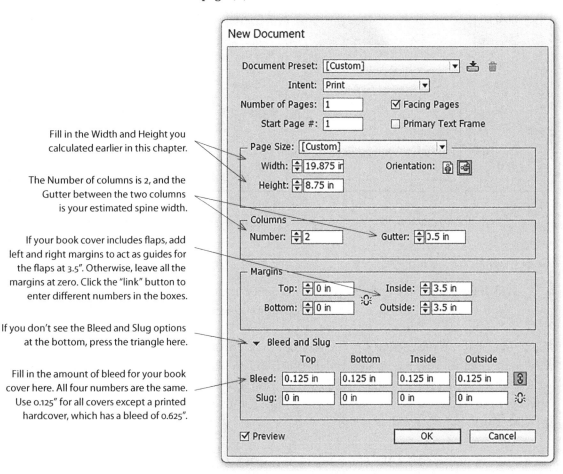

The cover template you've created will look similar to the template for your type of cover shown earlier in this chapter. (The example below is from the dust jacket template shown on page 417). Regardless of which template you've created, you'll see that the gutter between the two columns in the center forms the spine of your book. And, if you've created a template for a cover or dust jacket with flaps, the left and right margins show the fold of the flaps.

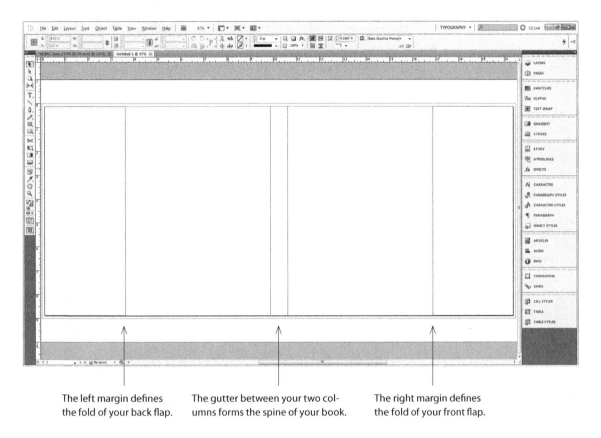

The left margin defines the fold of your back flap.

The gutter between your two columns forms the spine of your book.

The right margin defines the fold of your front flap.

If you've created a softcover template without flaps, then you're done! However, for any other cover template you'll want to add guides (see page 421) to show where the fold allowances lie, so you don't accidentally put any important information there.

If you want to copy and paste an existing front-cover design into your new template, follow the instructions on page 411.

Changing your existing front-cover InDesign file into a template

To change your existing InDesign file into a full cover template, you'll change your document dimensions in two places: in Document Setup and in Layout>Margins and Columns. Here are the steps:

1 Make sure you're in Normal view by selecting the Selection Tool and pressing W. That way you can see the margins and columns.
2 Select File>Document Setup and change the Width and Height to the numbers you calculated for your template. Add your bleed. Click OK.
3 Select Layout>Margins and Columns. Change the Number of columns to 2 and add your spine width to Gutter. Click OK.

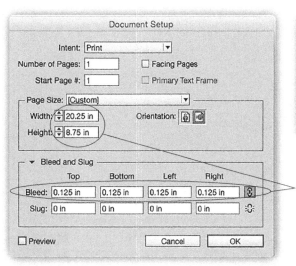

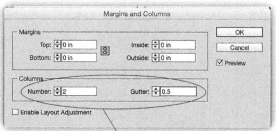

Change the Number of columns to 2, and add the spine width you calculated (or estimated) to Gutter.

Fill in the Width and Height figures you calculated earlier in this chapter, then add the amount of bleed (0.125" for any cover except a printed hardcover, which has a bleed of 0.625").

4 Now select and drag your front cover design into the appropriate position on the right side of your template (remember the front cover is on the right and the back cover is on the left).
5 And finally, save your whole cover with a new name.

If you're creating a cover with flaps or a spine width allowance, you'll want to add some guides to show where those allowances are and avoid putting any important information there (see next page).

3 Add guides to show fold and spine allowances (if needed)

Adding guides to the fold and spine allowances is a handy reminder of which parts of your cover won't be readily visible when your book is bound.

Guides are easy to set and won't show either on your printed document or when you view your document in Preview mode. Here's how to set them:

If your book-cover template is for a softcover, you won't have any fold or spine allowances and so won't need to add guides for them.

1   To add a vertical guide, click anywhere in the ruler on the left side, and drag to the right. Release the mouse at the place you want the guide to be on your template.

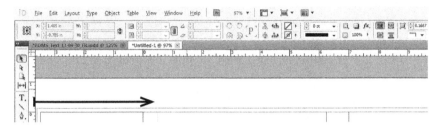

Press Ctrl/Cmd while dragging, and the guide will extend across the pasteboard, too.

2   To add a horizontal guide, click anywhere in the ruler across the top, and drag a new guide down.

You may want to add a guide a specific distance from something, such as a guide to show a fold allowance 0.5″ from the fold of a dust-jacket flap. To do this, set the ruler to zero at the fold by dragging from the crosshairs where the rulers meet. Then drag a guide to 0.5″ away from the fold to show the fold allowance.

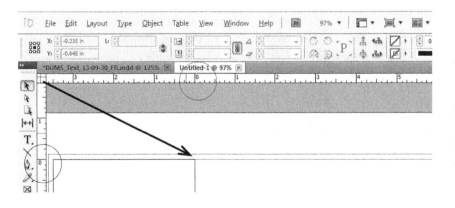

Set your ruler to zero in the place you want to measure *from*. Then drag a guide to the correct distance from it.

Later, you can return your zero point to its original position by double-clicking on the intersection of the rulers at the top left of your screen.

Planning your back cover

Front covers grab and back covers sell . . . this is where you make your sale! Plan what you need to include on your back cover, and keep it simple. When deciding what to include on your back cover:

- Ask yourself what the main benefits are to your target readers. Leave out everything else.
- Don't clutter your back cover with too much information and a busy background.
- Presenting less information in an easy-to-read type size is better than cramming in lots of information with a small type size.

Remember, your back cover copy can be just as powerful a marketing tool as your front cover. Be clear about the benefits of buying your book, and you'll deliver an irresistible message.

Use this chapter to decide what you'll include on your back cover, then write your copy and compile your testimonials and images. You'll add them to your cover template and typeset them in chapter 64.

Assemble your back-cover copy in Word. Then you'll be able to place your Word document into your cover template in InDesign.

Tagline

Grab your reader's attention by placing a catchy tagline at the top of your back cover. Don't just repeat your book's title on the back cover. Your tagline can be a short phrase or a whole sentence, or it can pose a question. Just make sure it's to the point and will draw your reader in.

Summary

Don't give away the entire plot or all the contents; just offer an enticing taste of what's inside. If your book is nonfiction, tell your readers what a great benefit your book will be to them. It'll be easy to use, or fast to use, or it'll keep your reader up to date. It'll simplify your reader's life or make him/her an authority on the subject. Write advertising text that blends with a summary of your book. Not many bookstore browsers are going to read the whole thing and wish for more, so one or two paragraphs should be enough. And remember that this is not the same style of writing as inside the book; this is ad copy.

Testimonials, endorsements, reviews, blurbs

Gather comments from other authors, people in your field, or celebrities, if you happen to know any. Always print an attribution after the reviewer's name. If he or she is an author, give the name of their most relevant book. This is the major way to reward them for writing your review.

Someone may want to give you a testimonial but be unsure about what to write. In this case, write a good testimonial and ask permission to use their name with it.

On the back cover, use your best testimonials (best description or author), and just use the phrase or sentence of each testimonial with the most impact. Make the testimonials as short as possible while retaining the key words and intent. Keep it honest, too. If a reviewer says, "This book is the best example of garbage I've seen this year," don't edit it down to "This book is the best I've seen this year." Ask the reviewer's permission to edit their copy if necessary so that it fits nicely on the page. (The full testimonials can be printed on the first page or two inside the book.)

If you don't have any testimonials yet, consider printing some advance review copies to give to potential reviewers.

What if you get a bad review? You don't have to put it on your cover, and who would? But take the reviewer's words seriously, and see whether there is a way to improve your book. Thank the reviewer for his or her candid views and suggestions.

Author biography

Just a short bio will do, including only relevant information (why you are an expert on the book's subject). You can include a more complete bio on the last page inside the book if you want to.

Author photo

Everyone likes to see what the author looks like. In most cases a professional photo works best, but don't rule out snapshots taken by friends, as a candid shot can be very charming. Narrow the choice down to a few images, then poll your friends and family about which one they like best. Make sure that *you* are the main feature in the photo; unnecessary extras can be distracting. If your book is about lion taming, it's fine to show a lion nearby, but probably not with your head inside its mouth! Be sure to include a credit for the photographer under the picture or on the copyright page.

For a fiction work, the author bio can be lighthearted and vague, or it can list education, career, and family details, especially if they are relevant to the book's topic. For nonfiction, and especially a how-to book, the author's credentials are essential. Keep the biography short (one paragraph) and to the point.

Publishing information and bookstore categories

QR code

Your publishing information is usually placed at the bottom of your back cover. This includes a barcode with ISBN and price (see chapter 70), your publishing name and logo (optional), your website URL (if you have one), and a QR code (optional, see below).

List one or two catagories so that bookstore staff will know where to shelve your book. The categories are usually shown at the top left corner of your back cover but can instead be placed at the bottom with your publishing information. Find your category at bisg.org.

Create a QR (Quick Response) code

A QR code is programmed with a website URL address and, when scanned with a mobile device, opens the specified website in a browser.

To create a QR code in InDesign, click Object>Generate QR Code with

your Selection Tool. Choose Web Hyperlink from the Type drop-down menu, then enter the URL of your home page (or Buy the Book page) on your website, then click OK. The QR code will load onto your pointer. Click anywhere on your page or pasteboard to place the QR code, and it can be placed at any size since it is a vector image (based on math rather than pixels).

Designing your back cover

There are as many ways to design a back cover as there are books out there. So start by keeping it simple, and embellish later when you see how much space you have available.

The steps you'll take are:

1   Typesetting your back cover copy
2   Typesetting your bio and adding your photo
3   Adding your barcode and publishing information
4   Fine-tuning your back cover

Keep in mind there are no hard and fast rules for designing back covers. If a different kind of design suits your book, feel free to deviate from the guidelines in this chapter.

1 Typesetting your back-cover copy

Start by placing your back-cover copy onto the Text layer on your back cover. Using your Selection Tool, click File>Place, browse for the Word document containing your back-cover copy, and click Open. When your pointer is loaded with the text, drag a frame to fill your back cover to flow the text in.

The keyboard shortcut for Place is Ctrl/Cmd+D.

Drag the edges of the text frame so they are approximately 0.5″ in from the edges of the cover. (This leaves an ample area between the text and the edges of the back cover, and you can decrease the amount of space later if needed.)

Next, create and apply paragraph styles for your tagline, summary, testimonials, and testimonial attributions, following the guidelines on pages 426–429. Make sure the text fits nicely into the top two-thirds of the back cover. If you discover you have too much copy and your back cover looks crowded, simply edit it to fit.

Organize your existing paragraph styles

If you need a refresher on creating paragraph styles, see chapter 10 and/ or the box on page 61.

Before creating new paragraph styles for your back cover, take a moment to organize your paragraph styles. You probably have some unused ones left over from your front-cover designs. Remove unused paragraph styles by clicking the fly-out menu on the Paragraph Styles panel then choosing Select All Unused. Click on the trash can icon at the bottom right, and you'll see the Delete Paragraph Style dialog box (shown below). Choose the option shown, then click OK.

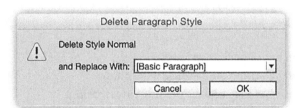

Now open your Basic Paragraph style by double-clicking it, and select Basic Character Formats on the left. Make sure the typeface chosen for Font Family is the same typeface used in the main narrative for your pages. That way your back-cover copy will be set in the same typeface and your cover will complement your pages.

Creating and applying your back-cover copy styles

On pages 427–428 are sample paragraph styles for your tagline, summary, and testimonials. These are very general paragraph styles to get you started, and you'll need to tweak them to suit the amount of back-cover material and style of book *you* have. For now, just create the styles and apply them to your text. When you're finished, your Paragraph Styles panel should look like the one shown to the right.

To sort your paragraph styles alphabetically, click the fly-out menu and choose Sort by Name.

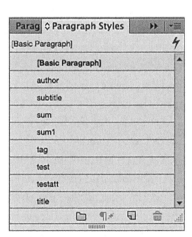

☐ **Tagline [tag]**
General:

Parent = [Basic Paragraph]
Style Name = **tag**
Based On = [Basic Paragraph]

Changes from the [Basic Paragraph] style:
Basic Character Formats:

Font Style = Semibold Italic
Size = 18 pt

Indents and Spacing:

Alignment = Center
Space After = 14 pt *or* 0.1944 in

Design your own book with confidence!

Do you want to create your book cover and/or pages yourself? Well, now you can! Follow this simple step-by-step guide to design and typeset your own book using Adobe InDesign.

Learn the basics of book design from experts. We'll help you through every stage of your book's design, from getting started in InDesign to uploading your digital files to your printer.

Here's what your tagline looks like using the Tagline [**tag**] style above. Later you can change it to suit *your* back cover by changing its typeface, size, color, and/or alignment.

☐ **Summary, First Paragraph [sum1]**
General:

Parent = [Basic Paragraph]
Style Name = **sum1**
Based On = [Basic Paragraph]

Changes from the [Basic Paragraph] style:
None

☐ **Summary [sum]**
General:

Parent = **sum1**
Style Name = **sum**
Based On = **sum1**

Changes from the [Basic Paragraph] style:
Indents and Spacing:

First Line Indent = 0.2 in

Apply the **sum1** style to your first summary paragraph and **sum** to subsequent paragraphs. These paragraphs currently match the main narrative in your pages.

Do you want to create your book cover and/or pages yourself? Well, now you can! Follow this simple step-by-step guide to design and typeset your own book using Adobe InDesign.

Learn the basics of book design from experts. We'll help you through every stage of your book's design, from getting started in InDesign to uploading your digital files to your printer.

☐ **Testimonials [test]**

Parent = [Basic Paragraph]
Style Name = **test**
Based On = [Basic Paragraph]

Changes from the [Basic Paragraph] style:

Basic Character Formats:

Size = 10 pt
Leading = 12 pt

Indents and Spacing:

Alignment = Center

☐ **Testimonial Attributions [testatt]**

Parent = **test**

General:

Style Name = **testatt**
Based On = **test**

Changes from the Testimonials style:

Basic Character Formats:

Size = 8 pt
Leading = 10 pt

Indents and Spacing:

Space Before = 0.0625 in
Space After = 0.125 in

Apply the **test** style to your testimonials and **testatt** for the attributions. Later you'll make sure the testimonials with more than one line split in appropriate places, and you'll add small caps and italics to the attributions.

A testimonial goes here, saying how wonderful the book is!

—Attribution, author of *Another Book*

A second testimonial goes here, with lots of kudos about the book . . . really a spectacular endorsement.

—Testimonial Name, CEO of Great Company

A third testimonial goes here.

—Testimonial Attribution, book designer

Now that you've set up your back-cover copy with paragraph styles, it should fill the top two-thirds of your book cover, leaving room for your bio, photo, publishing info, and barcode below.

2 Typesetting your bio and adding your photo

Place your bio in a new text frame below the text frame containing your back-cover copy. It's handy to keep your bio in a separate frame so it can be moved and sized independently from the back-cover copy. Create the Bio [bio] paragraph style shown below and apply it to your bio.

If your book cover is a dust jacket or soft-cover with flaps, your bio will go on your back flap (see page 436).

☐ **Bio [bio]**

Parent = [Basic Paragraph]
Style Name = **bio**
Based On = [Basic Paragraph]

Changes from the [Basic Paragraph] style:
Basic Character Formats:

Size = 10 pt
Leading = 12 pt

Next, place your photo (see page 288) on your Text layer, and apply a text wrap to it (see page 296). Your photo is placed on the same layer as your text rather than the Graphics layer so that the text wrap affects the text (text wrap doesn't affect text on a layer above it).

Fiona Raven and Glenna Collett are book designers who share a keen interest in all things relating to book design. The question arose, "Why isn't there a book that explains step-by-step how to create a book in InDesign?" We have shelves full of books that explain part of the process—books about design, typography, InDesign, image optimization, publishing, and so on—but not a single book that walks you through the whole process of creating a book from start to finish in simple terms.

Apply the **bio** style to your bio, then place your photo and make it a suitable size using the Free Transform Tool. Then apply a text wrap (see page 296) to your photo and move it next to your bio.

3 Adding your barcode and publishing information

If you already have your barcode (see chapter 70), place it at the bottom of your back cover on the Graphics layer. With the frame selected, open your Swatches panel and select [Paper] for the fill color (see page 259). Most printers allow light-colored backgrounds for barcodes; however, some POD printers require a white background, so start with that.

If you don't have a barcode yet (and this is most likely the case), create a placeholder by drawing a 2″ wide × 1.25″ high white rectangle using your Rectangle Tool (see chapter 33), and add your barcode to it later.

Always place a barcode at actual size, and don't resize it. If you need a slightly bigger box behind it, use the Selection Tool to enlarge the frame without changing the size of the barcode.

Possible placement of category for bookstores

If your barcode doesn't come with a human-readable price, you must add one yourself.

human-readable price
ISBN
encoded price

Adding your other publishing information is optional and depends on what you have available:

- **Publishing name** Create a new text frame on the Text layer, type your publishing name, and create a new paragraph style for it. Or, if it's an established brand, typeset the name using the colors and typeface of your brand, or place an image of your brand name there.

- **Publishing logo** If you have a logo for your publishing company, place it at the bottom of your back cover on the Graphics layer.

- **Website URL** If you have a website, type the URL in a new text frame on the Text layer, and create a new paragraph style for it.

- **Category** If you want to let bookstores know where to shelve your book, create a new text frame on the Text layer, type your category, and create a new paragraph style for it. Put it at the top left of your back cover or at the top left corner of your barcode box (see above).

The Book Industry Study Group lists book subject categories at bisg.org.

4 Fine-tuning your back cover

Now that you have all your information laid out on your back cover, you'll need to make it all fit nicely and add some color.

Look at the examples below to get some ideas for your back cover. Put what you feel is most important at the top. If you'd prefer to have your testimonials above your tagline and back-cover copy, just cut and paste them at the top.

If you're designing a dust jacket or softcover with flaps, your bio and author photo will go on the back flap rather than the back cover (see page 436).

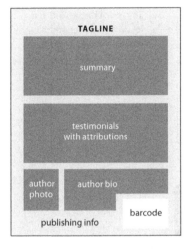
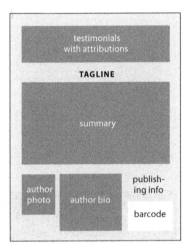
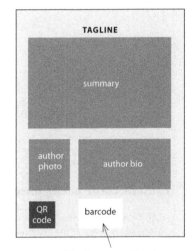

Distributors and bookstores usually require that barcodes be placed in compliance with Book Industry Study Group standards (a minimum of 0.25″ and a maximum of 0.75″ from the bottom edge of the back cover).

Experiment with your paragraph styles to make your type larger or smaller to fit the space. If your type is too small to read comfortably, consider rewording some of your material to make it more concise. Think about your potential readers . . . what will appeal most to them? Make sure you are speaking to them directly. Make it clear and easy to read.

You'll need to give credit for the cover design and images, including the author photo. Credits usually go on the copyright page (see page 226), with two exceptions: if your cover is separate from the book (i.e., a dust jacket), then the credits go on the back flap (see page 436), and if you're designing the cover but not typesetting the pages, you should add the credits to the back cover.

See pages 432–433 for ideas on embellishing your back cover.

Simple back cover

Tagline set in all caps to fit the width of the text block

Summary is longer as there are no testimonials.

Publishing name/logo and website URL

The red of the tagline, bullet paragraph separators, and title on the front cover are all taken from the red of the publishing logo.

From *Mastering Massive Complexity* by Don Johnson

Gradient color background

Tagline set in yellow and fits on one line in width of the text block

Summary set in white

Testimonials set in yellow with attributions in turquoise

Bio set in white with author's name set in yellow

No publishing info or website URL

Gradient background fades from dark blue at the top to light blue at the bottom to match front cover. See page 262 to learn to make a gradient.

From *All The Way Home* by David Berner

Box around testimonials

Tagline set in green italics in typeface used on front cover

Summary set in black, with book title set in pink used on front cover

Testimonials set in black, attribution names set in green small caps

Website URL set large in green

Green is brought around spine from front cover and repeated on both sides of back cover to add color

Green box around testimonials with inverse round corners and a Thick-Thin 3 pt stroke

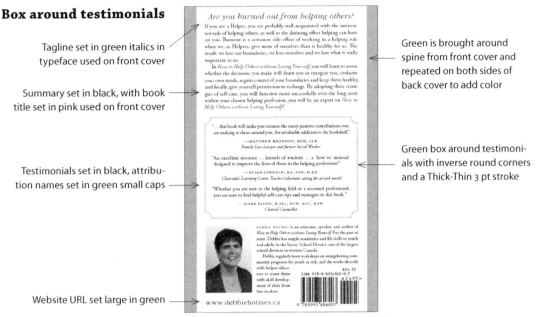

From *How to Help Others Without Losing Yourself* by Debbie Holmes

Color bars top and bottom

Tagline set in white in top color bar

Headings for bulleted lists set in red in same typeface used on front cover

Bio does not include a photo

Publishing info in bottom color bar, inluding publisher's contact info in black and website URL in white

Orange color bars are continued from front cover, around spine, and onto the back cover

Starburst draws attention to bullet points with yellow fill and 2 pt black stroke (polygon shape with 13 pt star and 40% inset)

Rotate by selecting the frame with the Selection Tool and then entering a Rotation Angle value into the field in the Control panel (shown below). Or use the Free Transform Tool.

Bookstore category set in white down right side of barcode box

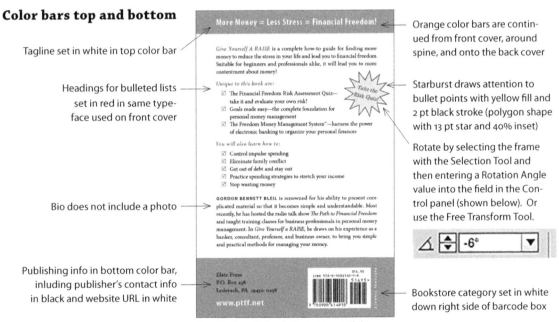

From *Give Yourself a Raise* by Gordon Bennett Bleil

Typesetting tips for your back cover

Here are some ideas for making the type on your back cover look great:

- If you've used a different typeface for type on your front cover, or for the titles and headings in your pages, consider using that typeface for your tagline, author's name, and other special type on your back cover.
- It's best to use black ink for your summary, but consider using another color for your tagline, testimonial attribution names, author's name, website URL, and so on. Choose a color that ties in with your front cover or publishing logo.
- When typesetting testimonials and attributions, you don't need to include the quotation marks around the testimonials. Try center justifying the testimonials and centering the attributions (shown below), or left aligning the testimonials and right aligning the attributions.

A testimonial goes here, saying how wonderful the book is!

—FIONA RAVEN, coauthor of *Book Design Made Simple*

Try placing an em dash before the attribution. Try setting the attribution author's name in small caps, bold, and/or a different color, to make it stand out. If there is a book title in the attribution, be sure to set it in italics.

- You might choose to dispense with your publishing name and logo on the back cover and simply feature your website URL. Try making the URL larger, and set it in a color taken from your front cover (shown below). If you have several words in your URL, capitalize the first letter in each word to make it easier to read at a glance. Adding a QR code to your back cover will simplify steering viewers directly to your website, or to the "Buy the Book" page on your website.

www.BookDesignMadeSimple.com

Embellishing your back cover

Just having type filling the space can be a bit uninspiring. Consider adding a few other embellishments, as long as they don't make the back cover too crowded or hard to read.

Keep in mind the colors, typefaces, and graphic elements you've used on your front cover and in your pages. Can you use the same colors on your back cover?

You can add:

- A background color for your back cover that complements your front cover. Choose a pale color that type will show nicely against. Or, if your front cover is dark, consider a dark background color with light-colored boxes between the background and your type (put those shapes on your Graphics layer)
- Color bars across the top and/or bottom of the back cover, or down both sides to bring those colors around from the front cover (like the examples on page 433)
- A color box between your text and background images, to make the text easier to read (see example to the right, from page 404)
- A box around text to separate it visually from other text (see top example on page 433)
- Paragraph separators or paragraph rules between text to separate different sections, especially if you used paragraph separators in your pages (see top example of bullets on page 432)
- A bulleted list to simplify your summary using special bullet points to add color and interest, such as arrows, checkboxes, or even just colored dots (see bottom example on page 433)

A color box between text and background images helps the text to stand out.

If your book doesn't have a lot of back-cover copy, you can really use colored shapes and paragraph separators to your advantage, to add color and interest to your back cover and to help fill space. If you have a lot of back cover copy, then separate the sections of text visually by using different sizes of type, colored backgrounds, and/or paragraph separators.

The most important issue is that your back cover draws your reader in by being uncluttered and inviting to read.

Back cover and flaps for dust jacket or softcover with flaps

Dust jackets and softcovers with flaps have a slightly different back-cover layout because they include flaps.

The author's photo and bio goes on the back flap (on the left in your InDesign file). For a dust jacket (where the cover can be separated from the rest of the book) be sure to add your design and image credits, and especially the country where your book was printed, at the bottom of the back flap. Put "Printed in [Country]." This is required by customs if your book is shipped across a border.

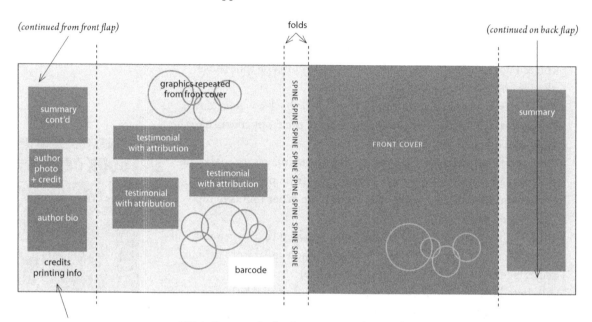

(continued from front flap)   folds   *(continued on back flap)*

Jacket design by Jane Doe
Cover photo by John Smith
Author photo by Moe Curly
Printed in the USA

With flaps and a back cover, you have a lot more cover space available to you. Use the front flap for a straightforward summary or synopsis of the book—no direct marketing. If you need more space, continue it at the top of the back flap, and add "*(continued . . .)*" at the bottom of the front flap and top of the back flap as shown above.

On the back cover, put your testimonials with attributions. You might also choose to include your marketing summary. Look at other dust jackets in your genre to get ideas of what will be best for *your* back cover. And see pages 431–435 for ideas on embellishing your back cover and flaps using typefaces, colors, and graphic elements from your cover and pages.

Designing your spine

The spine may be the first part of your book that a reader sees, and it also connects the front and the back covers. Try to keep both of these factors in mind as you decide how to present your book to the world.

Consider the following as you think about your spine:

- If your front cover has an overall background color, do you want to use that same color on the spine?
- What solid color would appeal to your target audience and also match the color on the rest of the cover? (For POD printing, it's not recommended that a color be placed *just* on the spine, as often the binding is slightly off, and this will make binding flaws very obvious.)
- If your front cover has an image, do you want it to spill over onto the spine and perhaps onto the back cover too? If you do so, will the spine type be readable? (If not, consider a color box behind the type.)
- Is there a small image you could place at the top, middle, or bottom of the spine to entice a reader to pick your book off the shelf?
- If you use the same typeface as for the title on the front cover, will it be legible from a distance? If your title is long, you may need to use a sans serif (even a condensed one) to make your title fit and be easy to read.
- If you're producing a series of books, plan ahead. You'll want all of them to have a similar spine design so they'll look like a set. Try the same placement and type treatment for the title and author's name, but vary the colors of the background and/or type. If you plan to number the series, add a number to the top, middle, or bottom of the spine.

The spine is an important part of the cover that'll help to sell your book because unless you're lucky enough to have your book facing out on a bookstore shelf or table, the spine will be the first thing a customer sees. So make the most of this valuable marketing opportunity!

Books are displayed lying face up on a table, so the front cover and spine must look good together. The type on the spine should be right side up when a book is in this position.

Test the longest and shortest titles in your series to see how well they fit in the space. If both look fine, then your medium-length titles will work, too.

As a corollary to this, the words in your book's title should have immediate impact. Not even a great design will make up for a weak title.

Choosing elements to include on your spine

Here is a list of things you can choose to add to your spine. You'll probably want your book title and author's name as a minimum, but there are other options too:

A spine measuring 0.125" or less is too narrow to have type on it. The printer cannot guarantee that the type would not slide over onto the front or back cover in the binding process.

- ☑ book title
- ☑ author's name (or just surname if you prefer)
- ☐ subtitle
- ☐ publishing name
- ☐ publishing logo
- ☐ small image
- ☐ series number
- ☐ graphics (rules, bullets, and so on) used elsewhere on your cover or pages

Adding a background to the spine

It's more common to carry an image or color onto the spine from the front cover than from the back cover. That way, when the book is lying on a table with the front cover up, the front cover and spine appear seamless.

Before adding any elements to your spine, choose a background image or color. Consider wrapping your front cover image onto the spine (and possibly ¼–½" onto the back cover as well) if there is enough image available. If the image creates a busy background and makes your type too hard to read, you can add a white or color box between the type and the background image. Screen the box back to 20–30% (see page 404) or however much is needed to make the type easy to read.

If you've used a solid color on the front or back cover, it could be extended onto the spine. If your books will be printed digitally, keep in mind that your books will be bound one at a time, and the binding machine will not be adjusted specifically for *your* book. This means that the cover may shift slightly side to side or up or down during the binding process. So avoid putting a separate color *just* on the spine, as the spine could shift in the binding process. If you do want a separate color on the spine, make it narrower than the spine width (use the allowable width for text, as explained on page 439). You'll notice on *this* book there is a color bar down the spine, narrower than the actual spine width, and that's specifically for digital printing, in case the spine isn't perfectly lined up during the binding process.

Adding guides for spine-text clearance

Most printers require a minimum clearance of 0.0625" (¹⁄₁₆") between anything on the spine and the edges of the spine. Here's how to add two guides as a reminder to keep all your spine elements inside the clearance space.

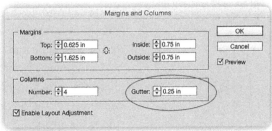

Click Layout>Margins & Columns and in the Columns section see what your spine width is set at (the Gutter number). Subtract 0.125" from that number, put the resulting number in the Gutter box, and click OK. Drag guides from the left ruler (see page 421) onto your two new column guides, then go back into Margins & Columns and change the Gutter number back to your proper spine width.

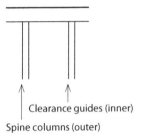

Clearance guides (inner)
Spine columns (outer)

Adding type sideways down the spine

Here's an easy way to add your title sideways down the spine. Select Basic Paragraph style in your Paragraph Styles panel, and create a new text frame by dragging the Type Tool on your Text layer. Type your title in the text frame, then select the title and create a new paragraph style (see page 61) called Spine Title [**sptitle**].

Switch to the Selection Tool, select the text frame, and click the Rotate 90° Clockwise icon in the Control panel. After your text frame rotates, drag it onto the spine, and line up the edges of the text frame with the sides of the spine. With the frame still selected, click Object>Text Frame Options, then under Vertical Justification change the Align drop-down menu to Center and click OK.

Rotate 90°
Clockwise icon

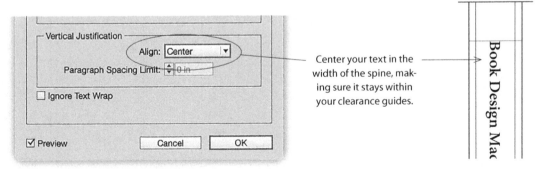

Center your text in the width of the spine, making sure it stays within your clearance guides.

Fitting everything onto the spine

Create separate text frames and paragraph styles for the other text on your spine, and place any images you intend to include. Then change the size of your type and images to fit on the spine.

Sometimes a book title is too long, or there's more than one author, making it difficult to fit everything in. Rather than crowding it all onto one line, try stacking names or the title on two lines. Study other book spines for options. Your main goal is to make the most important information clear and readable from a distance.

Most of the time, spine type reads down from the top. If the spine is wide enough, though, you can place some of the elements horizontally.

Below are some ideas on how to fit everything onto the spine.

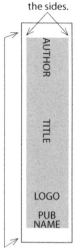

Leave 0.0625" or your printer's specified amount of space without type on the sides.

Leave at least 0.25" of space without type or logo at top and bottom.

You may notice that some of your type doesn't look centered on the spine. You can shift the type left or right (actually up or down) using Baseline Shift, found under the Advanced Character Formats tab in your paragraph style.

Style Name: sptitle
Location:
Advanced Character Formats

Horizontal Scale: 100%
Vertical Scale: 100%
Baseline Shift: 1 pt
Skew: 0°

1 pt baseline shift applied to "AUTHOR"

Don't even think about hyphenating the title to get this effect! If the words don't fit, set them vertically.

Designing extras for hardcovers

If you've designed a dust jacket for your hardcover book, then you'll need to create a digital file for the foil stamping on the hardcover's spine, as well as choose colors for the foil stamping, headbands, and hardcover wrap (the paper or cloth that covers it). You'll also decide whether to create custom endsheets or simply use white paper.

Creating a digital file for the spine imprint

Hardcover books are stamped with foil on the spine. Create an InDesign file for your spine by clicking File>New>Document. Fill out the dialog box as shown to the right, then click OK.

Open your dust jacket file, select the text and images you want on your hardcover spine, and copy them (click Edit>Copy or press Ctrl/Cmd+C). Now go back to your new document, and Paste in Place those elements into your spine (click Edit>Paste in Place or press Ctrl/Cmd+Shift+Alt/Opt+V). Save your new file.

Your new digital file for foil stamping can only contain 100% black ink, with no shades of gray. So open your Swatches panel and select all of the colors except the defaults in square brackets. Then click the Trash icon to delete them all, and the Delete Swatch dialog box will appear as shown to the right. Replace all the swatches you're deleting with default [Black].

If you have a logo or image on the spine that cannot be translated into one solid color, you may need to leave it off the hardcover spine or substitute a more suitable image.

Put the spine width from your dust jacket in the Width box and the height of your dust jacket in the Height box (and you may need to set your margins to zero).

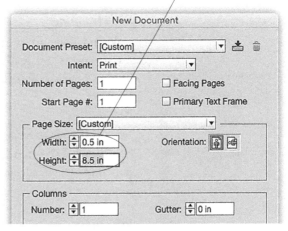

Choosing colors for your hardcover

You'll need to choose colors for the foil stamping on the spine, your hardcover wrap (the paper or cloth that covers the hardcover), the headbands, and a ribbon (if you decide to include one). You can request samples of these from your printer. All of these color choices are included in the cost of printing your hardcover book. There is usually an extra charge for using a cloth hardcover wrap (instead of paper) and always for adding a ribbon.

Hardcover wrap

You'll probably choose a colored paper wrap, but cloth is available for an extra cost if you're so inclined. Look through the color samples from your printer, and choose one to complement your dust jacket. You might choose a color that you've used in your cover design, a neutral color (such as black, gray, taupe, or white), or an accent color, like bright red or yellow, to make a statement.

Foil stamping

Gold and silver are the most common choices for foil stamping, but there are several colors available as well, such as red, green, blue, yellow, and black. Choose a color that complements your hardcover wrap.

headband   endsheet

cloth- or paper-wrapped board

Headbands

The headband (see diagram at left) adds a decorative touch to the book binding. It is the small, ribbon-like cloth band attached to the top and bottom of the hardcover spine. Choose your headband color to complement your hardcover wrap and/or dust jacket.

Ribbon(s)

Ribbons are used as place markers, and you can choose to add one or two. They come in a variety of widths (usually ¼" or ½" wide) and colors. Choose from your printer's samples.

Paper color for the pages

You'll have a choice of white- or cream-colored paper for your pages and can probably choose from thicker (60 lb) or thinner (50 lb) paper.

Endsheets: white, colored, or printed?

All hardcover books automatically come with white endsheets at no extra cost. Or, for a small extra cost you can choose to have endsheets made from colored paper (and choose from a number of standard colors).

If your printer doesn't have a suitable color in their colored papers, you could choose to have the endsheets printed with a color wash (a solid color of your choice, printed on the endsheets). This will cost a bit more than colored-paper endsheets, but you'll get the exact color you want. You can choose from a CMYK color or a spot color (such as a metallic or neon color, or a bright color that can't be duplicated using CMYK colors).

A more expensive option is to design printed endsheets. The cost will depend on the number of ink colors (one color is cheaper than four) and whether you create different endsheets for the front and back of the book or use the same one for both. Keep in mind that the flaps of your dust jacket will obscure part of the endsheets, which might influence your decision.

Create an InDesign file for printed endsheets by clicking File>New>Document. Add two columns with no gutter so you can see where the endsheet will fold (and keep any crucial parts of your design away from the fold). Note there is a bleed of 0.125" on all four sides. Fill out the dialog box as shown to the right, then click OK.

Create an endsheet on page 1 of your document. If you choose to have different endsheets at the front and back of your book, then put the front endsheet on page 1 and the back endsheet on page 2. Consider placing a guide (see page 421) where the flap of your dust jacket will overlap the endsheet, as that area will be covered.

Be aware that endsheets are always made from uncoated paper so that glue will be absorbed into them. After all, the endsheets are glued to both the hardcover and the pages to hold the book together. Uncoated paper absorbs more ink, so colors will look less intense than they will on coated paper.

In the Width box, put the width of your page times 2. So if your book is 5.5" wide, your endsheets will be 11" wide.

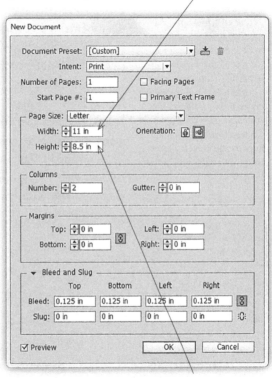

In the Height box, put the height of your page.

67

Printing color cover proofs

You'll want to get color proofs of your cover printed *before* your book goes to press to make sure the colors are perfect for your book and that they print as expected. You certainly don't want any surprises after you've uploaded your book to your printer. An easy way to check your colors is to send a PDF to your local copy store and ask them to print your cover.

To create a PDF, click File>Export, and check that the name of your PDF is okay (InDesign will use same name and file folder as your cover document, except with the file extension .pdf). Choose Adobe PDF (Print) from the Save as type (PC) or Format (Mac) drop-down menu. Click Save to get the Export Adobe PDF dialog box. Choose High Quality Print from the Adobe PDF Preset drop-down menu at the top, then select Marks and Bleeds from the menu on the left, and fill out that section as shown below. All the other sections can remain the same. Then click Export to generate your high-resolution PDF.

Send the PDF to your copy store by email, use FTP transfer, upload it to their website, or hand-deliver a memory stick. For softcovers, ask them to print your cover on 11" × 17" glossy cardstock (coated one side, or

> If you're not sure about a color, try a few options in the same InDesign file. In your Pages panel, drag your cover page icon onto the Create New Page icon at the bottom to duplicate your cover, then try some variations of colors on the new page. Duplicate as many pages as you need to experiment with different colors.

C1S). For dust jackets, ask them to print on 28 lb paper (or their equivalent). If the dust jacket is too wide to fit on one sheet of paper, ask them to tile it (print it on two pieces of paper), with the spine showing on both pieces. Later you'll be able to trim and fold it using the crop marks. Now take the proof to your local bookstore, wrap it around a similar-sized book, and set it on the shelf to see how it fits in with other books.

Congratulations, you've finished your cover!

Part IX:
Preparing to Publish

Obtaining and assigning ISBNs

One of the things you'll need to do as a publisher is obtain a block of International Standard Book Numbers (ISBNs) for your books. Some printers, print-on-demand publishers, and ebook vendors will offer to provide you with an ISBN, but it's better to get your own. Part of the ISBN includes a "publisher number," which is assigned to a specific publisher. Therefore, if you allow another company to provide the ISBN, then that company will be listed as the publisher of your book. ISBNs are easy to obtain online, and using your own numbers means that you'll retain control over your books.

Pages 448–449 offer more details to help you decide how many ISBNs you'll need.

ISBNs are assigned by the ISBN agency in your country. They usually come in blocks of 10, 100, or 1,000, and you'll need a separate ISBN for each edition of your book. If you're publishing one book, be sure to get more than one ISBN as you'll probably produce more than one edition (for example, a softcover edition and a Kindle edition). You might even have other editions, such as hardcover, EPUB, and PDF.

Getting ISBNs in the United States

U.S. publishers can purchase ISBNs from R. R. Bowker LLC at myidentifiers.com.

Go to the U.S. ISBN Agency website and click on the "buy your ISBNs today!" button to get to their purchase page. ISBNs are available one at a time, or in blocks of 10, 100, or 1,000. It's best not to buy just one, as you'll need a unique number for each edition.

Once you've purchased a block of numbers, you can assign the ISBNs to your books as they're published.

Getting ISBNs in Canada

Canadian publishers can purchase ISBNs at bac-lac.gc.ca/eng/services/isbn-canada/Pages/isbn-canada.aspx.

ISBNs are free to Canadian publishers and are issued in 10 days. Go to the Library and Archives Canada ISBN website, where you'll see the steps to register explained. Once approved, you'll receive a user ID and password by email, together with instructions for using your online account. You'll then be able to assign a unique ISBN from your block to each edition of your book through your online account.

Getting ISBNs outside North America

Go to the International ISBN Agency website and click the "Find an agency" button. Select your country from the drop-down menu and you'll see information there on how to obtain your ISBNs.

What do the numbers in the ISBN stand for?

In North America, most retail products are marked with a UPC symbol. The corresponding barcode symbol in use outside North America is the European Article Number (EAN). Every EAN begins with a two- or three-digit prefix, which indicates the country of origin. EANs for companies registered in France, for example, might begin with the prefix 34; Australia's prefix is 93. Since the book industry produces so many products, it has been designated as a country unto itself and has been assigned its own EAN prefix. That prefix is 978, and it signifies Bookland, that wonderful, fictitious country where all books come from.

The publisher number is a unique seven-digit number assigned to your publishing company. All the books you publish will have the same country prefix, country indicator, and publisher number. The only digits that will change from book to book are the title number and check digit.

You'll assign a unique title number to each edition of each book you publish (see page 448).

Getting your own ISBNs is easy to do online, and allows you to retain control of your books after they're published. You might choose to get your books printed somewhere else down the road or produce an updated version or second edition. When you have your own block of ISBNs, you'll be in control of your books' destiny.

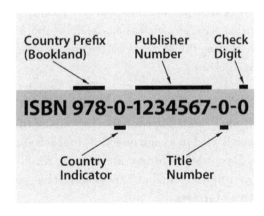

Country Prefix (Bookland) · Publisher Number · Check Digit

ISBN 978-0-1234567-0-0

Country Indicator · Title Number

Assigning ISBNs to print books

When you've obtained your block of ISBNs, you'll need to assign a unique ISBN to each edition of every book you publish. Let's say your first book is a novel called *Raven* and it's a hardcover book. That means your first ISBN number will be assigned like this:

ISBN 978-0-1234567-0-0 / BookTitle1 / Hardcover Edition

The second-last number is 0, the first digit in your block of ISBNs. This number is always assigned to the first edition (in this case the hardcover edition) of your first book. The last number is automatically calculated by an algorithm, and it's called the "check digit." (Sometimes the check digit is an X, so don't worry if you get an X as the check digit in one of your ISBNs.)

Let's say you also release a softcover edition of your book. You'll assign the next ISBN in your block of numbers to your softcover edition:

ISBN 978-0-1234567-1-7 / BookTitle1 / Softcover Edition

The second-last number is 1, the next digit in your block of ISBNs. And the last number is the check digit. So far so good, right?

Assigning ISBNs to ebooks

There are three main formats for ebooks: MOBI (for Kindle), EPUB (for other ereaders, such as Nook, Kobo, iBooks), and PDF. And this is where assigning ISBNs gets a bit trickier, as it depends on how you intend to *sell* your ebooks.

Selling ebooks yourself through different ebook retailers

If you'll be selling your ebooks yourself through different ebook retailers, you'll need to assign one ISBN for each ebook format. For example, if you sell your MOBI format at Amazon's Kindle Direct Publishing (KDP) and your EPUB format at Barnes and Noble, you'll assign one ISBN for each of those formats, like this:

ISBN 978-0-1234567-2-4 / BookTitle1 / Digital Edition (Kindle)
ISBN 978-0-1234567-3-1 / BookTitle1 / Digital Edition (EPUB)

Selling ebooks through an ebook service

Several companies will act as a sales channel for all your digital editions. BookBaby, Smashwords, and Vook are examples of these services. If you're using one sales channel for all your digital editions, then you'll need to assign one ISBN for that sales channel, like this:

ISBN 978-0-1234567-2-4 / BookTitle1 / Digital Editions (BookBaby)
or
ISBN 978-0-1234567-2-4 / BookTitle1 / Digital Editions (Smashwords)

Can your ebook be published without an ISBN?

Yes. If you are only publishing a Kindle edition through Amazon's Kindle Direct Publishing, you can use their internal ASIN tracking number to track your sales instead of an ISBN. Or, if you are only selling ebooks from your own website, you can choose not to assign ISBNs to them.

Keep in mind that publishing ebook editions using your own ISBNs means that you'll be listed as the publisher in the appropriate Books in Print database, and that may help readers search for your ebook online.

How do I tell whether my updated book is a reprint or a second edition requiring a new ISBN?

If you are ordering another print run of your book with no substantial changes (just fixing a few typos, for example), then you don't need to assign a new ISBN. If you've changed the cover but not the text, you can continue to use the same ISBN.

If you've changed the content of your book or added new material (another chapter, preface, appendix, or other content, for example), then you'll need to assign a new ISBN. A new edition is considered a different product and therefore gets its own ISBN.

Setting your book's retail price

Determining your book's retail price can be nerve-wracking. If it's too expensive, your book may be priced out of the market. If it's not expensive enough, you won't even recover your costs. How do other publishers decide? Consider three things: cost per book to print, pre- and post-printing expenses, and the price of similar books in the marketplace.

One way to calculate your book's retail price is to take your printing cost per book and multiply it by five. That may seem like a lot, but consider this: if you sell to a distributor or online retailer, they usually take 65% off your retail price, and you pay the shipping; and if you sell directly to a bookstore, they often take 50% off your retail price, and you pay the shipping. You need to have enough left over to cover your pre- and post-printing costs, and then some.

You are not paying just for printing books. Your pre-printing costs can include editing, proofreading, book design and typesetting, images, indexing, and your ISBN number and barcode. These are all expenses you'll have paid before your book goes to press.

Also see our blog post at BookDesign MadeSimple.com/ how-to-price-your-book.

After your book is printed, you could have any or all of the following expenses: packaging, shipping, postage, advertising, website design and maintenance, web hosting, book marketing, editorial reviews, and contest fees. Plus your time. Don't forget you'll also be giving away free books to your reviewers and to stores and distributors as samples to generate sales, as well as paying for the return of any books damaged in shipping or unsold in stores.

What are books like yours selling for in the marketplace? Your book's price should be in the same ballpark. If your book is thicker, printed in color, has more images, or is unique in subject, people will pay more for it.

Before you decide on a retail price for your book, consider carefully all of the costs to produce it, and anticipate your future costs as well. Then compare prices of similar books in bookstores, and you'll be on track to setting the right price for your book.

Obtaining a barcode

Barcodes are scannable codes that allow booksellers to automatically capture an ISBN (and retail price, if encoded). The Bookland EAN is the barcode used by the book industry. It's actually two barcodes side by side. The larger barcode to the left is the encoded ISBN, and the smaller barcode to the right is the encoded price.

encoded ISBN →

$12.95 ←—— human-readable price
ISBN 978-0-9896511-0-3 ←—— ISBN
51295> ←—— 5-digit price add-on

←—— encoded price

9 780989 651103

You might find later on that your book distributor, if you use one for printed books, requires the price to be encoded. So if you are certain of your price, you might as well include it with the barcode.

Before obtaining a barcode, you'll need to decide whether to encode your retail price. If you choose to encode your price, you'll decide what the five digits will be in the five-digit price add-on. The first digit is the currency indicator. Five is the designation for U.S. dollars, and six is the designation for Canadian dollars. An add-on of 51095 encodes the price $10.95 in USD. A book priced at $3.00 in USD would have the add-on 50300. Books priced at $99.99 or higher use the add-on 59999. If you choose not to encode your retail price, the add-on is 90000. This indicates there is no data encoded.

A free barcode is included on any cover template from POD printers such as Amazon KDP and IngramSpark. Place the cover template on your book cover a second time, then using your Selection Tool, drag the frame sides in to fit around the barcode (this will hide the rest of the template). Move the barcode into position, but take care not to enlarge or shrink it, as doing so may affect its scanning readability. For tips on placing a barcode on your back cover, see page 430.

If you order a barcode from an encoding service, choose EPS or PDF format. The minimum EAN size allowed for book covers is 80% of the barcode's original size, and 2350 resolution is standard. See BookDesignMadeSimple.com/resources for links.

71

Packaging for your printer

Preparing your InDesign file for the printer involves four important steps:

1 Finalizing your InDesign file
2 Checking for errors
3 Packaging your InDesign file
4 Generating a printer-ready PDF

1 Finalizing your InDesign file

If you are using the Book feature to package, see our blog at BookDesignMade Simple.com/using-the-book-feature-in-indesign.

Finalizing your InDesign file involves getting rid of extraneous colors, styles, master pages, and fonts. Here's how:

☐ Open your Swatches panel and from the fly-out menu click Select All Unused. If any swatches are highlighted, delete them by clicking the trash icon. If there are any RGB or spot colors in the Swatches panel, convert them to CMYK by double-clicking the color then changing Color Type to Process.

☐ Open your Paragraph Styles panel and from the fly-out menu click Select All Unused. If any paragraph styles are highlighted, delete them by clicking the trash icon.

☐ Open your Character Styles panel and from the fly-out menu click Select All Unused. If any character styles are highlighted, delete them by clicking the trash icon.

☐ Check at the bottom of the Pages panel to make sure the total number of pages is correct. You should have an even number of pages. If not, add a blank page after the last page.

☐ Go to Type>Find Font and look at the list. Make sure that all the fonts you used are listed and that there are no warnings or question marks next to any of them. If you're using Typekit, all the fonts you've used should be listed. If any are missing or have a warning, select the font, then find it using the Replace With drop-down menus. If the font isn't listed there, you'll need to install it. If there are fonts listed that you didn't mean to use (they might have been imported with your manuscript), click on each one and enter the name of the correct font in the Replace With box below. Go to Find First, then click Change or Change All, and the substitutions will be made. Repeat for each unwanted font.

☐ In the Layers panel, click the eye icon next to any layers you don't want to print so that they become invisible.

If you discover that the unwanted or missing font is used in one of your paragraph or character styles, click here and the style setting will change when you click Change All.

2 Checking for errors

By the time you've finished with the steps listed above, it's unlikely that you will still have anything to fix. But take a look at the bottom of your screen and you might see a red dot and some number of errors next to it. Double-click on this error list to open the Preflight dialog box. It will show you the details of each problem and where it appears, so simply click on the page number shown to jump directly to the trouble spot. You might see any one of the following:

Click on the page number to go directly to the problem.

☐ **Missing font** You have already taken care of any font troubles in step 1, so there should be no warnings, but if there are, go through that step again.

☐ **Missing link** If any images have come unlinked, select each one, click the Relink button, and link it up again (see page 317).

The highlighted error is explained in the Info box.

☐ **Overset text** The text frame has words that don't fit in the frame. Stretch the text frame down to see the words, then either find a way to fit them on the page, or delete them. When you are finished there should no longer be a red "⊞" icon (out port) at the bottom right side of the text frame. Remember to restore the text frame to the right size.

☐ **Other errors** Each is explained in the Info box. Click on the listed page number to go to the problem and correct it.

3 Packaging your InDesign file

Don't forget to go through the packaging process with both your pages and your book cover (the process will be the same for both).

Now that your entire book is organized, everything is gathered together, and all errors are corrected, you will package it all one last time. Packaging a file creates a folder that contains the InDesign file, all fonts (except those used in Typekit), all links, and a customized report.

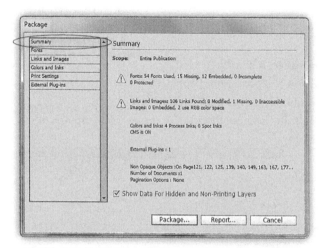

Summary

Save your InDesign file using today's date, then click File>Package. The first section of the resulting dialog box is Summary. If you see a warning symbol, go to the relevant section in the dialog box and find out what the problem is. In this example, there are problems with the fonts and the links.

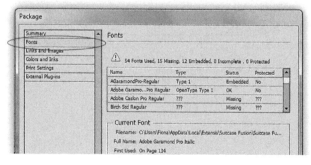

Fonts

In this example, fonts are missing. Click on Cancel, then install the missing fonts, or substitute another font by going to Type>Find Font, selecting the problem font, and replacing it with another one.

Links and Images

This is the final test of all of your graphics and photos. As you can see, the book in the example has images that are improperly linked or are missing (see the Status column). Select a missing link, then click the Relink button. You'll be able to find the problem link and relink or update it. Don't worry about RGB images showing as problems. You'll convert them to CMYK when you create a PDF.

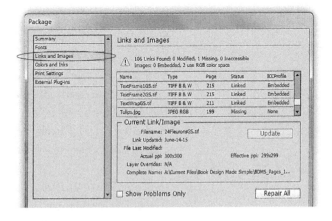

Colors and Inks

In this box you should only see the four CMYK colors: cyan, magenta, yellow, and black. If any other colors are listed, such as spot colors, you'll need to convert them to CMYK in your Swatches panel (see page 452), and do the same for any images coming from another application, such as Photoshop or Illustrator.

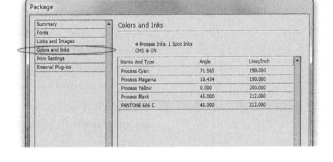

Print Settings

These specifications relate to the printer at the top of the list. This is probably the one you've been using to check your layouts. This information is irrelevant to the final printing of the book, so just ignore it.

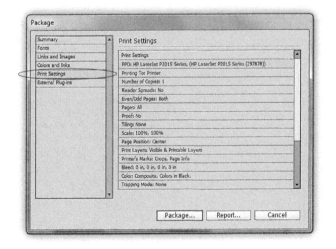

External Plug-ins

Most likely, this box will be blank. If you purchased a plug-in, though, it should be listed.

The final steps

Now click on Package and the next dialog box is Printing Instructions. You may ignore this page and click Continue to get the Package Publication (PC) or Create Package Folder (Mac) dialog box.

Browse for a suitable place to save your new folder, and type a name for the folder in the Folder Name field at the bottom (PC) or Save As field at the top (Mac). Check the boxes shown below. Here is a quick explanation of what these features do:

- **Copy Fonts** InDesign creates a subfolder called Document Fonts and copies all the fonts used in your document into this folder, except for Typekit fonts, Chinese, Japanese, and Korean (CJK) fonts, and any fonts that do not include copying in their license. If you've used any fonts that aren't included (besides Typekit fonts), add them to the packaged folder yourself. No need to worry about Typekit fonts.
- **Linked Graphics** InDesign creates a subfolder called Links and copies all the graphics used in your document into this folder. You want InDesign to copy linked graphics and to make sure the graphics are the updated versions, so check the second and third boxes.
- **Hyphenation** The prepress or printer's computer might have a dictionary program that's different from yours, and it might make the

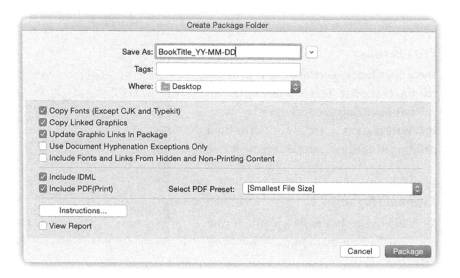

hyphenation in your book change, causing lines of type to move. You don't want this to happen, so check this box if you're going to send your InDesign file (rather than a PDF) to a service provider before printing.

- **Hidden and Non-Printing Content** If you have graphics and fonts on your pasteboard or on a layer that is not visible, and you want those graphics and fonts to be included in your package, then check Include Fonts and Links From Hidden and Non-Printing Content. If you don't want them included, leave it unchecked.
- **Include IDML** IDML is a file extension for an InDesign file format that can be opened by earlier versions than Creative Cloud. It's good to have an IDML file of your book, in case you ever want to open it in an earlier version.
- **Include PDF (Print), Select PDF Preset** This automatically creates a PDF of your InDesign file, which can be handy to have. Choose Smallest File Size for the Preset; that way you can easily email your PDF if needed.
- **View Report** If you check this box, you'll see the complete packaging report in a text editor program immediately after packaging. You can review the report later, so there's no need to check this box.

Click Package to continue. If you've included fonts in your book that aren't from Typekit, you'll see a warning screen like this one (right) explaining how you may use the fonts. Any reputable printer will be happy to explain their font rights and policies to you.

Click OK, and in a few moments your entire book will be grouped into the folder that you named. Now close the InDesign file you were just working on, and open the new file in the packaged folder. Check your Links panel once again to make sure all your images are linked, and click Type>Find Font to make sure your fonts are used properly, and that everything still looks the way it did a moment ago in your original file. From now on this is the file you'll be using.

Note that when you package your files, your library will not be included in the package (though the objects in the library will). If you want to include your library for future use, simply locate it on your computer and add it to the packaged folder.

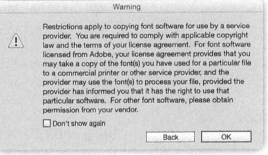

The font legal issues are irrelevant if you're going to send a PDF to the printer instead of sending your InDesign file with fonts. But if necessary, review page 132 for more about fonts and their legal use.

4 Generating a printer-ready PDF

If you haven't done this already, you should now obtain your printer's instructions for making a PDF they can work with. Often you can get this information from your printer's website, but if not, contact your customer representative. The instructions may be available in a PDF you can download, or they may simply instruct you to use an Adobe PDF Preset.

Whichever method you use, you'll be generating a high-resolution PDF using the InDesign file you most recently packaged.

Click File>Export (or press Ctrl/Cmd+E) to open the Export dialog box. Browse to the same packaged folder your InDesign file is saved in (the one you just created). In the Save as type (PC) or Format (Mac) drop-down menu, choose Adobe PDF (Print). In the File name (PC) or Save As (Mac) field, type a name for your file. Your printer may have specific instructions on how to name your book files. CreateSpace and IngramSpark require your book's ISBN plus "txt" for pages and "cvr" for covers, like this:

9780123456700_txt.pdf (for your pages)
9780123456700_cvr.pdf (for your cover)

Then click Save, and you'll see the Export Adobe PDF dialog box. The settings you choose in this dialog box will depend on whether you are using an Adobe PDF Preset or custom settings.

Using a PDF preset

Look in the Adobe PDF Preset drop-down menu at the top of the Export Adobe PDF dialog box (see next page). You'll see there are several choices. Find the one that your printer has specified. Do not change any of the default settings. Be sure you are saving the file as single pages and not spreads. Click Export, and you are done! Your PDF should automatically open in Acrobat; however, not all of the presets have the View PDF after Exporting box checked, and if not, you may need to open Acrobat and then open your file.

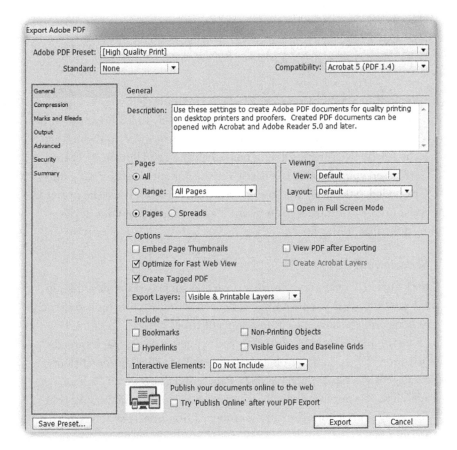

This Export Adobe PDF dialog box shows a typical preset used by printers.

Generating a custom PDF

If your printer has given you specific custom PDF settings, don't panic. This won't be difficult. There are two ways that printers can give you their settings for PDFs: by providing instructions to create a custom preset, or by providing a .joboptions file.

1   **Instructions to create a custom preset** Simply follow the printer's instructions, dialog box by dialog box, and copy every setting precisely. If you run into trouble, the customer rep is there to help. When you've created all the settings, save the printer's settings as a custom preset. Click Save Preset at the bottom left of the Export Adobe PDF dialog box, and name the preset for the printing company, such as

If you are using the Book feature, see our blog at BookDesignMade Simple.com/using-the-book-feature-in-indesign to create a single PDF from multiple documents.

Amazon KDP or IngramSpark. Next time you make a PDF for that printer, you can simply select the preset from the drop-down menu at the top and click Export.

2 **Providing a .joboptions file** This is a small file that your printer can provide to you, containing their custom preset. To load this file into your preset list, click File>Adobe PDF Presets>Define, and you'll see the Adobe PDF Presets dialog box. Click the Load button on the right side, and you'll be able to browse for the .joboptions file your printer provided. Select the file, then click Open. Now you'll see the preset in the Adobe PDF Preset drop-down menu at the top of your Export Adobe PDF dialog box.

Checking your PDF

Check this PDF over very carefully. Don't be surprised if you suddenly spot mistakes that you never noticed, even though you've looked through the book and checked the cover dozens of times before!

You might find it helpful to view your pages PDF as 2-page spreads. With your PDF open in Acrobat, go to View>Page Display and click on Two Page View, Show Gaps Between Pages, and Show Cover Page in Two Page View. The pages will display in spreads so you can make sure that each 2-page spread has the same number of text lines, the folios are in the right place, etc.

You can even get the PDF printed at your local copy store if you prefer to proof a hard copy. Have it printed double-sided and trimmed to size, then bound with VeloBind, Cerlox, or spiral binding.

Take your time, and make sure that every single thing is right before you upload the PDF to your printer.

Uploading to your printer

Every printer has a slightly different process for file delivery. When you're ready to upload your PDFs, contact your printer to find out the procedure. There are a few different ways of uploading to a printer:

1 **Uploading to their website** POD printers such as Amazon KDP and IngramSpark will have you log in to your account on their website, then upload the PDFs in the appropriate place within your account. Usually you'll upload the pages PDF first and then you'll upload the cover PDF, and both will run through a file checker. You'll wait for 24 hours to get an email confirmation that the files are ready to go. You can order a printed proof at this time too (the first printed copy of your book!).

2 **Uploading via FTP** Your printer may provide instructions together with an FTP address, username, and password. You'll be able to upload your two PDFs to their FTP site. Once the files are uploaded, confirm with the printer by email that you've uploaded the files, and let them know what your file names are.

3 **Uploading to a printer's production site** Some printers use specific software, such as Insite or MyBooks, to exchange files, proof files, and track your book's production. Your printer will provide you with a login and password, together with instructions for using the site.

Sometimes printers ask you to send the packaged files for your book cover: the InDesign file, linked images, fonts (if you used any outside of Typekit), and high-resolution PDF. This is requested just in case they need to adjust your book's spine width to accommodate a change in paper stocks.

The easiest way to provide your packaged files is to create a .zip file, which compresses all the files and folders into a single file.

Creating a .zip file in Windows

To create a .zip file in Windows, open Windows Explorer. Find the folder containing the files you want to place into your .zip file. Click once on the folder to select it. Right-click your mouse, go to Send to, and click Compressed (zipped) folder. A new .zip icon or file will appear, and you can type in a name for it. To view the contents of the .zip file, simply double-click it to display its contents in Explorer.

Creating a .zip file on a Macintosh

To create a .zip file on a Macintosh, select the packaged folder, then click File>Compress. The resulting file name will end with .zip.

Reviewing printer's proofs

When your printer sends the proofs, check them carefully. Here's what to look for:

- Pages in the right order, all right side up
- See-through issues—hold the pages up so they are backlit and check to see whether the lines of type that are visible through the paper line up with the ones on the other side of the page
- Spots, marks, or streaks on the pages
- Spelling issues on the cover—one last careful check
- Cover colors—they should be very close to what you expect
- Book spine on center
- Dust jacket spine centered and flap copy properly placed

Avoid making any changes to the words in your book at this point. Changes will be expensive.

Congratulations! You're a published author!

Ebook editions: EPUB and MOBI

73

In this book we are not going to describe how to create an ebook from your InDesign file because the methods are improving and changing all the time, and the topic is big enough to fill another book. This chapter will explain what to expect from an ebook edition and how to prepare your file for conversion.

In this chapter you will learn:

- What EPUB and MOBI files are and why you need both
- What you will lose in a reflowable ebook edition
- What you will gain in a reflowable ebook edition
- When a fixed layout ebook edition is more practical
- How your book is protected against excessive downloads
- How to prepare your InDesign files for conversion

We recommend sending your well-prepared InDesign file to an ebook conversion service.

What are EPUB and MOBI files?

An EPUB file is an ebook that can be read on all ebook readers (except the Kindle), and on computers or mobile devices using an EPUB-reading app. A MOBI file can be read on a Kindle device or the Kindle ebook reader on a computer or mobile device. InDesign exports only to EPUB (with a choice of reflowable or fixed layout), and the EPUB file can then be further converted to create a MOBI file.

A **reflowable** EPUB means the text and images will reflow depending on the screen size and orientation of the device and the size of text the reader chooses.

A **fixed layout** EPUB is similar to a PDF in that the text is not flowable, nor can the reader choose the size of text. The pages remain the same as in the print edition, and the reader is able to zoom in and out, use hyperlinks, search text, and view the book on a mobile device.

What you will lose in a reflowable ebook edition

Some of the features that you designed with great care are going to disappear in your ebook. Similar to a website, the way an ebook looks depends on the device that's being used to view it. Most ebook readers have color screens, but some don't. Some have built-in proprietary designs that take over all books and simply display them all the same. The only thing that's guaranteed to remain in the ebook is the words. Once you come to terms with this idea, you'll feel better about losing the features in the list below.

Of course you can leave all of these features in your print book. But you might need or want to go back and make a new version for EPUB. Remember to give it a different file name.

- **Folios and running heads** In an ebook, your folios and running heads become irrelevant.
- **The back cover** Sadly, this is not needed in an ebook. All that great information that you gathered for the back cover can go on your book's website and in the online bookstore's description instead. You can use it for your ebook's and website's metadata descriptions, too.
- **Extra word spaces and linespaces** Remember that we advised you not to use multiple linespaces or word spaces? This is why. Ebook coding cannot recognize multiple spaces and will use only one. If you need to, go back and find all the multiple word spaces and change them to en, em, or other fixed spaces. Also, add Space Before and Space After in your paragraph styles.

If you need to change your list styles, carefully review each list afterward to see how it turned out.

- **Tabs** Believe it or not, EPUB does not recognize tabs. Go back and convert your tabbed lists to tables or put them in multicolumn text frames. For numbered lists, use the Bullets and Numbering area of the Paragraph Styles panel to change your numbered list styles. Bulleted lists, if styled as described in this book, will be fine the way they are.
- **Small caps and oldstyle figures** In an ebook, small caps are difficult to achieve (see page 92), and oldstyle figures are next to impossible, so use lining figures instead. Change your paragraph styles accordingly.
- **All your careful typesetting** In your ebook you will see widows and orphans everywhere! But try not to fret because someone else will see different ones—it all depends on their device and the size of the text on their screen. If there is some type that simply must sit just so on a page, alert your conversion service. They will isolate that section and treat it like a piece of art, placing it where you want it.

If you've set some display type in a very specific way and are concerned the font won't show properly in your ebook, change the type to an image using InDesign's Create Outlines feature. Select the type using your Type Tool, then click Type>Create Outlines (Ctrl/Cmd+Shift+O). The top line of text below is type, and the bottom line is converted to outlines. Can you tell the difference?

FONT OR IMAGE?

FONT OR IMAGE?

What you will gain in a reflowable ebook edition

In some cases, ebooks can give the reader a better experience than a print book. One reason is that they can see color versions of your illustrations (on a color device). For some people, being able to greatly enlarge the type makes ebooks the only viable way to read a book at all. Other readers simply like the fact that they can loads dozens of books onto their device at once. Also, because ebooks usually cost less, people tend to buy more of them. And don't forget that reading ebooks saves trees, too.

Specifically, here's what you'll gain in your ebook edition:

- **Color** If your book is printed in black only and you have illustrations, save RGB color versions of the illustrations and use them here. Even without illustrations, your book can be made more appealing with color in your headings, chapter openers, sidebar backgrounds, and so on. You can go back now and create a new RGB color version of your book by making a few changes in your paragraph and object styles. (Aren't styles wonderful?)

- **Hyperlinks** InDesign automatically creates links to websites (from URLs in the text) or email addresses (if they are spelled out in the text) when the file is converted to EPUB. If the device is able, it will jump to the link on the Internet while the reader is still on the book page; this is indisputably very handy. Also you can add links to web-sites, to other places in your book, or to your glossary. If your book has an index, you will fill it with hundreds of hyperlinks to pages. And finally, your automatic table of contents (see chapter 28) links to the places listed there.

Review how to convert from one color mode to another in chapter 46.

When a fixed layout ebook edition is more practical

Reflowable ebooks are the preferred format for material that is text based and linear in nature—beginning to middle to end—like a novel. But many books depend on the juxtaposition of text and images to get their message across and, in these cases, a fixed layout ebook is more practical:

- **Children's books** Many children's books include text set on top of illustrations that span 2-page spreads, and the flow of the story is lost if the text is separated from the illustrations.

- **Many illustrations** Heavily illustrated books, such as art and photo-graphy books, are often designed to showcase the illustrations to their best advantage. The illustrations are displayed in pleasing groups, with captions placed to balance the pages. Sometimes a background

Creating hyperlinks

A hyperlink has two parts: a destination (a website or a phrase in the text) and a source (the text or image you want to jump from to get to the destination). To make a hyperlink in InDesign, you must create the destination first and then link to it from the text. Destinations can be used multiple times, but each source can link to only one destination.

Destination

Open the Hyperlinks panel by going to Window> Interactive>Hyperlinks. Select New Hyperlink Destination from the fly-out menu. Choose Text Anchor (specific words somewhere in your text), or URL (web address) destination type. Choosing a Page destination is only practical in a fixed-layout ebook because with reflowable text, you won't know what ebook page any of your text will be on.

- **To make a Text Anchor destination,** highlight the destination word(s) (the anchor) in your text, open New Hyperlink Destination, choose Text Anchor from the Type list, then name the anchor carefully, keeping in mind other destinations that might have similar names. Keep a record of your anchors—the text itself, the anchor names, and where they are located.
- **To make a URL destination,** open New Hyperlink Destination, choose URL from the Type list, and type (or paste) the address in the URL field. You may also give the URL a name in the Name field. If you have used this URL as a destination before, the name will appear in the drop-down list at the top of the Hyperlinks panel.

Source

Select the source in the text—the words or image you want to jump from to get to the destination. Open the Hyperlinks panel and go to New Hyperlink in the fly-out menu. Specify the kind of destination in the Link To list: Text Anchor or URL (or files or email). Then choose the name of the specific destination from the drop-down list. Make sure you are linking to the correct document, too.

If you've made a hyperlink character style, you can apply that style in the lower part of the dialog box.

Click OK and your hyperlink is in place. To delete your link, highlight the source, then click on the trash can on the main page of the Hyperlinks panel.

To find out about some of the other hyperlink functions, complete an InDesign tutorial.

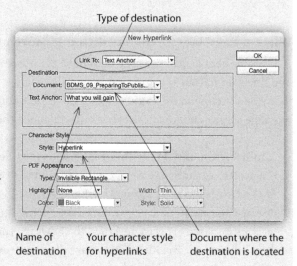

Type of destination

Name of destination

Your character style for hyperlinks

Document where the destination is located

color is placed behind illustrations to enhance them. Keeping all of these design features is possible in a fixed layout ebook.

- **How-to books** Many how-to books, such as cookbooks, textbooks, and *this* book, rely on presenting information one whole page at a time. For example, a cookbook might show a recipe with ingredients, method, and image all on one page. How-to books also tend to have more complex layouts, containing charts, tables, sidebars, pullout quotes, and images, which remain intact in a fixed layout ebook.

The fixed layout ebook format works very well for books where it's important to retain the original design and layout of the book, yet still be available in digital format.

This book has been converted to a fixed layout EPUB.

Protection from excessive downloads

Your ebook file is not automatically protected by DRM (Digital Rights Management). This protection is added by your vendor, if you choose to use one. For example, when your MOBI file is uploaded to your Amazon Kindle Direct Publishing account, Amazon will add DRM protection and sell your ebook to the public in their AZW format. This format restricts the number of downloads by the same user to six different devices.

How to prepare your InDesign files for conversion

If you have carefully followed the instructions in *Book Design Made Simple,* your files should be almost ready for conversion now. Did you:

- create a paragraph style for every single paragraph in your book?
- create a character style for every single character in your book (except those that are [None])?
- use em, en, and other set spaces in place of multiple word spaces?
- use Space Before and Space After in place of multiple linespaces?
- avoid using tabs? EPUB does not recognize tabs. (This might affect your numbered lists but probably not your tables.)
- change small caps to caps and oldstyle figures to lining figures?
- generate an automatic table of contents (if you have one)?

If you've answered "yes" to all of the above, good for you! You now simply need to consider a few more things—we mentioned these earlier:

- You may use color illustrations in place of your grayscales ones. Most images start out in RGB mode, but if you need to convert from CMYK, return to chapter 46 to review how to do that. If necessary, go back to page 317 to learn how to replace the old images with new ones by relinking.
- You may make color headings, chapter openings, and sidebar backgrounds if you like. To do this, change your paragraph and character styles. Go to the Character Color area of the Paragraph Styles and/or Character Styles panels and specify RGB colors in the Character Color area and/or the Paragraph Shading area.
- You may add hyperlinks. See the sidebar on page 466 for instructions. Make a new character style for the link sources. Often they are set in a different color (usually R0_G0_B255).
- You should tell your conversion people about anything that you need to cement in place on a page. For instance, you might have some display type that needs to be positioned just so, like this:

You can create outlines from the type (see page 464), and your conversion service will anchor it to the page just where it belongs.

Visit BookDesignMade Simple.com/resources for recommended providers.

There may be other ways that you can redesign certain elements that would conform better to ebook requirements—consult with your conversion provider. Good, direct communication with your provider is very important. For the simplest books, one of the less expensive services might be all you need, but for those with higher levels of complexity, we recommend using a conversion provider with personal service and a good reputation.

References

Glossary

The page on which each term is defined or first mentioned is listed in parentheses.

2-up (14)   With both pages of a 2-page spread visible at once.

anchored object (350)   A graphic or photo that is locked in place in a line of text. In this book we refer to these as *inline objects*.

autoflow (48)   An InDesign feature that allows text to flow from one page to all of the rest of the book pages automatically. To use autoflow, with the Selection Tool, click on the **out port** on the current last page of text, and you'll see the loaded text icon. Go to the next page, press the Shift key, and click the left mouse button in the upper left corner of that page. The remainder of your text will automatically flow onto the rest of the pages of the book.

back matter (23)   All the material that comes after the last page of regular text in a book. Also called *end matter*.

banding (263)   In a gradient, the appearance of bands of color.

bitmap (303)   A format for art files that are only black and white with no grays or color. Can be abbreviated .bmp in filename extensions but is also supported by **TIFF** format.

bleed (275)   Anything that runs off the edge of the page when printed. In your InDesign document, this material should overlap the edge of the page by 0.125".

book block (414)   After the pages are printed on large sheets of paper and folded into **signatures**, the signatures are assembled into a book ready for binding. The set of signatures for one book is called a book block. Another name for this is **F&Gs** (folded and gathered).

bottom margin (124)   White space at the bottom of the page. Optimally, this space should be quite large, allowing plenty of room for the reader's thumb to hold the book without blocking any of the text.

bounding box (298)   The rectangular **frame** that surrounds a graphic object or image. The box has eight handles for editing its shape and size. Also referred to as a **frame**.

caption (27)   Text commentary related to an illustration, photo, or chart. A caption is usually placed just above, below, or to the side of the illustration.

cardstock (444)   Thick paper that is used for soft-cover book covers.

casebound (409)   *See* **hardcover**.

chapter title (27)   The name given to a section of a book.

character (80)   Unicode is an international system that organizes and names every symbol in each of the world's writing systems. Each symbol (e.g., T, a, &, ġ, ÷) is called a character. *See also* **glyph**.

character style (80)   A collection of attributes applied to a type character.

CMYK (257)   Cyan, magenta, yellow, and black, the four ink colors that make up a regular "full-color" printing job. *See also* **RGB**.

coated (444)   A paper surface with a smooth material applied to it. Not the same as a protective coating.

concealed Wire-O® (408)   A **Wire-O®** binding in which the wires are concealed by the cover material so that the spine can be printed.

Control panel (18)   The panel across the top of the InDesign workspace. It displays most of the type or object settings that are currently in use.

crash (171)   When two characters touch each other it's called a type crash. Usually the characters should be separated; use **kerning** (for two characters) or **tracking** (for a series of characters), or add leading for crashes between two lines.

crossover (293)   A single shape or image that spans both pages of a spread.

digital press (22)   High-quality laser press that uses toner rather than ink to apply type and images to paper.

dingbat (220)   Nonalphabetic type symbol , such as ■, ③, ✗, or ➔. Dingbats are often made up into their own font (e.g., Wingdings or ITC Zapf Dingbats). *See also* **ornament**.

discretionary hyphen (359)   A hyphen inserted manually (Type>Insert Special Character>Hyphens and Dashes>Discretionary Hyphen) that remains invisible unless needed to break a word. Also called a soft hyphen.

dot leader (233)   A tab function that creates a horizontal line of dots from the cursor to the next tab stop. Commonly used in tables of contents, charts, or lists, to connect information visually for the reader.

dots per inch (dpi)   In printing, the number of dots of ink in a one-inch line that make it possible to print **grayscale** or **CMYK**; also called lines per inch. In digital printing, dpi is the output resolution of the printer—as opposed to the input resolution, or **ppi**, of an image. "150 dpi" is actually 150 × 150 (22,500) dots in a square inch.

drop cap (40)   A large initial uppercase letter with its baseline aligning with the base of the second, third, or lower line of the paragraph. *See also* **initial cap**.

em   A horizontal measurement that is equal to the size of the type. An em in 11-point type is 11 points; in 24-point type it is 24 points.

em dash (340)   A dash that is approximately equal to the width of an **em**.

em space (185)   White space that is equal to the width of an **em**.

en   A horizontal measurement equal to one half of an **em**. An **en** in 11-point type is 5.5 points; in 24-point type it is 12 points.

en dash (340)   A dash that is approximately equal to the length of an en. En dashes are used primarily between two numbers (e.g., 12–27).

en space (185)   White space equal to the width of an **en**.

endnotes (25)   Numbered notes that are gathered at the end of the book or chapter instead of being set as footnotes.

endsheets (410)   The paper pasted to the inside of the front and back covers of a **hardcover** book. The sheets serve to hide the turned-in parts of the cover material and to attach the pages to the cover. Also called *endpapers*.

epigraph (24)   A quotation that appears at the start of a book.

EPS (303)   Encapsulated Postscript format that can contain vector and bitmap graphics produced in Illustrator or Photoshop.

F&Gs   Stands for folded and gathered. *See* **book block**.

fly-out panel (17)   A menu that appears when a topic is selected in the set of panels on the right side of the InDesign workspace.

figures (numbers, digits) (42)   Arabic numerals.

folio (26)   Page number.

font (131)   The electronic mechanism that delivers a **typeface**. Each typeface may consist of several different fonts, such as italic, bold, bold condensed, etc. *See also* **typeface**.

footnote (348)   Explanatory note that appears at the bottom of a page.

frame (47) Every object in an InDesign document is contained in a frame. Even if you do not draw a frame, InDesign will make a box around type or graphics. *See also* **bounding box**, **text frame**.

front matter (23) All the material before page 1 in a book.

GBC (408) This type of binding holds the pages together with a cylindrical plastic comb, requiring rectangular holes to be punched near the inside edges of the pages. The spine can be printed on. The name comes from the company that introduced the technique: General Binding Corporation. Also called Cerlox®.

GIF (287) Graphics Interchange Format (pronounced "jiff"). This file format is used mainly for solid-colored graphics on the Internet. The files are compressed to the smallest possible size. Usually not compatible with book printing unless used very small.

glyph (337) A specific design of a type character. For instance, the Q character has a different glyph in each typeface: Q, Q, Q, etc. *See also* **character**.

gradient (262) A smooth transition between two or a series of colors or tints, such as black to white, or orange to purple to blue.

grayscale (303) The term for what used to be called "black and white," as in photos. Grayscale includes all shades of gray as well as black and white and so is a more accurate description.

GREP (51) A type of search used in the Find/Change function that looks for patterns rather than specific words or characters. The term comes from an application designed in the early 1970s for a Unix computer system and stands for Global/Regular Expression/Print.

gutter (126) The space between columns. Also, the inside margin where facing pages meet.

H&J (39) Hyphenation and justification.

hanging indent (65) An indent with the first line sticking out to the left more than the lines that follow it. The glossary you are reading is set using hanging indents.

hard page break *See* **page break**.

hard return (50) A line return that forces a new paragraph; also called an end-of-paragraph return. Place the cursor where you want the break, then press Enter/Return. *See also* **soft return**.

hardcover (407) A book binding with a cloth- or paper-covered board on the front and back. Also known as *casebound*.

headband (409) A decorative cloth band fastened under the spine at the top and bottom of a hardcover book.

heading (26) Title of a section of text.

hyphen (39) A short dash used to break a word between lines or parts, or between digits in a phone number. Do not confuse with an **en dash** or **em dash**.

ICC color profile (307) The International Color Consortium develops international color standards (profiles) that are vendor-neutral. This makes the color data for a book both understandable to and portable among printers.

imposition (321) The arrangement of pages on a printing sheet so that they will be in the correct order when folded.

in port (49) A small box that appears near the upper left corner of a text frame in InDesign, visible when the text frame is selected with the Selection tool.

initial cap (165) A large letter set at the beginning of a section. An initial cap aligns at base with the first line of regular text. *See also* **drop cap**.

ink density (401) The total amount of ink that is on the printing press in any one spot. This is measured by adding up the percentages (tints) of the C+M+Y+K inks in that spot. Also called **total area coverage**, or TAC.

inside margin (124)   The margin next to the inside edge, where facing pages meet. Also known as the gutter margin.

JPEG (.jpg) (305)   Joint Photographic Experts Group photo file format commonly used by digital cameras and on the web. These files can be used for printing, although **PSD** is a surer bet.

justification (40)   This refers to the way text lines align with each other. The most common examples are *left* (aligning at left but not on the right—also known as **ragged right**), *center, right* (aligning at right but not on the left), *left justify* (aligning both left and right, but the last line of a paragraph can be short), and *full justify* (aligning both left and right, including the last line of the paragraph). In InDesign, letter and word spacing preferences related to text alignment can be specified (File>Preferences>Justification on a PC, or InDesign>Preferences on a Mac). *See also* **justified**.

justified (37)   The common name for type that is left justified. *See also* **justification**.

kerning (337)   Adding or subtracting space between any two type characters. *See also* **tracking**.

keyboard shortcut (67)   A combination of keys that can be used instead of selecting a menu item. See page 477 for a list of common shortcuts.

leading (36)   (rhymes with "heading") Space between lines of type, measured in points from the base of one line to the base of the next. The term comes from the days of metal type, when thin bars of lead were placed between lines of type for spacing.

letter spacing (358)   The space between letters in the same word. You can set values for this in the Justification area of the Paragraph or Paragraph Styles panel. Letter spacing is also affected by **kerning** and **tracking**.

ligature (36)   Two letters tied together in the same character for better appearance. The most commonly seen are *ff, fi, fl, ffl,* and *Th*.

line art (310)   Black and white images with no grays. Also called a **bitmap**.

lines per inch   *See* **dots per inch (dpi)**. *Compare with* **ppi (pixels per inch)**.

lining figures (42)   Arabic numerals that are the same size as the uppercase letters of the same font. *See also* **oldstyle figures**.

master page (119)   A special page in an InDesign document on which all the standard margins and elements that will appear on the actual book pages are set up. A book can have one or many master pages.

normal view (16)   A view that shows margins, columns, and text and object frames in the InDesign document. Toggle back and forth between normal view and preview (which shows no margins, columns, or frames) by pressing W when nothing else is selected.

offset press (22)   A press that uses plastic plates and rollers to print ink on paper. Most efficient for 1,000 or more copies.

oldstyle figures (42)   Arabic numerals that are the same size as the lowercase letters in a font. *See also* **lining figures**.

opening quote (27)   A quotation that appears at the start of a part or chapter. Usually followed by a **quote attribution**.

OpenType (42)   A type font format that is interchangeable between Windows and Macintosh systems. OpenType fonts have several useful features, such as built-in small caps, oldstyle numerals, ligatures, and easily built fractions. OpenType faces with "Pro" in the name include European letters with accents; those with "Std" in the name do not. In the InDesign Control panel, each typeface in the list at the upper left has an icon next to its name. A two-color italic "O" is the OpenType icon.

ornament (105)   A decorative symbol used most commonly as a paragraph separator. Ornaments may be included as part of a font character set, or they may be gathered into a font of their own.

orphan (224)   1) A single word on a line by itself at the end of a paragraph; 2) the first line of a paragraph, positioned at the bottom of a page. Both kinds of orphans should be avoided whenever possible. *See also* **widow**.

out port (49)   The small box at the bottom right corner of a page frame, indicating that there is more text. When the out port has a red "+" in it, the text has nowhere to go and should be flowed, or threaded, to the next page. *See also* **overset text**.

outside margin (124)   The margin next to the outer edge of a page.

overset text (454)   Text that does not fit in a text frame or table cell. Change the shape of the text frame or table cell to accommodate the overset text, or use the **out port** to thread the text to another page or text frame.

page break (330)   This forces everything that follows onto the next page. Place the cursor where you want the break, then press Enter/Return on your numeric keypad, or choose Type>Insert Break Character>Page Break.

paragraph separator (26)   A graphic, **dingbat**, **ornament**, **rule**, or series of asterisks between paragraphs, indicating the passage of time or a change of topic.

paragraph shading (211)   A color or shade that appears behind the type in a paragraph. Shading can be applied in the Paragraph Styles panel or Control panel.

paragraph style (56)   A collection of type style, size, spacing, and color attributes assigned to a paragraph.

pasteboard (14)   In the InDesign workspace, the area outside of the pages. Use this area for experimenting and for storing objects or type. Nothing that is on the pasteboard will appear in the book.

PDF (Portable Document Format) (301)   A file format that preserves the layout, type, and images just the way you created them in InDesign or another program. Your work is "cemented" in place and can be shared with anyone who has the freely distributed Acrobat Reader. To make a PDF, go to File>Export and choose Adobe PDF.

pica (33)   A traditional typesetting measurement unit equal to one-sixth of an inch; 1 pica = 12 points. *See also* **point**.

PNG (315)   Portable Network Graphics image file format, best used on the web (RGB color).

point (33)   A typesetting unit equal to one 72nd of an inch. 12 points = 1 pica. Abbreviated as pt. *See also* **pica**.

PostScript Type 1 (132)   One of the two type "flavors" of OpenType. In the upper left of the Control panel, PostScript font names are shown next to a red lowercase "a" icon. *See also* **OpenType** and **TrueType**.

ppi (pixels per inch) (306)   For most book printing, 300 is the optimal ppi for photos, and 800–1200 ppi is recommended for line (bitmapped) art. *Compare with* **dots per inch (dpi)**.

preflight (453)   Checking an InDesign document for errors prior to going to press. The Preflight panel is a live checker showing errors at the bottom of the screen.

prepress (302)   The work that the printer does to an InDesign, PDF, or Photoshop file to get it ready to go on press.

print-on-demand (POD) (21)   A method of digital printing that makes it possible to print one book at a time, as it is needed.

pt (33)   Abbreviation for **point**.

quotation (27)   Words attributable to a writer or

speaker other than the author; usually followed by an attribution (*see* **quote attribution**).

quote attribution (27)   The writer or speaker of the words in the quotation.

ragged right (37)   Type **justification** with all lines aligning on the left but not on the right (such as throughout *this* book).

recto (24)   Right-hand page.

resample (303)   An action in Photoshop that rearranges the pixels of an image in order to change its **resolution** while maintaining its physical size.

resolution (306)   *In digital images,* the amount of detail the image holds, measured in **pixels per inch (ppi)**—this is the input resolution. 72 ppi is standard for a computer, phone, or camera screen. 300 ppi is standard for printing. *In printing,* the number of ink **dots per inch (dpi)** that the offset or digital printer can produce—this is the output resolution.

RGB (257)   Red, green, and blue, the three colors used by digital cameras, scanners, and computer monitors to display "full color." RGB is not used in printing on a press. *See also* **CMYK**.

rich black (401)   A combination of black and other color(s) of ink that enhances the appearance of large areas of black on a printed page. 100K + 60C is a popular choice.

rule (57)   A straight line in any style (dashed, dotted, etc.) that is drawn or typeset.

run-in subhead (26)   A heading that appears at the start of a paragraph, with text following it on the same line.

running head or foot (26)   Information about the book, placed above or below the text block. It can be used for navigation of the book, or it can simply show the book author and title.

saddle stitch (408)   A binding for books consisting of only one **signature**. Two or three staples hold the pages together at the fold.

sheet-fed press (22)   A printing press that prints ink on single sheets of paper. *See also* **offset press** and **web press**.

shortcut (67)   A keyboard shortcut can be created and used to apply character or paragraph styles to text. See a list of commonly used shortcuts on page 477.

short-run printing (22)   Printing in small quantities (usually 50–999).

sidebar (70)   Supplemental material that is designed differently and placed apart from the rest of the text on the page.

signature (321)   Group of book pages that are printed on the same sheet and folded so that they form a booklet. Signatures are then gathered together and bound. The number of pages in a signature varies according to the dimensions of both the paper and the book pages. Common numbers of pages in a signature are 16 and 32 (for sheet-fed presses), and 24 and 48 (for web presses).

small caps (80)   Capital letters that are approximately the same height as the lowercase letters in a font. Commonly used for acronyms and terms such as A.M., P.M., BCE, and CE.

Smyth-sewn (408)   A type of binding that involves sewing signatures together before putting the cover on.

soft hyphen (359)   *See* **discretionary hyphen**.

soft return (147)   A line return that forces a new line but keeps it within the same paragraph. Place the cursor where you want the break, then press Shift+Enter/Return. *See also* **hard return**.

softcover (407)   Commonly called a paperback, but softcovers can also be made of a plastic material.

spiral (408)   A type of binding that uses one continuous metal wire (plastic coated or not), curled into a spiral, to hold the pages together. Also called *coil*.

stamping (442)   The process of using ink or metal foil to apply lettering or other designs to a cloth-bound hardcover book. With blind stamping (also called *blind embossing*), the design is pressed into the cover with no ink or foil.

story (97)   All the text that is connected by the same series of text **threads**.

swatch (258)   A small sample of a color. The Swatches panel in InDesign lists all the named colors in the document.

tabular figures (42)   Numerals, either **lining** or **oldstyle**, that are spaced evenly so that they can be aligned in columns.

text block (46)   The area on a page in which the main body of text is placed. The text block does not include the **running head**, **running foot**, or **folio**, or any material in a side column.

text frame (16)   A box in which type is placed.

text wrap (296)   The means for allowing type to run around the edges of a graphic shape or image rather than flowing in front of or behind it.

thread (49)   In InDesign, a link from one text frame to the next. Text threads can be made visible by going to View>Extras>Show Text Threads, then selecting any text frame with the Selection tool.

TIFF (.tif) (303)   Tagged Image File Format. A flexible image format that supports all color modes. Easily imported into InDesign, it is a popular file format used in printed books.

tint (259)   Less than 100% of a color. For example, a light gray is actually 10% black.

top margin (124)   The margin at the top of a page; also known as the head margin.

total area coverage (401)   *See* **ink density**.

tracking (36)   Adding or subtracting space between groups of letters. Not the same as **kerning**.

trade paperback (407)   A paperback produced for the general public, as opposed to a textbook, an academic book, or other specialized book.

trim size (20)   The size of the pages of a book, measured in inches, horizontal × vertical, after the book has been trimmed to its final size.

TrueType (132)   One of the two typeface "flavors" of OpenType. In the upper left area of the Control panel, TrueType fonts have a blue double "T" icon next to them. *See also* **PostScript Type 1** and **OpenType**.

turnover line (205)   A line in a list entry or a heading that continues after the first line. Also called *turned line* or simply *turn*.

typeface (5)   A group of related styles of type. Garamond and Minion are two examples of typefaces; each has many instances, such as italic, bold, semibold, etc. *See also* **font**.

uncoated (443)   Paper that has not been treated with any substance to make it smoother.

vector image (303)   A drawing in which shapes are described with mathematical expressions called vectors. Vector images generally have a flatter appearance than photographs. They can be printed at any size without loss of quality. Anything drawn in Adobe Illustrator is a vector image.

verso (24)   Left-hand page.

web press (22)   A very large printing press that prints from rolls of paper and is used to print great quantities of books. *See also* **digital press, sheet-fed press,** and **offset press**.

weight (192)   Thickness.

widow (38)   The last line of a paragraph that is positioned at the top of a page. Widows are forbidden in bookmaking. *See also* **orphan**.

Wire-O® (408)   A type of binding that is similar to **spiral** but sturdier. The wires are paired and parallel to each other. *See also* **concealed Wire-O**.

word spacing (40)   The amount of space between words, controlled in the Justification section of the Paragraph or Paragraph Styles panel.

Keyboard shortcuts

InDesign provides many, many keyboard shortcuts. Below are some of the ones you'll use most often.

File functions

New . . . . Ctrl/Cmd+N
Open . . . . Ctrl/Cmd+O
Close . . . . Ctrl/Cmd+W
Quit/Exit . . . . Ctrl/Cmd+Q
Print . . . . .Ctrl/Cmd+P
Export (to PDF) . . . . .Ctrl/Cmd+E
Save . . . . .Ctrl/Cmd+S
Save As . . . . Ctrl/Cmd+Shift+S

Navigation

Page view—Normal to Preview, Preview
    to Normal . . . . W
Zoom in . . . . .Ctrl/Cmd+=
Zoom out . . . . Ctrl/Cmd+- (hyphen)
Fit page view to window . . . . Ctrl/Cmd+0 (zero)
Actual size . . . . Ctrl/Cmd+1
Jump to page . . . . . . .Ctrl/Cmd+J, then page number

Type and objects

Switch from Type Tool to Selection Tool. . . . . Esc
Switch to Selection Tool. V
Switch to Type Tool. . . . . T
Switch to Free Transform Tool . . . . E
Undo . . . . .Ctrl/Cmd+Z
Redo . . . . Ctrl/Cmd+Shift+Z
Find/Change . . . . .Ctrl/Cmd+F

Show Tabs panel . . . . Ctrl/Cmd+Shift+T
Select all . . . . .Ctrl/Cmd+A
Group . . . . Ctrl/Cmd+G
Ungroup . . . . .Ctrl/Cmd+Shift+G
Em space. Ctrl/Cmd+Shift+M
Em dash . . . . Alt/Opt+Shift+- (hyphen)
En space . . . . .Ctrl/Cmd+Shift+N
En dash . . . . .Alt/Opt+- (hyphen)
Opening double quotation mark . . . . .Alt/Opt+[
Closing double quotation mark . . . . Alt/Opt+Shift+[
Opening single quotation mark . . . . .Alt/Opt+]
Closing single quotation mark . . . . . Alt/Opt+Shift+]
Forced line break. . . . . .Shift+Enter/Return
Nonbreaking space . . . . .Ctrl/Cmd+Alt/Opt+X
Copy . . . . .Ctrl/Cmd+C
Cut . . . . .Ctrl/Cmd+X
Paste . . . . .Ctrl/Cmd+V
Paste in Place. . . . . Ctrl/Cmd+Alt/Opt+Shift+V
Place (image or text). . . . . Ctrl/Cmd+D
Bring to the front . . . . .Ctrl/Cmd+Shift+]
Send to the back . . . . .Ctrl/Cmd+Shift+[
Bring forward . . . . Ctrl/Cmd+]
Send backward . . . . Ctrl/Cmd+[
Text frame options . . . . .Ctrl/Cmd+B
Select frame on master . . . . . . Ctrl/Cmd+Shift+click
Quick scroll to a new typeface
    in the Control panel. . . . . .Type first letter
                           of typeface name

The self-publishing process

Note that several activities can be going on simultaneously. The items in gray boxes are discussed in this book, with chapter references noted in parentheses.

1	Begin your market research (chapters 5 and 55).	Create your book's website (with blog) and social media.	Write the book.
2	Lease Adobe Creative Cloud package (chapter 3).	Design your front cover (chapters 56–59) for marketing.	Ask for permission to borrow material (chapters 28 and 41).
3	Work with an editor until your copy is finished.	Plan your pages for design (chapter 6).	
4	Design and lay out your main text (chapters 1–54).	Design your front and back matter (chapters 28 and 29).	Obtain your ISBN, CIP, and/or LCCN (chapters 28 and 68).
5	Send your pages out for proofreading (chapter 53).	Obtain your permissions (see step 2).	Make arrangements for a book launch (physical or virtual).
6	Polish your cover (and dust jacket) (chapters 55–67).	Obtain your barcode (chapters 64 and 70).	Order and send out advance review copies for review.

| 7 | Typeset your proof-reader's corrections (chapter 53). | Send your chapters out to an indexer (chapter 54). | Make arrangements with distributors or online vendors. | Create an online media kit, sell pre-publication copies. |

| 8 | Add testimonials to book cover (chapters 63 and 64). | Finish cover and jacket (chapter 67). | Complete your copyright page (chapter 28). |

| 9 | Add your index (chapter 54). | Prepare final PDFs and send to printer (chapter 71). | Prepare your files for an ebook edition (chapter 73). |

| 10 | Review printer's proofs (chapter 72). | Get ebook file converted to EPUB and MOBI editions. |

| 11 | Receive printed books, EPUB and MOBI files. | Provide all editions to distributors and online vendors. | Announce book launch on website and social media. |

Congratulations, you're a published author! Way to go!

Bibliography

Adobe® InDesign® CC Classroom in a Book (2017 Release). Berkeley, CA: Adobe Press, 2017.

Adobe® Photoshop® CC Classroom in a Book (2017 Release). Berkeley, CA: Adobe Press, 2017.

Birdsall, Derek. *Notes on Book Design*. New Haven: Yale University Press, 2004.

Bringhurst, Robert. *The Elements of Typographic Style*, 4th ed. Vancouver: Hartley & Marks, 2013.

The Chicago Manual of Style: 16th Edition. Chicago: University of Chicago Press, 2010.

Craig, James, and William Bevington. *Designing with Type*, 5th ed. New York: Watson-Guptill Publications, 2006.

Eckersley, Richard, et al. *Glossary of Typesetting Terms*. Chicago: University of Chicago Press, 1994.

Felici, James. *The Complete Manual of Typography*, 2nd ed. Berkeley: Peachpit Press, 2012.

Haslam, Andrew. *Book Design: A Comprehensive Guide*. New York: Abrams, 2006.

Hendel, Richard. *On Book Design*. New Haven: Yale University Press, 1998.

Holleley, Douglas. *Digital Book Design and Publishing*. New York: Clarellen and Cary Graphic Arts Press, 2001.

Kelby, Scott. *Photoshop 7 Down & Dirty Tricks*. New Riders Publishing, 2002.

Lee, Marshall. *Bookmaking: The Illustrated Guide to Design & Production*. New York: R.R. Bowker, 1965.

Lupton, Ellen. *Indie Publishing*. New York: Princeton Architectural Press, 2008.

Lupton, Ellen. *Thinking with Type*, 2nd ed. New York: Princeton Architectural Press, 2010.

McClelland, Deke. *Adobe Photoshop CS5 One-on-One*. Sebastopol, CA: Deke Press/O'Reilly Media, Inc., 2010.

Mitchell, Michael, and Susan Wightman. *Book Typography: A Designer's Manual*. Somerset, UK: Butler & Tanner Ltd., 2005.

Rafaeli, Ari. *Book Typography*. New Castle, DE: Oak Knoll Press, 2005.

Ross, Marilyn, and Sue Collier. *The Complete Guide to Self-Publishing: Everything You Need to Know to Write, Publish, Promote and Sell Your Own Book*, 5th ed. Cleveland: Writers Digest Books, 2010.

Spiekermann, Erik, and E.M. Ginger. *Stop Stealing Sheep & Find Out How Type Works*. Berkeley: Adobe Press, 2003.

Williams, Robin. *The Non-Designer's Type Book*, 2nd ed. Berkeley: Peachpit Press, 2005.

Wilson, Adrian. *The Design of Books*. San Francisco: Chronicle Books, 1993.

Index

32-page signatures, 322

thumbnails, moving pages by
dragging, 332

thumb space, 123

TIF/TIFF format, 303
optimizing images in, 305
Photoshop, saving files in, 315

Tint feature, 261

title page, 23
designing, 222–224
half title pages, 24, 224
as mandatory, 24
repeat elements on, 223

titles. *See also* chapter titles
decreasing page count by
changing, 325
design document, setting up,
388
interesting layouts, finding,
386–387
layouts, experimenting with,
383–387
modern sidebar with graphic
and title, 212–213
in running heads, 219
typefaces, choosing, 384–385

TOC (table of contents). *See* table
of contents (TOC)

Toolbox. *See also* specific tools
working with, 16

tracking
for balancing lines on facing
pages, 357
front cover visual element, 391
letter and word spacing, adjusting, 358

trade paperbacks, bindings for, 407

traditional printers and printing
explanation of, 22
page count for, 321–326
trim sizes for, 21

Transcontinental, trim sizes for, 21

transparency. *See* screening

trim size
changing, 121–122
decreasing to reduce page count,
326
New Document dialog box, setting in, 34
page count and changing, 324
printer specifications for, 21–22
selecting, 20–22
standard printing sizes for, 122

two-digit numbered lists, values
for, 200–201

.txt files, importing, 44

typefaces. *See also* display type;
front cover
Basic Paragraph style for, 36
categories of, 129
colors to shapes, applying,
259
with Creative Cloud, 5
fonts compared, 132
Glyphs panel for finding, 338
gradients, applying, 262
history of, 134
Illustrator, converting type to
outlines in, 312
for main text, 133
main typeface, changing,
129–134
margins and, 125
modern headings with two
typefaces, 190–191
repeat elements for, 143
shapes, adding to, 259
terminology for, 134
for titles, 384–385

Typekit, 5
legal use of fonts, 132
turning on, 8

warning for non-Typekit fonts,
457

typesetting
back cover copy and text,
425–429
charts and tables, 342–347
Create Outlines, 312, 464, 468
in ebooks, 464
footnotes, 348–349
indexes, 373
inline art, adjusting, 350
kerning, 337
math and fractions, 141,
350–351
for poetry, 352–355
punctuation for, 339–341

type size
Basic Paragraph style for, 36
decreasing to reduce page count,
326
examples of, 137
for folios, 221
increasing to add page count,
324
margins and, 125
for running heads/feet, 221
setting, 135

Type Tester, Typekit, 10

Type Tool, 16, 18

Typographer's Quotes, 45

typographic elements, 26–27
and paragraph styles, 57

U

UI scaling, 30

underline options, 42

undoing
margin changes, 127
mistakes, 86

unnumbered/unordered lists,
designing, 201–203

About the authors

Fiona Raven, of Vancouver, Canada, has designed hundreds of books for small presses, independent publishers, and self-publishing authors since 1995. Fiona is a self-taught book designer, having learned her craft from reading and examining countless books on typography, design, layout, and software. Every now and then she still gets a hankering to create a book the old-fashioned way—by printing on handmade papers, illustrating with woodcuts or watercolors, and creating a binding by hand.

Glenna Collett has been a book designer in the Boston area for over forty years. She created her first book by hand using metal type, a letterpress, silkscreen illustrations, and a sewn binding. Since then, she has designed more than 100 textbooks for large publishers and dozens of books for individual authors. Glenna also teaches self-publishing workshops, and now that she is an author herself, she brings a deeper understanding of the issues her students may face.

Join us on social media

Follow us on Twitter
@BookDesignBook

Keep up on LinkedIn
www.linkedin.com/company/
book-design-made-simple

Like us on Facebook
www.facebook.com/BookDesignMadeSimple

Subscribe to our YouTube channel
via BookDesignMadeSimple.com/videos

Visit us and our blog at
www.BookDesignMadeSimple.com
and subscribe to our newsletter for updates.

Made in the USA
Las Vegas, NV
17 January 2021